FAMINE, LAND AND POLITICS

British Government and Irish Society

1843–1850

In memory of Winston Breen

FAMINE, LAND AND POLITICS

British Government and Irish Society

1843–1850

PETER GRAY

IRISH ACADEMIC PRESS
DUBLIN • PORTLAND, OR

First published in 1999 by
IRISH ACADEMIC PRESS
44, Northumberland Road, Dublin 4, Ireland,
and in the United States of America by
IRISH ACADEMIC PRESS
c/o ISBS, 5824 NE Hassalo Street, Portland, OR 97213-3644.

website: http://www.iap.ie

British Library Cataloguing in Publication Data
Gray, Peter
Famine, land and politics: British Government and Irish Society, 1843-50
1. Ireland – History – Famine, 1845-1852 2. Great Britain – Politics and government – 1837-1901
I. Title
941'.081

ISBN 0-7165-2564-X-hb
ISBN 0-7165-2642-5-pb

Library of Congress Cataloguing-in-Publication Data
Gray, Peter, 1965–
Famine, land and politics: British government and Irish society, 1843-1850 / Peter Gray.
p. cm.
Includes bibliographical references and index.
ISBN 0-7165-2564-X (hc.)
1. Ireland—History—Famine, 1845-1852. 2. Great Britain—Foreign economic relations—Ireland—History—19th century. 3. Ireland—Foreign economic relations—Great Britain—History—19th century. 4. Great Britain—Politics and government—1837-1901. 5. Land tenure—Ireland—History—19th century. 6. Ireland—Social conditions—19th century. 7. Famines—Ireland—History—19th century. I. Title.
DA950.7.G72 1998
941.5081—dc21 98-42975
CIP

Typeset in 10.5 pt on 12.5 pt Adobe Garamond by
Carrigboy Typesetting Services, County Cork
Printed by Creative Print and Design (Wales), Ebbw Vale

Table of Contents

PREFACE vii

1 *Irish land and British politics* 1

i The problem of Irish land 1
ii Economic orthodoxy and its critics 7
iii Varieties of Whiggism: Foxites, moderates and moralists 17
iv The politics of 'Justice to Ireland', 1830–41 26
v Peelites and Tories 37

2 *Agitation and inquiry, 1843–6* 41

i The 'landlord and tenant question', 1843 42
ii The Commission and its critics, 1843–4 58
iii 'A cart-load of cross-examinations': the response to the Devon Commission report 69
iv 'As mysterious as the bricks of Babylon': Peel's land legislation 78

3 *The coming of the blight: land and relief, 1845–6* 95

i Potatoes and Providence 96
ii Free trade and food policy 107
iii Relief works, land and coercion 125

4 *Whiggery and the land question, 1846–50* 142

i Bessborough's administration, 1846–7 143
ii Clarendon, clearances and coercion, 1847–8 168
iii 'Free trade in land', 1847–50 196

5 *'The visitation of God': the Whigs and famine relief, 1846–7* 227

i The Whigs and the blight: strategies and tensions 227
ii Public works and 'sound principle', 1846–7 240
iii Providence and the Poor Law, 1847 256

6 *'Between the censure of the Economists and the Philanthropists': the Whigs and famine relief, 1847–50* 284

i Cutting the 'Gordian knot', 1847–8 285
ii 'Natural causes', 1848–9 304
iii 'Disposed of by a higher Power', 1849–50 322

CONCLUSION 328

BIBLIOGRAPHY 339

INDEX 366

LIST OF ILLUSTRATIONS

facing page

1 The New Lord Mayor of Dublin (That is to be) by HB, March 1836 1

2 *Naturam expellas furca*, Joe Miller the Younger, 7 June 1845 114

3 The Minister's dream, *Pictorial Times*, 22 November 1845 115

4 Paddy! Will you now, take me while I'm in the humour? *The Puppet-Show*, 9 September 1848 210

5 Yankee Doodle's Corn Exchange, *Yankee Doodle*, 21 November 1846 211

6 While the crop grows Ireland starves, *The Puppet-Show*, 13 May 1849 318

7 The new Irish still: showing how all sorts of good things may be obtained (by industry) out of peat, *Punch*, August 1849 319

Preface

Historical anniversaries have a tendency to focus the minds of historians and the public alike. The sesquicentenary of the Great Famine has stimulated a wide-ranging debate on the causation, nature and consequences of the catastrophe. After a long drought, a torrent of monographs and essays have appeared, the best of which – including Ó Gráda, Mokyr and Solar on the economy, Bourke on potato blight, Kinealy on administration, Kerr on the Church, Scally on peasant society and emigration, and Donnelly on clearances – have profoundly enhanced our perceptions of western Europe's most acute peacetime social crisis in the modern era. In the wake of such scholarship few can now dispute the centrality of the Famine to the historical experience of modern Ireland. Its demographic, economic and political legacies shaped the 'new' Ireland of the later nineteenth century and the Irish diaspora communities overseas, and moulded the collective memory of both.

In the public arena the anniversary has seen, alongside the predictable reassertion of reductionist nationalist and revisionist polemics, a largely sophisticated and dignified commemoration of the Famine. President Mary Robinson's inclusivist and internationalizing speeches went far to focus public attention on the past and continuing roots of famine in poverty and the denial of basic human rights. The process of commemoration has not been without surprises. The decision of Prime Minister Tony Blair to issue an 'apology' for Britain's role in the Famine – in fact an acknowledgment that 'those who governed in London at the time failed their people through standing by while a crop failure turned into a massive human tragedy' – provoked an outraged reaction from conservative commentators in Britain and Ireland. The political motivations behind this unprecedented declaration do not concern us here, but the accuracy of the statement does. This book is a contribution to the debate on responsibility which the reaction to Blair's statement demonstrates is very much alive.

This book is not a general history of the Great Famine. Its intention is rather to unravel and interpret a specific dimension of the crisis: the response of British government and public opinion to the disaster in the light of contemporary debates about the nature and future of Irish society. If the politics of the Famine are to be understood, contextualization is vital. The British political system of the 1840s was a complex structure, subject to considerable flux. Ideological differences were rife, cutting across party lines and appealing to the validating pillars of 'scientific' political economy, natural or revealed religion, and shared political inheritance. This study brings together two key aspects; the first is the articulation and construction of 'the problem of Ireland' by British policy-makers and opinion-formers in the 1840s. Reports of direct observation of the potato blight from autumn 1845 were filtered and interpreted through pre-existing ideological lenses, and official conceptions of the famine in Ireland were shaped by established linguistic systems, such as providentialism.

The second, and less fashionable, element is close political analysis, or 'high politics'. Insofar as this book is a study in the history of the use of power – with regard both to the transformation or reinforcement of the structures of rural society, and the more basic matter of the allocation of resources at a time of acute shortage – it must incorporate a mechanism for evaluating and assessing the influence and power of these ideological constructions. The necessity of such analysis arises from the basic assumption that there was a plurality of responses within the British political elite (and indeed its Irish counterpart). Such ideological differences were not marginal, despite the similarities in class background of the political protagonists. Even the British press stressed the sheer range of attitudes that were generally identified as 'political economy': 'If all Her Majesty's ministers, all the writers in buff and blue, all the professors of the science, had each a political economy of his own, there could not be more variety.' (*Times*, 19 March 1847).

While all British commentators were far removed from the pre-modern world view of the Irish peasantry, and infected by some degree of colonialist perception, there was by the early 1840s some degree of blurring between 'native' and 'colonial' assumptions, not least as a consequence of the politicizing activities of Daniel O'Connell. Politics has to be taken seriously not only to appreciate the dynamics of O'Connell's relationship with British government and the possibility of land reform in the 1840s, but to answer the more basic questions of what viable choices were available to policy-makers in the face of Famine, and to what degree can individuals be held culpable for acting as they did.

The contention of this book is that the political reaction to the Great Famine in Ireland cannot be understood entirely as a question of the limits and structures of relief. The Irish 'question' as it evolved in the early 1840s had acquired a high political and public profile in Britain by 1845, and was already dominated by issues relating to land. The Famine obliged the state to react, but the broad lines of response had already been sketched out in the preceding years. What seemed to be at stake in 1845–50 was the future of Irish society. For most of the politicians, activists and commentators who observed the 'act of God' implicit in the potato failure, the reconstruction of that society on a radically altered pattern was to be the primary objective of policy. Humanitarian or welfarist responses were not entirely absent, but were severely curbed by the greater force of ideas of Irish 'regeneration'.

My first thanks are to Boyd Hilton, for his inspiration, encouragement and patience in supervising the writing of the Ph.D. dissertation on which this book is based. I also owe a particular debt of gratitude to late Angus Macintyre for advice and guidance when these were most needed. Brendan Bradshaw and the Cambridge Group for Irish Studies provided stimulating opportunities for the discussion of Irish history (and historiography), as did the Institute of Irish Studies at Queen's University Belfast, which elected me to a fellowship in 1991–2. This book owes a great deal to the opportunity to pursue postdoctoral research granted me by the British Academy and the Master and Fellows of Downing College, Cambridge, in 1993–6. Financial support is also gratefully acknowledged from the Department of Education, Northern Ireland, and the Thirlwall Fund at Cambridge University. I would like to thank Theo Hoppen, Donal Kerr, Cormac Ó Gráda, Virginia Crossman, Oliver MacDonagh, Jim Donnelly and Paul Bew for reading and commenting on parts of this text at various stages of its evolution. All errors remain the sole responsibility of the author. Many debts have been accrued in the writing of this book, and only a few can be acknowledged here. Particular thanks are due to my colleagues at the University of Southampton, to Jon Parry, Derek Beales, Margaret O'Callaghan, Hiram Morgan, Janice Holmes, Kathleen Nutt, Melissa Calaresu, Joan Pau Rubies, Chas and Sarah Geiger, John Weste, John and Pádraicín McCafferty, and, most especially, to Sara Jan.

I am grateful to the staff of the following libraries, record offices and archives for their assistance and for permission to quote from collections in their keeping: the Bodleian Library, Oxford; the British Library; Cambridge University Library; the Devon Record Office; Durham University Library; the Hartley Library, University of Southampton; the Linen Hall Library, Belfast; Liverpool Record Office; the National Library of Ireland; the National Library of Wales; Nottingham University Library; the Public Record Office, London; the Public Record Office of Northern Ireland, Belfast; Queen's University Library, Belfast; the Surrey Record Office; the West Yorkshire Archive Service, Leeds. I am grateful to the Earl of Clarendon for permission to quote from the Clarendon Deposit, and to the Earl of Bessborough for the use of quotations from the Bessborough Papers at the West Sussex Record Office. Quotations from the Castle Howard Papers and from the Palmerston Papers are by kind permission of the Howard family and the Trustees of the Broadlands Archives, respectively. I must also thank the Earl of Derby for permission to quote from the Derby Papers, and the Earl of Harewood for the Clanricarde Papers.

PETER GRAY
Southampton, February 1998

1. The New Lord Mayor of Dublin (That is to be) by HB, March 1836. John Doyle, the Irish born Tory cartoonist, produced a series of 'political sketches' in the 1830s lampooning what he alleged was Whig subservience to O'Connell's political bullying. Here the Irish Municipal Corporations reform is portrayed as calculated to aggrandize O'Connell (centre) while reducing the Whig ministers (from left, Russell, Melbourne, Morpeth, Normanby) to the role of his flunkies.

CHAPTER ONE

Irish Land and British Politics

The Irish question is a mighty maze, it is a vast babel of conflicting opinions, and hostile passions and prejudices. In the great divisions of party there are innumerable sub-divisions upon all Irish matters; there are vast masses of opinions, jostling with other masses, intermingling in a confused conflict, not arranged in one compact body against another compact body, with one distinguishing banner over each; and out of this confusion it is impossible to look for any satisfactory and reasonable solution of all the difficult questions that are afloat.

Charles Greville, 26 January 1844[1]

Ireland is still clay under the potter's hand: the elements of society in that country are still floating in chaos, and await the hand of power to fix and fashion them. In England and Scotland the form of society is . . . firmly established . . . But it is otherwise in Ireland. Improvement and civilization must there descend from above; they will not rise spontaneously from the inward workings of the community. Hence it is above all things to be hoped, that all who may now be said to hold in their hands the destinies of that important country, will take a connected view of its entire condition; that they will deliberately frame a consistent scheme of policy with reference not to present exigencies, but to the future welfare of Ireland, and its relation to this country; that they will seek to guide events, not wait upon them . . .

George Cornewall Lewis, 1836[2]

I THE PROBLEM OF IRISH LAND

The politics of land has been a contentious matter throughout most of Ireland's modern history. The experience of colonization and plantation cast a long shadow over Irish economic and social development, and left a legacy of agrarian resentment and animosity that went deeper than the class tensions usual in the European countryside. Gaelic popular tradition identified the dispossession of the Catholic elite with the grievances of the rural poor, and co-existed uneasily with agrarian combinations formed to attain more specific objectives. The abandonment in the

1 Charles Cavendish Fulke Greville, *The Greville memoirs (second part): a journal of the reign of Queen Victoria, from 1837 to 1852*, edited by H. Reeve, 3 vols., (London, 1885), II, 221.

2 George Cornewall Lewis, *On local disturbances in Ireland; and on the Irish Church question* (London, 1836), pp. v–vi.

later eighteenth century of the economic penal laws against Catholics enacted in the 1690s–1720s did nothing to reverse the near-monopoly of land ownership and local political power in the hands of the Protestant elite. If anything, the deep political polarization of Ireland in the 1790s and the religious revivals which swept the country in the following decades reinforced the centrality of land as a focus of confrontation.

Land-related conflict had a number of dimensions. Rapid economic change from the mid-eighteenth century stimulated class friction throughout the country, often as virulent within the Catholic community between farmer and agricultural labourer or cottier, as it was between landlord and tenant. Nevertheless, in the Irish context the cultural and political gulf between the landowning elite and the bulk of the land-occupying masses laid the foundations for the fusing of nationalism and agrarianism in the nineteenth century. This in turn posed problems as well as opportunities for nationalist leaders; class enmities had to be carefully circumvented, the utopian expectations and boisterous energies of the rural poor restrained, and (for constitutional nationalists) a working relationship with often recalcitrant British ministers and public opinion constructed. Balancing this unruly mass proved difficult, but by the 1840s no nationalist movement could afford to ignore the pressing question of land.[3]

The 1800 Act of Union gave the British parliament and executive direct responsibility for Irish social policy, but the state's interest in legislative intervention was at first decidedly muted. Only when the Irish economy entered serious difficulties after 1815 was substantial attention directed towards it. The early decades of the Union witnessed an increasing economic divergence between the two countries that by the 1840s had rendered Ireland extremely vulnerable to social disaster. The 'Irish problem' had hitherto been constructed primarily as a matter of military security and political control; with growing perceptions of agricultural malaise, proto-industrial collapse and rural over-population, British observers began to search for the roots of Irish instability in the 'backward' structure of Irish society.

While the politics of the Irish land question in the post-Famine period has been subjected to considerable historical analysis, both the pre-Famine and the Famine period itself have been somewhat neglected. Surveys of the political struggles over Irish land have tended to begin around mid-century,[4] partly because of the great discontinuities in social and economic conditions produced by the Famine, which transformed the nature of the land question, and partly because of the political discontinuities in both Ireland and England which coincided with

3 James S. Donnelly, 'The land question in nationalist politics', T.E. Hachey and L.J. McCaffrey (eds.), *Perspectives on Irish nationalism* (Lexington, KY, 1989), pp. 79–98.

4 See, for example, W.E. Vaughan, *Landlords and tenants in Ireland, 1848–1904* (Dublin, 1984); Paul Bew, *Land and the national question in Ireland, 1858–82* (Dublin, 1978). Philip Bull's recent *Land, politics and nationalism: a study of the Irish land question* (Dublin, 1996), the first general history of the subject since the 1930s, also concentrates on the period after 1848.

the agrarian catastrophe. The significance of the 1840s has been overlooked, and the central events and debates of these years – the politicization of the land question in the early 1840s, the formation and report of the Devon Commission in 1843–5, the abortive landlord-tenant bills of 1845–50, and the role of the land question in delimiting famine-relief policy – have rarely been given the weight they deserve. Only the 1849 Encumbered Estates Act has attracted much attention, although more for its effects than for the motivations that underlay it.

The Famine years formed a watershed not only in socio-economic conditions, but also in Irish politics, with the assertive and self-confident O'Connellism that had characterized the pre-Famine decades giving way to a defensive localist politics, dominated by the landlord, 'strong farmer' and the Catholic Church in the 1850s and 1860s.[5] In Great Britain, the same years witnessed the fading of the ideological conflicts of the 1830s, and the reformulation of parties that was to underlie the mid-Victorian liberal consensus. Both these changes produced major alterations in the character of Anglo-Irish relations and hence in the parliamentary politics of Irish land.

If we are to understand the dynamics of this relationship on the eve of the Famine, and the circumstances of its redefinition during the cataclysm of the later 1840s, sufficient weight must be given to the attempts, however abortive, to analyse and resolve the land question during that decade. In the 1840s the traditional elements of the 'Irish question' as understood and debated at Westminster were increasingly supplemented by agrarian issues, to the extent that the Lord Lieutenant could declare in 1848 that 'the question of land is the question of Government in Ireland'.[6]

For the purposes of the present study, the 'Irish land question' will be understood as encompassing those problems associated with the structure and relations of landownership, landholding and the productive use of the soil which were articulated politically in Ireland, and which entered the deliberations of British policy-makers in the 1840s. The politics of land must, however, be approached in the context of the broader Irish policies of British governments; to the leaders of both main parties land was a central component of the larger set of problems raised starkly by the crisis of 1843. Thus Sir Robert Peel established the Devon Commission of inquiry as part of his 'new direction' in Irish policy in late 1843, and legislation on Irish land became part of the 'comprehensive measures' mooted by Lord John Russell from 1845. Land issues intertwined with other elements of policy, such as Catholic endowment and franchise reform; the maintenance of public order and the prevention of violent outrage – both agrarian and political – were equally inseparable. Most importantly of all, the response of the British state to the Great Famine of 1845–50 cannot be fully comprehended without an

5 K. Theodore Hoppen, *Ireland since 1800: conflict and conformity* (Harlow, 1989), ch. 5.

6 Clarendon to Lansdowne, 16 July 1848, Clarendon Deposit Irish, Bodleian Library, Oxford, letterbook III.

understanding of how the debate over the structure of Irish rural society merged with and dominated relief policy-making.

At the core of the Irish land question in the 1840s lay four interconnected elements – the relationship of landlord and tenant, the structure of landholding and landownership, the development of the Irish agricultural economy, and the connection of the land system with poverty and over-population. Contemporary theorists and politicians tended to stress one or more of these elements as the key to solving, or at least mitigating, the socio-economic problems of Ireland.

The relation of landlord and tenant was the element most actively agitated in Ireland itself. Most modern analyses of the Irish land question have tended to downplay the 'land tenure thesis' as the central issue in the economic history of nineteenth-century Irish agriculture, and although evidence on the nature of tenurial relations is more fragmentary for the pre-Famine period than for the later nineteenth century, it appears that poor landlord-tenant relations may have been of less economic significance than many contemporaries and earlier historians assumed.[7] Joel Mokyr concludes that poor landlord-tenant relations probably acted as a 'second-order effect' in restricting agricultural capital formation and retarding economic development, while James Donnelly suggests that in County Cork falling farm income after 1815 was a more important factor in constraining investment in agriculture.[8]

Whatever the judgment of hindsight, from 1843 the questions of tenant security, compensation for agricultural improvements and the protection or extension of 'tenant right' came to the forefront of Irish political agitation. Conversely, landowners complained of tenant negligence or obduracy, criticized the existing legal structure as hampering the exercise of the 'rights of proprietorship' and demanded a strengthening of legal powers to facilitate efficient estate management.[9] The contending stereotypes of the predatory landlord and the bloody-minded tenant concealed a vast range of individual experience even on neighbouring estates. However, recent economic writing suggests that the land-tenure system did impose a certain general pattern on Irish economic development. Most Irish landowners invested little money on the provision and upkeep of the farming infrastructure or on substantive agricultural improvements, preferring to spend on more socially prestigious but largely unproductive projects such as houses, demesnes and urban development. Even the most highly regarded northern landowners invested less than a quarter of the proportion of rental income sunk by the larger English proprietors

---

7 B.L. Solow, *The land question and the Irish economy, 1870–1903* (Cambridge, MA, 1971), pp. 10–13; Joel Mokyr, *Why Ireland starved: a quantitative and analytical history of the Irish economy, 1800–1850* (London, 1985 edn), pp. 81–7.

8 Ibid., p. 103; James S. Donnelly, *The land and the people of nineteenth-century Cork: the rural economy and the land question* (London, 1975), pp. 62–8.

9 [Mortimer O'Sullivan], 'Ireland – Repealers and landlords', *Dublin University Magazine*, XXI (Feb. 1843), 156–67.

in improving their estates. For the majority, maximizing rental income remained their chief priority, and, facilitated by rising population and intense land-hunger, rents rose in real terms until the Famine.[10]

Inevitably the landlord-tenant debate drew upon many non- or semi-economic concepts, reflecting the history of the ethno-religious divisions which were superimposed upon the class structure in much of Ireland. The adoption by Daniel O'Connell's nationalist movement of a rhetoric that articulated what Oliver MacDonagh has termed the 'communal concept of Irish land rights' put the question firmly on the national political agenda.[11] The strength of this agitation forced British politicians to consider the matter seriously, and partisans adopted various positions reflecting more general tactical and ideological divisions over Irish questions. For British legislators the landlord-tenant question raised profound difficulties concerning the legitimacy of government interference in the law of contract and in the legal regulation of economic activity. The absence of any effective legislation on landlord and tenant relations in this period may appear to confirm MacDonagh's argument that there was a steady divergence of British and Irish concepts of land law between 1800 and 1865, but a closer examination of events reveals a greater range of attitudes within the British political elite of the 1840s, some foreshadowing the better known Gladstonian 'conversions' of the 1860s and 1880s. There was, in fact, no uniformity of belief in the efficacy of a greater contractualization of economic relationships to solve the problems of tenurial relations in Ireland.

A second element of the land question in the 1840s involved the structure of landholding and the ownership of land. A number of issues fell under this head – the subdivision of holdings and the consolidation of farms, landlord encumbrances and the efficiency of the land market, the legitimacy of state intervention in that market, and the possibility and practicability of peasant proprietorship. All these were discussed by economists, politicians and the press, and were addressed by parliamentary bills and legislation. In Britain there were calls for government intervention in the land market to provide opportunities for facilitating peasant proprietorship through the division and sale of estates, or through state reclamation of waste lands. Though these issues failed to attract the same strength of opinion in Ireland as did landlord-tenant relations, for many British writers and politicians they offered a better basis for legislation.

Differences of opinion on the structure of landholding in Ireland frequently arose from conflicting approaches to the third element of the land question – the stimulation and development of the economy. Most observers agreed with the

10 W.A. Maguire, *The Downshire estates in Ireland 1801–1845* (Oxford, 1972), pp. 75–8; Cormac Ó Gráda, *Ireland: a new economic history 1780–1939* (Oxford, 1994), pp. 121–30.

11 Oliver MacDonagh, *States of mind: a study of Anglo-Irish conflict 1780–1980* (London, 1983), pp. 36, 39–45.

agriculturalist John Pitt Kennedy that the acknowledged Irish malaise arose from 'the usual agricultural practice in Ireland [which] is defective in the highest degree',[12] but ameliorative strategies varied. Orthodox economists held that the solution lay in the anglicization of the structures of Irish society, and that government policy should seek to bring Irish realities into line with English models.[13] Yet beyond the provision of security for capital investment there were uncertainties as to which forms of intervention might be applicable amid the 'backward' conditions of Ireland. In the mid-1840s, radical economic criticism of the traditional assumptions, based on a recognition of the impracticability of the English agrarian capitalist models in Ireland and a sense of the applicability of continental-style small-farm structures, emerged to complicate the debate further.

Closely linked to overall economic development was a fourth element associated with the land question, that of the alleviation of poverty and distress. Underlying much of the debate on Irish economic matters were concerns about over-population and underemployment.[14] At the heart of the controversy was the search for a mechanism that would promote the growth of productive resources and food output at a rate exceeding that of the growth of population. For many economists in the 1840s the preconditions for growth (and thus for the alleviation of poverty) dictated that the land structure be altered as a means of stabilizing or reducing the population. The radical critique of orthodox economics challenged the assumptions on which these prescriptions were based, while retaining a concern for over-population; in John Stuart Mill's words: 'the people are there, and the problem is not how to improve the country, but how it can be improved by and for its present inhabitants'.[15]

The coming of the Famine forced the question of Irish poverty to the head of the political agenda. Insofar as the debate on relief was inseparable from prescriptions for preventing the continuation *ad infinitum* or the repetition of the famine crisis, it was also overwhelmingly a question of land and thus drew on the three other elements outlined above. The poverty question was, however, more than solely economic in character; political, moral and religious considerations profoundly influenced the thought of policy-makers and coloured legislative activity.

This is the context in which the politics of Irish land must be examined. Economic theory, while obviously of great significance, cannot solely account for the attitudes and responses of British politicians and administrators, and excessive

---

12 John Pitt Kennedy (ed.), *Digest of evidence taken before Her Majesty's Commissioners of Inquiry into the state of the law and practice in respect to the occupation of land in Ireland* (2 vols., Dublin, 1847–8), I, 13.

13 R.D. Collison Black, *Economic thought and the Irish question, 1817–1870* (Cambridge, 1960), pp. 15–27.

14 To Kennedy, the latter was 'the root of all misery', Kennedy, *Digest*, I, 126–7.

15 John Stuart Mill, *Principles of political economy with some of their applications to social philosophy*, edited by J.M. Robson, in *Collected works of John Stuart Mill: Vol. III*, (Toronto, 1965), p. 991.

concentration on its role and influence can obscure much of the complexity of the debate in the 1840s. Irish policy was part of a complicated pattern of inter- and intra-party conflict, and, as an integral part of the wider 'condition of Britain' debate, attracted the attention of an increasingly vociferous and powerful British middle-class public opinion. Extensive analyses of the problems of Irish land were published in numerous pamphlets and in leading newspapers both before and during the Famine.[16] Public debate drew not only on orthodox economic arguments, but on more pervasive popular and Christian concepts of economic laws, which were in turn heavily laden with moral, religious, and political presuppositions and concerns. Some of these elements had long existed at the policy-making level, but with the mobilization of middle-class political activity in the 1840s, popular opinion became an important force in the making of Irish policy. The repeated potato failures from 1845 and the ensuing famine drew these developments to a head and added a new dimension of urgency; policy decisions could no longer be deferred when thousands began to perish.

II ECONOMIC ORTHODOXY AND ITS CRITICS

Most political economists followed Adam Smith in arguing that the political union of Ireland with Britain was the essential precondition for Irish economic progress.[17] This confidence in the Union was never seriously challenged after 1800, but the economic problems of Ireland began seriously to concern British observers from around 1815, when the collapse in grain prices exposed the precariousness of the massive and mutually-reinforcing expansion of tillage and rural population that had occurred in the preceding decades. The pre-war expansion of commercial output in Ireland, intensified from 1793 by the war-time boom in British demand, had transformed Ireland into a 'small open economy', subject to fluctuations in the British and world economies. The process was completed with the achievement of internal free trade and monetary integration between Ireland and Britain by 1826.[18] The sudden end to war-time conditions, brought about by the collapse of grain prices and intensified by monetary deflation and a squeeze on bank credit in 1819–20, put severe pressure on the Irish economy and exacerbated the threat of famine in the following decades.[19]

While the capacity of the Irish economy to grow in absolute terms under these difficult circumstances, and the ability of at least part of the population to attain

16 E.g. [Thomas Campbell Foster], 'The condition of the people of Ireland', *Times*, August 1845–January 1846; [John Stuart Mill], 'The condition of Ireland', *Morning Chronicle* October 1846–January 1847.

17 Adam Smith, *An inquiry into the nature and causes of the wealth of nations*, edited by Kathryn Sutherland (Oxford, 1993), p. 461.

18 Mokyr, *Why Ireland starved*, p. 279.

19 L.M. Cullen, *An economic history of Ireland since 1660* (2nd edn, London, 1987), pp. 101–2, 109–10.

a better standard of living, should not be underestimated, it is undeniable that the conditions of the large proportion of the poor living on the land were deteriorating as a result of the reversal of the country's economic fortunes.[20] This vulnerability was brought to the attention of the British governing class in stark fashion by the partial famines of 1816–17 and 1822. Agricultural malaise was compounded by the contraction of the domestic textile sector. Cottage production of linen had boomed in the later eighteenth century and further stimulated population expansion, but mechanization from the 1820s devastated the far-flung linen area, reducing significant production to the industrialized triangle around Belfast.

This growing awareness of the problem of Irish economic stagnation and widespread poverty came in the context of an explosion of concern and debate about the 'problem of poverty' in Britain.[21] By 1815 T.R. Malthus's thesis on the connection of population growth, poverty and 'positive checks' such as famine had entered both the mainstream of economic debate and popular perceptions, and had stimulated argument on his 'principle of population' along a number of lines. While Malthus's target in England had been the Poor Law – which in his view had promoted gross misery by encouraging the poor to procreate beyond the available means of subsistence – in Ireland, where there was no Poor Law, he located the great evil in a land system that had permitted the numbers of the poor to multiply to dangerous levels, and sustained them with a 'low' diet of cheap potatoes.[22]

Starting from these premises, the solution appeared straightforward. The consolidation of holdings, and the conversion of the cottier into a wage-labourer, would impose a deterrent on improvident marriages and thus check population growth. By denying the labourer his traditional subsistence, he would be given new incentives to work. Both Malthus and David Ricardo feared Ireland could not support its current population on the land, and looked to the development of manufacturing industry and the subsequent redeployment of population.

The problem was reconsidered by a younger generation of economists, notably J.R. McCulloch, Robert Torrens, and Nassau Senior, who recognized the incapacity of Irish industry to compete with British output by the 1820s and thus raised the

20 Increasing inequalities in income distribution are suggested in Joel Mokyr and Cormac Ó Gráda, 'Poor and getting poorer? Living standards in Ireland before the Famine', *Economic History Review*, 2nd series, LXI (1988), 209–35, and in Ó Gráda, *Ireland: a new economic history*, pp. 80–5, 158–67.

21 Gertrude Himmelfarb, *The idea of poverty: England in the early industrial age* (London, 1984), pp. 130–44.

22 Despite its seeming attraction as a case study in the 'primitive' principle of population, Ireland was never at the centre of Malthus's thought on population and, it has been argued, his study of its problems was both superficial and inconsistent, Cormac Ó Gráda, *Ireland before and after the Famine: explorations in economic history 1800–1925* (Manchester, 1988), pp. 1–8; Cormac Ó Gráda, 'Malthus and the pre-Famine economy', in Antoin E. Murphy (ed.), *Economists and the Irish economy from the eighteenth century to the present day* (Dublin, 1984), pp. 75–95.

question of the 'surplus' Irish population afresh.[23] By questioning Ricardo's law of diminishing returns, these writers suggested the possibility of the development of agricultural resources and productivity in Ireland at a rate greater than that of the increase of population. This partial optimism about the prospects of Ireland as an agricultural producer and exporter reflected a modest revival in corn production by the early 1830s, but the economists believed this improvement would be stifled in the absence of any structural change.[24] Capital investment in land was for them a high priority, and required guarantees of security for freedom of outlay and certainty of return. To be successful, a re-organization of landholding sweeping away the cottier system remained essential, for they were convinced that only large-scale capitalist farming could be efficient. Greater productivity would provide increased and more regular employment for labour, and the advantages of higher expectations and greater consumption of goods would be made possible by the replacement of subsistence cropping by cash wages.[25]

The anglicization of Irish society and the agricultural economy was central to the vision of the classical economists. What they intended was not the extension to Ireland of all existing English institutions – Senior attacked the 'blind imitation . . . and enforcement of British legislation by a mere spirit of system'[26] – but the replication of those conditions which had permitted England to progress and thus to improve the condition of her own working population. The core of anglicization lay in the extension to Ireland of the tripartite division of labour between landlord, capitalist tenant farmer, and landless wage-labourer. This was the shared aim of all orthodox economic writers, and divisions existed only over the best mode of implementing this structure and of guaranteeing the inflow of capital that would make the system work. Criticism was directed at all those elements of Irish society which stood in the way of this progress, including landlords who failed to grasp the nettle of improvement.[27]

The prescriptions of the classical economists struck a chord with many 'improving' Irish landlords in the post-war period who sought greater control over their estates amid adverse economic conditions. Arguments critical of the middleman class which had emerged in the eighteenth century, and for measures to control or reverse population growth, were persuasive to many landowners for practical reasons as much as any desire to submit to protective English ideologies.[28] Less

---

23 Black, *Economic thought*, pp. 134–40.

24 D.P. O'Brien, *The classical economists* (Oxford, 1975), p. 48. For Senior's more optimistic view as to the possibilities of social progress, see Himmelfarb, *Idea of poverty*, pp. 157–8.

25 The most effective popularization of this orthodoxy was provided by J.R. McCulloch, 'Cottage system', *Encyclopedia Britannica Supplement* (Edinburgh, 1824), III, 378–9.

26 [Nassau W. Senior], 'Proposals for extending the Irish Poor Law', *Edinburgh Review*, LXXXIV (Oct. 1846), 267–8.

27 Black, *Economic thought*, pp. 20–4.

28 Donnelly, *Land and people*, pp. 52–63; MacDonagh, *States of mind*, p. 38.

optimistic than the economists about the prospects of 'high farming' (mixed agriculture utilizing capital-intensive techniques), many landowners began to look to a restoration of tilled land to pasture to take advantage of improving export prices for livestock. The removal of middlemen tenants when their long leases fell in and the 'clearance' of the cottier sub-tenants who had occupied the land in the interim thus appeared economically desirable. The concerns of landowners and economists were reflected in an act of 1826 which prohibited the subletting of a property by a lessee, and in other measures facilitating consolidation. The Subletting Act failed to solve the essential problem, however, as in many areas consolidation was met with the threat or reality of agrarian violence from those facing eviction. Official inquiries suggest that consolidation was limited in extent before the 1840s, and that the proportion of land under crops may even have increased to the 1830s.[29] The limits of voluntary action to alleviate the problems of Ireland, as perceived in orthodox terms, had become clear by the late 1820s.

Pure *laissez-faire* was never the classical prescription for Ireland. There was a consensus that the country could not be expected to follow the English path to development without assistance. The problem lay in finding ways of stimulating the apparently underdeveloped economy which would not contribute to the causes of stagnation. Education appeared one function suited to the state, and had been advocated by Adam Smith and Malthus. Nassau Senior identified the state of Irish society in 1843 as one representing 'proof of the grossest IGNORANCE', expressed in the people's systematic opposition to law and apparent incompetence in their daily occupations.[30] A national system of education was desirable to teach the masses not only literacy, but also the rationality of the rule of British law, the basics of political economy and useful practical skills in equal measure.

The acceptable extent of public works programmes as a means of promoting development was a matter of greater contention. Adam Smith had endorsed the undertaking by government of large-scale works that were beyond the capacities of individual entrepreneurs, but had stressed that such projects be profitable and that the outlay be repaid over time. Most classical economists followed him in this basic premise, but the application to Ireland was problematic.[31] Commentators agreed that any grant of funds from imperial resources for Irish public works would have to be accompanied by strict supervision and tight fiscal discipline, particularly as the county grand juries of leading landowners (the main organs of local government in the countryside) had acquired a reputation in Britain for irresponsibility and wastefulness. Nevertheless, in the 1830s, public works schemes organized by the state-controlled Irish Board of Works became the favoured transitional aid. In 1831 Senior recommended advances for building roads, canals, railways and harbours,

29 Ó Gráda, *Ireland: a new economic history*, pp. 117–18.

30 Nassau W. Senior, 'Ireland in 1843', *Journals, conversations and essays relating to Ireland* (2 vols., London, 1868), I, 45–6.

31 Black, *Economic thought*, pp. 159–68.

as well as assistance to landlords in drainage and waste-land reclamation.[32] Archbishop Whately's Poor Inquiry Commission of 1834–6 came to the similar conclusion that remunerative public works, if combined with government-sponsored emigration schemes, could make a reversal in Ireland's fortunes possible.[33]

The unavoidable fact of widespread poverty provoked frequent debates on the desirability of a poor law. Senior strongly opposed the extension to Ireland of the English Poor Law, believing that even in its reformed 1834 form it would be disastrous for the country, and could not assist in the process of transition to a fully capitalized agrarian society. While accepting the safety of legal provision for the sick and insane, he rejected it for the able-bodied and the old, on the grounds that that the extreme poverty of the Irish countryside rendered the workhouse test of 'less-eligibility' inapplicable.[34]

The majority of orthodox economists initially agreed with this view, but some became persuaded that a strict administration of the test of incarceration in the workhouse would have the desired effect on a people notorious for their love of personal liberty. This case was put most cogently by George Cornewall Lewis in 1836. Senior and Lewis disagreed over tactics rather than ultimate objectives. Both identified the real obstacles to the process of socio-economic re-organization in Ireland as lying in the resistance of strong elements in Irish society to change, and in the insecurity resulting from agrarian and political unrest. Lewis condemned landlord rackrenting as a contributory factor in popular disturbances, but traced the root of the problem to the poverty and lack of employment caused by the cottier system. Outrage perpetuated the vicious circle of under-employment and under-capitalization in the countryside; the only solution lay in speeding the transition from peasant to proletarian by means of a poor law.[35]

Senior was also well aware of the difficulty of enforcing social change on a recalcitrant population, but looked instead to the Catholic clergy as agents of social control in the countryside. The clergy had been the vital mobilizing force in O'Connell's emancipation campaign in the 1820s, and in the following decades threatened to extend their support *en masse* to the politically destabilizing Repeal campaigns. If the clergy could be neutralized, or converted into the agents of social order, preaching submission to the law and the sanctity of property rights, their flocks would surely follow. He suggested the appropriation of the 'excessive'

---

32 Nassau W. Senior, *A letter to Lord Howick on a legal provision for the Irish poor; commutation of tithes, and a provision for the Irish Roman Catholic clergy* (London, 1831), pp. 45–6.

33 *Third report of the Commission for inquiring into the condition of the poorer classes in Ireland*, P.P. 1836 [43], XXX, 1.

34 Senior, *Letter to Lord Howick*, pp. 11–54; *Letter from Nassau W. Senior, esq., to Her Majesty's principal Secretary of State for the Home Department, on the third report from the Commissioners for inquiring into the condition of the poor in Ireland. Dated April 14th 1836*, P.P. 1837 (90), LI, 241.

35 Lewis, *On local disturbances*, pp. 45–92, 318–38.

endowments of the established Church of Ireland as the most expedient fund for providing for the Catholic priests. Endowment was defensible on the grounds of utility and the national interest: 'Troops are more expensive than priests . . . We are not proposing a new expenditure . . . the Catholic priests exist, and are paid. We propose that their payment should be borne by the whole nation, which would scarcely feel it, instead of falling exclusively on a portion, and that the very poorest portion of the community, whom it demoralizes and crushes.'[36] Senior would bring these propositions before the Whig-Liberal governments of the 1830s and 1840s as the resident ideologist of the Bowood circle.[37]

Orthodox economists also devoted serious attention to the possibility of large-scale assisted emigration from Ireland. While reluctant to declare Ireland excessively over-populated in regard to its potential resources, most believed some emigration desirable as a transitional aid. However, divisions were particularly sharp over the optimum mode of state intervention. Senior was wary of advocating an extensive state mechanism, and Whately, while much more favourable to this in his 1836 report, was vague as to details. Part of the problem lay in the existence of a long-running controversy over the issue of colonization.

R.J. Wilmot Horton had in the 1820s advocated the settlement of large numbers of British and Irish paupers – a 'redundant population' at home – as pioneering yeomen in Canada. Horton failed to translate his scheme into legislation, and in the 1830s was countered by the more vigorously propagandist 'systematic colonization' plans of Edward Gibbon Wakefield. Whereas Malthus was hostile towards both schemes on the grounds that the 'vacuum' created by emigration would soon be filled, Senior was more sympathetic towards the principle. Yet the arrogant self-assurance with which the Wakefieldians dismissed alternative schemes and defended their own allegedly self-financing proposals led many to withhold complete adherence.[38] Robert Torrens was one of the few leading economists to give whole-hearted support to Wakefield, and became a consistent advocate of colonization to create a 'New Erin' on the settlement frontier of the empire.[39] By the early 1840s, however, 'systematic colonization' was still at an experimental stage, and its advocates were concerned more with establishing viable British settlement colonies in the antipodes than resolving the problems of Ireland.

The heterodox challenge to economic orthodoxy evolved partially out of the classical tradition. William Thomas Thornton retained an essentially Malthusian

---

36 Senior, *Letter to Lord Howick*, pp. 54–80. Nassau W. Senior, *On national property and on the prospects of the present administration and of their successors* (2nd edn, London, 1835), pp. 117–18.

37 See below, pp. 22–4.

38 R.N. Ghosh, 'The colonization controversy: R.J. Wilmot-Horton and the classical economists', *Economica*, n.s. XXXI (1964), 375–400; R.N. Ghosh, 'Malthus on emigration and colonization: letters to Wilmot-Horton', idem, n.s. XXX (1963), 45–62.

39 Robert Torrens, *Systematic colonization: Ireland saved, without cost to the imperial Treasury* (2nd edn, London, 1849).

concern about over-population and an insistence on the deterrent powers of the reformed English Poor Law,[40] while John Stuart Mill was as vehement as Senior in his opposition to an extensive Irish poor law.[41] George Poulett Scrope, on the other hand, drew more on the popular-radical tradition; he was resolutely anti-Malthusian and defended the old Poor Law in England while calling for a more comprehensive one for Ireland.[42] What united these writers, despite their differences over poor relief, was their rejection of the orthodox insistence that the tripartite agrarian division of labour in the context of large capitalized farms was the only means of facilitating economic growth and of averting stagnation and potential catastrophe. Drawing on the pioneering anti-Ricardian work of Richard Jones, and on the writings of continental commentators, Thornton and Mill overturned the theory of the unproductivity of peasant smallholdings by pointing to examples of prosperous and demographically stable peasant communities in continental Europe, and advocating 'the magic of property' as the best incentive to self-exertion and improvement.[43]

Thornton's and Mill's work on Ireland became well known only from the mid-1840s and had no influence on policy before the Famine,[44] but the radical MP Poulett Scope's more populist and less theoretical arguments became well known through a series of treatises and pamphlets published from the early 1830s. He rejected the doctrine of diminishing returns as empirically refutable, and denounced the Malthusian law of population as 'that most pernicious dogma which has long been palmed upon the public as the most fundamental axiom of political economy'. An admirer of the Elizabethan Poor Law and advocate of 'welfare economics', Scrope also came to adopt a relativist and historicist approach.[45]

Scrope's advocacy of the principle of smallholdings in Ireland was at first implied rather than stated; in his robustly argued 1834 polemic *How is Ireland to be governed?* he adopted a stance at first sight similar to Lewis's of 1836, stressing the agrarian nature of violence and unrest in Ireland, and arguing that an extensive poor law would undermine the activities of the secret societies. It is clear, however, that Scrope did not intend to advocate an increase in clearances facilitated by the introduction

40 William Thomas Thornton, *Over-population and its remedy: or, an inquiry into the extent and causes of distress prevailing among the labouring classes of the British islands, and into the means of remedying it* (London, 1846), pp. 1–6, 267–86.

41 [John Stuart Mill], 'The proposed Irish poor law', *Morning Chronicle*, 17, 19 March 1847.

42 Black, *Economic thought*, pp. 96–7.

43 Clive J. Dewey, 'The rehabilitation of the peasant proprietor in nineteenth-century economic thought', *History of Political Economy*, VI (1974), 17–47.

44 Mill had made his first forays into the Irish land question in the 1820s, criticizing landlord rhetoric and the 1826 subletting act, but made no extended comment on the subject until 1846, see [J.S. Mill], 'Ireland', *Parliamentary History and Review*, II (1827), pp. 600–2. For a detailed account of the development of Mill's thinking about Ireland, see David Martin, *John Stuart Mill and the land question* (Hull, 1981), pp. 7–24.

45 Samuel Hollander, *The economics of John Stuart Mill* (2 vols., Oxford, 1985), I, 52–3; Redvers Opie, 'A neglected English economist: George Poulett Scrope', *Quarterly Journal of Economics*, XLIV (1929), 101–37.

of a poor law. If, he maintained, 'God gave the land of Ireland to the people – to the many – but law had given it *unconditionally* to the few', then the land law should be changed to place conditions on those landowning few – the state should act to curtail rack-rents, coerce landlords into providing greater employment by the threat of a large poor-rate, and use the new structures to engage in large scale public works to provide employment and increase the productive powers of the country.[46] The postscript added in early 1846 was more explicit: the 1838 Poor Law had failed because of its inadequacy (it merely '*pretends* to be a Poor Law'), but even if it was extended, large ancillary measures would also be required, including the reclamation of the Irish waste lands. He defended the viability of small farms (of around ten acres in extent), and advocated the legalization of tenant right on all other existing farms.[47]

Scrope adopted a perspective on Irish matters similar to such diverse figures as Bishop James Doyle of Kildare and the Ulster radical William Sharman Crawford.[48] Crawford's opinions on the land question had a considerable influence on Scrope, and the two men also shared similar perspectives on the English Poor Law and the general problem of unemployment. Both were hostile to the workhouse system, and Crawford advocated the granting of small plots (of five to six acres) to agricultural and industrial labourers in both countries. The object of political economy, he argued, should be to 'decrease as far as possible the proportion of the population dependent upon hired labour'.[49]

Recent work by Boyd Hilton, Peter Mandler and others has revealed that the relationship between classical political economy and the policy actually implemented was more complex than some historians have assumed. With the professionalization and secularization of political economy under Ricardo and his followers, the forms of economic thought holding sway among the ruling classes, though drawing on the language of the classical writers (particularly Adam Smith), were in large part inspired by different intellectual strands. Perhaps the most significant group influencing policy making in this period were the 'Christian economists'.[50]

Centred in the English and Scottish universities, churchmen such as Thomas Chalmers, J.B. Sumner and Edward Copleston had a deep influence on the upper echelons of a British society saturated by evangelical Protestantism. Concerned more with the moral nature of economic laws – and with adapting the moral

46 George Poulett Scrope, *How is Ireland to be governed?: a question addressed to the new administration of Lord Melbourne in 1834* (2nd edn, London, 1846), pp. 8–10, 26–8, 34–9.

47 Ibid., pp. 40–66.

48 See below, pp. 32, 49–50.

49 William Sharman Crawford, *A defence of the small farmers of Ireland* (Dublin, 1839), pp. 30–48.

50 Boyd Hilton, *The age of atonement: the influence of evangelicalism on social and economic thought, 1795–1865* (Oxford, 1988), pp. 36–70. See also A.M.C. Waterman, *Revolution, economics and religion: Christian political economy 1798–1833* (Cambridge, 1991), pp. 1–14.

philosophy of Smith's economics to a Malthusian world – Christian economists encouraged government to remove all restrictions on economic life so as to reveal the operation of the natural moral law, rather than to stimulate economic growth. There were varieties and degrees within the world of Christian economics, but Hilton has argued that the dominant strand stressed the static and cyclical, retributive and purgative world view of 'moderate' or Claphamite evangelicalism, and looked to competition as a means to moral education, and to the mechanisms of the free market to nurture the economic conscience.[51] Relying on a providentialist theory which held that the divine will usually operated 'generally' through the natural laws of cause and effect (as opposed to the pre-millenarian evangelical view of direct paternalist intervention), this doctrine appealed most strongly to the 'moderate evangelical' liberal Tories such as Peel and Goulburn promoted by Lord Liverpool in the 1820s.[52] It is difficult to identify the direct effect of Christian economics on policy decisions in the early nineteenth century, as their prescriptions frequently mirrored those of the classical economists and Benthamites (although arrived at from different premises), but Peter Mandler has advanced a convincing case for the effectiveness of evangelical thinking in the making of the new English Poor Law of 1834.[53]

Some Christian economists were less conservative in their views than Thomas Chalmers and his followers. Richard Whately, an important political economist in his own right, tutored Nassau Senior at Oxford and shared many of his student's economic doctrines.[54] While not an evangelical in theology and favouring a complacent economic optimism over Malthusian pessimism, his priorities were, however, somewhat different to Senior's, being primarily to disseminate orthodox political economy in a morally didactic form. Whately used his position as Anglican Archbishop of Dublin from 1831 to crusade for the conversion of Ireland to true economic doctrine, in the belief that such an ideological assimilation would promote Irish development.[55] Yet increasingly he found himself the defender of

---

51 Hilton, *Age of atonement*, pp. 69–70.

52 Ibid., pp. 13–15, 218–236.

53 Peter Mandler, 'The making of the new Poor Law *redivivus*', *Past and Present*, 117 (1987), 131–57; 'Tories and paupers: Christian political economy and the making of the new Poor Law', *Historical Journal*, XXXIII (1990), 81–101.

54 Brent has identified a Whatelian 'Oxford school' of economists who drew optimistic economic conclusions from their belief in the self-regulating dispensations of a benign Providence, Richard Brent, 'God's Providence: liberal political economy as natural theology at Oxford 1825–1862', in Michael Bentley (ed.), *Public and private doctrine* (Cambridge, 1993), pp. 85–107.

55 Thomas A. Boylan and Timothy P. Foley, *Political economy and colonial Ireland: the propagation and ideological function of economic discourse in the nineteenth century* (London, 1992), pp. 2–6, 124–30; D.H. Akenson, *A Protestant in purgatory: Richard Whately, Archbishop of Dublin* (Hamden, CT, 1981), pp. 18–19, 54–76; J.M. Goldstrom, 'Richard Whately and political economy in school books 1833–80', *Irish Historical Studies*, XV (1966–7), 131–46.

orthodoxy and the interests of Irish property against what he believed to be dangerous deviations in government policy.[56]

Hilton has argued that those most resistant to the various forms of Christian political economy widespread in the broadly evangelical cultural environment of early nineteenth-century Britain were groups with an alternative conception of time, including those with a Whiggish perception of history or a radical-utopian confidence in future progress. Yet there were many ideological tendencies contained within the broad Whig-Liberal coalition. Some leading figures, such as the third Marquess of Lansdowne, were deeply attracted by the secular tenets of Ricardianism. Other Whig-Liberals such as Lord Monteagle appear to have held orthodox economic opinions more from Whateleian than from Ricardian premises. The Whig-Liberals also had a number of prominent evangelicals in their ranks, and their response to economic questions seems to have been complex. Certainly an evangelical providentialism played a large part in determining the 'moralist' response to the famine crisis in the 1840s and was strongly in evidence in the words and actions of Charles Trevelyan, Charles Wood and Sir George Grey.

Beneath the political elite, in the ranks of the increasingly politicized middle classes in the 1830s and 1840s, economic ideas took different forms. Christian economics had a powerful influence on many, and was disseminated by the clergy of several denominations. Optimistic approaches – based on classical economy and disseminated by such heavyweight journals as the *Edinburgh Review* – also became widespread among the middle classes, if in an increasingly radicalized form. The *Edinburgh* itself promoted the popularization of economic doctrines stressing the desirability of the progress of commercial society, economic expansion and the pursuit of individual liberty, at the cost of classical intellectual rigour.[57]

The economic ideas of the 'Manchester School' of the 1840s diverged from orthodoxy in both objectives and tone – and were as much motivated by moral feelings as by calculations of middle-class economic self-interest.[58] Radical politics combined with a stridently commercial and industrial ideology to produce uncompromising hostility not only to the Corn Laws, but to the existing land system (in both Britain and Ireland) – and in particular to the laws of primogeniture. A moral antagonism to the perception of entrenched landed power lay behind the adoption of the politics of 'free trade in land' by the Manchester school radicals in the later 1840s.[59] This class hostility was quite alien to orthodox writers, whose connections with 'progressive' landowners were often close. The economic ideas of these middle-class radicals, as manifested in their burgeoning parliamentary

---

56 Whately to Lady Osborne, n.d. (1843?), E. Jane Whately (ed.), *Life and correspondence of Richard Whately, late Archbishop of Dublin* (2 vols., London, 1866), II, 47–8.

57 Biancamaria Fontana, *Rethinking the politics of commercial society: the Edinburgh Review 1802–1832* (Cambridge, 1985), pp. 183–5.

58 William D. Grampp, *The Manchester school of economics* (Stanford, CA, 1960), pp. 1–5, 16–38.

59 F.M.L. Thompson, 'Land and politics in England in the nineteenth century', *Transactions of the Royal Historical Society*, 5th series, XV (1965), 23–44.

presence in the mid- and late-1840s, were to be of considerable significance during the Famine.

III VARIETIES OF WHIGGISM: FOXITES, MODERATES AND MORALISTS

As a survey of the politics of Irish land and famine relief in the 1840s, this study focuses primarily on the Westminster political elite and its policy advisers. Within that elite a plurality of political attitudes can be identified, making it necessary to analyze decision-making in terms of the ideological and factional divisions between and within the political parties. Consequently, much attention has been given to the competing perceptions, interpretations and prescriptions current in governing circles.

The system within which Irish policy was made was, however, never closed. There was a widespread popular perception in Britain that the conditions responsible for the widespread agrarian disorder that threatened property and the social hierarchy, and the political agitation that potentially endangered the security of the empire, should receive an urgent response. The dialogue between the classical formulae advanced for Irish reform and reconstruction and the intractable realities of Irish conditions has been dissected by a number of historians. What has attracted less attention is the responsiveness to certain forms of 'public opinion' that was part of the political self-definition of several high-political groupings. This openness to popular grievances and aspirations was regulated in each case by attitudes to the legitimate limits of state action and the constraints imposed by the strength of other systems of ideas, but the changing political circumstances of the decade placed a premium on responding to mobilized outdoor opinion in both Ireland and Great Britain. The relationships between members of the governing elite and outdoor agitations were complex and variable, but the making of Irish policy in this period is incomprehensible without some understanding of their dynamics and development.

As the internal politics of the Whig-Liberal Party must play a considerable part in this account, some attempt must be made to provide an analytical taxonomy. The historiography of early nineteenth-century Whiggery has in recent years seen something of a renaissance. Perhaps the most important work on this subject is Peter Mandler's *Aristocratic government in the age of reform*, a book which seeks to identify a vibrant and confident Whig ideology at work in the 1830s and 1840s, and to 'tease apart' that aristocratic and reformist creed from the emerging ideology of liberalism. In rejecting what has become the orthodoxy of the Whigs as 'trimmers', manoeuvring between radicals and Conservatives and doomed to be eclipsed by a united Liberalism in the 1850s,[60] Mandler argues for a distinctively Whig political style and substance, especially in the fields of political and social reform.[61]

---

60 See, for example, Norman Gash, *Reaction and reconstruction in English politics, 1832–1852* (Oxford, 1965), pp. 186–9, 199–200; F.A. Dreyer, 'The Russell administration, 1846–1852', (unpublished Ph. D. thesis, University of St Andrews, 1962).

61 Peter Mandler, *Aristocratic government in the age of reform: Whigs and Liberals 1830–1852* (Oxford, 1990), pp. 6–8.

Mandler's taxonomy of Whig-Liberal groupings has been employed, in modified form, in the present study, having been found to be particularly applicable to the politics of Ireland in the 1840s. Two of the three major categories employed here for party factions, the 'Foxites' or 'true Whigs', and the 'moderate liberals', follow Mandler's usage. However, it has been necessary to employ a third category, that of the liberal 'moralists', to describe the ideological tendencies of the group centred on the third Earl Grey in the 1840s.[62]

Factions served several functions, as extended connections promoting the interests of families or individuals, as well as interest groups pursuing shared policy objectives. It should also be stressed that there was not always a sharp edge of division between the Whig-Liberal party factions, which overlapped to some degree in programme and personnel. Political necessity dictated that the Whig-Liberals in the 1830s and 1840s remain a broad church defined by shared opposition to Toryism, suspicion of radicalism and advocacy of reform. Nevertheless, strong differences over aims and governing style were evident to contemporaries. These divisions were not absolute – some individuals maintained an ambiguous position between groups, and there was some fluctuation of allegiances over time – but they represent distinct tendencies which were frequently identifiable over such issues as Irish land and social policy.

The 'Foxite' Whigs of the 1830s–40s inherited and redefined the 'true Whig' tradition of the later eighteenth century which had been focused on the personality and career of Charles James Fox. Their political style was founded on a sense of the cultural distinctiveness of the Whig aristocracy as the trustees of popular rights and liberties in parliament. Metropolitan and cosmopolitan by social orientation, these self-conscious heirs of Fox legitimized their political stance by appealing to a powerful Whig mythology that was strongly reinforced by the Party's virtually total exclusion from power between 1784 and 1830.[63] Enemies to both royal despotism and to riotous democracy, they felt themselves elevated above mere class interest as landowners by their separation from the actual management of their estates and by their self-identification as the representatives of the popular interest.[64]

---

62 R.J. Montague, in an excellent but unpublished dissertation on the politics of the Great Famine, proposes a dichotomy of 'environmentalist' and 'moralist' responses to the Irish crisis. While the latter categorization in particular is useful, Montague's thesis is limited by too heavy a reliance on classical writings and a neglect of the importance of partisan traditions, R.J. Montague, 'Relief and reconstruction in Ireland, 1845–1849: a study in public policy during the Great Famine' (unpublished D. Phil. thesis, University of Oxford, 1976).

63 Austin Mitchell, *The Whigs in opposition 1815–30* (Oxford, 1967), pp. 4–14.

64 Mandler, *Aristocratic government*, pp. 13–22. Mandler describes the rise in the late eighteenth and early nineteenth century of a landed gentry class in Britain increasingly drawn to liberal commercial ideas. The 'professionalization' of estate management and the associated attitudes towards landholding and rural society typical of this interest could be rejected by those elements of the older aristocracy who were more insulated from agricultural fluctuations by their great wealth or who chose to abandon the management of their estates to stewards and agents, and by those heirs and younger sons who devoted themselves to political careers.

Mandler follows Leslie Mitchell in identifying Fox's nephew, the third Baron Holland, as the heir to his uncle's political tradition, and in regarding the Holland House salon as the centre of Foxite Whiggery from 1807 to 1840.[65] Holland was no orator and lacked a taste for political power; his achievement lay in conditioning and nurturing a new generation of Whig politicians as his protégés in the Foxite tradition, at a time when Party fortunes were low and many of the younger members of the Whig aristocracy were defecting to other political groupings.

The political code of Holland House is described by Mitchell as a commitment to government for 'the people' – who should be adequately represented in parliament (although not by a democratic franchise) – with governing initiative being exercised by the whig aristocracy on their behalf. Whigs were thus obliged to heed the voice of 'the people' when this was expressed in a constitutional form. They pursued 'balance', encouraged and patronized political ability, and promoted 'party' as a necessary counterweight to the politics of class and faction. Foxites were committed to opposing Toryism at every opportunity, and promoting a series of reforms including the elimination of electoral corruption, the extension of the parliamentary franchise, the restraint of executive power and the protection of civil rights, the abolition of slavery, and the granting of full equality of rights to Dissenters and Catholics.

Of Holland's protégés the first and most important was Lord John Russell, second son of Fox's colleague, the sixth Duke of Bedford. Russell acquired from Holland the political code that was to carry him through his long political life, along with the confidence and sense of purpose that was to make him leader of the Party and defender of its distinctive role in the 1840s.[66] As an essayist and historian also, Russell set about refurbishing the Whig tradition, idealizing Fox and his Whig forbears as upholders of popular liberties. Implicit in the 'Foxite' position was a criticism of the less inspirational leadership of the Party after 1806; indeed, for Russell in 1810, Holland was 'the only true Whig in England'.[67] Party, in Russell's opinion, remained the chief guarantor of political morality in Britain.[68]

Holland's other pupils came both from within and from outside the traditional circles of grand Whiggery. Viscount Duncannon, a scion of the Ponsonby clan of Irish Whigs, was cousin to the Duke of Devonshire and heir to the Kilkenny and Carlow estates of his father, the third Earl of Bessborough. An MP from 1805 to 1834 (initially for a Devonshire pocket borough), he emerged in collaboration with his mentor Holland as the Party's most effective indoor organizer and manager, preferring regular activity at Westminster in and out of season to tending his Irish

65 L.G. Mitchell, *Holland House* (London, 1980), pp. 39–59.

66 Ibid., pp. 27–8; John Prest, *Lord John Russell* (London, 1972), pp. 8–17.

67 Richard Brent, *Liberal Anglican politics: Whiggery, religion and reform 1830–1841* (Oxford, 1987), pp. 42–3.

68 Lord John Russell (ed.), *Correspondence of John, fourth Duke of Bedford* (3 vols., London, 1842–6), III, lxii.

estates.[69] He was an energetic Whig-Liberal chief whip 1816–30, using the position to inject fresh life into a nearly moribund Party.[70] His fellow Foxite, Viscount Ebrington (heir to Earl Fortescue), had, on the other hand, started his political career under Tory patronage before espousing parliamentary reform and constitutional Whiggism in 1817, and coming under the political mantle of Holland and Bedford. Likewise Viscount Normanby (later Earl of Mulgrave and Marquess of Normanby) found his inherited Tory connections uncongenial. In 1821 he joined Russell in promoting an ambitious scheme of parliamentary reform and moved to a Whig borough seat. In the 1820s and 1830s these four came to form a coherent leadership group under Holland's guidance.[71] Other individuals were added to the Foxite stable in the 1820s, the most important being Viscount Morpeth, heir to the Earl of Carlisle.[72]

Imposing a taxonomy on a political system in which political identities were implicitly recognized rather than explicitly articulated inevitably gives rise to numerous problems, but is unavoidable if the political dynamics of the period are to be uncovered. I have followed Mandler in applying the apparently anachronistic term 'Foxite' to describe the Russell group, as much of their political mentality was shaped by the agenda and outlook inherited from Fox as mediated (and no doubt sanitized) by Holland. Consequently, Richard Brent's use of this term to denote only the older generation of Whig religious sceptics, including Lansdowne along with Holland and the second Earl Grey, has been rejected. While it is clear that the evolution of 'liberal Anglican' religious beliefs by Russell and others of his generation, as described by Brent, did have a significant impact on their political principles, it seems equally clear that such religious opinions were of limited importance regarding matters other than ecclesiastical policy, and that cross-generational links (between Holland and Russell in particular) were often stronger than a shared 'liberal Anglicanism'.[73]

These men formed the core of the Foxite Whig group who, under the parliamentary leadership of Russell in the 1830s and 1840s, sought to preserve the inherited

69 Mandler, *Aristocratic government*, pp. 59, 62–3. Duncannon nevertheless acquired a reputation in Ireland as an indulgent and popular landlord.

70 Mitchell, *Whigs in opposition*, pp. 38–9.

71 For the enthusiastic participation of Duncannon, Normanby and Ebrington in party organization in the 1830s, see Ian Newbould, 'Whiggery and the growth of party, 1830–1841: organization and the challenge of reform', *Parliamentary History*, IV (1985), 137–56. Despite his presentation of evidence to the contrary, Newbould concludes that 'Whiggism was a creed whose Foxite cause . . . looked back to an earlier age' in terms of organization and popular appeal.

72 Mandler, *Aristocratic government*, pp. 59–61, 63.

73 Brent, *Liberal Anglican politics*, pp. 40–64; Mandler, *Aristocratic government*, p. 59. As Hilton has indicated, a number of Mandler's 'Foxites', such as Ebrington, William Cowper and to some degree Morpeth, were drawn to a form of pre-millenarian evangelicalism, Boyd Hilton, 'Whiggery, religion and social reform: the case of Lord Morpeth', *Historical Journal*, XXXVII (1994), 829–59.

values of Whiggery and anti-Toryism within the wider Whig-Liberal Party. Foxites remained hostile to Peelite liberal Toryism, and generally resistant to the idea of coalition or liberal convergence.[74] For Russell, adherence to an inherited party identity was essential to political morality; 'the true party-man', he wrote in 1823, 'finds in his own mind certain general rules of politics, like the general rules of morals, by which he decides every new and doubtful case. The belief that those principles are just, enables him to withstand the seductions of interest, and the ingenuity of projects: his conduct acquires somewhat of the firmness of integrity and wisdom.'[75]

Ireland had a special place in the Foxite political credo. Edmund Burke's polemics in favour of the removal of the penal laws had entered the rhetoric of Rockinghamite Whiggery from the 1760s, and links had been forged with Grattan and the Irish 'patriot' party in the 1770s. The connection between Irish liberties and Whiggism appeared further strengthened by Fox and Grattan's co-operation in the granting of 'legislative independence' to the Irish parliament in 1782. This event entered Whig mythology as a great peaceful revolution against executive tyranny carried in response to manifested popular opinion. Its failure to resolve the developing Catholic question was attributed to the intolerance and corruption of the Protestant ascendancy, whose misgovernment and cruelty provoked the bloody insurrection of 1798.[76]

Fox's lieutenant (and future Party leader), Charles Grey, vigorously opposed the Union Bills of 1799 and 1800 on the grounds that any Union based on coercion and bribery, and which failed to grant religious liberty, could not win the support of the Irish people.[77] Foxites subsequently came to accept the Union as a positive institution only on the condition that Catholic emancipation be implemented. Holland had opposed the coercion of Ireland in 1798, and came to regard the Catholic question as the personal political property of the Foxite connection.[78] The Catholic question dominated British politics at the time when Holland's protégés were finding their parliamentary feet. Taught to see the question as one founded on first principles of religious and civil liberty, they were led to draw conclusions about Pittite duplicity and the futility of coercion that were to prove

74 See, for example, Normanby's delight at what he took to be a 'general rout' of the Peelites in the 1847 general election, Normanby to Russell, 29 July 1847, Russell Papers, Public Record Office, London, PRO 30/22/6D, fols. 236–7.

75 John, Earl Russell, *An essay on the history of the English government and constitution from the reign of Henry VII to the present time* (new edn, London, 1865) pp. 150–1.

76 Lord John Russell (ed.), *Memorials and correspondence of Charles James Fox* (4 vols., London, 1853–7), I, 430–1, 471; John, Earl Russell, *Recollections and suggestions 1813–1873* (London, 1875), pp. 335–40; *Hansard's Parliamentary Debates*, 3rd series, LXX, 1011, [11 July 1843: Russell]. Russell exaggerated Fox's commitment to Irish reform, see L.G. Mitchell, *Charles James Fox* (Oxford, 1992), pp. 250–2.

77 E.A. Smith, *Lord Grey 1764–1845* (Oxford, 1990), pp. 72–6.

78 Mitchell, *Holland House*, pp. 110–4.

long-lasting. As a young man Russell had experienced the matter at first hand, when in 1806 his father became Lord Lieutenant of Ireland in the 'All Talents' ministry. Bedford's pressing of the Catholic question (in response to insistent Irish petitions) against intolerant royal opposition led to the government's collapse and the return of Ireland to 'that monopolizing ministry, who, by intolerance, corruption and oppression, kept her in miserable subjugation'.[79] The manner in which Catholic emancipation was ultimately attained in 1829 – reluctantly and ungraciously out of fear of rebellion – was regularly referred to by Foxite Whigs as the model for how not to govern Ireland, and as evidence of the impossibility of a just and satisfactory Tory administration of that country.[80] Ireland was more of more than theoretical interest to the Foxites; the intimate friendship between Duncannon and Daniel O'Connell drew the faction into active participation in the struggle over Irish policy in the 1830s.[81]

The second major section of the Whig-Liberal Party were the 'moderate liberals'. The core of moderate liberalism within the Party was the circle attracted by the third Marquess of Lansdowne as the heir of the Shelburnite or non-Foxite tradition of Whiggery, which emphasized commercial and financial reform along the lines prescribed by orthodox political economy. In marked contrast to Holland House, Lansdowne's 'Bowood set' of advisers and protégés were more austere in their economic and speculative orientation; Edinburgh Reviewers such as Thomas Spring Rice (later Lord Monteagle), Francis Horner and Nassau Senior were patronized and economic debate welcomed.[82] Spring Rice, a liberal Protestant and 'improving' landowner in County Limerick, was Lansdowne's most important political protégé, serving as his Under-Secretary at the Home Office during the Canning coalition in 1827, and as Secretary to the Treasury 1830–4. Centrist figures in the Party including Lord Auckland and Sir Francis Baring were also drawn under the Lansdowne aegis, as were the next generation of economic liberals such as George Cornewall Lewis and Henry Labouchere.

The 'moderate' core also attracted the 'Young Whigs' Lords Althorp, Milton and Tavistock (heirs respectively to the Spencer, Fitzwilliam and Bedford peerages). Never happy with partisan conflict, these three withdrew from government in the

79 Prest, *Russell*, pp. 8–17; S.J. Connolly, 'The Catholic question, 1801–12', in Vaughan (ed.), *N.H.I., V*, pp. 28–35; Russell, *Recollections*, pp. 22–3.

80 Russell, *Essay on the history of the English government*, pp. xix–xxi; *Annual Register*, LXXXVI (1844), 67.

81 Duncannon 'sincerely rejoiced' at O'Connell's electoral victories in County Clare and gave him the credit for extracting Catholic emancipation, while the Irish leader described Duncannon as 'the most popular person that ever belonged to the party of the Whigs . . . whom everybody esteems and respects . . . [and] to whom the Catholics owe a debt of gratitude and in whose personal qualities everybody places unlimited confidence.' Duncannon to O'Connell, 4 Aug. 1829, O'Connell to Duncannon, 27 Nov. 1831, Maurice R. O'Connell (ed.), *The correspondence of Daniel O'Connell* (8 vols., Dublin, 1972–80), IV, 86, 365.

82 Mandler, *Aristocratic government*, pp. 101–4.

mid-1830s, disappointed that parliamentary reform had not led to an age of enlightened equipoise. They remained influential figures and looked increasingly to Lansdowne as their spokesman in cabinet.[83] Canningite Liberals with an interest in commercial reform such as George Villiers (fourth Earl of Clarendon from 1838) were drawn to Lansdowne in the course of the 1830s. The more sceptical and pragmatic Canningites, Viscounts Melbourne and Palmerston, avoided explicit commitment to any faction, but they too were deeply hostile to radicalism and attracted to orthodox economic ideas, and gravitated towards the moderates. Palmerston himself had studied political economy under Dugald Stewart at Edinburgh, and remained attached to orthodox economics throughout his political life.[84]

Although a considerable bloc within the Whig-Liberal administrations of the 1830s–40s, the 'moderates' were hampered by the lack of political energy exhibited by such senior figures as Lansdowne and Melbourne. They were also undoubtedly weakened by the defection in 1834 of the 'Derby Dilly', the group around Lord Stanley with whom the Lansdownites shared much common ground on economic matters. Without Stanley the moderates lacked a dynamic younger leadership figure to muzzle Russell.

Moderates looked primarily to orthodox classical models for resolving the problems of Ireland. They shared common ground with the other Party factions on the utility of Church reform and Catholic endowment, but stressed the imposition of social control in the unruly Irish countryside rather than winning hearts and minds through pursuing 'justice for Ireland'. Several of their number, including Lansdowne, Monteagle, Palmerston and the Marquess of Clanricarde, were major Irish landowners totally committed to maximizing the productivity of their estates, and impatient with obstacles to such 'improvements'. While critical of Peel's hesitancy over Irish reforms, moderates increasingly favoured a bipartisan approach, and were hostile towards O'Connell and populist politics. Their stance was clearly expressed by Charles Greville, who as Clerk of the Privy Council was ostensibly 'neutral' in politics, but in practice was an intimate of the moderate liberal grandees. Writing to Clarendon in 1844, he denied that the grievances of Ireland were the work of either party, or that the 1835–41 Whig government had made any permanent impact on the state of the country. O'Connell should be confronted rather than conciliated:

> I would much rather have this great question fought out at once, and at all cost and hazard, than let it remain in a constant state of abeyance and recurring danger – a vast recognized power in always ready to be called into action, and is only kept quiet by means no government ought to be reduced to employ . . .

83 Ibid., pp. 87–96. Tavistock (seventh Duke of Bedford from 1839) retained a sense of familial loyalty to his brother Lord John Russell, but differed frequently with him over the tone and content of policy. See, for example, Greville, *Journal*, II, 161 [6 June 1843].

84 Muriel Chamberlain, *Lord Palmerston* (Cardiff, 1987), pp. 15–16.

> You and I (I am sure) look to the great and the permanent consideration, and not to the immediate or the party one.[85]

This represented a fundamentally different attitude towards Irish policy and reflected a distinct underlying diagnosis. Moderates were keen to 'break the [Irish] people in to habits of a less lawless and pernicious character',[86] and lacked the Foxite aversion to the use of coercion for this purpose.

In the 1840s a third, 'moralist', tendency in Whig politics also needs to be taken into consideration. Politically this group centred on the Grey family connection. As the second Earl Grey's heir, Lord Howick was inevitably placed in a position of rivalry to Russell and the Holland House set for the future leadership of the Party from the early 1830s. Charles Wood was Howick's brother-in-law, his father's private secretary in 1830–2, and Howick's closest political associate after the second Earl's retirement in 1834. A usual ally was Sir George Grey (Howick's cousin), and a more regular one Edward Ellice (brother-in-law to the second Earl). Several of the group had strong evangelical beliefs: George Grey was well known for his 'steadfast piety' and belief in the doctrines of atonement; Charles Trevelyan, the moralist Assistant Secretary to the Treasury and partisan Whig, was a devout member of the Clapham sect for whom 'Evangelicalism was the family religion'.[87]

Howick's political career was erratic and inconsistent, and he frequently irritated his colleagues by his behaviour. He tended increasingly towards bidding for the support of middle-class radicals and taking up their economic demands, particularly for free trade and financial retrenchment (although he opposed further political reform or religious voluntarism). His attachment to Whiggery became increasingly attenuated in the 1840s, as his sympathy grew for a 'real liberal Government' that would embrace Peel and Cobden but displace Russell.[88] Bitter personal rivalry with Russell, whom Howick dismissed as a 'little animal engrossed by an inordinate ambition of the most narrow and selfish kind', led to his resignation (with Wood) from the government in 1839 and continuing tensions thereafter.[89] If Howick remained a member of the Whig-Liberal Party throughout his political career, it was from a conviction that party was an evil necessary for the operation of parliamentary government, rather than from any transcendent belief in the Whig tradition.[90]

---

85 Greville to Clarendon, 26 Jan. 1844, Clarendon Deposit, Bodleian Library, Oxford, c.520.

86 Greville to Clarendon, 20 Jan. 1848, ibid., c.521.

87 Mandell Creighton, *Memoir of Sir George Grey, Bart.* (London, 1901), pp. 123–6, 133–7; G.M. Trevelyan, *Sir George Otto Trevelyan: a memoir* (London, 1932), p. 14.

88 Diary of the third Earl Grey, 24 May, 2 June 1846, Grey of Howick Papers, University of Durham. Wood agreed, see Wood to Howick, 7 January 1843, ibid.

89 R. Job, 'The political career of the third Earl Grey' (unpublished M.Litt. thesis, University of Durham, 1959), p. 319.

90 For an analysis of Grey's 1858 essay 'Parliamentary government considered with reference to reform of parliament', see Angus Hawkins, '"Parliamentary Government" and Victorian political parties, *c.*1830–*c.*1880', *English Historical Review*, CIV (1989), 657–61.

Howick took an early interest in Ireland and, along with Wood, became a self-proclaimed 'expert' on Irish affairs. A religious radical concerned more with attacking the established Church in Ireland than with responding to Catholic grievances, he also adopted a distinct stance on Irish economic and social matters that is best described as 'moralist', and which contributed to the contemporary view that Howick had a tendency to push the doctrines of political economy too far.[91] Deeply interested in poor law reform and attracted to the Benthamite idea of using it as a mechanism for enforcing moral improvement, Howick pressed Senior to consider an investigation of the Irish poor law question in 1831 and kept a close and critical interest in the subject thereafter.[92] Howick, Wood, and their associates were eager students of political economy, but preferred more popular forms to the more reserved and cautious tones of Bowood orthodoxy; they were optimists with a genuine belief in the liberating potential of free trade. The moralists' confidence that the Irish wages fund was large enough to allow rapid growth if that society was exposed to moral stimuli, distanced them from many others in the governing class. Something of this optimism is suggested in a letter from Howick to Wood in 1844, in which the former ridiculed the Ricardian theory of diminishing returns, arguing that with sufficient investment and improvement there were virtually no limits to productivity growth (and raised living standards for labourers):

> [P]olitical science is eminently a practical science, and what we want is to know how in the actual state of things the interests of different classes of society are affected. Progressive improvement in agriculture as well as in every other art, I believe to be the law of human society and that it will always go on if not arrested by violence.

What was needed was the creation of conditions (in England by the abolition of the Corn Laws) in which moral imperatives would compel individuals to act in a progressive manner in their own and others' interests.[93]

Wood was more reluctant than his colleague to dispense with the classical doctrine of rent, but he too was concerned to build moral incentives into economic policy.[94] Despite his gentry origins, as MP for the West Riding industrial town of Halifax, Wood became conscious of the increasing redundancy of traditional Whiggery. He was obliged to work in tandem with urban radicals and the Anti-Corn Law League at a local level, and advocated a similar alliance nationally.[95]

---

91 G.H. Francis, *Orators of the age* (London, 1847), pp. 178–81.

92 S. Leon Levy, *Nassau W. Senior, 1790–1864* (Newton Abbot, 1970), p. 74.

93 Howick to Wood, 26 Dec. 1844, Hickleton Papers, Cambridge University Library (microfilm), A4/55/1.

94 Wood to Howick, 14, 22 Dec. 1844, Grey Papers.

95 John Anthony Jowitt, 'Sir Charles Wood (1800–85): a case study in the formation of Liberalism in mid-Victorian England' (unpublished M.Phil. thesis, University of Leeds, 1981), pp. 15–89, 97–8. Howick was MP for the industrial borough of Sunderland 1841–5.

More than any other grouping, the moralists complied with Marx's stereotype of Whigs as 'the aristocratic representatives of the bourgeoisie'.[96]

TAXONOMY OF BRITISH WHIG-LIBERALS[97]

Foxites	*Moralists*	*Moderates*
Earl of Bessborough (*Viscount Duncannon*)	Edward Ellice	Lord Auckland
Earl Fortescue (*Viscount Ebrington*)	Earl Grey (*Viscount Howick*)	Sir Francis Baring
Earl of Minto	Sir George Grey	Duke of Bedford (*Marquess of Tavistock*)
Viscount Morpeth	Thomas Babington Macaulay	Marquess of Clanricarde
Marquess of Normanby (*Earl of Mulgrave*)	Charles Wood	Earl of Clarendon
Lord John Russell	Charles Trevelyan	John Cam Hobhouse (*Lord Broughton*) Earl Fitzwilliam (*Viscount Milton*) Henry Labouchere Marquess of Lansdowne Lord Monteagle Viscount Palmerston

IV THE POLITICS OF 'JUSTICE TO IRELAND', 1830–41

The factional tensions that were so important in the 1840s were already accentuated following the Whigs' return to power in 1830. In the coalition ministry

96 Karl Marx, 'Tories and Whigs', *New York Daily Tribune*, 21 Aug. 1852, cited in Mandler, *Aristocratic government*, p. 2

97 This is solely a rough guide to political orientations in the mid to late 1840s. Several other categories might be employed for members of the 1846–52 administration, such as 'Irish' (Somerville, Redington, Sheil, More O'Ferrall), and 'Radical' (Buller, T.M. Gibson), but all cabinet ministers can be placed into the three main categories.

formed by Earl Grey, the leading ministerial posts went to moderate liberals and former Canningites. Edward Stanley, the young high-churchman from the Party's right, was appointed Chief Secretary for Ireland and set about implementing an Irish policy broadly consistent with classical prescriptions. Neither of his key Irish measures – the establishment of the National Board of Education and the Board of Works (both 1831) – were distinctively Whig in character; Peel had been considering both in the later stages of the Wellington ministry.[98] The connection between orthodox thought and Irish policy was highlighted by the appointment of Richard Whately, former Drummond Professor of Political Economy at Oxford, to the archbishopric of Dublin in 1831, and subsequently to the National Board and to the Poor Inquiry Commission.

Stanley's policy in Ireland was parallel to Melbourne's as Home Secretary in England; both sought to encourage economic growth in the context of greater social discipline. Stanley believed that the repression of both political agitation and the widespread agrarian agitation against tithes in the early 1830s was essential to provide security for the investment of capital. His approach was two-pronged; alleviating social unrest by starting reproductive public works, while at the same time rigorously putting down political agitation. He was delighted at the prospect of cabinet approval for his public works initiative in Ireland, and wrote to Lord Lieutenant Anglesey in 1831: 'If only we can only effect this, we may laugh at O'Connell'.[99] Anglesey's own suggestions for a more popular reform policy were quashed by his assertive Chief Secretary.[100] The law officers of the Wellington administration were retained or promoted, Catholics were passed over for patronage, and coercive legislation was prepared.

The Foxites gained some leverage as several cabinet ministers became aware that O'Connell's 'tail' would be useful in the struggle to pass the Reform Bill, and for this reason Stanley's coercion measures were suspended in 1831–2.[101] However, sporadic attempts to buy off O'Connell, interspersed with Stanley's threats to prosecute him and dissolve his political organization, only further embittered relations between O'Connell and the government and encouraged him to fall back on the rhetoric of Repeal.[102] Despite this harassment, and the disillusionment of finding that the new government lacked the good intentions he had expected in 1829, when he told the Knight of Kerry, 'if I get in I will be a Whig [and] certainly

98 Norman Gash, *Mr Secretary Peel: the life of Sir Robert Peel to 1830* (Harlow, 1985 edn), pp. 511–13, 605–7, 670.

99 Cited in R.B. McDowell, *Public opinion and government policy in Ireland, 1801–1846* (London, 1952), p. 143.

100 A.D. Kriegel, 'The Irish policy of Lord Grey's government', *English Historical Review*, LXXXVI (1971), 29.

101 Virginia Crossman, 'Emergency legislation and agrarian disorder in Ireland, 1821–41', *Irish Historical Studies*, XXVII (1991), 317–21.

102 Oliver MacDonagh, *The emancipist: Daniel O'Connell 1830–1847* (London, 1989), pp. 42–5, 56.

one "des plus prononcés"',[103] O'Connell was still reluctant to break off all communications.

The ascendancy of Stanley, coupled with their own exclusion from major offices in the first years of Grey's administration, was galling to the Foxite group, who found the unmitigated coercion of Stanley's policy particularly offensive.[104] Russell threatened resignation from the government in 1832 in protest at the refusal to adopt a radical solution to the tithe issue, and the insistence on upholding 'a system which I think unjust, leading to an effusion of human blood, and the insecurity of life and property in Ireland'.[105] O'Connell's alienation from the ministry was offset by his continued good relations with his personal friend Duncannon, with whom he worked closely during the Reform Bill crisis.[106] The developing rapport between O'Connell and the Foxites depended not merely on hatred of a common enemy – Stanley – but on some degree of shared attitudes respecting Ireland.[107]

While O'Connell's politics always involved a strong element of Irish nationalist feeling, they were also flexible and creatively ambiguous. His realistic political aim was less a simple repeal of the Union than the achievement of Irish and Catholic political, civil and religious equality within a reformed (and preferably decentralized) British polity – a programme that could be summarized by the phrase 'justice to Ireland'. Precisely what should be encompassed by 'justice' was never fully agreed between the parties, but what differentiated the Foxites from other groups prepared to flirt with killing Repeal with kindness was a degree of acceptance of O'Connell's legitimate position in British and Irish political life, and a degree of responsiveness to the grievances of Irish mass opinion as articulated by O'Connell and other popular representatives.

Russell's unilateral declaration in 1834 in support of the appropriation of 'surplus' revenue from the Church of Ireland for non-denominational purposes amounted to a bid for the reformulation of the ministry along distinctively Foxite lines. Irish policy was to be the touchstone; 'Justice for Ireland', he announced, required 'an actual transfer of resources from the Protestant Church to the Catholic people'.[108] The resulting resignation as Prime Minister of the exhausted Grey, the fierce internal struggle leading to the secession of Stanley, Graham and Ripon from the

---

103 O'Connell to Knight of Kerry, 6 Feb. 1829, O'Connell, *Correspondence*, IV, 7.

104 Mandler, *Aristocratic government*, pp. 123–8; McDowell, *Public opinion and government policy*, pp. 142–3. Russell, like O'Connell, was not averse to all coercion, but thought it should be proportionate and tied to conciliatory measures.

105 Russell to Grey, 20 Oct. 1832, Russell Papers, PRO 30/22/1C, fols 35–6.

106 O'Connell to Bennett, 7 Feb. 1831, O'Connell, *Correspondence*, IV, 269; MacDonagh, *Emancipist*, pp. 47, 53, 57–60.

107 O'Connell expected Duncannon to agree with his observation that the 'insanity of delivering this country to so weak a man as Lord Anglesey and so obstinate a maniac as Stanley, is unequalled even in our annals.' O'Connell to Duncannon, 14 Jan. 1833, O'Connell, *Correspondence*, V, 3.

108 *Hans.*, XXIV, 796–804 [23 June 1834].

Party, and the antagonism of the crown to such an extent that William IV was prepared to dismiss the ministry in November 1834, were all seen by Russell as unavoidable steps clearing the way for a redefinition of Whig government.

To the dismay of moderates such as Lansdowne, the frenetic organizational activity of the Foxites in opposition resulted in a shift in the Party's orientation.[109] Duncannon was active, on Russell's behalf, in the skilful manoeuvrings that led to the Lichfield House 'compact' that subordinated O'Connellite and radical demands to the new Whig-Liberal programme.[110] The second Melbourne government formed in April 1835 was thus qualitatively different from the Whig-Liberal administrations of 1830–4. What made such changes possible was the advancement of Foxites to positions of dominance. Russell took the Home Office and the leadership of the House, Mulgrave went to Dublin as Lord Lieutenant with Morpeth as his Chief Secretary; Duncannon returned to his old position at the Woods and Forests, while Ebrington, content at first with a junior ministry, went on to succeed Mulgrave in 1839. Ireland was the key area for all these ministers; indeed it became what they had hoped for, 'a kind of Foxite fiefdom'.[111]

At the heart of the politics of 'justice to Ireland' lay the relationship between the ministers and O'Connell. It would be easy to see the Lichfield House compact as a cynical compromise made to guarantee Irish support for a minority Whig-Liberal administration, but this is belied by the publicly and privately expressed opinions of the participants. O'Connell's commitment to the alliance entailed the surrender of most of his political independence, which he privately argued was necessary 'to realise as much good for Ireland as I possibly can'. He argued that continuing 'the cry for Repeal', in such circumstances, would 'only give increased strength to the vile Orange faction'.[112] The pact was also expensive for the Whigs, as their political friendship with one of the most reviled men in British political life gave their opponents the opportunity to ride the wave of reviving popular anti-Catholicism.[113]

---

109 Lansdowne to Russell, 1 Feb. 1835, Rollo Russell (ed.), *Early correspondence of Lord John Russell, 1805–40* (2 vols., London, 1913), II, 81–2.

110 Holland to Duncannon, 20, 23 Jan. 1835, Bessborough Papers, West Sussex Record Office, Chichester, F. 150. While accepting Brent's argument that appropriation was a specifically Whig rather than O'Connellite or radical objective, his contention that 'the Lichfield House meeting . . . did not cement an alliance between O'Connell and the Whigs, but forestalled its occurrence', cannot be sustained. O'Connell's allegiance was not to appropriation *per se* but to what it jointly symbolized to him and the Foxites – the commitment of the new government to giving priority to measures of 'justice to Ireland'. Brent, *Liberal Anglican politics*, pp. 92–103; MacDonagh, *Emancipist*, pp. 120–2; Mandler, *Aristocratic government*, pp. 157–61; A.H. Graham, 'The Lichfield House Compact, 1835', *Irish Historical Studies*, XII (1960–1), 209–25.

111 Mandler, *Aristocratic government*, p. 162.

112 O'Connell to FitzPatrick, 4 Sept. 1835, O'Connell, *Correspondence*, V, 329.

113 MacDonagh, *Emancipist*, pp. 124–6; Macintyre, *Liberator*, pp. 146–9, 155–8. For the graphic representation of this relationship by Tory critics, see J.N. McCord, 'The image in England: the cartoons of HB', in Maurice R. O'Connell (ed.), *Daniel O'Connell: political pioneer* (Dublin, 1991), pp. 57–71.

The Foxite conviction of the necessity of co-operation with O'Connell, despite some personal doubts raised by the excesses of some of his speeches, was based on an awareness that feeling for Repeal was legitimate (if misguided) and that good government would have to 'please the people of that country', the 'only way of governing Ireland [which] had not yet been tried'.[114] The only way of doing so was by responding to the demands of 'the people' as articulated through their spokesmen.[115] Their objective was thus to govern 'upon the principles laid down by Mr Fox in 1797'; in Russell's words, to have 'the Irish government regulated by Irish notions and Irish prejudices . . . [for] I am convinced, the more Ireland is under Irish government, the more she will be bound to English interests'.[116]

The Foxite achievement in Ireland in 1835–41 lay not in its limited legislative record but in the revolution carried out in the personnel and practice of the Irish executive and administration. The branches of government worked with a rare harmony in their desire to demonstrate the positive value of the Union by winning the sympathies of the Catholic Irish, distancing themselves from the ascendancy, and seeking to rule 'justly and impartially'. It was subsequently Russell's proudest boast to have 'pacified' Ireland without undue recourse to coercion.[117] Foxites were convinced that Ireland's 'backward' and violent character was due to past misgovernment and that progress could only be made in the context of the popularization of the instruments of administration leading to a revival of confidence in the rule of law. Their aim was the advancement of Ireland to occupy an integral and equal position within the United Kingdom, accompanied by the full realization of Catholic emancipation by the promotion of Catholics to responsible positions under the crown, especially to the key legal positions in Dublin Castle. This was also one of O'Connell's priorities, and Mulgrave's appointments in April 1835 led him to state privately that 'there is a fixed determination to do justice to Ireland'.[118] Russell and Mulgrave ignored protests from Melbourne and the King over their intimacy with the Irish leader.[119]

Paradoxically, the Whigs intended to use precisely those institutional features that made Ireland different from England to pursue the object of integration; the quasi-colonial lord lieutenancy, although intended for early abolition, was seen as invaluable in the short run as a reforming instrument (Mulgrave theatrically transformed it into a popular totem), while the expanded scope of the Dublin

114 Russell to Holland, 20, 30 Sept. 1833, cited in Mandler, *Aristocratic government*, pp. 152–3.

115 The precedent of the relationship between Fox and Grattan may have occurred to Russell. For his impression of this *entente*, see Russell, *Charles James Fox*, I, 471.

116 W. Torrens McCullagh (ed.), *Memoirs of the Rt. Hon. Richard Lalor Sheil* (2 vols., London, 1855), II, 249–50.

117 *Annual Register*, LXXXV (1843), 139.

118 O'Connell to Duncannon, 2 Sept. 1834, O'Connell to FitzPatrick, 21 April, 1835, O'Connell, *Correspondence*, V, 170–3, 293–4.

119 Melbourne to Russell, 20 Oct. 1835, Russell Papers, PRO 30/22/1E, fols. 223–4.

Castle departments, already substantially more interventionist than their English counterparts, provided a means of circumventing ascendancy obstruction, resistance and incapacity. The appointment of Thomas Drummond as Under-Secretary ensured that vigorous and efficient reforming administration would be allied to Whig popular flourishes.[120]

The politics of 'justice to Ireland' in 1835–41 was concerned primarily with responding to political, legal and religious grievances. In legislative terms the greatest struggles were over the municipal corporations and tithes bills, both middle-class Catholic concerns close to O'Connell's heart and political interests. Yet there was a recognition that the tithe issue involved more demotic concerns, and that 'justice' should also extend into the economic sphere. In 1835 the government turned its face firmly against assisting tithe-owners in obtaining arrears.[121]

The most significant part of the developing Foxite position on Irish economic questions was its attitude towards the system of Irish landholding, and in particular its critique of Irish landlordism. Foxite hostility to the mass of Irish landlords had primarily a political rather than an economic root. As the landed Protestant ascendancy had abused its powers and alienated the Catholic masses, 'justice' could not be expected from this class, and would have to be imposed on them from without. The relative hostility to orthodox economics it inherited from Holland, also gave Russell's circle a degree of openness to heterodox ideas.[122] Russell's initial instincts were strongly reinforced when he visited Ireland in 1833 to observe conditions at first hand. He concluded from what he saw that in order to put an end to the system whereby exorbitant rents were extracted 'by the distress of the landlord, from the distress of the tenant', a scheme should be devised enabling the state to purchase and improve land on a large scale.[123] Little came of this in the 1830s beyond a number of limited reclamation experiments on crown lands,[124] but Russell's statement was significant for being so much at odds with the orthodoxy of the day.

Russell and his colleagues interpreted Irish grievances in the 1830s not solely in terms of the need to grant 'justice' to the middle classes or the Catholic clergy, but also to secure the peasant 'justice' against his landlord. This was implicit in the attempt to change the administration of justice in the countryside from its traditional role of imposing landed property rights on a recalcitrant peasantry. This

---

120 For the popularization and 'Catholicization' of the Irish legal structure from 1835, see MacDonagh, *Emancipist*, pp. 127–31; for the harmonious and balanced operation of the Irish executive, see M.A.G. Ó Tuathaigh, *Thomas Drummond and the government of Ireland, 1835–40* (Dublin, 1978).

121 Macintyre, *Liberator*, pp. 188–9; Russell to Mulgrave, 27 May 1835, Russell, *Early correspondence*, II, 115–16.

122 At his parliamentary debut Russell had written off political economy as 'an awful thing', urging statesmen to 'first be Englishmen, and then economists', cited in Mandler, *Aristocratic government*, p. 27.

123 Memorandum on Irish policy, 18 Oct. 1833, Russell, *Early correspondence*, II, 43.

124 See below, p. 159.

reform involved the creation of a centralized, non-sectarian Irish Constabulary in 1836, and a great increase in the numbers of stipendiary magistrates, supposedly independent of the local power networks. The tone of the ministry towards landlords was expressed in Drummond's celebrated answer to the Tipperary magistrates' demand for extra coercive powers in 1838:

> Property has its duties as well as its rights. To the neglect of those duties in times past is mainly to be ascribed that diseased state of society in which such crimes take their rise; and it is not in the enactment of statutes of extraordinary severity, but chiefly in the better and more faithful performance of those duties, and the more enlightened and humane exercise of those rights, that a permanent remedy for those disorders is to be sought.[125]

That the government had no intention of trusting the performance of those duties of property to the paternal feeling of the landowners became clear with their adoption of the Irish Poor Law.

In choosing to disregard the orthodox conclusions of the Whately Commission in 1836, Russell and the Irish government believed themselves to be responding to the demands for legal relief as an act of justice made by Bishop Doyle and such polemicists as Sadler, Poulett Scrope and Sharman Crawford.[126] When Russell consulted Mulgrave on the Whately report, the Lord Lieutenant questioned the suitability of assistance to irresponsible proprietors, while Drummond attacked their 'cold blooded indifference to the sufferings of their tenantry'.[127] The Irish government and Russell were not opposed to public works in principle, but were impatient to demonstrate that they were prepared to legislate directly on behalf of the people. Whately himself was incensed by their behaviour, believing the government was sacrificing sound doctrine 'for the sake of a temporary popularity'.[128]

Russell's decision to endorse Lewis's criticism of Whately's report, and to adopt Nicholls' plan for an Irish poor law, has been criticised by some historians as representing the choice of a 'conventional' option over a radical one.[129] It would, however, be a mistake to regard the decision as originating in a simple desire for institutional anglicization. Whereas the 1834 Act had severely curtailed the old English Poor Law, the Irish Act of 1838 was seen as a move in the opposite direction,

---

125 Drummond to Donoughmore, 22 May 1838, G. Locker Lampson, *A consideration of the state of Ireland in the nineteenth century* (London, 1907), pp. 242–3.

126 James W. Doyle, *Letter to Thomas Spring Rice, esq., MP, on the establishment of a legal provision for the Irish poor, and on the nature and destination of Church property* (Dublin, 1831), pp. 72–81; George Poulett Scrope, *How is Ireland to be governed?: a question addressed to the new administration of Lord Melbourne in 1834* (2nd edn, London, 1846), pp. 8–10, 26–8, 34–9; Macintyre, *Liberator*, pp. 205–7.

127 Mulgrave to Russell, 13 Sept. 1836, Drummond to Morpeth, 21 June 1836, cited in Diana Davids Olien, *Morpeth: a Victorian public career* (Washington, 1983), pp. 167–173.

128 Whately to Senior, 6 Dec. 1835, Senior Papers, National Library of Wales, Aberystwyth, C.548.

129 McDowell, *Public opinion*, pp. 192–3.

creating a social provision where none had previously existed. Russell used Lewis and Nicholls to provide the necessary administrative and economic gloss without which an Irish Poor Law Bill could not pass, but Foxite thinking was based on a different agenda. Morpeth commented that the conclusions expressed in Nicholls' 1836 memoranda, were 'very satisfactory, very much . . . because they coincide with those which I have ventured to form',[130] and Duncannon and Drummond agreed. This suggests a coherent Foxite position on the poor law, parallel with, but not identical to, the premises of Lewis and Nicholls. The language used to defend the Bill was a far cry from Nicholls' rationalization of the Bill as an aid to economic transition.[131] Russell declared that he did not seek to 'please either the Irish landlords, or farmers, but to do good in Ireland', and Morpeth argued that the Bill was to defend the rights of the inarticulate, as 'the cry of him that was ready to perish did not find its way to their table'.[132] While the measure that passed was something of a compromise, and stopped well short of Doyle's demands, Russell believed it contained the seeds of the right to relief. He was optimistic that 'In ten years more . . . much good will be effected by this decried and restricted law, if it is not set aside'.[133] For his part, Senior reluctantly conceded defeat, and turned to lobbying for the enactment of the anti-vagrancy clauses which had been dropped from the 1838 Act.[134]

The Poor Law was one area of Irish policy on which the Foxites were prepared to flout O'Connell's opposition; but it too was intended, at least in part, as a component of 'justice to Ireland'. O'Connell's opposition was inconsistent and at first somewhat muted, indeed Sharman Crawford thought O'Connell's initial silence due to his concern to follow rather than lead popular opinion.[135] When O'Connell eventually did express opposition, his rhetoric drew heavily on an idealization of Christian paternalism and a repetition of the wages-fund fears expressed by many Irish landowners. His party was deeply divided, but much of the Catholic clergy and a substantial cross-section of Irish MPs, including his former Catholic Association ally, Richard Lalor Sheil, strongly favoured the Bill.[136] In fact, the Act

---

130 Morpeth to Russell, 29 Sept. 1836, Russell Papers, PRO 30/22/2C, fol. 186.

131 G. Nicholls, *Poor laws – Ireland: three reports* (London, 1838), pp. 15–16.

132 Russell to Morpeth, 10 Feb. 1838, cited in Olien, *Morpeth*, pp. 173–5.

133 Russell to Monteagle, 25 Nov. 1843, Monteagle Papers, National Library of Ireland, Dublin, MS 13,394/3. Scrope denounced the 1838 act as a 'pretence', but he later expressed confidence in Russell's 'reputation for just policy' and expected him to introduce comprehensive amendments, Scrope, *How is Ireland to be governed?*, p. 46; Scrope to Russell, 2 May, 23 June 1846, Russell Papers, 30/22/5A, fols 201–4, 267–74.

134 [Nassau W. Senior]. 'Mendicancy in Ireland', *Edinburgh Review*, LXXVII (April 1843), 391–411.

135 W.S. Crawford to J.S. Crawford, July 1835, 31 Dec. 1835, 5 April 1836, Sharman Crawford Papers, Public Record Office of Northern Ireland, Belfast, D.856/D/37, 44, 47. In the 1830s O'Connell wavered on the question of a compulsory poor law, see Michael MacDonagh, *Bishop Doyle 'J.K.L.': a biographical and historical study* (London, 1896), pp. 154–9.

136 MacDonagh, *Emancipist*, pp. 157–8; Macintyre, *Liberator*, pp. 209–10; McCullagh, *Sheil*, I, 78–9, 110–16.

not only gave legal force to the slogan that 'Irish property must support Irish poverty', but in establishing elected boards of guardians it marked yet another step away from ascendancy control of local administration through the grand juries.[137] The opportunity this created for popular pressure was not lost on the young radical Thomas Davis, who argued that the guardians could be incited into acting as obstacles to evictions.[138]

Some of the parliamentary success of the 1838 Bill can be attributed to the massive expense of Whately's proposals, and the objections raised to these in parliament. The government's rejection of his report, however, did not mean a rejection of public works; commitment to a major programme was demonstrated in the railway construction proposals drawn up by Drummond in 1836–8. The scheme introduced into parliament by Morpeth in 1839 had both economic and humanitarian objects, and was in flagrant violation of the principles of *laissez-faire.* It was coolly received by Lansdowne and Baring in the cabinet on the grounds that few Irish railways could be profitable, and was killed by Peel's insistence in the House of Commons on fiscal orthodoxy.[139]

If the spirit of the politics of 'justice to Ireland' was anywhere coherently expressed, it was in Russell's speech of 15 April 1839 in vindication of Normanby's administration against a Tory assault in the Lords on the government's alleged softness on agrarian 'outrages'. Russell acknowledged the continuing rural crisis in parts of Ireland, but put the blame for outrage firmly on previous misgovernment and the past and present activities of landlords.[140] Irish difficulties were, he asserted, the inevitable outcome of the alienation of the Catholic masses by palpably unjust laws. Russell declared that the experience of the fifty years before 1830 had taught them that concessions would only be granted to political agitation and the threat of force, and hence he could understand and empathize with O'Connell's motivation:

> Had he [Russell] been an Irishman, and in the position of the hon. and learned member for Dublin [O'Connell], it was very likely, that notwithstanding upon calm consideration he must disapprove of such political associations, he would, on the spur of such an insulting provocation, have enrolled himself as a member of a political society.

The enmity of the past could only be alleviated by a government embodying a disposition of mind favourable to the Irish people. It was the case, as Burke had

---

137 Oliver MacDonagh, 'Politics 1830–45', in Vaughan, *N.H.I., V,* p. 180.

138 [Thomas Davis], 'Emigration – no remedy', *The Citizen,* I (Dec. 1839), p. 82.

139 Olien, *Morpeth,* pp. 207–12 .

140 [Lord John Russell], *The government of Ireland: the substance of a speech, delivered in the House of Commons, on Monday, April 15th, 1839* (London, 1839), pp. 15–17, 21. For the political context of this speech, see Virginia Crossman, 'The politics of security: a study of the official reaction to rural unrest in Ireland, 1821–41', (unpublished D. Phil. thesis, University of Oxford, 1989), pp. 70–84.

observed, that 'the most favourable laws can do very little towards the happiness of a people when the disposition of the ruling power is adverse to them. Men do not live upon blotting paper. The favourable or the hostile mind of the ruling power is of far more importance to mankind for good or evil than the black letter of any statute.'[141]

Normanby's administration had shown just such a conciliatory disposition, and the situation in Ireland had rapidly improved with increasing confidence in the law. There was still too much rural crime, but the causes for this lay not in the Irish character, but in the system of landholding, and specifically in the landlords' misuse of their powers to eject their tenantry ruthlessly. The Poor Law had given some rights to these destitutes, and had to be given a fair trial,[142] but while no government could end the outrages immediately, it could hope to eliminate gradually the root causes by seeking to 'show a determination to administer impartial justice to all classes . . . to promote laws tending to diminish poverty and misery; they might show confidence in the people and reliance on their affections'. This was the ideal that lay at the root of the Foxite interpretation of 'justice to Ireland', and for which they were prepared to go beyond rhetoric and make considerable political sacrifices.[143]

O'Connell's path was difficult during this period. He had simultaneously to maintain the popular political activity in Ireland that was necessary to exert pressure on parliament, while at the same time moderating agitation so as to retain the tangible political benefits of Whig-Liberal government. This became more awkward after 1839 as parliamentary interest in Irish issues declined. Russell moved to the Colonial Office and became obsessed with colonial and international crises, Drummond's early death in 1840 removed a driving force from the Castle, and Morpeth (despite promotion to the cabinet) found it impossible to proceed with major Irish legislation in the face of Melbourne's studied indifference, the precariousness of the government's Commons majority and constant hostility from the Lords.[144] As the Whig-Liberal majority in the Commons suffered attrition, and the threat of a return to Tory rule increased, O'Connell's outdoor activities escalated. In 1840 he launched the Loyal National Repeal Association, although agitation was initially constrained by Ebrington's strong warnings against Repeal, and the threat of the loss of patronage.[145]

141 [Russell], *Government of Ireland*, pp. 36–7, 42–3.

142 Russell's use of the phrase 'in the spirit of the laws of Elizabeth, for the subsistence of the poor' to describe the Act (ibid., p. 18), indicated again the difference of his approach to the problem of poor relief from that of the orthodox Lewis and the Benthamite Nicholls. For orthodox hostility to the spirit of the Elizabethan Poor Law, see Himmelfarb, *The idea of poverty*, pp. 160–3.

143 [Russell], *Government of Ireland*, pp. 40, 45–6.

144 His plans included the 1839 railways bill and a major Irish franchise bill in 1841, which the moderate Fitzwilliam feared would open 'a door . . . which no man will be able to shut', Fitzwilliam to Morpeth, 8 Feb. 1841, cited in Olien, *Morpeth*, pp. 220–5.

145 MacDonagh, *Emancipist*, pp. 185–91.

O'Connell's commitment to Whig government in Ireland remained strong right up to their loss of power in 1841. Writing to Morpeth he praised the administration's record amid surrounding problems:

> [T]hey are placed as a kind of moral promontory between the people of Ireland and that furious and fanatical party, who have so often driven a kindly and naturally faithful people to the very verge of actual rebellion and into the gulf of agrarian crimes and of local but sanguinary outrages. It seems to me to be a sacred duty which they owe as well to the Queen . . . as to the people of Ireland to protect both from the disastrous results of that just irritation that must follow from the restoration to power of the Orange faction.[146]

Yet for all this, the elections of 1841 demonstrated the limitations of 'justice to Ireland'. The Whig-Liberals in Ireland reaped the benefits of six years of conciliatory government and emerged as the largest Irish party. O'Connell, unable to excite his popular constituency over Repeal, retained only eighteen followers and suffered a number of embarrassing defeats.[147] The return of Peel left him marginalized and rendered his tactics of 1834–41 irrelevant; the Whig alliance had always been dependent on results and broke down rapidly. The impotence of the parliamentary opposition in 1841–3 led him to write them off completely and encouraged a radicalization of his politics.[148]

The Repeal agitation in Ireland was temporarily subdued as O'Connell savoured the fruits of municipal reform during his term as the first Catholic Lord Mayor of Dublin in 1841–2. It accelerated with his self-conscious rejection of the Whigs, which pushed relations to a low point by 1843. Nevertheless, on the Whig side there had been no desire for an immediate rupture in 1841. While he eventually decided that he could have 'no party concert' with any group fully committed to Repeal, Russell agreed with Palmerston that the initiative for any break should not come from them.[149] The politics of 'justice to Ireland' appeared to have collapsed ignominiously in the two years after 1841, but were dormant rather than extinct. They remained at the core of the self-defining credo of a Foxite group seeking to preserve a traditional Whiggish identity within the Party. As the politics of Irish land entered a critical period from 1843, this agenda re-emerged, but found itself in conflict with other, more orthodox, ideas and policies.

---

146 O'Connell to Morpeth, 7 May 1841, O'Connell, *Correspondence*, VII, 48–9.

147 Macintyre, *Liberator*, pp. 65–9.

148 O'Connell to Smethwick, 12 May 1841, O'Connell to FitzPatrick, 19 May 1841, O'Connell, *Correspondence*, VII, 56–7, 62–3.

149 Palmerston to Russell, 12 October 1841, Russell to Lansdowne, 12 November 1841, G.P. Gooch (ed.), *The later correspondence of Lord John Russell, 1840–78* (2 vols., London, 1925), I, 47–8, 49–50.

V PEELITES AND TORIES

While tensions also existed within the Conservative Party over Ireland, these were less often evident within the Party's leadership in the 1830s–40s. Despite continuing suspicion on the part of his anti-Catholic backbenchers, Sir Robert Peel remained the undisputed arbiter of Conservative Irish policy in these years. Peel's attitude towards the problem of how Ireland should be governed had changed substantially over time. Apprenticed as Irish Chief Secretary in 1812–18, he excelled in the narrow range of administrative activities carried on from Dublin Castle – particularly the wielding of patronage and the use of coercion against rural disturbance and Catholic political agitation. He also proved adept at organizing the effective state response to the partial famine resulting from the defective potato crop of 1816. This talent for management and intervention existed, however, in a relationship of increasing contradiction with his maturing liberal Tory beliefs, which stressed the moral superiority of *laissez-faire* and the promotion of 'natural' self-regulating systems.

At the Home Office in the 1820s Peel became increasingly critical of the Irish governing class and insistent that it take upon itself the moral obligations of landownership.[150] Disillusionment with the Protestant ascendancy may have contributed to Peel's declining resistance to Catholic emancipation in the later 1820s, but he still hoped to avoid the obloquy of 'betraying' his anti-Catholic commitments by resigning from the government before it was obliged to give way over emancipation. O'Connell's victory at the Clare by-election in 1828 denied him this luxury, and forced him into a cathartic crisis, from which he emerged a fully-fledged liberal.[151] Peel's 'intellectual conversion' led him not only to take responsibility for formal ending of Catholic political exclusion, but also to advocate measures to promote Irish self-reliance. In the aftermath of the Emancipation Act he wrote to the Chief Secretary, 'we must seriously consider some extensive and decisive system of measures for the permanent civilization of Ireland'. He insisted that England should not be expected to meet the expense of Irish development: 'The time is come when it is unnecessary any longer to pet Ireland. We only spoil her by very undeserved flattery, and by treating her to everything for which she ought to pay.'[152]

The collapse of the Wellington ministry in 1830 denied Peel the opportunity to implement a liberal Irish policy, although much of what he envisaged was implemented during Stanley's tenure as Chief Secretary. He subsequently opposed Treasury financing of extensive Irish improvement projects, particularly those regarding railway construction. He did welcome a degree of private railway development in

150 Norman Gash, *Mr. Secretary Peel: the life of Sir Robert Peel to 1830* (Harlow, 1986 edn), p. 378.

151 Boyd Hilton, 'The ripening of Robert Peel', Bentley, *Public and private doctrine*, pp. 63–84.

152 Peel to Leveson Gower, 30 July 1829, C.S. Parker (ed.), *Sir Robert Peel from his private papers* (3 vols., London, 1891–9), II, 122–3.

Ireland, not least for its role in promoting the rapid assimilation of the Irish and British markets and economies. This, for Peel, was the desired end of Irish policy by the 1840s, to be attained in tandem with the reconciliation to the British state of moderate landed and bourgeois Catholics. Irish development could be promoted only by quelling the partisan conflicts that threatened the Union, and the task of government was to do this by winning the support of the political centre ground. Peel told his new Lord Lieutenant, Baron Heytesbury, in 1844: 'the old party distinctions engendered – and necessarily engendered – by monopoly and exclusion are fast wearing away – and there is a great mass of public opinion not tinged by Orange or by Green – of public opinion, Protestant and Roman Catholic, wearied out by agitation and acrimonious controversy.' With equitable treatment, this interest would gravitate towards a moderate policy. The Prime Minister also pointedly warned of the trap into which he himself had fallen in 1812: 'Do not believe any who tell you on arrival that the Lord Lieutenant must belong to one local party or another – and who warn of the fatal consequences of being left without support.'[153]

While the government could assist in creating the best conditions for economic improvement, it was not its initiative, but that of landowners, that would bring about regeneration. In September 1843 Peel upbraided Sir Valentine Blake on the consequences of his flirtation with the Repeal movement:

> The real obstacles to the improvement of Ireland and to the legitimate and permanent employment of her people, are interposed by those who from unmanly weakness and love of worthless and very fleeting popularity, lend such influence they possess to the encouragement of mischievous agitation – and by countenancing Repeal divert the application of English capital from undertakings beneficial to Ireland.[154]

This criticism was equally valid against those who perpetuated sectarian conflict by seeking to uphold a bankrupt Orange 'monopoly' against moderate Catholic demands.[155] If Peel's attitude towards the mechanisms of Irish government had altered, his fundamental belief in the Union did not. The political bond was the only hope for Irish advancement, and was the result of the natural law ordained by God. He warned Repealers in 1834:

> Beware how you act in the presumptuous confidence that you can restore, by artificial devices, the equilibrium that has been disturbed – that you can launch the new planet into the social system – can set bounds to its vibrations – can so adjust the antagonist forces which are to determine its orbit, that it shall neither be drawn back into violent contact with the mass from which it has been severed, nor flame across the void of space a lawless and eccentric meteor. To do

153 Peel to Heytesbury, 1 Aug. 1844, ibid., III, 114–15.
154 Peel to Blake, 3 Sept. 1843, Peel Papers, British Library, London, Add. MS 40,532, fols. 387–8.
155 Peel to Croker, 17 Dec. 1844, Parker, *Peel*, III, 130–1.

this is far beyond the grasp of your limited faculties – far beyond the intelligence of any save that of the Almighty and Omniscient Power which derived light from darkness, and ordained the laws which regulate in magnificent harmony the movements of countless worlds.[156]

From 1832 to 1844 Conservative Irish policy was virtually dictated by Peel and acquiesced in by most of his followers. Latent contradictions existed between the views of Peel and his closest colleagues and those of Tory landlords (many with Irish connections) on the backbenches, but these were obscured by a shared hostility towards Whig-Liberal policy before 1841, and by Peel's cautious 'safety-first' policies of 1841–3. The increasingly bitter dissension that arose over Peel's new Irish policy in 1844–6 brought some of these conflicts to the surface, but essentially the clash was between leadership and the backbenches, and not between different strands within the cabinet.

Other leading Conservatives had considerable experience of Ireland. Henry Goulburn had been a 'furious Protestant' as Chief Secretary in 1821–7, but had followed Peel's path into pragmatic Conservatism in the 1830s. Although coming from an Whiggish gentry background, Sir James Graham had also fallen under Peel's spell after 1836 and became his closest political confidant. Graham's Irish experience had been acquired largely during his de facto responsibility for the partial western famine of 1831, which led him to be wary of Irish habits of 'dependency'.[157] Of the Conservative front bench in the 1840s only Lord Stanley retained any substantial degree of independence from the Party's leader. Stanley's approach to the economic development of Ireland was not dissimilar from Peel's, and his achievement as Chief Secretary from 1830 to 1833 had been considerable. Two things set Stanley apart from both Peel and his former 'Derby Dilly' associates who joined the Conservatives in 1836. Firstly he was an extensive Irish landlord who took an intense interest in his County Tipperary estates, and was thus more sympathetic to Irish landed concerns than was the aloof Peel.[158] Secondly, he combined a residual Whiggish reverence for the principle of party with the zeal of a political convert towards his adopted Conservative Party, believing it to be an indispensable bulwark against the British and Irish radicalism that threatened the body politic.[159]

156 Peel speech, 25 April 1834, cited in Camille de Cavour, *Considerations on the present state and future prospects of Ireland* (London, 1845), pp. 84–5.

157 See below, pp. 126–7.

158 Stanley was anxious to see the 1831 non-denominational Education Act implemented on his own estate, and instructed his agent to co-operate with the local Catholic curate in managing the school. His object was to create 'good citizens, good subjects, good Christians and I will add good Catholics', by means of a tightly controlled National Board curriculum, Stanley to Thomas Bolton, 19 Jan. 1845, Derby Papers, Liverpool Record Office, 920 DER (14), 176/2, fols. 63–5.

159 Angus Hawkins, 'Lord Derby and Victorian Conservatism: a reappraisal', *Parliamentary History*, VI (1987), 280–301.

In the aftermath of the 1846 Conservative split, Protectionist leaders made a bid to contribute to the making of Irish policy, but with the exception of Stanley (who was in many ways closer to Peel than to his own followers) they were largely incoherent and opportunistic when proposing positive measures, and defensive and uninfluential in opposition to government measures. In contrast, Peel was to remain a dominant political presence, even in opposition, and was in large measure responsible for the success of the encumbered estates legislation of 1849.

CHAPTER TWO

Agitation and Inquiry, 1843–6

Land they will have, honestly, if possible, but at all risks, they will have land. In other words, they will try to live. All this has been the work of the landlords. They have dug a pit for themselves, large enough to swallow the property of England with their own. We appeal to the representatives of Great Britain. We entreat them to attend to what is pressing in Ireland. Are they so insensate, or so indifferent, as not to have perceived that the effect of a union must either tend to raise Ireland, or to lower England? The scales must be balanced.

Remarks by a junior to his senior, 1844[1]

Indolence – the last of the causes to which we have attributed the existing misery of Ireland – is not so much an independent source of evil, as the result of the combination of all the others . . . The indolence of the agricultural labourer arises, perhaps, principally from his labour being almost always day-work, and in great measure a mere payment of a debt – a mere mode of working out his rent. That of the occupier may be attributed to a combination of causes. In the first place, a man must be master of himself to a degree not common even among the educated classes, before he can be trusted to be his own task-master . . . The Irish occupier, working for a distant object, dependent in some measure on the seasons, and with no one to control, or even to advise him, puts off to to-morrow what need not necessarily be done to-day – puts off to next year what need not be necessarily done this year, and ultimately leaves much totally undone.

Nassau Senior, 'Ireland', 1844[2]

The year 1843 was one of mass political excitement in Ireland and of crisis in Anglo-Irish relations. The unprecedented scale of popular mobilization created by O'Connell's Repeal movement alarmed British politicians and forced the government to reconsider its Irish policy and attempt to defuse a situation which many feared was degenerating towards civil war. This chapter will examine how in their bid to further the Repeal mobilization, the movement's leaders articulated the agrarian demands of the tenant farmers and cottiers, and incorporated these into the Repeal Association programme alongside more established objectives.

1 [Anon.], *Remarks by a junior to his senior, on an article in the Edinburgh Review of January, 1844, on the state of Ireland, and the measures for its improvement* (London, 1844), p. 74.
2 [Nassau Senior], 'Ireland', *Edinburgh Review*, LXXIX (Jan. 1844), 206–7.

This politicization of agrarian questions forced them on to the British political agenda, and into the field of party political conflict at Westminster. The Peel government's considered response – the establishment of the Devon Commission of inquiry in November 1843 – did not have true cross-party support, and was itself politically contentious. Peel's instincts pointed away from state interference in the law of contract and towards the commodification of land; his efforts at land legislation in 1845–6 were not wholly serious. At the same time, the Devon Commission stimulated an intense debate in Britain on the future of Irish society that would continue into the Famine years and have an important bearing on the state's response to that catastrophe.

I THE 'LANDLORD AND TENANT QUESTION', 1843

The complex of tensions, antagonisms and grievances that existed in the Irish countryside before the Famine contained latent political elements. In an age of religious polarization, it was inevitable that the broad sectarian divide between Protestant landlords and Catholic tenants and labourers should have been the cause of much antipathy. Moreover, the ambiguous legacy of the 1790s left its mark on the structure and codes of agrarian secret societies in some areas.[3] In general, however, the 'agrarian law' enforced by secret societies appears not to have been overtly political, but concerned with the preservation of a 'moral economy' based on traditional concepts of reciprocal rights and duties. What this entailed was extremely variable, and could embrace a range of conflicts between landlord and tenant, farmer and labourer, and between and within kinship groups, in different areas and at different times.[4]

The changing socio-economic circumstances of the late 1830s and early 1840s altered the general nature of rural grievances and disturbances. The condition of the rural poor in Ireland was deteriorating still further, and while the rate of population increase was slowing, the problems of underemployment and excessive competition for land were continuing to increase. A period of acute agricultural distress coincided with the British commercial and industrial depression of 1839–43, which severely reduced the demand for Irish migrant labour, and pushed the Irish cottage textile industry further towards its ultimate demise.[5] The reduced

3 'Ribbonmen' in the northern half of Ireland had such a political strand, but the less coherent 'Whiteboy' societies of the south and south-west were motivated mainly by economic stimuli, Tom Garvin, 'Defenders, Ribbonmen and others: underground political networks in pre-Famine Ireland', *Past and Present*, 96 (1982), 133–55; Joseph Lee, 'The Ribbonmen', in T.D. Williams (ed.), *Secret societies in Ireland* (Dublin, 1973), pp. 26–35.

4 For a summary of the debate on this subject, see David Fitzpatrick, 'Unrest in rural Ireland', *Irish Economic and Social History*, XII (1985), 98–105.

5 M.A.G. Ó Tuathaigh, *Ireland before the Famine 1798–1848* (Dublin, 1972), pp. 140–2; Liam Kennedy, 'The rural economy', in Liam Kennedy and Philip Ollerenshaw (eds.), *An*

earnings of those smallholders who had doubled as proto-industrial workers further increased the pressure on the land and the sense of rural crisis. As rents fell into arrears, some landowners responded harshly; evictions on the Ranfurly estate in Tyrone in early 1843 were attributed to 'the appalling distress to which these unfortunate people are reduced by the decay of trade, and the ruinous price to which agricultural produce has fallen'.[6] Under such conditions of agricultural depression the social composition of Irish rural unrest tended to emphasize a 'peasant' collectivity against landlords and graziers intent on 'improving' by clearances and consolidation.[7]

The 'Repeal Year'

Daniel O'Connell's political campaigns, while drawing occasionally on the energies of the peasantry, had not been greatly concerned with questions of land before 1843. His core supporters were drawn from the ranks of the Catholic and liberal Protestant gentry, large farmers and middle-class professionals, who were often also interested in the 'improvement' and commercialization of their estates and the security of their investments. The potential conflict of interest that existed between these practitioners of constitutionalist politics and the defenders of the agrarian moral economy was made clear by the assassination of several improving Catholic landlords, including O'Connell's friend James Scully, as a result of land disputes.[8]

Nevertheless, the Repeal movement was flexible enough to respond positively to the popular challenge of the land question in the early 1840s. This was due to both the complexity of O'Connell's economic ideas, and to the influx of young radicals into the movement. O'Connell was himself a small landowner and middleman in County Kerry, but was not dependent on his rentals for the bulk of his income, which came from the infamous 'Repeal rent'. His approach to proprietorship was traditional; he valued an easy-going, even negligent, paternalism over the maximization of economic opportunities, and sought to preserve a tribal-feudal relationship with his tenants.[9] While O'Connell firmly opposed agrarian

---

economic history of Ulster 1820–1940 (Manchester, 1985), pp. 8–11; Cormac Ó Gráda, *Ireland: a new economic history 1780–1939* (Oxford, 1994), pp. 166–7.

6 *Dublin Evening Post*, 2 Feb. 1843, in *Cases of tenant eviction, from 1840 to 1846, extracted from the public journals* (n.p., n.d.) pp. 7–8.

7 For this general pattern, see James S. Donnelly, 'The social composition of agrarian rebellion in early nineteenth-century Ireland: the case of the Carders and Caravats, 1813–16', in P.J. Corish (ed.), *Radicals, rebels and establishments* (Belfast, 1985), pp. 151–69; Michael Beames, 'Rural conflict in pre-Famine Ireland: peasant assassinations in Tipperary 1837–47', *Past and Present*, 81 (1978), 75–91.

8 Michael Beames, *Peasants and power: the Whiteboy movements and their control in pre-Famine Ireland* (Brighton, 1983), pp. 142–4, 194–7; Angus Macintyre, *The liberator: Daniel O'Connell and the Irish party 1830–47* (London, 1965), pp. 72–83.

9 Oliver MacDonagh, *The hereditary bondsman: Daniel O'Connell 1775–1829* (London, 1988), pp. 187–90.

violence, he was receptive to his tenants' complaints, and was able on his own property to avoid the upheavals that accompanied so many of the 'improvements' carried out or planned on so many early nineteenth-century estates. The consequent 'backwardness' of his Derrynane estate shocked English observers in 1845.[10]

O'Connell's economic ideas were not entirely coherent, being composed of four disparate intellectual elements. His clannish paternalism reflected his Gaelic background and upbringing; his scapegoating of the Union and of absentee landowners as the cause of Ireland's economic stagnation was derived from eighteenth-century 'patriot' rhetoric; and his concern to promote individual liberty and his belief in the liberating potential of free trade was pure Benthamism.[11] Perhaps the most important element, however, was the sense of social justice he derived from his liberal Catholic identity. In the 1830s his identification of 'justice' with the removal of Catholic disabilities in law and practice seemed straightforward; his personal interest in professional advancement, the interests of the aspirant Catholic gentry and middle class, and the interest of the Catholic peasantry in the removal of the 'Orange clique' from control of the administration and enforcement of the law, all appeared complementary.[12] The continuation of rural disturbance, and the eclipse of 'Whiggism . . . [which] has passed by never to return',[13] pointed towards a radicalization of his tactics and demands from 1841. The mobilization of the Catholic masses behind the banner of 'simple Repeal' involved the broadening of what was understood by 'justice' in response to popular feeling. Emancipation, O'Connell admitted in 1843, had been 'chiefly beneficial to the opulent upper classes', but Repeal, accompanied by a series of sweeping social reforms, would be to the advantage of all.[14]

Peel's return to office led to the revival of agitation and contributed to the politicization of the land question. The appointment of the 'Orange' Lord de Grey as Lord Lieutenant and of Edward Lucas as Under-Secretary was only partially offset by that of the liberal Tory, Lord Eliot, as Chief Secretary. This coupling, arising from a vain attempt to balance the liberal and high Tory wings of the Party, had disastrous consequences.[15] The restoration to senior legal positions of O'Connell's old adversaries, Sir Edward Sugden and Francis Blackburne, and the adoption of

10 *Times*, 10 Nov., 20 Dec. 1845.

11 Joseph Lee, 'The social and economic ideas of O'Connell', in Kevin B. Nowlan and Maurice R. O'Connell (eds.), *Daniel O'Connell: portrait of a radical* (Belfast, 1984), pp. 70–84.

12 O'Connell's popularization of the legal system was central to his popular image. His reputation as 'the Counsellor' was particularly resonant with the peasantry, Diarmaid Ó Muirithe, 'O'Connell in Irish folk tradition', in Maurice R. O'Connell (ed.), *Daniel O'Connell: political pioneer* (Dublin, 1991), p. 74.

13 O'Connell to Ray, 6 August 1842, Maurice R. O'Connell (ed.), *The correspondence of Daniel O'Connell* (8 vols., Dublin, 1972–80), VII, 172.

14 Speech to the Drogheda Repeal meeting, 5 June 1843, *Nation*, 10 June 1843.

15 Norman Gash, *Sir Robert Peel: the life of Sir Robert Peel after 1830* (Harlow, 1986 edn), pp. 393–401.

a provocatively 'Protestant' patronage policy, presaged both a renewed attack on O'Connell and his supporters, and dramatized the abandonment of the Whig policy of popularizing the institutions of law and the police.[16] The return of the Tories appeared to herald a restoration of unbridled landlord authority in the countryside and hence raised proprietorial expectations. Elizabeth Smith, the Scottish-born wife of a resident proprietor in County Wicklow, noted in her diary in December 1841:

> This vigorous government has brought peace already, agitation now is such a mere farce that it soon must cease altogether, every one appearing tired of it . . . There is a great change coming over the Irish minds most certainly, the most remarkable move being among the priesthood with whom alone any great change for good can originate; those of us who live for twenty years will see better times arising.[17]

Such hopes would soon be dashed.

The popular Irish press did much to politicize the land question by articulating peasant fears in the language of constitutionalist politics. Evictions were regularly reported in an emotive manner, and sectarian and political motives were frequently attributed to proprietors. The nationalist *Newry Examiner* claimed that the evicted were 'driven from the land of their fathers, after being stripped of every particle of property, and then left to wander, pennyless, without a home, as exiles, in the land of their birth; merely because they bore the proscribed cognomen of *Catholic*.' In March 1843 the same paper warned that 'peaceable' Ulster could not remain calm 'if reckless tyranny continues to trample the lives and affections of men who have all the passions of humanity as strongly mixed in their nature as their brethren of the south'.[18] Such comments were more than idle threats. When the 'improving' land agent W. Steuart Trench took on the management of the Shirley estate in County Monaghan in March 1843 he was faced with mass demonstrations for rent reductions followed by intimidatory violence.[19]

Similar accounts and comments appeared throughout the popular provincial and national press, which was widely disseminated through the network of Repeal reading rooms. The *Nation* in particular articulated a language of collective

---

16 Oliver MacDonagh, *The emancipist: Daniel O'Connell 1830–47* (London, 1989), pp. 200–1. Discrimination against Catholics in police appointments became a point of embarrassment for the government in 1843, Eliot to Graham, 26 Aug. 1843, Graham Papers, Cambridge University Library (microfilm), bundle 10 IR.

17 David Thomson and Moyra McGusty (eds.), *The Irish journals of Elizabeth Smith 1840–1850* (Oxford, 1980), p. 40 [9 Dec. 1841].

18 *Newry Examiner*, 6 Dec. 1841, March 1843, in *Cases of tenant eviction*, pp. 5, 8. Religious discrimination by Protestant landlords and agents was not unusual in the polarized conditions of the early nineteenth century, see W.A. Maguire, *The Downshire estates in Ireland 1801–1845* (Oxford, 1972), pp. 229–231.

19 W. Steuart Trench, *Realities of Irish life* (London, 1866), pp. 20–43.

peasant mobilization and resistance to the 'system'. While warning of an incipient 'war that will shake landocracy to its centre', the paper cautioned the peasantry against the 'meshes of Ribbonism', and urged constitutionalist agitation behind the Repeal banner.[20] The *Nation* perceived itself as a 'new light' penetrating the 'Cimmerian darkness of ignorance and want', disclosing 'to the People the horrors of their own fate and the crimes of their oppressors', but it was probably less widely read in the countryside than was the local O'Connellite press.[21]

The Young Ireland radicals associated with the *Nation* raised the profile of the land question in the Repeal Association from 1841. Thomas Davis was inspired by the romantic concept of the peasantry as the bearers of the true national culture, and attacked economic anglicization as heralding the 'extermination' of both. Davis' rhetoric was radical, idealizing a Norwegian 'udalist' model of peasant proprietorship, but his practical prescriptions were more muted. While the question of tenure was 'a matter of life and death with the people', he believed that 'the adoption of any particular plan for Irish tenure [would be] . . . mischievous because premature'. He thought the matter would be settled simultaneously with the national question, and in co-operation with patriotic landowners.[22] This vagueness over details reflected the range of opinion within the Young Ireland group, which ranged from the vigorous agrarianism of John Dillon (and later the more social-revolutionary position of John Mitchel and James Fintan Lalor) to the more cautious reformist attitudes of Charles Gavan Duffy and William Smith O'Brien.[23]

The Repeal agitation was slow to take off after its revival in 1841, but O'Connell sought to extend its appeal beyond the range of traditional activists by developing a platform attractive to smallholding tenants and labourers. He was assisted by two parallel but contradictory campaigns connected with the Poor Law which contributed to the politicization of the peasantry in the early 1840s. The often fiercely contested elections for boards of guardians – in which O'Connellite priests were believed to wield a 'decisive influence' over Catholic ratepayers – brought popular politics into the localities from 1839.[24] At the same time the anti-poor rate agitation of 1842–3 mobilized the smallholders in many areas, and was endorsed by O'Connell. The campaign was successful in 1843 in extracting the removal of the direct burden of poor rates from tenants on holdings valued under £4 per annum, but this

20 *Nation*, 10, 24 June 1843.

21 Ibid., 19 Aug. 1843; Sean Ryder, 'Reading lessons: Famine and the *Nation*, 1845–1849', in Chris Morash and Richard Hayes (eds.), *Fearful realities: new perspectives on the Famine* (Blackrock, 1996), pp. 153–4.

22 Thomas Davis, 'Udalism and feudalism', in T.W. Rolleston (ed.), *Prose writings of Thomas Davis* (London, n.d.), pp. 44–75. This article first appeared in the *Citizen* in March-April 1842.

23 Richard Davis, *The Young Ireland movement* (Dublin, 1987), pp. 187–9; D. George Boyce, *Nationalism in Ireland* (London, 1982), p. 171; John N. Molony, *A soul came into Ireland: Thomas Davis 1814–1845, a biography* (Dublin, 1995), pp. 46–53, 59–61.

24 G.C. Lewis to G. Grote, 11, 29 Jan. 1843, Sir Gilbert Frankland Lewis (ed.), *Letters of the Rt. Hon. Sir George Cornewall Lewis, Bart., to several friends* (London, 1870), pp. 128–30.

merely tended to increase landlord-tenant conflict as it gave landlords an added incentive to clear small tenants.[25] Popular agitation was thus transferred to the cry of 'fixity of tenure'. The network of local Repeal committees set up and controlled by O'Connell in 1842–3 investigated perceived problems and proposed legislative remedies. The questions of land policy and the demands of the small tenants thus began to enter serious constitutionalist debate as part of the total community mobilization, envisaged in O'Connell's plan for a series of 'monster meetings' and for an alternative administrative structure in early 1843.[26]

'Fixity of tenure' was thus one of the 'five great measures' associated with Repeal in O'Connell's manifesto of January 1843, but it was at first defined vaguely as opposition to 'the clearance system'.[27] More constructively, O'Connell presented to the Repeal Association in April a series of propositions drawing on the rival programmes for land reform advanced by William Conner, who had been engaged in sporadic agitation for 'tenant right' in south-west Leinster from the early 1830s,[28] and by the Ulsterman William Sharman Crawford. O'Connell rejected the former's proposal for 'dual ownership' based on 'a valuation and a perpetuity', firstly because it would deny the landowner those 'just rights' that followed the fulfilment of the 'duties of property', and secondly because he believed the plan would widen and perpetuate social cleavages within the lower classes, as it would do nothing for the labourers:

> The present tenantry would get their land at a valuation, and by that means shut out the rest of the community; that was only shifting the monopoly from the landlord to the tenant, and in such a state of things what were the labouring classes to do? They could not get a farm – they were completely shut out; and could anything be more cruel than to adopt any plan which would produce such an effect?[29]

---

25 Gerard O'Brien, 'The establishment of Poor-Law Unions in Ireland, 1838–43', *Irish Historical Studies*, XXIII (1982), 97–120; L. McCaffrey, *Daniel O'Connell and the Repeal year* (Lexington, KY, 1966), pp. 20–3, 34–9. Nassau Senior supported the alteration, not least because it involved a substantial reduction in the electorate of boards of guardians, [Nassau W. Senior], 'Mendicancy in Ireland', *Edinburgh Review*, LXXVII (April 1843), 411.

26 MacDonagh, *Emancipist*, pp. 219–21.

27 Repeal Association meeting, 5 Jan. 1843, *Freeman's Journal*, 6 Jan. The other measures included abolition of tithes and the replacement of the Poor Law with a more acceptable form of public charity.

28 See William Conner, *The true political economy of Ireland: or, rack-rent, the one great cause of all her evils, with its remedy* (Dublin, 1835); R.D. Collison Black, *Economic thought and the Irish question, 1817–70* (Cambridge, 1960), pp. 24–6; T.P. O'Neill, 'The Irish land question, 1830–50', *Studies*, XLIV (1955), 325–36.

29 Repeal Association meeting, 11 April 1843, *Nation*, 15 April. Conner was expelled from the Repeal Association in September after proposing a rent and rates strike against both government and landlords.

O'Connell's conception of social justice centred on the idea of securing the 'just rights' and enforcing the mutual 'duties' of all classes. Landlordism was to be maintained, but in the context of a social reformation as fundamental as that undergone by Prussia under the Stein-Hardenberg land reforms a generation previously. The social distinction between tenant and labourer was to remain blurred, to allow social mobility and prevent class polarization. To implement these objectives, O'Connell looked to Sharman Crawford's legislative proposals for 'compensation for improvements', supported by his own suggestions for compulsory twenty-one year leases and the penalizing of absenteeism.[30]

O'Connell was at this point anxious not to alienate the 'patriotic gentry', and assured them that the endorsement of his plan by the clergy was proof of its moral propriety.[31] Nevertheless, the desire for land reform was explicit in the feelings of the rural masses who flocked to the 'monster meetings' of 1843, and could not be ignored. O'Connell's dialectical relationship with this popular voice was noted by a the German liberal Catholic Jacob Venedey: 'The peasant below thinks aloud – the Liberator above him on the platform catches the thought from beneath, and flings it back with redoubled force, or tosses it high in the air, and plays with it as long as it suits his fancy to do so.'[32]

Naturally the interconnection between O'Connellite nationalism and agrarian agitation alarmed British and Irish Conservatives. Many were aware that for the rural poor attendance at the monster meetings was as much a gesture of defiance to their landlords as an endorsement of nationalist sentiment, and some Irish landowners penalized those tenants who attended.[33] Others expressed frustration when attempts to impede the meetings failed in the absence of government support. The Tipperary landlord Thomas Storey sought in vain to convince the populace that self-interested agitation was at the root of all misery, and that social quietism would bring tangible rewards,[34] but most despaired of such appeals and pleaded for coercion. De Grey endorsed these cries, but Peel, aware of the political

---

30 'To the people of Ireland', *Nation*, 10 June 1843. The reforms in Prussia, which had transferred the ownership of farms to the occupying tenantry in return for ceding a portion to the landlords, was a subject of considerable controversy. Repeal publications remarked favourably on European, and particularly the Prussian, models of peasant proprietorship, while apologists for Irish landlordism denied that there was any parallel between the two countries, and attacked the Prussian system as diverting 'the attention of all classes from true sources of wealth to false ones', 'Fee', John O'Connell, *The Repeal dictionary, part I* (Dublin, 1845), pp. 48–50; [Bancroft], '"Fixity of tenure" historically and economically considered', *Dublin University Magazine*, XXIII (May 1844), 605–15.

31 Speech at the Tara Repeal meeting, 15 Aug. 1843, *Nation*, 19 Aug. 1843.

32 Jacob Venedey, *Ireland and the Irish during the Repeal year* (Dublin, 1844), p. 49.

33 Thomson and McGusty, *Journals of Elizabeth Smith*, p. 63 [14 May 1843].

34 Thomas George Storey, *A short address as a word of advice to the small farmers and peasantry of the County of Tipperary* (Dublin, 1843).

dangers in Britain and Ireland, was careful not to over-react, waiting until he deemed the situation expedient.[35]

Few doubted that the 'Repeal year' had brought Ireland to the brink of agrarian revolution. The liberal-conservative *Spectator* was sure that, 'it requires but a word or a secret whisper from O'Connell or the Irish clergy, to put a stop to the payment of rent over the greater part of Ireland. "Fixity of tenure" would then mean, that everyone should keep what land he had got.'[36] This exaggerated the revolutionary intent of the Repeal movement, but reflected the alarm of orthodox observers at the coalescence of nationalism and the campaign for land reform.

Sharman Crawford's proposals

A progressive County Down landowner and the radical MP for Rochdale since 1841, Sharman Crawford was a consistent critic of liberal economic orthodoxy. He had championed the idea of an Irish poor law in the early 1830s on humanitarian grounds, and was the leading parliamentary defender of Ulster tenant right.[37] Crawford's interest in the landlord-tenant question was long-standing, and he had originally introduced bills on the subject into parliament in 1835 and 1836.[38] Irish Tories had fiercely denounced these proposals, but O'Connell offered belated and ambiguous support once Crawford had demonstrated that it had popular support in north-east Ulster.[39] Morpeth, then Chief Secretary, had agreed in principle to such a measure, but the subject was dropped to give way to the Poor Law Bill.[40] Crawford subsequently took on the theorists of agrarian anglicization in print, denouncing consolidation and the 'compulsory expatriation of the small holders'. He defended the productivity and social utility of the small farm system, as long as the tenant was given security, and was not over-rented.[41]

Crawford proposed compulsory compensation to the tenant for 'improvements' made to his holding as an indirect mode of bringing about 'fixity of tenure'. His commitment to the other parts of what later became known as the 'three Fs' was clear from his defence of the 'free sale' of the tenant's interest in his holding inherent in the 'Ulster custom', and from his call for 'fair' rents to be set in line with a government valuation.[42] He also argued that excessive powers of distress

---

35 De Grey to Peel, 6 May, Peel to de Grey, 12 June 1843, Peel Papers, British Library, London, Add. MS 40,478, fols. 39–44, 79–84.

36 *Spectator*, 8 July 1843.

37 Black, *Economic thought*, pp. 27–9; Macintyre, *Liberator*, pp. 151–2, 206–7.

38 *Hansard's Parliamentary Debates*, 3rd series, XXIX, 218–9, [2 July 1835: Sharman Crawford].

39 W. Sharman Crawford to J. Sharman Crawford, 31 Dec. 1835, 5 April 1836, Sharman Crawford Papers, Public Record Office of Northern Ireland, Belfast, D.856/D/44, 47.

40 *Hans.*, XXXII, 188 [10 March 1836: Morpeth].

41 William Sharman Crawford, *A defence of the small farmers of Ireland* (Dublin, 1839), pp. 3–15.

42 On some Irish estates the system of 'canting' or auctioning tenancies to the highest bidder had already been replaced by letting at a rent set by the agent's valuation. On the Downshire estates in the 1840s these private valuations were about 25 per cent higher than the official Griffiths valuation then in progress, Maguire, *Downshire estates*, pp. 41–3.

and eviction be removed from the landlord. These demands were expressed in a language that stressed reward for merit and encouragement to individual exertion: 'My view always has been, that any increased length of tenure should be founded upon the degree of improvement made by the tenant. I have always considered that it would be very unjust to place the improving tenant and the unimproving tenant upon the same footing.' The aim of his bill was thus to, 'produce a practical prolongation of tenure, founded upon the tenant's improvement, without compelling, by any legal enactment, the prolongation of tenure; but by giving the tenant the power of claiming value for improvements, he would, thereby, acquire a practical fixity'.[43] 'Improvement' was understood by Crawford as the provision of those parts of the essential farming infrastructure, including houses and agricultural buildings, fences, drains and soil improvements, that in England, but not in Ireland, were generally provided by the landlord.[44] The crux of Crawford's argument lay in his belief that it was preferable such tasks be left to the tenant:

> a system [of landlord improvements] would not be suitable to the circumstances of Ireland, because the effect of that would be . . . to tend to increase the dispossessment of the small tenantry; for, if the landlord was compelled to make buildings and improvements, he would naturally desire to reduce the number of those buildings and improvements as much as possible, and he would, therefore, feel it his interest to dispossess the small tenantry in order to consolidate farms; and I am of the opinion that, under the present circumstances of Ireland, the greatest possible evil would be the rapid or injudicious dispossessment of the small holders.[45]

Crawford's aim was to justify and articulate peasant demands for 'tenant right' in a form and language acceptable to a British parliamentary audience. He sought to square the circle, granting security to the tenant, while also providing incentives to exertion that would stimulate development. Legislative intervention was justified on the utilitarian principle that land differed from other descriptions of property, as 'the state never gave an absolute right of ownership to individuals in land'.[46]

---

43 *Report of Her Majesty's Commissioners of Inquiry into the state of the law and practice in respect to the occupation of land in Ireland (Devon Commission)*, part I, P.P. 1845 [606], XIX, 253–8, 270–5. This optimistic view of the inherent industriousness of the small tenant was typical of liberal landlordism in Ulster, see William Blacker, *An essay on the improvement to be made in the cultivation of small farms, by the introduction of green crops and housefeeding the stock thereon* (tenant's edn, Dublin, n.d.), pp. 5–6.

44 *A Bill to amend the law of landlord and tenant in Ireland*, P.P. 1843 (490), III, 223–4.

45 *Devon Commission*, part I, P.P. 1845 [606], XIX, 274–5.

46 Ibid., p. 273. Crawford continued to advocate this scheme through the Famine years. See William Sharman Crawford, *Depopulation not necessary: an appeal to the British members of the imperial parliament against the extermination of the Irish people* (2nd edn, London, 1850), pp. 3–10.

'Fixity of tenure' in parliament

The greater attention devoted at Westminster to the land question in 1843 was a direct result of the Repeal campaign. Many of the Irish Whig-Liberals returned in 1841 owed their places to the weakness or tacit support of O'Connellites, and were aware of their increasing vulnerability amid the revival of popular political excitement. For many of the Whig-Liberals, the renewal of the politics of 'justice to Ireland' in a form that took account of these new circumstances was imperative for their political survival. Thus it was the Irish Whig-Liberals Richard Lalor Sheil and Lord Clements, along with the radical William Smith O'Brien, who took the lead in resisting Peel's 1843 Arms Bill and in calling for measures of conciliation as the only way of quieting Ireland.[47]

'Fixity of tenure' became the focus of the debates on the condition of the Ireland in 1843. The Irish Attorney General attributed its prominence to O'Connell's rhetoric and denounced it as 'a transfer of the fee simple of the landed property of Ireland from the landlord to the occupying tenant'.[48] Richard More O'Ferrall, a liberal Catholic landowner who had been a Lord of the Treasury in 1835–41, felt obliged to qualify this: 'for the tenant to wish to possess himself of all the rights of a proprietor, was too absurd a thing to be even discussed . . . it was no less certain that there was much in the existing law between landlord and tenant that required alteration.' The situation was now critical, 'and if it was not attended to, the consequence would be, that the attention of a large part of the population would be so much fastened on the absurdity . . . that it would afterwards be difficult to dispose them to accept of a more reasonable arrangement.'[49]

Inevitably, the issue played a prominent role in the full-scale debate in July on Smith O'Brien's motion for a commission of inquiry into the condition of Ireland.[50] O'Brien made a powerful speech outlining the grievances which underlay the social crisis and which invalidated the Union in the minds of many. Most of these grievances had been well rehearsed; the indefensible privileges of the Irish Church, an anti-Catholic bias in the administration of justice, the resort to coercion and the suspension of civil rights, and the inequalities between Ireland and Britain in taxation and franchise, were all stock subjects of radical and Irish complaint.

---

47 *Annual Register*, LXXXV (1843), 134–46.

48 *Hans.*, LXIX, 1056 [29 May 1843: Smith].

49 Ibid., 1245–6 [2 June 1843].

50 O'Brien was not yet a member of the Repeal Association, but in May had resigned from the magistracy in protest at government policy. The July 1843 debate was, for him, the last test of the government's intentions towards Ireland. Its failure to produce what he considered an adequate response led him to conclude that 'the Ministry, instead of applying themselves to remove the causes of complaint, have resolved to deprive us of even the liberty of discontent . . . Slowly, reluctantly convinced that Ireland has nothing to hope for from the sagacity, the justice and the generosity of the English Parliament, my reliance shall henceforth be placed upon our own native energy and patriotism', Smith O'Brien to the Repeal Association, 20 Oct. 1843, cited in Macintyre, *Liberator*, pp. 274–5.

O'Brien added to these the relation of landlord and tenant and proposed 'fixity of tenure' as the solution. In introducing the question he admitted the laxity of definition surrounding the term, but went on to reject Conner's construction, and to endorse the general principle of Sharman Crawford's scheme.[51]

Most Irish Whig-Liberal MPs followed O'Brien's lead in the subsequent debate. Thomas Wyse defended the principle of peasant proprietorship, the success of which he had witnessed in other countries:

> [There] the cultivator and the proprietor were, it must be observed, one. What he sowed he felt he was sure to reap. To attain this security, to inspire this conviction was indeed a matter of utmost moment, and worthy of the attention of the greatest statesmen. It was obvious it was not compatible with a system, which exposed the cultivator at every turn to the caprices of a landlord, as ignorant of his own interests in many instances as that of his tenants.[52]

Despite this, he was hesitant to propose legislative intervention in the existing law of contract except to prevent gross abuses. Sir D.J. Norreys went further than most Whig-Liberals in stressing the importance of land reform, by declaring that 'all other questions in comparison with this, were of minor consideration.' He believed that the time was rapidly approaching when 'it would become imperatively necessary to discuss the law of landlord and tenant in a manner which had not hitherto been attempted in that House, and in a way that might startle the principles of any man who considered that he had a right to do what he liked with his own.'[53] He was hesitant to intervene in existing contracts, but thought that the solution might lie in a compulsory and comprehensive waste-lands reclamation scheme designed to provide extra means of subsistence and security to the peasantry. O'Brien's motion of inquiry failed, but the British party leaders could no longer ignore the urgency of the land issue. Sharman Crawford, still determined on extracting 'equal rights' for Ireland, re-introduced his Landlord and Tenant Bill in August as a focus for Irish protest, and agreed to abandon it only on Peel's announcement of a public inquiry into Irish land.[54]

Meanwhile, the Irish Whig-Liberals maintained their campaign, and on 18 July persuaded Russell to call a joint Party meeting at the Reform Club. Russell and the English members dissuaded them from organizing public meetings in England to draw attention to the needs of Ireland, but also entered into serious discussions

---

51 *Hans*, LXX, 630–77 [4 July 1843].

52 Ibid., 685. Wyse was MP for Waterford and had been a junior minister in 1839–41; he was one of the most Whiggish of the Catholic Irish MPs. See Macintyre, *Liberator*, pp. 55–6, Peter Mandler, *Aristocratic government in the age of reform: Whigs and Liberals, 1830–1852* (Oxford, 1990), pp. 68–9.

53 *Hans.*, LXX, 778, [7 July 1843]. Norreys seconded Sharman Crawford's land bill later in the session.

54 Ibid., 943–4 [11 July], 1088–92 [12 July]; LXXI, 412–20, [9 August: S. Crawford, Peel]; S. Crawford to Peel, 8 July, 5 Aug. 1843, Peel Papers, Add. MS 40,531, fols. 14–15, 18–19.

with the Irish over measures of reform.[55] At the end of the session an address of protest to the government was drawn up by Wyse and Smith O'Brien and signed by twenty-nine Irish MPs. This 'solemn remonstrance' listed again the reforms they thought necessary to alleviate the critical state of the country. Along with Church reform, a wider franchise, local government reform and equality of opportunity for Catholics, they pointed to the disordered condition of Irish society, in which the landlord-tenant relationship had been 'deranged . . . by a long course of vicious legislation', and reiterated the demand for legal adjustments.[56]

The British Whig-Liberal leadership, while engaging enthusiastically in the attack on the government, expressed a mixed and cautious interest in the land question. Russell welcomed the suggestions of the Irish members as worthy of debate and consistent with real property rights. He thought the topics discussed 'were not taken up as themes of complaint, but adduced with a view to redress grievances which press hardly upon the people',[57] and had come to the conclusion earlier in the session that coercion was no adequate response to the 'irregular and midnight legislation which has existed for so many years [and] takes no account of justice or injustice'. Parliament was obliged to consider the real grievances that lay behind the agitation for 'fixity of tenure': 'there is the case of tenants being suddenly turned out, contrary to all justice and all principles of charity and kindness, by their landlords into the waste without sustenance and habitation, and deep schemes of revenge and murder and destruction of houses and property are resolved upon.'[58] He ended the session convinced not only that a Peel government could do nothing to conciliate Ireland, but that the Whigs should prepare a programme of 'just and kind' measures for Ireland.[59] Earl Fortescue, the Foxite former Lord Lieutenant, also condemned government policy and called for the legislative redress of Irish grievances, including that of the law of landlord and tenant.[60]

Moderates like Palmerston were more qualified in their language, and advocated reliance on public opinion alone to prevent landlord abuses.[61] Palmerston's reluctance to admit government interference in Irish land was based on more than abstract political economy. He had long taken an active interest in the improvement of his own extensive estates in County Sligo, and since the 1830s his agent had been

---

55 Russell to Palmerston, 15 July 1843, Palmerston (Broadlands) Papers, Southampton University Library, GC/RU/74; Russell to Lansdowne, 19 July 1843, G.P. Gooch (ed.), *The later correspondence of Lord John Russell 1840–1878* (2 vols, London, 1925), I, 64–5.

56 *Morning Chronicle*, 24 Aug. 1843; Macintyre, *Liberator*, pp. 274–5.

57 *Hans.*, LXX, 1003 [11 July 1843].

58 Ibid., 58–9 [16 June]. Russell acknowledged that the landlord had a right to protection from the actions of bad tenants, but that it was necessary to reconcile the peasantry to the rule of law.

59 Russell to Palmerston, 24 July, 19 Aug., Palmerston Papers, GC/RU/75/1–2, 76/1–2.

60 *Hans.* LXX, 1132–3 [14 July]. Ebrington had succeeded as the second Earl Fortescue in 1841.

61 Ibid., 1067 [12 July]. This argument was echoed by Irish Tories, ibid., 946 [11 July: Bateson].

engaged in extensive reorganizations, consolidating and squaring the lands formerly held by middlemen, insisting on payment of rent arrears and ejecting the defaulters.[62]

The 'moralists' Wood and Howick used the 'condition of Ireland' debate to assert their claims to expertise in Irish policy. Both lamented the state of landlord-tenant relations, but passed over the question of legislation in order to concentrate on measures to promote long-term economic improvement. Employment was the great aim, and could be boosted by inducing property to perform its duties, and by removing obstacles to investment. The introduction of a more effective poor law, and the ending of Catholic alienation through sweeping reforms of the Church establishment and the franchise, were the necessary instruments. Some government action in the economy was required, including a pump-priming of the economy by a scheme of public works, and the alleviation of population pressure by assisted emigration along the lines proposed by Charles Buller.[63] Howick's distinctive 'moralist' attitude was evident in his assertion that Ireland's problems were not 'owing to want of capital . . . He believed that Ireland could very soon obtain all the capital she required, and he knew that even if she could not, there was always capital in this country seeking a profitable investment.' Unlike other opposition leaders, Howick criticized his own party's record in government, and believed that Peel had been called by providence 'to the high task . . . of re-organising the disjointed frame of society in Ireland'.[64] These words drew praise from the parliamentary radicals; Roebuck singled him out as being free from the rest of the Whigs' quibbles and narrowness, and Joseph Hume echoed the fervour of his attack on the Irish Church and landlords.[65]

The 'condition of Ireland' debates in 1843 revived Whig-Liberal interest in Ireland as a political priority, even if relations with O'Connell remained cool. The common Whig belief that the maintenance of the Union was the *sine qua non* of Irish progress and British security, remained unchanged. O'Connell's disgust at Russell's inflexibility over this, which he expressed in strong language to Buller,[66] appeared to widen the rift. Nevertheless, the Foxites were confident that O'Connell's monster meeting campaign was tactical, and that he would 'do all in his power to keep the peace'.[67] Russell urged Wyse to persuade O'Connell that the suspension of Repeal agitation would create a public climate favourable to substantial reforms.[68] Contemporaries

---

62 Kenneth Bourne, *Palmerston: the early years 1784–1841* (London, 1982), pp. 257–8; Kincaid to Palmerston, 1 May 1839, Palmerston Papers, BR/146/Sligo 1839.

63 *Hans.*, LXX, 711–18, [4 July 1843: Wood], 877–93, [10 July: Howick]. For the debate on Buller's 'colonization' proposals, which were denounced by Sharman Crawford as 'the transportation of the people', see *Annual Register*, LXXXV (1843), 60–70.

64 *Hans.*, LXX, 881, 893 [10 July 1843].

65 Ibid., 963 [11 July: Roebuck], 1053–4 [12 July: Hume].

66 O'Connell to Buller, 9 Jan. 1844, O'Connell, *Correspondence*, VII, 234–7.

67 Broughton Diary [30 June, 28 July 1843], Broughton Papers, British Library, London, Add. MS 43,745, fols. 161, 176.

68 Russell to Wyse, 21 Jan. 1844, James Johnston Auchmuty, *Sir Thomas Wyse 1791–1862* (London, 1939), p. 195.

were aware that a new direction had been taken in Whig politics. Charles Greville was shocked and indignant at Russell's attempting 'to turn the alarming state of Ireland to a mere party account', and his joining 'the senseless and unmeaning rant about Irish insults and injuries'.[69] His fears were echoed in the centrist liberal press.[70]

The genesis of the Devon Commission

Peel's preferred approach to Irish policy was, in Greville's words, 'to do gradually and safely all he can venture to do, to feel his way . . . to reconcile those prejudices and those interests by degrees to the changes which times and circumstances and the progress of sound systems have put in motion'.[71] The political and social upheavals of 1843 rendered this minimalist policy untenable, and necessitated a 'new departure in the management of . . . Irish affairs'. Peel believed that social peace and security for private investment were vital prerequisites of any real improvement in Ireland, but that under the pressure of the immediate crisis, the government should not appear indifferent to moderate Irish concerns. Senior ministers regarded O'Connell and the bulk of his followers as beyond conciliation, but thought many of the liberal Catholic gentry, middle classes and clergy might be reconciled to the state by concessions.[72]

Although the alleviation of religious grievances was paramount in ministerial deliberations, it was impossible for them to ignore land agitation. Their instincts were decidedly hostile to intervention. Graham publicly condemned the idea of 'fixity of tenure' as 'neither more nor less than confiscation of the land, and the erection of a tribunal of tenants to decide what rent should be paid, and what allowance made for outlay on land'. It was, 'a direct interference with the rights of landlords, which could not take place without the greatest danger, and without an entire overthrow of the existing laws and institutions framed for the protection and defence of property'.[73] Peel agreed:

> any alteration of the law which seriously affected what I understand by the right of property – namely, the free possession of property – any alteration of that great principle which distinguishes civilized from barbarous communities, would be most injurious to the interests of Ireland. If we tell the possessor of wealth that in Ireland the purchase of land will not be uncontrolled, we shall, in my opinion, strike a fatal blow at property.

---

69 Charles Cavendish Fulke Greville, *The Greville memoirs (second part): a journal of the reign of Queen Victoria, from 1837 to 1852*, edited by H. Reeve, 3 vols. (London, 1885), II, 188, 195 [1, 11 Aug. 1843]. Greville and Bedford reluctantly acknowledged the importance the debates had given the landlord-tenant question, ibid., 197–8 [10 Sept.].

70 *Spectator*, 21 Oct. 1843.

71 Greville, *Journal*, II, 199–200 [10 Sept. 1843].

72 Graham to Peel, 15 July 1843, Peel Papers, Add. MS 40,448, fol. 350; Gash, *Sir Robert Peel*, pp. 411–14.

73 *Hans.*, LXX, 816–18, 822 [7 July 1843].

Yet both declared they would not oppose an inquiry into the abuse of landlord powers, particularly with regard to compensation for improvements.[74]

There were several reasons for this decision. Peel and Graham were concerned that the social condition of Ireland should not become a party question, and were angry at the dangerous lengths to which Russell appeared prepared to go 'to conciliate the good will of the Catholic majority'. Graham was convinced that Russell's words on the Church establishment and 'fixity of tenure' would have 'the effect of stimulating the wild hopes and expectations of the most lawless and desperate portion of the Irish agitators'. They were under pressure to act, both from the liberal British press, and from their supporters in Ireland, who were anxious for an inquiry as a means of undermining agitation.[75]

It is apparent that ministers were primarily concerned with containing agitation and neutralizing a dangerous subject, rather than seeking to redress grievances. In July Graham began consultations with George Alexander Hamilton, the strongly Orange MP for Dublin University, but one of the Irish Tories prepared to advocate a non-party investigation.[76] Both Graham and the Prime Minister also found time to read material on the land question, including what Peel thought a 'very curious' letter from the then unknown James Fintan Lalor.[77] Peel drew further encouragement from an article in the *Dublin Review*, a journal close to the Irish Catholic hierarchy, which had suggested that an inquiry and moderate alterations in the law of ejectment would satisfy Catholic opinion.[78]

Ministers were convinced that the landlord-tenant issue was a distraction from the real problems of Irish land. In Graham's opinion, 'the real seat of the evils of Ireland is in the bankrupt condition of the landlords and the severance of the religion of the people from all connection with the state. We cannot heal this gangrene; but we may probe it, and purpose to administer decisive remedies'.[79] A commission of inquiry would be desirable in the short term, to 'open a distinct

---

74 Ibid., 979–81, 983–4 [11 July].

75 Graham to de Grey, 17 June 1843, Graham Papers, bundle 3 IR; *Times*, 16 May, 1 Aug. 1843; J. Morgan to Peel, 26 July, Peel Papers, Add. MS 40,531, fols 339–42.

76 Graham to Peel, 15 July 1843, Peel Papers, Add. MS 40,448, fols 350–1; *Hans.*, LXX, 1033–43 [12 July 1843: Hamilton].

77 Peel thought that Lalor's attack on O'Connell's 'series of wretched agitations', and his argument that Repeal could be safely suppressed if coercion was accompanied by agrarian reforms, displayed more 'dispassionate and comprehensive' views than most of his Irish correspondence. Graham, however, found the details vague and allusive. He sarcastically dismissed Lalor's claim that his plan 'will "not only effect a reconciliation and establish good feelings between landlords and tenants, but will suppress the present and prevent any future agitation". This nostrum, if it be genuine, would be worth a great price', Lalor to Peel, July 1843, Peel Papers, Add. MS 40,530, fols. 399–400; Peel to de Grey, 21 July, ibid., Add. MS 40,478, fol. 93; Graham to Peel, 18 July 1843, ibid., Add. MS 40,448, fol. 360.

78 Peel to Graham, 4 Sept. 1843, ibid., Add. MS 40,449, fol. 18; [Patrick McMahon], 'Depopulation – fixity of tenure', *Dublin Review*, XIII (Nov. 1842), 512–60.

79 Graham to Peel, 6 Sept. 1843, Peel Papers, Add. MS 40,449, fols. 27–8.

view of the causes of discontent in Ireland'. He was pessimistic as to the practical outcome, fearing that 'the remedies are beyond the reach of legislative power'. Like Hamilton, he thought that the inquiry would have a beneficial moral effect, as 'sympathy with the sorrow of an entire people will be evinced by the Government, and the public mind may be satisfied and soothed in some degree by kindness of purpose and the exposure of injustice.'[80]

The public character of the inquiry was thus of paramount importance. Sugden and de Grey feared that it might raise popular expectations by appearing to legitimize Sharman Crawford's 'inadmissible' plan, and thus provoke further agitation, but their preference for a quiet and cautious investigation into the practicability of a series of moderate reforms was overruled.[81] Eliot was more optimistic that in the wake of a good harvest in 1843 a public gesture could help wean respectable farmers from a movement now dominated by labourers 'excited almost to madness by the language of agitation'.[82] The Commission was from the start primarily an exercise in public relations, expected to hold the line while other initiatives came to fruition.

Peel and Graham went to some lengths to ensure that the personnel of the Commission were amenable to their own pre-conceptions while appearing non-partisan. The Earl of Devon, an Irish landowner of liberal Conservative politics, offered advice to Peel on the subject, and was prevailed upon to accept the chairmanship.[83] Devon's attitudes made him ideal for the post. He recognized the need for a 'counter irritation' to O'Connell's agitation, but believed the only effective solution to the underlying crisis was a greater provision of private employment on land improvement. 'Proper conduct on the part of individuals' was the remedy; the role of 'a prudent Commission' would be to expose malpractices and, 'to dissipate many errors, and perhaps assist you towards some little amendment of the law. Much cannot be done by legislation.'[84] Devon was joined by Hamilton, whose Orangist sympathies and respected position on the back-benches would allay Irish Tory suspicions of a sell-out on tenant right.[85] John Wynne, another Irish Conservative and owner of 28,000 acres in Sligo and Leitrim, was de Grey's suggestion for the third Commissioner.[86] Graham was anxious that the inquiry be

---

80 Graham to Peel, 17 Oct. 1843, ibid., fols. 91–3.

81 Graham to Eliot, 11 Sept., Sugden: 'Draft of a suggestion for a plan of proposed inquiry into the operation of the relation of landlord and tenant in Ireland', Sugden to Graham, 16 Sept., de Grey to Graham, 18 Sept., Graham Papers, bundle 5 IR.

82 Eliot to Graham, 2 Sept., ibid.; Eliot to Graham, 15 Nov., ibid., bundle 11 IR.

83 Graham to Peel, 24 Sept. 1843, Peel Papers, Add. MS 40,449, fols 55–6; Wellington was consulted and approved the appointment, Wellington to Peel, 10 Oct. 1843, C.S. Parker (ed.), *Sir Robert Peel from his private papers* (3 vols., London, 1891–9), III, 64.

84 Devon to Peel, 1 Sept., Peel Papers, Add. MS 40,533, fols 1–3; Devon to Eliot, 8 Sept., Graham Papers, bundle 5 IR.

85 Irish Tory opinion was as divided on the idea of an investigation into landholding as it was on Peel's 1843 policy generally, see McCaffrey, *O'Connell and the Repeal year*, pp. 93–105.

86 De Grey to Graham, 11 Oct. 1843, Graham Papers, bundle 6 IR. Wynne, who became Irish

initiated as soon as possible, but finding two suitable Whig-Liberal improving landowners proved difficult, and it was not until mid-November that Sir Robert Ferguson and Thomas Redington agreed to serve. The accession of the latter, a signatory to the Irish Whig-Liberal remonstrance of August, was regarded as a good omen.[87] The choice of secretary to the Commission was left to Devon, who selected John Pitt Kennedy, a former Royal Engineers officer, expert on public works, progressive farmer, and subsequently land agent on Devon's estates in County Limerick.[88] Following suggestions by Stanley and Graham, the Commission's terms of reference were carefully worded to avoid giving any commitment to reform. The Commission was to inquire into the state of the law and practice of the occupation of land in Ireland, and into local taxation, and to suggest any legal amendments, 'which, having due regard to the just rights of property, may be calculated to encourage the cultivation of the soil, to extend a better system of agriculture, and to improve the relation between landlord and tenant in that part of our United Kingdom.'[89] This order of priorities, implying the subordination of tenurial adjustment to the greater aim of agricultural development, revealed the true intentions of government policy.

II THE COMMISSION AND ITS CRITICS, 1843–4

The appointment of the Devon Commission was only partly successful in defusing the land question as a political issue. O'Connell was unimpressed, and told FitzPatrick: 'the Commission, formed as it is, can be nothing but a bubble. It is perfectly one-sided – all landlords and no tenants. I do not think it should have the confidence of the people.'[90] Yet while attacking the commissioners as 'a board of foxes deliberating gravely over a flock of geese', he was prepared to correspond with Devon and to give evidence before him.[91] As usual, O'Connell responded to

---

Under-Secretary under Derby in 1852, was particularly conscious of the difficulties facing Irish landowners, as his estates were mortgaged to the value of over £100,000. His father had acquired a reputation as one of the most ruthless rent-extractors in the county, Winston Guthrie-Jones, *The Wynnes of Sligo and Leitrim* (Manorhamilton, 1994), pp. 73–8; Henry D. Inglis, *A journey throughout Ireland* (3rd edn, 2 vols., London, 1835), II, 125.

87 De Grey to Graham, 25 Oct., Graham to de Grey, 27 Oct., Graham Papers, bundle 6 IR; de Grey to Graham, 2, 8, 14 Nov., Graham to de Grey, 4, 6 Nov., ibid., bundle 11 IR. Ferguson was the 'moderate' MP for Londonderry City; Redington was a Galway landowner, MP for Dundalk, and, most importantly, a Catholic.

88 Kennedy's approach to Irish social problems was epitomized by the title of a pamphlet he had published some years before, *Instruct, employ, don't hang them: or, Ireland tranquillized without soldiers and enriched without English capital* (London, 1835).

89 Graham to Peel, 13 Oct. 1843, Peel Papers, Add. MSS 40,449, fols. 81–2; Graham to de Grey, 13 Oct., Graham Papers, bundle 6 IR; *Devon Commission*, part I, P.P. 1845 [605], XIX, 3. The inclusion of 'a better system of agriculture' was made at Stanley's prompting, Stanley to Graham, 8 Oct. 1843, Derby Papers, 920 DER (14) 174/1, fols. 54–5.

90 O'Connell to FitzPatrick, 13 Dec. 1843, O'Connell, *Correspondence*, VII, 228.

91 O'Connell to Mahony, 17 Dec. 1843, O'Connell to Ray, 15 Dec. 1843, ibid., pp. 231–2; *Devon Commission*, part III, P.P. 1845 [657], XXI, 939–48.

the challenge posed by the Commission at two levels. In Ireland he established a Repeal Association committee to shadow and criticise the government body's activities.[92] At the same time he was ready to take the first tentative steps towards a rapprochement with the British opposition. Writing to Lord Campbell in September 1843, he was severely critical of what he saw as a Whig failure of leadership, and demanded that they support measures 'to mitigate the statute law as between landlord and tenant', alongside other parliamentary and corporate reforms and an abatement of 'the Church nuisance in Ireland'.[93] In January 1844 he wrote to Charles Buller, a Benthamite radical with close ties to the Whig-Liberal leadership, stressing ecclesiastical reform as the first priority, closely followed by agrarian reform.[94] While including his long-standing demands for a punitive income tax on absentees, and the restoration of the (idealized) former balance between landlord and tenant through the abolition of seven post-Union laws which had increased the landlord's powers of distraint and eviction, O'Connell went on to say that 'the question of fixity of tenure should be taken into the most deliberate consideration'. What exactly this amounted to remained imprecise, but he denounced the 'present humbug Committee' [the Devon Commission] and called for a real inquiry including representatives of the tenants.[95]

Some British Whig-Liberals shared his dislike of the Commission. Russell's opinions on the landlord-tenant question were somewhat opaque, but his bias was firmly Foxite, conceiving of the matter in terms of rights and 'justice', and he was deeply suspicious of Peel. He commented to Lansdowne: 'This Commission to enquire into the conduct of Landlords is a curious affair, especially on the part of a man who so gravely censured Drummond for saying, "Property has its duties as well as its rights".'[96] Russell began to give serious consideration to agrarian reform in autumn 1843. His first thought was to suggest to Duncannon legislation on compensation for improvements authorized by the landlord, with an extra poor rate charge on the estates of those who ejected their tenantry.[97] Duncannon, with more experience of Irish conditions and of popular demands, endorsed the latter, but questioned the effectiveness of the former: 'It may be possible to frame a bill

---

92 For the work of this committee, see below, pp. 72–4.

93 O'Connell to Campbell, 9 Sept. 1843, O'Connell, *Correspondence*, VII, 223–4.

94 Buller, who had long been on good terms with the Irish leader, had inquired as to what O'Connell now considered necessary to give 'Justice to Ireland'. See D.A. Haury, *The origins of the Liberal Party and liberal imperialism: the career of Charles Buller, 1806–1848* (New York, 1987), pp. 223–4.

95 O'Connell to Buller, 9 Jan. 1844, O'Connell, *Correspondence*, VII, 234–7. O'Connell had in mind particularly the Acts of 1816 and 1820 which had reduced the expense to the landlord of the civil process for ejectment on holdings rented under £50 yearly, *Devon Commission*, part III, P.P. 1845 [657], XXI, 939–40.

96 Russell to Lansdowne, 11 Nov. 1843, Gooch, *Later correspondence*, I, 69.

97 Russell to Duncannon, 17 Sept. 1843, Bessborough Papers, West Sussex Record Office, Chichester, F. 250.

giving compensation to an outgoing tenant . . . but that will not redress the great grievance which has been the cause of half the murders and outrages in Ireland.' The real crisis lay in the eviction of large numbers of families who had been subtenants under a middleman whose lease had expired, who now lacked any legal rights, and for whom nobody would take responsibility:

> The landlord says he will not accept possession unless it is delivered up to him as his ancestor let it . . . The lessee answers that during the first 40 years of the lease he was impelled by the agent or family of his landlord to divide his land to swell the amount of rent, or to make 40 shilling freeholders for parliamentary influence, and that it is hard 360 innocent persons should be thrown on the road, because the policy is changed . . . The landlord however is obdurate, the under-tenants are turned out because they are nobody's tenants, although put there with the concurrence of the agent and knowledge of the landlord, and are left with their families to starve on the road. This has been since 1825 a common occurrence . . .

The plight of these people, wrote Duncannon, was the key problem; even Sharman Crawford's Bill could not ameliorate their condition.[98] He could see no immediate remedy (although agreeing with Russell's idea of a punitive poor rate), but began work on a suitable bill that could be introduced should the Whig-Liberals return to office.[99]

The government's decision at last to abandon its 'do nothing' policy and to prosecute O'Connell after banning the Clontarf 'monster meeting' in October 1843 began the process of clearing the air between O'Connell and the Whigs. The coercive action taken by the government was only superficially a defeat for O'Connell, as it allowed him to don a cloak of martyrdom, to shift his tactics and attempt to expend the political capital amassed through his mobilization of popular discontent. Palmerston and Russell both welcomed the government's action, if for different reasons; Palmerston believed that O'Connell 'has had a flooring', and decided he would 'not be sorry if the prosecution succeeds'. Russell, on the other hand, thought that the government had bungled, and that O'Connell was probably 'delighted' at the government's action as 'it answers his purpose perfectly'. For his part, Duncannon believed that the agitation had gone beyond what O'Connell had expected or wished, and that he would be 'glad of having a stop put to his proceedings by the government, to relieve him from his embarrassment'.[100]

This difference reflected not only temperamental dissimilarities, but conflicting attitudes towards Irish reform. Palmerston was more alarmed at the state of Ireland,

---

98 Duncannon to Russell, 29 Sept. 1843, ibid., F. 26.

99 Bessborough to Russell, 10 Jan. 1845, Russell Papers, Public Record Office, London, 30/22/4D, fols. 111–12.

100 Palmerston to Russell, 22 Oct. 1843, Gooch, *Later correspondence*, I, 65–7; Greville, *Journal*, II, 206 [31 Oct. 1843]; Duncannon to Charlemont, 5 Sept., Bessborough Papers, F. 26.

sceptical as to the value of conciliatory reform, and disposed to leave the initiative to others.[101] Russell, meanwhile, was in correspondence with D.R. Pigot, effectively the Party's Irish co-ordinator, on a programme for the next session. He told Lansdowne, 'whatever the peril may be . . . I shall not think to have done my duty unless I contribute when Parliament meets the best advice I can give to set things right. The concessions must be large, and must be undertaken in a friendly and not a grudging spirit.' It was the impossibility of Conservatives ever showing such generosity of spirit that made 'Peel and the good government of Ireland . . . a contradiction in terms'.[102]

From 1843 Russell and his Foxite colleagues sought to revivify the deeply dispirited Party on the question of Irish reform. As Grey had been forced aside in 1834 as a result of his conservatism over Ireland, so Russell now thought it necessary to break finally with the aged Melbourne, whose advocacy of harsh coercion was 'a sad proof of his inability to judge correctly the present state of affairs in Ireland'.[103] Other Foxites rallied energetically to the cause; Normanby determined to make full use of his improved health to wage 'a good fight for the removal of [Ireland's] real grievances', and was much shocked by Melbourne's implication that the Irish were beyond the reach of good government.[104]

The immediate point at issue was a classic Foxite issue – the suspension of British liberties during the prosecution and trial of O'Connell for sedition. Whatever his excesses, the Irish leader was entitled to a fair trial by an impartial jury. Russell was sure this would not happen, and that the excitement of the trial would be counterproductive. Moreover, he believed the real criminals were now to escape retribution:

> [I]f Lord Lyndhurst and Lord Stanley, who denounced the Irish as aliens and perjurers were put upon their trial as well as O'Connell, I might think somewhat like equal justice was done. But that those who have been feeding animosity and national ill-will against Ireland for the last eight years should expect that we, who implored them not to do so, should now join in their indignation at finding that contumely and calumny produce anger and hatred is rather too much.[105]

---

101 Lord Broughton, *Recollections of a long life*, edited by Lady Dorchester, 6 vols., (London, 1909–11), VI, 81–2 [3 July 1843].

102 Russell to Lansdowne, 9, 31 Oct. 1843, Gooch, *Later correspondence*, I, 65, 67.

103 Russell to Duncannon, 7 Dec. 1843, Bessborough Papers , F. 250; Russell to Clarendon, 28 Jan. 1844, Clarendon Deposit, Bodleian Library, Oxford, c.523.

104 Normanby to Monteagle, 1 Dec. 1843, Monteagle Papers, National Library of Ireland, Dublin, MS 13,394/2; Diary of Lord Morpeth, 1 Dec. 1843, Castle Howard Papers, Castle Howard, N. Yorkshire, J19/8/1.

105 Russell to Senior, 9 Dec. 1843, Nassau Senior Papers, National Library of Wales, Aberystwyth, C364.

The miscarriages of justice associated with the trial of O'Connell and his fellow 'traversers' strengthened these sentiments.

Russell's success in interesting the Party in Ireland was due at least in part to the willingness of Lansdowne and his associates to participate in a new Irish reform campaign. Monteagle and Clanricarde, the leading Irish moderates, were anxious for 'healing measures' and were sceptical of Peel's tardy 'plausible claptraps'.[106] Consensus on economic matters was unlikely, so it was probable that these 'healing measures' should concern themselves primarily with the question of the established Church and Catholic rights. The Party leaders were able to achieve some degree of cohesion through their mutual endorsement of Nassau Senior's article in the January 1844 number of the *Edinburgh Review.*

Senior on Ireland

The initiative for the article came from Senior and Lansdowne, who agreed that a statement of Whig-Liberal intentions was expedient at a time when Irish agitation was 'making the whole empire shake'. Senior's starting points were the remodelling of the established Church, a provision for the Catholic clergy from an imperial fund, the improvement of national education, and the abolition of the lord lieutenancy. There would be no appeal to the Repealers, 'for they are no more to be treated with than a wolf can be treated with by a shepherd', but Senior hoped his proposals would also be acceptable to 'moderate Tories'.[107] The last comment brought a rebuke from the *Edinburgh's* editor Macvey Napier, who refused to countenance a coalition ministry, and was anxious to keep his journal a Party organ.[108]

The article was from the outset a Bowood project. Monteagle and Whately read the early drafts, and Lansdowne gave it his imprimatur.[109] Monteagle had some reservations about the final draft, fearing that Senior's lack of local knowledge had led him to be somewhat rash in his language and to exaggerate his criticism of the Catholic Church, and regretting that he omitted to deal with the Poor Law and tenure issues, but Senior admitted to seeing 'less clearly' the means of improving the condition of the people, and privately endorsed the Devon inquiry.[110] However, some of Monteagle's suggestions were adopted, and he was always in agreement with the main points and principles.[111] Since 1836 the moderate agenda had shifted

106 Clanricarde to Monteagle, 10 Nov. 1843, Monteagle Papers, MS 13,394/1.

107 Senior to Napier, 5, 12, 14 June 1843, Macvey Napier Papers, British Library, London, Add. MS 34,623, fols. 589–92, 622–3, 624–6.

108 Napier to Senior, 29 July, Senior Papers, C309.

109 Senior to Napier, 27 Aug., 9 Nov., Macvey Napier Papers, Add. MS 34,624, fols. 64–8, 207–8.

110 Monteagle to Napier, 7 Dec. 1843, Monteagle Papers, MS 13,394/4; Senior to Napier, 12 June, Macvey Napier Papers, Add. MS 34,623, fol. 623; Senior to Napier, 14 Nov., ibid., Add. MS 34,624, fols. 715–16.

111 Napier to Monteagle, 25 Dec. 1843, Monteagle Papers, MS 13,394/4; Empson to Monteagle, 25 Dec. 1843, ibid., MS 13,394/1. Monteagle's relationship with the leading figures in the

away from developmental intervention towards the promotion of agencies of social control and economic stimulation.

Napier had doubts about practicality of Senior's proposals, and insisted it be seen by Russell before publication. In late November and early December copies of the manuscript were circulated to Party leaders for their comments. Napier was concerned about the forcefulness of the section on Church reform, but when Russell and Fortescue added their support to Lansdowne's, he felt he could not object.[112] Russell took a keen interest in the paper, believing it 'able, calm and judicious'; but his detailed objections reveal the disparity of perspective lying behind the superficial consensus. Senior argued that Catholic endowment was necessary to separate the clergy from the unruly masses and the 'revolutionary' party. This was argued from first principles with rigorous logic:

> 1. I trace the physical evils of Ireland to the concurrent want of capital and of small proprietors. I trace the want of capital to insecurity, ignorance and indolence; and both of these to insecurity. 2. I trace insecurity to the hatred of the law. I say that the law cannot be popular till the institutions of Ireland are just, and justice requires the two churches be put on equality. Therefore the Catholic priests must be paid.[113]

Russell's defence of the Whig-Liberal government's record from 1835 to 1841 – when he had postponed endowment on finding the Catholic prelates averse to it – and the tone of his comments on future policy, expressed a different priority: 'Unless the feelings of the Irish people, their national pride and ambition are satisfied, it is useless to propose stipends for their clergy or outlay of money. They will consider such offers as bribes to church them.'[114] Under pressure from the editor, Senior amended his draft slightly to take account of some of these cavils, but Russell did not press them. The Whig leader told Napier: 'I must repeat that although a general concurrence of views between the *Edinburgh Review*, and the bulk of the Whig Party is very desirable, it would injure both the Party and the *Review*, if the writers in the *Review* were checked in their general observations, or the Party bound to enforce practically all that is speculatively beneficial.' There was no point in trying 'to combine the expressions of various politicians into one crucible'.[115]

Edinburgh Review was intimate, as he was the chief Whig-Liberal commentator on government economic policy, see Russell to Monteagle, 22 Aug. 1843, ibid., MS 13,394/3; [Monteagle] 'Distress in the manufacturing districts – causes and remedies', *Edinburgh Review*, LXXVII (Feb. 1843), 190–227.

112 Napier to Senior, 18 Nov. 1843, Senior Papers, C316; Napier to Monteagle, 14 Dec. 1843, Monteagle Papers, MS 13,394/2.

113 Senior to Napier, 14 Nov. 1843, Macvey Napier Papers, Add. MS 34,624, fols. 216–17.

114 Russell to Napier, 1 Dec. 1843, ibid., fols. 255–6.

115 Napier to Senior, 7 Dec., Russell to Senior, 7 Dec., Senior Papers, C318, C363; Russell to Napier, 9 Dec., Napier Papers, Add. MS 34,624, fols. 719–20. Senior deprecated this 'running the gauntlet of party leaders', but thought it worthwhile if it tied the party to certain favoured policies, Senior to Whately, 8 Dec. 1843, Senior Papers, C632.

For Russell and his circle, the *Edinburgh Review* article was of value as a reformist manifesto that would be broadly acceptable to most elements of the Party, but their commitment did not extend to the ideological premises from which Senior and Lansdowne drew their version of 'justice to Ireland'. For Senior the moral evils of Ireland (i.e. the absence of the structural and internalized instruments of 'civilization' consequent on clerical authority in society) were at the root of the physical ones, and Catholic endowment and additional education expenditure were thus essential to further the economic development along orthodox lines.[116] Senior believed it worthwhile to conciliate only the clergy and the gentry, for O'Connell and his 'revolutionary party' were beyond the pale. Indeed in his earlier drafts Senior had included a character sketch denigrating the Irish leader as intellectually shallow, morally dishonest and (worst of all) inadmissible to good society.[117]

The 1843 debates led Senior to go beyond his original intentions and address (in passing) the land question in his paper. He had acquired information about Ulster tenant right from the land agents of Lord Lurgan and Sir Robert Ferguson, but chose to ignore this phenomenon in his article;[118] 'fixity of tenure' he denounced as the desire of the social revolutionaries in the Repeal movement to confiscate the property of Ireland. In his description of the material evils of Ireland he was, however, prepared to modify the orthodox theory so far as to admit that 'want of small proprietors' might be a problem of equal weight to 'want of capital'. A society could succeed if supplied with one and not the other, but his strong preference remained for an adequate supply of capital and a tripartite division of labour. Peasant societies lacked middle classes, making them deficient in civilization and less likely to achieve high labour productivity and a rapid accumulation of wealth. The achievement of social harmony under an improved system required considerable capital investment, but this would be forthcoming from England once the principal moral evil of insecurity was removed. Senior did not rule out the desirability of 'small proprietors', but these were subsidiary to his main arguments, and bourgeois rather than peasant ownership was implied.[119]

Senior believed that the solution to Irish social conflict lay in the harmonization of interests inherent in a fully capitalized large-farm society. It followed that the existing land law was largely satisfactory, and that the problem lay in the ignorance and resistance to the law that characterized Irish rural society. While 'justice to Ireland' represented for the Foxites a positive response to the articulated grievances

116 Senior to Napier, 8 Sept. 1843, Napier Papers, Add. MS 34,624, fols. 79–80; Nassau W. Senior, 'Ireland in 1843', *Journals, conversations and essays relating to Ireland* (2 vols., London, 1868), I, 139.

117 Ibid., pp. 69–74, 121–2.

118 Miscellaneous notes on tenant right in Ulster (June 1843), Senior Papers, D46.

119 'Ireland in 1843', Senior, *Journals*, I, 20–52, 111. The reference to small proprietors appears to have been inserted in response to Fortescue's advocacy of the subject, Fortescue to Senior, 17 Nov., Senior to Fortescue, 24 Nov. 1843, Fortescue Papers, Devon County Record Office, Exeter, 1262M/FC 99.

of Ireland, Bowood was more interested in finding mechanisms to persuade the Irish to accept the justice of existing social institutions and economic relationships.[120]

Despite its 'party' character, the article was well received by centrist liberal opinion. The *Spectator* welcomed what it perceived as the Whigs' belated renunciation of O'Connell, praised the comprehensiveness of Senior's scheme and hinted that Peel could enact much of it.[121] This rapture was not universal. One Irish observer who favoured an enhanced grant to the seminary at Maynooth found Senior's treatment of Irish national feeling 'flippant' and thought his proposals amounted to a crude bribe.[122] The radical pro-Catholic author of another hostile pamphlet rejected the endowment proposal as impractical and offensive to the clergy. The 'happy accident' of Normanby's viceroyalty was recalled, but comprehensive popular reforms were now the only way to pacify Ireland. It was the gentry – 'the spoiled children of the state' – who were at the root of the problem; their privileges needed to be curbed if English and Irish property was not be swallowed up in a common ruin.[123] This was closer to traditional Foxite thinking than Senior's paper; it remained to be seen which path Russell would follow.

The 1844 session

The centre-piece of the Whig assault on the government in the following session was Russell's motion on the state of Ireland, introduced on 13 February 1844. Russell embraced this task with moral fervour. Hobhouse recorded a private conversation:

> He spoke in the strongest terms of reprobation against the Government doings in Ireland; and when I said that I feared the people of England would not sympathise with him in that respect, said he was sorry for it, but that would not reconcile him to injustice or silence him; quite the contrary . . . If people were wrong they ought to be put right.[124]

Reflecting the shared Party programme, Russell's speech concentrated on the Church, the franchise and the administration of justice. He was, however, prepared to denounce 'the wholesale massacres of the clearance system', along with the retaliatory murders that this produced, although for the time being he could only recommend a more impartial administration of justice to combat it. While not

120 Russell and Bessborough remained sceptical of Catholic endowment, and it emerged as a government priority only in later 1848 when Russell's social policies for Ireland had been exhausted, Russell to Palmerston, 28 Dec. 1844, Palmerston Papers, GC/RU/87/1–2. See below, pp. 209–10.

121 *Spectator*, 30 Dec. 1843.

122 Philip Reade, *Whig and Tory remedies for Irish evils, and the effects a repeal of the Corn Laws would have on the legislative union* (Dublin, 1844), pp. 22–3.

123 [Anon.], *Remarks by a junior to his senior, on an article in the Edinburgh Review of January, 1844, on the state of Ireland, and the measures for its improvement* (London, 1844).

124 Broughton, *Recollections*, VI, 88 [27 Jan. 1844].

straying beyond the recommendations of Senior's manifesto, Russell's tone was markedly different, and he went out of his way to praise O'Connell's exertions to prevent the government's lazy and careless conduct leading to a bloody disaster, and to roundly denounce the state trials then in progress in Dublin. Russell again invoked the spirit of his political idol, quoting 'The words of Mr Fox . . . in behalf of oppressed Irishmen'.[125] While Russell strove to co-ordinate the Party's energies against Peel, and to initiate what Greville considered 'a new war of principles', it was clear to contemporaries that the Party was not fully united on its Irish policy.[126] This was most evident in the area of land policy, which the Whigs raised in parliament despite the government's plea that the issue be postponed whilst the Devon Commission was sitting.

Normanby led his assault on the 1844 Queen's speech, in which the Commission's appointment was formally announced, with a frontal attack on its principle and activities. He was not alone in doing so in the Lords, for Clanricarde and Fitzwilliam stated that the investigations conducted so publicly could only raise 'mischievous expectations' among the tenantry by implying that the government was prepared to make extensive alterations to the land laws.[127] Unlike his 'moderate' colleagues, however, Normanby clearly felt that legislation was desirable, and suspected that the Commission would be used to prevent consideration of measures on the subject introduced by others.[128] With Sharman Crawford's Bill in cold storage and Duncannon still at work on his own draft, the Commission appeared to Normanby as an attempt to frustrate measures necessary to remove from the landlord the 'monopoly of the means of existence, and . . . [the] power of enforcing his bargains . . . [by] the power of starvation.' Still, he was prepared to admit that it might be beneficial in drawing to the attention of England the wants of the Irish people, and hence dissipating its 'utter ignorance' of Ireland.[129] Normanby's scepticism may well have been bolstered by the views of Lord Headley's land agent John Wiggins, whose opinions on rack-renting were quoted in his speech. Wiggins had doubted that the inquiry could be impartial: 'What tenant will dare to complain of his landlord or his agent? Alas . . . all that can be expected, is a record of such facts and opinions as may tend to rebut what have been called "calumnies" against the Irish landlords.'[130]

---

125 *Hans.*, LXXII, 683–726 [13 Feb. 1844].

126 Greville, *Journal*, II, 229 [17 Feb. 1844].

127 *Hans.*, LXXII, 32–6 [1 Feb. 1844: Clanricarde, Fitzwilliam].

128 Ibid., 18–19.

129 Ibid., 630–2 [13 Feb. 1844].

130 John Wiggins, *The 'monster' misery of Ireland: a practical treatise on the relation of landlord and tenant* (London, 1844), p. 284. The Headley estate in County Kerry was well known for waste-land reclamation and the comfortable condition of its tenantry, see Inglis, *Journey*, pp. 233–5, Lord John Manners, *Notes of an Irish tour in 1846* (new edn, Edinburgh and London, 1881), p. 75; *Spectator*, 17 Oct. 1846.

Fortescue also thought an inquiry would be useful in enlightening those 'Saxons [who] cannot duly appreciate the extent of the misery produced by the ejectment of the Irish cottier tenantry'. While not personally hostile towards Devon, he thought that:

> the objections which are felt by landlords of all parties to the admission of any interference with proprietary rights, will render the performance of [the Commissioners'] duty impossible without the strongest call on public attention to the proceedings of the Commissioners, and the strongest expression of public opinion in support of such an enquiry as may expose fully the nature and extent of grievances . . . [131]

Normanby believed that it was vital to raise such questions, and to express some sympathy for Irish political demands in parliament, if Whig influence in Ireland was to be preserved. Non-Foxites like Clarendon objected strongly that this was irresponsible and inexpedient, and urged that 'generalities liable to misconstruction, and expectations incapable of fulfilment, should be most carefully avoided'.[132]

The consequence of the Foxite initiative was a growing rapprochement with O'Connell in the course of 1844. In the interval between being found guilty of sedition on 10 February and receiving a sentence of one year's imprisonment on 30 May, O'Connell toured England, and was feted by Whigs in parliament and radicals outdoors. When finally committed to Richmond Penitentiary in Dublin, he wrote to Sheil contrasting the feeble stance taken by the Irish Whig-Liberals with that of Russell, who, he was 'bound to say . . . readily and gratefully . . . has behaved exceedingly well respecting these trials'.[133] Indeed, O'Connell's unexpected early release in September was the result of Whig pressure for an appeal and a partisan vote by the Whig Law Lords.[134] Despite his good treatment in prison, O'Connell was grateful for his release. His first speech to the Repeal Association on regaining his freedom paid tribute to the Whigs, and sought 'atonement' for his previous unfair censure of them.[135] This volte-face was a major step away from the rhetoric of the 'monster meetings' and paved the way for a renewal of the Lichfield House alliance.[136] Much of the credit for this lay with Russell and his

---

131 Fortescue to Senior, 17 Nov. 1843, Fortescue Papers, 1262M/FC 99.

132 Normanby to Clarendon, 17 Dec., Clarendon to Normanby, 22 Dec. 1843, Herbert Maxwell (ed.), *The life and letters of George William Frederick fourth Earl of Clarendon* (2 vols., London, 1913), I, 249–52.

133 O'Connell to Sheil, 19 June 1844, O'Connell, *Correspondence*, VII, 256–7.

134 The Whig Law Lords were more united than the party leadership: Russell and Normanby supported Wyse, Sheil and Wilde in their parliamentary efforts on O'Connell's behalf, while Hobhouse, Bedford and the Duke of Leinster were opposed to any such initiative, and Howick was doubtful, Broughton Diary, Add. MS 43,746, fols 137–8, 144–6 [8, 9, 12 June 1844].

135 *Nation*, 14 Sept. 1844; MacDonagh, *Emancipist*, p. 252.

136 Conservative commentators were, predictably, outraged at the prospect, and accused both O'Connell and the Whigs of hypocrisy, [J.W. Croker], 'Repeal agitation', *Quarterly Review*, LXXV (Dec. 1844), 222–92.

closest colleagues for their restraint under provocation, yet great obstacles remained. Peel's Irish reform initiative of 1844–5 confused the clear party lines Russell desired, and large elements within the opposition were hostile to any renewed O'Connellite pact. O'Connell was himself hampered by the need to mollify the anti-Whig Young Irelanders who had acquired greater prominence in the Repeal ranks, and was under pressure from the intransigent Archbishop John MacHale of Tuam to adopt a more pronounced 'Catholic' line. As a result, the situation at the close of 1844 was not greatly altered from the 'vast babel of conflicting opinions' which Greville had observed at the start of the year.[137]

The Devon Commission at work

While O'Connell and the Whig-Liberals were redefining their positions, the investigations of the Devon Commission proceeded apace. The body spent much of 1844 amassing evidence: general information on the management of estates was taken first by examination of assistant barristers, land agents and others with expertise who were resident in Dublin. A series of letters and circulars was then sent out to boards of guardians and to the Church of Ireland and Catholic bishops and Presbyterian moderators requesting information and contacts. A 'paper of queries' was circulated to those who expressed interest, pointing out the principal subjects of investigation; these included the state of local agriculture, the size and conditions of farms, the levels and types of rent, the forms of tenure and the prevalence of 'tenant right', the state of improvement and consolidation, the condition of the farming population, and the charges on the land.[138] The Commissioners then proceeded in the summer and autumn of 1844 to tour the country, travelling 3,126 miles, sitting in 90 towns and examining 1,100 witnesses of all classes (although cottiers and smallholders were poorly represented). These were chosen mostly by the corresponding guardians and clergy, but the Commissioners insisted on hearing all who tendered evidence, and published all that was recorded on oath at length, 'to avoid the dangers of a partial selection'.[139]

Despite some frustration at the slowness of the Commission's proceedings, the Irish executive was pleased by what it saw as the generally benign popular response and the readiness of people to testify.[140] Eliot continued to believe that only increased employment could provide an antidote to the 'poison' of Repeal agitation, but was confident that the Commission's activities had induced 'many landlords desirous of making a good figure' in the report to improve their estates and the condition of their tenants.[141] The Irish press attributed reported incidents of landlord-tenant

137 Greville, *Journal*, II, 221 [26 Jan. 1844].
138 *Devon Commission*, part I, P.P. 1845 [605], XIX, 46–7, Letter no. 4.
139 Ibid., XIX, 5–6; part V, *Index*, P.P. 1845 [673], XXII, 225–8.
140 Eliot to Graham, 30 Nov. 1843, Graham Papers, bundle 11 IR; de Grey to Graham, 14 Feb. 1844, ibid., bundle 14 IR.
141 Eliot to Graham, 3 Oct. 1844, ibid., bundle 17 IR.

co-operation, involving mutual concessions, to the operations of the inquiry.[142] Yet the gulf between popular expectations and government intentions widened during the course of the inquiry, and the increasing interest expressed in the subject by the liberal and radical press and pamphleteers in Britain created great anxiety in Irish landlord circles. O'Connell's renewed alliance with the anti-Corn Law movement in 1843–4 led to something of a juncture between the British and Irish anti-landlordist campaigns, epitomized in a sympathetic history of Ireland written by the free-trade polemicist Samuel Smiles.[143] Landlord apologists found themselves thrown onto the defensive by a stream of '"monster pamphlets" and "monster paragraphs", all marked by "monstrous" assertions and "monstrous" ignorance', which were believed to be the product of Whig and radical political manoeuvring. Appeals made to Peel for assistance in promoting agrarian anglicization now included desperate calls for the suppression of the political agitation thought still to be convulsing the country.[144] If Peel's policy in 1843–4 had succeeded in containing and delaying confrontation on the land question, the problems to be encountered in the 1845 session were formidable.

III 'A CART-LOAD OF CROSS-EXAMINATIONS': THE RESPONSE TO THE DEVON COMMISSION REPORT

The outcome of the Devon inquiry reflected the manner of its inception. Two faces were presented; the first, in the shape of the report and its three massive volumes of evidence, was formal, public and didactic, and was intended to allay anxieties in Britain and Ireland. The second, recorded in the informal private correspondence between the Commissioners and the ministry, expressed their real concerns and priorities. The failure of the report to achieve the desired effect on public opinion in either country placed increased pressure on the government to resort to legislation.

The Commissioners finally submitted their report in February 1845. As anticipated, they stressed the necessity for further agricultural improvement, but pointed to 'unequivocal symptoms of improvement' already evident throughout the country.[145] The chief problem lay in the absence of any corresponding advance in the comforts and conditions of the labouring classes, who remained dependent on casual and precarious employment, and who patiently endured sufferings worse than any

142 *Galway Vindicator* (Dec. 1844), cited *Times*, 4 Jan. 1845.

143 Samuel Smiles, *The history of Ireland and the Irish people under the government of England*, (London, 1844), pp. iv–x, 470; MacDonagh, *Emancipist*, p. 246.

144 [J.D. Brady], 'Ireland: the landlord and tenant question', *Blackwood's Edinburgh Magazine*, LV (May 1844), 638–64; W.W. Simpson, *A defence of the landlords of Ireland, with remarks on the relation between landlords and tenant* (London, 1844), pp. 5, 25–6. Brady was particularly scathing on Normanby and his 'protégé' Wiggins.

145 *Devon Commission*, part I, P.P. 1845 [605], XIX, 12.

similar class in Europe. A number of causes for this state of affairs was noticed: there were too few landlords, and many were severely encumbered and hence unable to take responsibility for their tenantry's welfare. Leases were rare and the country still suffered from the consequences of excessive subdivision by middlemen. Above all, the mutual distrust separating landlord and tenant prevented all classes from uniting their exertions for the common benefit. The report argued that the sweeping charges levelled against the landlord class were exaggerated, and that exposure to the censure of public opinion was the best check to the abuse of property rights. Farm consolidation was declared to be an economic imperative, although the accompanying clearances should be made in a humane fashion, assisted by subsidized emigration and waste-land reclamation.[146]

While thus placing the chief burden for improvement on responsible landlords, the Commissioners conceded that some remedial legislation was required. They suggested an encumbered estates measure to facilitate the investment of mercantile capital in land improvement and remove estates under the courts from the gross mismanagement of official receivers. One of the more striking passages questioned the suitability of latifundia style agriculture to Irish conditions, and recommended the sale of estates in small lots. It was hoped that a 'yeoman' farmer-proprietor class would emerge from the present tenants-for-life, tenants in tail and other 'men of small capital', and that this would encourage tenant farmers to exert themselves in the hope of improving their social status. This deviation from the classical model was probably inspired by John Pitt Kennedy, a believer in the viability of 'small farms'. The rather allusive comments in the 1845 report (the size of such 'small lots' was not discussed), were later elaborated in a more vigorous and sustained manner in Kennedy's 1847 edition of the Commission's *Digest of evidence*.[147]

The report regarded long-term improvement and growth as dependent on a more co-operative relationship between the landlord and his tenants, and argued that the creation of such confidence required a review of peasant demands for increased security. The Commissioners found the 'Ulster custom' of tenant right tolerable only where proprietors had been able to restrict it by limiting the sums paid for 'sale of goodwill'. Its immediate abolition was impossible, but such an 'anomalous' infringement of the rights of property could not be legally recognized.[148] They agreed that the universality of the demand for 'fixity of tenure' throughout Ireland, and the paralysis caused by tenurial uncertainty in a context where day-

146 Ibid., pp. 20–1.

147 Ibid., p. 27; John Pitt Kennedy (ed.), *Digest of evidence taken before Her Majesty's Commissioners of Inquiry into the state of the law and practice in respect to the occupation of land in Ireland* (2 vols., Dublin, 1847–8), I, 393–403, II, 860–9. See also below, p. 154.

148 *Devon Commission*, part I, P.P. 1845 [605], XIX, 14–15. The Commissioners summarized this notoriously amorphous practice as the exercise of the tenant's claim to dispose of his holding for a valuable consideration, irrespective of whether he was a tenant-at-will or had made permanent improvements.

to-day 'improvements' were generally left to the tenant, made some legislation necessary. They believed that despite the extreme demands that had been made, the mass of tenants would accept something more moderate, namely, compensation for 'improvements', payable by the landlord on eviction. This recommendation appeared to emulate Sharman Crawford's scheme, but its emphasis was fundamentally different. While Crawford urged his Compensation Bill as a mechanism to provide fixity for smallholders, the Commissioners hoped to induce landlords to carry out improvements (of a more substantial nature) by means of voluntary agreements with their tenants. This meant in effect the encouragement of the English model of the provision of 'improvements' on farms by the landlord himself.[149]

In general, the Devon report offered little to cottiers and labourers beyond greater landlord paternalism, and concluded by trusting that 'the exposure of such a state of things may lead to its remedy'. While several legislative enactments were expedient, it was through the patience, perseverance and mutual forbearance of all classes that social improvement would be achieved.[150] The report combined concern for economic anglicization with fears of diminishing an already precarious wages-fund. The Commission's defence of the institution of conacre (payment for labour through the yearly grant of small plots for a single potato crop), albeit in an improved and regularized form, reflected an assumption that mass dependence on potato cultivation would continue to underlie Ireland's economic structure for the foreseeable future.

The Devon report's general optimism about future prospects was not entirely unfounded, as commercial agriculture was recovering and production increasing in 1844–5. Many 'improving' landowners were convinced that prosperity would advance in the absence of agitation, and distributed agriculturalist literature to their 'better farmers'.[151] As confidence returned, however, the willingness of proprietors to tolerate any state interference fell away.

Irish reactions

The report went some way towards reassuring the government's Irish supporters. The *Dublin Evening Mail* found it 'not only exculpatory of, but highly creditable to, the great body of Irish landlords'. Yet while observing with approval that the Commission had targeted such favourite landlord bugbears as 'receivers', 'grinding middlemen' and 'tin-canister agents', the *Mail* was critical of some proposals as

149 *Devon Commission*, part I, P.P. 1845 [605], XIX, 15–18.

150 Ibid., pp. 36, 43–4.

151 See, for example, William R. Townshend, *Directions on practical agriculture, originally addressed to the working farmers of Ireland* (2nd edn, Dublin, 1843); [Anon], *The farmer's guide: compiled for the use of the small farmer and cottier tenantry in Ireland* (2nd edn, Dublin, 1842).

dangerous innovations foisted on the 'irresolute' Ferguson and the 'ignorant' Devon by the quasi-Repealer Redington.[152] The *Dublin University Magazine* was less critical of the recommendations, but thought the Commissioners had lost sight of the central problems – the eradication of agrarian outrage, and the priority of the moral regeneration of the peasantry. Its conclusion was uncompromisingly Malthusian: the physical improvement of the people was impossible until they grasped the truth of the 'Law of God that men cannot multiply like brutes without foregoing the benefits and blessings of social progress.'[153]

O'Connellite opinion was more forthright in its condemnation. To the *Freeman's Journal* the report was a 'bitter mockery' of the hopes of the people. While agricultural improvement was desired by all, 'how it was to be done, and by whom, was the problem.' The Commissioners had assumed 'that it must be done for the sole and exclusive benefit of the landlords, and that the good of Ireland has no other meaning than the improving the properties of Irish landowners!'[154] Even their admission of the 'good principle' of the tenant's right to compensation for improvements was due not their own inclinations, but to popular pressure. It would have needed 'bolder, and, indeed worse men than these to have lied down the truths which . . . every witness carried in his mouth. [They] . . . could not hope to choke this universal outcry down'. Even so, the *Freeman* was concerned that this principle had been expressed in impracticable terms, and that it was overshadowed by hostility to the practice of Ulster tenant right.[155]

The Repeal Association responded formally to the Devon report through its parliamentary committee. Three reports were drafted by O'Connell, assisted by Davis and Dillon, and adopted as a coherent land policy by the movement. Drawing heavily on the Commission's volumes of evidence, the Association's reports lamented the conditions of the cottiers and labourers, condemned the clearance system as 'the natural and necessary propagator of disease and death', and defended Ulster tenant right.[156] The third report listed thirty-five measures necessary 'in order to improve the condition of the people, stop outrage, and prevent the danger of agrarian war'. These included full compensation to tenants

---

152 *Dublin Evening Mail*, 18, 21 Feb. 1845.

153 [Samuel O'Sullivan], 'Land Commission in Ireland', first and second parts, *Dublin University Magazine*, XXV (April–May 1845), 471–85, 616–30.

154 *Freeman's Journal*, 21 Feb. 1845. This criticism was reflected throughout the nationalist press. To the *Belfast Vindicator* the conclusion of the report implied that 'tenants must live at the mercy of the landlords, for we are told that their extermination in many cases is *"necessary"*,' quoted in *Freeman's Journal*, 24 Feb. 1845.

155 *Freeman's Journal*, 24 Feb. The paper held that the evidence proved the viability of the 'Ulster custom', but warned northerners of the threat posed by 'the doctrine of assimilation', ibid., 6, 8 March 1845.

156 'First report . . . on the land question', *Report of the parliamentary committee of the Loyal National Repeal Association of Ireland* (2 vols., Dublin, 1845), II, 296–9; Mahony, *Davis*, pp. 243–4, 305.

for improvements on eviction, compulsory granting of conacre plots by large graziers, changes favourable to the tenant in the laws of distress and ejectment, and the abolition of the stamp duty on leases. The report followed the Devon Commission in calling for encumbered estates legislation, but placed greater emphasis on the sale of small lots, with the right of pre-emption to the occupier. O'Connell praised Ulster tenant right, but left the desirability of its extension to the south an open question, and stipulated that if adopted it would have to be accompanied by guarantees against any injustice to landlords. Proprietorship was not prominent on the agenda, but the report recommended 'efforts to effect reclamation of waste lands under such arrangements as would allow each poor family located on a portion, to become the eventual possessor in fee'. Major public works schemes for the immediate alleviation of under-employment were also demanded.[157]

This represented a major advance in O'Connell's position. His concern for urgent land reform was genuine, if partly based on the fear of an imminent outbreak of 'such a servile war in Ireland as has been unknown since the days of the French *Jacoterie*'. This dangerous situation made radical reform imperative: 'skin-deep remedies will not do . . . The occupying tenant is the "Hamlet left out by special desire" from the Land Commission Report. He must be relieved, or depend on it, . . . he will go mad.' O'Connell admitted to Pierce Mahony the limits of his own control over the situation:

> Nothing will do but giving some kind or other of fixity of tenure to the occupiers; and especially an absolute right of recompense for all substantial improvements. I am ready to take (as to the security of tenure) as mitigated a measure as is consistent with the principle . . . I know well how unpalatable such a system would be to the landlords, especially to the absentees, but in truth unless something be done the people will slip out of my hands and the hands of those who like me look for peaceful amelioration; and they will operate a 'fixity of tenure' for themselves with a vengeance.[158]

By 1845 measures of land reform – particularly those relating to landlord-tenant relations – had come to the forefront of O'Connell's conception of 'justice to Ireland', not least because he believed that failure to grant meaningful concessions could result in the outbreak of bloody social revolution. He was fully aware that attempts by the Repeal Association and the Catholic clergy to stem the growing tide of agrarian outrages were having little success.[159]

---

157 'Third report . . . on the land question', *Repeal Association report*, pp. 319–27. Other popular pamphleteers followed this line, placing particular emphasis on waste-land reclamation, John Henchy, *Observations on the state of Ireland, with remarks on her resources and capabilities* (Dublin, 1845).

158 Daniel O'Connell to Mahony, 25, 26 April 1845, O'Connell, *Correspondence*, VII, 312–16.

159 *Tipperary Vindicator*, 28 Jan. 1845, *Roscommon Journal*, n.d., quoted *Times*, 31 Jan., 3 April 1845.

The decisiveness with which Peel pressed through the Maynooth Bill in spring 1845 led some to expect something similarly imaginative with respect to land. Even O'Connell was, for a time, optimistic; writing to Mahony he declared, 'something substantial must be done and this is just the time to do it. The *manner* of the Maynooth grant has put the people into good humour; and the effect of really good measures would be unmixed by any querimonious disposition with respect to the details but the measures *must* be *substantially good measures*.'[160] If O'Connell ever really expected positive action from the government, he was soon expressing disillusionment. The government's temporizing delay followed by a weak land bill forced him to take a more cynical view of Peel's true objectives: 'Stanley's Bill is laughed at. No other efficient measure this session simply because they think they have established a feud in our camp. They shall find themselves mistaken.'[161]

O'Connell regarded his third Repeal Association report as an invitation to the British parties to treat. Presenting it to the Association on 19 May he explained the sociological basis of the Repeal movement and its role as the container of social disintegration: 'Were it not for their buoyancy of spirit amidst all their misfortune, and their hopes of obtaining a domestic legislature the miseries of the country would burst asunder the bonds of society, and the people would become unwilling anarchists.' While he expressed scepticism regarding the government's intentions, O'Connell declared that, 'on the question of landlord and tenant we are in a precursor state'. The use of a term reminiscent of the period of Whig-O'Connellite alliance was deliberate. O'Connell took as his 'text' for the speech an editorial from the *Morning Chronicle* critical of the government's failure to 'settle and pacify that large class whose disaffection springs from their stomachs rather than their feelings, the exacerbation of one following from the emptiness of the other'. If the government was indeed hoping to escape their obligations to act in the wake of the Devon Commission report, O'Connell saw in the response of the British radical and Whig publications sufficient grounds to 'call upon the people of England to arouse and assist in affording relief to the people of Ireland'.[162]

O'Connell was not without grounds for believing that a positive Whig-Liberal response was possible. The Foxites had remained suspicious of the Commission throughout its inquiry, and Bessborough had anticipated that:

160 O'Connell to Mahony, 25 April 1845, O'Connell, *Correspondence*, VII, 312–15. Mahony was in communication with the government at this time, and O'Connell's letter may have been intended as an oblique warning to ministers on the necessity of strong measures. However, Graham was highly suspicious of Mahony's motives and thought him a 'dangerous man', Mahony to Graham, 21 April 1845, Graham Papers, bundle 88; Graham to Heytesbury, 23 April, ibid., bundle 21 IR.

161 O'Connell to Fitzpatrick, 21 June 1845, O'Connell, *Correspondence*, VII, 320.

162 Speech at the Repeal Association meeting, 19 May 1845, *Freeman's Journal*, 20 May 1845. The 'Precursor Society' had been established by O'Connell in 1839 as an instrument for extracting 'justice to Ireland'.

> there will be nothing whatever in it, indeed I hardly see how there can be much, and it has done the mischief of raising fresh expectations here which I always felt would not be realized. The commission has passed over every part of Ireland, they will probably give an account of what is complained of in each district, forbear to suggest any remedy, whitewash landlords a little, make a few recommendations, and so leave the matter.[163]

He believed that the Commission had been cynically issued to gain time, and that it had cruelly and unfairly raised tenant expectations by its connection with the suspension of Sharman Crawford's Bill. Bessborough urged Russell to consider introducing, alongside the planned 'condition of England' programme, the Bill he was preparing to strike at the root of the problem: 'the clearances of land, and the manner in which landlords have formerly treated their tenantry in this country.'[164] Normanby made similar accusations in parliament, and warned that unless some more 'comprehensive' scheme of justice were prepared, 'they never would be able to secure the affections of the Irish people, and never could . . . calculate on the permanent tranquillity and progressive improvement of Ireland.'[165]

The *Morning Chronicle* also adopted an advanced position on the land question. The Devon report, the paper declared, completely confirmed its opinion that the Commission had been intended as a 'mere delusion upon the people of Ireland'. The facts were well known from previous inquiries, and the appointed Commissioners were far from impartial. The *Chronicle* bitterly attacked the tone of the report: 'such is the language in which the Commissioner-landlords describe the continued practice, by their Irish brother landlords, of wholesale, unmitigated murder – we can designate the "system" by no other term – which has converted Ireland into a lazar-house of disease and destitution, and a charnel-house of death'. Ejectments and consolidation were at the heart of this system, and it was evident that their facilitation was the Commissioners' true object.[166] In the course of the year the paper adopted progressively stronger language against Irish landlordism, denying the applicability to Ireland of English contractual modes of land-letting, and endorsing the principle of legislative interference between landlord and tenant.[167]

Other elements of British liberal opinion were also critical of the Devon report. The *Economist* condemned landlord 'monopolists', but pointed to free-trade in food rather than any state interference in tenurial relations as the sole panacea for the ills of the Irish and British masses.[168] This doctrinaire adherence to *laissez-faire* was

---

163 Bessborough to Russell, 10 Jan. 1845, Russell Papers, PRO 30/22/4D, fols. 110–12. Duncannon had succeeded as fourth Earl of Bessborough in February 1844.

164 Ibid.

165 *Hans.*, LXXVII, 17–21 [4 Feb. 1845].

166 *Morning Chronicle*, 22 Feb. 1845. The *Morning Chronicle*, owned by Sir John Easthope and edited by John Black, was the leading Whiggish daily in the capital, with a circulation of around 3,500, A.P. Wadsworth, *Newspaper circulations, 1800–1854* (Manchester, 1955), pp. 8–9.

167 *Morning Chronicle*, 4 Oct., 6 Nov. 1845, 23 Jan. 1846.

168 *Economist*, 9 Aug. 1845.

symptomatic of the beliefs of the journal's proprietor James Wilson, who was profoundly optimistic about Ireland's economic prospects once aristocratic 'misgovernment' was lifted, religious equality assured and Ireland morally and socially integrated with Britain. He was sure that self-reliance was the key to unlocking the potential riches of the country.[169]

'The condition of the people of Ireland'

The *Times*, by far the most influential newspaper of the day, sneered at the Commission's 'cart-load of cross-examinations', and demanded an accessible and straightforward analysis carried out by someone personally disinterested and impartial.[170] Not waiting for the government to respond, it dispatched Thomas Campbell Foster, a legal writer who had previously produced similar inquiries into the Scottish Poor Law and the Rebecca riots in South Wales, as a '*Times* commissioner' to tour Ireland from August 1845. His findings were published in a series of articles on the 'Condition of the people of Ireland'.[171]

Foster's views were grounded on a combination of crude ethnographic theory and an unboundedly positive belief in the power of private enterprise which owed much to the optimistic 'common sense' economics of the Manchester school.[172] He started from the assumption that all Irish problems stemmed from an economic malaise which manifested itself in the lack of employment and consequently in the lack of the means of subsistence. Assuming that productive labour was the source of all wealth, and that the capital essential for the development of industry could be accumulated within the community by an excess of productive labour over consumption, he asserted that Ireland was capable of accumulating sufficient capital by maximizing its productive labour. Accumulation had hitherto been paralysed, firstly by the absence of the due rewards of labour, and the acclimatization of the tenants to the lowest possible level of subsistence as a result of the activities of predatory landlords; secondly, by the removal of the surplus product of the soil and its investment elsewhere; and thirdly, by a lack of skills and knowledge on the part of the labourers.[173] He presupposed that the Irish wages fund was large and elastic, but that resources had been misdirected or squandered by inefficient land-

---

169 Ibid., 28 Oct. 1843, 28 June 1845. See also Ruth Dudley Edwards, *The pursuit of reason: The Economist 1843–1993* (London, 1993), pp. 48–55.

170 *Times*, 21 Aug. 1845. For a more detailed account of the influence of the liberal press on Irish policy in the 1840s, see Peter Gray, 'British public opinion and the Great Irish Famine 1845–49', in Breandán Ó Conaire (ed.), *Comhdháil an Chraoibhín conference proceedings 1995* (Boyle, 1996), pp. 56–74.

171 These were later republished as *Letters on the condition of the people of Ireland* (London, 1846). For the popularity this book with the British political class, see G. Elliot to Russell, 21 June 1846, Russell Papers, PRO 30/22/5A, fols. 255–6.

172 See William D. Grampp, *The Manchester school of economics* (Stanford, 1960), pp. 1–5.

173 *Times*, 26 Aug. 1845.

lordism. It was thus the moral framework of society that needed to be altered if the economic malaise was to be eliminated. Foster insisted that:

> When Irishmen, as a nation, learn that true spirit of independence which looks for help to no man, and which does not lie in blustering, but in the quiet evidence of self-supporting strength, then, and not till then, they and their concerns will command respect, and will have every attention.[174]

This statement contained the kernel of the popular 'moralist' stance that was to play an important role during the Famine. Foster's combination of a labour theory of value with the idea of an elastic wages fund became the touchstone of the paper's Irish commentary.[175]

Foster argued that social change could only come from above, from a resident and active landlord class using all the benefits of its intelligence and station, for nothing could be expected from the corrupt middlemen or the degraded tenantry. He denied the legitimacy of any alternative conception of property rights or obligations held by the peasantry, and deprecated as an obstacle to progress any 'tenant right' beyond the narrow limits of a degree of compensation for improvements.[176] The landed classes, he concluded, had largely neglected their duties for reasons of wilful negligence, financial embarrassment, and intimidation. Remedial measures had to be directed at these faults; further legislative prohibitions on subdivision would compel the remaining middlemen to either give up their positions or become proper landlords, and the problem of embarrassments should be met with legislation to facilitate the transfer of land. Such a measure would 'let the life-blood and energy, and enterprise of capitalists into the lifeless masses of large, encumbered, unimproved, helpless estates. They will become real owners of the land, and will give employment upon it, and stimulate industry. Employment will bring peace. Industry will bring wealth.' The most important task of the state, however, would be to provide the security necessary for all to fulfil their duties and to realize their economic potential. This could be provided only by firm coercion.[177]

Foster's articles were more widely read than the Devon report and aroused greater controversy. Extracts from the letters with favourable commentary were printed in many journals, although his taste for 'forcing' the peasantry into more

---

174 Ibid., 4 Sept., 28 Aug. 1845.

175 'It is ridiculous to say that there is no capital in Ireland where there is labour and land. A country which exports the means of millions can of course pay for its own improvement.' *Times*, 19 Aug. 1846.

176 Ibid., 12 Sept. 1845. Parts of Ulster he thought were prosperous in spite of the custom of tenant right. It was the 'industrious habits of the people', which he attributed to the racial superiority of eastern Ulster's 'Saxon' stock, that made the difference. He thought this separation should be encouraged, if possible by a legal differentiation between the 'Saxon' and 'native' regions, and with the former alone being governed on English precepts, *Times*, 28 Aug., 16 Sept. 1845, 10 Jan. 1846.

177 *Times*, 20 Jan. 1846.

'civilized habits' was attacked by the *Morning Chronicle*, and his denunciations of O'Connell both as politician and landlord incensed the Repeal press.[178] In England, however, they had the effect of moulding opinion on Irish land and society at a time when interest in the economic character of the 'Irish question' was growing and was about to be propelled to the centre of the political agenda by economic catastrophe.[179] Just in case any of its readers had misunderstood, the *Times* highlighted the moral of Foster's articles: Irish rents should be regarded as 'an infamous source of profit, a base and immoral traffic, or at least as something unbecoming of a gentleman', at least until the system was reformed at the behest of English public opinion.[180] This populist moralism contrasted strongly with the moderate liberalism common to Devon and Senior, and posed a threat to their policy prescriptions.

IV 'AS MYSTERIOUS AS THE BRICKS OF BABYLON': PEEL'S LAND LEGISLATION[181]

Between the establishment and the termination of the Devon inquiry, the government's Irish policy had been transformed. Peel intended this 'new direction' in policy to serve both strategic and tactical ends. From the 1820s he had become progressively disillusioned with the Protestant ascendancy and inclined towards a reconciliation between landed and bourgeois Catholics and the state. By 1844 he was anxious to govern Ireland through the co-operation of the 'great mass of public opinion not tinged by Orange or by Green . . . [who are] wearied out by agitation and acrimonious controversy'.[182] This necessitated the abandonment of traditional Conservative hostility towards the Catholic Church.

It was, however, the tactical problems thrown up by the political crisis of 1843–4 that induced Peel to take the risk of antagonizing the ultra-Protestants in his own Party. The shift in emphasis was symbolized in early 1844 by the replacement of the pro-Orange de Grey by the former diplomat and loyal Peelite, Baron Heytesbury,

---

178 *Spectator*, 6, 13 Sept. 1845, 24 Jan. 1846, *Morning Chronicle*, 4 Nov. 1845, *Times*, 18, 25 Dec., *Nation*, 1 Nov. 1845. For the antipathy of John Walter, proprietor of the *Times*, to O'Connell, and its part in this controversy, see [Stanley Morison], *The history of The Times: Vol. II, The tradition established, 1841–84* (London, 1939), pp. 8–9.

179 The *Times*, with a circulation expanding both numerically (to over 40,000 by 1850), and geographically as a result of the railway revolution in communications, far outstripped its rivals as both a mirror and a moulder of middle-class public opinion. In the opinion of *Mitchell's Press Directory* (1846): 'Other papers may be preferred by particular classes, but *all* read the *Times* who can, just because it is not possible to predict its course on any question as regulated by the interests of any party or any class . . . the moderate common sense side of the case is almost certain to be taken up in this paper.' Cited in Donald Read, *Peel and the Victorians* (Oxford, 1987), p. 38.

180 *Times*, 27 Aug. 1845.

181 *Freeman's Journal*, 22 June 1846.

182 Peel to Heytesbury, 1 Aug. 1844, Parker, *Peel*, III, 114–15.

as Lord Lieutenant. The measures of 1844–5, creating a new Charitable Bequests Board, augmenting the grant to the Catholic seminary at Maynooth, and establishing the three non-denominational Queen's Colleges, were intended to detach the 'moderate' from the 'extreme' adherents of Repeal, and to sow dissension in O'Connell's ranks.[183] This policy met with mixed, but not inconsiderable, success in undermining the broad national front of the Catholic clergy and laity.[184] What has been less often observed by historians is the fact that Peel's policy was also successful in attaining a second tactical aim, the disruption of the Whig-Liberal 'justice to Ireland' initiative of 1844. Peel's measures fell short of those advocated by Senior, but were proposed in much the same spirit. By boldly taking the legislative initiative, Peel had challenged the Whig claim to be the only political force capable of responding to Irish popular grievances.

This 'new direction' had profound political implications, not least in undermining traditional certainties and opening up the possibility of further constructive reform. While many ultra-Tories were outraged at the 'betrayal' of the Protestant cause, the 1844–5 legislation did much to blur the partisan barriers that had previously separated liberals of various hues, and made possible the liberal convergence realized in the 1850s.[185] At the end of the 1845 session Greville noted that while Peel was unpopular, he was secure as Prime Minister and people now thought him capable of anything: 'everybody expects that he means to go on and to knock the Corn Laws on the head, and endow the Catholic Church; but nobody knows how or when he will do these things.' Party politics was out of fashion: 'there is no party distinguished by any badge of principle, with a distinct colour, standing in open and defined antagonism to any other; none with any great object to advance. All is confusion, intermingling, political and personal antipathy.'[186]

Peel's volte-face left Russell in some disarray. While it was impossible for him to refuse co-operation on measures drawn from Whig prototypes, Russell embarrassed some of his colleagues by accompanying his support with bitter attacks on Peel's insincerity.[187] One significant consequence of the events of 1844–5 was Russell's

---

183 Peel, cabinet memo, 11 Feb. 1844, Peel Papers, Add. MS 40,540, fols. 19–25.

184 Donal A. Kerr, *Peel, priests and politics: Sir Robert Peel's administration and the Roman Catholic Church in Ireland, 1841–1846* (Oxford, 1982), pp. 269–83; Kevin B. Nowlan, *The politics of Repeal: a study in the relation between Great Britain and Ireland, 1841–50* (London, 1965), pp. 81–3; MacDonagh, *Emancipist*, pp. 259–63.

185 Both Prince Albert and Lansdowne approved of this development, Le Marchant to Russell, 20 Sept. 1844, Russell Papers, PRO 30/22/4C, fol. 151; Minto to Russell, 6 Dec. 1844, ibid., 4D, fol. 24.

186 Greville, *Journal*, II, 290–1 [21 Aug. 1845]. Greville himself had written a book earlier in the year (assisted by Clarendon, Lewis, and Bedford), in which he had advocated Irish Church reform. It appeared simultaneously with the announcement of the government's measures, and was praised by Peel and Graham, as well as by 'moderate men of neither party', *Journal*, II, 259–63, 275–6 [12, 16, January, 29, 30 March 1845]; [Charles Cavendish Fulke Greville], *The past and present policy of England towards Ireland* (London, 1845).

187 *Hans.*, LXXVII, 71–3 [4 Feb. 1845], LXXIX, 1227–30 [23 April 1845]; Broughton Diary,

growing conviction that the Catholic question could only be settled after full consultations and agreement on both sides, and that this would not be possible until the broader grievances of Ireland had been resolved. He did not believe Peel's strategy stood any chance of success so long as O'Connell could continue to 'organize the democracy of Ireland'.[188] In his summing-up of the 1845 session, Russell accused the government of inconsistency, defended O'Connell's campaign for 'justice to Ireland', and stressed the necessity of granting civil and political equality and introducing effective land legislation before the ecclesiastical question could be settled.[189] This was in itself another victory for Peel, for in forcing the Foxites to define their conception of 'justice to Ireland' in terms of popular political and socio-economic reform, in the place of the more comprehensive and religiously-oriented definition of 1843–4, he had deprived them of the political centre ground, and exposed the Whig-Liberal Party's internal fissures over Irish policy.

While the possibility that Peel might also adopt an advanced land policy seemed plausible to some contemporaries, it appears unlikely in retrospect. The Irish measures of 1844–5 were based on the assumption that the Emancipation and Reform Acts were irreversible, and that this fact rendered desirable the conciliation of moderate Catholics. Major concessions to peasant demands would counteract the Burkean strategy of consolidating propertied interests behind Conservative government in Ireland. Peel's general approach to economic problems was determined by the rigid and mechanistic outlook of his liberal Toryism, which stressed the moral superiority of *laissez-faire*, and the desirability of promoting 'natural' self-regulating economic systems.[190] He did not find it necessary to formulate a distinct Irish economic policy before the Famine, but relied instead on general non-intervention, combined with occasional marginal assistance and encouragement to 'improving' proprietors. He was confident that the growth stimulated in Britain by his liberal economic policy would also revive the Irish markets, and was sure that the geographical integration of England and Ireland resulting from the 'wonderful applications of science' embodied in steam-powered transport would lead to unprecedented improvements in Irish conditions.[191] If social tranquillity could be created, Ireland's social advance would be more rapid than any other part of the empire.[192] To Peel, any unnecessary direct intervention by government in the realm of private enterprise was not only likely to be counter-productive, but was immoral. Arguing that Ireland could not be exempt from the normal rules of

---

Add. MS 43,747, fols. 50, 91, 97–8 [4 Feb., 14, 23 April 1845]. Hobhouse and Palmerston disapproved of the partisan language employed by Russell and Macaulay.

188 Russell to Lansdowne, 5 Jan. 1845, Gooch, *Later correspondence*, I, 77; Russell to Palmerston, 25 Jan. 1845, Palmerston Papers, GC/RU/93. O'Connell revived the monster meeting campaign, albeit on a smaller scale, in spring 1845.

189 *Hans.*, LXXXII, 1454–81 [5 Aug. 1845].

190 Boyd Hilton, 'Peel: a reappraisal', *Historical Journal*, XXII (1979), 585–614.

191 *Hans.*, LXXIII, 254–5 [23 Feb. 1844].

192 *Annual Register*, LXXXVI (1844), 84.

economic activity, he attacked the idea of a state railway scheme in 1843 as merely an artificial and temporary stimulus to the Irish economy. The belief that this sort of state interference could only exacerbate Irish difficulties was at the core of his thought.[193]

Peel's Irish policy of 1844–5 was thus concentrated on the indirect assistance the state could provide through the creation of security for private investment. Undermining of the Repeal movement appeared the vital precondition for social progress. In 1843 the Prime Minister warned Catholic property-owners that their flirtation with democratic agitation would 'divert the application of English capital from undertakings beneficial to Ireland'.[194] He expected concessions designed to alleviate the grievance of Catholic religious inequality to appease such moderate men. The establishment of provincial colleges, each equipped with a chair of political economy, offered the additional attraction of continuing Stanley's 1831 policy of educating the Irish into embracing the logic of the market.[195]

Peel and the Devon report

Peel's moral commitment to the precepts of *laissez-faire* extended as strongly to land as it did to public works policy. His approach to the problem of landlord-tenant conflict was not to concede tenant demands, but to exhort landlords to fulfil their duties and improve the cultivation of their estates. Both Peel and Graham were advocates and practitioners of scientific agriculture or 'high farming', and patronized the theorists of this movement.[196] They considered it possible to increase productivity through the capitalization of agriculture, without disturbing the hierarchical structure of rural society, and believed that the key to improvement lay in the willingness of landlord and tenant to co-operate in investment. Individual exertion was the mainspring of improvement, and the role of the state was confined

193 *Hans.*, LXX, 981–2 [11 July 1843]. The 1844–5 boom in railway development in Ireland that followed that in England appeared to justify Peel's views. However, his opinions on the inadmissibility of interference to advance or restrain development in the railway market were determined as much by moral as by economic considerations, Peel to Goulburn, 21, 27 Aug. 1845, Goulburn Papers, Surrey Record Office, Kingston, SHS 304, box 42. For the 'evangelical' assumptions underlying Peel's views see Boyd Hilton, *The age of atonement: the influence of evangelicalism on social and economic thought, 1785–1865* (Oxford, 1988), pp. 115–25.

194 Peel to V. Blake, 3 Sept. 1843, Peel Papers, Add. MS 40,532, fols. 387–8.

195 Stanley enthusiastically endorsed the idea of the provincial colleges and a remodelled Maynooth providing a 'liberal' education to Irish Catholics, Stanley to Peel, 18 Feb. 1844, Peel Papers, Add. MS. 40,468, fol. 132. For the establishment of the chairs of political economy at the Queen's Colleges, see Thomas A. Boylan and Timothy P. Foley, *Political economy and colonial Ireland: the propagation and ideological function of economic discourse in the nineteenth century* (London, 1992), pp. 44–66.

196 Norman Gash, *Sir Robert Peel*, pp. 678–82; David Spring, 'A great agricultural estate: Netherby under Sir James Graham, 1820–1845', *Agricultural History*, XXIX (1955), 73–81. For Peel's endorsement of the 'high farming' polemicist James Caird, see below, p. 221–2.

to removing obstacles to investment and educating the rural classes to recognize their own best interests.[197]

The Devon inquiry itself had embodied the extension of high-farming doctrine to Ireland. Devon and Pitt Kennedy were both high farmers close to the Prime Minister's ideal of innovating landownership, and the Commission report was primarily an exercise in didacticism strongly in keeping with Peel and Graham's own preconceptions. Devon's personal views as to the obstacles in the way of agricultural progress, and his priorities for reform, were expressed in his private correspondence with the ministers. He believed that coercion was a vital prerequisite to the betterment of Ireland, and ought to be directed specifically against the class which was most strongly resistant to the anglicization of Irish rural society:

> It is important and I believe it is practicable, gradually to amend the social condition of Ireland by removing some of those causes which have remotely led to the present state of things; but the outrages of the present day are rarely to be traced to any tangible cause – neither are they committed by the lowest and most miserable of the people. That class which has certainly suffered the greatest hardships, have been wonderfully patient and forbearing. The idle extravagant small farmer, bankrupt in means and in character, is usually the instigator if not the perpetrator of the worst crimes of which we hear.[198]

The greatest remediable cause of this state of society was the prevalence of absenteeism among proprietors. It followed that corrective legislation should concentrate on providing encouragements to active resident landlords.[199] Devon urged that the government's attention should be more immediately drawn to his recommendations relating to the financial burdens placed on improving landlords and substantial tenants, 'under the heads of stamp duties, public works, county cess and . . . the duty on glass.'[200] These were the grievances most frequently mentioned in correspondence from Irish landlords such as the Tipperary proprietor, Lord Glengall. Peel was reluctant to accede to any additional public works, but commented: '. . . We must humour these gentlemen who profess to have the public interest at heart. Lord Glengall is an improving resident nobleman, and that consideration entitles him to be heard.'[201]

Devon's recommendation on local taxation attracted the government's closest interest as this dovetailed neatly with coercion through the question of the financial support of the Irish Constabulary. The report suggested that this burden be removed

---

197 D.C. Moore, 'The Corn Laws and high farming', *Economic History Review*, 2nd series, XVIII (1965), 544–61.

198 Devon to Peel, 2 Feb. 1845, Peel Papers, Add. MS 40,559, fols. 23–6.

199 Ibid.

200 Devon to Peel, 10 Feb. 1845, ibid., fol. 258.

201 T. Lynch to Sir J. Young, 8 March 1845, Newcastle Papers, University of Nottingham Library, NeC 9,502; Glengall to Peel, 10 March 1845, Peel Papers, Add. MS 40,562, fols. 164–6; Peel to Fremantle, 13 March 1845, ibid., Add. MS 40,476, fols. 416–17.

from the county cess and shouldered by the state.[202] The Lord Lieutenant, however, expressed concern about the constitutional implications of removing the entire cost of the police to the consolidated fund, fearing that 'such a measure [would] take away from the force the character of a constabulary, and approximate it very much to a standing army.'[203] Graham agreed that the entire transfer of the charge to the Treasury might be inexpedient, but was convinced of the importance of making local districts bear the cost of the extra police sent to quell insurrection or agrarian outrage. The government hesitated to take this step in 1845, but adopted the recommendation as the central element of its plan of concession to Irish landed property in return for the removal of the Corn Laws.[204] There is no doubt that devising a systematic and self-regulating system of coercion had been prominent in Peel's thinking long before 1845. However, he was concerned that the state should not relieve the local landowners and gentlemen of their personal responsibilities for maintaining social order.[205] In the spring of 1845 Graham believed that despite the admitted existence of a 'Jacquerie of revolutionary character . . . subversive of law, property and order', ad hoc state repression would be against Ireland's true interests, for, 'if magistrates and country gentlemen have not the courage to do their duty, the fatal consequences must rest on their own heads – they will be over-powered because they do not have the manliness to defend their position.'[206] A systematic form of coercive law, incorporating the moral responsibilities of individuals, would be the object of future legislation.

One of the Commission's most important recommendations was for some form of encumbered estates bill to promote a greater degree of 'free trade' in

---

202 *Devon Commission*, part I, P.P. 1845 [605], XIX, 37–8. The report rejected the recommendation of the 1844 Townland Valuation Committee that all tenants should have the power of deducting a portion of the cess from their rent, as was the case with the Poor Law rate. Despite the fact that only occupiers paid the cess, by the 1840s it was a grievance more strongly expressed by landlords than by the tenantry, not least because of the antagonisms raised by the vagaries of applotment, and local resistance to payment, Memorial of the Cork Grand Jury, 18 March 1845, Peel Papers, Add. MS 40,563, fol. 50; Kennedy, *Digest*, II, 943–1024; Beames, *Peasants and power*, pp. 113–14.

203 Graham to Heytesbury, 13 Feb. 1845, Heytesbury to Graham, 15 Feb. 1845, Graham Papers, bundle 20 IR.

204 See below, pp. 117, 139. It is also probable that the government sought to avoid parliamentary confrontation with the Irish members and the Whigs at a time when the Maynooth and Colleges Bills were endangered in the Commons.

205 Peel had argued in 1829 that 'some severe discipline must be permanently administered, and discipline for which Ireland ought to pay . . . Why should England pay the charge of civilizing Ireland [?] . . . Let Ireland, as is but just, pay the charge of suppressing her own disorders, and have therefore an inducement to keep the peace.' Peel to Wellington, 27 July 1829, Parker, *Peel*, II, 120–1.

206 Graham to Heytesbury, 22 March 1845, Graham papers, bundle 87. Peel agreed that 'there is sheer cowardice in dealing with the disturbers of the public peace . . . Proprietors should be at home setting examples, not issuing appeals from the Carlton Club.' Peel to Graham, 25 March ibid.

land.[207] The encumbrance of land by a complex web of mortgages and 'judgments' was a universal phenomenon on the estates of England and Ireland. The greater over-extension of Irish landowners, their dependency on a more vulnerable agricultural base and the added difficulties of obtaining cheap credit on the security of Irish land in the cautious English capital market, rendered their position more exposed. Consequently, a high proportion of Irish estates had by the 1840s fallen under the receivership of the notoriously inefficient Court of Chancery. Irish laws designed to protect the interests of encumbrancers, heirs and the beneficiaries of family settlements rendered it difficult for the nominal owners of land to realize their assets through sale and thus avoid bankruptcy.

Peel took the opportunity presented by a letter from a King's County proprietor to put the question of facilitating land sales before the Irish government law officers, but the Attorney General and Lord Chancellor were hostile, and wrote off the proposals as 'impracticable'. With such strong objections from the Irish legal establishment, it was clear that the introduction of encumbered estates legislation would be problematic.[208] The Prime Minister was, however, increasingly convinced that this path offered the only effective means of advancing Irish agriculture.

Stanley's Compensation Bill

The legislative response to the Devon report preferred by Peel was low-key and would require time, yet the continuing Irish crisis made a more immediate and prominent initiative expedient. The government was as embarrassed in taking up the compensation proposal as the Commissioners were in suggesting it, but given the commitment made in 1843, and the continuing pressure of public opinion, there appeared little alternative. In the spring of 1845 ministers became increasingly alarmed at the deteriorating social state of Ireland, and in particular at the putative juncture of agrarianism and Repeal agitation. The Lord Lieutenant's sources attributed the upsurge in agrarian disturbances directly to the high levels of peasant expectation:

> The general idea seems to be that many of the present agrarian outrages are due to the exaggerated notions which have been circulated, with respect to measures which are likely to be recommended by the Land Tenure Commission. The common people believe, that all those found in possession of the land, will have that possession confirmed to them, subject to certain not very serious conditions. Hence the eagerness to possess themselves of land, either by fair means, or foul.[209]

---

207 *Devon Commission*, P.P. 1845 [605], XIX, 12–14, 27.

208 Magawly to Peel, 17 March , Peel to Fremantle, 19 March, Attorney General to (Fremantle), 25 May 1845, Newcastle Papers, NeC 9,498/1–4.

209 Heytesbury to Graham, 17 Feb., Graham Papers, bundle 20 IR. 'Ribbonism' in disturbed counties such as Leitrim and Roscommon appeared to have taken on a new aggressiveness:

Graham appreciated this danger and promised immediate publication of the report to dispel 'the false impression on the minds of the peasantry'.[210] Yet two days later Heytesbury observed that the furious attack on the report in the *Freeman's Journal* indicated that the issue would replace the Bequests Act as the focus for popular political clamour in the new session.[211]

In late March work began on the drafting of the tenants' compensation measure, with Graham at the Home Office as the moving force. The blueprint contained in the Devon report was found too difficult by the Irish administration's lawyers, and a bill drawn on a less extensive principle was suggested.[212] Graham was also dissatisfied with Devon's recommendation; the Commission, in his view, had 'only skimmed the surface but did not dive to the real depths and difficulties of the subject'. He doubted if it would be possible to frame a practicable bill, but thought the government was obliged to make the attempt.[213]

The parliamentary priority of the Maynooth and the Colleges Bills led to some delay, and in early May Devon expressed to the Lords his anxiety that the government was not responding promptly enough to public pressure. He complained of being inundated with petitions from all parts of Ireland, which 'pointed particularly at one measure as of paramount importance – that was some measure which should secure to industrious tenants the benefit which was desired for the improvement which they made on the land which they occupied'.[214] The announcement of 'some measure' for this purpose would, he hoped, 'satisfy some impatient spirits on both sides of the water'.[215]

Copies of the Tenant's Compensation Bill were printed and privately circulated in the first week of May. The response was mixed; Lord Granville Somerset was critical of the alterations proposed to the power of distraint for arrears, and Graham accepted the justice of his observations. The Home Secretary agreed that landlords might be granted a greater facility for objecting to improvements which were considered unnecessary, and for which they might be compelled to pay compensation.[216]

'armed bands are traversing the country, dividing fields into allotments, and digging them up without resistance from the occupiers', Heytesbury to Graham, 23 March 1845, ibid., bundle 21 IR.

210 Graham to Heytesbury, 19 Feb., ibid., bundle 20 IR.

211 Heytesbury to Graham, 21 Feb. 1845, Graham Papers, bundle 20 IR.

212 Fremantle to Graham, 25 March 1845, ibid., bundle 21 IR.

213 Graham to Fremantle, 25 March 1845, ibid.

214 *Hans.*, LXXX, 225–7, [6 May 1845]. For an example of tenant demands, see 'Petition of the farmers and landholders of the Union of Ennis and adjoining districts', *Clare Journal*, 17 April 1845, Peel Papers, Add. MS 40,566, fol. 118. Fortescue also pressed the subject in the Lords, *Hans.*, LXXVIII, 426–7 [7 March]; Wellington to Graham, 26 May 1845, Graham Papers, bundle 89.

215 Devon to Stanley, 5 May 1845, Derby Papers, 920 DER (14) 137/3.

216 Granville Somerset to (Graham), May 1845, Graham to Fremantle, 6 May 1845, Newcastle Papers, NeC 9,517, 9,504/2. The proposed clauses referring to ejectment and distress were dropped from the 1845 Bill and introduced separately in 1846.

Lord Farnham, the leading Conservative proprietor of the disturbed county of Cavan, rejected the Bill entirely, and argued that agrarian agitation was 'not against real or practical grievances, but against the very existence of the rights of the landlord'. It was axiomatic that tenant right was landlord wrong, and that any legislative interference under the circumstances was dangerous.[217]

The task of preparing the final version of the Compensation Bill was entrusted to Stanley. Peel and Graham were pre-occupied with other matters in the Commons, and as an ex-Chief Secretary and an Irish landlord close to the agricultural interest, Stanley appeared to combine the administrative experience and the sympathy to landlord opinion essential for the success any such bill. In 1843 Stanley had declared his hostility to tenant demands more stridently than any other minister, and had announced himself averse to interference with the 'sacred' rights of property. He thought Irish landlords possessed not too much, but too little power to enforce their rights, and that 'the relative positions of landlord and tenants are such as to impede those improvements which, without depopulating the country, a wise and judicious landlord might wish to introduce, but which, from the attachment of the Irish to the land of their forefathers, a landlord in that country finds it very difficult to introduce.'[218]

Stanley's speech introducing his Compensation Bill in June 1845 was less an argument for the rights of tenants than an orthodox analysis of the problems of the Irish economy and a survey of possible remedies. Righting the population-capital imbalance in Ireland was the aim of the legislation; reducing the population by extensive emigration would be expensive and of limited viability, and hence it was necessary to encourage employment by improving agriculture and mobilizing under-utilized resources. While all facilities should be given to encourage landlords to invest, it was, Stanley argued, illegitimate to expect significant assistance from the state. Effective internal capital inputs could be made by the tenantry, who had concealed considerable amounts of dormant capital.[219] Interference in legitimate property rights by the proposed Bill was to be minimal, and those made would be in the landlord's interest only because of the peculiar circumstances of Ireland. Nothing like the 'gross injustice' of Ulster tenant right was to be considered, but Stanley hoped that illegal agrarian combinations would be undermined by the granting of compensation. Those who sought 'fixity of tenure', however, would be disappointed: 'Nothing could be more ridiculous, more suicidal, and I might almost say criminal, on the part of any Government, than to propose such a measure.'[220] His

---

217 'Lord Farnham's Memo: Tenant Improvement Bill', n.d. (May 1845), ibid., NeC 9,506. Farnham was one of the Irish peers whom the government sought to conciliate in 1845, see Peel to the Queen, 1 Oct. 1845, Peel Papers, Add. MS 40,440, fol. 249.

218 *Hans.*, LXX, 1084–6 [12 July 1843].

219 *Hans.*, LXXXI, 211–16 [9 June 1845].

220 Ibid., 221–2. Graham appreciated the importance of the manner in which the Bill was presented. He told Stanley, 'when you introduce it, it will be quite necessary to go at large

intention was, he explained privately, to narrow the scope of the bill to improvements which increased the letting value of the land.[221]

The most striking point about Stanley's Bill was the proposal that the machinery for implementation was to include a 'commissioner of improvements' with an office in Dublin and a staff of temporary assistants in the counties. Despite his assurances that the facilities for registration would primarily encourage voluntary agreements between landlord and tenant, it was this proposed centralization that focused the indignation of Irish landlords against the bill. The inclusion of this provision, which was at variance with both Sharman Crawford's and Devon's preference for local machinery and the assistant barrister's court as the mechanism of claim and enforcement, led some observers to suspect that the government had deliberately sabotaged their own Bill. Stanley's apparent eagerness to inter the Bill in a select committee does indeed cast doubt on his own commitment to it.[222] In the event Stanley explained to Devon that the Bill had proved too cumbrous and complicated to continue with, and that it would have to be entirely recast.[223]

The Bill found enthusiastic support only from Devon himself, although it was pointed out in debate that the Commissioners had not supported the proposed form of machinery.[224] Nineteen, mostly Irish, peers signed a protest against the Bill's principle; the Irish Whig-Liberal moderates Monteagle and Clanricarde joined the Tories Londonderry and Roden in denouncing the principle of intervention in the law of contract. Monteagle also took a critical line, arguing that improvement of social relations by act of parliament would be as counter-productive as any statutory attempts to improve morals or religion. Real economic improvement could not be achieved on the scale envisaged in the terms of the Bill: 'to consider it possible that any effectual system of draining would originate from the holders of twenty, ten, or

---

into the subject, and to make our plan clearly intelligible and its limits clearly understood. The first impression on this subject is most important.' Graham to Stanley, 24 May 1845, Graham Papers, bundle 89.

221 Stanley to Sir R. Brooke, 28 June, Derby Papers, 920 DER (14) 176/2, fol. 216.

222 *Hans.*, LXXXI, 1017, 1115–16 [23, 24 June 1845]. This 'sabotage' theory was developed in the leaders of the *Freeman's Journal* after the withdrawal of the Bill. It had been introduced, the paper alleged, solely as a misleading exercise in public relations: 'Lord Stanley introduced this Bill with a good name into the House of Lords, knowing that he had there no chance of an effective support for the principle on which it was put forward.' The government had been anxious to 'have Downing-street scattered over with good intentions, that the nerves of the cabinet might not be shaken by the rolling on of Irish agitation without.' But Stanley's deception would not succeed: 'This failure [of the Bill] seems designed. He will succeed in his failure, but Irishmen understand him.' In short, 'never has a Bill been so traitorously dealt with by its author in the little it contained that was worth betraying.' *Freeman's Journal*, 30 June, 5 July 1845.

223 Stanley to Devon, 10 Oct. 1845, Derby Papers, 920 DER (14) 176/2, fol. 295.

224 *Hans.*, LXXXI, 1117, 1136 [Londonderry, Normanby]. Ferguson and Wynne had questioned the centralizing clause when the draft was circulated, Ferguson to Fremantle, 26 May 1845, Newcastle Papers, NeC 9,507/1.

even five acres of land, was the most consummate absurdity of which any man could be guilty.'[225]

Foxites were less hasty to deny the principle of the Bill. Normanby and Fortescue thought tenant expectations would be dashed by Stanley's Bill, but welcomed the principle of compulsory compensation. Fortescue declared his opinion that Peel had held out a 'sort of promise' in 1843 to bring in the kind of compensation contemplated by Crawford. The present Bill, however, offered little in the way of 'justice' to the tenant. Bessborough, who was a rare speaker in the Lords, also publicly supported the compulsory powers.[226]

If the government had any hopes that Stanley's Bill might win at least a degree of support from Irish popular opinion, they were soon dashed. While the Bill's acknowledgment of the 'sound principles' of tenant compensation was welcomed, its terms were declared grossly inadequate. Again, it was the machinery of the central commissioner, which was 'utterly at variance with the free institutions of the country', that was found most offensive. The *Freeman* expressed the fear that its dictatorial power would be used against the tenantry. The definition of improvement was:

> to depend upon the capricious whim of some coxcombe official who has picked up the materials of his judgement in the drawing-room or at the dinner table. At best, the tenant will have permission to improve, or not, according to the ever-shifting vapours of agricultural doctrines that flit across the upper and fickler regions of society. If not at once, the doctrine will soon prevail that the buildings and homesteads upon small farms are only incumbrances and obstructions to a superior economy of agriculture, and improvements by small tenants will be steadily and effectually discountenanced.[227]

The paper's other main objections to the Bill were that it made no provision for retrospective compensation for existing 'improvements', that it strictly limited the sort of works covered, the amount claimable by the tenant, and the period allowed before the claim became exhausted, and that it threatened the existence of tenant right in Ulster.[228] However, the paper concluded that while the threat of agrarian outrage remained the tenant's greatest protection against landlord depredations, the government's acknowledgment of the principle of compensation represented an advance. The initiative now returned to the tenants and their outdoor agitation.[229]

---

225 *Hans.*, LXXXI, 1128. Lansdowne and Clanricarde played on English landowners' fears that the Bill would prove a precedent for similar measures in Great Britain, ibid., 1147–50.

226 Ibid., 1124–6, 1202 [26 June].

227 *Freeman's Journal*, 11, 12 June 1845.

228 Ibid., 12, 17, 18 June. On 20 June the *Freeman's Journal* reprinted critical comments on the Bill from the *Derry Standard*, *Banner of Ulster* and *Northern Whig* on the latter point, and published a favourable review of W. Neilson Hancock's *The tenant-right of Ulster, considered economically* (Dublin, 1845), an apologia for the Ulster custom.

229 *Freeman's Journal*, 9, 19 July 1845.

British liberal opinion was no more indulgent. The *Times* condemned the proposed machinery as one of 'the most unmanageable bits of blundering that [was] ever manufactured', and objected to the idea that the British tax-payer would be obliged to meet the expense incurred as a result of the landlords' failure to do their duty. The Bill was, the paper concluded, an exercise in political cynicism: 'The title of the act is not bad . . . but it is the old trick of a "cry" to go to the country with – it is not until the hollowness of the thing is seen that any reasonable person would think of opposing it.'[230]

While Stanley's Bill disappeared, as expected, into a select committee, pressure for legislation remained strong. Sharman Crawford went on prodding Peel to act in the Commons, and extracted a promise that the Bill would be re-introduced once amended.[231] Fortescue kept the matter open in the Lords in the new session,[232] and the *Morning Chronicle* demanded a substantial landlord-tenant bill.[233] The Devon Commissioners continued to work on their own initiative in preparing a number of bills that would embody the recommendations to which they had put their names. Some confusion arose from the parallel processes of official and semi-official drafting of legislation. Ferguson, writing to Devon, was unsure of the government's intentions regarding the Tenants' Compensation Bill, but thought the commissioners should press ahead with bills regarding ejectments, leases and the grand juries.[234]

Devon's favourable impressions of the Ballinasloe livestock fair in 1845 convinced him that agricultural improvement had now become a 'fashionable object', yet he felt that the measures recommended in his report were still looked to with great anxiety in Ireland. After communicating with the Dublin Castle administration, he informed Ferguson of the government's assumption of responsibility for the Compensation Bill, but he noted that little progress had been made on it.[235] He impressed on ministers the necessity of further action.[236] Under such pressure, Peel finally agreed to re-commit the government to promoting the Bills. One

---

230 *Times*, 27, 28 June 1845.

231 *Hans.*, LXXXII, 621–2 [17 July 1845].

232 Ibid., LXXXIV, 1391–4 [23 March 1846]. He declared that the great evils of Ireland were to be found, 'in the circumstances attending, not merely the relation of landlord and tenant, but the tenure and possession of land in Ireland'. He advocated the replication in Ireland of what the Anti-Corn Law League had pioneered in England – the creation of smallholding properties which united the relation of landlord and tenant. This could be facilitated by encumbered estates legislation and franchise reform.

233 *Morning Chronicle*, 23 Jan. 1846.

234 Ferguson to Devon, 7 Oct. 1845, Newcastle Papers, NeC 9,483/1–2; Heytesbury to Graham, 9 Oct. 1845, Graham Papers, bundle 24 IR.

235 Devon to Ferguson, 28 Oct. 1845, Newcastle Papers, NeC 9,487/2. 'Ballinasloe' was a term of abuse in Repeal circles, signifying mass clearances by the grazing interest, O'Connell, *Repeal dictionary*, p. 7.

236 Devon to Peel, 27 Oct. 1845, Stanley to Devon, 19 Oct., Devon to Fremantle, 22 Oct. 1845, Newcastle Papers, NeC 9,486/1, 9,484, 9,485/1.

reason for this may have been the risk of embarrassment to the administration arising from Devon's collaboration with Pierce Mahony in the semi-official drafting process. Devon was aware that Mahony's name was 'apt to excite suspicion', but thought that his enthusiastic co-operation might be useful. The government, however, thought otherwise.[237] Peel insisted that a proper distance be kept and that anything proposed by Mahony should be treated as the suggestion of a private individual. Mahony's bills were savaged by the Irish Attorney General, who expressed surprise that Devon had promoted these schemes, and thought it 'quite clear that some very great deception must have been practised on his Lordship'.[238]

If the risk of political embarrassment on such a sensitive subject tended to propel the administration into legislative preparation in late 1845, the rising fear of social disruption in the wake of the potato failure of that autumn was another and much more serious motivation. Fremantle reported in late October a growing disposition on the part of the small tenants to resist the payment of rents, and he feared 'that if the distress is severe the people will not submit to privation so patiently as they have done in former years, particularly in 1822. There will not be wanting agitators who . . . will stimulate them to violence and outrage.' In the context of the continuing popular agitation of the land question, the potato failure threatened to provoke widespread agrarian warfare. Reports were already coming in of Catholic priests urging the morality of a rent strike, and O'Connell's brinkmanship appeared very dangerous.[239]

Landlord-tenant measures had to give way in the session of 1846 to the pressing priorities of the Corn, Famine Relief and Coercion Bills. Despite the conviction of Peel, Graham and Fremantle that some such measure was necessary under the circumstances, little progress was made. Stanley, the Bill's erstwhile proposer, was out of the government, Fremantle was on the brink of resigning as Irish Secretary, and Graham was complaining of over-work and was apprehensive of 'the difficulty of framing a Landlord and Tenant Bill . . . which in the present state of Ireland will not add fuel to the flame'.[240] The matter received more attention from March, partly due to the appointment of the more active and ambitious Earl of Lincoln as Chief Secretary, but perhaps more as a result of the scandal of the

237 Peel to Fremantle, 5 Nov. 1845, Peel Papers, Add. MS 40,476, fol. 524; Devon to Fremantle, 22 Oct. 1845, Newcastle Papers, NeC 9,485/1; the Commissioners had been warned about Mahony's unreliability after he had appeared drunk at the London Law Club boasting about his drafting of several Irish land bills on behalf of the government, Sir J. Young to Peel, 9 May 1845, Peel Papers, Add. MS 40,566, fol. 277.

238 Peel to Fremantle, 3 Nov. 1845, ibid., Add. MS 40,476, fol. 510; (Irish) 'Attorney General's Memo', 11 Nov. 1845, Newcastle Papers, NeC 9,490.

239 Fremantle to Peel, 28 Oct., 20 Nov. 1845, Peel Papers, Add. MS 40,476, fols. 492–3, 556–9. Irish landlords attributed the upsurge in agrarian disturbances directly to Repeal doctrine and activity, R. Daly to Peel, 4 Oct. 1845, ibid., Add. MS 40,575, fol. 136.

240 Graham to Peel, 28 Dec. 1845, ibid., Add. MS 40,452, fol. 83; Graham to Fremantle, 3 Jan. 1846, Graham Papers, bundle 98; Graham to Heytesbury, 25 Feb. 1846, ibid., bundle 27 IR.

notorious Gerrard evictions in County Galway. The scale and severity of this incident, in which 270 people were cleared to create a bullock pasture, coming at a time of heightened tensions in Ireland, led to critical questions in parliament from Tories, Whigs and radicals, and provoked considerable controversy in the press.[241] This was deeply embarrassing to a government pledged to the encouragement of 'humane' improving landlords. Graham was genuinely angered at the reports and wrote an indignant letter to Heytesbury stating that, under the circumstances, Mrs Gerrard's actions had been 'fearfully injudicious and pregnant with fearful consequences'. Graham thought that:

> If the landlords of Ireland will neither learn prudence, nor exercise forbearance towards their tenantry, the strong arm of the law must be interposed to put down crime and insurrection on one hand, and to prevent oppression and reckless harshness on the other. I have the greatest respect for the rights of property and am earnest in my desire to uphold them; but British feelings are outraged by these sweeping ejectments, and the imperial parliament cannot be persuaded to maintain in their integrity powers which are so abused while the land is exempted from all forced contribution for the relief and support of the destitute.[242]

Other ministers were also irritated by these events, but felt a greater need for caution.[243] Peel approved an inquiry, but was most concerned at the risk this bad publicity posed to the safe passage of his Irish Coercion Bill. The Lord Lieutenant declared that he was not aware of any way in which the government could intervene to prevent such an incident.[244] Graham accepted these arguments, and shared Peel's fears about the implications of the Coercion Bill, yet the incident appears to have had a deep effect on him, and he pressed the Irish Office to produce quickly a workable version of the Compensation Bill, as a means of overcoming the Irish 'Pandemonium'.[245]

The reintroduction of the Compensation Bill by Lincoln in the Commons in June 1846 was the outcome of these considerations, and a reflection of Peel's

241 *Hans.*, LXXXV, 274, 278 [30 March 1846: Londonderry, Clanricarde], ibid., 485 [2 April: Smith O'Brien], ibid., 1076 [27 April: Poulett Scrope]; *Freeman's Journal*, 27 March. The *Times* thought such incidents ought to be prevented by 'penal consequences to the ejector', and asked, 'How long shall the rights of property in Ireland continue to be the wrongs of poverty, and the advancement of the rich be the destruction of the poor?' Graham was castigated along with the landowners, and an extension of the Irish Poor Law demanded, *Times*, 31 March, 4 April 1846.

242 Graham to Heytesbury, 3 April 1846, Graham Papers, bundle 29 IR; Graham's anger reflected his own experience of having removed half of the tenants on his own estate without 'inhumanity' or disturbance, Spring, 'A great agricultural estate', pp. 77–8.

243 Lincoln to Peel, 30 March 1846, Newcastle Papers, NeC 12,129.

244 Peel to Lincoln, 4 April 1846, ibid., NeC 11,982; Heytesbury to Graham, 10 April 1846, Graham Papers, bundle 29 IR.

245 Graham to Heytesbury, 13 April 1846, ibid.; A. Brewster to Lincoln, 23 March, 18 April 1846, Newcastle Papers, NeC 9,285, 9,288.

concern to avoid repeating the 1843 experience of bringing in coercion without any accompanying remedial measures. The Devon Commission report had pointed out that agrarian outrage arose mostly from questions of land, and it was on these issues that Whig criticism of the coercive legislation tended to concentrate.[246] Introducing his Bill, Lincoln felt it unnecessary to explain its principle, but stressed its very limited scope, and emphasized that much would remain to be done by the landlords as a class, without state assistance. Parliament's task was merely to see justice done between the two parties, if necessary by intervening to break the vicious circle of want of employment – turbulence – want of security – want of capital. Compensation would encourage tenants with capital to improve, but far more commonly, it would facilitate voluntary agreements combining the landlord's capital and the tenant's labour. The 1846 Bill dropped Stanley's contentious central commissioner and opted for Devon's local enforcement machinery, but Lincoln stressed that landlord consultation remained the first step of the legal process, and that at all stages the proprietor would retain the power to take on the 'improvement' himself and to inspect the work in progress.[247]

Lincoln's Bill met with a more favourable reception than its predecessor, and gained the support of the Irish Tory Shaw, the radical Bernal Osborne, and the Repealer M.J. O'Connell. Those most closely connected with tenant right demands, however, found it wanting. Sharman Crawford, Poulett Scrope and Daniel O'Connell all identified its purely prospective nature as the key failing of the Bill. Only retrospective compensation could satisfy the tenants, by providing sufficient protection against immediate landlord oppression. Crawford objected to the limitation of the amount of compensation to the value of three years' rental, and O'Connell thought that the object of 'fixity of tenure' could not be achieved by this measure. Nevertheless, they were not prepared to oppose what would still be a precedent-setting interference in the law of landed property.[248]

Having initially made welcoming noises, the *Freeman's Journal* reverted to putting up another barrage of criticism against the revived Bill. While an improvement on Stanley's 'shapeless abortions', the scale of compensation remained inadequate, and the period covered too brief.[249] A closer examination of its details revealed that even the altered arbitration machinery was exceedingly complex and would operate in the landlord's favour. The measure was based on premisses totally alien to Irish circumstances:

---

246 *Hans.*, LXXXV, 630–2 [6 April 1846: Morpeth]; LXXXVII, 508–14 [15 June: Russell]. For the Coercion Bill, see below, pp. 143–6.

247 *Hans.*, LXXXVII, 279–87, [11 June 1846].

248 Ibid., 291, 293 [11 June 1846: Sharman Crawford, Poulett Scrope], ibid., 397 [12 June: D. O'Connell].

249 *Freeman's Journal*, 13 June 1846. Lincoln's Bill envisaged a reduction in the scale of compensation by one quarter of its value every seven years, expiring completely at the end of 28 years; the *Freeman* demanded at least 40 years to give a semblance of justice.

> Such legislation may do well enough for England; but the constitution of society in Ireland – power on the one side – dependency and poverty on the other – renders such a remedy impossible of execution even if it were sanatory of the disorder which it does not even touch. Tenants with large capital, and filling an independent position, may stand face to face with the landlord in the county court, and demand arbitrators, and certificates, and awards! But the poor Irish tenant . . . would as soon think, and with as much justice, of ordering his coffin![250]

From the other end of the political spectrum, the very principle of such legislation was denounced as a concession to peasant trickery and unprincipled agitation.[251]

The Bill was lost on the fall of Peel's ministry on 29 June. Questioning Russell on his intentions, Crawford alluded to the growing impatience of the people and stressed the necessity of adopting retrospective clauses. Russell stated that he had found some parts of Lincoln's Bill objectionable, and that it was better dropped and reconsidered over the recess. Lincoln's other measures, an Ejectments and a Leases Bill (both embodying Devon's recommendations) were taken up by the new government and passed, though Russell expressed interest in a stronger measure against ejectments, to be brought in at the start of the next session.[252]

Conclusion

Peel's government passed without realizing its three-year commitment to enact legislation on Irish land. It is doubtful that there was ever any great enthusiasm for the idea of government intervention in this field on the part of ministers. Suffused with orthodox economic preconceptions, they saw legislation on landlord-tenant relations as a political irritation, and ultimately as marginal to the solution of Irish problems. The proposals of 1845–6 combined a degree of concern for the investment activity of the larger tenant with a rhetorical gloss intended to defuse an increasingly politicized praedial agitation. This latter concern explains the paradox of the government's simultaneous advocacy of a tenant protection measure in Ireland, and rejection of Portman and Pusey's tenant right proposals in England.[253] In both countries, Peel looked primarily to a landlord-led introduction of high-

250 Ibid., 22 June 1846.

251 [J.D. Brady], 'Ireland – its condition – the Life and Property Bill – the debate, and the famine', *Blackwood's Edinburgh Magazine*, LIX (May 1846), p. 602.

252 *Hans.*, LXXXVIII, 282–4 [3 Aug. 1846: Sharman Crawford, Russell, Labouchere].

253 There was little co-operation between the English and Irish tenant right campaigns. Portman opposed Stanley's Irish Compensation Bill, while Lord Wharncliffe opposed Portman's and supported Stanley's, both on the grounds that Irish conditions were vastly different from English, *Hans.*, LXXXI, 389–92, 1205–7 [4 June, 7 July 1845]. Ministers read and rejected the ideas proposed in several English agriculturalist publications on 'tenant right'. See Fremantle to the Attorney General, 3 June 1845, on G.M. Williams' *On the tenant's right to unexhausted improvements, according to the custom of North Lincolnshire,*

farming techniques to meet the problems of agricultural development. His convictions were reinforced by the challenge posed by free trade in 1846.

Peel's government could claim success in defusing the threat evident in the broad movement for reform of 1843, and in reconciling at least some of the Irish Whig-Liberals to Conservative government. This sea-change is evident in the words of More O'Ferrall in 1846, when he urged Russell to unite with Peel to pursue 'the regeneration of this country' through further Maynooth-style Church reforms, and vigorous legislation on the lines of the Devon report.[254] It was a measure of how far Peel had taken politics in the three years since the 'state of Ireland' debates that this Catholic liberal could now say that 'it would be impossible to return to the government of Lord Normanby with the same success, not even if you placed an Irishman in every office, and bestowed the patronage of the empire.'[255] Whatever the feasibility of O'Ferrall's ideas, the profound shock to Ireland and Britain alike of the potato failure which began in 1845 dislocated norms and expectations and compelled politicians to concentrate their attention on the problems of Irish land.

Newcastle Papers, NeC 9,509/1–2, and the handwritten marginal note on the Irish government copy of *'What should constitute tenant right?': Resolutions of the Northamptonshire Agricultural Book Club, 16 August 1845*, ibid., NeC 9,513. D.C. Moore suggests that Peelite hostility to English tenant right arose from the fear that the granting of contractual equality would destroy the cohesion of the rural interest, 'The Corn Laws and high farming', pp. 557–9.

254 More O'Ferrall to Russell, 17 March 1846, Russell Papers, 30/22/5A, fol. 167.

255 More O'Ferrall to Russell, 26 March 1846, ibid., fols. 177–8.

CHAPTER THREE

The Coming of the Blight: Land and Relief, 1845–6

At the very instant when the imagination of the community is rapt in a sort of frenzy by the discoverers of some new mode of creating inexhaustible wealth, we are reminded that these great magicians of the age are powerless against the canker-worm or the palmer-worm, which are emphatically called God's army for the chastisement of mankind; and whilst they are proclaiming their recent victory over space and time, a blast of wind or a grub may deny subsistence to the world . . . The Irish peasant starves because his whole subsistence depends on the produce of his own patch of ground, and that failing he has nothing to offer in exchange for the necessaries of life elsewhere . . . In England, on the contrary, the laws of commerce operating fairly . . . will preserve us from this horrible affliction . . . it is not in breaking the laws of commerce, which are the laws of nature and consequently the laws of God, that we are to place our hope of softening the Divine displeasure to remove any calamity under which we now suffer or which hangs over us.

The Times, 3 November 1845

I thought the matter of the colleges of primary importance, but potatoes have quite superseded it, and my anxiety at the present moment is almost concentrated in the question: How is Ireland to be fed? A famine there is a calamity for which I was not prepared: it alone was wanting to fill the measure of sorrow and of difficulty which ever attend the government of that ill fated country.

Sir James Graham, 18 October 1845[1]

The debate on the Devon Commission report was overshadowed by the first major potato failure in autumn 1845, and the consequent threat of widespread famine. The scale of the crop failure naturally led contemporary commentators to speculate on the meaning of the catastrophe. A variety of factors informed the debate, amongst them Christian providentialism, political economy in its various strands, Irish and British nationalism, anti-Catholicism, and the land debate that had been raging since 1843. The coming of the blight appeared to many to precipitate the dissolution of existing Irish social relationships, and few observers believed that it was possible for Irish society to return to the *status quo ante*. Rival

1 Graham to Heytesbury, 18 Oct. 1845, Graham Papers, Cambridge University Library (microfilm), bundle 94.

models for Irish reconstruction and regeneration lay behind the policy conflicts of the Famine years.

This chapter will analyze the response of the state and the British political classes to the first season of what became known as the Great Famine. The emphasis will fall less upon orthodox political economy and more upon political motivations arising from partisan traditions, the pressure of public opinion, the balance of political forces, and the religious considerations inseparable from many people's interpretations of famine in the early nineteenth century. The first section of this chapter considers the mental impact the potato failure of 1845 had on ministers and public opinion. The second section looks in more detail at the relationship between the potato failure and the Corn Law crisis of 1845–6, and at Peel's food policy more generally. The final section evaluates the measures adopted for relief by public works, and concludes by considering the significance of the Irish Coercion Bill on which Peel's ministry fell in June 1846.

I POTATOES AND PROVIDENCE

The reaction of Peel's government to the 1845 potato failure has generally been praised by historians for its promptness and efficiency, and relative absence of ideological motivation, at least in contrast to that of its successor.[2] Yet Woodham-Smith expressed the important reservation that Peel had allowed the Irish crisis to become mixed up with and overshadowed by the political controversy surrounding the Corn Laws.[3] The two issues cannot, however, be separated. The scepticism with which many historians have treated Peel's claim that he had been compelled to act by 'that great and mysterious calamity' is understandable, for it is undeniable that by the mid-1840s many other considerations were pushing him towards the removal of agricultural protection. Yet if the threatened famine is seen merely as a contingent opportunity and not as an imperative to grasp the political nettle, its full significance may be missed.[4]

2 See Cormac Ó Gráda, *The Great Irish Famine* (London, 1989), pp. 50–1. See also James S. Donnelly, 'Famine and government response, 1845–6', in W.E. Vaughan (ed.), *A new history of Ireland, vol. V: Ireland under the Union, I, 1801–70* (Oxford, 1989), pp. 276–7.

3 Cecil Woodham-Smith, *The great hunger: Ireland, 1845–1849* (London, 1987 edn), p. 50.

4 The claim that the Irish potato failure merely provided a tactical opportunity to implement a premeditated plan to avert the political dangers posed by the Anti-Corn Law League campaign is made in Betty Kemp, 'Reflections on the repeal of the Corn Laws', *Victorian Studies*, V (1961–2), 198. Prest also emphasizes the perceived political threat of the League's campaign to enfranchise radical forty-shilling freeholders in the counties, but acknowledges that this was but one of a number of cumulative causes in play in 1845–6. In contrast, Fairlie has argued that Corn Law repeal was essentially a rational response to secularly changing economic circumstances, resulting from a recognition that protection was becoming a national economic liability from the later 1830s and intensified by the general European shortages of the mid-1840s, John Prest, *Politics in the age of Cobden* (London, 1977),

Peel shared with his closest colleagues, Graham and Goulburn, a Huskissonian economic outlook which regarded the Corn Laws as an impediment to the operation of a 'natural' economic system regulated solely by the operation of providential laws. This belief, which Peel held from the 1820s, dictated that protection be abandoned whenever political circumstances made this possible. Returning to power in 1841 at the head of a party committed by constituency pledges to resisting the Whig-Liberal initiative for a low fixed duty on corn, Peel was constrained by the necessity of maintaining his party as a unified governing instrument. He envisaged a ten-year process of educating his followers as to in the virtues of free trade, during which he would gradually scale down the protective duties. Their ultimate repeal could take place only after he had distanced himself from any implicit protectionist pledge at the general election due in 1847 or 1848. While he allotted his party a subordinate and instrumental role in government, Peel was conscious that it continued to provide a bulwark against radical innovation, and that it offered the means of educating the landed class as to what was in its own, and the state's, best interest.[5] His decennial plan was common knowledge among ministers, and was intended to avoid any repetition of the party dislocation and attacks on his personal honour that had followed the 'conversion' of 1829. Naturally, he subsequently cited his original intentions in justification of his own consistency.[6] Despite considerable political set-backs in the 1845 session, the plan was not abandoned. There was speculation that the Maynooth grant would be followed by something equally spectacular in tariff policy, but the Prime Minister gave no public or private indication in the summer of that year that there would be any alteration to his gradualist policy.[7] He expressed little concern about the Anti-Corn Law League's activities, and expected its campaign to prove counter-productive in a period of general prosperity.[8]

Nevertheless, food supply was uppermost in the minds of Peel and Graham during the summer, as poor weather gave much cause for concern. The tone of

---

pp. 88–97; Susan Fairlie, 'The nineteenth-century Corn Law reconsidered', *Economic History Review*, 2nd ser., XVIII (1965), 562–75.

5 This didactic process continued after the die had been cast in 1846, Peel to the electors of Tamworth, July 1847, Sir Robert Peel, *Memoirs*, edited by Lord Mahon and Edward Cardwell, 2 vols. (London, 1856–7), II, 102–6. For Peel's attitude to party, see Angus Hawkins, '"Parliamentary Government" and Victorian political parties, *c.*1830–*c.*1880', *English Historical Review*, CIV (1989), 647–8, 652–5.

6 Boyd Hilton, 'Peel: a reappraisal', *Historical Journal*, XXII (1979), p. 604; Peel, *Memoirs*, II, 318–21.

7 Gladstone memo, 6 Dec. 1845, M.R.D. Foot and H.C.G. Matthew (eds.), *The Gladstone Diaries, vol. III, 1840–1847* (Oxford, 1974), pp. 500–1; Charles Cavendish Fulke Greville, *The Greville memoirs (second part): a journal of the reign of Queen Victoria, from 1837 to 1852*, edited by H. Reeve, 3 vols. (London, 1885), II, 290–1 [21 Aug. 1845].

8 Peel to Graham, 16 Aug. 1845, Peel Papers, British Library, London, Add. MS 40,451, fol. 185; see also *Illustrated London News*, 14 June 1845.

their correspondence reflected fear of an impending crisis rather than any anticipation of political opportunity. Graham wrote on 15 August that 'under no law will it be found easy to feed twenty-five millions crowded together in a narrow space, when Heaven denies the blessings of abundance. The question always returns, what is the legislation which most aggravates or mitigates this dispensation of Providence?'[9]

Graham's pessimism was derived from his evangelical religious faith. The state of the harvest was a recurrent concern for him, and he tended to regard both bounty and dearth as signs of specific providential action in the natural world. In 1843 he had reminded Peel of this truth, telling him 'how fruitless are all our endeavours and most anxious cares without that divine blessing, which alone gives prosperity!'[10] Despite their close political bonding from the later 1830s, Graham and Peel did not share identical religious outlooks. Peel's beliefs were rarely expressed in public, but he did make known his admiration for the theology of the evangelical Bishop, J.B. Sumner, and had publicly stated his belief that scientific knowledge would 'make men not merely believe in the cold doctrines of natural religion, but . . . so prepare and temper the spirit and understanding, that they will be better qualified to comprehend that great scheme of human redemption.' Such statements of 'moderate' and 'rational' evangelicalism were shared by many of his fellow liberal Tories. A more rationalistic and mechanistic interpretation of the workings of providence, holding that suffering was imposed on man only as an instrument of divine mercy, distinguished this from the premillenarian eschatology of more extreme evangelicals.[11] Although differing in tone, the doctrinal opinions of the two chief ministers were ultimately compatible, and produced a powerful synthesis in response to the crisis of 1845–6.

Despite their concerns over the prospective harvest, and experience of previous partial potato failures in Ireland, neither man could have foreseen the scale of the loss which Ireland was to experience in that season. The potato blight of 1845 was a disease new to Europe and unknown in its characteristics. However, the experience of North America, where the blight had been active since 1843, led some observers to predict the worst once 'the American potato cholera' was identified as having reached Europe in summer 1845.[12]

9 Graham to Peel, 15 Aug. 1845, C.S. Parker (ed.), *Life and letters of Sir James Graham, 1792–1861* (2 vols., London, 1907), II, 21.

10 Graham to Peel, 6 Sept. 1843, Peel Papers, Add. MS 40,449, fol. 28. In this respect, Graham was closer to the ultra-Protestant Sir Robert Inglis than to Peel, who had rejected Inglis' proposal for a public thanksgiving for the harvest of that year, Peel to Inglis, 9 Oct. 1843, ibid., Add. MS 40,533, fol. 202.

11 Evangelical providentialism in this period is analyzed in Boyd Hilton, *The age of atonement: the influence of evangelicalism on social and economic thought, 1785–1865* (Oxford, 1988), pp. 7–25, 249–50. The eschatological differences between Graham and Peel are outlined in the light of the 1845–6 crisis in 'Peel: a reappraisal', pp. 609–14. I have sought to develop the ideas suggested by Dr Hilton through a more extensive study of the Famine crisis.

12 *Economist*, 6 Sept. 1845.

The first intimations of a potential potato failure came in early August, but it was not until 10 October that the Lord Lieutenant began to express serious concern for the Irish crop.[13] Heytesbury's warnings prompted Graham to answer his own rhetorical question of 15 August: the threat of famine pointed inexorably to the need for free trade. In coming to this conclusion he mixed the practical concerns of food supply and the balance of political forces with an awareness of an underlying providential causation.[14] Peel drew the same conclusions, but was more cautious and conditional. Irish reports had a tendency to exaggerate, but he foresaw 'the necessity that may be imposed upon us at an early period of considering whether there is not that well-grounded apprehension of actual scarcity that justifies and compels the adoption of every means of relief which the exercise of the prerogative or legislation might afford.'[15]

Perhaps the most surprising aspect of the Peel-Graham correspondence of autumn 1845, given the opportunistic interpretation favoured by many historians, is the reluctance of either to grasp at the possibility of a potato failure as an excuse to implement the removal of agricultural protection. Both were hesitant to admit the threat until reliable evidence was forthcoming, although Graham was the more pessimistic of the two. This caution reflected in part an awareness of the need for certainty in the formulation of a persuasive political argument for any alteration of the Corn Laws,[16] but the tone of their correspondence betrays little sign of overt political calculation and suggests instead a genuine belief that the threat of famine in Ireland, and its inevitable ramifications in Britain, compelled a response incompatible with the maintenance of protection. The Home Secretary wrote of the government being 'driven' to this action by the urgency of the evil.[17]

This involuntary aspect of Graham and Peel's response to the potato blight has not received sufficient attention. For a man of Graham's eschatological pre-occupations, famine could not be understood in purely pragmatic and secular terms. Once convinced that the Irish situation did indeed indicate such a danger, he declared to Peel:

> It is awful to observe how the Almighty humbles the pride of nations. The sword, the pestilence, and famine are the instruments of his displeasure; the canker-worm and the locust are his armies; he gives the word: a single crop is blighted; and we see a nation prostrate, stretching out its hands for bread. These are solemn warnings, and they fill me with reverence; they proclaim with a voice not to be mistaken, that 'doubtless there is a God, who judgeth the Earth'.[18]

---

13 Peel, *Memoirs*, II, 111–13; Heytesbury to Graham, 10, 12 Oct. 1845, Graham Papers, bundle 24 IR.

14 Graham to Peel, 13 Oct., Peel, *Memoirs*, II, 114–16.

15 Peel to Graham, 13 Oct., ibid., 113–14.

16 Peel to Heytesbury, 15 Oct., Peel Papers, Add. MS 40,479, fols. 499–505.

17 Graham to Peel, 17 Oct., Peel, *Memoirs*, II, 117.

18 Graham to Peel, 18 Oct., Peel Papers, Add. MS 40,451, fols. 400–1. Peel had intended this extract to be published in full in his memoirs, yet all but the first sentence was excluded by

Graham's comments were not made in a passing moment of theological abstraction – the next paragraph of his letter commented on the Bank of England's interest rate, and reminded Peel of the urgency of government preparation. Nor was this his only use of such striking language. He had written to the Chief Secretary, Fremantle, several days earlier: 'Potatoes at the present moment engross my thoughts. I never looked forward to any winter with such gloomy forebodings, and all the hopes in which I had ventured to indulge are dashed by one foreseen evil, which is decay at the root of a single plant: so praised is statesmanship, so inscrutable are the ways of the Almighty!'[19]

While his perception of this direct intervention of divine providence in human affairs led Graham to express the need for personal abasement and humiliation before God, it also pointed towards atonement for the sin of national pride. Graham's tutelage under Peel from the later 1830s had led him to modify his views as to the ends illuminated by providential visitations, even if he retained a different idea of the means whereby they operated.[20] Convinced of the moral superiority of free trade over protection, he interpreted the blight as an indication that temporizing was no longer tolerable.[21] From this point forward, Graham's obsession with the coming famine in Ireland suffused his correspondence, and his pessimism led him to dismiss out of hand any suggestions that the scale of the crisis might be over-estimated, or that any 'practical' remedy short of Corn Law repeal might be sufficient.[22] He also sought strenuously to convince other ministers of the seriousness of the situation, and told the cabinet that 'Ireland will be decimated by the famine'.[23] Returning to office after the political crisis of December 1845, he stated his sense of the 'mission' now imposed upon the government: 'The Irish potato case is now *beginning* to develop itself in its awful magnitude . . . I am not disheartened; and I will do all I can – but we have a nation to carry, as it were, in our arms, and no very great assistance, on which we can rely.'[24]

---

the editors in 1857. This omission reflected the rapidly changing religious mores of mid-nineteenth-century England, and the decline of orthodox evangelical providentialism, Hilton, 'Peel: a reappraisal', p. 613. Graham's quotation was a paraphrase of the book of Joel, ch. 1, v. 4; for the use of such prophetic metaphors in botanical writing, see George Weightman, *A treatise on the true nature and cause of the present destructive disease of potatoes, with the means of cure* (London, 1846).

19 Graham to Fremantle, 15 Oct. 1845, Graham Papers, bundle 24 IR.

20 Graham admitted his debt to Peel in the letter of 18 October by adding 'You have been my master', Peel Papers, Add. MS 40,451, fol. 401.

21 Graham to Heytesbury, 18 Oct. 1845, Graham Papers, bundle 94.

22 Graham to Peel, 8 Nov., Peel Papers, Add. MS 40,452, fol. 3.

23 'I have spoken *here* of nothing but the extent of the potato disease in Ireland and of the serious consequences which I apprehend. I do not think the full measure of our difficulties is felt or comprehended.' Graham to Peel, 14 Nov., ibid., fol. 15; Thomas Wemyss Reid (ed.), *Memoirs and correspondence of Lyon Playfair* (London, 1899), p. 99.

24 Graham to Peel, 31 Dec., Peel Papers, Add. MS 40,452, fol. 90.

Graham's alarm had a considerable impact on Peel, for while the latter may have been responsible for channelling Graham's premillenarian alarms towards a specific temporal focus, the influence was not all in one direction. The Premier's language was always more restrained, but contemporaries saw him as coming under the spell of Graham. Evelyn Denison told Gladstone in December that 'Graham had been frightened and had frightened [Peel]' over Ireland, and both Lincoln and Wharncliffe shared this opinion.[25] A more sympathetic account of Peel's motivations – significantly from a man sceptical of any connection between the Corn Laws and the Irish crisis – was Wellington's defence of Peel's conduct to the hostile Croker: 'I cannot doubt that which passed under my own view and frequent observation day after day. I mean the alarms of the consequences in Ireland of the potato disease. I never witnessed in any case such agony.'[26]

It would be wrong to attribute Peel's convictions as to the nature of the Irish crisis solely to Graham's apprehensions. It was indicative of the temperamental differences between the two men that Peel placed so much weight on the activities of the Scientific Commission he set up in October 1845 to inquire into causes and extent of the disease, and to recommend practical measures. This was required not only to convince sceptical colleagues that the extent of the failure was on a scale that made traditional relief responses inadequate,[27] but to ensure that all human endeavours to halt the spread of the rot should be attempted before further measures were taken.[28]

The Commission produced no surprises. Its chair, the eminent chemist and advocate of scientific agriculture, Lyon Playfair, shared Peel's gloom before taking up the position, and from the start did not expect to find a remedy.[29] The Commission's final statement that at a low estimate, 'one-half of the actual potato crop in Ireland is either destroyed or remains in a state unfit for the food of man', was based on a survey of the worst-hit eastern counties of Ireland, and thus exaggerated the

25 Gladstone memo, 20 Dec. 1845, Foot and Matthew, *Gladstone diaries*, III, 504–6; Greville, *Journal*, II, 318–19 [13 Dec. 1845]. Gladstone's initial incomprehension and his reluctance to abandon his protectionist pledge of 1841 were also overcome on reading the official Irish papers. Only after seriously revolving the matter in his mind, under the guidance of 'the Holy One', did he consent to accept office, *Gladstone Diaries*, III, 503, 506–7.

26 Wellington to Croker, 6 April 1846, Lewis J. Jennings (ed.), *The correspondence and diaries of the late Rt. Hon. John Wilson Croker* (3 vols., London, 1884), III, 65.

27 Peel to Goulburn, 18 Oct. 1845, Peel Papers, Add. MS 40,445, fols 228–31; Goulburn to Peel, 21 Oct., ibid., fols. 234–6.

28 Peel to Graham, 18 Oct., Heytesbury to Peel, 20 Oct., Peel, *Memoirs*, II, 118–19, 129–30.

29 Reid, *Playfair*, p. 98. The government distributed via the parish clergy 70,000 copies of the Commission's second report recommending drying the tubers in kilns, but did not expect much success from this. Playfair admitted that kiln-drying would be of only marginal utility, while Fremantle drew attention to the inability of the rural poor to afford such measures and their general apathy. Peel to Fremantle, 2 Nov. 1845, Parker, *Peel*, III, 227–8, Fremantle to Peel, 6 Nov., ibid., 229, Playfair to Peel, 4 Nov., Peel Papers, Add. MS 40,578, fols 28–30, Fremantle to Peel, 4 Nov., ibid., 40,476, fols. 520–1.

national impact somewhat, but it appeared to provide incontrovertible scientific confirmation of Peel and Graham's worst fears.[30] More generally, the inability of the Commission and the leading European botanists to agree on a convincing diagnosis of the disease encouraged the tendency to look for supernatural causation.[31] Even some of the minority who correctly identified the rot with the action of 'a minute parasitical fungus' attributed its appearance to divine direction. One Irish horticulturalist declared the fungus 'a part – a little part – of the mighty magazine of the great "I Am". Well, then, may puny man exclaim, "How unsearchable are his judgments, and his ways past finding out!".'[32]

Public perceptions of the blight

Religious opinion in Britain reflected these varied responses to the potato failure. Peel's interpretations were mirrored in the words of some evangelical clergymen. One anonymous 'dignitary of the English Church', a self-declared Peelite, warned that the Corn Laws were impeding the providential destiny of the empire. Rejecting vulgar Malthusian arguments as a denial of God's natural laws, this author warned that the crisis could not be regarded as a special visitation so long as man-made laws continued to impede the feeding of the country's population. 'Partial scarcities', he concluded, 'may perhaps be regarded as warnings that God does not intend that his children should live apart from each other in sullen independence, but should feel themselves part of a great whole, requiring from each other mutual aid and sympathy.'[33]

In contrast 'extreme' evangelicals clung to prophetic interpretations of crop failure as the punishment of an angry providence. For premillenarians the blight was a 'national judgment' sent to punish Ireland and Britain for the sin of idolatry embodied in the Maynooth Act passed several months earlier. The initial blow would fall most heavily on Ireland, but clergymen warned that this might be the 'harbinger of some heavier calamity' to be visited upon England if she did not change her ways.[34]

---

30 *Copy of the report of Dr Playfair and Mr Lindley on the present state of the Irish potato crop and on the prospect of the approaching scarcity, dated 15 November 1845*, P.P. 1846 (28), XXXVII, 33. In fact around one third of the main potato crop was lost in 1845.

31 C.E. Trevelyan, *The Irish crisis* (London, 1848), pp. 44, 201. On the scientific debate on the blight, see Austin Bourke, '*The visitation of God'? The potato and the Great Irish Famine* (Dublin, 1993), pp. 129–39.

32 N. Niven, *The potato epidemic and its probable consequences* (Dublin, 1846), p. 13.

33 [Anon.], *God's laws versus Corn Laws: a letter to his grace the Archbishop of Canterbury. From a dignitary of the English Church* (London, 1846). The pamphlet was welcomed in the radical press, see [Christine Johnstone], 'God's laws *versus* Corn Laws', *Tait's Edinburgh Magazine*, XIII (May 1846), 284–8.

34 Edward Pizey, 'National sins, the cause of national judgments; or, Israel and England compared. A sermon . . . preached at St Peter's Church, Saffron Hill, on . . . Nov. 16, 1845', *Pulpit*, XLVIII (1845–6), 348–53.

Much of the Prime Minister's private correspondence from Ireland reinforced his apprehensions. Some leading Irish landlords continued to play down the extent of the failure for political reasons, yet even the optimistic Lord Glengall admitted that he thought some relief would be necessary in the following summer.[35] Other writers, of more evangelical inclinations, tended to echo and elaborate Graham's alarms. One of the first serious reports received was from John Dillon Croker, a County Cork proprietor, who warned in an apocalyptic tone of 'what must be looked forward to as a result of the direful calamity it hath pleased the Almighty to visit us with'.[36] Other individuals wrote in a similar vein. George Newson of Newry called Peel's attention to the 'awful prospect before this country, from the scourge the Almighty is apparently about to inflict by the disease of the potato crop'.[37]

These providentialist interpretations of the failure did not all point to the same remedial response, but most of these correspondents appear to have been favourable to connecting the Irish crisis to the Corn Law question. Newson, although 'an advocate of your Corn Law', urged Peel to open the ports and purchase food supplies in America while prices remained low. G.N. Whately, a merchant in Cork, observed that the failure had completely discredited agricultural protection. Here, he argued, was a 'glorious . . . opportunity' to set the country free from the 'incubus that has so long prayed upon her resources and paralysed . . . for years her commerce and manufactures'. The opportunity was providentially inspired, and would allow all interests, including the agricultural, to revive and flourish.[38] These communications to the Prime Minister were merely a fraction of the flood of unsolicited correspondence on the potato failure received in autumn 1845. Their importance lies in the support they offered to conclusions already drawn by the two chief ministers, and as evidence that at least some sections of public opinion shared their preoccupations and concerns.

Perhaps of greater significance than the private letters was the public debate in the British press on the meaning of the failure. The *Times* declared Ireland to be 'in a perpetual state of famine', and ought not to be exporting her entire grain crop merely to pay the rents of absentee landowners. England could and should not rely on this 'broken reed' for a considerable portion of its annual supply.[39] Protectionist and absentee landowners had encouraged the 'most precarious of crops and meanest of foods' in an attempt to circumvent the natural moral laws of the economy, but 'Providence, which made us and the land we till, evidently

---

35 Glengall to Peel, 26 Oct., Peel Papers, Add. MS 40,577, fols. 8–11.

36 Dillon Croker to Fremantle, 8 Oct., ibid., Add. MS 40,575, fols. 249–51.

37 G. Newson to Peel, 11 Oct., ibid., fols 346–7. See also F.S. Trench to Peel, 11 Oct., ibid., fols. 352–5; J. Robinson to Peel, 25 Oct., ibid., Add. MS 40,576, fol. 406.

38 G.N. Whately to Peel, 3 Nov., ibid., Add. MS 40,577, fols. 409–10.

39 *Times*, 1 Sept. 1845. For the unreliability of Irish grain supplies for the English market, see Susan Fairlie, 'The Corn Laws and British wheat production, 1829–76', *Economic History Review*, 2nd series, XXII (1969), 93, 99.

intended another subsistence'. Diet was the bench-mark of civilization, and those dependent on the potato were in a debased and savage state, equalling that of the 'untutored Indian' and 'ocean islander'. The potato's bulk and perishability made it unsuitable for the 'prudent accumulations' typical of 'higher' foodstuffs, but the Irish diet would never be raised to the English level so long as agricultural protection continued to distort the price of corn.[40]

The *Times* was not entirely consistent in its analysis. On 30 October a leader commented on the work of the Scientific Commission, and praised the value of scientific learning and its usefulness in the present situation:

> An universal famine is a scourge of GOD, such as Divine mercy seldom suffers to be inflicted on a nation. But a partial famine – a dearth – is soon magnified by the fears and superstitions of a half-starved people into the most awful of calamities; and this prostration of the popular mind paves the way for the very evil which it apprehends. The labourer's arm is paralyzed and his heart appalled by that which he deems to be a judgment of Heaven.

It was hoped that the Scientific Commission would show that there were human means at hand for preventing the diffusion of a greater calamity.[41] Yet within three weeks the paper turned savagely against the 'Potato Triumvirate' pronouncing 'their researches vain, their suggestions idle, and their information unsatisfactory'.[42]

On 3 November it reverted to an extreme providentialist interpretation in an apocalyptic leader which argued that the Irish crisis had brought into question the very basis of English prosperity. The Irish calamity, arising from 'the stern incurable deficiency of the most essential products of nature', raised in the writer a 'wondering fear' at England's 'intemperate pursuit of artificial wealth', its 'imaginary opulence' and its 'excesses of unreal luxury'. Present prosperity had augmented the danger of scarcity by encouraging indulgence and driving off 'the day of privation and self-denial'. The Irish case proved that scientists were powerless against 'the canker-worm or the palmer-worm, which are emphatically called GOD'S army for the chastisement of mankind'. In such circumstances, all were obliged to atone individually, but the visitation also called for public wisdom and virtue. The Irish would be preserved by their 'habitual abstemiousness', but England could only survive by holding firm to the laws of commerce, which were 'the laws of nature and consequently the laws of God'.[43]

---

40 *Times*, 10 Oct. 1845.

41 Ibid., 30 Oct.

42 Ibid., 18 Nov. Some Irish evangelicals clung to the hope that once the alarm had been sounded and all had exerted themselves to preserve the crop, the danger would abate, Dillon Croker to Peel, 11 Nov., Peel Papers, Add. MS 40,578, fols. 282–3.

43 *Times*, 3 Nov. 1845. This was a quotation from Edmund Burke, who had warned in 1795 that 'the people, ought to be made sensible, that it is not in breaking the laws of commerce, which are the laws of nature, and consequently the laws of God, that we are to place our

A synthesis of these two different but related providentialist views pointed to the removal of the Corn Laws in their entirety. The *Times* called on Peel to humble himself, and sacrifice his 1842 Corn Law, which was the cause of excessive and unnecessary fluctuations in the food supply. He was reminded that 'state necessity is more powerful than self-love or self-delusion. It works by signs and by wonders – by the popular voice, by the operations of nature, by the distress of nations.' Nature had provided a pretext for action by creating a prospective dearth in England and a present calamity in Ireland. Ireland could not be relieved separately, for if the ports were opened to allow in maize and coarse grain to feed that country, and money supplied by the Treasury to give employment, then England would also be entitled to compensatory relief. It was neither 'safe nor pious' to oppose this chance to draw good from the evil of the threatened famine.[44]

Even after making some allowance for an element of rhetorical flamboyance, the consistency of language and the ideological power of this interpretation is striking. The *Times'* explanation of the meaning of the famine crisis was in an idiom comprehensible to the paper's readers and expressed conclusions shared by many of them. One correspondent wrote to the editor describing the potato failure as a retribution on the Premier and the nation, in punishment for the luxury and selfishness of the rich. More positively, if somewhat blandly, Lord Devon suggested that 'this visitation of Providence may teach us all some useful lessons'.[45]

Similar language was to be heard at meetings of the Anti-Corn Law League. Richard Cobden warned of the 'gaunt spectre' of Irish famine and argued that 'Providence has stepped in, and by famine . . . set at naught all the contrivances and delays and moderations of statesmen'.[46] W.J. Fox, the fiery Unitarian preacher, elaborated on this theme. Fox's providentialist interpretation was more benign than that of many Anglicans. He held men to be responsible for perverting the designs of a beneficent providence, but made allowance for a specific, if not retributive, visitations to expose the corruption of protection:

> Providence never yet sent an universal famine; there is no such thing on record, for when the crop fails in one quarter of the globe there is a superabundance in another . . . It is wicked – we might say blasphemous – that those who raise the

---

hope of softening the Divine displeasure to remove any calamity under which we suffer, or which hangs over us'. It was to be regularly quoted in the ensuing years of famine, Edmund Burke, *Thoughts and details on scarcity* (London, 1800), p. 32.

44 *Times*, 6, 22 Nov., 1 Dec. 1845.

45 Ibid., 22, 27 Nov.

46 Anti-Corn Law League meetings, Manchester, 29 Oct., *Spectator*, 1 Nov.; Covent Garden, 17 Dec., *Times*, 18 Dec. This language was not new to Cobden, who had informed Gladstone in 1841 that the Corn Laws 'are an interference with the dispensation of divine Providence as proved by the revealed word of God and the obvious laws of nature, and . . . they ought to be totally and immediately repealed', H.C.G. Matthew, *Gladstone 1809–1874* (Oxford, 1986), p. 56.

> price of corn should thus attempt to transfer the opprobrium of their own iniquitous doings to the Divine Government, and to represent Providence as not less oppressive and tyrannical than themselves . . . such is their abuse of the goodness of Providence, that they . . . would attribute their own bad feelings to the author of all blessings – to him who said, 'he who withholdeth the corn the people shall curse him'. Providence acts differently, and by the smallest things often effects the greatest objects for the good of man, as it has shown in the present instance, where a failure in the crop of the lowest vegetable in a small portion of the globe will provoke the occasion of the destruction of the mightiest monopoly that ever plundered humanity, or revelled in its sufferings.[47]

This aspect of the critique of protection, as much as the more familiar expressions of free-trade theory, dominated the discourse of liberal public opinion during the political crisis of 1845–6. Moral revulsion at the Corn Laws was not new,[48] but the threat of Irish famine concentrated the minds of many of the public, and indeed of the Prime Minister and Home Secretary. It underlay the sense of self-righteousness with which Graham was to console himself after the fall of the ministry:

> I consider it the most fortunate event of my life to have been enabled in any degree, however slight, to contribute to the attainment of this national good, which compensates for a severe dispensation of Providence. And you will think of this and be comforted, when friends forsake you, when enemies assail you, and when the tinsel of the vanities of public life become tarnished in your estimation.[49]

This attitude also contributed to the view taken by many in 1846 of Peel's prophetic role, as an agent 'specially designated by Divine Providence for [the] great work of social improvement and moral improvement'.[50]

---

47 Anti-Corn Law League meeting, Manchester, 10 Dec., *Morning Chronicle*, 12 Dec. Fox's speech ended with one of the great rallying cries of nineteenth-century political nonconformity, 'trust in Providence, and keep your names on the registration list'. The effectiveness of his words is suggested by the *Chronicle* reporter's observation: 'the vast assembly, who had been perfectly enchanted by this brilliant peroration, here rose *en masse*, and burst into one of the most tremendous shouts of enthusiasm we ever heard. It was many minutes before anything like silence was restored.'

48 See Anti-Corn Law League pamphlets such as *Corn Laws: selections from a plea for the poor, by the hon. and rev. Baptist W. Noel* (Manchester, 1842), *Corn Laws: selections from Mrs Loudon's Philanthropic Economy* (Manchester, 1842).

49 Graham to Peel, 4 Sept. 1846, Parker, *Peel*, III, 463.

50 Thomas Ensor, *Ireland made happy and England safe: two letters addressed to the Rt. Hon. Sir Robert Peel, Bart., MP, and a letter to Daniel O'Connell., esq., MP* (London, 1846), p. 7. Ensor's hoped for the 'Christianizing' of Ireland by means of a moral revolution led by a disinterested supra-party government. For the popular idolization of Peel in the course of 1846, see Donald Read, *Peel and the Victorians* (Oxford, 1987), pp. 186–241.

II FREE TRADE AND FOOD POLICY

Once convinced that the potato failure necessitated the immediate abandonment of the original timetable for implementing free trade, Peel and Graham stuck rigidly to their new policy.[51] Their continual rejection of compromise was incomprehensible to many ministers, including some who recognized the full seriousness of the potato failure in Ireland.[52] Peel's inflexibility has subsequently been attributed to his greater foresight and grasp of the political situation. While there is some truth in this, his retrospective comment that 'there are many occasions, and this was one of them, on which it is wise to consider the temper of the public mind, as well as the abstract reasonableness of a particular proposition', takes on a particular resonance when considered in the light of the perspective he shared with some of the most vociferous and weighty elements of that 'public mind'. Both the undoubted scale of the Irish crisis and the intensity of British public response pointed to the inevitability of following any immediate suspension of import restrictions with a major revision, leading to an early repeal of the Corn Law.[53]

A number of ministers were unhappy with this line of reasoning, and feared the consequences of a further 'betrayal' of party commitments. Most would follow Wellington in deferring ultimately and reluctantly to Peel's authority, but one, Lord Stanley, refused to budge. Stanley was in receipt of private information from his Tipperary agents and other Irish correspondents, and refused to accept the veracity of the official government inquiries. In mid-October his Irish sources had led him to fear a total failure, but he later argued that the large oat crop in Ireland meant there was no need for serious alarm. He was unmoved by Playfair and Lindley's figures on the scale of the loss, which Graham forwarded to him in exasperation, and he believed that part of the potato crop could be salvaged by drying.[54]

The deadlock in the cabinet was broken by the publication of Lord John Russell's 'Edinburgh letter' on 26 November.[55] This letter heralded Russell's bid for the leadership of the popular campaign against the Corn Laws and it vindicated Peel's argument that any suspension was bound to be followed by a parliamentary assault on the 1842 Corn Law. Russell commented on the evil raised by the potato disease, which he feared would 'tell with fearful force in the spring',[56] but he

---

51 For a more detailed account of the cabinet infighting over Corn Law policy in later 1845, see Norman Gash, *Sir Robert Peel*, pp. 538–61; Peel, *Memoirs*, II, 140–251.

52 Ibid., pp. 165–6.

53 Cabinet memo, 2 Dec. 1845, ibid., pp. 214–20.

54 Stanley to Peel, 14 Oct., Peel Papers, Add. MS 40,468, fol. 374, Stanley to Peel, 2 Nov., Peel, *Memoirs*, II, 160–1, Graham to Stanley, 11 Nov., Graham Papers, bundle 95A; Stanley to John Browne, 3 Nov., Derby Papers, 920 DER (14) 176/2, fol. 297.

55 Lord John Russell to the electors of the City of London, 25 Nov. 1845, *Morning Chronicle*, 26 Nov.

56 Russell to Lansdowne, 17 Nov. 1845, G.P. Gooch (ed.), *The later correspondence of Lord John Russell 1840–78* (2 vols., London, 1925), I, 80.

argued for repeal primarily on the grounds of social justice and the national interest. The government feared that this meant a Whig alliance not only with the League, but also with O'Connell, who was now demanding Corn Law repeal on the grounds of 'justice to Ireland'.[57]

Whole-heartedly supported by only a handful of his colleagues, and confident now that an incoming Whig government would repeal the Corn Laws, Peel took the opportunity to resign on 5 December, and expressed relief at his liberation from 'certain party doctrines, to be blindly followed, whatever new circumstances may arise'.[58] When Russell failed to form a ministry, he returned to office imbued with a sense of mission, and determined that his position as 'the Queen's minister' had placed him above the constraints of party. His task was 'to purify the remaining tariff', and to 'put the finishing stroke to this good work'.[59]

The Corn Bill in parliament

In the 1846 session Peel lectured the landed interest on the potential benefits free-trade would bring to high-farmers,[60] but it was the 'great and mysterious calamity' of the potato blight to which he attributed the timing and form of his legislative plan. This 'great visitation of Providence' had compelled the government to act without delay, and it had done so in good faith.[61] Peel argued that the precautionary measures taken against Irish famine were 'inconsistent with the determination to maintain untouched the present Corn Law'. Two factors made this the case; the first was the import of food supplies for Ireland at the cheapest rate. The second was compensation to England for expenditure on Irish relief, which could only take the form of a uniform removal of agricultural protection.[62] Graham made the latter point explicit: 'to give this aid to the Irish people, and at the same time to

57 For the response of the Whigs to Russell's initiative see below, pp. 142–4.

58 Peel to Fremantle, 19 Dec. 1845, C.S. Parker (ed.), *Sir Robert Peel from his private papers* (3 vols., London, 1891–9), III, 254–5. Aberdeen, Herbert, and later Gladstone had backed Peel and Graham. Lincoln saw no reason to abandon the original timetable, and thought there was greater political danger in acting during a time of crisis and agitation, Lincoln to Peel, 5 Nov., Peel Papers, Add. MS 40,481, fols. 322–8.

59 Peel to Goulburn, 27 Dec. 1845, Goulburn Papers, Surrey Record Office, Kingston, SHS 304, box 42.

60 *Hansard's Parliamentary Debates,* third ser., LXXXIII, 255–70 [27 Jan. 1846]. For the depth of Peel's commitment to the development of high-farming as the salvation of British agriculture, see D.C. Moore, 'The Corn Laws and high farming', *Economic History Review,* 2nd series, XVIII (1965), 544–61. Peelites were aware of the costs of agricultural transition but thought these were outweighed by the advantages: 'there will be another class of sufferers for whom our sympathies must be strong and whose number will be great – the small farmers with little capital – These will be swept away – but on the other hand the removal of the present state of suspense will attract capital to the soil and before long another race of men, aided by the annual addition of 300,000 mouths, would be earning a livelihood where others had starved.' Lincoln to Peel, 5 Nov., 1845, Peel Papers, Add. MS 40,481, fols. 326–7.

61 *Hans.*, LXXXIII, 78 [22 Jan. 1846].

62 Ibid., 90–2.

enhance the price of the food . . . of England . . . is a proposition which I could never have maintained.'[63]

Peel's speech of 16 February 1846 was directed at the landed interest through their parliamentary representatives, whose 'credit and honour' he sought to defend. State charity was, he argued, compelled by the Irish crisis; without it, the landed and clerical orders in Ireland could hardly be expected to exert themselves, and all efforts unaccompanied by the admission of cheap grain would prove counter-productive. If charity demanded some form of legislative suspension, policy urged that it should be made permanent. Ireland pointed the way – the removal of the maize duty was now imperative – and the voice of British public opinion demanded equity with regard to 'higher' grains. The threatened famine in Ireland served also as a sign and warning for England that 'the years of plenteousness may have ended', and the 'the years of dearth may have come'. It aroused 'that provident fear, which is the mother of all safety', and urged the need for action now, while England still basked in 'this present hour of comparative prosperity', and before the country suffered a return to the awful conditions of 1841–2, when 'again you may have to offer the unavailing expressions of sympathy and urgent exhortations to patient resignation'. The imminence of the Irish catastrophe was explicit in Peel's call to the landed interest to embrace the task of removing 'every impediment to the free circulation of the Creator's bounty'. He concluded:

> When you are again exhorting a suffering people to fortitude under their privations, when you are telling them, 'These are the chastenings of an all-wise and merciful Providence, sent for some inscrutable but just and beneficent purpose – it may be, to humble our pride, or to punish our unfaithfulness, or to impress us with the sense of our own nothingness and dependence on His mercy'; when you are thus addressing your suffering fellow subjects, and encouraging them to bear without repining the dispensations of Providence, may God grant that by your decision of this night you may have laid in store for yourselves the consolation of reflecting that such calamities are, in truth, the dispensations of Providence – that they have not been caused, they have not been aggravated by laws of man restricting, in the hour of scarcity, the supply of food![64]

The Prime Minister adhered to this line of argument throughout the remainder of the corn debates, despite the increasing certainty that the bulk of the Conservative Party was immune to such rhetoric and becoming irrevocably antagonistic. The majority of the Party chose to believe the continuing claims of the Irish Tory press that the crop failure had been exaggerated for political purposes and that Ireland faced no real danger.[65] The loyal Irish Peelite, William Gregory, was one of the

63 Ibid., 716–17 [10 Feb. 1846]. See also, ibid., LXXXV, 177–8 [27 March].

64 Ibid., LXXXIII, 1014–43. Hilton has described this speech as encapsulating the mechanistic and providentialist fatalism of liberal Tory social policy, *Age of atonement*, p. 250.

65 *Carlow Sentinel*, reprinted in *Illustrated London News*, 13 Dec. 1845.

few Conservatives to echo Peel's words. Speaking in the corn debate he praised the way the Irish people had received the visitation; they had been 'meek, patient, and resigned', and shared the last of their food as they 'bowed themselves humbly beneath the chastisement of Heaven'. The Irish crisis was a warning to England of her own vulnerability, and hence compelled a positive response from parliament. The legislature could not 'preserve their restriction upon the people's food, and then preach resignation . . . to an angry and terrified nation . . . That would not do. They would never drive it from them, but that, smitten as they were by the heavy hand of God, they had, in addition, crushed them with the iron hand of man.'[66]

Amidst the furious denunciations of the Corn Bill from the Tory backbenches and editorial offices, some 'moderate' evangelical voices continued to support Peel. The Claphamite *Christian Observer* welcomed the Bill for arranging 'losses and gains . . . in equitable adjustment', although it thought any encouragement thus given to manufacturing and commerce would have to be accompanied by measures to raise the moral and spiritual condition of the people.[67] Like Peel, it was certain that the visitation would herald the rejuvenation of Irish society:

> The present heavy calamity will not be destitute of ultimate advantage, if it lead to a freer use of grain, and a less perilous dependence upon the potato crop; so as to elevate the physical condition of the people; to call forth improved habits; to force the legislature, the landowners, and all classes of persons in Ireland, upon devising such laws, and carrying out such social improvements, as may be requisite to raise the wretched peasantry from their present degraded and precarious lot, to the decent comforts of farmers, fairly remunerated labourers, and thriving artisans.[68]

Free trade and Irish society

Most commentaries on the relief measures adopted by Peel's government have stressed the continuities with the policies adopted by Tory ministries in 1816 and 1822. Yet it was the elements of discontinuity that produced the greatest controversy in 1845–6.[69] Even if they accepted that repeal was politically expedient in Britain,

---

66 *Hans.*, LXXXIII, 680–95 [10 Feb. 1846]. Peel rewarded Gregory by offering him the Irish Lordship of the Treasury, Brian Jenkins, *Sir William Gregory of Coole: a biography* (Gerrard's Cross, 1986), pp. 66–8.

67 *Christian Observer*, Feb. 1846, p. 128, March 1846, pp. 191–2. The paper also upbraided the government for failing to call a day of humiliation to atone for 'the mysterious injury which Divine Providence has permitted to fall on the food of millions of people'.

68 Ibid., April 1846, pp. 254–5.

69 In 1816–17 detailed statistics were accumulated at Dublin Castle, the duty on maize and rice suspended for a year, distilling discouraged and arrangements made for the importation of seed oats to distressed areas. A commission of professionals was established in Dublin to administer the £50,000 relief fund, and to regulate the activities of voluntary local relief committees. Gash stresses Peel's pragmatism in initiating these relief measures, but notes

the idea that free trade was essential to the relief of Ireland was doubted by some ministers. Chancellor of the Exchequer, Henry Goulburn, while also seeing the hand of providence in the potato failure, did not see any immediate connection with the principle of protection, and recommended only the reintroduction of the relief scheme over which he had presided as Chief Secretary in 1822.[70] He remained unconvinced by the process of reasoning Peel expounded in the November cabinets, and could 'not see how the repeal of the Corn Law is to afford relief to the distress with which we are threatened'.[71]

Goulburn's criticism has been taken up by some historians to illustrate the expedient role of the Irish crisis in Peel's free trade policy in 1846.[72] This argument is open to criticism. Providentialist concerns prioritized the potato failure in policy deliberations to a degree that makes a purely opportunistic reading of the political crisis unsustainable. In addition, it is clear that Peel thought free trade in food would bring practical benefits to Ireland. Peel's Irish relief policy was determined by two complementary priorities. The first was the preservation of the social and political advances (and their economic concomitants) for which the government had laboured in 1844–5. The second was the acceleration of the process of social and moral change vital for the anglicization of Irish society. Both required the introduction of free trade, although for different reasons.

The government's investment of considerable political capital in its Irish reform programme of 1844–5 reflected the importance it awarded to defusing the O'Connellite threat to the Union, and providing a stable basis for Irish economic development. Peel was certain that progress was underway by the eve of the Famine, claiming in the Queen's speech of 1845 that the improvement of Ireland had advanced as 'political agitation has gradually abated, and as a natural result, private capital has been more freely applied to useful public enterprises, undertaken through the friendly co-operation of individuals interested in the welfare of Ireland.' But by the summer of that year it appeared that the physical improvement of the country had outrun political progress, and was threatened by a renewed surge of party warfare.[73] Despite the Prime Minister's assurances to the Queen that the Irish Repeal movement was on the wane, and that the 'foundations have been laid not only for present tranquillity – but for a permanent improvement in the state of affairs in that unhappy country',[74] the government was uneasy about future prospects. Orangeism remained active and was bitterly hostile to any

that Peel found the repetition of such intervention 'most distressing' by the 1820s, Norman Gash, *Mr. Secretary Peel: the life of Sir Robert Peel to 1830* (Harlow, 1985 edn), pp. 218–25; Peel to Goulburn, 17 Aug. 1826, cited in ibid., p. 377.

70 Goulburn to Peel, 21 Oct. 1845, Peel Papers, Add. MS 40,445, fols. 234–6.

71 Goulburn to Peel, 30 Nov., Peel, *Memoirs*, II, 202.

72 Kemp, 'Reflections on the repeal of the Corn Laws', pp. 196–8.

73 *Annual Register*, LXXXVII (1845), 3; Peel to Lifford, 25 Aug. 1845, Parker, *Peel*, III, 187.

74 Peel to the Queen, 28, 31 Aug. 1845, Peel Papers, Add. MS 40,440, fols. 214, 215.

conciliatory policy, while the monster meeting at Thurles in September, attended by over 100,000 people, appeared to herald the revival of mass O'Connellite agitation.[75] Moreover, it appeared that agricultural improvement had not halted agrarian disturbances in Ireland. Graham despairingly wrote that he could 'see no cure for the evils, which render the impartial government of that country almost impossible'.[76]

One of the greatest dangers posed by the potato failure was the consolidation of what had been regarded as the opposite sides of the equation of Irish agitation, 'Ribbonism' and O'Connellism, in a common campaign against landlordism.[77] It was this potentially revolutionary political context, as Fremantle pointed out, that marked 1845–6 off from previous Irish subsistence crises.[78] The incidence of agrarian outrage began to increase rapidly in counties with a tradition of disturbance in the later months of the year.[79] Ministers were certain that the renewed outbreak now had a political character, an interpretation that was enthusiastically endorsed by the nationalist press.[80] Most alarmingly, it now appeared to have the sanction of at least some of the lower Catholic clergy. Lord Clare wrote to the Lord Lieutenant that 'violent priests' were at work:

> advising the labourers not to thresh the farmers' corn, or allow it to go to market at Limerick – as strangers will be eating it in England while we starve at home. You can imagine the effect of such language on an excitable population . . . [Some] think the multitude only wait for the command to begin an attack on property, I fear this is true – the labouring population is alarmed and reckless. The Cabinet should be alarmed in advance for agitators, who will take advantage of a scarcity or a want of provisions in any district, to let loose the masses.

Clare added that the British public could no longer be expected to make charitable donations for Ireland, and the Treasury would have to bear the burden.[81] Attacks on the 'subversive' character and activities of the priests were common from Irish landowners, but Clare was respected by ministers and thought 'too sensible to write this without cause for alarm'. Fremantle confirmed reports of priests calling on their flocks to withhold their rents, 'and hinting that when famine comes they may help themselves, the law of nature being superior to the law of man'. Such

---

75 O'Connell's speech at the meeting included an extended denunciation of the '*Times*' commissioner', *Spectator*, 4 Oct. 1845.

76 Graham to Peel, 2 Oct. 1845, Peel Papers, Add. MS 40,451, fols. 340–1.

77 Fremantle to Graham, 23 March, Graham Papers, bundle 21 IR; Peel to Graham, 5 Oct., ibid., bundle 94.

78 Fremantle to Peel, 28 Oct., Peel Papers, Add. MS 40,476, fols. 492–3.

79 Tipperary, Westmeath and Cavan were particularly convulsed, Heytesbury to Graham, 14, 28 Nov., Graham Papers, bundle 24 IR.

80 The *Nation* urged the people to take advantage of the opportunities created by the crisis, and was sure that 'out of the peril and humiliation of the prosperous shall come the good of the poor.' *Nation*, 8 Nov. 1845.

81 Clare to Heytesbury, 30 Oct., Graham Papers, bundle 24 IR.

reports confirmed Graham's apprehensions that the policy initiatives of the previous two years were now in jeopardy.[82]

O'Connell's shift of emphasis from the monster meetings to the Dublin Corporation Committee on the potato failure in November 1845 was equally ominous. This 'Mansion House Committee' was ostensibly non-partisan, but Peel and Graham regarded it as a platform for O'Connell and his supporters. While they declined its offers of advice and information, they felt politically compelled by its existence to mobilize the relief machinery.[83] Graham wrote to Peel that he would assemble a relief commission in Dublin without delay, as it would 'not do to surrender to O'Connell the credit of this measure of anxious precaution'.[84] The crisis thus posed the greatest test of the government's sincerity in its 'new departure'. Graham thought that 'harsh injustice to the Irish people on the part of the imperial parliament in this extremity of their need would justify almost any effort to obtain emancipation from misrule', and he expressed shock at Wellington's *sang-froid* in the face of threatened mass starvation.[85]

Direct interference by the state in the economy remained undesirable, but Graham thought it clear that 'we have but to choose the least of great and manifold dangers'.[86] What was required was the provision of food supplies and employment to the poor, to be supervised by an expert commission, and funded jointly by the state and by Irish charity. The prospect of a massive outlay for Irish distress pointed inexorably to the need for 'compensation' to British tax-payers, a point readily conceded by the Home Secretary to parliament. The demand for compensation was made incessantly by liberal newspapers throughout the corn law crisis, with the *Times* in particular putting great emphasis on the sacrifices being demanded of the English poor to assist the ungrateful Irish.[87] This consideration tied the Irish crisis directly to the debate over agricultural protection.

The potato and Indian corn

The political uncertainty surrounding the suspension of the Corn Laws led Peel to authorize the secret purchase of £100,000 worth of American Indian corn (maize) through Baring Brothers' agency in mid-November.[88] This sort of

---

82 Heytesbury to Graham, 31 Oct., Graham to Heytesbury, 2 Nov., ibid.; Fremantle to Peel, 20 Nov., Peel Papers, Add. MS 40,476, fols. 557–8.

83 Heytesbury to Graham, 2 Nov., Graham Papers, bundle 24 IR; Cloncurry to Peel, 7 Nov., Peel to Cloncurry, 10 Nov., *Report of the Mansion House Committee on the potato disease* (Dublin, 1846), pp. 4–7.

84 Graham to Peel, 9 Nov., Peel Papers, Add. MS 40,452, fol. 5.

85 Graham to Heytesbury, 13 Oct., Graham Papers, bundle 94; Wellington to Peel, 17 Oct., Parker, *Peel*, III, 225; Graham to Peel, 22 Oct., Peel Papers, Add. MS 40,451, fol. 420.

86 Graham to Peel, 14 Nov., Peel Papers, Add. MS 40,452, fol. 15.

87 *Times*, 6, 8, 22 Nov. 1845, 14 March 1846.

88 Goulburn to Peel, 11, 13 Nov., Peel Papers, Add. MS 40,445, fols 258–9, 264–5. Goulburn thought this course 'right though at variance with general principles', and succeeded in

intervention was not novel – food imports had been made at government expense during previous subsistence crises – but Peel's justification for it in his memoirs placed it in a different light:

> I should greatly have preferred the introduction of this additional supply of food through the ordinary medium of private adventure, stimulated as it would have been by the suspension of the import duty. I considered it, however, of so much importance to provide, *by any means*, for an increased supply of food, and to habituate the Irish people to the consumption of a novel species of food as a substitute for their ordinary subsistence, that I did not hesitate . . .[89]

The importation was intended to tide Ireland over until the full benefits of the opening of the ports could be realized, by securing for Irish use at least a part of the transatlantic supply before it was too late in the season. It was never intended that the state should take direct responsibility for feeding the destitute. The maize purchased from America was ground and distributed to a network of official storage depots set up by the army Commissariat, assisted in some remote areas by the Coast Guard and constabulary. Ministers hoped that the existence of the depots would regulate the price of food in the private markets, but issues to relief committees from the depots were not to begin until mid-May 1846.

It was recognized that the state purchase would meet only a fraction of Irish needs. By late December Peel had abandoned the idea of immediate suspension of the Corn Law in favour of the early introduction of a Bill that would include the summary admission of Indian corn at a nominal duty. Graham concurred with Peel's argument that the announcement of a legislative repeal of the duty would be sufficient to secure private orders for grain that would arrive once the Bill was passed.[90] The Prime Minister's concern for Irish food supplies was less for the immediate situation than for the summer months ahead, traditionally the time of greatest food shortage in Ireland. Yet he believed that the vital decisions affecting that supply had to be taken urgently. When it became clear that the Corn Bill would be delayed by protectionist obstruction, Peel shifted course to allow for Irish necessity. In early March he declared that Indian corn and rice were to be dealt with in a separate resolution in the Tariff Bill, and would be admitted free by Treasury order as soon as the Bill passed the Commons.[91]

While Ireland might be expected to share in the benefits that Corn Law repeal would bring to the British economic system as a whole, Peel was convinced that it would also be a beneficiary in a number of specific ways. Ireland's particular

---

overcoming the reluctance of Barings, and the preference of his Treasury subordinate, Charles Trevelyan, for open dealing.

89 Peel, *Memoirs*, II, 173.

90 Graham to Peel, 26 Dec. 1845, Peel Papers, Add. MS 40,452, fol. 75.

91 *Hans.*, LXXXIII, 261–2 [27 Jan. 1846]; 1018 [16 Feb.]; LXXXIV, 784, 787 [9 March].

"NATURAM EXPELLAS FURCA."

Hor.

You think you have me *treed?* cried Dan to Bob,
But soon you'll find I'll extricate my nob.
Tho' you *fork* out the blunt to gay Maynooth,
Your fork shan't throttle me, my handsome youth.

P——L.

Arthur, don't mind his chaffing, here we have him,
In such a fix—salt water couldn't save him;
I'll hold Maynooth *dilemma* 'bout his ears,
So come be active, and apply the shears.

W——GT——N.

Its easier said than done Bob—for I'm *cust*
If I can use them, they're so eat with rust;
And had they e'en been whetted sharp enough,
They couldn't cut—his Irish tail's too tough.

2. *Naturam expellas furca,* Joe Miller the Younger, 7 June 1845. Peel's failure to subdue O'Connellite agitation in 1845 was satirized in the London press. While the Prime Minister temporarily restrains O'Connell with the Maynooth Grant, Wellington still finds it impossible to sever the 'tail' of the Repeal Party.

3. The Minister's dream, *Pictorial Times*, 22 Nov. 1845. In this allegory the potato failure combines all Peel's problems into a single nightmare. Chained corn and English radicals occupy the foreground, but behind stand the Irish Catholic clergy and agrarian secret societies, and above all, the shade of O'Connell.

problem was its excessive dependence on the potato, a crop that had long attracted considerable prejudice in England, and whose future reliability had been called into question. Despite the Scientific Commission's rather anodyne conclusion that adverse climatic conditions were the cause of the blight, there was a widespread belief in the 'degeneracy' of the potato plant.[92] Much of the press believed the disease to be of modern origin,[93] and after some confusion, Graham also became convinced that 'the disease is a new and unknown one – at least in Europe'.[94] This shift in opinion had major implications; an existing disease made dangerous by freak weather conditions posed great immediate dangers but was unlikely to recur, but a new disease which had proved extremely virulent on its first appearance threatened to prove a permanent threat. Graham's pessimism and scepticism about the Scientific Commission may have inclined him towards the latter view, and he certainly believed a second failure a strong possibility in the following season.

Two fields of policy were directly affected by the this debate. The first was that of the supply of 'untainted' seed potatoes for the next season. Peel was instinctively hostile to any state intervention by purchase or import bounty,[95] and Graham firmly rejected such measures as impracticable. He also held out little real hope of this being done by private speculation. Potatoes were 'not a cargo well suited in large quantities for transportation by sea', and were hence not viable as an international commercial commodity. In their place he thought 'corn and maize if necessary may be imported'.[96] In addition, Graham's belief in the novelty of the blight led him to abandon the idea of local seed depots in Ireland.[97] If providence acted through an unknown disease of a reviled plant, and not merely through adverse weather conditions, any state policy encouraging propagation of the potato became questionable.

The potato's unpredictability also heightened fears of its reliability as the staple food and pointed to the importance of promoting corn consumption not only as a short-term substitute for that season's shortfall, but as a permanent subsistence

92 P.M. Austin Bourke, 'The scientific investigation of the potato blight in Ireland, 1845–6', *Irish Historical Studies*, XIII (1962–3), 26–32; Playfair to Peel, 28 Oct., Peel Papers, Add. MS 40,577, fol. 92. Kane, a member of the Potato Commission, believed the 'lumper', which was consumed by the poor, to be degenerate. Lincoln agreed that this thesis was 'highly probable', Fremantle to Peel, 16 Nov., ibid., Add MSS 40,476, fol. 554; Lincoln to Peel, 26 Nov. 1845, Newcastle Papers, Nottingham University Library, NeC 12,099.

93 *Times*, 14 Nov., *Economist*, 6 Sept., 8 Nov.

94 Graham to Heytesbury, 15 Dec., Graham Papers, bundle 96B.

95 See his marginal annotation to B.E. Cole's paper recommending bounties for potato seed imports from South America, 29 Oct. 1845, Peel Papers, Add. MS 40,577, fols. 151–4.

96 Graham to Heytesbury, 3 Jan. 1846, Graham Papers, bundle 26 IR.

97 Twisleton to Graham, 18 March 1846, ibid., bundle 100. He also rejected as unworkable the proposal that workhouses be employed as centres for the extraction of edible starch from tainted tubers, Graham to Peel, 8 Nov. 1845, Peel Papers, Add. MS 40,452, fols. 3–4.

food.[98] This had important sociological implications. In early November Playfair pointed out to Peel the providential possibilities presented by the crisis – if the dietary habits of the peasantry were altered, 'it would go a great way to improve their social and therefore their political habits'.[99] This idea was attractive to the government. In introducing the Corn Bill, Peel declared:

> I wish it were possible to take advantage of this calamity for introducing among the people of Ireland the taste for a better and more certain provision for their support, than that which they have heretofore cultivated; and thereby diminishing the chances to which they will be constantly, I am afraid, liable, of recurrences of this great and mysterious visitation, by making potatoes the ordinary food of millions of our fellow subjects.

Maize appeared the best substitute and its importation would be facilitated only by repeal of the duty. Peel was careful to avoid the impression that this dietary transition could be achieved overnight, and to encourage the continued efforts of the Irish gentry to preserve potato seed, but he suggested a reasonably rapid process of change: 'You may think the potato an insufficient article of subsistence; but you cannot, for a period of two to three years to come, dispose of your reliance upon the potato.'[100] This time-scale was similar to that envisaged for English agricultural transition from protection to the rigours of free trade in wheat.

This leads to the central question of whether, leaving the question of relief to one side, Peel sacrificed the interests of Ireland as a grain producer to the greater good of the English urban consumer in 1846. The danger posed by the repeal of the Corn Laws to Ireland's economy and social stability had long been pressed by Irish landowners, and was taken up at length by both English and Irish Tories in the 1846 debates.[101] Even liberal free traders admitted privately that any gain to Ireland would be 'doubtful and remote'.[102] The original 1815 Corn Law had been the fruit of Irish-led lobbying and that country's commercial grain producers had been the chief beneficiaries in the period of its existence.[103] In the course of 1846

98 It was widely believed that almost unlimited amounts of maize would be available for import from America if it was admitted free of tariff, *Spectator*, 15 Nov. 1845.

99 Playfair to Peel, 7 Nov. 1845, Peel Papers, Add. MS 40,578, fols. 175–6.

100 *Hans.*, LXXXIII, 261 [27 Jan. 1846]. The shortness of the time available was more strongly emphasized after Lindley's belated recognition that the disease could be transmitted through the seed. This led Peel to admit that precaution, although necessary, could not guarantee the prevention of the progress of the blight in the next year, ibid., 1263 [20 Feb.].

101 Philip Reade, *Whig and Tory remedies for Irish evils, and the effect a repeal of the Corn Laws would have on the legislative union* (Dublin, 1844); *Hans.*, LXXXIII, 123 [22 Jan. 1846: Northland], 179–83 [26 Jan.: Beaumont], 1113–16 [17 Feb.: Shaw].

102 Clarendon memo, 'Peculiar position of Lord John Russell', n.d. [Dec. 1845], Clarendon Deposit, Bodleian Library, Oxford, c.555.

103 Boyd Hilton, *Corn, cash, commerce: the economic policies of the Tory governments 1815–1830* (Oxford, 1977), pp. 3–4. For the real benefits of the Corn Laws in the post-1815 period to

Stanley and the protectionist press continued to deny that Ireland faced any real danger of famine, and to accuse the government of exploiting exaggerated fears to attain their political objectives.[104]

Peel acknowledged that Ireland would be the part of the United Kingdom that might suffer most from the withdrawal of protection, but he argued that this disadvantage would be overcome by major fiscal concessions.[105] Irish land was to be relieved of the substantial burdens of the national education system, the payment of Poor Law officials and the ordinary expense of the constabulary. Given Peel's commitments since 1829 to ensuring that Ireland herself took responsibility for such 'improving' items of expenditure, this amounted to a major article of compensation, and was considerably more important than the tax relief offered to England and Scotland. Peel evidently expected Irish proprietors to respond to the challenge of free trade in the same manner of their English brethren – by adopting the techniques of high farming and implementing large-scale agricultural improvement. If in 1846 there was little sign of many responding voluntarily to his call, the potato crisis seemed to leave the government little alternative but to initiate the process of putting Irish agriculture on a less 'artificial' basis. Graham stressed the importance of British manufacturing prosperity to the betterment of the condition of the Irish peasantry – already emigration had been promoted and the greater demand for Irish agricultural produce had stimulated increased productivity.[106] Both would be increased as the benefits of free trade in food made themselves felt throughout the British economy.

This argument drew the support of Irish free traders. Sharman Crawford noted that the only prosperous part of Ireland was that where the manufacturing interest was united with agriculture in mutual co-operation, and he expressed a hope that an increase in wages and employment would prosper equally the people and the landlords.[107] Even more striking was O'Connell's acknowledgement of the priority of the free-trade measure for the relief of Ireland. O'Connell had long been committed to the abandonment of the Corn Laws on the grounds both of liberal theory and of moral indignation against a monopoly which he believed acted against the interests of the poor.[108] In 1845–6 he pressed for the suspension of the Corn Laws

Irish landowners and commercial farmers, see Cormac Ó Gráda, 'Poverty, population and agriculture, 1801–45', Vaughan, *N.H.I., V,* 132–3.

104 Stanley to John Browne, 29 May 1846, Derby Papers, 920 DER (14), 176/2, fol. 355; [W.E. Aytoun], 'Ministerial measures', *Blackwood's Edinburgh Magazine,* LIX (March 1846), 378, 382–3.

105 *Hans.*, LXXXIII, 264 [27 Jan.]. This was consistent with his previous statements on the subject. See ibid., LXX, 982 [11 July 1843].

106 *Hans.*, LXXXIII, 1071 [17 Feb. 1846].

107 Ibid., 657 [10 Feb.].

108 Daniel O'Connell, *Observations on the Corn Laws, on political pravity and ingratitude, and on clerical and personal slander* (Dublin, 1842); Joseph Lee, 'The social and economic ideas of O'Connell', in Kevin B. Nowlan and Maurice R. O'Connell (eds.), *Daniel O'Connell: portrait of a radical* (Belfast, 1984), pp. 70–84.

to mitigate the 'dispensation of Providence', and his authority was sufficient to hold in check any scepticism in the Irish popular party and press as to the utility of the Corn Bill.[109] O'Connell was influenced by practical considerations – in March 1846 he instructed his son Maurice to purchase several tons of maize at Cork to support his own tenants.[110]

O'Connell and Sharman Crawford shared the belief that the chief result of the removal of protection would be a large and immediate fall in the price of grain, produced by large-scale importation into Great Britain from abroad. This would, they hoped, allow the Irish poor to consume the produce of their own soil, as was already to some degree the case in the oatmeal-consuming north. Along with many British radicals, they believed that any immediate loss of income this involved could and should be borne by the landlords in the shape of sharply reduced rentals. This view was completely at odds with Peel and Graham's vision of the results of free trade in Ireland; indeed, Graham declared that he had no regrets over the rise in Irish food exports to England, as this was the only means whereby Ireland could accumulate wealth and improve its modes of production. Peel's hope was that the Irish masses would henceforward live mostly on imported maize – the 'lowest' and cheapest grain – and that Ireland would continue to export the bulk of its produce.[111] Neither he nor Graham believed that their Corn Bill would lead to any sudden collapse in corn prices. This division illustrates the more fundamental rift over the future of Irish society. O'Connell envisaged the prevalence of secure smallholders living largely off their own produce. Peel looked to the proletarianization of the smallholder and conacre peasant, who would henceforth live on imported corn purchased through the wages of labour.

Indian corn was not an entirely unknown commodity in Ireland in 1845–6, but previous imports had been relatively small and intended solely as temporary food relief in times of scarcity.[112] In early November 1845 Commissary-General Hewetson urged Peel to promote its use, as maize was 'the cheapest substitute for the potato, equally, if not more substantially, nutritious, and as simple in its mode of preparation'.[113] These claims were deeply flawed – maize was in fact nutritionally poorer than the potato and dependency on it made people prone to vitamin-deficiency diseases, and it required intensive grinding and lengthy cooking – but ignorance

109 D. O'Connell to Smith O'Brien, 20, 22 Dec. 1845, Maurice R. O'Connell (ed.), *The correspondence of Daniel O'Connell* (8 vols., 1972–80), VII, 351–3; *Hans.*, LXXXIII, 1050–68 [17 Feb. 1846]; Heytesbury to Graham, 1 March, Graham Papers, bundle 28 IR.

110 D. O'Connell to M. O'Connell, 26 March 1846, O'Connell, *Correspondence*, VIII, 10.

111 *Hans.*, LXXXIII, 1071, [17 Feb.: Graham], LXXXV, 693–5 [8 April: Peel].

112 E. Margaret Crawford, 'Indian meal and pellagra in nineteenth-century Ireland', in J.M Goldstrom and L.A. Clarkson (eds.), *Irish population, economy and society* (Oxford, 1981), pp. 113–33.

113 Hewetson to Peel, 5 Nov. 1845, *Correspondence explanatory of the measures adopted by Her Majesty's government for the relief of distress arising from the failure of the potato crop in Ireland (Commissariat series)*, P.P. 1846 [735], XXXVII, 53.

and prejudice blinded its advocates to its limitations.[114] One of the most striking aspects of the Commissariat's activity in administering and distributing the 20,000 tons of maize imported by the government, was the long-term view of their operations taken by many of its officers. Most not only agreed with the Prime Minister that maize should be permanently integrated into the Irish economy as an article of consumption, but felt a sense of mission in forwarding this end. Hewetson hoped 'that Indian corn and meal will, before another six months, become . . . a primary article of food among the peasantry and poorer classes'.[115] Sir Randolph Routh, the head of the army Commissariat Department and one of the Relief Commissioners, apprehended that 'as a food the potato will never be what it has been, nor can the people ever place the same confidence in its growth. It will in time resume its proper station as a vegetable, and cease to be a staple article of food.' The importance of securing that maize supplanted oatmeal as well as the potato led Routh to propose a temporary management of the market to prepare Ireland for the operation of free trade and to accustom the peasantry to the new foodstuff. Routh was convinced that potato cultivation was morally debilitating: 'The little industry called for to rear the potato, and its prolific growth, leave the people to indolence and all kinds of vice, which habitual labour and a higher order of food would prevent. I think it very probable we may derive much advantage from this present calamity.' Indian corn would be the basis of Irish 'regeneration', and was preferable to 'oatmeal, which has not the same moral effect'.[116] These views were shared by members of the government. Speaking in the Commons, Edward Cardwell quoted Routh's letter and endorsed its sentiments:

> [I]f, while they diffused amongst [the Irish] a taste for a higher kind of food, they could also introduce amongst them habits of industry and improvement calculated to furnish them with the means of procuring that higher food, they would be effecting one of the greatest practical improvements which this country was capable of accomplishing. Even in the most afflicting dispensations of Providence there was ground for consolation, and often even occasion for congratulation.[117]

The transformation of Irish society was to follow directly from Corn Law repeal.

---

114 E. Margaret Crawford, 'Food and famine', in Cathal Póirtéir (ed.), *The Great Irish Famine: the Thomas Davis lecture series* (Cork, 1995), pp. 60–74.

115 Hewetson to Trevelyan, 27 Feb. 1846, *Corr. explan. (Comm. ser.)*, P.P. 1846 [735], XXXVII, 102. The Commissariat was also involved in the preparation of cheap pamphlets for distribution in Ireland on the modes of cooking Indian corn, see [Anon.], *Memorandum in regard to the use of Indian corn as an article of food* (Dublin, 1846).

116 Routh to Trevelyan, 6 March, 1, 15 April, *Corr. explan. (Comm. ser.)*, P.P. 1846 [735], XXXVII, 108–9, 139, 157.

117 *Hans.*, LXXXIV, 792 [9 March 1846].

The Commissariat and the Treasury

Charles Trevelyan, the Assistant Secretary to the Treasury, was resistant to the agenda shared by ministers and the Commissariat officers. In his opinion, any permanent benefits that might accrue to Ireland as a result of the scarcity were incidental; the first object of relief activity was to teach the people to depend upon themselves for developing the resources of their country. Encouragement given to the consumption of Indian corn from government stores threatened to jeopardize this spirit of self-reliance.[118] He was, if anything, more convinced than his colleagues that the blight was a providential visitation against the corrupt state of social morality founded upon potato subsistence.[119] His disagreement with the government and Commissariat was not over the character or place of the potato in the diet, but over the legitimacy of intervention during such a visitation to privilege maize as a specific replacement. However, Trevelyan's control over relief policy was not yet as extensive as it would become later under the Whigs. During the first half of 1846 the Commissariat generally got its way regarding the management of the depots, but while Graham endorsed Routh's use of his discretion, he also shared Trevelyan's concern for the dangers of interference.[120]

There was considerable division within the administration over Routh's requests for further purchases of supplies for the depots. What forced the government's hand was the outbreak of food riots at Carrick-on-Suir, Clonmel and other places in April.[121] Routh attributed these to the indisposition of the richer classes to exert themselves for the relief of the poor in these towns, and after investigation Assistant Commissary-General Dobree agreed, although adding that the trouble had been triggered by 'a set of able-bodied vagrants from Tipperary and Kilkenny, who recruited [local] idlers'. Military vigilance and the use of sound discretion by relief committees should prevent its recurrence.[122] The Earl of Lincoln, who had become Chief Secretary the previous month, was considerably more alarmed at these attacks on 'mills, bakeries and convoys', and blamed Treasury obstruction for exacerbating

---

118 Trevelyan to Routh, 3, 20 Feb., *Corr. explan. (Comm. ser.)*, P.P. 1846 [735], XXXVII, 77, 95.

119 This was the central theme of his 1848 apologia: 'the only hope for those who lived upon potatoes was in some great visitation of Providence to bring back the potato to its original use and intention as an adjunct, and not as the principal article of national food; and by compelling the people of Ireland to recur to other more nutritious means of aliment, to restore the energy and the vast industrial capabilities of that country', Trevelyan, *Irish crisis*, pp. 8–9.

120 Trevelyan to Routh, 26 Jan. 1846, *Corr. explan. (Comm. ser.)*, P.P. 1846 [735], XXXVII, 67; Graham to Heytesbury, 16 Feb., Graham Papers, bundle 27 IR.

121 These often took the form of raids on food convoys on the roads and rivers, *Illustrated London News*, 18, 25 April 1846.

122 Routh to Trevelyan, 7 April, Dobree to Trevelyan, 24 April, *Corr. explan. (Comm. ser.)*, P.P. 1846 [735], XXXVII, 144, 174–5. Heytesbury added that he believed Bianconi, the O'Connellite Mayor of Clonmel, had dragged his heels in an attempt to throw the whole expense of relief on the state, Heytesbury to Graham, 16 April, Graham Papers, bundle 29 IR.

an already tense situation. He declared to Graham that, 'the danger is frightful if Trevelyan is allowed to be the judge of what is to be done'. On his own authority he ordered Routh to purchase 400 tons of oatmeal in Tipperary, and put pressure on the Treasury for additional supplies of maize.[123] Goulburn sprang to Trevelyan's defence, arguing that his subordinate was only implementing the agreed policy of delaying all further purchases until exceptional circumstances made them expedient. Despite this, he gave in to Lincoln's demands, but insisted that the Indian corn cargo to be bought at Liverpool should again be 'made apparently on private account in order not to raise the market'.[124] Goulburn was concerned that local purchases made in Ireland in the wake of riots would prove an additional incentive to violence, but Lincoln thought the example of the rise in wages on the public works extorted by the rioters at Carrick proved the greater danger.

The importance of the geographical focus of these riots should be borne in mind. South Tipperary was not only a centre of agrarian disturbance and political agitation, but an area of commercial grain production. Dobree described the importance of the river Suir to commerce, and the measures taken to ensure internal free trade: 'The barges leave Clonmel once a week for [Waterford], with the export supplies under convoy which, last Tuesday, consisted of 2 guns, 50 cavalry and 80 infantry escorting them . . . as far as Carrick.'[125] In this and similar areas, anger and alienation had been stirred up by the sight of large-scale exportation of food in time of dearth and threatened famine. Smith O'Brien sought to force this onto the attention of the Commons: 'The circumstance which appeared most aggravating was, that the people were starving in the midst of plenty, and that every tide carried from the Irish ports corn sufficient for the maintenance of thousands of the Irish people. Was it not, then, surprising that there should not, under such circumstances, be more attacks on property?'[126]

Lincoln was successful in April 1846 because he was able to enlist the support of Peel and Graham. The Prime Minister stressed to Goulburn the urgency of the situation: 'I think something worse is at hand than we have yet calculated upon and that no time should be lost in providing for these extraordinary and unexpected difficulties.'[127] What Peel found so alarming was not only the deteriorating famine situation, but the response of parts of Irish society to it. Reports from the Lord Lieutenant in April spoke of growing restiveness in several regions of Ireland, due less

---

123 Lincoln to Goulburn, 15 April, Newcastle Papers, NeC 9,235, Lincoln to Graham, 18 April, ibid., NeC 9,284.

124 Goulburn to Lincoln, 17 April, ibid., NeC 9,242.

125 Dobree to Trevelyan, 24 April, *Corr. explan. (Comm. ser.)*, P.P. 1846 [735], XXXVII, 174–5. Lincoln believed the special character of Clonmel as a major export centre made it unusually suitable for local grain purchases, as these would not adversely affect the market for local consumers, Lincoln to Goulburn, 19 April, Newcastle Papers, NeC 9,236.

126 *Hans.*, LXXXV, 707 [17 April].

127 Peel to Goulburn, 26 April, Goulburn Papers, SHS 304, box 42.

to extreme distress than to a burgeoning 'spirit of insubordination'.[128] Heytesbury blamed political agitation: 'The people are so excited by the Repeal press and orators, and the ill-disposed part of the priesthood, are ripe for any mischief – they believe they have the right to call on the government for employment, on their own terms, and for the supply of a better description of food. It is only in a crisis like the present that the evils arising from Repeal agitation are fully developed.'[129] What concerned the Lord Lieutenant was exemplified by articles such as that in the *Freeman's Journal* of 15 April, which threatened the government with the consequences of their failure. To the *Freeman*, the people were in a state of misery:

> mingled with the last stern resolves of despair, not to perish from the earth while there is food on its surface. We would repress the dangerous spirit which seeks the plunder of the innocent few without bringing relief to the famished many; but despair is a passion which halts at no ordinary considerations, and will not subside by exhortations or lectures . . . There is but one mode of curbing its wayward violence – *let the people be fed*.[130]

Graham took these warning seriously and was worried about 'the danger of a servile insurrection before we are well prepared to resist it'; yet he thought it vital that these 'attacks on stores, mills and ships . . . be put down with a high hand – there is mercy in doing it at once'.[131] The political campaign waged by the Repealers made repression difficult unless accompanied by a renewed commitment to fulfil the promises to relieve Ireland made in January. Under these extraordinary circumstances, Peel also decided that the loosening of relief regulations would be the lesser of two evils. Writing to Goulburn about another disturbed region, he thought that:

> [U]nder ordinary circumstances it might not be advisable to interfere with the maize market – but when Sir R. Routh says that 'the people in Galway are in so excited a state that it would be impossible to contain them, unless a depot is immediately established there', considerations connected with such a state of things, and the example of any successful outbreak, appear to me to overrule other more ordinary considerations.[132]

Yet there were limitations of this interference, for Peel too was concerned that excessive and open intervention in the market would prejudice private trade. He told parliament, 'the measure that might be justified in December, might be very unwise and injudicious now . . . if it were known that Government was in the market as a great purchaser of Indian corn, the first effect would be greatly to

128 Heytesbury to Graham, 16, 18 April, Graham Papers, bundle 29 IR.
129 Heytesbury to Graham, 17 April, ibid.
130 *Freeman's Journal*, 15 April.
131 Graham to Heytesbury, 20 April, Graham Papers, bundle 29 IR.
132 Peel to Goulburn, 15 April, Peel Papers, Add. MS 40,445, fol. 336.

enhance the price, and the next to embarrass the trade.' Further government action, it was implied, would be both marginal and discreet.[133] Peel may also have been alarmed by the temporary deterioration in Anglo-American relations over the Oregon boundary dispute in April 1846. Peaceful relations between the powers were central to his scheme, and he had hoped that free trade would in turn promote amicable relations with the United States. The rumour of war raised prices, threatening the whole edifice of the Irish relief and regeneration policies and suggesting the need for emergency intervention in the markets.[134] This crisis had dissipated by June 1846, reducing the justification for 'extraordinary' intervention.

The two imperatives of relieving short-term distress and securing the 'permanent' supply of Indian corn by private trade thus found themselves in sharp conflict. This question was unresolved on the fall of Peel's government in late June. In terms of the government's intention of promoting the consumption of imported maize, the operation was deemed a success. Although there had initially been resistance to the unpalatable 'Peel's brimstone', by June Commissariat officers were reporting a general preference for Indian meal, and the abandonment of the opposition to it by 'even the radical papers'.[135] The success of the experiment was thought so complete that Edward Twisleton, the Irish Poor Law Commissioner, believed free trade would also promote the introduction of maize to England as the subsistence of the lowest classes there.[136] At the same time, it also appeared in the summer that the Commissariat operation had succeeded in priming the pump of private trade; Baring informed Trevelyan in late June that 'a whole fleet of ships laden with Indian corn has arrived', and Routh reported the establishment of a major private depot at Limerick.[137]

Perhaps most important for the ministerial plan, the transformation of agrarian society envisaged as the natural consequence of the catastrophe appeared to have begun. In April Griffith reported the planting of potatoes well down on the previous year – with less than one quarter the usual quantity of land being taken in conacre, and oats being planted by farmers instead. Griffith was concerned about the provision of employment in the following year necessary to keep the cottiers and conacre peasants alive, but Routh thought the disappearance of conacre desirable: 'In ordinary years, from that conacre system, there is no such thing literally as wages; labour is an affair of barter . . . they . . . often refuse the employment if offered to them. This life of indolence is enough to demoralize any nation.'[138] Heytesbury

133 *Hans.*, LXXXV, 722–4 [17 April].

134 Peel to Lord Francis Egerton, 6 Jan., Parker, *Peel*, III, 323–4; Heytesbury to Graham, 16 April, Graham Papers, bundle 29 IR.

135 Coffin to Trevelyan, 30 March, Routh to Trevelyan, 17 June, *Corr. explan. (Comm. ser.)*, P.P. 1846 [735], XXXVII, 136, 218–19.

136 Twisleton to Graham, 9 July, Graham Papers, bundle 103.

137 Trevelyan to Routh, 29 June, Routh to Trevelyan, 30 June, *Corr. explan. (Comm. ser.)*, P.P. 1846 [735], XXXVII, 235, 237–8.

138 Griffith to Lincoln, 18 April, Routh to Trevelyan, 28 May, ibid., 161–2, 195. Other officers

was notably less sanguine, but while he feared that a decline in potato cultivation raised a 'very gloomy prospect' for the coming year, he found it difficult to determine in what way the evil should be met. The healthy state of the early potatoes in May led to greater demand for conacre in some areas, but the Lord Lieutenant remained apprehensive.[139] The government did not survive to face the consequences of its ambiguity on this question.

Reports of a second failure of the potato were received in late June. Graham took this as confirmation of his anticipations and believed it vindicated the course of policy embarked upon in 1845. He wrote in self-justification in September:

> I entertained from the first a very unfavourable opinion of the potato disease. I was satisfied in my own mind that reliance could no longer be placed on potatoes as the staff of life for one third of our whole population, and failing the potatoes, I always foresaw, that it would be difficult to draw from the whole world suddenly an adequate supply of bread corn as the substitute for the potato on which our dense and increasing population so much depended . . . Events have justified and will continue to justify this foresight.[140]

A consensus had by now emerged that Ireland must in future rely on privately imported grain for much of its food requirements, and policy shifted to avoid any interference that might damage the private trade. Trevelyan and Routh agreed that Commissariat operations should be brought gradually to an end, and that in the following season state purchases should be limited to what was available in the British market, deposited in a greatly reduced number of depots on the western seaboard, and subjected to a much more stringent distribution policy.[141]

The food policy of Peel's government has been frequently been contrasted favourably with Russell's for its relative lack of ideological commitment to *laissez-faire*.[142] Yet if the transitional character of this interference as an interim measure tiding the country over until the ports could be opened by legislative act, and the bi-partisan support for the November 1845 maize purchase are taken into account, the distinction becomes more difficult to sustain.[143] Peel stated clearly that the

---

were optimistic as to the transformation of the Irish economy – Captain Perceval reported from Westport: 'I think that the people are beginning to see the mistake of depending altogether on their potato; and a peasant told me yesterday, unsuggested, that he should sow more green crops in future, and buy meal, which is the advice I endeavour to give.' Perceval to Trevelyan, 11 July, ibid., 256.

139 Heytesbury to Graham, 23 April, Graham Papers, bundle 29 IR; Heytesbury to Graham, 24 May, ibid., bundle 30 IR.

140 Heytesbury to Graham, 23 June, ibid., bundle 102; Graham to Sanders, 17 Sept. 1846, ibid., bundle 103.

141 Trevelyan to Routh, 21, 24 July, Routh to Trevelyan, 31 July, *Corr. explan. (Comm. ser.)*, P.P. 1846 [735], XXXVII, 264, 266, 274.

142 See, for example, Mary E. Daly, *The Famine in Ireland* (Dundalk, 1986), p. 71.

143 The Indian corn purchase of 1845 was endorsed by the Whig-Liberal leadership; Russell thought the government had shown 'sound discretion' in this as a relief measure, and

purchase was purely a temporary measure and that once the duties were lifted, interference in the food trade would be illegitimate. He assured the Commons that, 'it is not from any fear of incurring the expense that has deterred us from going further . . . but it is a fear of too great an intervention with the ordinary course of commerce, and of thus ultimately aggravating the evil which we meant to remove.'[144]

Graham as well as Trevelyan found guidance in Edmund Burke's *Thoughts and details on scarcity*, and quoted the warning against breaking the laws of commerce, which were 'the words of wisdom . . . [and] the moving principle with me'.[145] The cross-party liberal orthodoxy was made even more clear in Lincoln's speech in answer to the new government's declaration of policy, which included the termination of state purchase of supplies, in August 1846. Lincoln defended the Conservative government's record, but went on to state that:

> If the late government had remained in office, it by no means followed that they would have persevered in the course they had, for a time, felt bound to adopt; and he must say, that he fully approved of the intentions of Her Majesty's present advisers on this subject. The circumstances under which the late government interfered on this subject, differed very materially from those of the present time.

He agreed that 'if government was now to import provisions, it would paralyse trade and prevent the exertions on which the country must depend for its permanent reliance.'[146] If the Peelite and Whig-Liberal versions of Irish relief policy diverged, it was not on the question of free trade as the guarantor of the food supply and as the basis of Irish social regeneration. The Corn Law crisis, with its political and ideological ramifications, set the parameters for subsequent thinking on the Irish Famine.

III RELIEF WORKS, LAND AND COERCION

The history of the relief measures adopted by the Peel government in 1845–6 has been the subject of a number of studies.[147] What remains to be examined in

Labouchere agreed with Peel that in the longer term it would 'raise the people from the lowest condition, caused by their habitually living on potatoes', *Hans.*, LXXXIV, 765 [6 March], 803 [9 March].

144 Ibid., LXXXV, 722–6 [17 April]. This opinion was reiterated in a private letter to Monteagle during the summer, Peel to Monteagle, 18 Aug. 1846, Monteagle Papers, National Library of Ireland, Dublin, MS 13,396/4.

145 *Hans.*, LXXXV, 178 [27 March]. Trevelyan circulated copies of Burke's tract to Commissariat officers in early 1846. Most declared their belief in the 'general truth of the principles', but expressed doubts about its strict application to existing Irish conditions, Coffin to Trevelyan, 11 April, Dobree to Trevelyan, 24 April, *Corr. explan. (Comm. ser.)*, P.P. 1846 [735], XXXVII, 151, 175.

146 *Hans.*, LXXXVIII, 784–90 [17 Aug. 1846].

147 T.P. O'Neill, 'The organization and administration of relief, 1845–52', in R.D. Edwards

greater detail is the relationship between the politics of land and relief policy, taking into consideration the government's long-term hopes for Irish development, the threats posed by political and agrarian agitation, and the debate over the duties and responsibilities of landed proprietors.

Obligation and assistance: the debate on relief

While the food policy adopted by the government in 1845–6 was controversial and novel, other aspects of famine-relief policy drew on established precedents. The models of Peel's relief policy in 1816–17 and 1822 have been the subject of much historical attention, but considerably less has been devoted to the more recent case of the policy adopted to meet the partial famine of 1831. This year was of particular importance as it marked the first sustained interest displayed by Sir James Graham in Irish affairs. As First Lord of the Admiralty, Graham was given charge of the relief of western seaboard in that year. Working in co-operation with Stanley, Graham ordered John Hill, a naval officer, to superintend the expenditure of the £40,000 government advance for the relief of distress in such a manner as to eliminate the endemic peculation believed to have characterized previous relief efforts.[148] Graham's instructions to Hill laid down the strict principle of proportional aid:

> In a country where by law no fund is raised for the maintenance or employment of the poor, the surest guide to the exercise of sound discretion is the limitation of the assistance afforded out of the public funds to contributions in aid of private charity, and of local exertions made by the rich proprietors to relieve the wants of their poorer neighbours.[149]

The outcome of Hill's mission appeared to vindicate the government's suspicions of the Irish landlords. Graham noted that exaggerated statements had been made 'with a view of obtaining aid in the shape of money for purposes neither pure nor disinterested'. He proposed that Hill be knighted as proof of the government's approval of his course, and to reward him for suffering the abuse of the landlords, 'whose hands he kept with difficulty out of the public purse'.[150] Hill's activities in 1831 set the pattern for government relief of regional distress in Ireland for the remainder of the 1830s. In 1835 and 1837 Thomas Drummond directed the relief measures of the Coast Guard and constabulary on the western coast; Hill himself

---

and T.D. Williams (eds.) *The Great Famine: studies in Irish history, 1845–1852* (Dublin, 1956), pp. 209–52, remains the clearest account.

148 Graham to Grey, 5 June, Graham to Stanley, 6 June 1831, Graham Papers, bundle 5.

149 Graham to Hill, 8 July 1831, Newcastle Papers, NeC 9,142. Stanley agreed that Hill should be warned not to disclose the extent of his resources to the local resident gentry and magistrates, as 'there is *hardly* one of them who will not have an object in drawing the relief, and employment, to some particular point', Stanley to Graham, 8 June, Graham Papers, bundle 5.

150 Graham to (Grey), 25 August 1831, ibid., bundle 6.

was dispatched again in the summer of 1836 to Donegal, and in 1839 Captain Chads, another naval officer, was sent on a similar mission to the west.[151] In 1836 Hill noted that in very few of the places he had visited had he found the representations made to the government to have been borne out by the facts. Chads, a man of similar temperament, was equally critical of the local notables in 1839. Describing the reality of dearth in the west, he reported, 'all these evils were gradually approaching and must have been foreseen by all those interested and possessing properties in the country; and yet with few honourable exceptions, no steps were taken to avert them; this has been so long the accustomed indifference and coldness of many of the Irish landlords, that the poor do not look up to them as their natural protectors; but both landlords and tenants trust to the intervention of Government.'[152]

It is hardly surprising that Graham, having had his first taste of governing Ireland in 1831, should have taken this as his precedent when faced by a similar crisis in 1845. Graham's role was pivotal in policy making, for once the broad outlines of policy had been determined, Peel left the detail of Irish administration to his trusted Home Secretary. Hill was consulted on the potato crisis in late October 1845, and consequently the Irish government was ordered to collect and study the records of 1831 and 1836.[153] Once ministers had agreed on the expediency of immediately forming a relief commission, Peel proposed that Hill should go to Ireland to assist it with his local knowledge, if this was thought necessary.[154] In the end Hill did not go over, but the instructions to the Commission drawn up by Graham drew heavily on the experience of the 1830s. In his official letter of 3 November, he included for the guidance of the Commissioners the confidential instructions issued to Hill in 1831 and 1836, and recommended in particular the 'statement of principles and caution' laid down in the former. On the orders of the government, Under-Secretary Richard Pennefather drew up a memo of previous responses which stressed the relief rules enforced by Chads in 1839; these included giving no gratuitous relief, making government donations only in aid of proportional local subscriptions, and the publication of the names of local proprietors who failed to contribute. He noted that Chads' recommendations had been adopted on a smaller scale in the west in 1842, although he also added that the distress expected

151 *Correspondence and accounts relating to the different occasions on which measures were taken for the relief of the people suffering from scarcity in Ireland between the years 1822 and 1839*, P.P. 1846 [734], XXXVII, 3–4.

152 'Copy of a letter from Sir John Hill . . . to the Chancellor of the Exchequer', 3 Oct. 1836, 'Copy of a letter from Captain Chads to the Chancellor of the Exchequer', 22 Aug. 1839, ibid., 17–19, 21–2.

153 Peel to Fremantle, 31 Oct. 1845, Peel Papers, Add. MS 40,476, fol. 500. Monteagle also wrote to the Prime Minister to suggest such a course. Heytesbury saw this letter and endorsed the plan, Monteagle to Peel, 24 Oct., ibid., Add. MS 40,576, fols 322–6, Heytesbury to Graham, 4 Nov., Graham Papers, bundle 24 IR.

154 Peel memo, 1 Nov., Peel, *Memoirs*, II, 142–3. For the political pressure to form a relief commission, see above, pp. 111–13.

in the coming year would be different from that previously met with in its scale and distribution.[155]

The importance of the 1831 model was not that it was the sole determinant of relief policy in 1845–6, but that it was a significant element in the policy-making equation, and a reminder of the degree of continuity between Conservative and Whig-Liberal responses to Irish distress. Important differences may indeed have existed, but it is too simple to praise in an unqualified manner a greater 'compassion' and freedom from doctrinal rigidity on the part of the Peelites. It may also be possible to use the model of 1831 as a template for analysing the deviations of the government from the consensus on relief policy of the 1830s.

The relief policy of Peel's government can best be described as the outcome of the tensions between a number of competing and sometimes conflicting imperatives. The danger of relieving Irish landlords from their just responsibilities was an important consideration, and the instructions issued to the Relief Commission made it quite explicit that 'the real power of relieving distress and ministering to the wants of the people is in the hands of the owners of the soil'.[156] Government assistance in aid of local exertions was thus to be kept under strict Treasury control, as a security against 'fraud and maladministration'. Routh was to operate under its instructions, and was chosen in preference to others less accustomed to Whitehall control. It was recognized that Routh might seek to increase the role of the state, but a balance was to be created between his indulgence in '*large views*' and the necessary financial checks from London. As Graham commented 'we shall hold the purse-string here: no large outlay can be made without the previous sanction of the Treasury.'[157]

Unlike previous occasions when a single relief commissioner had been appointed, it was decided that Routh should not act as the sole agent of government. This decision was to some extent made necessary by the unprecedented scale of the catastrophe – the heads of all the relevant departments were to share the load of relief – but perhaps as importantly, it was dictated by the government's preoccupation with the politics of relief. Ignoring Pennefather's recommendation of an efficient commission of three ('an engineer, a Commissariat officer; a third person of practical experience . . . like Captain Chads . . . in 1839'), the government opted for a larger and politically balanced group. Edward Lucas, the recently retired Under-Secretary, an Irish landlord and a high Tory, was chosen as chairman of the Relief Commission, despite Fremantle's doubts about his ability.[158] Graham was concerned that while the 'nobility and gentry should be made to feel that at this

155 Graham to Heytesbury, 3 Nov., Pennefather memo: 'Distress in Ireland', 4 Nov., Graham Papers, bundle 95A.

156 Graham to Heytesbury, 26 Nov., ibid., bundle 95B.

157 Graham to Heytesbury, 15 Dec., ibid.; Graham to Peel, 12 Nov., ibid., bundle 95A.

158 Pennefather memo: 'Sir Robert Peel's questions, with answers', 4 Nov., ibid., bundle 24 IR; Fremantle to Peel, 5 Nov., Peel Papers, Add. MS 40,476, fol. 523.

juncture they have great duties to fulfil . . . and that the eye of the Government and public is fixed upon them . . . their cordial cooperation and assistance should be courted and encouraged.'[159] Lucas was balanced by the Catholics Robert Kane and Theobald McKenna. John Pitt Kennedy was made secretary, partly to enlist his experience on the Devon Commission, but also because he was 'well thought of in the Liberal party'.[160] These additions were intended to give the Commission a 'popular character', but the government was aware of the drawbacks. Graham observed to Peel that, 'we shall be involved in great future mischief if Irish notions should be pushed to an extreme in this Commission and if we should be driven to stand out against recommendations emanating from a body of our own creation. There is a great advantage, as it appears to me, in the decisive preponderance of official influence and control.'[161]

The relationship between the Relief Commission and the Irish government was somewhat ambiguous. Graham believed that the state could only palliate and not remedy a scarcity arising from 'natural causes'. It followed that caution would be necessary in all the Commission's proceedings, which were to 'aid in the discharge of duties which are beyond the sphere of government in ordinary times'. Nevertheless, Graham added that 'in the last extremity of want, especially where it arises from a dispensation of Providence, these rules must frequently be relaxed'.[162] Graham's providentialist interpretation of the crisis appeared to him to legitimize extraordinary state intervention in the short term, and the Irish government was the body he entrusted with these overriding powers.[163] He hoped that his instructions were 'consistent with prudence and limit the violation of general principles within restrictions so narrow as the peculiar circumstances of Ireland and the pressure of present necessity admit'.[164] This inevitably gave rise to differences of interpretation.

A serious clash between the government and the Commissioners occurred in early December 1845, when Lucas approved a plan to base the relief of extraordinary destitution on an extended Poor Law structure, on the grounds that relief should be connected with local taxation to give local administrators a direct interest in avoiding fraud and imposition. Graham was quick to declare his decided opposition to the proposal, arguing that 'the claim of the able-bodied for relief from the poor rate, when once admitted in Ireland, the locust will devour the land, and the concession once made can never be withdrawn.'[165] The essence of the govern-

159 Graham to Heytesbury, 7 Nov., Graham Papers, bundle 95A.
160 Peel to Graham, 11 Nov., Peel Papers, Add. MS 40,452, fol. 9; Fremantle to Graham, 16 Nov., Graham Papers, bundle 24 IR; Fremantle to Peel, 6 Nov., Peel Papers, Add. MS 40,476, fols. 527–8.
161 Graham to Peel, 12 Nov., Graham Papers, bundle 95A.
162 Graham to Heytesbury, 26 Nov., ibid., bundle 95B.
163 Graham to Heytesbury, 23 Jan. 1846, ibid., bundle 98.
164 Graham to Twisleton, 2 Dec., ibid., bundle 96A.
165 Fremantle to Graham, 6 Dec., Graham to Fremantle, 9 Dec., ibid., bundle 25 IR.

ment's measures lay in their *ad hoc* character, as 'an extraordinary remedy to meet an extraordinary state of things'; it would be impossible to withdraw outdoor relief once granted, and it was essential that central government should retain absolute control over expenditure.

Graham's objections to any extension of the Poor Law rested on the government's preoccupation with promoting Irish development. The concession of outdoor relief to the able-bodied would, in his view, be recognized in Ireland as 'an agrarian law of the worst form'; it would require the imposition of a direct rate on proprietors and place local control over that rate in the hands of the boards of guardians, dominated by the representatives of the tenants and by O'Connellite radicals. This was just the sort of opportunity for social conflict which the government sought to prevent. Even more importantly, Graham raised the issue of the inadequacy of local funds. It was a 'perilous uncertainty' that the resources of most rural unions would be sufficient to meet the present emergency.[166] This concern for the pressure of rates for relief on the Irish wages fund may seem to conflict with Graham's insistence on proprietorial responsibility, but it should be remembered that what differentiated the crisis of 1845–6 from its predecessors was not only its scale, but its interrelation with the Corn Law crisis. If Irish agriculture was to face the same rigours as that of England following the removal of protection, and if this national transformation had been prompted by a special visitation on the Irish staple crop – meant as a warning to the whole country – it followed that Irish property had a right to transitional state assistance to help it weather the short-term crisis. The limited capital available to Irish proprietors needed to be invested in agricultural improvements designed to increase productivity, and not sucked into the relief of the destitute population. Moreover, compulsory charity would remove the moral example of voluntary action.

At the same time, the government refused to be drawn into the alternative of a large-scale state-led reproductive works project advocated by John Pitt Kennedy. If the state provided organization and sufficient loans, Kennedy told the Commission, the self-interest of landlord and tenant alike could be relied upon to secure their co-operation on drainage, although stronger action would be necessary on entailed or encumbered estates.[167] Kennedy's recommendations, which were echoed by Irish pamphleteers anxious to extract the maximum benefit to Ireland from the

166 Graham to Heytesbury, 15 Dec., ibid., bundle 96B.

167 'Report and suggestions, addressed to the Irish Government in November 1845, in reference to the mode of meeting the evils attending the failure of the potato crop of that year', 'Draft of a manifesto, suggested for the adoption of the Relief Commissioners, at their first meeting in 1845, intended to explain to the public, that the principle of Government assistance would be chiefly that of stimulating private exertion, by affording facilities for improvement and drainage of land, etc.', John Pitt Kennedy, *Correspondence on some of the general effects of the failures of the potato crop, and the consequent relief measures* (Dublin, 1847), pp. 3–12.

crisis,[168] were declined, and the government opted for a limited and voluntary drainage bill.

The Home Secretary's official declaration on the Poor Law did not end the controversy over that subject in 1845–6. In January 1846 Routh drew up a proposal for a one-year 'labour tax' of sixpence in the pound for public works employment, to be collected through the Poor Law machinery. He argued that the terms under which he had been sent to Ireland made such a plan essential; it arose from 'the great and almost insuperable difficulty of obtaining pecuniary aid at present from the landed proprietors'.[169]

Despite pressure from the Irish government, the Commission agreed to Routh's plan and suggested the heads of a bill to embody it. Graham again responded angrily to such a 'labour rate', and feared considerable political embarrassment would follow the formal proposal of the plan.[170] The land tax amounted, he argued, to an extension of the Poor Law along the lines of the worst aspects of the pre-1834 Law of England. It threatened to reverse the improvement of agriculture, as 'the claim of the able-bodied to Poor Law relief in Ireland . . . if now admitted, the subdivided occupation of land and the consequent multitude and poverty of the inhabitants, will break down all restraints on demand . . . and the beneficial enjoyment of the soil will ultimately be transferred from the owners to the occupiers.' It would cause bitter resentment among the landed interest – the 'heart of Ireland would be estranged from England' – and the opportunity of demonstrating to the Irish people the generosity of parliament and the 'paternal care of British Government' would be lost. He reiterated his previous view that it would seem unjust to impose an additional burden at the moment 'when Providence has inflicted a severe national calamity and the power of bearing a greater impost is necessarily reduced'.[171]

The government had previously urged the Commissioners to use their own initiative in drawing up relief plans, but the consistency with which they overstepped the bounds led to Lucas being removed and the Commission restructured in late February. Graham ordered its reduction to an efficient body of three, with the Irish contingent marginalized and weekly reports to the Lord Lieutenant made obligatory.[172] Neither Kane, Routh nor Twisleton were initially happy with the new

168 Martin Doyle, *The labouring classes in Ireland: an inquiry as to what beneficial changes may be effected in their condition by the legislature, the landowner and the labourer respectively* (Dublin, 1846), [William Graydon], *Suggestions on the best modes of employing the Irish peasantry as an anti-famine measure* (London, 1845).

169 Heytesbury to Graham, 21 Jan. 1846, Graham Papers, bundle 26 IR.

170 Heytesbury to Graham, 22 Jan., ibid., Fremantle to Graham, 4 Feb., Graham to Heytesbury, 4 Feb., ibid., bundle 27 IR.

171 Graham to Heytesbury, 6 Feb., ibid., bundle 99.

172 Graham to Fremantle, 21 Jan., ibid., bundle 26 IR, Graham to Twisleton, 16 Feb., ibid., bundle 99; Graham to Peel, 5 March, ibid., bundle 100.

arrangements, but they were pacified by the retention of the general Commission in name, and accepted places on the active executive committee.[173]

The relief system favoured by the government placed a premium on stimulating local co-operation. In the first instance responsibility for relieving destitution was to lie with *ad hoc* relief committees, composed of local magistrates, gentry, clergy and some ex officio members. These were to prepare lists of the destitute, imposing labour tests in all but exceptional cases, and raising local subscriptions for the purchase of food from the depots.[174] The government pledged itself to assist the committees with donations in aid, but sought also to balance 'voluntary' exertions with regulations preventing abuses. The landlord-dominated committees succeeded in raising over £98,000 by August 1846, but were the subject of constant criticism from British liberal opinion and relief officials.[175]

The remodelling of the Relief Commission and its subjection to closer government control ended internal divisions on the mechanisms of relief. Nevertheless, Graham found himself facing growing pressure for an extended Poor Law, as Sharman Crawford and Poulett Scrope waged a vociferous campaign for Irish outdoor relief in parliament.[176] This demand was taken up by the *Times* which attacked the existing system of relief as merely a form of hand-outs to Irish landowners: 'Whatever we give to the peasant passes through that hungry sieve right into the pocket of the landlord. Benevolence is wasted on those who neither need nor deserve it.' This abuse would be removed by giving the Irish peasantry a statutory right to employment, or in the case of those with disabilities, to direct relief.[177] This campaign took on added resonance in the wake of the widely publicized Irish clearances of spring 1846; the Gerrard evictions provoked the *Illustrated London News* into a diatribe that would be reiterated with increasing intensity in the liberal press in the following years: 'Englishmen cannot see such barbarities practiced at the very moment they are paying enormous sums out of the taxes to support those whom the landlords thus plunge into destitution . . . if the landlord makes paupers he must also maintain them.'[178]

Graham was alarmed by the growing strength of opinion in both England and Ireland, and in late April noted fatalistically that 'if this sad state of affairs be prolonged beyond the current year, permanent enactments of a decisive character charging the land of Ireland will become inevitable.'[179] However, he reaffirmed his

---

173 Heytesbury to Graham, 17, 25 Feb., Graham to Heytesbury, 20 Feb., ibid., bundle 27 IR.

174 *Instructions to committees of relief districts, extracted from minutes of the proceedings of the Commissioners appointed in reference to the apprehended scarcity*, P.P. 1846 (171), XXXVII, 1.

175 *Times*, 2 April 1846.

176 *Hans.*, LXXXIII, 727–9 [11 Feb. 1846]. Peel declared his firm opposition to the extension of the Poor Law as a remedy for Irish social disorder, ibid., LXXXV, 1125–6 [27 April].

177 *Times*, 19 March, 2 April 1846.

178 *Illustrated London News*, 4 April 1846.

179 Graham to Heytesbury, 7 May, Graham Papers, bundle 30 IR, Graham to Heytesbury, 25 April, ibid., bundle 101.

position in an official letter to the Lord Lieutenant. The two central themes in Graham's policy were again stressed; firstly, the extraordinary character of the crisis, and secondly, the threat to the Irish wages fund posed by outdoor relief, and the social unrest that putting pressure on this fund would create.[180] Yet with the government in an increasingly precarious position, the likelihood of a further potato failure apparently increasing, and pressure being put upon the Whig leaders by the promoters of an extended Irish Poor Law, Graham's pessimism in mid-1846 was justified.

The public works system

The government's preferred mode of relief was employment by public works. Graham's instructions stressed the importance of developmental works, and he cited the Devon report's argument that these would be well supported and beneficial to society. The general rule should be 'to encourage the utmost private contributions for the improvement of labour by public aids which the existing laws permit'. In the marginal areas where such co-operative improvement was not feasible, the state was to undertake more direct relief using local relief works as a test of destitution.[181] Two parallel systems were envisaged – one in the commercialized sector encouraged and supported by the government and directed at agricultural improvement; the second in the impoverished subsistence sector, to keep the poorest alive. Both were organized by the Board of Works in co-operation with local initiative, supervised by the Commission, with all expenditure subject to Treasury ratification. Confusion was inherent within this system, for while the government insisted on the Commission ensuring that proprietors met their obligations before assistance was made to private improvements,[182] the more flexible emergency relief works were to be administered by the same body and with the same degree of Treasury overview.

The legislative structure for the public works was rushed through parliament early in the 1846 session. Two pieces of legislation dealt specifically with emergency relief; the Public Works Bill and the County Works Presentments Bill. The former was based on the pound for pound subscription-donation system, with up to £50,000 available from the Treasury in aid of local road-building and repairs.

180 Graham to Heytesbury, 7 May, *Corr. explan. (Comm. ser.)*, P.P. 1846 (735), XXXVII, 183–4.

181 Graham to Heytesbury, 26 Nov. 1845, Graham Papers, bundle 95B. The government's willingness to support private undertakings contrasted with its position earlier in the year. In July, Peel had told a landlord deputation that 'I would not give a sous of public money during the present session – would promise none for the future – that I would never ask for public money for local improvements in Ireland, without being satisfied that the public as opposed to local and pecuniary interests would be really benefited by it – and that the latter if the benefit was a joint one, would contribute their fair share of the expense.' Peel to Fremantle, 19 July 1845, Peel Papers, Add. MS 40,476, fol. 428.

182 Graham to Fremantle, 27 Nov., Graham Papers, bundle 24 IR.

Under pressure from British radicals, led by Joseph Hume, the Prime Minister committed the government to vigorous supervision and a finite period of operation. At the same time, the Bill was attacked by Irish landlords and Repealers alike as offering insufficient sums. To Sir Winston Barron it was 'a mere drop of water in the sea', insufficient to meet 'the severe visitation of Providence'. The Peelite Richard Monckton Milnes agreed, but argued that it should be taken as 'a sign and token of English sympathy and interest', for the crisis 'ought not to be met by English charity or Government assistance, but by the cordial sympathy and aid of the landed proprietors in Ireland'.[183] The County Works Bill, which had been suggested by Lucas, and designed to preserve local autonomy, allowed baronies to bring forward their presentment sessions for general works, and made further sums available as loans.[184]

Important as these measures were, the government put greater store by the other two pieces of legislation passed at the same time – the Drainage and Harbours Bills. Although the potato crisis was used as an opportunity to introduce them, and it was hoped both would add substantially to the available employment during the crisis, these Bills were aimed at long-term development and were permanent in character. Peel had previously been cool towards drainage loans, but the potato failure, and more importantly the decision to repeal the Corn Laws, made him more amenable.[185] Fremantle was certain that amendments to the law would lead to the private outlay of several hundred thousand pounds in the course of 1846.[186] It is significant that while a separate Irish Bill for procedure was introduced in early 1846, the government insisted on a single Drainage Loan Bill for the entire United Kingdom.[187] This suggests the government's concern was to prepare Ireland as much as England for the transition to free trade in food by promoting high farming.[188] The Drainage Bill offended some Irish members by its 'arrogation of excessive powers' to the Board of Works, and upset others by leaving too great a veto power to the individual proprietor.[189] It was passed, along with the less

183 *Hans.*, LXXXIII, 162, 183–6, 332–6 [23, 26, 28 Jan. 1846].

184 Fremantle to Graham, 14 Jan., Graham Papers, bundle 26 IR.

185 Fremantle to Peel, 11 June 1845, Peel to Fremantle, 12 June, Peel Papers, Add. MS 40,476, fols. 424–5, 426–7.

186 Fremantle to Graham, 23 Nov., Graham Papers, bundle 24 IR.

187 Graham to Lincoln, 8 Jan. 1846, Newcastle Papers, NeC 11,913.

188 Lincoln thought the Drainage Loans Bill would be a real boon to land and would offset the Corn Bill, Lincoln to Peel, 15 Jan., ibid., NeC 12,107. The importance of the drainage measure for England is emphasized by Moore. The loan was an intrinsic part of Peel's 'general scheme' and the two million pounds proposed (Ireland was to have an additional million) 'was primarily a psychological measure designed to popularize high farming by facilitating the pre-requisite land drainage on those estates on which . . . there was a "natural reluctance of proprietors to expend capital upon the permanent improvement of the land".' It appears that ministers had similar hopes for Ireland, D.C. Moore, 'The Corn Laws and high farming', pp. 553–7.

189 *Hans.*, LXXXIII, 428–31 [2 Feb.: French, Ferguson]; ibid., 726–7 [10 Feb.: Somerville].

contentious Harbours Bill, but drainage in Ireland subsequently fell well short of government expectations.[190] Under pressure to find work for the destitute, and attracted by the half-grant system, most landowners turned instead to the Public Works Act.

These Acts became law in March, and were put into practice by the Board of Works. The mechanism for initiating works was complex and required the recruitment of additional skilled personnel; delays were the inevitable consequence.[191] The conflict between ministers, and particularly between Lincoln and the Treasury over the interpretation of the public works legislation of 1846, is well documented. It has been argued by some historians that this tension 'prevented the smooth and complete execution of the ministers' measures for the relief of famine-plagued Ireland'.[192] Charles Trevelyan indisputably played a wilful and destructive role in the relief administration of 1846, and was clearly motivated by his own policy agenda. Nevertheless, his frequent depiction as the *bête noire* of the period has been allowed to obscure the government's policy errors. The relief structure created in 1846 wove together a number of disparate strands and conflicting priorities in a manner that could not fail to create substantial confusion. A Relief Commission had been formed to advise, yet its recommendations had been dismissed as unacceptable, and the primary burden of relief placed on a body widely regarded as incapable of efficiently meeting this challenge – the Board of Works. Moreover, in intermingling works for direct relief with those for long-term development, and placing the control of both under the same mechanism, the government had created a recipe for confusion and tied relief to a matter of political sensitivity in Great Britain – the special treatment of the landed interest.

From the outset the Treasury made clear the rules by which grants in aid would be made for local works. The full sum for each work under the Public Works Act (half of which was to be repaid) would be advanced only where the Lord Lieutenant was satisfied that no local landlords would benefit who had not subscribed an appropriate private sum for the work. Exceptions were to be made where proven to be necessary, but Trevelyan added that 'discretion ought . . . to be exercised with great caution in a time of serious scarcity; and cases may occur in which proprietors who both ought to contribute, and have the means of doing so, may nevertheless

190 Landowners blamed its failure on Treasury obstruction, but this needs to be contrasted with the success of the measure in Great Britain, see H.C. White (ed.), *Sixty years' experience as an Irish landlord: memoirs of John Hamilton, DL, of St Ernan's, Donegal* (London, n.d.), pp. 217–19, J. Bailey Denton, 'On land drainage and improvement by loans from government or public companies', *Journal of the Royal Agricultural Society of England*, 2nd ser., IV (1868), 123–43.

191 The structure of public works administration is outlined in A.R.G. Griffiths, 'The Irish Board of Works in the Famine years', *Historical Journal*, XIII (1970), 634–9.

192 F. Darrell Munsell, 'Charles Edward Trevelyan and Peelite Irish Famine policy, 1845–1846', *Societas: a review of social history*, I (1971), 299–315. This article argues forcibly that Trevelyan's activities constituted 'a systematic attack upon ministerial policy'.

presume upon the knowledge they have that the Government cannot, *under any circumstances*, allow the people to starve.'[193] Trevelyan's fears that the generous terms of the Public Works Bill would be exploited by proprietors were endorsed by the government. Fremantle thought the Treasury requirement 'not unreasonable' and its object desirable – although it was not necessary to press the conditions too far.[194] Trevelyan and his allies in the Board of Works considered their apprehensions justified by the vast sums applied for under the Public Works Act (£478,000 by 9 April, of which only £70,000 had been sanctioned), and declared the half-grant system a failure. Trevelyan was sure that 'instead of *a test of real distress*, we have a bounty on interested exaggeration . . . there has been an exclusive application to this particular means of relief, not for the sake of the *remedy*, but for the *sugar in which it is offered*, to the neglect of the other and less objectionable means provided.'[195] The Board followed Trevelyan's instructions and carried out detailed surveys of proposed works, causing considerable delays.

On his arrival as Chief Secretary in late March, Lincoln made alarmed reports to the cabinet on the state of Ireland and the dangers of Treasury obstruction. With the support of Peel and Graham he proceeded to expand and remodel the Board of Works by bringing in Richard Griffith and Thomas Larcom from the Ordnance Survey office to head a special new relief works section. Both Trevelyan and Colonel Harry Jones (chairman of the Board of Works) resisted these alterations, and a confrontation with Lincoln ensued.[196] While some of Trevelyan's practices, in particular the use of private correspondence to convey important instructions to his subordinates, deserved the criticism they received from the administration, an excessive concentration on these can obscure the real divisions within the government over his activities. In answer to Lincoln's criticisms, Goulburn strongly echoed Trevelyan's concerns, and absolved him of any blame 'beyond any which may be supposed to attach to the phraseology in which the instructions received from me were expressed'.[197] Peel defended Lincoln and urged Goulburn to allow for a greater discretionary authority on the part of the Lord Lieutenant and Chief Secretary in initiating relief works, but the Chancellor pointed

193 Treasury minute, 17 Feb., Trevelyan to Fremantle, 26 Feb. 1846, *Correspondence explanatory of the measures adopted by Her Majesty's government for the relief of distress arising from the failure of the potato crop in Ireland (Board of Works series)*, P.P. 1846 [735] XXXVII, 319–20, 321–4.

194 Fremantle to Trevelyan, 26 Feb., ibid., 321.

195 Jones to Lincoln, 9 April, Trevelyan Memo: Grants for the relief of distress in Ireland, 15 April, ibid., 355–6.

196 Munsell, 'Trevelyan and Peelite Irish Famine policy', pp. 305–9. See also F. Darrell Munsell, *The unfortunate duke: the life of Henry Pelham, fifth Duke of Newcastle, 1811–1864* (Columbia, MO, 1984), pp. 67–78, for a very sympathetic account of Lincoln's period as Irish Chief Secretary.

197 Goulburn to Lincoln, 3, 15 April 1846, Newcastle papers, NeC 9,238, 9241. Goulburn quoted correspondence from Antrim and Kerry that indicated that the proprietors meant 'to make hay while the sun shines, to execute all the roads . . . at no charge'.

out that under the original instructions such latitude to override Treasury rules had always existed in cases of immediate distress.[198] Graham, who shared Lincoln's fears, conceded that the Treasury's stance proceeded from an honest intention to prevent corruption (Lincoln attributed it to Trevelyan's Whiggish sympathies), but argued that as the government had committed itself to relief by public works, it should be given full effect, regardless of any minor evils that would arise. Large discretionary powers for the Lord Lieutenant were re-confirmed, and an unlimited emergency credit granted to him to prevent starvation.[199] Many of the works initiated after Easter 1846 were authorized by the Lord Lieutenant, yet tensions remained between the Chief Secretary's office and the still sceptical Board of Works.[200]

It is undeniable that Peel's administration took very seriously the need to override the relief mechanism it had created when this was demanded by the urgency of preventing mass mortality. Peel's motives were, however, more complex than the 'liberal compassion' suggested by some historians. As with the simultaneous crisis in food supply, the government's greatest fears in April 1846 were concentrated in the effects of the potato failure on political and social order.[201] The Prime Minister was concerned with the continuing need to conciliate Catholics, and Lincoln acknowledged the significance of the Catholic clergy in preserving social stability.[202] Peel's appeal to Goulburn for greater laxity in granting relief suggested his hierarchy of concerns: 'we may have on our hands not merely a suffering, but an outrageous multitude having broken the bounds of law. One example of successful turbulence may be very injurious in its consequences for it may be very contagious.'[203] The government's response to the agitation for commencing public works in the spring of 1846 reflected these fears and the Lord Lieutenant's belief that although 'impositions probably will be sanctioned . . . the risk must be run, rather than that of outbreak caused by misery and starvation.' Even where absolute distress was not apparent, he thought it might be expedient to restore tranquillity by giving employment to the people.[204]

---

198 Peel to Goulburn, 10 April, Peel Papers, Add. MS 40,445, fols. 317–20, Goulburn to Peel, 12 April, ibid., fols 325–8.

199 Graham to Heytesbury, 13, 25, 27 April, Graham Papers, bundle 101; Lincoln to Goulburn, 19 April, Newcastle Papers, NeC 9,236–7.

200 Jones to Trevelyan, 21 May, Treas. Min., 16 June, *Corr. explan. (Bd. of Works ser.)*, P.P. 1846 [735], XXXVII, 370, 378; Pennefather to Lincoln, 4 June, Newcastle Papers, NeC 9,345.

201 See above, pp. 111–13.

202 Peel to Lincoln, n.d. (March 1846), Lincoln to Graham, 10 April, Newcastle Papers, NeC 11,980, 9,234.

203 Peel to Goulburn, 10 April, Peel Papers, Add. MS 40,445, fol. 318. Such fears continued to haunt Peel after leaving office, Peel to Goulburn, 14 Aug. 1846, Goulburn Papers, SHS 304, box 42.

204 Heytesbury to Graham, 10, 15 April, Graham Papers, bundle 29 IR.

The Coercion Bill and the fall of Peel

The decision to end agricultural protection in 1846 made social stability doubly important. In 1845 the government had strenuously resisted landlord demands for increased coercive powers,[205] but in 1846 it staked its existence on just such a measure. The explanation for this reversal can be traced only partly to an upsurge in agrarian disturbance in the immediate aftermath of the potato failure; the government acknowledged that outrages had increased substantially in only five counties, and violence had declined in most others.[206] It was also acknowledged that specifically famine-related crimes could easily be put down without recourse to extraordinary powers. The government's insistence on proceeding with the Bill after unrest had passed its peak in the spring of 1846 lost it the support of a number of landed Whig-Liberals, and confirmed that its character was less an emergency measure than a permanent element in Peel's 'general scheme'.

In early December Peel revived the idea of a district fine and a detective police force for use in disturbed districts.[207] This may have been in part a response to calls from some of the 'improving' landlords favoured by the government for the provision of greater security for the lives and property of those who invested in the land,[208] for, as with other aspects of Irish policy, Peel demonstrated an increasing indulgence towards landlord sensitivities as he moved towards Corn Law repeal. Graham observed that it was 'desirable to meet the outcry for coercion with such a Bill', and that it was defensible in principle. Local responsibility would be imposed by local fines, and property would be relieved from taxation by the implementation of Devon's recommendation for the removal of the ordinary constabulary charge.[209]

There was little chance that landed opinion might be won back by any government coercion measure. Harsh and permanent coercive powers for Ireland had been advocated by the British press for years. Some polemicists argued that Ireland was not sufficiently civilized to enjoy the benefits of the British constitution. 'Trial by jury itself', claimed *Fraser's Magazine*, 'palladium though it be of an Englishman's liberties, [is] as little suited to the actual condition of the Irish people as they are to the condition of a horde of Bedouin Arabs or a tribe of Red Indians.'[210] Peel was incapable of satisfying such baying with any systematic legislation; his Coercion Bill sought primarily to deal with the moral causes of crime rather than its symptoms.

---

205 Heytesbury to Graham, 3 Dec. 1845, Graham Papers, bundle 25 IR.

206 *Hans.*, LXXXV, 338–9 [30 March 1846: Graham].

207 Peel to Graham, 3 Dec. 1845, Peel Papers, Add. MS 40,452, fol. 46; see above, pp. 82–3.

208 Heytesbury forwarded a letter from the ex-Devon Commissioner, George Hamilton, which insisted that tranquillity or security must be the foundation of any economic and social improvement, Heytesbury to Graham, 2 Dec., Hamilton to Heytesbury, 4 Dec., Graham Papers, bundle 25 IR.

209 Graham to Heytesbury, 9 Dec., Graham Papers, bundle 25 IR, Fremantle to Graham, 12 Jan. 1846, ibid., bundle 26 IR.

210 'What is to be done with Ireland now?', *Fraser's Magazine*, XXVIII (Dec. 1843), 731.

The Protection of Life Bill was introduced into the Lords in February 1846 as a permanent measure, but for the sake of political consensus at a time when the Corn Bill was threatened in the Commons, a Whig-Liberal amendment limiting its duration to three years was accepted.[211] Irish landlords and the protectionist press were not fully satisfied, but the inclusion of harsh provisions for the breaking of curfew in proclaimed districts gave some satisfaction.[212] Graham acknowledged the agrarian character of many of the outrages, but argued that only agricultural improvement over time could remove its causes. However, recent attacks on landlords and capitalists showed 'that unless you put down this state of things, not only will there be no influx of capital into the country, but the social evils of Ireland will be aggravated by the spread of murder and rapine.'[213]

Peel's speech on the first reading was one of his clearest statements on the Irish land question. He defended the Bill's constitutionality and its regard for precedent, and denied that it would be used to assist landlords in promoting the 'clearance system'. He declared his hope that the Bill would act as a deterrent and lie dormant until needed – encouraging a self-regulating system of social relationships by the very threat of its presence. Remedial measures were vital for Irish regeneration, but would be futile until crimes were repressed, prevented and punished. Peel observed that there was a crisis in the Irish land system, but he denied that the government could do much beyond creating the conditions for security of investment and improvement. Any fundamental interference in the law of landlord and tenant would compromise Peel's solution for what he considered the greatest problem relating to Irish land:

> A great number of estates are wholly unprofitable to their nominal owners, being in the hands, not of proprietors, but of receivers; and it is impossible to contemplate the number of estates in this position, and their unfruitfulness either to the creditor or the proprietor, without being forcibly convinced of the absolute necessity of some change in the law. I entertain the strongest opinion that there is no country where the maintenance of the great principles of property is more important than in Ireland. I do not believe that you could hope to establish prosperity in any country, to afford encouragement to industry, to excite a desire to realise the fruits of labour, if you violated any of the great principles of property.[214]

---

211 *Hans.*, LXXXIV, 716 [6 March 1846]. The bill for transferring the constabulary charge to the consolidated fund was introduced separately and passed in August.

212 [J.D. Brady], 'Ireland – its condition – the Life and Property Bill – the debate, and the famine', *Blackwood's Edinburgh Magazine*, LIX (May 1846), p. 572.

213 *Hans.*, LXXXV, 348 [30 March 1846]. While this argument was close to that of Thomas Campbell Foster, the *Times* was cool towards Graham's speech, and claimed that landlords had been treated too leniently and that the remedial measures had been both wrong-headed and inadequate, *Times*, 4 April 1846.

214 *Hans.*, LXXXV, 1106–31 [27 April, 1846].

Such an encumbered estates measure would be effective only if interference with proprietorial rights was kept to a complete minimum, and if those rights were upheld by the authority of the state.

To this commitment to coercion and the maintenance of the rights of property, Peel added an impassioned exhortation to the Irish landlords. The government had gone as far as was possible, and the onus for pacifying and improving Ireland, he argued, lay now with them. If some voluntary provision was made for the victims of (inevitable) evictions, great benefits could be conferred on the country; the success of Lord George Hill's paternalist improvements in Donegal was a model for all landowners. 'Immediate practical improvements', in contrast, were mostly outside the realm of legislation and beyond the reach of government sanction.[215]

Despite the decreasing incidences of outrage and the increasing likelihood of defeat on the second reading of the Bill, the government persevered; Graham believed there could be 'no better opportunity for a decorous retirement from office'.[216] Peel emphasized the benevolence with which his government had met the immediate pressure of famine, and congratulated himself on the political results: 'I say, that these measures, as might have been expected in a generous and kind-hearted people, have produced a corresponding good. I believe that there does pervade amongst the people in the wilds of Connaught, and in Munster . . . a feeling of grateful acknowledgement towards Her Majesty's Government.' Although he did not think this change of mood sufficient for the Coercion Bill to be dispensed with as a permanent measure, it was clearly the outcome which the government had sought to promote in its relief policy at this critical period.[217] The political and social implications of relief policy were recognized by the relief officers in the field, and were the source of consolation and satisfaction to the Irish government.[218]

Important as this change of mood was, it should not be exaggerated. Many in Ireland attributed the response of the government less to its own motives than to the popular pressure placed upon it. Captain Pole – officer in charge of a depot in the highly politicized area of the midlands – protested perhaps too strongly when he wrote that, 'some of the poor, in ignorance, anxious to bestow the

---

215 Ibid. Hill's activities were a contemporary *cause célèbre* and frequently cited as a model for improving landlordism. Yet they were not without controversy, and a tenant backlash forced him to discontinue his work in 1856. See Lord George Hill, *Facts from Gweedore* ([1845], facsimile edn, Belfast, 1971).

216 Graham to Heytesbury, 4, 11 June, Graham Papers, bundle 102.

217 *Hans.*, LXXXVII, 423–4 [12 June].

218 Coffin noted of the ordinary people that 'facts live long in their minds, and though the feeling which arises out of them may for a time yield to newer impressions, a solid ground of confidence can never be wholly effaced from recollection. I know it to be an opinion among reflecting Irishmen that more will have been done in these few months to counteract the efforts of agitation, than years could have accomplished under ordinary circumstances.' Coffin to Trevelyan, 24 June, *Corr. explan. (Comm. ser.)*, P.P. 1846 [735], XXXVII, 277; Heytesbury to Graham, 12 June, Graham Papers, bundle 102.

highest honour on the person to whom they think they owe the greatest gratitude, attribute to Daniel O'Connell the supplies of food thus sent into the country.' It was only in retrospect, in the wake of the Whig-Liberal government's failure to respond adequately to the catastrophic shortfall of 1846, that nationalist opinion began to give qualified praise to Peel.[219]

219 Pole to Trevelyan, 6 July, *Corr. explan. (Comm. ser.)*, P.P. 1846 [735], XXXVII, 245–6, *Freeman's Journal*, 5 April 1847. However, some moderate O'Connellites remained critical of Peel's failure to attempt any permanent improvements, [W.B. McCabe], 'Measures for Ireland', *Dublin Review*, XXII (March 1847), 232–6.

CHAPTER FOUR

Whiggery and the Land Question, 1846–50

> My objection is that the law allows [the landlord] to do such an act as this. In England public opinion would prevent his doing it, but I am sorry to say that powerful engine is wanting in Ireland both in respect to this and many other cases in which the poorest classes of person are concerned. This must be altered somehow or other before Ireland can be quiet . . . As it is all the laws affecting the poor appear to have been framed for the protection of the rich.
>
> *Lord John Russell*, April 1846[1]

> [I]t would be a violation of . . . sacred maxims to appropriate the entire crops of the husbandman without compensating him for the seed or the labour expended on the cultivation of the soil. Yet laws sanctioning such unnatural injustice, and, therefore, injurious to society, not only exist but are extensively enforced with reckless and unrelenting vigour, whilst the sacred and indefeasible rights of life are forgotten amidst the incessant reclamation of the subordinate rights of property.
>
> *Memorial of the Catholic bishops and archbishops of Ireland*, 21 October 1847[2]

In hindsight it seems a cruel irony that the return of the Whigs to power in 1846 should have been so warmly welcomed in Ireland. The events of 1846–50 went far to vindicate Young Ireland's denunciation of Russell's Party as inveterate enemies to Ireland, and to discredit O'Connell's optimistic predictions about the fruits of a renewed Whig alliance.[3] Yet the fateful outcome of these years was contingent on the Famine continuing and intensifying from summer 1846, and this eventuality was not foreseen by O'Connell or Russell. Both were pre-occupied by the negotiation of a reformist agenda, and allowed themselves to be lulled into false security by the previous pattern of Irish famines (which had rarely lasted into a second year) and perhaps also by the dominant tendency to regard free trade as the 'solution' to the crisis of 1845–6. To understand the full magnitude of the

1 Russell to (Bessborough), n.d. (April 1846), Russell Papers, Public Record Office, London, PRO 30/22/5G, fols. 129–30.

2 *Freeman's Journal*, 26 Oct. 1847.

3 Kevin B. Nowlan, *The politics of Repeal: a study in the relations between Great Britain and Ireland, 1841–50* (London, 1965), pp. 98, 108–9.

Whigs' Irish failures in the later 1840s, it is necessary to trace both the collapse of their reform initiatives and the gross mishandling of the Famine emergency.

From 1846 to 1850 the elements of what constituted the 'land question' were transformed by the catastrophic social consequences of the potato failures. A greater sense of urgency was injected into the debate, as the risks of uprooting, destitution and death forced many tenants and labourers into a more aggressive assertion of agrarian demands, while landlords felt obliged to proceed more rapidly with the restructuring of their property along the lines prescribed by economic orthodoxy. The Whig government, faced with the heightened expectations regarding land reform which some of its leaders had encouraged while in opposition, but feeling compelled to meet the famine crisis with measures that would prevent its perpetuation or recurrence, found itself pulled in contradictory directions. These unresolved tensions had a divisive impact on the politics of the later 1840s.

I BESSBOROUGH'S ADMINISTRATION, 1846–7

A 'golden age for Ireland'?: the formation of Russell's government

Peel's Coercion Bill proved the ideal focus for the reformulation of a Whig-O'Connellite alliance during the 1846 session. By early that year leading elements of both parties were keen to promote a return to the politics of Lichfield House. Russell was anxious to conciliate Ireland by means of a 'large and comprehensive scheme' of reforms, and publicly regretted that his failure to form an administration in December 1845 had denied him the opportunity to do so.[4] His private denunciation of the Conservatives as 'a mere party of officials . . . [having] neither authority nor affection',[5] and his idealistic vision of introducing a 'golden age for Ireland',[6] suggest that his public statements were sincere. Lady Russell shared and endorsed his Foxite inclinations. She assured him in January that: 'Your mention of the dreams which you had of happiness for Ireland made me sad, and you know how I shared in those dreams.'[7]

For his part, O'Connell was also anxious to re-establish the alliance, and indicated his intention to 'rally round the old standard and sustain, in the season of difficulty, the public men with whom the Irish popular party have often contended in common for benefits to Ireland.'[8] He defended his toning down of the Repeal

4 *Hansard's Parliamentary Debates*, third series, LXXXIII, 109 [22 Jan. 1846].

5 Russell to Lansdowne, 27 Dec. 1845, 1 Jan. 1846, G.P. Gooch (ed.), *The later correspondence of Lord John Russell, 1840–1878* (2 vols., London, 1925), I, 99.

6 Lady John Russell to Melgund, n.d. (1846), cited in Frederick August Dreyer, 'The Whigs and the political crisis of 1845', *English Historical Review*, LXXX (1965), 530.

7 Lady John Russell to Russell, 26 Jan. 1846, Desmond MacCarthy and Agatha Russell (eds.), *Lady John Russell: a memoir, with selections from her diaries and correspondence* (London, 1910), p. 79.

8 Pigot to Russell, 15 Dec. 1845, Russell Papers, PRO 30/22/4E, fols. 159–61.

agitation to the sceptical William Smith O'Brien: 'If we could have managed to play our cards well in Lord John's Government, we should have *squeezed out* a great deal of good for Ireland without for one moment . . . postponing Repeal but on the contrary advancing that measure. Every popular concession . . . advances the cause of Repeal.'[9] Michael Staunton, editor of the *Dublin Weekly Register* and a confidant of the Irish leader, confirmed the eagerness of many moderate O'Connellites to see such a political development. He wrote to Morpeth that O'Connell was heartily disposed to co-operate, and that the 'country will go with him either for Repeal or any substitute that may be devised'. Staunton declared himself a Repealer largely from convenience, but reminded the Whigs that Repeal 'never will, or should, be got out of the hearts of the people without complete and ample justice, and a great improvement in the condition of the people.' Popular legal administration and political reforms remained desirable, but these would have to be supplemented by measures of social amelioration.[10]

In the aftermath of the December debacle, Russell committed himself politically to a renewed compact through his stance on the Coercion Bill. There were considerable political difficulties involved in his doing so, particularly the threat to the Corn Bill posed by any overt opposition to the Coercion Bill's first reading. This was initially the source of much frustration for Russell, who stated to his colleagues that he felt himself obliged by parliamentary circumstances 'very reluctantly' not to oppose the first reading. Greville recorded that having done so, he 'broke out with a bitterness beyond description against the Government, which he said was the greatest curse to Ireland, and that while they were in office no good was possible there.'[11] His next action was, 'with bile still flowing', to give notice of a motion on the state of Ireland. This alarmed many of his colleagues, and when Peel threatened to make it a question of confidence, Russell was forced to postpone it.[12]

Much of Russell's frustration stemmed from the deep division within Whig-Liberal ranks over the coercion issue. Certain peers, especially those with Irish estates such as Lansdowne, Clanricarde and Monteagle, were firmly in favour of repressing disturbances,[13] while the O'Connellites and many Irish liberals had

---

9 O'Connell to Smith O'Brien, 22 Dec. 1845, Maurice R. O'Connell (ed.) *The correspondence of Daniel O'Connell* (8 vols., Dublin, 1972–80), VII, 353.

10 Staunton to Morpeth, 15, 20 Dec. 1845, Castle Howard Papers, Castle Howard, N. Yorks., J19/1/40/70, 79. Staunton personally favoured a major scheme of state waste-land reclamation for this purpose.

11 Charles Cavendish Fulke Greville, *The Greville memoirs (second part): a journal of the reign of Queen Victoria, from 1837 to 1852*, edited by H. Reeve, 3 vols. (London, 1885), II, 375 [18 March 1846].

12 Broughton Diary, Broughton Papers, British Library, London, Add. MS 43,748, fol. 65 [14 March 1846].

13 *Hans.*, LXXXIII, 1367–70, 1376–8 [23 Feb.]. Clanricarde had the additional incentive of being the subject of a recent agrarian death threat, Anon. to Capt. Burke, 3 March 1846, Clanricarde Papers, W. Yorkshire Archive Service, Leeds, bundle 71; Clanricarde to Russell, 11 March, Russell Papers, PRO 30/22/5A, fols. 164–6.

publicly declared opposition to the Bill as their primary political priority. Russell's greatest headache lay in the initial support afforded to the Bill by his allies Bessborough and Normanby. This division within the Foxite ranks proved a considerable embarrassment.[14] Bessborough's visit to Ireland in late 1845 had left him in 'a state of great uneasiness and uncertainty', distrustful of the influence of Conciliation Hall and convinced that the scale of disturbance required some form of coercive check.[15] He looked, however, to a purely temporary and limited measure, and was active in promoting mediating amendments to Peel's Bill in the Lords.[16] Russell felt that he could not simply throw out the Bill so long as it had Bessborough's support.[17]

Bessborough's convictions made him uneasy about the expedient agreed by the party in the Commons of supporting Somerville's motion for the postponement of the Coercion Bill until after the Corn Bill had passed,[18] but by late April, a major shift of attitudes had taken place, as Bessborough and Clanricarde recognized that the Bill would now be counterproductive. The reasoning behind their conversions was outlined by Greville: 'If it was necessary at all, the necessity was urgent . . . if the country can go on without it for three or four months . . . it may as well go on for ever.'[19] This was not Bessborough's only reason for abandoning coercion; he was increasingly convinced of the viability of an alternative mode of 'pacifying' Ireland.

O'Connell and his followers had taken an active role in the opposition party meetings in the course of the session, much to the annoyance of liberal 'moderates' such as Lansdowne.[20] For all the continuing flourishes of the Repeal press, it was evident that O'Connell was sympathetic to Russell's difficulties.[21] The entente was re-established through parliamentary co-operation, and consolidated at the party meeting of 6 June, which determined the course to be pursued with respect to the second reading of the Coercion Bill. At this meeting, reminiscent of the Lichfield House gatherings, Russell declared that he would oppose the second reading, and O'Connell committed his followers to support the Whig leader. It was still uncertain

---

14 Broughton Diary, Add. MS 43,748, fol. 63 [9 March].

15 Bessborough to Grey, 2 Jan. 1846, Grey of Howick Papers, Durham University Library; Greville, *Journal*, II, 352–4 [14 Jan. 1846].

16 *Hans.*, LXXXIV, 841 [10 March]; Graham to Heytesbury, 5 March, Graham Papers, Cambridge University Library (microfilm), bundle 28 IR; Diary of third Earl Grey, 23 Feb., 24 March, Grey Papers.

17 Russell to Lady John Russell, March 1846, MacCarthy and Russell, *Lady John Russell*, p. 86.

18 Bessborough tactfully kept quiet at the party meeting on 27 March, and it was Ellice who took the brunt of Russell's anger for suggesting that the Bill be left unmolested, Broughton Diary, Add. MS 43,748, fol. 73 [27 March 1846].

19 Greville, *Journal*, II, 381–2 [23 April]. Normanby now also attacked the government over the Coercion Bill, Grey Diary, 22 May 1846, Grey Papers.

20 Broughton Diary, Add. MS 43,748, fol. 51 [21 Feb.].

21 The *Freeman* remained suspicious of the 'old Whigs', but hoped that the 'friends of Lord John Russell' would commit themselves to 'justice to Ireland', *Freeman's Journal*, 23 Dec. 1845.

what the consequence of this step would be, for the Protectionists had not declared themselves, but it was decided that the coercion debate be deliberately protracted to ensure the safe passage of the Corn Bill through the Lords.[22]

The government was bitterly hostile towards these developments. Graham thought Smith O'Brien correct in fearing that O'Connell intended to sell out Repeal to the Whigs, and he cynically added that the price would not be exorbitant. Heytesbury was also convinced that the new pact was the outcome of some sharp political dealing:

> That Lord Bessborough, having made his bargain with O'Connell, may now be willing to undertake the Government of this country, without the Coercion Bill he is said to have insisted upon, three months ago, is very possible. No doubt O'Connell and the parish priests would do a great deal more to check agrarian agitation and other outrages than any Coercion Bill, however wisely framed, but there must be the *quid* for the *pro*, and nothing short of the whole patronage of the Government yielded to O'Connell and his partisans would induce the first to put his shoulder to the wheel, or the latter to assist him.[23]

Lord George Bentinck's declaration shortly thereafter that he and many of his Protectionist colleagues would oppose the second reading of the Coercion Bill sealed the government's fate. As in 1835, Peel fell on an Irish question made dangerous by the force of Russell's Foxite principles. Not surprisingly, the assumption of power on an Irish issue, and particularly on the rejection of coercion, was found objectionable by liberal moderates, and Monteagle thought it 'inexcusable'.[24]

There was, however, to be no resurrection of the ministry of 1835–41, for while the administration formed in July 1846 was at first sight similar to Lord Melbourne's, the balance of power had shifted. The events of the 1846 session, and particularly divisions over the proposal of a compromise fixed corn duty, had undermined the unity of the Foxite group and dissipated its strength. Bessborough and Normanby, not convinced free-traders, were concerned at Russell's pact with the League, and feared that the choice of ground exposed the Whigs to being out-manoeuvred by Peel. More particularly, Bessborough had suggested a fixed-duty compromise as a tactical concession to Bentinck in return for his support for Irish reforms. He reminded Russell that in the current conditions of parliamentary uncertainty, an alliance with 'liberal Protectionists' could secure a Whig government against Peelite machinations. Bentinck's membership of an 'old Whig family' would augment his

---

22 Broughton Diary, Add. MS 43,748, fols 123–7 [6 June 1846]; Morpeth Diary, 6 June 1846, Castle Howard Papers, J19/8/11.

23 Graham to Heytesbury, 28 May, Heytesbury to Graham, 31 May, Graham Papers, bundle 30 IR. Heytesbury drew some consolation from the thought that Young Ireland's intransigence would disrupt this arrangement.

24 Frederick August Dreyer, 'The Russell administration, 1846–52' (unpublished Ph. D. thesis, University of St. Andrews, 1962), p. 56.

claims to a seat in the new cabinet.[25] Russell was not slow to point out the major flaw in this argument – that the relatively liberal Bentinck was far from representative of his party – and Bessborough and Normanby reluctantly acquiesced.[26]

Ill-health and personal sensitivities of several of the group also added to Foxite weakness, but Russell was anxious to make the best use of the remaining materials. Earl Fortescue, loyal but plagued by sickness, accepted the place of Lord Steward of the Royal Household, but continued to offer advice to his chief on Irish affairs.[27] Normanby – whom Russell had considered for another stint as Lord Lieutenant – cited personal reasons as well as doubts over the Corn Law policy for declining a seat in the cabinet, and was granted the Paris embassy he desired.[28] Bessborough accepted the Irish viceroyalty after much persuasion, to the irritation of the moderate Fitzwilliam, but to the delight of many Repealers.[29] Morpeth was deeply disappointed not to be offered the Home Office, but this was hardly surprising in view of his absence from active politics since 1841. He grudged the low formal status of the office of First Commissioner of Woods and Forests, and was increasingly frustrated at Russell's reluctance to move him to a more prestigious post. However, this was not necessarily the slight Morpeth took it to be, for the Woods and Forests was evolving into 'the public works department of the early Victorian age', and had been made a centre of interventionist activity in both England and Ireland by Duncannon in the 1830s. Morpeth's appointment would facilitate Bessborough's plans for Irish improvement, as well as Russell's intentions for social reform in England.[30]

Much of the cabinet weight lost by the Foxites was taken up by what Prince Albert termed the 'Grey Party'.[31] Earl Grey accepted office as Colonial Secretary

---

25 Broughton Diary, Add. MS 43,748, fol. 67 [18 March]; Bessborough to Russell, 7 April (1846), Russell Papers, PRO 30/22/6C, fols 31–2. Bessborough's interest in 'liberal Protectionists' may not have been as misplaced as it appeared; some romantic Conservatives favoured both Catholic endowment and a 'small farm' system in Ireland. See Lord John Manners, *Notes of an Irish tour in 1846* (new edn, Edinburgh and London, 1881), pp. 102–11.

26 He lectured Bessborough: 'your liberal Protectionists must seriously consider whether they can bear to see franchises equal to those of Englishmen bestowed upon Irishmen; offices given to Catholics as well as to Protestants; the Irish landlords compelled to act fairly by their tenants; the national revenue maintained by adequate taxes; crime put down by vigilance and exertion rather than shutting honest people up all night . . . and when measures of severity are necessary, taking care to give them soothing as well as drastic medicine.' Russell to Bessborough, 11 April 1846, Russell Papers, PRO 30/22/5A, fols. 184–6.

27 Conscious of the Peelite leanings of the Court, Russell regarded this as a political appointment, Russell to Fortescue, 3 July 1846, Fortescue of Castle Hill Papers, Devon Record Office, Exeter, 1262M/FC 102.

28 Normanby to Russell, 24 Jan. 1846, Russell Papers, PRO 30/22/5A, fols 86–9; Morpeth Diary, 17 Dec. 1845, Castle Howard Papers, J19/8/10.

29 Fitzwilliam to Bedford, 30 June 1846, Russell Papers, PRO 30/22/5A, fols 318–22; *Freeman's Journal*, 6 July 1846.

30 Morpeth Diary, 2 July 1846, Castle Howard Papers, J19/8/12; Diana Davids Olien, *Morpeth: a Victorian public career* (Washington, 1983), pp. 280–90; Mandler, *Aristocratic government*, pp. 237–8.

31 Memorandum by Prince Albert, 6 July 1846, A.C. Benson and Viscount Esher (eds.), *The*

after muting both his objections to Palmerston and his insistence on immediate and radical Irish Church reform.[32] Charles Wood emerged from Grey's shadow to a dominant place in the cabinet as Chancellor of the Exchequer. Russell preferred him to the 1841 incumbent, Francis Baring, whose moderation and 'independence' he disliked.[33] Sir George Grey, whose administrative skills and parliamentary popularity were widely recognized, became Home Secretary. Despite his close family connections with Wood and Grey, Sir George was an occasional rather than an invariable collaborator in their plans – although his strongly moralistic and evangelical beliefs usually led him towards similar conclusions. Clarendon, who took the Board of Trade, also held some moralist opinions on Ireland, but to a much lesser extent and without the religious underpinning. As Mandler suggests, Russell may have promoted the Grey faction in the belief that they would act as counter-balance to the cabinet conservatives.[34]

The ballast of the cabinet was made up of men of moderate opinions. Lansdowne and Palmerston retained their traditional weighty positions, Auckland and the ex-radical Hobhouse usually sided with them, and they were now joined by the Irish landowner Clanricarde. Russell was obliged to adopt the role of moderator over this uneasy assemblage – united by shared political experience rather than by any ideological cohesion or policy objectives. Ironically, his position as Prime Minister may have left him less free to pursue his own political aims than he had been as Home Secretary under the indolent Melbourne or as opposition leader.

The Irish appointments of the new government were carefully made. The choice of the young moderate Henry Labouchere as Chief Secretary appeared to balance Bessborough, but Russell took account of Labouchere's malleability as well as his administrative ability and cabinet rank. Labouchere accepted the position only on the understanding that his Irish inexperience would be 'remedied by having Lord Bessborough over me'.[35] Labouchere also had extensive consultations with Morpeth before going over to Ireland, and reached agreement with his predecessor on many 'points of principle'.[36] He was clearly expected to act as Bessborough's mouthpiece in the cabinet. Other ministers believed that the Irish offices had been sewn up

---

letters of Queen Victoria: a selection from Her Majesty's correspondence between the years 1837 and 1861 (3 vols., London, 1907) II, 101–3.

32 Grey Diary, 30 June 1846, Grey Papers. Grey had cited Russell's coolness on the latter point as one reason for refusing to join the proposed cabinet in December, Grey to Russell, 19 Dec. 1845, Russell Papers, PRO 30/22/4E, fols. 223–4.

33 Grey Diary, 27 June 1846, Grey Papers.

34 Mandler, *Aristocratic government*, pp. 232–3, 238.

35 Pigot's suggestion of an Irishman like Somerville or More O'Ferrall, and Sheil's recommendation of himself for this post, were turned down on the grounds of their insufficient weight in cabinet, Labouchere to Russell, 21 June, Sheil to Russell, 20 June, Russell Papers, PRO 30/22/5A, fols. 257–8, 253–4. The choice of Labouchere over Somerville was unpopular in Ireland, *Freeman's Journal*, 6 July.

36 Morpeth Diary, 20 Dec. 1845, 1 July 1846, Castle Howard Papers, J19/8/10.

by Russell; Grey developed an instant dislike for the two Irish ministers, and the moderates also soon began to see their fears of a vigorous Bessborough administration being realized.[37] Given his close relationship with Russell, the Lord Lieutenant's cabinet opponents were left with only the resort of spreading malicious gossip about his liaison with Katherine Maberley, romantic novelist and wife of the Secretary to the Post Office.[38]

The subordinate Irish offices were allocated by traditional Foxite practice, mostly on Pigot's advice. Thomas Redington, a man with extensive knowledge of Irish social conditions, was chosen as the first Catholic to hold the post of Under-Secretary. Morpeth strongly approved of this appointment, and of the offers to Corry Connellan and Thomas Larcom (the experienced Ordnance Survey officer) of private secretaryships to Bessborough and Labouchere.[39] Larcom declined this offer, and the latter post went to the Irish radical (and associate of Thomas Davis), William Torrens McCullagh.[40] The law offices and legal appointments went to 'friends of O'Connell' – Pigot, Moore, Brady and Monahan.

O'Connell himself was anxious to co-operate with Pigot in facilitating the change of administration and according it a degree of popular legitimacy. He made efforts to secure the safe electoral return of a number of government nominees, acting 'in an under channel' for Monahan, but being obliged to draw the line at Redington, who despite being 'a most excellent appointment' had declared himself too strongly against Repeal for it to be possible to withdraw the Association's candidate at the Dundalk by-election. Even so, O'Connell informed Whig contacts that he was angry that the Association had forced his hand at Dundalk, and declared that it was his intention to purge the 'physical force men'. One observer remarked to Russell, that 'Old Dan was never in better humour and more inclined to remove difficulties in the way of the Government.'[41] O'Connell also approved Russell's continuation of the practice of the later 1830s of integrating Irish liberals into positions of junior rank in the British government. Sheil was

37 Grey Diary, 6 July 1846, Grey Papers. Clarendon also thought Labouchere 'timid and vacillating', and incapable of dealing with the Irish, Clarendon to Lewis, 1 Oct., Clarendon Deposit, Bodleian Library, Oxford, c.532/1.

38 Grey Diary, 1 July 1846, Grey Papers; Broughton Diary, Add. MS 43,750, fol. 44 [12 May 1847]; Greville to Clarendon, n.d. (1847), Clar. Dep., c.520. Despite her protestations of innocence, Mrs Maberley later came close to exploiting her notoriety by publishing a pamphlet on the Irish question. Her 'remedy' – mass emigration – owed more to conventional wisdom than to Bessborough's economic views, Mrs. Maberley to Russell, 19 June 1847, Russell Papers, PRO 30/22/6D, fols. 64–7; Katherine C. Maberley, *The present state of Ireland, and its remedy* (2nd edn, London, 1847), p. 12.

39 Morpeth Diary, 3 July 1846, Castle Howard Papers, J19/8/12.

40 The last appointment was particularly popular with the O'Connellite press, *Freeman's Journal*, 27 July 1846.

41 O'Conor Don to O'Connell, 6 July, O'Connell to Pigot, 8 July, O'Connell, *Correspondence*, VIII, 62–3; A. Bannerman to Russell, 25 July, Russell Papers, PRO 30/22/5B, fols. 226–7.

made Master of the Mint, Somerville and Wyse Under-Secretaries at the Home Office and Board of Control, and the O'Conor Don became a Lord of the Treasury.

O'Connell was also insistent that the government alter the pattern of patronage to attract popular support. The administration again proved compliant, advancing numerous Repealers and conceding a number of colonial positions,[42] but this policy became a subject of acrimonious debate in the cabinet when objections were raised to the reinstatement of the 'Repeal magistrates' dismissed by Peel in 1843. O'Connell put pressure on the government to restore them to the bench, and Bessborough and Russell pushed this through cabinet against the opposition of Clarendon, Hobhouse and Lansdowne, and to the consternation of Bedford and Leinster.[43] The policy was then rapidly implemented by the Irish Lord Chancellor Maziere Brady, and O'Connell and his son Maurice were among those restored.[44] Conflict arose again over the appointment of Repealers to tidewaiterships in the customs department, but Bessborough was successful in forcing Wood to agree to arrangements allowing the Irish government to go on in a 'tolerant spirit'. For the Lord Lieutenant, liberal concessions were essential to bolster '[O'Connell, who] has, I assure you, a difficult game to play here as he is much watched and suspected'.[45]

These concessions were intended by the Foxites in the government to restore the relationship with Irish popular politicians which had existed in the later 1830s. Their success in the early months of Bessborough's administration was striking. Moderate Repealers including the Lord Mayor of Dublin believed the government sincere in its expressed desire to give Ireland 'satisfaction', and Morpeth's Irish Quaker correspondent Jacob Harvey was convinced of the benefits both sides would receive from this strategy:

> Fortune favours you beyond all precedent . . . I was delighted to find your Cabinet making no distinction between Repealers and Anti-Repealers in your appointments and that you contemplate the restoration of the Repeal magistrates – go on in this way and introduce your practical measures of relief, and you will succeed in killing Repeal . . . with kindness . . . It would seem as if Dan's last days are to be his best.[46]

42 Grey to Bessborough, 7 Sept., Bessborough to Grey, 10 Sept. 1846, Grey Papers; Oliver MacDonagh, *The emancipist: Daniel O'Connell, 1830–1847* (London, 1989), p. 297.

43 O'Connell to Pigot, 14 Aug. 1846, O'Connell, *Correspondence*, VIII, 83; Greville, *Journal*, II, 407 [18 July 1846].

44 Broughton Diary, Add. MS 43,749, fols. 6, 8 [17, 21 July]; Brady to Labouchere, 24 July 1846, Bessborough Papers, West Sussex Record Office, Chichester, F. 338; D. O'Connell to M. O'Connell, 19, 27 Aug., O'Connell, *Correspondence*, VIII, 86–7.

45 Bessborough to Wood, 2 Sept., Labouchere to Wood, 14, 18 Sept., Wood to Labouchere, 22 Sept. 1846, Hickleton Papers, Cambridge University Library (microfilm), A4/99, A4/102, A4/185/1; Bessborough to Grey, 10 Sept., Grey Papers.

46 Bessborough to Russell, 11 Sept., Russell Papers, PRO 30/22/5C, fols 116–19; Harvey to Morpeth, 28 Aug., Castle Howard Papers, J19/1/42/56.

In the late summer of 1846 the political situation did indeed appear to merit some of this optimism.

For his part, O'Connell did his utmost to knit the movement into the Whig alliance. Young Ireland opponents of this policy were forced out of the Association on the pretext of their refusal to renounce 'physical force' in principle.[47] He pointed to the Whig appointments and to the restoration of the magistrates, and spoke of his confidence in Bessborough as 'the man who gives fair play to all', and of the consistency of seeking immediate reforms without renouncing Repeal as an end in itself.[48] The rapid souring of this relationship and the profound disillusionment consequent on the gross inadequacy of Russell's famine relief policy later tarnished O'Connell's political reputation. Yet it may be unfair to place excessive blame on him for failing to foresee the future course of events in the summer of 1846. The second potato failure, and the consequent social crisis in the autumn of that year, destroyed O'Connellism partly because it encouraged the rise of radical political forces in England which were to strengthen the moralists and undermine the viability of Foxite Irish policies.

Waste lands and peasant proprietors

The evolution of the Irish social question in the 1840s made any simple return to the politics of 1835 impossible. O'Connell was reminded of the urgent need for land reform by his lieutenant P.V. FitzPatrick in May: 'respecting the "Tenant Right" question. It behoves you *most particularly*, now that you are in attendance in Parliament, to put your views on this momentous subject *practically* on record.' Calls in the nationalist press for a 'Tenant League' modelled on the triumphant Anti-Corn Law League emphasized the movement of popular opinion.[49] O'Connell took this seriously and assured Smith O'Brien that the Whigs would deserve support only if they brought in '*sweeping* measures'.[50] He set out in a letter to the Repeal Association the reforms on which he would base his support for the government. In addition to the long-standing civil and ecclesiastical grievances, O'Connell demanded the 'coercion of the Irish landlords, by compelling a new system of landlordism'. This new system should include the extension of the Ulster tenant

---

47 Nowlan, *The politics of Repeal*, pp. 108–10.

48 Speech to the Repeal Association, 3 August, *Freeman's Journal*, 4 Aug. 1846. The *Freeman* remained sceptical as to Whig intentions, but praised O'Connell as 'the sole and only political guide of the Irish people'. English conditions were declared to be right for Irish amelioration: 'the temper of England is wholly favourable to an enlarged and overflowing system of redress. O'Connell has beaten the impression into the English heart . . . [the Whigs] have a blank receipt, and may fill it up for any reasonable amount of justice.' Ibid., 8 July.

49 *Cork Examiner*, 3 July, 2 Dec. 1846.

50 FitzPatrick to O'Connell, 7 May, O'Connell to Smith O'Brien, 30 June 1846, O'Connell, *Correspondence*, VIII, 21, 61.

right to the other provinces and retrospective compensation to tenants for all the solid and lasting improvements made during their occupation, which was to be combined with tenant right in such a way as to continue the period of the tenant's occupation, without prejudicing the interest of the landlord. To this was added the abolition of the power of distraint and ejectment except in cases were the tenant had been offered a 21-year lease, the replacement of grand juries by elected county boards and an absentee tax.[51]

Sympathetic statements from parts of the British press helped persuade O'Connell that such measures were feasible. Popular expectations had been stimulated in 1846 by a series of leaders in the *Morning Chronicle* which accused the landlords of causing the very crimes they called for coercion to put down. By April the paper had declared support for the legalization of the Ulster tenant right and the extension of something similar to the rest of Ireland.[52] Several other journals joined the campaign. 'Justice to Ireland', wrote William Howitt in *Tait's Magazine*, was central to British self-interest, and must now be extended to address the land question.[53] Publications by Irish 'practical improvers' supporting tenant right as the precondition for social progress appeared to bolster the reformers' case.[54]

Russell's public statements also gave hope that the government would indeed move some way towards fulfilling these expectations. His address to the electors of London in July contained a statement of his reforming plans, which gave priority to Ireland: 'recent discussions have laid bare the misery, the discontent and outrages of Ireland – they are too clearly authenticated to be denied; too extensive to be healed by any but the most comprehensive measures.'[55] His Commons speech of 16 July set out clearly the principles on which he intended to base his Irish policy:

> We consider that the social grievances of Ireland are those which are the most prominent, and to which it is most likely to be in our power to afford, not a complete and immediate remedy, but some remedy, some kind of improvement, so that some kind of hope may be entertained that some ten or twelve years hence the country will, by the measures we undertake, be in a far better state with respect to the frightful destitution and misery which now prevail in that country. We have that practical object in view . . . and we will not be led away

51 *Freeman's Journal*, 30 June 1846.

52 *Morning Chronicle*, 5 Dec. 1845, 21 Jan., 23 April 1846.

53 William Howitt, 'Visit to Mr O'Connell at Derrynane', *Tait's Edinburgh Magazine*, XIII (Jan. 1846), 1–13.

54 Thomas Bermingham, *Letter addressed to the Rt. Hon. Lord John Russell, containing facts illustrative of the good effects from the just and considerate discharge of the duties of a resident landlord in Ireland* (London, 1846), pp. 4–9, 16.

55 Russell, Draft resignation address, n.d. (July 1846), Russell Papers, PRO 30/22/5B, fols. 3–8. Russell had been shocked by the reports of the Gerrard evictions in March, and was convinced that Ireland could not be pacified before such events were curtailed. Only government intervention could do this in Irish conditions, Russell to (Bessborough), n.d. (April 1846), ibid., PRO 30/22/5G, fols. 129–30.

> from it by any differences on other subjects, not calculated to effect any immediate good.

Russell declared himself to be still in favour of Catholic endowment, but that he was convinced that widespread opposition in Britain and Ireland made it both impracticable and inexpedient at present. In contrast, political reforms, such as the extension of the rural franchise, had a strong social dimension and would accompany his social reforms.[56]

It was not thought possible to do much in the remains of the 1846 session beyond adopting the permissive Leases and Ejectments Bills already introduced by Lincoln,[57] but planning for the reform programme of 1847 began in September. Bessborough concentrated on four measures – bills to reform the Irish electoral franchise and corporations, a Waste-land Reclamation Bill, and a Landlord-Tenant Bill.[58] During the course of the recess, as the government in Ireland and England found itself increasingly overwhelmed by the crisis of Irish distress, it was the waste-land proposal that displaced the others at the head of the remedial agenda. This measure promised at least some assistance to the relief of distress in a way that would be both remunerative and popular.[59]

The practicability of waste-land reclamation and cultivation had been a subject of considerable interest in Ireland since the establishment of the Bogs Commission in 1809. Subsequent government reports pointed to this as a great potential resource, and the Devon report publicized Griffith's estimation that 1.4 million acres could be profitably reclaimed for tillage, and a further 2.3 million for pasture.[60] Devon proposed a modest programme of state loans to assist the reclaiming endeavours of individual proprietors. He was himself chairman of the private Irish Waste Land Improvement Society (founded 1842) and continued to request government support for its activities during the Famine.[61] Ominously for a larger project, the society's reclamation efforts in the west ground to a halt when the blight destroyed the 1846 potato harvest.[62]

---

56 *Hans.*, LXXXVII, 1179–82 [16 July 1846].

57 Ibid., 283–4 [3 Aug.]. For Irish discontent at the postponement, see *Freeman's Journal*, 5, 10 Aug.

58 Bessborough to Russell, 11 Sept., Russell Papers, PRO 30/22/5C, fols. 116–19.

59 Pigot had initially suggested a waste-land scheme that could be implemented without any legislative enactment, but its scope was substantially less than that which Russell favoured, Pigot to Russell, n.d. (1846), ibid., 5G, fols. 155–62.

60 *Report of Her Majesty's Commissioners of Inquiry into the state of the law and practice in respect to the occupation of land in Ireland (Devon Commission)*, part I, P.P. 1845 [605], XIX, 29–30, 48–53.

61 Colonel D. Robinson, *Practical suggestions for the reclamation of waste lands, and improvement in the condition of the agricultural population of Ireland, with an introductory letter . . . from the Earl of Devon* (London [1847]), pp. iii–ix. See also N. Ludlow Beamish, *Remedy for the impending scarcity; suggested by a visit to the Kilkerrin estate of the Irish Waste Lands Improvement Society* (Cork, 1846).

62 *Observer*, 14 March 1847; cf. the similar experience of dashed hopes for reclamation by potato cultivation in W. Steuart Trench, *Realities of Irish life* (London, 1868), pp. 44–6.

English and Irish radicals also took an interest in the waste-lands question and 'optimistic' commentators had long regarded it as a virtual panacea for Ireland's social problems.[63] Pitt Kennedy had from the mid-1830s expressed strong criticisms of proprietors who acted irrationally by neglecting this resource. It was the duty of government, he argued in 1835, to compel landowners to act as their own interest and social obligations demanded.[64] Kennedy's preoccupation with waste lands found much clearer expression in his *Digest of evidence* from the Devon inquiry, published in 1847–8. Kennedy used his editorial position to state authoritatively his own opinions on the subjects considered by the Commission and to give them something of a radical coloration. Again he urged the improvement of wastelands as the most cost-effective and productive mode of improving the social condition of the country, and of relieving immediate distress. Yet he declined to suggest a mechanism for enacting this, and implied that while the government should exhort and encourage, responsibility for action should lie with the proprietors and their agents.[65]

In the mid-1840s some more advanced radicals came to see in the wastelands the tools for a far-reaching, even fundamental reform of the Irish land system. In 1846 Poulett Scrope urged the necessity of taking up Devon's recommendation, but wanted something more than the mere temporary provision of additional employment. He called for a waste-land measure that would involve 'the *creation* out of these paupers [evicted from their holdings] of a *class of yeomanry* – so wanted in Ireland, *cultivating their own lands for their sole profit*'.[66] Scrope presented a Bill to the Commons in April 1846 which included the mechanism of compulsory state purchase with a fair compensation to the proprietor. The plan was endorsed by Sharman Crawford, who agreed that it would be 'an essential mode of ending

63 For the latter, see the enthusiasm of the Scottish travel writer Henry D. Inglis, *A journey throughout Ireland* (3rd edn, 2 vols., London, 1835), II, 54–60.

64 John Pitt Kennedy, *Instruct; employ; don't hang them: or, Ireland tranquillized without soldiers, and enriched without English capital* (London, 1835), pp. 106–26. Kennedy wrote of his own successes as an agent, and emphasized the self-funding character of this improvement: 'Those who maintain that we have not the means to improve our condition without external help, and who urge the doctrine that everything must be done with 'capital' alone – would do well to reflect. They would find that we have capital, which we are satisfied to waste not employ – they would see that the light of heaven, the barren waste, and *superabundant population* are capital . . . the mere co-operation of the bog proprietor and the pauper creates capital – more sufficient and certain than the numerous popular speculations daily leading the knowing world in pursuit of riches . . . Proprietors want *judgement*, reflection, knowledge, fellow feeling and right selection. Without these proprietors cannot ascertain the amount of capital they possess, or turn this to beneficial account.' Ibid., pp. 95–9.

65 John Pitt Kennedy (ed.), *Digest of evidence taken before H.M. Commissioners of Inquiry into the state of the law and practice in respect to the occupation of land in Ireland* (2 vols., Dublin, 1847–8), I, 563–74.

66 George Poulett Scrope, *How is Ireland to be governed?: a question addressed to the new administration of Lord Melbourne in 1834, with a postscript in which the same question is addressed to the administration of Sir Robert Peel in 1846* (2nd edn, London, 1846), pp. 46–61.

the horrors of the clearance system'. The Bill was also welcomed by Wyse, who approved of state intervention in the case of incapable proprietors, but was dismissed by Graham, who said he looked to private enterprise for such improvements, and pointed to the differences over points of detail between the Bill's sponsors. The Bill was dropped by Scrope on hearing Russell's declaration of support for the principle, and his promise to consider it over the recess.[67]

Scrope drew on the recently published work of William Thornton to give intellectual substance to his proposal. Thornton's *Over-population* was a landmark in the development of the new radical economics, and while Scrope did not share Thornton's neo-Malthusian concern with the danger of over-population, he felt that the positive, even optimistic, conclusions regarding peasant proprietors should be brought to a wider public.[68] Thornton believed it possible to amend the social structure in such a way that would prevent the operation of the Malthusian trap by encouraging prudential population restraint by the lower classes. He used comparative and local analysis to demonstrate his point. A survey of most west European peasantries suggested a relative degree of prosperity and industriousness, and the existence of voluntary restraints on the birth rate. This, he suggested, might indicate that misery was as much the cause as the effect of over-population.[69]

Thornton applied his comparative scheme directly to Ireland, arguing that the primeval poverty of the people had merely continued in a new form as they became potato-fed peasant occupiers. One peculiar social circumstance of the Irish peasantry marked them off from their European fellows: 'the *terms of tenure in land* prevented them materially from increasing their resources [and] merely enabled them to bring up more children amid accustomed misery.' Considering the possible reforms, he thought that long leases of smallholdings at fair rents would be desirable, but could not be forced on reluctant landowners besotted with orthodox 'large farms' dogma, and that such tinkering as Stanley's Compensation Bill would also prove useless. The least objectionable and most practicable way of bringing about such reform was by an extensive waste-land reclamation, but only if the reclaiming labourer was settled on the land as a free-holder or as a perpetual tenant on a quit-rent. Thornton believed that 200,000 families could be settled on small but viable plots as a 'body of yeomanry'; this would benefit the remainder of the peasantry by rapidly relieving the competition for land.[70]

---

67 *Hans.*, LXXXV, 1198–1210, [28 April 1846], ibid., LXXXVIII, 346 [5 Aug.].

68 For a more hostile radical attack on Thornton's residual Malthusianism and adherence to wages-fund theory, see [Edward Baines], 'Overpopulation and its remedy', *British Quarterly Review*, IV (August 1846), 115–42.

69 William Thomas Thornton, *Over-population and its remedy; or an inquiry into the extent and causes of the distress among the labouring classes of the British islands, and into the means of remedying it* (London, 1846), pp. 118–56.

70 Ibid., pp. 251–66, 413–39. Thornton later developed his views as to the viability of small owner-occupier farms in Ireland in *A plea for peasant proprietors, with the outline of a plan for their establishment in Ireland* (London, 1848), pp. 1–40, 186–254.

John Stuart Mill, like Thornton, had been influenced by the revisionist political economy propounded by Richard Jones at Haileybury in the 1830s.[71] Mill synthesized Jones' and Thornton's ideas with his own observations on continental peasant societies, in a series of forty-three articles published in the *Morning Chronicle* in the winter of 1846–7. The series reflected the paper's long-running critique of Irish landlordism and gave it a distinctive radical demand to counter the *Times*' campaign for an extended Poor Law.[72] The importance of these articles in Mill's own intellectual development – forming as they did the first draft of the Irish sections of his *Principles of political economy* – has been the subject of academic debate,[73] but it is important to remember that these were not only an expression of Mill's deeply-held concern for Irish moral regeneration, but a vigorous polemic directed at promoting a specific policy objective.

Mill's revisionist propaganda was aimed at both the mental 'spirit of routine' that rested on unquestioning public acceptance of the obsolete 'supposed facts of one section of English economists', and at the alternative agendas for Irish reform proposed by Poulett Scrope and Thomas Campbell Foster.[74] Mill's purpose was to build up public support behind a major scheme of waste-land reclamation, facilitated by the state, that would begin the reconstruction of Irish rural society. He was confident that Russell would recognize the shift in public attitudes and that some such measure would be introduced, but was concerned with ensuring that it did not stop short of settling peasants on small freehold plots.[75]

For Mill, the 'grand economical' and 'grand moral' evil of Ireland lay in the 'cottier-tenant system', which had produced over-population and savage competition for subsistence, but which was tolerated by a reckless and improvident landlord class. The system destroyed all motivation to industry and enterprise, and produced a habitual disaffection from the law. While English writers and some Irish landlords had come to recognize these evils, they had opted for the

---

71 Clive Dewey has suggested that the shared experience of these three men as officials of the East India Company may have inclined them towards favouring the idea of peasant proprietors in their writings on the British Isles, 'The rehabilitation of the peasant proprietor in nineteenth-century economic thought', *History of Political Economy*, VI (1974), 17–47. It is worth noting, however, that Trevelyan's experience of India led him to the opposite opinion, C.E. Trevelyan, *The Irish crisis* (London, 1848), p. 176.

72 Mill later noted that the *Chronicle* 'unexpectedly entered warmly into my purpose', John Stuart Mill, *Autobiography* (London, 1924 edn), p. 199.

73 See Lynn Zastoupil, 'Moral government: J.S. Mill on Ireland', *Historical Journal*, XXVI (1983), 707–717, Bruce L. Kinzer 'J.S. Mill and Irish land: a reassessment', idem, XXVII (1984), 111–27, and cf. E.D. Steele, 'J.S. Mill and the Irish question: the principles of political economy, 1848–1865', idem, XIII (1970), 316–36.

74 Articles in the *Morning Chronicle*, 15 Oct., 16 Nov. 1846, Ann P. and John M. Robson (eds.), *The collected works of John Stuart Mill, Vol. XXIV: newspaper writings, January 1835 – June 1847* (Toronto and London, 1986), pp. 898–901, 949–52; [Scrope], 'The *Edinburgh Review* and Mr P. Scrope', *Times*, 27 Oct. 1846. For Foster's views, see above, pp. 76–8.

75 *Morning Chronicle*, 29 Oct. 1846, Robson, *Collected Works*, XXIV, 919–22.

erroneous and counterproductive model of agrarian anglicization, the attempted implementation of which was both inhumane and dangerous:

> The introduction of English farming is another word for the clearing system . . . compared with what we should see then, all we have yet seen . . . is a bagatelle. No one has seen the systematic unpeopling of estates on the scale necessary for introducing a system of farming by hired labour . . . it is a thing which no pretence of private right or public utility ought to induce society to tolerate for a moment. No legitimate construction of any right of ownership in land, which it is for the interest of society to permit, will warrant it.[76]

Mill was more sympathetic towards the 'Irish' demand for 'tenant-right' as a means of mitigating the cottier system, and welcomed the belated adoption of land reform by Repeal agitators. He admitted the merits of 'fixity of tenure' as offering 'a real and thorough remedy', and justified it in terms of both abstract utility and the 'normal' structure of landholding in western Europe.[77] Yet he admitted that such a change would involve a violent disturbance of legal rights, 'amounting almost to a social revolution', and would require the prior permeation of new economic ideas throughout the British public mind before it could be politically feasible. Mill indicated that he too had some reservations about the expediency of introducing such measures at present, as 'the danger of tampering, in times of political and moral change, with the salutary prepossessions by which property is protected against spoliation', made such a measure appear an extreme remedy. Moreover, the opportunity presented by the waste lands would make such a revolutionary step unnecessary. The prime objective of creating a moral structure of tenancy could thus be attained with less opposition, and its benefits would rapidly be felt throughout the island: 'Property in the soil has a sort of magic power of engendering industry, perseverance, forethought in an agricultural people. Any other charm for producing these qualities we know not of, and should be thankful to any one who could point one out. All other schemes for the improvement of Ireland are schemes for getting rid of the people.'[78]

It is difficult to assess the effect of Mill's writing on the British political public, but he himself believed that his objective had been at least partially met by late November. He wrote that the articles 'have excited a good deal of notice and have

---

76 *Morning Chronicle*, 10, 13 Oct., idem, pp. 889–95.

77 He noted that to 'enlightened foreigners' land reform appeared the obvious solution, citing in particular the Prussian Frederick von Raumer, *England in 1835* (trans. H.E. Lloyd, 3 vols., London, 1836), and the French sociologist Gustave de Beaumont, *Ireland, social, political and religious* (trans. W. Cooke Taylor, 2 vols., London, 1839). For Mill's intimate knowledge of this strand of continental social thought, see David E. Martin, 'The rehabilitation of the peasant proprietor in nineteenth-century economic thought: a comment', *History of Political Economy*, VIII (1976), 297–302.

78 *Morning Chronicle*, 14 Oct. 1846, Robson, *Collected works*, XXIV, 895–8.

quite snatched the initiative out of the *Times*',[79] and Mill believed himself effective in providing a theoretical riposte to the orthodox criticisms.[80] His articles were also well received in the Irish popular press. The *Freeman* shifted its ground from initially suspecting that Scrope's proposal would deflect attention from tenant right, to whole-heartedly endorsing Mill's as a substantial measure of justice, and embracing the principle of peasant proprietorship.[81] Irish writers had already drawn attention to the peasant-proprietor system in the Low Countries as a model for Ireland, and in 1847 pamphleteers enthusiastically took up the cry for the settlement of smallholders on reclaimed lands.[82]

Mill was not alone in England in his propagandizing. Scrope put the evidence on the waste lands collected by the Devon Commissioners before the public in a cheap pamphlet in early 1847, and made his intentions quite clear by calling in his introductory essay for the urgent settlement of 'A PROPRIETARY CLASS – A BODY OF YEOMANRY' on reclaimed plots.[83] Scrope proposed this as the first of a series of measures including tenant protection, an encumbered estates bill and the extension of the Poor Law.[84]

Both Mill and Scrope believed Russell serious in the commitment he had made to the commons on waste-lands reclamation at the end of the 1846 session. Yet while the Prime Minister had declared that 'some great scheme with regard to cultivation, preparation and tillage of the waste lands would somewhat abate the severe competition for land, and diminish the causes of crime',[85] he had said

---

79 Mill to Bain, n.d. (Nov. 1846), 28 Dec. 1846, Ann P. and John M. Robson (eds.), *The collected works of John Stuart Mill, Vol. XIII*, 705.

80 *Morning Chronicle*, 17, 22 Dec. 1846, 6, 7 Jan. 1847, Robson, *Collected works*, XXIV, 1001–4, 1008–11, 1030–5.

81 *Freeman's Journal*, 3 July, 17, 20 Oct. However, it regretted that he had not also advocated an immediate concession of tenant right, ibid., 9 Nov.

82 One of the more important advocates was Thomas Skilling, agriculturalist to the National Board of Education and superintendent of the model farm at Glasnevin, *The science and practice of agriculture* (Dublin, 1846), pp. 19–39. See also Robert Meekins, *Plan for the removal of pauperism, agrarian disturbances, and the poor's rate in Ireland, by liberally providing for the destitute, free of expense* (Dublin, 1847), Daniel Desmond, *Project for the reclamation of one million acres of waste lands in Ireland, by colonies for her surplus and unemployed population* (Cheltenham, 1847).

83 George Poulett Scrope, *Extracts of evidence taken by the late Commission of Inquiry . . . on the subject of waste lands reclamation, with a prefatory letter to the Rt. Hon. Lord John Russell* (London, 1847). This was but one of a flood of pamphlets by British radicals advocating such measures, each varying in its details; see for example, John Douglas, *Life and property in Ireland assured as in England by a poor rate on land to provide employment for the destitute poor on the waste lands of Ireland* (London, 1846).

84 Despite their differences over the Poor Law, Mill and Scrope advocated broadly similar plans for the waste lands. Mill, however, criticized the principle of Scrope's proposals and suggested – unfairly – that the latter was interested only in increased production and cared little for the creation of peasant proprietors, *Morning Chronicle*, 23 Oct. 1846, Robson, *Collected works*, XXIV, 910–13.

85 *Hans.*, LXXXVIII, 346 [5 Aug. 1846].

nothing about proprietorship. Their efforts were thus directed as much towards indicating to him the logic of this further step, as they were at preparing public opinion for such a measure. Their success can only be inferred from the correspondence of the ministers involved in preparing the Bill.

Russell was certainly convinced that a measure such as that advocated by Devon would be useless, and made it clear to Bessborough that the Bill must include compulsory powers of purchase and improvement by the state.[86] Both he and the Lord Lieutenant were of the opinion that the reclamation operations should come under the control of the Department of Woods and Forests, and hence be free of the direct Treasury constraints that operated on the Board of Works. Bessborough's own experience of Irish waste-land reclamation on the crown lands in the 1830s inclined him to this opinion.[87] Charles Gore, Morpeth's subordinate in that department, was entrusted with drawing up the Bill,[88] but it was Bessborough who set the tone by declaring that he had no objection to any infringement of the rights of property in this matter. He also hoped that in the period before parliament met, the government project for the drainage of Phoenix Park might be a model school for reclamation techniques.[89] What precisely was to be embraced by the Bill at this point is unclear, but Fortescue hoped that the plan would promote facilitate the growth of 'small freehold proprietors'.[90]

The Reclamation Bill quickly ran into difficulties in the cabinet. Lansdowne objected strongly against such a dangerous interference in private property, and a majority insisted that control be vested in the Board of Works.[91] Russell next suggested a special commission under an Irish Privy Councillor, which would undertake the management of all Irish crown lands, and oversee all works of reclamation. Again the Prime Minister was over-ruled and the cabinet accepted Wood's scheme for Treasury control, and responsibility for the Bill also passed to the Chancellor of the Exchequer.[92] Bessborough clung to his insistence on management by the Woods and Forests department, and commented irritably: 'I should be afraid of

86 Russell to Bessborough, 15 Sept., Russell Papers, PRO 30/22/5C, fols. 164–5; Russell had been favourable to the idea of the state compulsorily taking land for improvement from Irish proprietors from the early 1830s. See above, p. 31.

87 For the reclamation and redivision 'experiments' carried out under his authority, see *Papers relating to improvements on crown estates at King William's Town, Cork*, P.P. 1836 (315), XLVII, 613; *Further report of Richard Griffiths, esq., dated 15 July 1839, to the Commissioners of Her Majesty's Woods etc., on the progress of the roads and land improvements on the crown estates of King William's Town, County Cork*, P.P. 1839 (515), XLVII, 553.

88 Bessborough to Russell, 23 Oct., Russell Papers, PRO 30/22/5D, fols. 234–8.

89 Bessborough to Morpeth, 22 Oct., Labouchere to Morpeth, n.d. (Oct. 1846), Castle Howard Papers, J19/1/42/91, 90.

90 Fortescue to Russell, 29 Oct., Russell Papers, PRO 30/22/5D, fols. 315–18.

91 Lansdowne to Russell, 1 Nov., Russell to Bessborough, 13 Nov., ibid., 5E, fols. 1–2, 98–9.

92 Russell to Bessborough, 22 Nov., Russell to Labouchere, 24 Nov., ibid., fols. 156–8, 174–7.

such an undertaking attempted in any other manner.'[93] His concern about Wood's intentions was not unwarranted, for the latter was in communication with Lord Devon (a man for whom Bessborough had 'no great admiration') on the proposed measures, and an alternative plan of Irish land policy was worked out by Wood, Devon, Clarendon and Lansdowne at Bowood in December.[94] Wood's antagonism to the proposals was based on the belief that they would distract from the moralist project of compelling Irish landowners to meet their moral obligations. Trevelyan later recorded his view that the plan would have allowed landlords to 'consider themselves absolved of all responsibility'.[95]

Despite adverse cabinet amendments, the Waste Lands Bill remained near the top of the legislative programme for the 1847 session. The Lord Lieutenant continued to regard it as the government's most useful proposal, even if he was not over-optimistic as to its parliamentary prospects.[96] Russell announced the terms of the Bill in his speech on Irish policy of 25 January. One million pounds was to be earmarked for reclamation, with the power of compulsory purchase of wastes valued under a certain amount being vested in the Commissioners of Woods and Forests. These lands would be transferred to the Board of Works, which would undertake drainage, road-making and building works. Lots of 25 to 50 acres in extent would be marked out, and these then either sold or let to tenants for a fixed period (with the intention of ultimate purchase by instalments in the latter case).[97] The Prime Minister declared to the Commons that:

> great advantages will gradually arise from this plan if it be adopted . . . a great number of persons who have hitherto been driven to despair, and many of them into crime, by the great demand for land, will be placed in those holdings and be able to earn a comfortable living by the produce of their labour . . . we shall . . . raise a class of small proprietors, who by their industry and independence will form a valuable link in the future social condition of Ireland.

---

93 Bessborough to Russell, 24 Nov., ibid., fols. 178–9, Bessborough to Labouchere, 23 Nov., Bessborough Papers, F. 336.

94 Bessborough to Russell, 25 August, ibid., 5B, fols. 429–30, Wood to Russell, 9 Dec., ibid., 5F, fols 113–16. Devon made the rather dubious observation at this time that 'C. Wood had a knowledge of Ireland such as few Irishmen possessed', Clarendon to Russell, 10 Dec., ibid., fols. 136–7.

95 Trevelyan, *Irish crisis*, pp. 172–4.

96 Bessborough to Russell, 18 Jan. 1847, Russell Papers, PRO 30/22/6A, fols 171–3. The enthusiasm of some Board of Works officers for waste-land reclamation may have cheered him, see William Henry Smith, *A twelve month's residence in Ireland, during the famine and public works, 1846 and 1847* (London, 1848), pp. 29–41, 47–8.

97 Russell favoured outright purchase, but Bessborough preferred to avoid the danger of minute subdivision by reserving to the government for a period the same powers of management that it had over the Irish crown lands. Neither contemplated returning the improved estates to their original owners, Bessborough to Russell, 28 Dec. 1846, Labouchere to Russell, 24 Dec., Russell Papers, PRO 30/22/5G, fols. 90–2, 47–8.

He argued that a glance at the state of a county like Armagh proved that small-holdings in themselves were not the cause of the social evils of Ireland.[98]

Attacks on the Bill began immediately after Russell's speech. In the Lords, Stanley declared that it was illegitimate for ministers to take 'on themselves the duties of landowners on one hand, and of land speculators on the other.'[99] In the Commons, free-trade radicals were particularly vociferous against the Bill. Bernal Osborne (himself an owner of Irish land) dismissed it as utopian and as 'the most complete bubble a Government had ever brought before Parliament.' He was most alarmed by the proposed size of the reclaimed plots, and stated that 'of all the most astounding doctrines ever laid down by a Minister of the Crown professing to know the condition of Ireland, the assertion that small holdings were not disadvantageous to the country was the most extraordinary.' Roebuck then took up the cry; he 'would protest against all attempts on the part of the Government to become a land-jobber, a corn-jobber, or a road-maker. All these things were beyond the province of a Government.' Hume endorsed this with the statement that waste-land reclamation was 'the wildest speculation ever heard of'.[100]

The Bill was welcomed by Smith O'Brien and by many other Irish MPs,[101] but its fate was sealed by two adverse speeches in the Commons. Replying to Osborne, Wood stated 'I do not attach so much importance to this measure as some hon. Gentlemen seem to do', and he described it merely as an expedient to provide additional employment for the destitute.[102] This was followed by Peel's speech on the government's measures, in which he warned Russell of the dangers of state interference in language strikingly similar to that of the free trade radicals and moralists:

> Let us be liberal – let us be just to Ireland; but depend on it that we shall be incumbering that country, and paralysing her exertions, if we teach her to rely too much on Government assistance. This is true in respect to the cultivation of land, as in respect to the feeling of the people . . . with respect to the cultivation of bogs and waste lands in Ireland, I cannot help thinking that, with the encouragement there has been to employ private capital in the cultivation of land that would repay the outlay, if the Bill for permitting the sale of incumbered estates should be effective, these enterprises for reclaiming waste lands will be

98 *Hans.*, LXXXIX, 442–3 [27 Jan. 1847].

99 Ibid., 383 [27 Jan.]. Irish landlord opinion was generally hostile, see [Isaac Butt], 'Measures for Ireland', *Dublin University Magazine*, XXIX (May 1847), 664.

100 *Hans.*, LXXXIX, 628–30, 647–8, 674 [1 Feb. 1847].

101 Ibid., 641, 719, 721, 737 [1 Feb.: S. O'Brien, 2 Feb.: J. O'Connell, Castlereagh, Barron]. O'Brien was conscious of the cost of reclamation, but followed Scrope in thinking it would prove remunerative, and that work and livelihood for half a million people could be provided, William Smith O'Brien, *Reproductive employment: a series of letters to the landed proprietors of Ireland; with a preliminary letter to Lord John Russell* (Dublin, 1847), pp. 18–23.

102 *Hans.*, LXXXIX, 688 [1 Feb.]. The obvious differences between Wood and Russell were the subject of press comment, *Morning Chronicle*, 4 Feb. 1847.

> undertaken by private individuals if they are likely to be profitable; and if not, then public money would only be thrown away on them.[103]

Commenting on these exchanges, Mill regretted that the government's proposals had fallen short of his recommendations in several regards, while going too far in others. Nevertheless, these errors could be overlooked when set against the criticisms made by the Bill's parliamentary opponents. He was disappointed that the objectors felt under no obligation to refute his (and by extension Russell's) arguments in defence of peasant proprietors, and that both the free-trade radicals and Peel had merely resorted to obsolete commonplaces respecting smallholdings and state intervention. Peel's arguments had no validity, as 'capital *will not* go into Ireland to undertake even the most promising speculations.'[104]

Faced with intransigent opposition in both houses, and with many cabinet ministers, including its supposed sponsor, at best lukewarm, the Bill was suspended and eventually dropped in suspicious circumstances.[105] The *Freeman's Journal* was sure this was the result of political cowardice:

> The Waste Land Improvement Bill was a gorgeous feather in the ministerial cap. The government organs penned a vast deal of social philosophy on the organization of a class of small proprietors; but all their philosophy is smoke before the jibes of Sir Robert Peel. The government has been slinking away from week to week, and at length taken its stand on the most perfect emasculation of the measure. We wish it had been crammed altogether under the table.[106]

The abandonment of the Bill was a victory for dogmatic orthodoxy and left a vacuum at the heart of Russell's remedial programme. This was not the end of the idea of waste-land reclamation; hope was kept alive by the belief of some of its advocates that although Russell had been forced to drop it due to landlord resistance, he would re-introduce it once political conditions were more favourable.[107]

---

103 *Hans.*, LXXXIX, 762–4 [3 Feb.]. This speech was well received in the liberal press, *Examiner*, 6 Feb.

104 *Morning Chronicle*, 5 Feb., Robson, *Collected Works*, XXIV, 1058–62. He had previously argued that Irish moral regeneration could be compromised by excessive state assistance or regulation of the reclaiming peasant, *Morning Chronicle*, 23 Oct., 15 Dec. 1846, ibid., pp. 910–13, 994–7.

105 Hobhouse noted that not all the cabinet had been informed of the decision when Wood announced it to the Commons. He also commented on Russell's unusual 'flatness' of tone when commenting on the matter, Broughton Diary, Add. MS, 43, 750, fols 31–3 [30 April, 1 May]; *Hans.*, XCII, 213, 231–9 [30 April 1846: Wood, Russell].

106 *Freeman's Journal*, 1 May 1847.

107 George Poulett Scrope, *Letters to Lord John Russell MP etc., on the further measures required for the social amelioration of Ireland* (London, 1847), pp. 24–35. In early 1848 the question was indeed reopened following the publication of J. Fagan's *Wastelands of Ireland* (Dublin, 1847), and Thornton's *A plea for peasant proprietors*. Russell declared himself 'still of the opinion that with a full Exchequer the experiment might be tried to the extent of half a

Sympathy for some such measure continued in some sections of the Party. Charles Buller, one of the most radical and able of Russell's junior ministers, was one of the few leading politicians to be converted by the debates of early 1847, and was not afraid to dismiss Peel's arguments with contempt. He believed an extended Poor Law essential but inadequate without the state reclamation of waste lands:

> as yet there are no capitalists in Ireland: as yet English capital will be shy of entering: we have to choose between the Government and the landlords: and such is my opinion of the latter that I would decidedly prefer entrusting the improvement of Ireland to the Boards than to the Landlords . . . improvement in Ireland requires courage: and the Government is at present the only body that will *possess* and will also *give* the necessary courage.[108]

Buller's premature death in 1848 robbed Russell of an important supporter of radical land reform in Ireland; isolated within his own cabinet and with Bessborough increasingly ill, the Prime Minister found his courage ebbing away. In the meantime, Trevelyan justified the moralist case against reclamation in his book *The Irish crisis*. Such substantial state intervention, he argued, not only infringed on property rights, but would turn the people away from self-exertion to dependence on the state. Peasant proprietorship was a delusion and certainly not applicable to Irish conditions; emulation of English social models should be the aim of all policy.[109]

The end of the Foxite era

The other remedial measures prepared by Russell and Bessborough were also swamped by the combined weight of the priority of relief legislation, conservative obstruction in the cabinet, and hostility in parliament. Bessborough and Fortescue remained keen on the old Foxite aim of a broad franchise reform, to be based on a simple occupancy test and a county poor-law rating of either £5 (which would have embraced all tenant ratepayers) or £8.[110] The economic significance of

---

million of money'. Fagan's and Scrope's proposals that poor rates be used for the purpose were, however, firmly rejected, Clarendon to Russell, 9 Jan. 1848, Clarendon Deposit Irish, Bodleian Library, Oxford, letterbook II; Russell to Clarendon, 15 Jan., ibid., box 43; *Hans.*, CII, 386–91, 415–20 [7 Feb. 1849: Scrope, Somerville].

108 Charles Buller, memo: 'Thoughts on the Irish measures of the Government', n.d. (1847), Grey Papers. This opinion was consistent with Buller's radical attitudes towards land policy in the colonies. In 1843 he had shocked Peel by proposing the compulsory purchase and regrant of Canadian lands held by absentees; the Prime Minister had immediately become concerned about the precedent this might pose for Irish land, Peel to Stanley, 25 Sept. 1843, Peel Papers, British Library, London, Add. MS 40,468, fol. 62. For Buller's close political associations with J.S. Mill, see D.A. Haury, *The origins of the Liberal Party and liberal imperialism: the career of Charles Buller, 1806–1848* (New York, 1987), pp. 68–75, 197–8.

109 Trevelyan, *Irish crisis*, pp. 172–8.

110 Bessborough to Russell, 11 Sept. 1846, Fortescue to Russell, 29 Oct., Russell Papers, PRO 30/22/5C, fols 116–19, 5D, fols. 315–18. Bessborough advocated enfranchisement at a fixed

franchise reform was not lost on the cabinet moderates, who believed that it would amount to a recognition of the political 'fixity' of the existing tenant and hence would prove an obstacle to consolidation. Lansdowne feared an encouragement would be offered to subdivision, and even Labouchere was perturbed at the scale of the reform contemplated by Bessborough and Lord Chancellor Brady.[111] Russell again pressed this measure against the opposition of the bulk of the cabinet, and found himself alone in urging that it should have equal priority with relief legislation.[112] Despite Russell's hopes, it was not until 1850 that an Irish franchise measure reached the statute book.

Although no landlord-tenant measure was presented to the cabinet, there is strong evidence that such a bill was prepared during the recess. Bessborough was convinced that this bill 'to be of any use must be on a much more extended scale than before and compulsory on landlords'. This would require very careful drafting, and he was anxious not to press it prematurely or to risk any delay to the progress of the waste lands and relief legislation.[113] Nevertheless, the Lord Lieutenant hoped that it would be ready for parliamentary consideration before Easter, and Brady had prepared a draft by January.[114]

News of this activity provoked Monteagle into lecturing Russell on the dangers of state interference and favouritism towards the tenant class. Social subordination, he wrote, was the firm ground on which English society was built; the task of government was solely to uphold and enforce this. In Ireland, however:

> no subordination exists – either in the sense . . . of the organic relation between different classes, nor in the sense of the moral quality which the existence of that relation produces in society at large. The long continuance of political evils, brought by legislation into every detail of life, has produced a social state in which every class of society is isolated and looks upon its neighbours with distrust. The labourer hates the farmer – The farmer fears the labourer, and alternatively bullies and cajoles the landlord – The gentry make their political grievances the stalking horse for their own jobbing; and the (so-called) Government panders in turn to the vices of every class: intoxicating the labourer at one time with promises of the wonders to be atchieved [sic] by conciliation, betraying the

---

rateable value to do away with the complicated and corrupt registration process, and hence to relieve the small farmer from the conflicting influences of landlord and priest, Bessborough to Russell, 20 Nov., ibid., 5E, fols. 170–1.

111 Lansdowne to Russell, 1 Nov., ibid., 5E, fols. 1–2, Labouchere to Russell, 6 Nov., ibid., fols. 30–1.

112 Broughton Diary, Add. MS 43,749, fols 60, 67 [31 Oct., 11 Nov.]; Grey Diary, 18 Nov., Grey Papers.

113 Bessborough to Russell, 11 Sept., 27 Oct., Russell Papers, PRO 30/22/5C, fols. 116–19, 5D, fols. 312–14.

114 Bessborough to Russell, 8 Dec., ibid., 5F, fols. 98–9, Redington to Labouchere, 12 Jan. (1847), Bessborough Papers, F. 337.

> farmers by hopes of impossible results of fixity of tenure and bribing leading politicians and demagogues on either side as may merit its short sighted policy.

State intervention thus threatened to destroy the very basis of the necessary post-Famine reconstruction.[115] Although Monteagle was becoming increasingly marginalized within the Party at this time, these sentiments were shared by many moderates.[116]

The outlines of Bessborough's Bill have not survived, but its contents can be inferred from the surviving correspondence. Its scope extended only to farming tenants and not to conacre holders or the smallest cottiers. He believed that the blight had eliminated conacre as a viable source of subsistence, but was convinced that remedial measures had been made all the more necessary as a result. Many of the destitute could be relocated on the reclaimed wastes, but the others would be dependent on increased employment offered by tenant farmers. Irish agricultural regeneration, on which employment was dependent, required a degree of confidence and co-operation between landlord and tenant previously unknown. Bessborough hoped that his Compensation Bill would assist in creating such an environment.[117] Compensation would lead directly to improvement, but this was not Bessborough's only aim; the inclusion, after some deliberation, of a retrospective clause indicated that the Bill was to provide some security for the existing tenantry.[118]

The priority of other parliamentary business, and then Bessborough's debilitating illness from April 1847, led to the Bill's postponement. The frustration felt by many of the Irish members at the government's failure to deliver on Russell's promise was voiced by Sharman Crawford, who introduced his 'Bill to secure the rights of occupying tenants in Ireland' in February. Like Bessborough, Crawford saw cottiers under middle-men and the holders of joint-tenancies as beyond the scope of such legislation, but he defended the small-holding class and spoke in general terms of extending the benefits of 'tenant-right' to them. This was some advance on his previous pronouncements, but his opponents pointed to a certain vagueness in his intentions.[119] Crawford sought to combine in this Bill for the first

115 Monteagle to Russell, 10 Dec. 1846, Monteagle Papers, MS 13,396/9.

116 Senior warned that any law permitting the ejected tenant to claim compensation for improvements made without the landlord's consent 'would undoubtedly produce a state of misery more extensive than that which now exists . . . and less remediable', [N.W. Senior],'Proposals for extending the Irish Poor Law', *Edinburgh Review*, LXXXIV (Oct. 1846), 278–80.

117 Bessborough to Russell, 1 Dec. 1846, 20 Feb. 1847, Russell Papers, PRO 30/22/5F, fols. 38–9, 6B, fols. 104–5.

118 Bessborough to Labouchere, 16 April, Bessborough Papers, F. 336.

119 *Hans.*, LXXXIX, 1157–70 [11 Feb.], XC, 502–3 [25 Feb.]. Some confusion existed in the contemporary debates over the meaning of the word 'cottier'. To Crawford (and presumably to Bessborough), these were men occupying very small subsistence plots and

time mechanisms to enforce both the compensation for improvements and the 'sale of goodwill' implicit in Ulster tenant right, and the regulation of 'fair rents' by valuation.[120] When it became clear that no government bill would be introduced in the session, Crawford decided to proceed with his measure and moved its second reading. Perhaps as a result of his own legislative frustration, Russell wrote to explain the reasons for this postponement, adding that Crawford had been 'very reasonable on the subject', and suggesting that he went on with his Bill.[121] In the Commons Labouchere and Monahan admitted the necessity of some form of intervention, but declared Crawford's proposals too severe on the landed interest. English radicals were divided, and it was defeated by 112 votes to 25.[122] Land reform was deferred yet again, and the radicalization of demands progressed with each delay. By September 1847, Crawford had become convinced that any compromise based on compensation for improvements alone would no longer be adequate.[123]

In May 1847 an era in Anglo-Irish relations came to an end with the deaths of O'Connell and Bessborough. O'Connell's health had been fading rapidly from late 1846, and his physical breakdown was compounded by the mental anguish of being obliged to witness the sufferings of his country while aware of his inability to induce the government to make greater exertions for its relief. The pathos of his last appearance in parliament in February 1847 – to plead for additional assistance for Ireland – has been much remarked upon,[124] but it would be mistaken to write off his political importance prematurely. Despite his growing disillusionment with government policy, O'Connell chose not to come out in opposition to the ministry. For their part, many leading Whigs were convinced of the continuing value of the O'Connellite alliance; Fortescue warned Russell of the danger of a hostile O'Connell, and the Prime Minister regularly defended to the cabinet the continuing (although modest) flow of patronage to the Irish leader.[125] If any complacency began to

---

dependent on day labour for obtaining rent and some food. To many English commentators, however, 'cottiers' meant all tenants under 20–30 acres.

120 *A Bill to secure the rights of occupying tenants in Ireland*, P.P. 1847 (127), IV, 85. Some southern tenants believed the latter demand of greater significance than compensation for improvements, 'Some tenant farmers of Co. Cork' to D. O'Connell, 10 Sept. 1846, O'Connell, *Correspondence*, VIII, 117–18.

121 Russell to Crawford, 26 April 1847, Sharman Crawford Papers, Public Record Office of Northern Ireland, Belfast, D.856/D/89.

122 *Hans.*, XCII, 55–7 [29 April], XCIII, 630–45 [16 June].

123 Crawford to the editor, *Dublin Evening Mail*, reprinted in the *Times*, 22 Sept. 1847. He had previously explained to the tenants of Ulster that while he had initially sought compensation for improvements as the most acceptable measure to parliament, Lincoln's Bill had convinced him that this principle had been conceded only as a means to eradicate the Ulster custom, 'W. Sharman Crawford to the occupying tenants of Ulster', 8 July 1846, *Freeman's Journal*, 11 July 1846.

124 *Hans.*, LXXXIX, 944–5 [8 Feb.]; MacDonagh, *Emancipist*, p. 312.

125 Fortescue to Russell, 17 Nov., Russell to Labouchere, 24 Nov. 1846, Russell Papers, PRO 30/22/5E, fols. 118–20, 174–6.

colour the government's attitude towards O'Connell, it was rudely shattered by Bessborough's warning of the perils of a post-O'Connell Ireland. The Lord Lieutenant's words were prophetic:

> You know that I have always said that during his life and influence nothing would ever occur really to disturb the peace of the country, but I am not at all sure that if he were out of the way Young Ireland with Smith O'Brien at its head would not be wild enough to attempt something by main force – This in the present state of the country would be very troublesome.

Bessborough thought that his son John could be depended on to try to keep things quiet, but that '[Daniel] O'Connell held unlimited power over the lower orders that no man can hold again'.[126]

Bessborough, meanwhile, had retained much of his personal popularity in Ireland. Russell defended him against those in the cabinet who complained of the Lord Lieutenant's 'popular proceedings', and was 'well satisfied that all the blame should be given to us, and all the praise go to you.'[127] The degree to which a distinction was drawn between Bessborough and the government was well expressed in John O'Connell's eulogistic obituary for the Viceroy.[128] The nationalist press also praised the Lord Lieutenant's patriotism, attributing the failure of his relief policy to the fact that 'he was thwarted and counteracted by the despotism of the Home Office, which . . . leaves no freedom of action to Lieutenant or Secretary'.[129]

The Lord Lieutenant's sudden illness and death on 16 May was a major blow to Russell and to his brand of Whiggery, for Bessborough was not only a close personal friend, but had embodied the Foxite tradition of Irish policy.[130] Yet even the moderates lamented his loss as an able minister and an irreplaceable peacemaker and fixer for the party. Hobhouse commented that, although no saint:

---

126 Bessborough to Russell, 20, 24 Feb., ibid., 6B, fols. 104–6, 123–4. Bessborough was sceptical about Clanricarde's call for the government to promote the 'raising up of a powerful liberal party' in Ireland based on landlord connections and the Kildare St Club in the place of Pigot and Redington's connections with popular politicians, Clanricarde to Bessborough, 16 March, Bessborough to Russell, 19 March, Russell Papers, 6B, fols. 254–7, 268.

127 Russell to Bessborough, 13 Nov. 1846, G.P. Gooch (ed.), *The later correspondence of Lord John Russell, 1840–1878* (2 vols., London, 1925), I, 160–1.

128 'Speech of John O'Connell to the Loyal National Repeal Association' (May 1847), in *Notices of the Viceroyalty of the late Earl of Besborough* (Dublin, 1847), pp. 72–5. Bessborough managed to combine his popularity with good relations with the Irish Tories, partly because of his genuine concern for alleviating the pressure of distress, but also for his pronounced hostility to Peel, ibid., p. 69; Greville, *Journal*, II, 426 [4 Nov. 1846].

129 *Freeman's Journal*, 18 May 1847; see also the summary of 21 May, which reprinted commendations of the Viceroy from the *Tipperary Vindicator, Kilkenny Journal, Galway Vindicator* and others.

130 Russell's late correspondence with Bessborough was more than usually emotional, particularly for a man notorious for the coldness and curtness of his letters. See Lady E. Ponsonby to Russell, n.d. (May 1847), Russell Papers, PRO 30/22/6C, fols. 205–6. Hobhouse recorded

> for . . . keeping the political body together, [he] had a tact and success, such as no man in my times has possessed. He leant to the most liberal section of the Whig Party, but being connected by birth and marriage with the most aristocratic and unpopular portion of it, he was of great use in going between the two and preventing dissension – he was exceedingly cool and collected in circumstances of difficulty and was not to be deterred, by scruples and trifles of any kind, from steadily pursuing the object in view.[131]

While his personal loss was regretted, not all ministers lamented the passing of the political principles that Bessborough had stood for.

Greville contrasted the display of popular respect at Bessborough's funeral with what he (inaccurately) dismissed as O'Connell's almost unnoticed demise, yet in political terms the two events were closely connected. With Russell's failure to legislate on any of the promised popular remedial reforms in 1846–7, the personal Bessborough-O'Connell alliance remained virtually the only support for the politics of 'justice to Ireland', and this was being fatally undermined as the effects of the social catastrophe intensified. Only radical popular reform on land and other matters, and a more sympathetic response to the Famine crisis, could have revivified it. O'Connell had placed his trust in this in July 1846, and Bessborough had done his utmost to fulfil his part of the bargain, but it was not enough. The deaths of these two protagonists symbolized the collapse of Foxism as a response to the 'Irish question'.

II CLARENDON, CLEARANCES AND COERCION, 1847–8

The appointment of the Earl of Clarendon as Lord Lieutenant in May 1847 marked a sharp break with the past. Clarendon was emphatically not one of the Foxite circle – his political background was Canningite, and he had risen under the patronage of Lansdowne and Palmerston. He was not close either politically or personally to the Prime Minister; indeed Russell doubted both his honesty and his attachment to Whiggism.[132] This coolness was reflected in the nature of Russell's offer, which, Clarendon confided to his brother-in-law George Cornewall Lewis,

---

that Russell related Bessborough's 'eternal farewell' to the cabinet 'with a faltering voice and much affected', Broughton Diary, Add. MS 43,750, fol. 48 [17 May], and *Hansard* took the rare step of commenting on a parliamentarian's emotional state in its report of Russell's announcement to the Commons of the Viceroy's death, *Hans.*, XCII, 1053 [18 May].

131 Broughton Diary, Add. MS 43,750, fols 49–50 [18 May], Greville, *Journal*, III, 82–7 [7 June]. Both Hobhouse and Greville described Bessborough as 'liberal' in his opinions, meaning that he lent towards the 'popular' side of the Party. This is not to be confused with the supra-party economic liberalism that was then drawing together men like Peel, Clarendon and Monteagle, and towards which Bessborough was hostile.

132 Morpeth Diary, 2 April 1849, Castle Howard Papers, J19/8/20; Mandler, *Aristocratic government*, pp. 215–17, 238–9, 250.

had been made 'in his most cold, short, abrupt, indifferent manner – much as if he was disposing of a tide-waiter's place to an applicant'. Clarendon added that he was only prepared to make the personal sacrifice involved in accepting the post because of the private expressions of confidence he had received from Graham and Peel.[133]

Why, then was he chosen? Prest has suggested that the choice was determined mainly by Russell's desire to win press approval for his Irish policy and at the same time to stem the flow of cabinet leaks to the *Times*.[134] This is plausible, for Russell had been stung by that paper's criticisms, and Clarendon was notorious for his intimacy with its editor, J.T. Delane.[135] The *Times* did become noticeably more friendly towards the government's Irish policy after Clarendon's arrival, although he was less successful in his attempts to get the paper to adopt a more nuanced attitude towards Irish landowners.[136] Yet this is insufficient reason why Russell should have altered course so fundamentally. Russell's correspondence with the parties concerned reveals two more important considerations. The first was his desire to abolish the Lord Lieutenancy and replace it with a fourth Secretary of State. Russell, in common with other leading Whigs and many radicals, had favoured such a reform in principle from the early 1830s; he considered the existing quasi-colonial structure constitutionally anomalous and inefficient in practice, and believed there would be little opposition to its removal after O'Connell's death.[137]

The Prime Minister's initial plan was that his brother the Duke of Bedford should play a ceremonial role during the transition. The Duke was suitable not only because he lacked political ambition and ministerial responsibilities, but perhaps also because Russell wanted to associate his family's name with a reform that he hoped would go far towards making the Union a reality.[138] Bedford, however, was more pessimistic about the timetable for abolition, and with Lansdowne's

---

133 Graham to Clarendon, 22 May 1847, Clar. Dep., c.561/2; Clarendon to Lewis, May 1847, Herbert Maxwell (ed.), *The life and letters of George William Frederick, fourth Earl of Clarendon*, (2 vols., London, 1913), I, 276. Clarendon had little experience of Ireland except for a brief stint in Dublin on customs business in the late 1820s. He had at that time expressed sympathy for Catholic emancipation, but had no ties with Irish popular politics, G.W.F. Villiers, *A vanished Victorian: being the life of George Villiers, fourth Earl of Clarendon 1800–70*, (London, 1938), pp. 61–3.

134 John Prest, *Lord John Russell* (London, 1972), pp. 252–3.

135 Bessborough to Russell, 14 Jan. 1847, Russell Papers, PRO 30/22/6A, fols 140–3; Tom Morley, '"The arcana of that great machine": politicians and the *Times* in the late 1840s', *History*, LXXIII (1988), 38–54.

136 Bedford to Clarendon, 23, 26 Aug. 1847, Clar. Dep. Ir., box 3; *Times*, 29 Sept. 1847; Clarendon to Reeve, 9 May, 19 July 1847, Clar. Dep., c.534/1.

137 Russell memo: 'On the post of Irish Viceroy', n.d. (1847), Russell Papers, PRO 30/22/6H, fols. 372–3; R.B. McDowell, *The Irish administration, 1801–1914* (London, 1964), pp. 65–8. Radical journals called for the ending of the colonial form of government and the firm education of Ireland into responsible local self-government, [James Godkin], 'Ireland and its famine', *British Quarterly Review*, V (May 1847), 504–40.

138 For Russell's opinion of the Viceroyalty of his father, the 6th Duke of Bedford, see above, p. 22.

support persuaded Russell of the inexpediency of taking such a step immediately.[139] Russell postponed but did not abandon his plan, and Clarendon was offered the post on the understanding that he would be the last Viceroy and that he was unlikely to occupy the post for more that three years. Seeing his task as preparing the Irish administration and the country for the belated removal of one of the remaining symbols of Ireland's colonial status, he immediately set about stripping the Viceroyalty of its 'theatrical pomp'.[140]

The question still arises as to why Morpeth, who was very willing to take the position, was passed over.[141] He had recommended himself in typically Foxite terms: 'I think possibly . . . I might be of some use as Lord Lieutenant, especially at such a period. I feel as if I might find in a strength of sympathy for the sufferings of the people a counterpoise to other deficiencies.' His disappointment at being rejected was considerable.[142] After making all allowances for Russell's desire to keep Morpeth at the Woods and Forests during the preparation of important public health reforms, it still appears that this amounted to a Foxite loss of nerve. The fault was not entirely Russell's, for on his deathbed Bessborough himself had recommended Clarendon as his successor.[143] Both feared that Ireland was on the verge of collapse into social and political turmoil and anarchy, and neither believed that the mild-mannered and conciliatory Morpeth was capable of facing this threat. It is also possible that Morpeth's increasing pre-occupation with religious pursuits may have damaged his political prospects.[144]

There was also another side to Clarendon besides his reputation for 'firmness'. As a highly respected and talented minister (with cross-party appeal to all free-traders), he had a degree of political weight in both parliament and the cabinet that Morpeth lacked. While the latter was credited by observers for his popularity and 'instinctive, unfailing honesty of purpose', he had the misfortune 'always to be thought young or immature . . . a sort of parliamentary pupil of Lord John Russell'.[145] Clarendon's position on economic affairs was complex; a moderate liberal linked to the Bowood circle, he was noticeably more optimistic about the benefits of free trade than Lansdowne, and on some matters, such as the Irish

---

139 Greville, *Journal*, III, 80–2 [2–3 May 1847]; Lansdowne to Russell, 5 May, Russell Papers, PRO 30/22/6C, fols 246–7.

140 Lady Clarendon to Clarendon, 13 May, Clar. Dep., c.561/2; Clarendon to Lewis, 24 Aug. 1847, ibid., c.532/1.

141 At one point the *Freeman* was certain that Morpeth would succeed Bessborough, *Freeman's Journal*, 15 May 1847.

142 Morpeth to Russell, 2 May, Russell Papers, PRO 30/22/6C, fols. 211–12; Morpeth Diary, 12 May, Castle Howard Papers, J19/8/14.

143 Duncannon to Russell, n.d. (May 1847), Russell Papers, PRO 30/22/6C, fols. 209–10.

144 Boyd Hilton, 'Whiggery, religion and social reform: the case of Lord Morpeth', *Historical Journal*, XXXVII (1994), 844.

145 G.H. Francis, *Orators of the age* (London, 1847), pp. 206–10.

Poor Law, he veered close to a moralist hostility towards Irish landlordism.[146] Russell may have hoped that, like Labouchere, he would 'go native' in Dublin Castle, and use his political weight to press the views of the Irish administration on the cabinet. Something of this sort did indeed take place in the course of his Viceroyalty, and he came to work closely with Redington and Somerville, two of the most able Irish Whig-Liberals. William Somerville had been close to Bessborough and an adviser on relief policy from early 1847, and replaced Labouchere as Chief Secretary in July, although he was not admitted to the cabinet.[147]

There was, nevertheless, a tangible change in the tone of the Irish administration in May 1847. Clarendon retained most of Bessborough's staff, but adopted a strongly anti-Repeal patronage policy, being keen to make O'Connell's successors 'feel their nothingness'.[148] This antagonism did nothing to offset the bitter electoral struggles between Whig-Liberals and Repealers during the summer of 1847. Administrators of Foxite sympathies, such as Alexander MacDonnell, expressed great disappointment at the change in policy. He told his old friend Morpeth that 'the feelings for you were very strong, especially with the common people – alas they have no voice.'[149]

Agitation revived, 1847–8

Clarendon found himself beset with problems on his arrival. External pressure forced the question of landlord-tenant relations to the forefront of political attention. In the course of 1847 the agitation for tenant right underwent a revival, as tenant associations sprang up in a number of localities and demands for land reform became ever shriller in popular newspapers and pamphlets. Many small farmers were determined to consume their own corn and withhold their rent as a means of avoiding being forced onto relief.[150] Tenant associations focused their

---

146 As early as October 1846 Clarendon had adopted a hard line on relief loans, having convinced himself that Irish landlords were 'unscrupulous selfish greedy needy jobbers', Clarendon to Lewis, 1 Oct. 1846, Clar. Dep., c.532/1.

147 Bessborough to Russell, 2 Jan. 1847, Russell Papers, PRO 30/22/6A, fols. 19–20. Somerville was known as a practitioner of tenant right on his County Meath estate, *Dublin University Magazine*, XXXI (April 1848), p. 512.

148 Clarendon to Clanricarde, 13 Aug. 1847, Clanricarde Papers, bundle 79.

149 MacDonnell to Morpeth, 24 May 1847, Castle Howard Papers, J19/1/43/89. MacDonnell, who had been appointed resident Commissioner of National Education in 1839, became increasingly disillusioned with the new style of Irish administration. He wrote in early 1849: 'The Government is composed of excellent and able men individually, but the Whigs, naturally censorious, complain that it wants a central soul to attract – to warm – to give system and motion to our party. There is some truth in this. The thing cannot stand long in this state.' MacDonnell to Morpeth, 17 Jan. 1849, ibid., J19/1/46/79.

150 Mr Russell to Mr Radcliffe, 15 Aug. 1846, *Correspondence from July 1846 to January 1847, relating to the measures adopted for the relief of distress in Ireland . . . (Board of Works series)*, P.P. 1847 [764], L, 60–1. This strategy was widely adopted from autumn 1846, but the consequence of direct confrontation with the landlords was delayed by the rules of legal process.

attention on demands for large abatements from the landlords, and for legislative interference to secure 'fair rents' and 'fixity'.[151]

Three elements gave added importance to this local agitation. The first was the support it received from much of the Catholic clergy. Not only were parish priests frequently involved in local organization, but the prelates as a body addressed a memorial to the Lord Lieutenant on the subject in October, declaring that tenant protection should have primacy over other measures for conciliation and relief, and invoking a social morality higher than that of the rights of landed property.[152] Clarendon observed that MacHale was the author of the paper and principal spokesman for the bishops on this subject, but that he and the rest of the deputation seemed most conciliatory and genuinely anxious to see the government act.[153] Nevertheless, the memorial embodied a more critical attitude towards the existing land structure widespread in Catholic thinking in both Ireland and England in the later 1840s.[154]

Disappointment at government inaction later pushed considerable sections of the clergy into agrarian agitation. This operated at a number of levels. The *Dublin Review*, the intellectual organ of Irish Catholicism, ran a number of articles calling for major land reforms. To Jonathan Duncan, the Famine had been 'wisely and mercifully inflicted to arouse us to a sense of duty', and to warn the government that the sin of indifference would be punished. He argued that the only way to prevent the complete disintegration of Irish society was for the state to promote the break-up of bankrupt estates into small plots within the reach of yeomen farmer-proprietors, to grant to the other peasant farmers perpetual leases at fair rents, and to guarantee allotments to the remaining agricultural labourers.[155]

At a more popular level, the clergy were energetic in promoting tenant organization in the countryside from later 1847. Archdeacon Laffan told a meeting at Cashel in November that 'landlordism was the demon that blasted what was meant for happiness – [a] landlordism which, without mercy, would level the hovels of the poor man – which had sent the bone and sinew of the land to fertilize and enrich the forests and prairies of America – which had sent the poor man to starve in workhouses, or to die by the road side beneath the canopy of Heaven.'[156] His insistence that his audience adhere to constitutional methods of protest was questioned by the Viceroy, and dismissed by the English press, which

151 T.P. O'Neill, 'The Irish land question, 1830–50', *Studies*, XLIV (1955), 332–5; *Times*, 4 Sept. 1847.

152 Memorial of the Catholic archbishops and bishops of Ireland, 21 Oct. 1847, *Freeman's Journal*, 26 Oct.

153 Clarendon to Russell, 26 Oct., Russell Papers, PRO 30/22/6F, fols. 223–6.

154 See also James Hole, 'Social science, lecture V: the land', *The Truth-Seeker and Present Age: a Catholic Review*, I (1849), 421–43. Hole echoed J.S. Mill, but preferred leasing by the state to peasant proprietory.

155 [Jonathan Duncan], 'Tenure of land in Ireland', *Dublin Review*, XXIV (June 1848), 350–80.

156 *Freeman's Journal*, 15 Nov. 1847.

denounced such language as incitement to murder.[157] No doubt the participation of some priests was motivated by a desire to deflect popular anger away from the seizure of crops and animals,[158] but the genuine attachment of many of the clergy to land reform should not be underestimated.

The second worrying aspect of the agitation was its strength in Ulster. Sharman Crawford's campaigns had directed attention in the north to the perceived threat to the Ulster custom, and in 1847 the northern movement took shape under the leadership of Dr James McKnight, editor of the *Londonderry Standard*. Although never fully united, the movement won strong support from many of the Presbyterian clergy and had a high political profile.[159] Concerns about social unrest led some landowners to attend tenant right meetings, such as that at Coleraine in March 1847, but it is evident that the majority of tenants sought not merely the defence of the 'custom', but the realization of Sharman Crawford's proposals for rents set by valuation.[160]

Making the case for the legalization of tenant right, McKnight argued from both the history of the plantation settlement and utilitarian social philosophy that the tenant had a right to claim legislative recognition of 'fair' or 'plantation' rents, fixed by the value of the unimproved land, as well as to the 'free sale' of his 'interest' on giving up his holding.[161] He advocated the extension of tenant right throughout Ireland as an act of social and moral justice, and as the only effectual way of curbing political agitation and agrarian outrage. This alone would unlock the productive powers of the soil and eradicate destitution.[162] His arguments were underpinned by a deeply held belief in the providential ordering of society. In the process of confiscating the divinely ordained right of the labourer and tenant to the fruits of their own labour, the landowner had abrogated his social trusteeship and invited retribution. Agrarian outrage, while regrettable, could thus be seen in the abstract

---

157 *Times*, 17 Nov. 1847; Clarendon insisted that this speech be brought to the attention of the Pope, Clarendon to Palmerston, 21 Nov. 1847, Palmerston (Broadlands) Papers, Hartley Library, University of Southampton, GC/CL/480.

158 'Ireland – open-air peasant demonstration', *Examiner*, 23 Oct. 1847.

159 B.A. Kennedy, 'The tenant-right agitation in Ulster, 1845–50', *Bulletin of the Irish Committee for Historical Sciences*, 34 (1944), 2–5.

160 *Freeman's Journal*, 23 March 1847.

161 McKnight claimed that northern landowners had broken the plantation contract and had sought illegitimately to assert a feudal conception of proprietorship, while the state had abrogated its duty to wield superintending powers. His reading may have relied on poor history, but provided a powerful legitimating myth for both the defence of the custom and the intervention of the state, James McKnight, *The Ulster tenants' claim of right, or, land ownership a state trust* (Dublin, 1848), pp. 25–36. For an orthodox critique of this account of the origins of the custom, see Conway E. Dobbs, *Some observations on the tenant-right of Ulster* (Dublin, 1849).

162 McKnight, *Ulster tenants' claim of right*, pp. 59–60. Similar claims were made by other advocates of extending 'tenant right', [W. Gray], 'A visit to the barony of Farney. What can the landlords do?', *Freeman's Journal*, 7 April 1847.

as divine judgement for landlord crimes. Indeed, the Famine might itself be a visitation against Britain for imposing the penal laws and subsequently failing to grant justice to the tenantry.[163]

North-eastern Ulster began to recover from famine conditions in 1848, but exhaustion of savings and falling prices combined to severely depress the market value of tenant right. McKnight's movement expanded as smallholder frustration increased and landlords took advantage of the situation to evict cheaply.[164] 'Tenant right' was always subject to a variety of definitions, but in the difficult conditions of the later '40s, it came to acquire a more advanced meaning to Ulster radicals (and their southern imitators). Agitators who demanded under this head that landlords 'grant to their tenantry, without exception, fixed tenures in their lands', aroused the anger of conservative Ulster commentators, who insisted on a strict and localized definition of the 'Ulster custom'.[165] Edward Maginn, the Catholic Bishop of Derry and one of the most radical members of the hierarchy, proposed an alliance of the Ulster and southern tenant movements in 1847,[166] but there was a lack of the organizational coherence in the south, and little co-operation before 1850.

A further cause for government concern was the danger of a coalescence of land agitation with the radical nationalism of Young Ireland. Attention was focused on the well-publicized meeting at Holycross, County Tipperary, in September 1847, organized by James Fintan Lalor and Michael Doheny. Lalor had already brought himself to national attention through a series of articles published in the *Nation* from April to June 1847, in which he called in apocalyptic language for a tenant-based social revolution.[167] The propositions Lalor advocated in Tipperary fell far short of this, but the *Times* still took the trouble to denounce them as spoiling any real case the Tipperary tenants had against their landlords.[168] What this 'extremism'

---

163 McKnight, *Ulster tenants' claim of right*, pp. 8, 60–1. Duncan echoed this providentialist point in the *Dublin Review*, 'Tenure of land', pp. 350, 356–7.

164 Frank Wright, *Two lands on one soil: Ulster politics before Home Rule* (Dublin, 1996), pp. 128–32, 165–76.

165 *Belfast Newsletter*, 12 Oct. 1847.

166 Maginn to W.H. Trenwith, 4 May, *Freeman's Journal*, 18 May 1847. Trenwith was honorary secretary of the Cork Tenant League.

167 L. Fogarty (ed.), *James Fintan Lalor: patriot and political essayist – collected writings* (Dublin, 1947 edn), pp. 7–50. Lalor argued that divine providence had now dissolved Irish society, and that failure to grasp the opportunity for revolution would be suicidal: '[T]his people has been for ages past . . . a dark spot in the path of the sun. Nature and Heaven can bear it no longer. To any one who either looks to an immediate directing Providence, or trusts to a settled course of natural causes, it is clear that this island is about to take existence under a new tenure; or else that nature has issued her decree – often issued heretofore against nations and races, and ever for the same crime – that one other imbecile and cowardly people shall cease to exist, and no longer cumber the earth.' Ibid., p. 11. These providentialist sentiments (if not the objects sought) bear an uncanny similarity to those of Trevelyan and Wood.

168 *Times*, 14, 22 Sept. 1847.

consisted of was a call to agitate for the extension of 'the tenant-right of Ulster' to the south as a means of securing fixity of tenure and fair rents to the tenants. Lalor's use of the term departed some way from Sharman Crawford's initial emphasis on 'improvement', and was based on his own highly personal agrarian philosophy.[169] This amounted to an escalation of tenant demands, and demonstrated how far Crawford's ideas had been disseminated throughout the country, but it was the call to agitate for security in general, and not Lalor's somewhat abstract resolutions, that the Holycross assembly found attractive. This was demonstrated by the rapidity with which the meeting broke up into conflicting factions when William Conner arrived, denouncing 'tenant-right' as a delusion, declaring Lalor's resolutions 'dubious', and advocating the attainment of 'security' through the arbitration of rents by valuation and enforcing 'perpetuity' through direct pressure on the landlords.[170] Lalor's career as a practical land agitator ended amid the ensuing fracas.

Paradoxically, some landowners expressed a degree of satisfaction at Lalor's language. Clanricarde commented that by defining 'tenant right' in terms which appeared to exclude the cottier and labourer (Lalor had appealed to these classes to give auxiliary support to the cause, but only in return for a promise of more secure employment), Lalor had avoided that 'vague declamation raising extravagant and undefined expectations' wherein Clanricarde perceived the real threat to property.[171] Conner also believed Lalor hostile to the interests of cottiers, and attacked him and his father as oppressive middlemen, a theme later echoed by Whig-Liberal spokesmen in the Commons.[172]

Despite its fissiparous tendencies, the land agitation of 1847–8 had considerable political impact. Although there was an initial hesitation on the part of both John O'Connell and most of the Young Ireland leadership, while both sought to conciliate the elusive 'patriotic gentry',[173] the developing agitation was of increasing significance locally, and played a role in the 1847 general election. Pressure was put on Irish Whig-Liberals to declare their support for the principle on the hustings. It was reported that Somerville at Drogheda, and Clarendon's private secretary,

169 David N. Buckley, *James Fintan Lalor: radical* (Cork, 1990), pp. 32–43.

170 *Freeman's Journal*, 20 Sept. 1847. Conner's inveterate hostility after 1843 to the 'swindlers' of both Young and Old Ireland played a part in causing this fracas. See William Conner, *Two letters to the editor of the Times on the rackrent oppression of Ireland* (Dublin, 1846), pp. i–xviii.

171 Clanricarde to Maunsell, 14 Sept., Clanricarde Papers, bundle 73.

172 *Freeman's Journal*, 20 Sept. 1847; *Hans.*, C, 1005 [29 July 1848: Somerville]. See also *Examiner*, 25 Sept. 1847.

173 Land was a divisive issue within the Young Ireland ranks, and Gavan Duffy in particular was hostile to Lalor's ideas. See Charles Gavan Duffy, *Four years of Irish history, 1845–1849* (London, 1883), pp. 476–7. Smith O'Brien, meanwhile, looked in vain for landlord agreement on an effective measure of tenant compensation, *Reproductive employment*, pp. 12–17.

Torrens McCullagh, at Dundalk, had endorsed 'tenant right'. Both had very tight contests, and the popular press made considerable efforts to mobilize the borough electorates in support of a tenantry reduced to the condition of 'mere serfs of the landlord'.[174] Somerville later argued that what he had said on the hustings had been distorted by the Irish press, which had made it appear 'as if I were impregnated with all the nonsense which is daily put forth by a hundred writers with reference to it'. Yet he insisted privately that 'something must be attempted' to satisfy public opinion.[175] Torrens McCullagh was prepared to go further at the hustings, declaring that 'on the question of tenant-right he perfectly coincided with Mr. Sharman Crawford'.[176]

The events of 1847, and particularly the growing Young Ireland challenge, also impressed the necessity of action on the land question on the 'Old Irelanders'.[177] John O'Connell, anxious to fill his father's mantle and aware of clerical approval for land reform, appeared in October with other leading Repealers at a tenant right meeting at Kilmacthomas, County Waterford, and called for the extension of 'tenant-right' throughout Ireland. He was joined by Sir Winston Barron, a landowning Whig-Liberal and defeated candidate for Waterford city in 1847.[178] Earlier in the year O'Connell had advocated in print the radical proposal of extending the principle of tenant right (which he defined as the payment by the outgoing to the incoming occupier of 10–20 years' purchase value of the holding) to sub-tenants under farmers, as part of a broader remedial package,[179] but he proved an uncertain leader, and lacked the political ability to establish himself at the head of the reform movement.

---

174 Maunsell to Clanricarde, 1 Sept., Clanricarde Papers, bundle 79; *Belfast Vindicator*, reprinted *Times*, 4 Sept. McCullagh was beaten by three votes, but seated after a petition.

175 Somerville to Clanricarde, 13 Sept., Clanricarde Papers, bundle 79. The *Times* had reported him as saying: 'He was not, he candidly admitted, in favour of what was termed tenant right. (Groans) Yet who would tell him that he was not in favour of the tenants' rights, when he told them that he was in favour of granting full compensation to tenants for all the improvements they made . . . he would turn his most earnest attention to the subject, and if he succeeded in accomplishing such an important task to the satisfaction of the country he would indeed feel that he had not held his office in vain. (Loud cheers)', *Times*, 4 Aug. 1847.

176 Ibid., 7 Aug. 1847. McCullagh's statement of independence proved to be more than rhetorical; in 1850 he spoke strongly and voted against a land bill that appeared to augment landlord powers, *Hans.*, CVIII, 897–9 [6 Aug. 1850].

177 See M.R. O'Connell, 'John O'Connell and the Great Famine', *Irish Historical Studies*, XXV (1986), 138–43.

178 *Times*, 27 Oct. 1847. Barron regained sufficient popular support to retake his seat in a three-cornered by-election the following March. Supporters of Thomas Wyse, the other defeated Whig-Liberal in 1847, had claimed that he too supported the 'wholesome principle of tenant right', Carew to Clarendon, 5 Sept. 1847, Clar. Dep. Ir., box 8.

179 John O'Connell, 'Ireland and her present necessities', *Tait's Edinburgh Magazine*, XIV (Jan. 1847), 39–44.

Interest in Irish land reform was also reviving in England. Poulett Scrope brought the specific question of tenant right before English public opinion in the autumn of 1847. He stated that 'having anxiously watched the progress of opinion and the current of events by which some immediate settlement of relations between landlord and tenant is rendered imperatively necessary to avert agrarian revolution or civil war', he was now prepared to go further than compensation for improvements. This would be useful if it embraced retrospective improvements and if landlord permission to improve was not required, but it should be combined with the principle of recognizing 'in Ulster at least' compensation for the tenant's goodwill.[180] Some English radicals went further; Thomas Alcock, MP for Surrey east, called for the universal legalization of the custom as a 'matter of "justice to England", considering the taxes spent for Ireland'.[181] Like McKnight, Alcock believed that land reform would remove the need for British financial aid to Ireland, but he agreed with Scrope that tenant right was not as a panacea, but an essential part of a programme of remedial measures, including an encumbered estates act.

The combination of Irish agitation with British radical sympathy alarmed landlords in both countries. Clanricarde was worried by Somerville's and McCullagh's speeches, and warned Clarendon that 'a good many of the cleverest men about "the Castle" know little of the rural life of Ireland . . . and I doubt that . . . they have deep respect for the security of Real-property, which is the basis of the entire British political, social and legal constitution.' Parliament could not be trusted to reject such dangerous legislation, as 'there is a feeling of exacerbation in this country against Irishmen, and especially against Irish landlords, which would enable Parliament to pass the most fatal laws, and to confiscate Irish property to any extent.'[182] Like many of his fellow landlords, Clanricarde believed that legal reform was required for the protection of landlords' rights against tenant evasions; legislation ought to define the contractual duties of each party more clearly, and facilitate their enforcement. He directed the Lord Lieutenant's attention to Lord Westmeath's memorial on the subject, fully conscious that Westmeath, with his supporters, Brougham and Beaumont, was quite candid in admitting that greater powers were required to clear cottiers from Irish estates.[183]

Many landlords saw themselves as victims of a hostile conspiracy in England, 'where public opinion is artfully and most unjustly governed to [their] prejudice',

---

180 George Poulett Scrope, *Letters to Lord John Russell MP . . . on the further measures required for the social amelioration of Ireland* (London, 1847), pp. 37–50 [letter iv, 15 Oct. 1847].

181 Thomas Alcock, *The tenure of land in Ireland considered* (London, 1848), p. 30.

182 Clanricarde to Clarendon, 6 Sept. 1847, Clar. Dep. Ir., box 9; Clanricarde to Somerville, 17 Sept., Clanricarde Papers, bundle 76.

183 Clanricarde to Clarendon, 16 Aug., Clar. Dep. Ir., box 9; *Hans.*, LXXXIV, 837–40 [10 March 1846], XCI, 1039–47 [20 April 1847]. Support for pro-landlord legal reform was voiced in [John Anster], 'The state of Ireland', *North British Review*, VI (Feb. 1847), 509–50, and 'Agrarian outrages in Ireland', ibid., VII (Aug. 1847), 505–38.

and they consequently sought to combine 'for the assertion of their rights'.[184] Even in the north there were fears that under the cover of 'tenant right' the tenants were conspiring for the complete abolition of rent.[185] While some polemicists upheld the necessity of high rents if employment in tillage was to continue,[186] others used providentialist arguments to justify the necessity of eviction. One pamphleteer was sure that the 'Gracious Being, who wounds that he may heal' had sent the 'present afflictive dispensation [which] will lead to progressive improvement in social conditions and even to national prosperity'. The disappearance of the potato had made possible the 'depopulation' of estates and the consolidation of all farms under 30 Irish acres, these being the essential precondition for improvement.[187] One ultra-Protestant Ulsterman expressed the same idea in more retributive terms in 1850; to punish the indolence of the squatters and the murders committed by the poor, 'God, the all-wise and all-powerful ruler of the earth, has stopped the growth of ignorance and crime, by suspending for a time the laws of vegetable life, and the potato will no longer grow to feed an uneducated and wicked population . . . we must be content with the wise arrangement of Providence, and adopt our course of action to the altered circumstances of society.'[188]

Whiggery and tenant right

Clarendon had initially expressed uncertainty about the issue, but with Russell's encouragement he now felt obliged to proceed with legislative interference.[189] He assured Clanricarde that the state of the public mind in Ireland made legislation unavoidable, and that it was best that the government take its time to draw up its plan and prepare public opinion to accept it. What he himself envisaged was a moderate measure, not dissimilar to Lincoln's 1846 Bill:

> My notion is to vitiate no existing contract, to give every facility to landlords for improving their estates whatever may be the tenure under which they are let but at the same time to encourage tenants to do so by securing to them just compensation for their outlay to define the rights of each with greater clearness than at present and to provide for those rights being more cheaply and quickly enforced.[190]

---

184 [Samuel O'Sullivan], 'Irish landlords – the Land Commission report', *Dublin University Magazine*, XXX (Oct. 1847), 481–96.

185 *Erne Packet*, cited in *Examiner*, 9 Oct. 1847.

186 [Anon.], *Ireland in reality, or the true interest of the labourer* (Dublin, 1848).

187 Henry Goold, *Thoughts on a judicious disposition of land in Ireland* (London, 1847); see also [Anster], 'The state of Ireland', p. 550.

188 [R. McCollum], *Sketches of the highlands of Cavan and of Shirley Castle, in Farney, taken during the Irish Famine* (Belfast, 1856), pp. 18–19. These sketches were first published in the Cavan *Anglo-Celt* in 1850–1.

189 Clarendon to Lewis, 24 Aug., Clar. Dep., c.532/1; Russell to Clarendon, 23 Sept., Clar. Dep. Ir., box 43.

190 Clarendon to Clanricarde, 9 Sept., ibid., letterbook I.

By the end of September the Irish executive had produced the heads of a bill on compensation for improvements which Clarendon thought steered successfully 'between the wild and ignorant exigencies of the tenants, and the reasonable alarm of landlords'.[191]

Divisions within the government over the proposed bill soon became evident. Lord Chancellor Brady was unhappy with the abandonment of the retrospective clauses of Bessborough's Bill (essential for the protection of existing tenants) and with the alteration of the arbitration system. Somerville's doubts were also evident to cabinet observers when he presented the Bill in October.[192] The cabinet's response was largely hostile; the compulsory clauses were struck out, and the remaining voluntary clauses were retained only because Clanricarde and Grey agreed it expedient that something be proposed. Russell appears not to have taken a major role in these discussions, but confessed his apprehensions to Clarendon. He felt unable to answer Lansdowne's firm objection to the removal of the landlord's right to veto any 'improvement' for which he would later be expected to pay compensation, and he could not see how the Bill could protect the small tenant from eviction.[193] Clarendon was deeply offended by what he took to be the summary rejection of his Bill, the first he had recommended as Viceroy. He wrote to Russell with bitter sarcasm (a register which was to become his preferred mode of expression when in Ireland), warning that Lincoln would outbid them if no restitution was made.[194]

The Clarendon-Russell correspondence of this period reveals their very different attitudes towards Irish policy in general, and land in particular. Both stood outside the cabinet mainstream and sought to impose their will upon the majority; both thought legislative interference essential, but they began from different premises and reached for conflicting solutions. Whereas Russell was open to heterodox economic views, and felt obliged to respond to popular political demands, Clarendon felt contempt for both. To the Lord Lieutenant, J.S. Mill's doctrines were 'pestilent and fallacious . . . he is half mad, but that is not known and his name carries a certain authority with it'; O'Connell and his allies had, he assured G.C. Lewis, taken up land agitation out of cynical opportunism.[195] Only their shared frustration with the cabinet and the Viceroy's conviction that inaction was not an option pushed Russell and Clarendon into an uneasy coalition.

---

191 Clarendon to Russell, 25 Sept., ibid. This draft was circulated to friendly landlords; Clanricarde declared it was 'very innocent and will be thought of little value', and called for stronger powers to enforce agreements. Other landlords were also lukewarm, Clanricarde to Clarendon, 9 Oct., ibid., box 9; Clancarty to Clarendon, 4 Nov., ibid., box 8. However, Lord Sligo recognized that it would do little for the smallholders of the west, and approved the draft as an aid to consolidation, Sligo to Clarendon, 29 Nov., ibid., box 57.

192 Brady to Clarendon, 12 Oct., ibid., box 2; Broughton Diary, Add. MS 43,751, fol. 33 [14 Oct.].

193 Ibid., fols. 33–4 [15 Oct.]; Russell to Clarendon, 10, 15 Oct., Clar. Dep. Ir., box 43.

194 Clarendon to Russell, 18, 23 Oct. 1847, ibid., letterbook I.

195 Clarendon to Lewis, 2 Aug. 1848, Clar. Dep., c.532/1; Clarendon felt more comfortable with an anti-tenant right article in the *Dublin University Magazine*, which he erroneously

Clarendon had been appointed as the man most capable of containing trouble in Ireland. His first months in the country were remarkably quiet, but as the autumn wore on, famine-related social tensions increased. Landlord-tenant conflict took two forms. Middling farmers, who had managed to retain savings from the sale of their grain, were anxious to avoid the demand for unabated rents due at the Michaelmas gale, which came on top of the unprecedented burdens of heavy poor rates and the payment of money wages for agricultural labour. Many were eager to emigrate to America and were prepared to fight to safeguard their remaining capital from landlord depredations until the sailing season of 1848. The second and much larger group consisted of smallholders and cottiers, many of whom were faced with wholesale eviction or clearance, often as 'middleman' leases fell in.

'Improving' landlords had long been keen to consolidate and re-organize their estates; the Famine appeared to many as an opportunity to implement these changes. Other landlords and agents who had previously shown less interest also now recognized a number of incentives to clearance, and mounting debts and encumbrances raised the threat of the loss of their properties and hardened many against making abatements or forgiving arrears. Landlords often blamed government policy, particularly the £4-rating clause of the Poor Law, for their own harshness.[196] Perhaps typical was the relatively humane Marquess of Sligo, who began clearing the pauper tenantry of his Mayo estate in autumn 1848. In such areas, he pleaded, 'ejectments may not be the voluntary act of a landowner but sure consequences of laws and famine'. Swamped with personal debt and finding himself in receipt of little rent, he felt himself 'under the necessity of ejecting or being ejected'.[197] Evictions rose rapidly to unprecedented levels in 1847, and then increased steadily to an all-time peak of over 100,000 persons in 1850 (nearly three quarters of whom were not re-admitted). These official government figures collected by the constabulary from 1849 did not include those who surrendered possession 'voluntarily' to emigrate or as a result of the quarter-acre clause.[198]

The two classes of tenant frequently found themselves in conflict. Middling to large farmers had some weight in the boards of guardians and an interest in keeping down the poor rates, while cottiers and labourers had an interest in combining to push up the price of their labour and (in the wake of the partial potato revival of

---

attributed to Samuel Ferguson, [Samuel O'Sullivan], 'Tenant Right', *DUM*, XXXI (April 1848), 498–512.

196 *Hans.*, C, 92–3 [4 July 1848: L. O'Brien].

197 Sligo to Clarendon, 19 Nov. 1848, Clar. Dep. Ir., box 57; Sligo to Monteagle, 8 Oct. 1848, Monteagle Papers, MS 13,398/5. Sligo had previously expressed sympathy for the plight of the cottiers, Marquess of Sligo, *A few remarks and suggestions on the present state of Ireland* (London, 1847).

198 See James S. Donnelly, 'Landlords and tenants', in Vaughan, *N.H.I.*, *V*, 336–42; 'Mass eviction and the Great Famine', in Cathal Póirtéir (ed.), *The Great Irish Famine: the Thomas Davis lecture series* (Cork, 1995), pp. 155–73.

1847) to demand the granting of conacre land. Yet middling farmers, smallholders and cottiers all faced the threat of eviction or distraint and perceived landlordism as a common enemy. Many had in common the political tradition of O'Connellism, with its evocative cross-class articulation of grievances under the umbrella of an inclusive Catholic nationalism. Newspapers stressed the broad social mix at the tenant right meetings of 1847 (the Holycross fracas being an exception owing much to personality clashes). The attraction of the slogan of 'tenant-right' was that it would give either 'fixity' at a fair rent to those who chose to stay, or guarantee a reasonable emigration dowry on surrender of a holding. However, as evictions increased in later 1847 it was inevitable that more direct action would accompany political agitation.

The targets of this agrarian hostility and violence were primarily landlords, their bailiffs and servants, and the incoming tenants on consolidated farms. The geographical concentration of agrarian incidents in Tipperary, Limerick and Clare was interpreted by contemporaries as the consequence of a particularly bitter struggle there between landlords eager to consolidate small farms for pasture, and smallholders seeking to preserve the tillage plots which alone prevented them from 'degenerating into the pauper class'.[199]

This escalating conflict altered the context of the landlord-tenant question. Both Russell and Clarendon believed it augmented the necessity of remedial legislation. Clarendon's aim was to divide the first class of tenants and their supporters from the second by offering the strong farmer a moderate but compulsory protection, and then 'guiding' Irish public opinion into accepting it. Only strong action could protect the rights of property in Ireland from a united anti-landlord agitation: 'Property here is not in a state to be dealt with in an ordinary manner', he confided to Russell, 'It must be roughly handled to be saved.' He believed that Irish landed opinion saw the necessity of such a compromise, and hoped that moderate land reform would 'knock Repeal on the head'.[200]

While Clarendon sought to revive the Peelite strategy of encouraging divisions within the popular movement by means of judicious concessions to moderate interests, Russell continued to see the land question in terms of the Whiggish language of 'justice', and sought to protect the tenantry as a whole from as the injustice of clearance.[201] He agreed with the Lord Lieutenant that the amended Compensation

---

199 *Hans.*, XCV, 332, 435–6 [29 Nov. 1847: Fagan, Scrope]; [Patrick McMahon], 'Measures for Ireland – tillage - waste lands – fixity of tenure', *Dublin Review*, XXV (Dec. 1848), 300–3.

200 Clarendon to Russell, 18, 23 Oct. 1847, Clar. Dep. Ir., letterbook I; Clarendon to Russell, 26 Oct., Russell Papers, PRO 30/22/6F, fol. 226.

201 Clarendon and other ministers were increasingly contemptuous of this Foxite tradition, but hesitated to attack it publicly. An element of farce was introduced in 1848 when the Duke of Bedford bought a horse at the Curragh which its O'Connellite owner had christened 'Justice to Ireland'. Bedford was keen to change the name to something less embarrassing, but felt it advisable to consult Clarendon first. When warned of the political

Bill could do little, but thought that 'yours would be likewise evaded – when the tenant holds at will, notice might be followed by notice to quit at any time.'[202]

By late October Clarendon was becoming convinced that the scale of agrarian outrage necessitated strong coercive legislation, and expressed sympathy for the '*permanent* severe police measures' recommended by his military advisers.[203] Russell was understandably reluctant to abandon the principle on which his government had been formed, and warned that 'this universal war between unfeeling landlords and barbarous tenants is not to be put down by Act of Parliament.'[204] However, as report followed report on the disturbed state of the country it became difficult for the government to remain inactive. Clarendon was aware of the power of the press to sway an uncertain administration, and used his connections with Delane and the *Times*' chief leader-writer Henry Reeve to push a coercive agenda to the forefront.[205]

A storm of British indignation was whipped up by the *Times* and other journals against the Irish 'incubus of terrorism', and for a time moralistic criticisms of Irish landowners took second place to the demand that the 'six millions of Irish . . . accessories both before and after the fact', be disciplined. The press found a *cause célèbre* in the murder of Major Denis Mahon in Roscommon in early November. Mahon, the 'improving' owner of the Strokestown estate, had assisted the emigration to Canada of several hundred tenants, and had evicted over 3,000 others who had refused the offer. His case appeared to unite the *Times*' preoccupations with the need to protect improving landowners, the complicity of the whole Irish community in crime, and the culpable instigation of the Catholic clergy and Repeal politicians.[206] The matter was taken up by more hard-line members of the cabinet; Palmerston expressed sympathy for the exemplary transportation or hanging of agitating priests, singling out as an example Fr McDermott of Strokestown, who was alleged to have denounced Mahon from the pulpit.[207]

---

inexpediency of doing so, he let the horse retain its name, but later found it difficult to suppress a certain glee when 'Justice to Ireland' fell in an English steeplechase, Bedford to Clarendon, 23 June 1848, Clar Dep. Ir., box 3.

202 Russell to Clarendon, 21, 28 Oct. 1847, ibid., box 43.

203 Clarendon to Russell, 30 Oct., ibid., letterbook I; Clarendon to Grey, 4 Nov., ibid.; Maj. Gen. T.E. Napier to Sir E. Blakeney, 14 Nov., Russell Papers, PRO 30/22/6G, fols. 116–23; Clarendon to Lewis, 21 Nov. 1847, Maxwell, *Clarendon*, I, 285.

204 Russell to Clarendon, 8 Nov., Clar. Dep. Ir., box 43.

205 Greville to Clarendon, 16, 24 Nov. 1847, Clar. Dep., c.521; Clarendon to Reeve, 20 Dec., ibid., c.534/1. Clarendon's mother, Theresa Villiers, was also active in informing Reeve of the Viceroy's desire for firm measures, Mrs Villiers to Reeve, 4, 29 Dec. 1847, ibid.

206 *Times*, 10, 17 Nov. 1847. See also *Examiner*, 13 Nov. 1847.

207 Palmerston to Minto, 3 Dec. 1847, Anthony Evelyn Ashley, *The life of Henry John Temple, Viscount Palmerston: 1846–1865* (2 vols, 2nd edn, London, 1876), I, 44–6; Palmerston to Clarendon, 13 Nov. 1847, Clar. Dep., c.524. For the significance of the Mahon-McDermott case in British-Vatican relations, see Donal A. Kerr, *'A nation of beggars'?: priests, people and politics in Famine Ireland 1846–52* (Oxford, 1994), pp. 92–100.

Not all were swept along on the retributive bandwagon. Russell denied that there was any escalation of violence in Ireland, and had Somerville state the case against Mahon to the cabinet.[208] He acknowledged only with great reluctance the strength of the calls for coercion, and declared that he could accept it only if it met 'some immediate purpose and at the same time a general groundwork can be laid for permanent improvement'. He was unwilling to suppress the 'violent symptoms' of an 'organic disorder' that had been raging since 1760, for this would only encourage proprietors to commit 'more atrocities than before'. It was not the place of government to save them from the consequences of their own actions as a class – the encouragement of a potato-fed pauper population for profit in the past, and the attempted clearance of these masses in the present. Yet, if the state was obliged to intervene to preserve order, it must be in a strictly even-handed way. Cottiers should be protected as a *quid pro quo* for any coercion, but compensation for improvements would be inadequate, as the 'improvements' of most small-holders were of negligible financial value. This is the context for Russell's often misquoted aside that 'you might as well propose that the landlord should compensate the rabbits for the burrows they have made on his land'. Russell instead grasped for a solution of startling radicalism:

> [I]t seems to me that a remedy for this evil must strike deeper and wider – it must embrace all who have occupied the land for a certain number of years (say five) and must give them something like the tenant right of Ulster. This, I know, is a transfer of property – But it is founded on a right acknowledged in the North, the most peaceful and orderly province of Ireland – It has therefore a foundation in custom, which is a great advantage.

This amounted to something less than the full concession of Ulster tenant right, but it was to extend to the poorest cottier, holding anything above a quarter of an acre. He admitted that his plan would be thought objectionable, but he reminded Clarendon of his own view that 'the evil is deep-seated, and by ordinary means irremediable'. Russell agreed that the separatist threat should be stifled 'in the cradle by large measures of redress', but he held that it was the poorer tenants – whose discontents had fuelled the popular politics of the 1840s – who must be conciliated.[209]

This amounted to a conceptual leap for a British minister, the acknowledgement of the 'Irish' principle of dual ownership in the soil and the limitation of private property in land. No member of the British political elite had previously

208 Somerville reported that 'Of the gentlemen lately murdered *one* was a good man – the others had made themselves hated for one cause or another. Major Mahon was harsh and fearless – he had sent 900 of his tenants to America of whom 300 were lost in one of the vessels – and this was imputed to design', Broughton Diary, Add. MS 43,751, fols 52, 54. [17, 19 Nov. 1847].

209 Russell to Clarendon, 10 Nov., Clar. Dep. Ir., box 43.

considered a land reform based on Ulster tenant right as even remotely acceptable, and none would do so again until Gladstone took up the matter in the later 1860s. Clarendon regarded Russell's conversion with horror, and thought his plan dangerous and absurd. He thought it impossible to conciliate a mass of peasantry so long the subject of a 'demoralizing agitation', for 'whether the pretext be repeal of the Union or separation from England, or Tenant Right, the purpose is always the same. The assertion of illegal rights or in other words war against property is the object both of priest and peasant.' Ulster tenant right was an evil in itself – a 'mischievous invasion of the rights of property' – and Russell's proposal would only unite the landed proprietors of Ireland and England in bitter enmity towards the government.[210]

The Prime Minister was loath to accept Clarendon's arguments and was ready to cite the comparative prosperity of Ulster and parts of the continent in support of his plan:

> I have always thought the tenant-right of Ulster took part of the property of the landlord to give to the tenant – But I imagine the result is that the landlord gets more rent, and is less shot at than the landlord of Tipperary – In Prussia there was a far more violent interference with property and the country has flourished since – In fact many landlords in Ireland allow it for the sake of peace.[211]

However, as on previous occasions, the decided coolness of the cabinet along with Clarendon's objections forced him unwillingly to accept something less offensive to the majority. Russell was no Gladstone, and the cabinet were prepared to call his bluff over his threats of resignation if conciliation was rejected.[212] Yet he continued to stress that he would insist on a strong bill tied tightly to any coercive measure:

> It is quite true that landlords in England would not bear to be shot like hares or partridges by miscreants banded for murderous purposes. But neither does any landlord in England turn out fifty persons at once, and burn their homes over their heads, giving them no provision for the future. The murders are atrocious, but so are the ejectments. The truth is that a civil war between landlords and tenants has been raging for 80 years, marked by barbarity on both sides. I am willing to finish the contest, if it can be finished by leaving the law to its operation, by the gradual influence of civilization, by introducing and fostering education. But if stringent laws are required, they must bear on both sides in the contest.[213]

The effect of Russell's radical *démarche* was to prod the cabinet towards accepting a stronger form of Clarendon's Bill as a lesser evil. Russell's price for the abandonment of tenant right was two-fold – the reinstatement of the retrospective clauses in the

210 Clarendon to Russell, 12, 17 Nov., ibid., letterbook I.
211 Russell to Clarendon, 21 Nov., ibid., box 43.
212 Broughton Diary, Add. MS 43,751, fol. 54 [19 Nov. 1847].
213 Russell to Clarendon, 10 Nov., Clar. Dep. Ir., box 43.

Compensation Bill, and the preparation of a separate measure to provide a degree of protection to smallholders through the legislative regulation of ejectments.[214]

Cabinet resistance to this compromise came from two directions. The first and most obvious was that of the moderates. Clanricarde warned the Prime Minister against alienating landlords further by removing the power of distraint for rent or by introducing the system of arbitration favoured by the Irish government. In alliance with Lansdowne and Palmerston he sought to guide the cabinet into approving only minor and symbolic concessions to the tenantry, while facilitating leases, voluntary agreements and the eviction of tenants at will.[215] Lansdowne was, however, fully aware of Russell's sensitivity on the question of smallholders and was prepared to offer only limited resistance to retrospective compensation if it was restricted to tenants at will and not offered to leaseholders.[216] The key battle was fought over compulsory arbitration. Palmerston was intransigent on this point, and saw little need to accompany coercion with any great remedial measure. In his view the 'most drastic black dose' of the Poor Law, already 'crammed down the throats of the Irish landowners', entitled them to state protection without further infringement of their rights.[217] The Land Bill threatened to undermine the very basis of government: 'If the principle of the right of property which is the very foundation of social order were to be lightly and for such little reason departed from, we should find ourselves at sea in many other respects without any fixed rule to steer by.'[218]

Had the moderates been isolated from the rest of the cabinet, they would have been unable to do much damage. But in 1847–8 they were joined by the moralists in their opposition to a substantial Landlord-Tenant Bill. The hostility of moralists towards Irish landlords made them unlikely allies, but once convinced that the combined effects of the extended Poor Law and 'free trade in land' would be the creation of a revitalized and moralized landlordism in Ireland, they became as concerned to protect the 'just' rights of property.[219] This is not to say that they were wholly insensitive to tenant claims. Grey was as convinced as Clarendon as

214 Russell to Lansdowne, 28 Nov., Russell Papers, PRO 30/22/6G, fols. 292–5.

215 Clanricarde to Russell, 25 Dec., ibid., 6H, fols 226–7; Clanricarde to Clarendon, 30 Dec., Clar. Dep. Ir., box 9. The moderates also pressed for the removal of the powers of distraint from middlemen as part of the drive to eliminate them; clauses to enact this featured in all versions of the Bill. For landlord hostility to that class, see James S. Donnelly, 'Landlords and tenants', pp. 333–5.

216 Lansdowne to Russell, n.d. (Dec. 1847), Russell Papers, PRO 30/22/6H, fol. 17, Lansdowne to Russell, 14, 27 Jan. 1848, ibid., 7A, fols. 94–7, 214–214A.

217 Russell to Clarendon, 28 Jan., Clar. Dep. Ir., box 43; Palmerston to Russell, 20 Nov. 1847, Russell Papers, PRO 30/22/6G, fol. 200.

218 Palmerston to Clarendon, 18 Nov. 1847, Clar. Dep., c.524.

219 Wood had come to this conclusion as early as September 1846, Wood to Bessborough, 18 Sept. 1846, Hickleton Papers, A4/185/1.

to the expediency of some measure at the time, arguing that if nothing was proposed, we 'shall lose and deserve to lose any credit we possess with the country'.[220] Grey shared More O'Ferrall's opinion that some limits to landlord powers were expedient, but in return for the codification and strict enforcement of the remainder. He argued that the extended Poor Law offered the greatest guarantee to the tenant against eviction, but was prepared to offer increased protection against the 'hanging gale' of unlimited rent arrears, against the double indemnity faced by a solvent under-tenant on the default of a middleman holding over him (which had been a particular concern of Bessborough) and against the confiscation of the value of a yearly tenant's improvements. Grey's remedy was the systematic enforcement of the reformed rights of property. This was in fundamental conflict with Russell's and Clarendon's sympathy for 'interposing the executive or judicial power between landlord and tenant'.[221] Wood also thought Russell's principle a dangerous precedent for state intervention, particularly when the Protectionists Portman and Pusey were preparing another English Landlord-Tenant Bill.[222] Close co-operation was secured between moderates and moralists at Bowood over the new year, when Devon joined Wood, Lansdowne and others in setting out a 'good course' on the Bill.[223]

This moderate-moralist entente left Russell in a precarious position, particularly on tying remedial to coercive legislation. On this matter the Prime Minister could not rely on an increasingly alarmed Clarendon, and was virtually isolated. Russell contended that there was nothing new in the present outrages, and that many might even be justified. He declared that in his opinion coercion was wrong in 'policy and justice', and feared that such 'ripening measures' could provoke an agrarian insurrection. Yet while he believed the cabinet's thirst for such a measure reflected the descent into a 'sudden madness', he found himself under intense pressure to acquiesce.[224]

Although acknowledged even by its Irish opponents as being relatively mild in its terms, the Crimes and Outrages Bill introduced in the emergency session of parliament in November 1847 was the source of acute embarrassment to the Prime

220 Clarendon to Grey, 29 Dec. 1847, Clar. Dep. Ir., letterbook II.

221 Grey to Russell, 24 Nov., Russell Papers, PRO 30/22/6G, fols. 239–40; Grey memo 'On the Irish law of landlord and tenant', 18 Dec. 1847, Grey Papers.

222 Russell to Clarendon, 16 Nov., Clar. Dep. Ir., box 43; Wood to Clarendon, 26 Oct., Hickleton Papers, A4/185/2. English tenant-right activists were familiar with Irish demands and some advocated a measure that would embrace the whole United Kingdom. See C. Newman, *On the importance of a legislative enactment uniting the interest of landlord and tenant to facilitate the culture of land and promote an increase of food and employment for the millions* (2nd edn, London, 1848). For a dogmatic liberal response in line with Wood's opinions, see C. Nevile, *The justice and expediency of tenant-right legislation considered, in a letter to P. Pusey, esq.* (London, 1848).

223 Wood to Russell, 4 Jan. 1848, Russell Papers, PRO 30/22/7A, fols. 29–30, George Grey to Clarendon, 20, 25 Jan., Clar. Dep. Ir., box 12.

224 Russell to Clarendon, 2, 5 Dec. 1847, ibid., box 43.

Minister, who did not speak in the debates.[225] The criticism of Russell's supporters was worse even than Peel's condescending speech in its favour. Horsman reminded him of Holland's principled opposition to coercion and of Russell's own previous commitments to giving 'the death blow to the coercive system'. Horsman declared, however, that he, along with British public opinion, would accept coercion as part of a 'comprehensive scheme' of Irish reforms.[226]

The Crimes Bill passed with large majorities, leaving expectations of remedial legislation high but Russell in a weaker position than before. The rift with the Irish Party was reinforced and Russell's main bargaining point in cabinet had been lost. By the turn of the year he was as anxious as ever to get an effective landlord-tenant measure, and expressed anger when Clarendon wrote that landlords were seeking to use the Crimes Act to promote clearances and extract rents.[227] Russell remained unhappy with elements of Clarendon's Compensation Bill, but saw no alternative.[228] The Irish government prepared a version which included both retrospective compensation for improvements made by leaseholders and tenants at will, and compulsory arbitration.[229] Clarendon relied heavily on Thomas Redington in the drafting of this measure. Redington's views were those of an improving Irish liberal landowner; he looked forward to a system of tenure based on 21-year leases of farms over twenty acres in extent, which would be preferable to the 'loose, slobbering habits now in vogue'. Although he believed letting should be 'a mercantile transaction', Redington believed certain regulations necessary to protect the tenant's interest. Rent should be set by an arbitrated valuation and not by public auction, and while abatements should be made if the prices of agricultural produce fell, the landlord should have a commensurate power to raise them if prices rose. The tenant, Redington believed, had no right to be the sufferer if the landlord made a bad purchase. While all this was perceived to be in the objective best interest of the landlord, he was inclined to make it compulsory.[230] The problems regarding legislation arose because Ireland was in a state of social transition:

---

225 *Hans.*, XCV, 312–16, 936–41 [29 Nov., 10 Dec. 1847: J. O'Connell, W. Verner]. Clarendon thought it too weak, and it was denounced by the Tory press as inadequate, Clarendon to Lewis, 2 Dec., Clarendon to Greville, Dec. 1847, Maxwell, *Clarendon*, I, 285–6; [J.D. Brady], 'Ireland and the ministerial measures', *Blackwoods*, LXIII (Jan. 1848), 113–26.

226 *Hans.*, XCV, 321–8 [29 Nov. 1847].

227 Clarendon to Russell, 27 Dec. 1847, Russell Papers, PRO 30/22/6H, fols. 244–53. Clarendon was pleased at the effectiveness of the Special Commission operating under the Act in convicting suspects and suppressing outrages, and Mrs Villiers observed that it had broken the conspiracy to prevent the payment of rents, Clarendon to Reeve, 21 Jan. 1848, Mrs Villiers to Reeve, 5 Feb. 1848, Clar. Dep., c.534/1.

228 Russell to Clarendon, 29 Dec. 1847, Clar. Dep. Ir., box 43.

229 Clarendon to Russell, 14 Jan., Clarendon to George Grey, 14 Jan. 1848, ibid., letterbook II.

230 Redington memo: Paper II, n.d. (1848), ibid., box 24/1.

> If you legislate to provide for things as they are, you perpetuate the worst possible system – if you legislate as they ought to be, you legislate for a fiction, an Utopia – but my conviction is that legislation there must be – and that Government must, for a while, interfere more than it would be advisable to do under a sound state of things . . . The Act should *make* the landlords begin, but *compel* the tenants to follow close.

For this reason, Redington insisted on restricting prospective compensation to farmers over ten acres. Farmers under this threshold should become labourers, but should retain a one-acre garden ('that is . . . what is called the "cottier system", where properly managed'), and also have a right to compensation for whatever improvements they had made when they surrendered their tenure. Compensation for improvements – but emphatically not for 'goodwill' – was an essential step in Ireland's transition to a liberal capitalist agrarian economy.[231]

The cabinet did not share this vision of Irish transition. When a bout of ill health, brought on in part by the strain of over-work, obliged Russell to be absent from cabinet on 21 January 1848, tensions came to a head. George Grey admitted that 'we rather ran riot in your absence today', and that the cabinet had thrown out virtually all the modifications added by Russell and Clarendon. Wood led the assault on the arbitration clauses, while Lansdowne and Palmerston pushed through the abandonment of the retrospective compensation to leaseholders, insisted on a reduction of the ceiling level of compensation, and an increase in the powers to be given to landlords.[232] Russell observed that he had no particular attachment to the arbitration clauses, for he had been sceptical as to their efficacy, but that he had been 'ready to pay [Clarendon] the great compliment of agreeing to the Bill against all my own convictions'. For his part, Clarendon dissociated himself completely from the rump of the Bill, which he thought a mere incitement to renewed agitation.[233] The Prime Minister took this message to heart and made some restitution for the damage done on 21 January. He reminded Lansdowne that 'the Bill was meant to be a boon to the tenants not the landlords', and that as 'it was against all principle . . . there was no use attempting to make it conform to principle.'[234]

231 Ibid. He believed that 'tenant right' should be discouraged as much as possible and ultimately made illegal.

232 G. Grey to Russell, 21 Jan. 1848, Russell Papers, PRO 30/22/7A, fols. 159–62, Lansdowne to Russell, 27 Jan., ibid., fols. 214–214A, G. Grey to Clarendon, 21 Jan., Clar. Dep. Ir., box 12.

233 Russell to Clarendon, 22 Jan., ibid., box 26; Clarendon to Russell, 23, 24 Jan., ibid., letterbook II. Redington had advised the Lord Lieutenant that without the compulsory clauses the Bill would be 'a delusion, a mockery and a snare . . . it will not in fact any longer deal with the landlord and tenant question', Redington memo: 'On the landlord-tenant question', ibid., box 24/2.

234 Russell to Clarendon, 3 Feb., ibid., box 43; Broughton Diary, Add. MS 43,751, fols. 78–9 [1 Feb.]. Hobhouse observed that the cabinet of that day was characterized by a mixture of levity and inattention.

Clarendon put pressure on Palmerston to restore balance to the Bill, and thanked the moralists for giving way after a 'scramble at the eleventh hour',[235] but the Bill retained a number of concessions to its critics – with regard to prospective improvements, landlords were to have the power of undertaking the works themselves, and compensation was to be limited to a maximum of three year's rent. Obsessed with upholding the sanctity of contract, and suspicious of the 'love of popularity' infecting Dublin Castle lawyers, Palmerston continued to whittle away at what remained of the measure.[236]

The compromise measure had few committed supporters, and when Somerville introduced it on 15 February 1848, the Commons responded with a torrent of criticism. Sharman Crawford dismissed the retrospective clauses as grossly inadequate. The Bill would, he argued, exclude most of the tenantry of Ulster, and provide a 'pretence to landlords to abrogate the custom'.[237] The *Freeman* denounced it as a sad delusion, offering the tenant no security against ejectment.[238] If Irish popular opinion was deeply dissatisfied, English opinion was openly hostile. From early 1848 the *Times* had been running a campaign against both Sharman Crawford's scheme and the very object of seeking to preserve the existing tenantry.[239] The continued existence of the smallholder class was the cause of social anarchy in Ireland and a running sore in the body politic. The 'medicinal force of nature' was beginning to remove it, but this might be delayed by Crawford's 'quack remedy' of the partnership in the soil of landlord and tenant. Such stirring up of 'the mud at the bottom of the social system' could only have disastrous consequences.[240] The Lord Lieutenant's supposed influence over the paper was insufficient to prevent it publishing a broadside against the Landlord-Tenant Bill he had fought so hard to introduce. In the *Times'* opinion, 'Sir W. Somerville's bill would create as much agrarian confusion, litigation, ruin and ill will as the veriest Revolutionist or Repealer could possibly desire.' The principle of any intervention was rejected; while the peasantry wanted 'to be created landlords, and the contemptible puppies of Conciliation-hall have cajoled some of them into the belief that they ought, and perhaps will be made landlords', British opinion would not tolerate such a 'revolution'.[241] Russell could not help remarking to Clarendon that this article contained the same objections to compensation for improvements that he had made in November; but there was no question of the radical alternative he

235 Clarendon to Palmerston, 26 Jan., Palmerston Papers, GC/CL/482/1–3; Clarendon to George Grey, 27 Jan., 2, 5 Feb., Clar. Dep. Ir., letterbook II.

236 Palmerston to Clarendon, 22 June 1848, Clar. Dep., c.524.

237 *Hans.*, XCVI, 673–99 [15 Feb.]. Smith O'Brien and Feargus O'Connor agreed.

238 *Freeman's Journal*, 18 Feb. 1848.

239 *Times*, 7 Jan. 1848. The paper declared that it had no intention of demanding the abolition of Ulster tenant right, but that the different racial character of the south made it inapplicable there.

240 Ibid., 10 Jan., 5 Feb.

241 Ibid., 16 Feb.

had favoured being taken up in its place. Clarendon lamented the paper's opinions, but hoped that opinions could yet be changed, 'if only to avoid more extreme projects'.[242]

In the wake of the February revolution in France and the upsurge in insurrectionary rhetoric and organization in Ireland that followed, Clarendon's attention was directed towards security matters. Without his impetus, the Landlord-Tenant Bill faltered, and Somerville proposed that it be referred to a select committee. This was not entirely a move to bury the Bill, for Clarendon saw it as an opportunity to bypass the cabinet and open the question up to Irish parliamentary opinion. The select committee would also consider Sharman Crawford's reintroduced Tenant Right Bill and remove it as the focus of popular agitation.[243] A number of Whig-Liberal Irish MPs welcomed the chance to alter the Bill in committee, and only Lincoln vociferously resisted on the grounds that it was 'a contrivance for decently interring' the measure.[244]

Under Somerville's chairmanship the committee proceeded to make a number of alterations, the most important being a clause stipulating that the Bill would not infringe on any customary rights at present enjoyed by Irish tenants.[245] Russell approved these amendments, and reminded Clarendon that 'I was ready to go much further than the Cabinet here, or you in Ireland approved . . . [but] I could not march alone.'[246] The Bill was returned to the house in early July, but was dropped by the government on the grounds of want of time.

Clarendon felt that the withdrawal was unnecessary, and claimed that: 'I would have made you a *present* of the men of "station and property" for so long as you pleased provided you even made progress in any bill likely to do good or produce content in Ireland.'[247] There may have been more than a touch of wishful thinking in this, as the improving landlords of the Royal Agricultural Society of Ireland

---

242 Russell to Clarendon, 19 Feb., Clar. Dep. Ir., box 43, Clarendon to Russell, 19 Feb., ibid., letterbook II.

243 Clarendon to G. Grey, 22 March, 5 April, ibid.; *Hans.*, XCVII, 311–2 [8 March].

244 Ibid., XCVIII, 60–6 [7 April]. The Home Secretary remarked acidly that he thought Lincoln 'not unwilling to pick up a little popularity in any quarter without compromising his prospects', G. Grey to Clarendon, 3 March, Clar. Dep. Ir., box 12.

245 Most of the other adjustments were relatively minor, except for the recommendation that the system of arbitration should feature a board of three commissioners with authority over an inspectorate. These officials, rather than the 'umpires' who were to be chosen by the local magistrates in the case of a dispute, were to form the backbone of the system. This suggests parallels with Stanley's Bill of 1845, but it is possible that it was believed that a Whig-appointed inspectorate might be more 'popular' than a Conservative one, and the Irish landlords would put up less resistance to it in their politically weakened state, *A Bill [as amended by the select committee] to amend the law of landlord and tenant in Ireland*, P.P. 1847–8 (459), IV, 53.

246 Russell to Clarendon, 2 May 1848, Clar. Dep. Ir., box 43.

247 Clarendon to G. Grey, 29 July, ibid., letterbook III.

remained hostile on the grounds that arbitration of any sort would merely antagonize the landlord against his small tenants. If state intervention was necessary, the best 'healing measures' would be a statutory obligation to grant 20-year leases to all tenants at a fixed rent set by valuation. This would not infringe on the Ulster custom but would undermine those who called for 'tenant right' as an excuse to avoid exerting themselves.[248] Most Irish landowners thus remained unreconciled to the principle of a measure that appeared to penalize them to the advantage of the 'tenant landlords' responsible for producing the masses of 'squatters and mock tenants' that encumbered the country.[249]

'Coercion bills and splendid promises'

Russell had always been somewhat sceptical about the efficacy of Clarendon's Land Bill, and the deteriorating social and political condition of Ireland in the spring of 1848 reinforced his belief that a bill to control ejectments would be of greater immediate significance. A number of experienced observers, such as Count Strzelecki of the British Association, were also of the opinion that in early 1848 the greatest social crisis arose less from want of food than from the want of shelter suffered by the evicted.[250] The Prime Minister thus put a bill which would 'show most concern for the real good of the people', at the head of his plan for conciliatory measures in March 1848.[251] Nothing could have as great an effect as curbing ejectments, and it was in this context that he told Clarendon: 'Of course Irish proprietors would dislike such measures very much; but the murders of poor cottier tenants are too horrible to bear, and if we put down assassins we ought to put down the Lynch Law of the landlord.'[252]

The Prime Minister may have believed that he could succeed with this measure while more structured interventions had met come to grief. British public opinion, it appeared, was still ready to respond angrily to highly publicized clearances. James Hack Tuke's expose of the human consequences of clearances by Mayo proprietors had already caused considerable public controversy by the end of 1847, and attention remained high in the new year.[253] Russell observed that the Commons was

---

248 'The Landlord and Tenant Bill considered', *Agricultural and Industrial Journal*, I, (Oct. 1848), 211–26. This opinion bears comparison with Redington's, but is notable for its neglect of the political expediency of compensation.

249 J.L.W. Naper, *An appeal to Irishmen to unite in supporting measures formed on principles of justice and common sense for the social regeneration of Ireland* (London, 1848), pp. 3–7, 10–14. Naper accused the government of seeking to appease the Repealers by its measures.

250 Strzelecki to S. Spring Rice, 23 Feb. 1848, Monteagle Papers, MS 13,398/8.

251 Russell cabinet memo: 'State of Ireland', 30 March, Russell Papers, PRO 30/22/7B, fols. 158–61; Russell to Clarendon, 29 March, Clar. Dep. Ir., box 43.

252 Russell to Clarendon, 27 March, ibid.

253 James Hack Tuke, *A visit to Connaught in the autumn of 1847: a letter addressed to the Central Relief Committee of the Society of Friends, Dublin* (London, 1847), pp. 10–30. Tuke's

'much moved' by reports of evictions on the Blake estate in Galway, and even the *Times* declared its wish that such incidents be dealt with by 'a Government which should inflict upon violence and injustice a penalty at once speedy, stringent and commensurate with the wrong done'.[254] No doubt he was cheered by the radical *Daily News'* condemnation of evictions in Connacht as counter-productive as well as inhumane:

> What the inscrutable decrees of Providence spared, the more pitiless decrees of the land-law now seek to effect. As short-sighted in their present crusade against population, as they formerly were in their desire to stimulate its increase, the proprietory imagine that they will thereby be enabled to elude the burthen of its support, and believe that in the green desert they are making, they at length will find irresponsibility and peace.

Russell was determined that landowners be penalized for such activities.[255]

His initial idea was that some form of compensation for loss of tenure might be inserted into a bill to regulate ejectments, thus 'giving some security and some provision to the miserable cottiers who are now treated as brute beasts'.[256] Clarendon, however, was hostile, and this was dropped in favour of a bill which aimed merely to slow down and make ejectments more expensive to the proprietor. Even this muted proposal met with a cool response in cabinet.[257] The moderates were openly hostile. Palmerston, who was engaged in clearances on his own County Sligo property, stated his opinions bluntly:

> Ejectments ought to be made without cruelty in the manner of making them; but it is useless to disguise the truth that any great improvement in the social system of Ireland must be founded upon an extensive change in the present state of agrarian occupation, and that this change necessarily implies a long continued and systematic ejectment of Small Holders and of Squatting Cottiers.

Clanricarde's equally ruthless statements brought what Hobhouse described as a 'general shudder' from the cabinet.[258]

---

description of the 'living skeletons' who survived the eviction of 150 families on the Walsh estate on the Mullet peninsula was denied by the proprietor. Following a second visit in February 1848 Tuke defended his allegations, which Poulett Scrope proceeded to raise in the Commons, Edward Fry, *James Hack Tuke: a memoir* (London, 1899), pp. 62–9.

254 *Hans.*, XCVII, 1006–14 [24 March]; Russell to Clarendon, 25 March, Clar. Dep. Ir., box 43; *Times*, 27 March. An inquiry into the Blake evictions found that they had been illegal, cruel and the cause of numerous deaths, *Illustrated London News*, 1 April 1848.

255 *Daily News*, 10 Jan. 1848.

256 Russell to Clarendon, 15 Nov. 1847, Russell memo: 'On ejectments', n.d., Clar. Dep. Ir., box 43.

257 Wood memo: 'State of Ireland', 31 March 1848, Grey memo: 'State of Ireland', 30 March, Gooch, *Later correspondence*, I, 222–3, 225–6.

258 Palmerston memo: 'State of Ireland', 31 March, ibid., pp. 223–5; Broughton Diary, Add. MS 43,752, fol. 3 [25 March 1848].

Russell persevered, and his Evicted Destitute Poor Bill was introduced and passed the Commons within a week. Poulett Scrope alone lamented its limitations, and thought that it would do 'nothing to prevent the spread of the terrible system of depopulation'.[259] Even so, it was savagely attacked by many Irish proprietors in the Lords, where it was managed half-heartedly by Clanricarde. Monteagle thought that 'Scrope and Sharman Crawford could not be stronger legislators' than Russell on this matter. The Bill would, he claimed, effectively curb the practice of using ejectment notices to compel the tenant to pay his rent, and surreptitiously extend the scope of the Poor Law. Worst of all, it would lead to a further politicization of land disputes, for if the proprietor was obliged to notify the board of guardians several days in advance of his intention to eject: 'the expediency, the humanity, nay even the legality of the proceedings will be questioned, in a meeting of small farmers, and of violent political partisans, having for the most part a bias and personal interest in the question.'[260] Monteagle succeeded in carrying several wrecking amendments against the Bill.

Clarendon was led after some hesitation into supporting Russell's Bill by reports of evictions he thought particularly '"horrible" for being legal'. He was suspicious of Clanricarde's 'Galwegian' views, and lectured Lansdowne:

> there are really among them men who so scandalously abuse the rights of property that their conduct has a political importance and endangers the tranquillity of the country by the just exasperation they create. The question of land is the question of Government in Ireland and proprietors who are utterly insensible of their duties must be curtailed of their rights – the public safety requires it and they should no more be permitted to endanger that than any other nuisance or obstruction should be tolerated.[261]

Russell consulted Scrope on what he should do, and found himself in agreement with the radical writer that the peers' amendments should be treated severely.[262] The government was able to overturn some of the amendments, but at the price

---

259 *Hans.*, XCVIII, 803–4 [8 May].

260 Monteagle memo: 'On Evicted Tenant Bill', n.d. (1848), Monteagle Papers, MS 13,397/11; *Hans.*, XCIX, 82–5 [30 May 1848]. Monteagle also accused the government of hypocritically ejecting tenants from crown lands at Ballykilcline. Redington defended the government's actions regarding the case in question. The tenants had not paid rents for eleven years, but even so the Woods and Forests department had used assisted emigration and not clearance to resolve the problem, Redington memo: 'On Lord Monteagle's letter', n.d. (1848), Clar. dep. Ir., box 24/2. For a full discussion of this case, see Robert James Scally, *The end of hidden Ireland: rebellion, famine and emigration* (New York, 1995), pp. 9–129.

261 Clarendon to G. Grey, 17, 18 June 1848, Clarendon to Lansdowne, 16 July, Clar. Dep. Ir., letterbook III.

262 Scrope to Russell, 8 July, Russell Papers, PRO 30/22/7C, fols. 226–7; Russell to Clarendon, 13 July, Clar. Dep. Ir., box 43.

of accepting a Peelite compromise of giving only forty-eight hours notice of eviction to the Poor Law authorities.[263]

Russell almost certainly overestimated the public support that an effective restriction of ejectments was likely to attract. While the *Times* loudly denounced clearances as landlord crimes, it displayed little sympathy for the peasantry *per se*, particularly in the wake of the Young Ireland rising in July 1848.[264] A fatal ambiguity was also discernible in the coverage of other British journals. The *Illustrated London News* was ready in December 1848 to express moral outrage (in graphic as well as verbal form) at the ejectment of cottiers, and even to print alongside its etchings the *Tipperary Vindicator's* attack on clearances as 'a mockery of the eternal laws of God – a flagrant outrage on the principles of nature'. Yet its editorial on the same subject expressed sympathy for the proprietors struggling under the weight of the Poor Law:

> If they were a wealthy body of men, they might lighten [the poor-rate] effectually, by draining and otherwise improving their estates, and converting their paupers into labourers. But, as they are an impoverished body of men, they will endeavour to improve their estates by the best means which they can employ. It does not require any very large or difficult expenditure of capital to clear them of the cottier population, or convert small holdings into large farms, to be cultivated in the English and Scottish style of agriculture. It is the easiest mode of improvement, and, therefore, poor landlords are compelled to resort to it . . . now that a Poor Law has been introduced, we have no right, how great soever the apparent or real hardship may be, to find fault with the landlord, or cry out against his cruelty for dispossessing and ejecting the miserable swarms who encumber his land, and drag him into pauperism as bad as their own.[265]

This was a deviation from true moralism, but indicates how a considerable portion of British opinion was prepared to rationalize the actual practice of the Irish landlords.

The 1848 Ejectments Act proved weak and had only a marginal effect in softening the blow of eviction. One English observer later noted that the Act was sometimes evaded by the local authorities, and that even when notice was given, the evicted were extremely reluctant to enter the workhouses until forced to do so by the extremities of hunger and disease.[266] In the wake of this failure, Russell could put up only a feeble and evasive reply to Sharman Crawford's motion of censure in

---

263 *Hans.*, C, 481–2, 1016–18 [14, 31 July]. Monteagle found even this weak formulation illegitimate, 'Protest of Lord Monteagle against agreeing with the amendments made by the Commons in the Evicted Poor Bill, 31 July 1848', ibid., 1321–2.

264 *Times*, 14 Nov. 1848.

265 *Illustrated London News*, 16 Dec. 1848. Paradoxically the paper continued to support the reclamation of waste lands by peasant proprietors, ibid., 10 Feb. 1849.

266 Sidney Godolphin Osborne, *Gleanings in the west of Ireland* (London, 1850), pp. 22–35.

July. Faced with speaker after speaker quoting his own words since 1843 to condemn him, the Prime Minister pleaded that delay was inherent in the parliamentary system, that Ireland's problems could only be resolved gradually, and that the political and economic crisis of that year had held up many planned reforms. There was a degree of truth in his complaint that the unruliness and obstructiveness of the new parliament had frustrated his intentions, for this was indeed one of the most fruitless sessions for many years. The *Times* observed that 'never did so many promises terminate in such miserable abortions', and blamed parliament and the ministry in equal measure, while Clarendon privately berated the Commons, which had become 'a monster machine for obstructing public business'.[267] Yet Bernal Osborne's barbed jibes at Whig hypocrisy must have hurt Russell much more than other ministers lacking his attachment to the Foxite heritage. Instead of comprehensive measures, Osborne remarked, Ireland had received only 'two Coercion Acts, splendid promises, and the suspension of the Habeas Corpus Act'.[268]

Osborne and other radicals deflected attention and debate away from the question of land to that of ecclesiastical policy, but Russell felt obliged to answer Sharman Crawford's challenge on this matter. The government's Landlord-Tenant Bill had been postponed but not abandoned, he told the House. The government was not prepared to go beyond it – there would be no legislative infringement of the Ulster custom where it presently existed, but there was no question of extending it to the rest of the country. 'If such a law were passed for Ireland', he stated, 'it would strike at the root of property in the whole United Kingdom.' This public statement amounted to a renunciation of the views he had expressed privately in late 1847, but Russell still clung to one element of land policy that suggested there was still something more to his thought than the mild humanitarianism of the Evicted Tenants Bill. He informed the Commons of his belief in the efficacy of a small-farm structure for Ireland. Questioned as to what he meant by this, he mentioned 'such a division of land as exists in Tuscany, where the farms do not exceed six or seven acres in extent', and stipulated only that the plots should not be too large for a garden and too small for a farm. Yet he was cautious about suggesting a mechanism to introduce and regulate such a system. Change, he observed, would depend not only on law, but, 'on the conduct of the landlords, on the ability of persons of small capital to purchase small portions of land, and on various other circumstances of that nature'. The Encumbered Estates Bill would promote this, but 'in Ireland you must leave those things to take their own course, and to be settled according to the habits of the people in the different parts of Ireland.'[269]

---

267 *Times*, 31 Aug. 1848; Clarendon to Wood, 27 Aug., Clar. Dep. Ir., letterbook III.
268 *Hans.*, C, 960–76 [28 July].
269 Ibid., 937–54. Russell also continued to promise political and ecclesiastical reforms when the time was ripe, and railway and waste-lands initiatives when there was 'a more flourishing state of the finances'.

Russell's speech reflected his own marginalization within the cabinet, and his withdrawal into wishful thinking about the capabilities of an encumbered estates measure to solve the Irish land problem. This was not entirely his own fault – the political upheavals at home and abroad in 1848, and the dissipation of the Foxite group within the government made the consistent adherence to policy principles in the face of strong ideological opposition very difficult. There was more than a touch of truth in the *Times*' comment that 'Whiggism has – for all purposes of a defined policy – virtually ceased to exist'.[270] Not surprisingly, Russell's personal inclination after the strains of the 1848 session was towards retirement from government.[271]

By mid-1848 Russell was becoming alienated not only from the cabinet but from those reformers who had previously placed great hopes in him. His political relationship with Poulett Scrope had always been tinged with ambiguity, but it is striking how much of Russell's ideas and language appeared to draw on Scrope's writings from 1846 to 1848. As late as April 1848 Scrope affirmed his personal loyalty to the Premier, to whom he wrote: 'I am anxious not to be thought to look up to any other leader than the one I have hitherto (more or less *rebelliously*, I fear) but not the less admiringly followed.'[272] By the summer, little of this professed admiration appears to have remained. Scrope warned parliament of the danger of abandoning Ireland to the revolutionary rhetoric of the *Irish Felon* (now the mouthpiece of James Fintan Lalor) in default of any substantial redress of grievances. He also turned self-consciously from addressing the Premier in his publications, to appealing to the British people to recognize their interest in Irish amelioration. As Foxite Whiggery expired, Scrope turned back to popular radicalism in the hope that 'the English people would seriously take into consideration the state of Ireland, and no longer trifle with a question which had attracted the attention of Europe'.[273]

III 'FREE TRADE IN LAND', 1847–50

'Opening the door to a middle class'

The idea of a legislative enactment that would inject fresh energy and capital into Ireland by facilitating land sales had caught the liberal imagination more than any other recommendation in the Devon Commission report. For Peelites, 'free trade in land' was the natural concomitant of 'free trade in corn' – both were concerned with the removal of unnatural obstructions to the free flow of capital, and both

270 *Times*, 31 Aug. 1848.
271 Broughton Diary, Add. MS 43,753, fol. 23 [26 Aug.]. Hobhouse was pleased that he had been talked out of this step by his wife, as the result would have been a damaging internal struggle over leadership.
272 Scrope to Russell, 17 April, Russell Papers, PRO 30/22/7B, fols. 310–11.
273 *Hans.*, C, 985–8 [29 July]; [George Poulett Scrope], 'Irish clearances and improvement of waste lands', *Westminster and Foreign Quarterly Review*, L (Oct. 1848), 163–87.

were required for the capitalization of Irish agriculture. In the wake of the introduction of the Corn Bill and with the need for greater investment made acute by the potato failure, Peel gave serious thought to the subject. A bill was prepared late in the 1846 session and circulated to interested parties, but the government fell before it could be introduced.[274]

Radical opinion also saw a clear connection between free trade in food and the liberation of the land market. To one Scottish observer writing in 1845, the existing land law of Scotland and Ireland was an impediment to the unfettered 'operation of those providential laws . . . [which are] one of the chief means by which the moral government of the world is carried on'. Any system of law which, by means of entail or obstacles to free sale, preserved a monopoly of land-ownership in the hands of the aristocratic few was both dangerous and in opposition to the 'natural' progress of society.[275] The Benthamite *Westminster Review* agreed, in more secular language, that land reform was vital throughout the United Kingdom, to 'transform our nobility into a commercial aristocracy, and enable the farmer and the tradesman to become the proprietor, instead of the tenant, of his farm or shop.'[276]

The incoming Whig government had no such reform in mind, but two circumstances combined to render legislation expedient.[277] The first was the practical problem of the escalating debts of Irish proprietors. Indebtedness rose particularly rapidly from 1846 when the added weight of famine relief was thrown on to landlord incomes, and rent rolls – particularly on encumbered estates under the courts – collapsed. This struck at the heart of government relief policy, which was premised on forcing proprietors to disgorge their accumulated capital on making improvements if they wanted to evade heavy rates. The second circumstance was the development of a more ideological critique of Irish landlordism. The moralist vision transcended Peel's interest in the capitalization of agriculture and ultimately envisaged the 'clearance' of the existing body of indigenous landowners, and their replacement by men of a different class. Wood was convinced that a 'social revolution' had to be promoted and guided in Ireland, and that the proprietors

274 *Hans.*, LXXXV, 1126–7 [27 April 1846: Peel]. W. Booth, the clerk of the Irish Ordnance Survey, summarized the Peelite view: 'society in Ireland can never be constituted on a safe basis until capital can freely combine with land, and work those improvements which would naturally flow from such a combination.' Booth to Lincoln, 19 June 1846, Newcastle Papers, Nottingham University Library, NeC 9,543.

275 [Anon.], *The emancipation of the soil and free trade in land, by a landed proprietor* (Edinburgh, 1845), p. 17.

276 [Anon.], 'Registration of landed property', *Westminster Review*, XCV (March 1846), 107–32.

277 For a detailed account of the background to the Encumbered Estates Bills, see Padraig G. Lane, 'The Encumbered Estates Court, Ireland, 1848–1849', *Economic and Social Review*, III (1971–2), 413–53. This is a perceptive analysis of Peel's approach to the subject, but wrongly assumes that Russell was 'Peel's political legatee', and that the motives behind Whig policy were exclusively Peelite.

should not be spared if they hesitated to make the necessary sacrifices. From September 1846 he pressed for some form of encumbered estates measure, but expected stiff legal opposition: 'The lawyers will be against it; and I dare say that the Chancellor will cry out against such innovating doctrines . . . [but] great evils must be dealt with by extraordinary remedies.' He believed such a bill would introduce 'a middle class of landed proprietors in Ireland – what we may call yeomen – [who] would be of great political advantage to the country.'[278]

Much turned on the definition of the rather vague term 'yeoman'. When employed by Scrope and Mill, the term denoted a class of peasant proprietors on plots not exceeding 20–30 acres.[279] Wood, however, clearly envisaged a rural bourgeoisie of mercantile origins. The ability to command capital was essential, for it was 'by means of private capital and private enterprise that all general and permanent improvement is effected, in all countries'.[280] While there was much common ground between Wood and Peel on the benefits of 'free trade in land', they differed sharply on the extent to which it should be pushed to the detriment of existing owners.

Wood's opinions met with the approbation of other moralists, such as Edward Ellice, who had made a fortune in the Canadian trade, purchased an estate in the Scottish Highlands and undertaken to relieve destitution there through reproductive improvements as an example to others.[281] Interest was not confined to that section of the Party. The Foxite, Lord Fortescue, thought such a bill desirable (although not to the exclusion of other remedial measures), and Clanricarde also favoured the facilitation of sales.[282] A decision to legislate was reached at Bowood in early January 1847, where Wood had the support of Devon, who had recommended such a measure in 1845. Russell, who was not present, appears to have acquiesced, but the low priority accorded to the Bill suggests a certain indifference on the part of the Prime Minister and the Irish administration.[283] Russell's announcement in January 1847 that the government was considering a bill came as something of an afterthought to the 'comprehensive measures' that featured waste-land reclamation and the extended Poor Law. The details he mentioned were vague, and more attention was given to the proposal for a Leasehold Tenure Conversion Bill, which he hoped would bring about a simplification of tenure, and help

278 Wood to Bessborough, 16 Sept. 1846, Hickleton Papers, A4/185/1.

279 Scrope, *How is Ireland to be governed?*, pp. 40–66.

280 Wood to Labouchere, 22 Sept. 1846, Hickleton Papers, A4/185/1.

281 Ellice to Wood, 27 Oct., ibid., A4/103; T.M. Devine, *The Great Highland Famine: hunger, emigration and the Scottish Highlands in the nineteenth century* (Edinburgh, 1988), pp. 90, 103.

282 Fortescue to Russell, 29 Oct., Clanricarde to Russell, 17 Dec. 1846, Russell Papers, PRO 30/22/5D, fols. 315–18, 5F, fols 207–10. Clarendon also thought it would be of great public benefit and would command cross-party support, Clarendon to Russell, 23 Nov., ibid., 5E, fols. 163–5.

283 Bessborough was aware of the difficult position of small landowners, but was cautious about such legislation, Bessborough to Russell, 8, 18 Jan. 1847, ibid., 6A, fols. 91–2, 172–3.

alleviate 'the frightful cases of destitution' where it is impossible to find the person on whom the obligation of real proprietorship rested.[284]

The 1847 Bill was entrusted to the Lord Chancellor of England, who sought to base it on a 'simple principle', but dragged his heels in preparing it.[285] The Bill was introduced just before the Easter recess and proceeded through the Lords without significant opposition. Cottenham's intention was, he argued, to lessen the expense of proceedings in the Irish Court of Chancery by abolishing the preliminary processes, but the Bill ran into trouble as a result of the laxity with which it was drafted.[286] English insurance companies, who were the prime creditors of Irish encumbered properties, feared for the security of their loans and mortgages if small creditors were to have the power of forcing sales and thus glutting the land market.[287] Concern was also expressed about the inefficiency of the Irish Chancery, and also about the deterioration of property inseparable from extended receivership.[288] The companies' threats to freeze or recall their advances, and the consequent alarm among landowners, forced the government to withdraw the Bill for reconsideration.[289]

This setback was only temporary, for in the course of 1847 the encumbered estates question acquired a greater resonance in British politics. This was due in part to the propagandist efforts of a number of advocates, particularly of Jonathan Pim, a Dublin manufacturer and merchant, and secretary of the Friends' Central Relief Committee. Pim attributed landlord-tenant conflict and agricultural underdevelopment in Ireland to the twin problems of insecurity of title and want of capital. Interference with the law of entail and settlement had long been desirable in the interests of social utility, but the providential visitation of the potato failure now compelled the re-ordering of society without delay. Middle-class entrepreneurs (modelled on the Quaker self-ideal) would then begin Ireland's reconstruction: 'land must pass into the hands of those who do possess the means of employing the people – of men who will carry on agriculture as a business, and bring there to occupation their capital, habits of business, energy and intelligence, which have raised the commerce and manufactures of this nation to their present pre-eminence.' An extensive encumbered estates bill, giving any encumbrancer the

---

284 *Hans.*, LXXXIX, 445–6 [25 Jan. 1847]. The latter Bill was drawn up by Bessborough, but did not pass until 1849.

285 Cottenham to Russell, 3 Feb., Russell to Bessborough, 28 Feb. 1847, Russell Papers, PRO 30/22/6B, fols. 21–2, 145–6 .

286 *Hans.*, XCI, 262 [22 March], ibid., XCII, 3–5 [27 April 1847]. Cottenham's caution were not unrelated to the fact that he was the mortgagee for a substantial sum on Lord Limerick's Irish estate, Clarendon to Russell, 26 July 1848, Clar, Dep. Ir., letterbook III.

287 Lane, 'Encumbered Estates Court', p. 427.

288 'Encumbered Estates Act: Counsel's opinion on insurance', 14 June 1847, 'Encumbered Estates Act (1847): Counsel's further opinion on insurance and security', 1 July, Russell papers, PRO 30/22/6D, fols. 44–5, 94–5.

289 *Hans.*, XCIII, 809–11 [23 June], 1192 [5 July 1847].

power to force a sale, was required to 'free the land'.[290] Pim argued that this would also lead to the distribution of property in fee among a much wider section of the people; the 'independent yeomanry' who would purchase estates broken up into small lots would, he hoped, emulate 'the careful garden cultivation of Belgium or Switzerland'. If Pim was aware of any fundamental contradiction between his belief that free competition in land would lead to the soil passing quickly 'into the hands of those who have capital and the ability to manage it with the greatest advantage', and his desire for the conversion 'as far as is practicable of small farmers into landed proprietors', he did not acknowledge it in this pamphlet.

Inspired by Peel's restatement of the priority of such legislation in the Commons, Pim made his social vision more explicit in a letter to the former Premier. He was confident that while free sale would induce tenant exertion by offering a goal of independence to the farmer, the purchasers would not be primarily of that class; no man would be legally excluded from landownership by his creed or social origins, but the moral superiority of the Protestant and mercantile virtues would soon reveal themselves. English involvement could only be beneficial, as settlers would introduce the 'habits, industry and energy' that were as necessary as capital.[291] Pim's advocacy of encumbered estates legislation was taken up by other Irish and English Quakers,[292] and in a moderated form the idea was favourably considered by other commentators.[293] By the end of 1847 even the staunchest advocates of tenant compensation had also come to accept the desirability of freeing estates for sale.[294]

Irish landowners had mixed feelings about such measures. Many, like the liberal Monteagle, looked on them with a degree of equanimity,[295] but others – particularly those who were both resident and in perilous financial straits – were alarmed by the threat of a mass eviction of landowners.[296] The opinions of the latter were expressed in print by John Anster, who endorsed the facilitation of sales of portions of estates through the removal of the obstructions of entails and legal formalities,

290 [Jonathan Pim], *Observations on the evils resulting to Ireland from the insecurity of title and the existing laws of real property; with some suggestions towards a remedy* (Dublin, 1847), pp. 5–17.

291 *Hans.*, LXXXIX, 762–4 [3 Feb. 1847: Peel]; Pim to Peel, 3 March 1847 (copy), Bessborough Papers, F. 339.

292 Tuke, *A visit to Connaught*, pp. 42–5. Tuke thought that it was not so much capital that Ireland needed as the 'permission to use' it. Another Quaker, Jacob Harvey, suggested to Morpeth that British philanthropy, its eyes opened to Irish realities by famine, would insist on 'free trade in land' as an essential measure of 'justice to Ireland', Harvey to Morpeth, 29 April 1847, Castle Howard Papers, J19/1/43/71.

293 Montague Gore, *Suggestions for the amelioration of the present condition of Ireland* (London, 1847), pp. 52–3; Earl of Rosse, *Letters on the state of Ireland* (2nd edn, London, 1847), pp. 34–5.

294 George Poulett Scrope, *Letters to Lord John Russell*, pp. 52–3 (letter v: 26 Oct. 1847).

295 Monteagle to Wood, 4 Oct. 1846, Monteagle Papers, MS 13,396/9. See also ['Anglo-Hibernicus'], *A letter to the Rt. Hon. Lord John Russell, on the future prospects of Ireland* (London, 1847), pp. 8–10.

296 *Hans.*, XCIII, 810–11 [23 June 1847: F. French].

but abhorred the idea of the compulsion of sales and the removal of the old proprietary. Anster argued, *pace* Wood and Pim, that 'in the reconstruction of Ireland . . . the new structure must be formed pretty much of the old materials.'[297]

This defensiveness reflected the growing polarization of opinion over the future of the indigenous Irish landowning class. In the wake of the Poor Law Amendment Act, the *Times* called for the summary removal of 'bankrupt' proprietors who could or would not meet their moral obligations. The 'special visitation of PROVIDENCE' directed against the ingrained morals and habits of the Irish, weighed most heavily on those whose positions of social responsibility were greatest; providence held the landowners to account not only for their individual sins, but collectively for those of their 'thriftless and improvident' ancestors.[298] Manchester-school radicals were equally hostile. Hume denounced state intervention and called for the facilitation of sales as a panacea. The forced removal of encumbered proprietors – as a class the true 'curse of Ireland' – was endorsed by Bernal Osborne and Roebuck.[299] John Bright made explicit their belief that Irish land reform was central to the British radical agenda; the proprietorial class was responsible for its own predicament, and deserved to forfeit both the land and the political power associated with it. The Irish land structure appeared to radicals the weakest link in the whole British system that sustained networks of privilege and corruption, and in the wake of the repeal of the Corn Laws, much of their rhetorical energy was directed against the Irish proprietary.[300]

The radicals were a small if vociferous group in the 1841–7 parliament, but their statements were an indication of the feeling building up in much of middle-class opinion. In the wake of the 1847 general election radical numbers rose to between 80 and 90, giving this independently-minded if somewhat diffuse group a balance of power in the Commons. In this altered context, their views on Irish land took on greater significance, a point pushed home by John Bright, now MP for Manchester, during the debates on the 1847 Irish Crimes Bill:

---

297 [Anster], 'Agrarian outrages in Ireland', pp. 509–12. See also the guarded welcome in [Samuel O'Sullivan], 'Condition of Ireland', *Dublin University Magazine*, XXXII (Aug. 1848), 228–43.

298 *Times*, 14, 24 Aug. 1847.

299 *Hans.*, LXXXIX, 469–70 [25 Jan. 1847]; ibid., 633, 646 [1 Feb.]. Osborne had himself married into Irish land in 1844 and drew on his personal experience in his advocacy of the need to open up land to capitalist investment.

300 Ibid., XCV, 986–8 [13 Dec. 1847]. For the broader land campaign, and its centrality to radical politics, see F.M.L. Thompson, 'Land and politics in England in the nineteenth century', *Transactions of the Royal Historical Society*, 5th series, XV (1965), 23–44, David Martin, 'Land reform', in Patricia Hollis (ed.), *Pressure from without in early Victorian England* (London, 1974), pp. 139–58, and H.J. Perkin, 'Land reform and class conflict in Victorian Britain', in J. Butt and I.F. Clarke (eds.), *The Victorians and social protest* (Newton Abbot, 1973), pp. 177–217.

> There is an unanimous admission now that the misfortunes of Ireland are connected with the management of the land. I have a theory that, in England as well as Ireland, the proprietors of the soil are chiefly responsible for whatever of bad legislation has been inflicted upon us. The ownership of land confers more political power than the possession of any other description of property. The Irish landowners have been willing parties to the past legislation for Ireland, and they have also had the administration and execution of the laws in that country. The encumbered condition of landed property in Ireland is the question most pressing at the moment.

Only by 'clearing away the fetters under which the land is now held', could Ireland be revived and the radical reform of the rest of British society begun. For radicals Ireland was the site of a proxy war in which the ultimate target was the structure of landed power in Great Britain.[301]

Under increasing pressure, and with many of its members sympathetic, the cabinet was obliged to give the subject more attention in 1848. Clarendon wrote to the insurance companies to establish their specific objections, while Wood lobbied hard for the inclusion of powers to break up estates for sale.[302] The cabinet agreed the heads of a bill in October as the most important remedial measure of the coming session, and decided it should have priority over the Landlord-Tenant Bill.[303] Yet they remained divided over the question of compulsory sales. Moderates were attracted to the idea of a limited bill which would permit landowners to liquidate part of their landed assets, and would distract attention from more threatening subjects. As Henry Maunsell pointed out to Clanricarde:

> Instead of a cry for 'tenant right' the popular clamour ought to be for 'free trade in land' – The lawyers would, of course, be the opponents of such a movement; but there is a disposition towards it in the public mind which professional opposition would rather stimulate, and if once set a going it would harmlessly and usefully supersede the other agitation which is likely to become very dangerous and which . . . can be more easily eluded than opposed.[304]

Clanricarde recognized this, but remained perturbed by the Irish administration's preference for a stronger measure.[305]

Clarendon and Russell agreed on the necessity of compulsory powers, but had different visions of the social consequences of the measure. Neither wanted the overnight transformation of Irish landownership favoured by Wood and the radicals,

---

301 *Hans.*, XCV, 986–8 [13 Dec. 1847].
302 Clarendon to Russell, 25 Sept. 1847, Clar. Dep. Ir., letterbook I; Wood to Russell, 28 Sept., Russell Papers, PRO 30/22/6F, fols. 126–9.
303 Russell to Clarendon, 21, 28 Oct., Clar. Dep. Ir., box 43.
304 Maunsell to Clanricarde, 26 Aug., Clanricarde Papers, bundle 73.
305 Clanricarde to Clarendon, 27 Oct., Clar. Dep. Ir., box 9.

but the Prime Minister was initially more positive about the embourgeoisement of proprietors. Russell looked forward to the substitution 'in many instances [of] Catholic merchants and tradesmen for Protestant noblemen and gentry', and to the termination of the political and cultural separation of landownership from the Catholic clergy and people. Sale of land in small lots appeared to promise the fulfilment of the Foxite aim of granting social equality to Irish Catholics, although it required the simultaneous endowment of the Catholic clergy to make this safe and prevent 'extreme vibrations shaking everything loose'. Clarendon, on the other hand, saw the Bill as a necessary evil, and expressed sympathy for the existing landlords and their dislike of the 'pestilent class' of attorneys. While believing 'a middle class landed proprietary' necessary, he had no time for the claimed virtues of bourgeois landowners, and was much less sanguine about the transfer of land to a Catholic proprietary.[306]

For all the debate over the effects of legislation on the structure of Irish society, in practice the Bill was prepared by the government's English legal experts, whose natural inclinations were against radical judicial change.[307] The 1848 Encumbered Estates Bill which was drafted by Lord Campbell and introduced into the Lords in February, was based on the same principles as Cottenham's Bill, seeking to combine the protection of mortgagees' interests with the speeding up of conveyances under the Court of Chancery. Campbell's Bill went further to calm the fears of the London companies, but its terms threatened only to irritate many Irish lawyers and landowners without producing a substantial increase in sales.[308] Roden welcomed it, but both Fitzwilliam and Monteagle thought that it could not meet the expectations placed upon it because of the continued insistence that all cases go through Chancery. Stanley was also sceptical as to its efficacy.[309]

Ministers, who had been under the impression that they had sanctioned 'a very strong Bill',[310] were somewhat taken aback by this response, and withdrew it. Meanwhile, out of parliament, popular demand for a strong bill continued to grow. The radical *Daily News* welcomed the Bill as the 'beginning of the end' of the Irish crisis, but warned it was too weak to overturn the 'close monopoly' of Irish landownership. To be effective, the Bill would have to recognize that most Irish encumbrances were not mortgages but judgements of debt in the form of

306 Russell to Clarendon, 13, 18 Dec., ibid., box 43, Clarendon to Russell, 15 Dec., ibid., letterbook II.

307 Russell was forced to admit that 'of legal machinery I know nothing', Russell to Clarendon, 21 May 1848, ibid., box 43.

308 Clarendon to Russell, 12 Jan. 1848, ibid. letterbook II; *A Bill intitulated an Act to facilitate the sale of Incumbered Estates in Ireland*, P.P. 1847–8 (319), III, 193. A detailed account of the terms and progress of the Bills of 1848 and 1849 can be found in Lane, 'Encumbered Estates Court', pp. 435–42.

309 *Hans.*, XCVI, 1249–53 [24 Feb. 1848].

310 Broughton Diary, Add. MS 43,751, fols. 79–80 [1 Feb. 1848].

bonds (requiring no transfer of title deeds to the creditor and therefore giving no power of sale under the Bill). It was only equitable, the paper asserted, that all major creditors be given the power to force a sale, and that the archaic privileges of landownership be stripped away:

> Why should there be a different law and a different standard of public morality for the wholesale dealer in land and the wholesale dealer in tea? Can it be right that the one should be allowed to occupy a position implying competence and solvency and specially conferred influence and power, notwithstanding his having irretrievably pawned all that constitutes his qualification, – while the other is liable at any moment to be challenged to state publicly upon oath every particular of his affairs?[311]

For middle-class radicals, the matter of Irish encumbrances was 'an English and Scots question in a very obvious and practical sense'. Without effective legislation, Britain could again be obliged to cope with Irish distress; with it, a further blow against feudal privilege would be assured.

For his part, Trevelyan robustly asserted the moralist case for an encumbered estates bill strong enough to end the 'vicious cycle of embarrassment and mortgage'. This 'master-key to unlock the field of industry in Ireland', he wrote in the *Edinburgh Review*, would begin the regeneration of Irish society and provide the only safe means of meeting distress. He favoured the breaking up of estates into lots, 'which opens the door to a middle class . . . better able to maintain the stability of property and of our political institutions, because they are themselves sprung from the people.'[312] What began as a useful auxiliary had thus become by 1848 the moralists' and radicals' panacea for the present and future problems of Ireland.[313]

The Prussian land model, 1848

After his experience as secretary of the Friends' Relief Committee in 1847, Jonathan Pim was far from believing an encumbered estates measure would prove such a panacea, but he reiterated in early 1848 his view that all the suggested remedies would be futile in the absence of a real 'free trade in land'.[314] Freedom of sale

311 *Daily News*, 9, 14 March 1848.

312 Trevelyan, *Irish crisis*, pp. 22–36, 197–8. This was first published in the *Edinburgh Review*, CLXXV (Jan. 1848).

313 One Trevelyanite relief official confirmed in 1849 his belief that 'Free Trade in land' was Ireland's panacea, and that 'the *heavy blow of friendly confiscation*' was vital, Capt. Pole to Trevelyan, 19 March 1849, Treasury Papers, T64/366A.

314 Jonathan Pim, *The condition and prospects of Ireland, and the evils arising from the present distribution of landed property: with suggestions for a remedy* (Dublin, 1848), pp. 135–9, 235–94. Pim later used the Quaker Relief Committee as a platform to repeat these suggestions, [Society of Friends], *Address to the public from the Relief Association of the Society of Friends in Ireland* (Dublin [1849]), p. 3.

would allow capital investment in Irish land and dissipate Catholic alienation, but, he warned Trevelyan, it would be futile to expect purchasers to come forward when the masses were disaffected and dying.[315]

Pim's ideas were circulated to the cabinet and met with differing reactions. Trevelyan, who had passed them on, recommended only a few minor relief concessions, a stronger encumbered estates bill, and more vigorous coercion.[316] Clanricarde endorsed the need to supplement the resources available for Poor Law relief, but objected to the proposal to amend the Encumbered Estates Bill in such a way as to promote the break-up of estates. It was, he declared with the assurance of a great Irish proprietor, a 'vulgar error' to believe that small estates could be better managed or more productive than great ones.[317] Russell, in contrast, found himself in agreement with most of Pim's views – even though he felt it necessary to accompany the admission with a diatribe against Irish 'improvidence'. He concurred with Clarendon's opinion that the Bill should proceed and be amended as much as possible in the Commons.[318]

Sir John Romilly, who had recently become English Solicitor General, undertook the radical reconstruction of the Bill and proposed that the owner, or in certain cases the first encumbrancer, could sell the property without going through the courts.[319] In spite of the addition of considerable restrictions, the Solicitor General's amendments drew the fire of Irish Protectionists. Lucius O'Brien feared that the Bill would 'shake the foundation of property, and expose Irish landlords to every annoyance to which creditors could expose them', and Joseph Napier declared that a more ruinous piece of legislation was unimaginable.[320] Protectionist alarms may have been aroused less by the actual terms of the amendments than by the aggressive triumphalism with which they were received by radicals. Bernal Osborne and Charles Villiers sought to turn the debate into an indictment of the 'aristocratic' system in Ireland in general, and of the principles of entail and family settlements in particular.[321]

The key Commons debates turned on whether the Bill should include greater facilities for splitting up estates for sale and whether the power to force a sale should be extended to all encumbrancers. These proposals were combined in an

---

315 Pim to Trevelyan, 31 March 1848, Russell Papers, PRO 30/22/7B, fols. 223–6. He also urged the government to grant emergency relief and make amendments to the Poor Law, such as the suspension of the quarter-acre clause.

316 Trevelyan memo: 'Ireland and the Chartists', 4 April 1848, ibid., fols. 217–22.

317 Clanricarde memo: 'On the state of Ireland', 1 April, ibid., fols. 192–5.

318 Russell to Clarendon, 21, 24 April, Clar. Dep. Ir., box 43; Clarendon to Russell, 23, 30 April, ibid., letterbook II.

319 *A Bill [as amended by the committee] intitulated, an Act to facilitate the sale of Encumbered Estates in Ireland*, P.P. 1847–8 (373), III, 217; G. Grey to Clarendon, 18 May 1848, Clar. Dep. Ir., box 12.

320 *Hans.*, C, 88–93, 104–5 [4 July 1848]. They were supported by some English Protectionists in these criticisms, ibid., 394–6, 588–91, 595–6 [11 July: Walsh, 20 July: Newdegate, Henley].

321 Ibid., 396–401, 596–9 [11, 20 July].

amendment proposed by Torrens McCullagh, who argued that only the adoption of the latter would create a genuine land market and facilitate sales in small lots.[322] The Solicitor General, supported by Graham, rejected this as too dangerous to landed interests, and it was dropped.[323] Nevertheless, the Lords reacted angrily to the return of what was substantially a new bill. Stanley led the Protectionists in denouncing the process as unconstitutional and demanded the Bill's reconsideration by a select committee, and Glengall claimed to see in it a Quaker plot to confiscate land for speculation.[324] However, the combination of Peelite support and Lord Langdale's legal opinion that Romilly's clauses had been so hedged with conditions that the power to sell outside Chancery would be ineffective, was sufficient to ensure that the Bill passed without any great alteration.

It is unclear whether McCullagh's intervention was made with Clarendon's support, but the Lord Lieutenant was evidently anxious for a more effective measure, although one that would not 'exterminate the present race of landlords'.[325] Clarendon made great efforts to persuade Russell of the folly of transferring estates to the 'low attorney or political middleman', but this left both men in a conundrum as to where the purchasers of small portions of estates were to come from and how the purchase of land was to be made an attractive proposition.

Answers to these problems were offered by Sir Robert Kane and Lord Devon. In April 1848 Kane wrote a very favourable review of Pim's pamphlet in the Royal Agricultural Society's journal, and then proceeded to propose a scheme of agricultural credit based on the system of land banks existing in Prussia. This state-regulated but popularly based system made cheap agricultural loans available to all who could offer land as security, and thus redressed the bias of credit markets against small borrowers. This system had secured the success of Prussian agriculture, with its large peasant proprietor sector, and could, Kane argued, be applied in a modified form to Ireland.[326] Russell and Clarendon were impressed by this suggestion – the Prime Minister urged the Viceroy to 'take some pains with Sir R. Kane – I am very fond of his books', and reminded him that on such subjects 'I do not want to stand rigidly in the beaten track of political economy.'[327] Clarendon had

322 Ibid., 474–6 [13 July].

323 Graham argued that the Bill was sufficient for its purpose, although a reduction in stamp duties would promote the sale of the small portions desirable for creating a landed middle class and increasing the proportion of Catholic landowners. Lincoln also defended the Peelite vision against landlord criticisms by distinguishing small estates from peasant ownership, ibid., 390–4 [11 July], 768–72 [24 July].

324 Ibid., 1019–30 [31 July].

325 Clarendon to Russell, 5 June, Clar. Dep. Ir., letterbook II. Wood remained insistent that no government policy should impede the natural process of bankruptcy and clearance of the Irish landlords, Wood to Russell, 20 May, Russell Papers, PRO 30/22/7C, fols. 69–72.

326 Robert Kane, 'The agricultural banks of Prussia', *Agricultural and Industrial Journal*, I (April 1848), 125–34.

327 Russell to Clarendon, 23 April, 2 May 1848, Clar. Dep. Ir., box 43.

already taken an interest in the Prussian case, and suggested that a bill to facilitate its replication in Ireland alongside the privately funded Farmers' Estate Society Bill proposed by Devon. A combination of these measures with the alleviation of repayments might at last offer some hope of killing agitation and giving the government some credit for promoting popular social reform, but Clarendon expected stiff opposition from Wood.[328] This concern was well justified, for Clarendon and Kane envisaged that as part of the plan the government should buy out the mortgages and judgements on estates and issue debentures with a first charge upon the land in their place. A guaranteed interest rate on these would, it was thought, help restore confidence to proprietors and farmers, and remove the interference of encumbrances on normal agricultural activity. Chancery receiverships would thus be sharply curtailed and the sale of encumbered estates facilitated.[329] All these interventionist proposals were anathema to the Treasury.

Russell expressed sympathy towards applying a European solution to an Irish problem. He told Clarendon: 'it is the doctrine I have been always preaching to Wood and to Trevelyan that the Irish are fashioned more like our continental neighbours than ourselves – that instead of detesting Government control they cannot well do without it – and that we cannot change the nature of a nation in this respect.' He saw considerable virtue in the Prussian system in its entirety.[330] Yet again, however, Russell's grand intentions came to nothing. Clarendon's reservations about introducing such a measure before the encumbered estates had been broken up, and his belief that neither the government nor parliament would accept a bill that could be portrayed as offering a life-line to encumbered landlords, led to the scheme being laid aside.[331]

The idea of a Farmers' Estate Society had been first proposed over a decade previously by Sir Matthew Barrington.[332] It took serious form in the spring of 1848 when a group of Irish landowners, including Lord Devon, proposed the creation of a joint-stock company which would purchase land under the Encumbered Estates Bill, divide it, and offer portions for sale on reasonable terms to 'yeoman proprietors' – preferably the existing occupiers – in plots of over twenty acres. They anticipated that a profit would be realized from the differential between the cost of the estate (particularly in the then depressed state of the property market), and the higher price per acre which a small proprietor would offer.[333] The proposed

---

328 Clarendon to Bunsen, 28 Dec. 1847, Clarendon to Russell, 6 May 1848, ibid., letterbook II. The political advantages to be derived from the conciliation of the priests and small gentry he thought outweighed any objections on grounds of political economy, Clarendon to Wood, 30 March, ibid.

329 Clarendon to G. Grey, 18 May, ibid.

330 Russell to Clarendon, 21 May, ibid., box 43.

331 Clarendon to Russell, 18 May 1848, ibid., letterbook II.

332 Barrington to Russell, 4 Aug. 1846, Russell Papers, PRO 30/22/5B, fols. 300–1.

333 *Freeman's Journal*, 15 Feb. 1848; *Report of the select committee on the Farmers' Estate Society (Ireland) Bill, together with minutes of evidence*, P.P. 1847–8 (535), XVII, 363–76 [Devon].

company represented a cross-section of Irish public life, although it was weighted towards liberals. It achieved the rare feat of winning the favour of both the *Freeman's Journal* and *Dublin Evening Mail*.[334]

Clarendon doubted whether the company would succeed, but believed it at least 'a step in the right direction' and of political importance as a demonstration of concern for the lower classes. If successful, it would give the farming classes an incentive to preserve the social order and exert themselves, and had the advantage of requiring only the sanction and not the active management or funding of the state.[335] Moreover, the scheme would complement his joint initiative with the Royal Agricultural Society of Ireland to raise the quality of Irish farming through the employment of peripatetic agricultural instructors.[336] Nevertheless, George Grey and the cabinet moralists were hostile towards the scheme as an infringement of *laissez-faire*, and Lansdowne and Palmerston were lukewarm and sceptical.[337]

Russell, while regarding it as second best to the Prussian land-bank scheme, was enthusiastic, and insisted on the suspension of standing orders to rush the Bill into the Commons in June. A select committee heard evidence (all favourable), and reported it with several alterations raising the minimum plot size at thirty statute acres and adding stronger punitive disincentives to sub-division by the purchaser. Poulett Scrope was highly critical of this minimum and feared that it would be used to clear the existing occupying tenantry holding smaller plots, but to Devon this was one of the attractions of the Bill.[338] Clarendon was not unaware of the danger posed by this aspect of the Bill, and feared the 'planting [of] little Tipperaries all over Ireland' if the plots were too small.[339] The Bill received the royal assent, but proved as abortive as the 1848 Encumbered Estates Act it paralleled.

---

334 Ibid., 391–3 [P.D. Jeffers]. Shareholders included Devon, Monteagle, William Monsell, Joseph Fagan, Henry Maunsell and Barrington, and it received statements of support from figures as diverse as Lord Sligo, Sir Robert Kane and the Catholic Bishop of Derry, *A Bill for the establishment of the Farmers' Estate Society, Ireland*, P.P. 1847–8 (534), II, 397.

335 Clarendon to Lansdowne, 12 May, Clar. Dep. Ir., letterbook II; Clarendon to Lewis, 12 May 1848, Clar. Dep., c.532/1.

336 By May 1848 there were around thirty agricultural instructors, mostly supported by charitable funds, preaching the advantages of 'green crops' to farmers throughout the island. Clarendon's other 'improving' initiatives included the promotion of model agricultural schools under the National Board, and the introduction of official agricultural statistics for Ireland in 1847, [M.W. Savage], 'Lord Clarendon's administration', *Edinburgh* Review, XCI (Jan. 1851), pp. 264–9, 276–80. British observers attributed the limited success of the instructors primarily to the demoralized dependency of the small farmers, *Illustrated London News*, 26 Aug. 1848.

337 G. Grey to Clarendon, 16 May, Clar. Dep. Ir., box 12; Palmerston to Russell, 15 May, Lansdowne memo: 'Notes on the Irish Land Bill', 15 May, Russell Papers, PRO 30/22/7C, fols. 36–7, 53–4.

338 *Hans.*, C, 1041–2 [31 July]; ibid., CI, 255–8 [18 Aug.]. Only four other MPs supported Scrope's amendment to lower the minimum, Sharman Crawford, Feargus O'Connor, and two English radicals.

339 Clarendon to Somerville, 4 Aug., Clar. Dep. Ir., letterbook III.

The failure of the 1848 legislation to offer a practicable or popular solution to the land question demonstrated both the limitations of Russell's thought on the subject and the difficulties of his position. He was prepared to ignore orthodox political economy and entertain radical and non-British models for Irish reconstruction, but he lacked the legal expertise and political weight and will to impose them on reluctant colleagues and an unruly parliament. Political weakness frequently forced him into supporting what he considered to be second-best options. Yet even if Russell had been able to have his own way, it is by no means certain that he would have been able to implement a popular land policy. His belief that those tenants who could not avoid pauperization should be deprived of their holdings – a belief he maintained throughout the Famine crisis – created a bitterness which no amount of facilitation of purchase or promises of compensation could salve.[340]

Endowment or plantation? Russell and Peel, 1848–9

In the aftermath of the failure of the 1848 programme, Russell turned his attention to Catholic endowment as the precondition for an effective remedial project in 1849. Whig government in Ireland could not be truly effective without the co-operation of popular Irish interests, but in the aftermath of O'Connell's death and the Young Ireland rebellion it was useless to attempt to conciliate the Repeal movement. Russell resisted calls from the right for the extension of coercive powers to close down Conciliation Hall, on the grounds that it would infringe the 'equality of privileges' inherent in the Union, but the Repeal Association was anyway clearly in its death-throes. It was to the Catholic Church, then, that Russell turned in his search for Irish allies. He told Clarendon: 'The Priests and we are in the same boat to row against the current of infidelity and communism setting in with Mitchel and Duffy. Anything which would unite us with the Priests would be good.'[341]

Russell was concerned more with mutual co-operation than attempting to manipulate the clergy as agents of social and political control in Ireland, but his party's record on this matter was ambiguous. The published opinions of Senior and the known views of several members of the cabinet tended towards the latter and aroused intense Catholic suspicions. The Prime Minister was aware that the scheme could succeed only with the full consent of the clergy, but he believed that in their present straitened circumstances, this would be forthcoming. In September 1848 he visited Dublin to consult with Clarendon and the Irish government on this and other reforms.[342] Agreement was reached on an Irish land tax which

340 Russell to Clarendon, 9 July, ibid., box 43. See below, p. 295–7.

341 Russell to Clarendon, 8, 11 Aug., Clar. Dep. Ir., box 43.

342 His reception there was characterized by popular indifference rather than overt hostility, *Times*, 4, 7, 11 Sept. 1848. Redington, the leading Catholic in the Irish government, agreed

would provide the finance for railways, drainage and emigration as well as (via a circuitous route to avoid the opposition of Protestant landowners) for the indirect endowment of the Catholic clergy.[343]

Russell was fully aware of the dangers of failure, but was sure that Peel would provide parliamentary support.[344] Indeed, there was an element of emulation of Peel's political martyrdom of 1846 in Russell's insistence to the cabinet that he would rather go out of government on the issue of this 'great remedy' than evade his political duty,[345] although he was denied this dubious honour by the refusal of the Irish bishops to countenance any form of endowment. This fiasco not only further undermined his standing within the cabinet, but cut the heart out of his remedial scheme for 1849. The remaining elements now lacked a unifying centre and had little chance of a popular reception in Ireland.[346] These proposals, including a simplified and strengthened Landlord-Tenant Bill, a Leasehold Tenure Conversion Bill, a uniform £8 Rating Franchise Bill, the facilitation of the sale of Church lands, and the land tax for public works, were rapidly shelved.[347] The government was left in the deeply embarrassing situation of having nothing to propose alongside the renewal of coercion.[348]

This was all the more serious in the context of a further escalation of the Irish social and economic crisis in the winter of 1848–9. The press recorded forced and voluntary clearances on an unprecedented scale, and in some places a resurgence of Ribbonism.[349] What appeared particularly disturbing was the eagerness of 'comfortable' farmers – the class on which great hopes had been placed for the reconstruction of the country – to abandon their holdings and emigrate with

---

that endowment was desirable and feasible, but argued against a stipend. Redington also pointed to the problems inherent in Russell's suggestion of an Irish land tax for endowment, and recommended that the project be accompanied by a thorough reform of the Anglican Church establishment. Russell rejected the latter as impolitic but agreed that the precise form of endowment should be left to the Catholic bishops and Rome, Redington to Russell, 7 Sept., Russell to Redington, 9 Sept., Russell Papers, PRO 30/22/7D, fols. 30–48, 51–4.

343 For the continuing anti-Catholic virulence of much of Irish Tory opinion, see [O'Sullivan], 'Condition of Ireland', pp. 230–5.

344 Graham explicitly made Catholic endowment the price for his support of the government, Greville to Clarendon, 9 Feb. 1849, Clar. Dep., c.522.

345 Broughton Diary, Add. MS 43,753, fols. 46–8 [24 Oct. 1848].

346 Prest, *Russell*, pp. 290–2. For a detailed account of the endowment fiasco, see Kerr, *'A nation of beggars'?*, pp. 166–95.

347 Russell memo, 8 Sept. 1848, Clar. Dep. Ir., box 43.

348 Greville, *Journal*, III, 266–7 [7, 9 Feb. 1849]. The cabinet was again divided over coercion. Russell and the moralists favoured renewing the suspension of Habeas Corpus for six months, while moderates demanded a full year.

349 One Irish paper called on the *Times* to send its 'commissioner' back to Ireland to report to the English people 'the fearful system of wholesale ejectment . . . which we daily behold . . . a mockery of the eternal laws of God – a flagrant outrage on the principles of nature', *Tipperary Vindicator*, cited in *Times*, 11 Dec. 1848.

4. Paddy! Will you now, take me while I'm in the humour? *The Puppet-Show*, 9 Sept. 1848. Lord John Russell's visit to Ireland in the wake of the 1848 Rising did nothing to enhance his image in England. 'Little Johnny' carrying little of substance in his Gladstone bag, appeared incapable of dealing with inveterate Irish political and agrarian violence.

5. Yankee Doodle's Corn Exchange, *Yankee Doodle*, 21 Nov. 1846. The American press was quick to draw moral lessons from the Irish Famine. The surplus of the New World, in the view of this New York magazine, would soon be made available to redress the deficiencies of the Old. The precise mechanism of exchange is left unclear.

whatever capital they could acquire.[350] A government survey of districts affected by the rebellion in 1848 also pointed to the restlessness and expectations of the middling farmer class. A resident magistrate at Thurles, County Tipperary, warned that the existing 'tranquillity' owed more to despondency than to any appearance of industrial habits, and that 'at present the great ambition of the majority of the population is expatriation – every man with sufficient means will leave Ireland in the Spring and Summer.' A report from Clare described the poor as 'quite apathetic [and] broken-spirited' and noted that with the collapse of competition for land the old 'system' of crime had collapsed. Land conflict had not ceased but acquired a different sociological character: 'though there is nothing to be apprehended from those who were small farmers and cottiers, most of whom are out of existence, at least as such . . . some of the better class of farmers, endeavouring to hold their position, complain of the severity of the landlords – and some crimes may be committed.'[351]

British public opinion continued to call for Irish land reform. The radical *Daily News*, which had taken up elements of the Millite economics cast aside by the *Morning Chronicle* when that paper passed to Peelite control,[352] demanded the removal of the 'pauper landlord [who] stands between the masses and the soil', and the granting of whatever form of tenure or proprietary that would engender sufficient security to 'keep the peasantry of the west in the west'.[353] The *Times* differed sharply with its junior rival on several points of policy, but was also convinced of the necessity of taking further the principle of the 1848 Encumbered Estates Act as a means of promoting the desired 'social revolution' in the countryside. It insisted that land be made liable for proprietors' arrears of poor rate, facilitating its 'transfer . . . from a negligent and embarrassed to a thrifty and energetic class. A confiscation of this kind would be a blessing, not an injustice, both to the peasantry and their landlords.'[354]

---

350 *Times*, 28 Nov., 11 Dec. This tendency was exacerbated by the simultaneous collapse of grain and livestock prices in 1849, see James S. Donnelly, 'Production, prices and exports, 1846–51', in Vaughan, *N.H.I.*, *V*, 286–93.

351 'Confidential reports on the state of lately disturbed districts by the Resident Magistrates' (Jan. 1849), Ribbonism, vol. III, Dublin Castle Records, Colonial Office Papers, Public Record Office, London, CO 904/9, fols. 326–52.

352 Sir John Easthope, irritated by Russell's reluctance to make the *Chronicle* the organ of government, sold his paper to a group of Peelites including Lincoln and Herbert in February 1848. The editorial line became highly critical of the government's Irish policy, but its position was now landlordist rather than radical, Broughton Diary, Add. MS 43,750, fols. 20, 112–13 [22 April, 17 July 1847]; Donald Read, *Peel and the Victorians* (Oxford, 1987), pp. 251–6.

353 *Daily News*, 1 Jan. 1849.

354 *Times*, 16, 22 Nov. 1848, 9 Feb. 1849. Such statements aroused the fury of landlord spokesmen, who denounced the government as the tool of ignorant public opinion in England, [Andrew John Maley], *Observations upon the inutility of exterminating the resident landlords of Ireland* (Dublin, 1849).

The political deadlock was broken by two powerful speeches made by Sir Robert Peel in the Commons, proposing a comprehensive programme for tackling the continuing crisis in the west of Ireland. The most striking element in Peel's speeches was the demand for the facilitation of the transfer of landed property, which he articulated as the revival of the historical principle of plantation – the system which had brought Ulster from a 'state of nature' to prosperity. The purpose of this new plantation would not be to bolster Protestantism, but to channel commercial investment from Britain to the west. It would introduce 'new proprietors who shall take possession of the land of Ireland, freed from its present encumbrances, and enter into its cultivation with adequate capital, with new feelings, and inspired by new hopes'. As the 1848 Act had palpably failed, he recommended a major departure from its principle in the establishment of a commission with powers sufficient to side-step the equity courts in the buying and selling of land. This would, if accompanied by a restriction on the maximum local rate, and forced sales for rate arrears, 'infuse new blood into Ireland, new enterprise, and a new division of property'.[355]

On 30 March, Peel took the idea of the commission further, recommending that it have not only the legal power of superseding the courts and granting indisputable title to land, but that it should be entrusted with the administrative superintendence of the poor relief and works activities in the west. It was, in effect, to be a 'general controlling authority', acting in concert with the government, but discharging its duties on the spot. The commission was to have the power of managing and making improvements on the encumbered estates surrendered to it.[356]

Like most of Peel's visions the proposal was not original. Edward Ellice had suggested in autumn 1848 an active commission that 'might work the redemption and regeneration' of Connaught,[357] and in November the *Times* had also explicitly approved the plantation principle for the west, arguing that 'with a well-selected infusion of Scotch or English labourers, an example might be set of good husbandry, which all Ireland would do well to imitate'.[358] It may appear surprising that Peel's thought should have been moving in parallel with moralist opinion, and that both had come to advocate a departure from strict *laissez-faire* policy by early 1849. An examination of motives reveals some shared pre-occupations. The former Prime Minister's 1849 *démarche* was by no means a party move; his refusal to countenance an organized Peelite opposition was at this time progressively alienating Gladstone and Lincoln,[359] and he had no intention of risking the

355 *Hans.*, CIII, 179–92 [5 March 1849]. This speech contained his first public criticism of Whig famine policy since 1846, and amounted to a call for a return to the works and poor relief (but not the food) policies of 1845–6.

356 Ibid., CIV, 87–117 [30 March].

357 Ellice to Wood, 27 Oct. 1848, Hickleton papers, A4/103.

358 *Times*, 16 Nov. 1848.

359 Munsell, *The unfortunate duke*, pp. 92–3, 99–101. All the leading Peelites except Peel and Graham opposed Russell's Rate in Aid Bill.

formation of a Protectionist or radical government by bringing down Russell.[360] There is no doubt that Peel felt genuine sympathy for the plight of the people of the west, but his proposals reflected his pre-conceptions of the underlying structural problem of landownership. Peel had long favoured an efficient encumbered estates measure as the paramount regenerative instrument for Ireland, and the proposal of a commission with autocratic powers was the consummation of this line of thought. The political context accounts for much of his unprecedented commitment to state intervention. From early 1849 the revived Protectionist Party launched a sustained attack on the free trade settlement of 1845–6, and Peel was particularly sensitive to Disraeli's charge that the repeal of the Corn Laws had caused much of the current Irish distress and posed an obstacle to that country's recovery.[361]

Peel's response was to contend that the 'plantation of Connaught' would complete the process begun in 1846 of introducing capitalist farming on English principles into Ireland. The results of the 1848 harvest had confirmed his confidence in the course he had taken in 1845–6, but it also pointed to the folly of leaving recovery to the gradual action of 'natural forces'. The renewed potato blight demonstrated that 'unless vigorous efforts be made to improve both the moral and physical condition of the people, they will continue to rely upon that which experience has shown to be a most deceitful article of food. We have the prospect before us of a recurrence of that calamity, which for anything we know may not be casual, but the result of some mysterious agency, permanent in its operation.' The potential agricultural resources of the west were, he believed, immense – but these could only be realized through the influx of new proprietors and managers, imbued with commercial principles.[362] It would be the task of these men to wean the populace from the potato and induce them to begin the necessary cultivation of grain crops. The commission should assist them by providing reproductive employment and promoting emigration from congested areas. This interference, of a temporary and curative character, could be legitimated by reference to the continuing providential visitation:

> It has pleased God to afflict us with a great calamity – which may, perhaps, be improved into a blessing, if it awakens us to a due sense of the danger which threatens us: without this warning, we might have gone on from year to year, with little thought of the future; still trusting to one precarious root for the subsistence of millions . . . Let us now profit by this solemn warning – let us deeply consider whether 'out of this nettle, danger, we may not pluck the

360 Graham opposed Peel's initiative on 30 March, Greville, *Journal*, III, 285 [2 April 1849]. Graham's growing indifference to the fate of Irish proprietors mirrored his similar fatalist attitude towards distressed West Indian planters, ibid., p. 175 [14 May 1848].

361 Robert Stewart, *The politics of protection: Lord Derby and the Protectionist Party, 1841–52* (Cambridge, 1971), pp. 139–61; *Hans.*, CIV, 204–11 [2 April 1849: Disraeli].

362 Ibid., CIII, 185–92 [5 March].

> flower, safety' – and convert a grievous affliction into a means of future improvement and a source of future security.[363]

Not to act in such an 'extraordinary' way, he confided to the former Devon Commissioner, John Wynne, would allow Irish society to slide back into its pre-Famine condition and 'in a very short time [give us] the same cause for repentance that we have not profited by the warning which should have stimulated us to break through the vicious circle of the past.'[364]

Peel's proposals caught the imagination of the British and Irish press. The *Times* initially thought the plan utopian and challenged Peel to settle in Connaught himself, but soon swung around to support the central theme of 'free trade in land'. This shift was assisted by a similar diagnosis of the Irish situation: 'Has not Providence, in the course of its mysterious dispensations, brought about again an extraordinary conjuncture of circumstances so near akin to those which opened Ulster to the British settler as to encourage a like attempt? . . . Has not the crisis come for a new "plantation" of Ireland?'[365] The paper was, however, selective in its praise and ignored the 'general controlling authority' aspects of the commission.[366] The *Daily News* was similarly selective, enthusing on the tone of Peel's intervention and his skill at minting a coin 'of the same metal that lay worthless in other hands'. Peel had given hope to Ireland by authoritatively challenging the 'natural causes' doctrine and exposing the 'miserable stop-gap, the Rate in Aid', but much of his plan was miscellaneous, vague in principle, and mystifying in detail. Echoing Mill's viewpoint, the paper held that the west should be 'colonized' by its own smallholding farmers, through the break-up and sale of small portions of estates, and the settling of peasant proprietors on reclaimed waste lands.[367]

Peel's speeches were reported to have made a 'profound sensation' in Ireland, and to have 'fallen like a thunder clap on all parties'. The *Freeman's Journal* was initially 'in a state of perfect bewilderment, blowing hot and cold and seeming not to know whether to praise or censure', while the *Evening Mail* saw the speeches as an attempt to 'conciliate the Moloch of Irish agitation' with a scheme aimed at the final destruction of the Irish landlords.[368] The *Cork Examiner* was most positive about the land proposals, arguing that 'it was insanity to expect the condition of the inhabitants of the country to be changed for the better, until the whole system was revolutionized.' Most Irish nationalist and liberal papers seem to have

363 *Hans.*, CIV, 98–101 [30 March 1849].

364 Peel to Wynne, 13 April 1849, in Winston Guthrie-Jones, *The Wynnes of Sligo and Leitrim* (Manorhamilton, 1994), pp. 66–7.

365 *Times*, 7, 9, 28 March 1849.

366 Ibid., 31 March, 2 April.

367 *Daily News*, 6, 12 March, 2 April; the *Illustrated London News* was less critical, and more enthusiastic about the abandonment of *laissez-faire*, but it too thought that an encumbered estates bill should have priority, *ILN*, 7 April 1849.

368 *Times*, 9 March; *Dublin Evening Mail*, 7 March.

eventually endorsed 'Peel's plan', but usually in a partial and confused manner.[369] Its limitations were only noted in more considered retrospective analyses.[370]

The government, predictably, was less welcoming. Russell thought it a 'hollow and unsound proposal', but was anxious for the success of his Rate in Aid Bill, and instructed Sir George Grey not to dismiss it.[371] Grey's private opinion was that the speeches would stir up unrealizable hopes and expectations among Irish tenants, indebted landowners (who would expect higher land prices as a result of state intervention) and English Cobdenites.[372] The most extreme reaction came, however, from the Lord Lieutenant, who exploded with indignation against Peel's 'blatherumskyte'. The former Premier had, in his view, abused his authority: 'A spouter at an Irish committee meeting might have put forward such a scheme but for a man in Peel's position who must be supposed to mean what he says it is absurd.' The central flaw lay in the enormous advances of public money required for land purchase and the auxiliary tasks of the commission; this, Clarendon noted, was politically out of the question.[373]

Peel's second speech did nothing to alter these opinions, but the evident strength of public response in Ireland and England to the proposals obliged the cabinet to consider some positive reaction.[374] Redington advised the government to endorse Peel's scheme as far as it could. Arguing that Peel was correct with regard to the danger of continued potato cultivation and the need to 'secure the consumption of cereal food', he warned that unless measures were taken to promote the investment of capital in drainage and farming improvements, many landowners would have no option but to turn their estates into sheep-walks. Yet while Redington as a western landowner sympathized with the plan, as an administrator he recognized it would require massive subvention. The most practicable elements of the plan were, to his mind, the suggestions for facilitating sales.[375]

---

369 *Cork Examiner*, reprinted *Times*, 9 March. The *Limerick Examiner's* comment that it would like to see the co-operation of Peel, Scrope and Twisleton in tackling Ireland's problems was representative. These three held widely diverging opinions on both the land question and the Poor Law, but enjoyed a popularity in Ireland that derived from their common denunciation of the lethargy and dogmatism of the government, *Limerick Examiner*, reprinted *Times*, 14 April 1849.

370 [Patrick McMahon], 'Ireland – spirit of recent legislation', *Dublin Review*, XXVII (Dec. 1849), 392–3.

371 Russell to Clarendon, 13 March, Clar. Dep. Ir., box 26; G. Grey to Clarendon, 9 March, ibid., box 13; *Hans.*, CIII, 218–29 [5 March 1849]. For the rate in aid, see below, pp. 311–17.

372 G. Grey to Clarendon, 12 March, Clar. Dep. Ir., box 13.

373 Clarendon to G. Grey, 7 March, ibid., letterbook III, Clarendon to G. Grey, 10 March, ibid., letterbook IV.

374 Broughton Diary, Add. MS 43,753, fols. 135–7 [30, 31 March].

375 Redington to Clarendon, 1 April 1849, Russell Papers, PRO 30/22/7F, fols. 112–17. The tension between Redington's two roles is evident in this letter. Significantly, he concluded that the interests of the estate and the tenantry must be put before those of the encumbered proprietor, however innocent as an individual. Somerville also appears to have

Clarendon's personal inclination was for an 'experiment' of specific state assistance to a company of English capitalists who were considering buying the huge Martin estate in Connemara, but he felt obliged to discuss Peel's general ideas with him in London. The former Prime Minister's tact and 'extraordinary cordiality' did much to disarm Clarendon's suspicion, and the Lord Lieutenant was convinced that he had persuaded Peel of the irresponsibility of the entire commission scheme. Clarendon's ire was now turned against his own colleagues. Greville recorded that: 'His indignation against his own political friends is boundless . . . he is equally indignant about the past and hopeless about the future; hopeless, because John Russell is so infirm of purpose, that he will not predominate over his Cabinet and prevent the chaos of opinions and interests which prevent anything Clarendon proposes being done.'[376] The Lord Lieutenant left with a memorandum putting the proposed commission into a practicable form, which he proceeded to lay before the cabinet.[377] He meanwhile placed considerable indirect pressure on Russell to adopt an advanced position.[378] For once the Viceroy was working in tandem with the cabinet moralists, who had long advocated a more advanced measure.[379]

Russell's defensive and pessimistic speech to the Commons on 2 April, in which he denied the existence of an Irish panacea and argued that the prevention of potato cultivation was beyond the power of government, went far to justify Clarendon's anger. Russell did, however, take advantage of the political situation to commit the government to overhauling the 1848 Encumbered Estates Act.[380] By early 1849 the government had been obliged to recognize that the Act had failed because of its conferment of incomplete titles and by being 'clogged up with technical preliminaries and safeguards'.[381] Brady, Romilly and Redington had been

---

become reconciled to the idea of a strong encumbered estates bill at an early point, Wood to Russell, 28 Sept. 1847, ibid., 6F, fol. 129.

376 Greville, *Journal*, III, 286–7 [6 April 1849].

377 Peel, memo, n.d. (April 1849), C.S. Parker, *Sir Robert Peel from his private papers* (3 vols., London, 1891–9), III, 513–16.

378 Grey and Wood believed that Clarendon had colluded with Delane in suggesting a *Times* attack on Russell's most vulnerable point, the loss of the reformist zeal of 'the historical Whigs'. According to the paper: 'The Whigs, at least, have exhausted their quiver . . . The faith which did once remove mountains, which cast a hundred ancient boroughs and as many corporations and a dozen Irish bishoprics to the bottom of the sea, fails before a gigantic nuisance which condemns vast districts of Ireland to perpetual uncultivation and pauperism. The courts of law govern Ireland, and Lord John is only the humble servitor of those courts, who goes about with his rate-book, his ink-bottle, and steel pen, to collect money from their victims.' *Times*, 14 April 1849; Grey Diary, 15 April, Grey Papers.

379 For moralist support for 'free trade in land' among Trevelyan's subordinates in Ireland, see Capt. Pole to Trevelyan, 19 March 1849, Treasury Papers, T64/366A.

380 *Hans.*, CIV, 211–27 [2 April].

381 Pierce Mahony, *Incumbered Estates Act (Ireland) . . . Case and opinion* (Dublin, 1849); Mahony to Clarendon, 24 Feb. 1849, Clar. Dep. Ir., box 34. Mahony had criticized the 1848 Act, but been rebuffed by Trevelyan, Mahony to Trevelyan, 12, 18 Sept., 26 Oct. 1848, Trevelyan to Mahony, 16 Sept. 1848, Treasury Papers, T64/366A.

preparing further reforms of real property law, but had not envisaged any major alterations to the equity courts.[382] These low key measures were unlikely to attract much political interest, and thus it was Peel's encumbered estates commission which was adopted as the keystone of the government's Bill in April.[383]

The limits of free trade, 1849–50

Russell's decision to place real property reform at the top of the legislative agenda in April 1849 clearly owed a great deal to Peel's forceful initiative, but it was taken up with a degree of enthusiasm, once it was shorn of expensive ancillary measures. Romilly proceeded to draw up a bill free of the hedging limitations of 1848; indefeasible title was to be granted to all purchasers under the Commission, and every encumbrancer was to be given the power of forcing a sale. Russell insisted that it should also contain powers for the Commission to undertake the sale of estates subject to Chancery suits.[384]

Peel's intervention also gave the 1849 Bill an authority it would otherwise have lacked. This was particularly the case with moderates, for it was widely known that Peel shared their concern about the strained Irish wages fund and did not advocate the measure out of any sense of social radicalism. Lansdowne declared himself willing to accept a bill that would have the effect of 'brushing away with a vigorous hand all legal hindrances to the transfer of property in Ireland', while Devon assured the Royal Dublin Society that sales at market value would attract vast capital investment, perhaps doubling the produce per acre of land.[385] Whig-Liberal malcontents, such as Monteagle and Hatherton, would have preferred the adoption of the Peel plan *in toto*, but the Bill had enough of his imprimatur to limit their objections.[386]

---

382 Brady's preferred approaches were the reform of Chancery receiverships, and the promotion of leases by means of a radical franchise bill. The others looked to an improved system of land registration and the granting of powers to lessees for life and in tail to charge their estates for improvements, Brady to Clarendon, 22 Jan., 2 April 1849, Clar. Dep. Ir., box 2; Romilly to G. Grey, 13 Nov. 1848, Redington memo, n.d. (Nov. 1848), ibid., box 24.

383 Russell to Clarendon, 7, 9 April 1849, ibid., box 26, Romilly to Russell, 7 April, Russell Papers, PRO 30/22/7F, fols. 144–5. The ministers considered not only Peel's proposal, but another by John Pitt Kennedy for granting parliamentary title to purchasers. Kennedy was deeply dissatisfied with government policy and anxious for 'comprehensive measures', but he differed sharply with Peel in his views on the reform of the Poor Law. See *First report of the select committee of the House of Lords, appointed to inquire into the operation of the Irish Poor Law, and the expediency of making any amendment in its enactments*, P.P. 1849 (192), XVI, 217–24.

384 Romilly to Clarendon, 16 April, Clar. Dep. Ir., box 23; *Hans.*, CIV, 892–900 [26 April: Romilly].

385 Lansdowne to Russell, n.d. (April 1849), Russell Papers, PRO 30/22/7F, fols. 99–102; Earl of Devon, *Paper on Ireland: read at the Dublin Society in March, 1849* (London, 1849).

386 Monteagle to Peel, 9 April, Parker, *Peel*, III, 516; Hatherton to Monteagle, 22 March, Monteagle Papers, MS 13,399/2.

Speaking for middle-class radicalism in the Commons, Bright condemned both Russell's inaction and Peel's call for increased expenditure. At the heart of the Irish problem, he contended, lay a structure of landholding based on the false doctrine of the 'sacredness of property'. The solution was obvious – 'to remove every obstacle in the way of the free sale of land'.[387] The opinion of Bright and his colleagues could not be ignored by the government in the wake of the 1847 election. Radical hostility had led to the mauling of Wood's budget in 1848, and in 1849 their retrenchment and reform campaign was augmented by the mass agitation of the Financial Reform Association.[388] In April the radicals forced the issue with Bernal Osborne's notice for a committee of inquiry into the management and sale of estates by the Court of Chancery. They received some support from the moralist wing of the Whig-Liberals; Ellice distrusted Osborne, but was also keen to make the proposed committee an engine of '*radical* reform', which would undertake the amendment of the Encumbered Estates Bill should it be watered down by the Irish law officers. He warned Russell that the initiative lay with the radicals, who would give great difficulty over money votes unless the government proved it was prepared to 'override old habits and . . . prejudices in effecting reforms'.[389] With the *Times* taking a similarly robust moralist stance,[390] the political climate made it virtually impossible for Russell to resist such a measure, even if he had been so inclined.

Despite its more radical character, the 1849 Encumbered Estates Bill had an easier passage through parliament. This was partly due to Peel's unreserved endorsement and quiet abandonment of the rest of his plantation scheme.[391] Only twelve MPs voted against the third reading, mostly English and Irish Protectionists violently opposed to Peel and his works, who claimed that the Bill fundamentally undermined the rights of property in both countries.[392] The most vociferous opposition came, however, from a small cross-party group who sought to defend the professional interests of lawyers and the 'integrity' of the Court of Chancery.[393] The majority of Irish liberals and Repealers did, as expected, give strong support to the Bill; for the English radicals, Bright declared the Bill faultless.[394] Russell had good

---

387 *Hans.*, CIV, 161–80 [2 April].

388 In January, up to 12,000 people at a Manchester meeting heard Bright attribute Irish suffering to 'the oligarchical government of this country', *Daily News*, 12 Jan. 1849.

389 Ellice to Russell, 9, 11 April, Russell Papers, PRO 30/22/7F, fols. 164–5, 169–70. In the event Osborne's committee was kept out of radical control, and recommended a series of practical equity reforms acceptable to Whig-Liberals and Peelites, *Second report from the select committee on receivers, Courts of Chancery and Exchequer (Ireland)*, P.P. 1849 (494), VIII, 645.

390 *Times*, 30 April 1849.

391 Peel to Clarendon, 6 April, Clar. Dep. Ir., box 42; *Hans.*, CIV, 910–15 [26 April].

392 Ibid., CV, 1103–4 [4 June: Henley].

393 Ibid., 766–7 [21 May: Grogan], 1095–8 [4 June: Napier]; CIV, 900–3 [26 April: Stuart], CV, 772 [21 May: Turner].

394 Ibid., CIV, 915–16 [26 April: Bright].

reason to remark with relief that the House's reaction was much more well disposed than in 1847 and 1848.[395]

Opposition was also more muted in the Lords. Brougham fractiously defended the interests of his profession, and Glengall resorted to absurd hyperbole about the dangers of 'communism and socialism' lurking in the Bill.[396] Monteagle made the only reasoned case against the Bill. His objection was not to its principle, but to the inclusion of a clause permitting the superior courts to impose judgements on estates for the arrears of poor rate. The potential consequence was that an estate would be forcibly sold by the Commission for the 'fraudulent' debts imposed on it by tenants who absconded without paying their rent or rates. In these circumstances, he argued, the Bill would amount to a declaration of 'legislative war against a class that was now the most suffering in Ireland'.[397] Monteagle was not, however, prepared to press this opposition, and was placated by a number of amendments proposed by Stanley and accepted by the government. Stanley's moderation and the government's tractability ensured that the Bill, along with auxiliary measures relating to judgments and registration, passed into law in July.[398]

The enactment of the Encumbered Estates Act of 1849 went far to stimulate the supply side of the Irish land market, but numerous doubts remained as to the existence of sufficient demand. The press had been replete with reports of offers of portions of estates, which had received 'no bidders at realistic prices' in the first half of the year.[399] In public ministers expressed confidence that once the Commission was operative, a large number of purchasers would come forward, although Campbell in the Lords conceded that this effect might at first be gradual.[400] In private, however, a number of ministers were more sceptical.[401] Clarendon looked to the auxiliary schemes of 1848 as the means of meeting this difficulty, and recommended a plan based on the principle of the Farmers' Estate Society. It was proposed that the state take over and enlarge the scheme, and add Brady's land consolidation clauses to compensate small tenants for the loss of their interest in the soil. The plan would be financed either by the issuing of debentures – an idea

---

395 Russell to Clarendon, 27 April, Clar. Dep. Ir., box 26.

396 *Hans.*, CV, 1343–51 [11 June: Brougham], 1351–60 [Glengall]. Ministers privately remarked that Glengall's position smacked of a certain hypocrisy, for he had endeavoured to secure the benefits of such a measure for himself through private legislation, Clarendon to G. Grey, 7 July, Clar. Dep. Ir., letterbook IV.

397 *Hans.*, CV, 1361–4 [11 June].

398 Ibid., CVI, 709–14 [22 June], 1040–2 [28 June], CVII, 960–2 [26 July]. Stanley proposed that the owner be given the power to veto a sale where less than half the value of his estate was encumbered. Clarendon and Lansdowne thought this amendment insignificant, but Romilly resisted anything more than the minimum concession, Clarendon to G. Grey, 3 July, Clar. Dep. Ir., letterbook IV, G. Grey to Clarendon, 7 July, ibid., box 13.

399 *Times*, 2, 9, 14 June 1849.

400 *Hans.*, CV, 1107 [4 June: Romilly], CVI, 1041 [28 June: Campbell].

401 Clarendon to Russell, 6 May, Clar. Dep. Ir., letterbook IV.

borrowed from the Prussian Land Bank plan – or through co-operation with a company of English capitalists. Clarendon believed this quite feasible: 'It would be something in the nature of the Peel commission but practical and as I believe, remunerative, and at all events entailing no great risk as it need not be commenced on too great a scale and might at any moment be suspended. It would moreover be bold and new and the moral effect would be good.'[402] Wood's hostility was, however, inevitable, and Russell lacked the nerve to withstand the stream of Treasury objections.[403] While the Prime Minister assured Clarendon that he would see if anything could be done with it, the plan was effectively shelved.[404]

Following this rebuff, Clarendon turned to the alternative strategy of giving specific assistance to a high-profile experiment of English corporate investment. Reports that groups of investors were beginning to take such an interest no doubt stimulated his hopes.[405] In late June Clarendon began a correspondence with the Lord Mayor of London on the subject. Abandoning his earlier expressions of sympathy for insolvent Irish landlords, Clarendon now declared his belief that 'an extensive change in the Proprietary class is a condition indispensable to the progress and prosperity of this country.' He assured the Lord Mayor that investment would be remunerative, and that in the present social and political state of Ireland, there would be little resistance to agricultural reform.[406] He simultaneously sought to persuade the cabinet that if assistance was forthcoming, such investment would prove the 'turning point of Irish futurity', and assured the sceptical Clanricarde that 'if we get a million or two laid out judiciously the price of land would soon rise and the people would be employed and political, social and religious grievances would redress themselves.'[407]

Despite Clarendon's claims to the contrary, the plans of the London Corporation to purchase Irish land smacked of Peel's 'new plantation'. This aspect of the plan was open to misinterpretation, particularly with regard to its religious connotations, and was a point of sensitivity for the Lord Mayor.[408] Ironically, it was precisely the

---

402 Clarendon to Wood, 9 May, ibid.

403 Trevelyan to Clarendon, 16, 26 Feb. 1849, ibid., box 60; Wood to Clarendon, 16 May, ibid., box 32.

404 Russell to Clarendon, 12 May, ibid., box 26, G. Grey to Clarendon, 5 July, ibid., box 13. One historian has observed in this abortive proposal the prototype of the Land Purchase Acts introduced from 1885, Lane, 'Encumbered Estates Court', pp. 440–1. Private attempts to establish a more popular 'Irish Peasant-Proprietor Joint Stock Association' were also abortive, *Freeman's Journal*, 30 Nov., 5 Dec. 1849.

405 In May it was reported that a joint-stock company of London investors might be formed for the purchase of the huge Martin estate in Connemara, *Leinster Express*, reprinted *Times*, 28 May 1849.

406 Clarendon to Duke, 26 June, Clar. Dep. Ir., letterbook IV.

407 Clarendon to G. Grey, 24 June, Clarendon to Russell, 26 June, ibid.; Clarendon to Clanricarde, 26 June, Clanricarde Papers, bundle 73.

408 Duke to Clarendon, 26 July, Clar. Dep. Ir., box 10. The *Times* did not help by welcoming the proposals in precisely these terms. It argued that: 'The City of London does nothing

legacy of the Irish Society's involvement in the seventeenth-century plantation of Ulster that led to a breakdown of talks with the government in the following months, for the Society demanded that its Ulster property be specifically excluded from the operation of the government's Leasehold Tenure Bill.[409] Ultimately the London scheme fell through and Clarendon had to admit that only harm had resulted from falsely raised expectations.[410] Huge encumbered properties in the west, such as the Martin estate in Connemara, proved deeply unattractive to individual or corporate purchasers for years to come.[411]

Some consolation for this failure was derived from the English interest in Irish land that was apparently stimulated by the Queen's visit in August. Clarendon and Russell had been anxious for a royal visit for some time on the grounds that it would boost the morale of the country and give symbolic resonance to the Union. Yet the degree of popular enthusiasm witnessed in Cork, Dublin and Belfast, surprised even the visit's organizers.[412] Privately, the visit stirred greater controversy; Archbishop MacHale was infuriated by Archbishop Murray's refusal to include a denunciation of government policy in the Catholic prelates' address to the Queen.[413] The Whig-Liberals themselves were divided; popular symbolism of the visit was of particular concern to Foxites, while ostentation was vigorously opposed by the Treasury moralists, and the whole affair was denounced as a 'great lie' by Monteagle and Fitzwilliam.[414] Clarendon hoped that the interest shown by the 'swarms of strangers now visiting Ireland' would produce permanent good, and urged the *Times* to promote this.[415] He sought to keep up this momentum by giving official sanction to the tour and investigative report of James Caird, a Scottish

---

more than propose to proceed with an old work, and to carry out an existing design. Having revived one extensive district from the desolations of war, it proposes to rescue another from the lingering and recurrent visitations of famine. It is a link of distant ages when we see a great work resumed.' *Times*, 7 July 1849.

409 Clarendon to G. Grey, 9 July, Clar. Dep. Ir., letterbook IV.

410 Clarendon to G. Grey, 27 Sept., ibid.

411 See Tim Robinson (ed.), *Connemara after the Famine: journal of a survey of the Martin estate by Thomas Colville Scott, 1853* (Dublin, 1995), pp. vii–xix.

412 Cecil Woodham Smith, *The great hunger: Ireland 1845–1849* (London, 1987 edn), pp. 384–406. For the liberal unionist depiction of the visit as a source of 'new hope' for Ireland, see [Savage], 'Lord Clarendon's administration', pp. 236–40.

413 [Anon.], *Correspondence between the most Revd Dr MacHale, Archbishop of Tuam, and the most Revd Dr Murray, Archbishop of Dublin, relative to an address to be presented to Her Majesty Queen Victoria, on the occasion of her visit to Ireland in 1849* (Dublin, 1885).

414 Fortescue to Russell, 7, 10 July, Russell Papers, PRO 30/22/8A, fols. 8–11, Col. Phipps to Fortescue, 7 July, Fortescue Papers, 1262M/FC 105, Fitzwilliam to Monteagle, 2 Aug. 1849, Monteagle Papers, MS 13,399/7.

415 Clarendon to Reeve, 7 July, Clar. Dep., c.534/1; Clarendon to Russell, 16 Aug., Clar. Dep. Ir., letterbook IV; *Times*, 3, 9, 11 Aug. 1849. As if to promote this agenda, the *Illustrated London News* depicted the Queen's visit in detail, and published in July 'An excursion to the lakes of Killarney' – an uneasy blend of picturesque travelogue and what has more recently been described as 'disaster tourism', *ILN*, 21, 28 July, 4, 11, 18 Aug. 1849.

high-farming expert recommended to him by Peel.[416] The Lord Lieutenant's initial euphoria was succeeded by bouts of pessimism. Despite his satisfaction with Caird's work he found his hopes 'fast fading away' by October, as agrarian conflict and agitation reasserted itself as strongly as ever.[417]

The Encumbered Estates Commission proved to be more active and successful from the start of its operations in the autumn of 1849 than many had anticipated. The selection of Commissioners, on which much of the fears of landowners had concentrated, proved to be non-controversial. The three Commissioners – Baron Richards, Mountifort Longfield and C.J. Hargreave – demonstrated an eagerness to engage in 'clearing the augean stables of Chancery'.[418] Within six weeks petitions for the sale of property worth three million pounds had been received, and sales began once the rules of the Commission had been sanctioned by the government in October. Yet Clarendon feared that real capital investment could not be assured until the burdens on land were lifted.[419]

The figures submitted to parliament relating to the work of the Commission up to April 1853 – that is, before Gladstone's first budget lifted the remaining Famine debts from Irish land – at first sight appear to confound Clarendon's fears. By that time, 917 estates (or portions thereof) had been sold to 3428 purchasers for a total sum of £8,790,917.[420] Yet on closer examination, not only do Clarendon's concerns prove largely justified, but the social effects anticipated from the measure by most of its advocates can be shown to have been illusory. Despite the early optimism of its partisans,[421] expectations of a major anglicization of Irish land-

---

416 Clarendon to Peel, 2 Sept., Clar. Dep. Ir., letterbook IV; Graham to Peel, 27 Oct., Parker, *Peel*, III, 518. Peel was an enthusiastic admirer of Caird's vindication of prosperous farming under free-trade conditions, Peel to Graham, 27 Oct. 1849, Graham Papers, bundle 106; James Caird, *High farming under liberal covenants the best substitute for protection* (3rd edn, Edinburgh, 1850). This tract was dedicated to the 'Great Statesman, who sacrificed power, and the regard of friends, to the safety of his country; and who, free from the responsibilities of office, has not ceased to devote himself to the regeneration of Ireland'.

417 Clarendon to Peel, 24 Oct. 1849, Parker, *Peel*, III, 517. Caird's report, claiming that the west was eminently suited to profitable high-farming enterprise, was published as *The plantation scheme: the west of Ireland as a field for investment* (Edinburgh and London, 1850). In a similar vein, see [Anon.], *Remarks on Ireland; as it is; – as it ought to be; – and as it might be* (London, 1849).

418 Biographical sketches of the Commissioners and a brief outline of the court's history can be found in W.L. Burn, 'Free trade in land: an aspect of the Irish question', *Transactions of the Royal Historical Society*, 4th ser., XXXI (1949), 61–74. For Longfield's previous interest in the question, see also [Samuel O'Sullivan], 'Irish proprietorship', *Dublin University Magazine*, XXXII (Sept. 1848), p. 361.

419 Clarendon to Russell, 1 Sept., 30 Oct., 29 Nov., Clar. Dep. Ir., letterbook IV, letterbook V.

420 *Return from the Court for the sale of Encumbered Estates in Ireland, up to the 1st day of April 1853*, P.P. 1852–3 (390), XCIV, 599.

421 John Locke, *Ireland's recovery, or, excessive emigration and its reparative agencies in Ireland* (London, 1853), pp. 6–10; Harriet Martineau, *Letters from Ireland* (London, 1852), pp. 109–16, 145–9.

ownership were not realized. By 1857 only 4 per cent of purchasers (responsible for some 14 per cent of the value of sales) had come from outside Ireland. A modern study has suggested that, of the Irish purchasers, most came not from the urban or rural Catholic middle classes (as Russell had initially hoped), but from the established landed and professional elites, and particularly from the landed gentry and the more substantial middlemen. Moreover, much of this activity, in the context of the depressed land prices of the early 1850s, was carried on for the purpose of speculation.[422]

The results of the Act amounted, however, to something more than a simple 'Darwinian selection' of the most efficient indigenous landowners. Another unexpected and even more serious consequence was observed by Romilly in January 1850; large numbers of proprietors, not personally bound for the debts on the land they held, were applying to the Commission for the sale of their own estates at as low a price as possible. They were then seeking to acquire new loans to repurchase the estate, gaining in the process a clear parliamentary title, the clearing at minimum expense of old charges and settlements, and the halving of their original debts. The *Dublin Review* also commented on this process, declaring such incidents of fraud against creditors to be 'intolerably and outrageously iniquitous', while the *Dublin University Magazine* had only praise for the efficiency of the new Commission and was confident that it would not undermine Protestant power in the countryside.[423] By April 1853, 173 of the 917 whole or part estates sold under the Act had been brought before the court on the owner's personal petition.[424] The use of this strategy by landlords goes far to explain the considerable problem of the post-Famine landed indebtedness which underlay much of the landlord-tenant conflict of the second half of the century.[425]

---

422 James S. Donnelly, *The land and the people of nineteenth-century Cork: the rural economy and the land question* (London, 1975), p. 131; Donnelly, 'Landlord and tenant', pp. 346–9. Enthusiastic partisans of the Act denied that land was being sold below its true value, and continued to trust that it would lead to Irish regeneration. The lack of British purchasers was attributed by one Irish observer to the absence of many 'bargains', and by a Frenchman to continuing fear of Irish *jacqueries*, and dislike of popery, W. Neilson Hancock, *Statistics respecting the sales of incumbered estates in Ireland* (Dublin, 1850), pp. 9–10, Leonce de Lavergne, *The rural economy of England, Scotland and Ireland* (Edinburgh, 1855), pp. 387–8.

423 Romilly to Russell, 23 Jan. 1850, Russell Papers, PRO 30/22/8C, fols. 272–7; [McMahon], 'Ireland – spirit of recent legislation', pp. 387–9; [J.F. Waller], 'Incumbered Estates Court', *Dublin University Magazine*, XXXVI (Sept. 1850), 311–28. For further evidence of the resort to subterfuge in dealings between existing landowners and the Court, see Padraig G. Lane, 'The impact of the Encumbered Estates Court upon the landlords of Galway and Mayo', *Journal of the Galway Archaeological and Historical Society*, XXXVIII (1981–2), 45–58.

424 *Return from the Court for the sale of Encumbered Estates*, P.P. 1852–3 (390), XCIV, 599.

425 L.P. Curtis, 'Incumbered wealth: landed indebtedness in post-Famine Ireland', *American Historical Review*, LXXXV (1980), 332–67.

The consequence of such speculative or consolidatory use of the Act was that the anticipated mass investment of capital in agriculture proved chimerical. Despite some optimistic expectations in Ireland of the dawning of a 'new era of progress',[426] the capital and labour-intensive high-farming practices advocated by Caird and endorsed by Peel, Clarendon and Trevelyan were largely ignored.[427] Instead, old and new proprietors alike turned to expansion of the grazing or ranch system in response to the rising trend in livestock prices in the 1850s. Most proprietors consequently found it to be in their interest to continue to clear the remaining smallholders from consolidated farms, and to bring in English and Scots livestock farmers as managers. The process of mass eviction, particularly in the west, was probably accelerated by the operation of the Encumbered Estates Act, and remained at extremely high levels in the early 1850s.[428]

This outcome was not at all what the government had intended. Romilly had included powers in the 1849 Bill to facilitate the break-up of estates and the purchase of portions by the middle class and farmers. As a last effort he urged Russell to consider giving assistance to a plan drawn up by James Pim, a banker and relative of Jonathan Pim, for a Quaker-based association that would undertake the functions of the Farmers' Estate Society.[429] Russell's neglect of this suggestion reflected the political impossibility of state intervention to assist occupier purchase by 1850. Other attempts to facilitate the emergence of small proprietors proved equally abortive.[430] As the resurgence of the tenant right movement in late 1849 forced attention back to the more immediate question of landlord-tenant relations the bankruptcy of the cry of 'free trade in land' as a solution to the perennial land problem appeared evident.

CONCLUSION

The attenuation of the Foxite tradition in Irish policy was long evident by 1850, when the Tenant League emerged to give a degree of direction and organization

426 [Anon.], *Ireland. Observations on the people, the land and the law, in 1851; with especial reference to the policy and practice of the Incumbered Estates Court* (Dublin, 1851).

427 Trevelyan had summarized the moralist attitude towards pasture in 1847 as 'rather a symptom than a cause of a backward state of cultivation'; it would be 'necessarily and properly diminished' as a proper rotation of crops advanced, Trevelyan to Routh, 7 Jan. 1847, Trevelyan Letterbooks, Bodleian Library, Oxford (microfilm), vol. 11, fols. 76–7.

428 Donnelly, 'Landlord and tenant', pp. 341–4; Padraig G. Lane, 'The general impact of the Encumbered Estates Act of 1849 on Counties Galway and Mayo', *Journal of the Galway Archaeological and Historical Society*, XXXII (1972–3), 44–74.

429 Romilly to Russell, 23 Jan. 1850, Russell Papers, PRO 30/22/8C, fols. 272–7; James Pim, *Ireland: 'Incumbered Estates Commission': a letter to Sir John Romilly* (London, 1850).

430 The clauses introduced by Torrens McCullagh into the 1849 Poor Law Amendment Act for the forced sale of small portions of estates for rate arrears proved a dead letter in practice, Russell: cabinet memo, 3 Dec. 1849, Clar. Dep. Ir., box 26; Clarendon to Russell, 8, 17 Dec. 1849, ibid., letterbook V.

not previously seen in Irish land agitation.[431] Predictably, the movement provoked a landlord reaction that demanded an intransigent rejection of all concessions, and favoured the suppression of tenant right even in its customary strongholds in Ulster.[432] Facing this renewed polarization, the government, under pressure from John Bright, who had just returned from an Irish tour,[433] agreed to revive Somerville's Compensation Bill. However, little serious attention was paid to the new draft, which was relatively mild and was aimed solely at heading off and wrong-footing the developing agitation.[434] While Somerville and Russell were prepared to make some concessions to the demands of the Tenant League, Clarendon made it clear that there could be none on the 'detestable tenant-right'; the Bill pleased nobody and was quickly abandoned.[435]

The Whigs had come full circle to embrace Peel's tactics of 1845–6. Russell remained convinced of the need to tackle the problem, but failed to find a 'new principle' on which to legislate. Frustrated and confused, he damned the Tenant League, put his trust in the tenantry succumbing to their lot, and abandoned the subject as 'impossible'.[436] At least part of his problem lay in the collapse of the continental model of agrarian development in the later 1840s. Despite the attempts of advocates such as Thornton, Mill and Samuel Laing to keep a favourable image of European peasantries before the public,[437] European distress and the 1848 revolutions damaged this model in British eyes.[438]

---

431 For the Tenant League see J.H. Whyte, *The Tenant League and Irish politics in the eighteen-fifties* (Dundalk, 1972); Wright, *Two lands*, pp. 165–207.

432 [Anon.], 'Tenant-right and the Tenant League', *Dublin University Magazine*, XXXVII (Feb. 1851), 159–76

433 R.A.J. Walling (ed.), *The diaries of John Bright* (London, 1930), pp. 98–106; Clarendon to Russell, 20 Nov. 1849, Clar. Dep. Ir., letterbook V. Bright's attitudes towards tenant compensation were modified by his visit, and he believed the Irish could be rallied to the radical cause on the question, but he remained more favourable towards the idea of tenant purchase and suspicious of the Tenant League, Bright to Cobden, 17 Sept. 1849, 12 Oct. 1850, Bright Papers, British Library, London, Add. MS 43,383, fols. 189–94, 199–202.

434 Clarendon to G. Grey, 11 Jan., June 1850, Clar. Dep. Ir., letterbook V. The retrospective clauses of the 1848 Bill had been dropped, *Hans.*, CVIII, 1021–4 [18 Feb. 1850].

435 Somerville to Russell, May 1850, Somerville Letterbook, Public Record Office of Northern Ireland, Belfast, fols. 107–11; Clarendon to Monteagle, 4 April 1850, Monteagle Papers, MS 13,401/5. The government added insult to injury by temporarily lending support to a bill drafted by Westmeath and the former Devon Commissioner, G.A. Hamilton, intended to increase the landlord's powers of ejectment, *Hans.*, CXIII, 595–602, 891–910 [31 July, 6 Aug. 1850].

436 Russell to Clarendon, 5 Sept., 27 Oct., 22 Nov., 28 Dec. 1850, Clar. Dep. Ir. box 26; Walling, *Diaries of John Bright*, pp. 106–7 [June 1850].

437 Laing's restatement of these themes in 1850 was more muted, but still held up Flanders as the best model for Ireland, Samuel Laing, *Observations on the social and political state of the European people in 1848 and 1849* (London, 1850), pp. 18–92.

438 'The land question in France and Ireland', *Illustrated London News*, 8 Sept. 1849. For the impact of the European famines, see Peter Gray, 'Famine relief policy in comparative perspective: Ireland, Scotland and North-Western Europe, 1845–49', *Éire-Ireland*, XXXII (1997), pp. 86–108.

The final throw of Foxite political reform in 1850 was no more successful; Russell's Irish Franchise Bill was mutilated in the Lords, and his long delayed bill to abolish the lord lieutenancy failed after meeting strong opposition in Dublin.[439] What little remained of Russell's reputation as an Irish reformer disappeared in the aftermath of his Durham letter and Ecclesiastical Titles Bill.[440] Russell's dream of a 'golden age for Ireland' perished amid the convulsions of famine, agrarian conflict and religious recrimination.

439 Clarendon to Lewis, 17 March 1850, Harpton Court Papers, National Library of Wales, Aberystwyth, C/1047.

440 Prest, *Russell*, pp. 307–8; Kerr, *'A nation of beggars?'*, pp. 329–32.

CHAPTER FIVE

'The Visitation of God': the Whigs and Famine Relief' 1846–47

For our part, we regard the potato blight as a blessing. When the Celts once cease to be potatophagi, they must become carnivorous. With the taste for meats will grow the appetite for them; with the appetite, the readiness to earn them. With this will come steadiness, regularity, and perseverance; unless, indeed, the growth of these qualities be impeded by the blindness of Irish patriotism, the short-sighted indifference of petty landlords, or the random recklessness of Government benevolence . . .

The Times, 22 Sept. 1846

What can be more absurd, what can be more wicked, than for men professing attachment to an imperial constitution to answer claims now put forward for state assistance to the unprecedented necessities of Ireland, by talking of Ireland being a drain upon the *English* treasury? The exchequer is the exchequer of the United Kingdom . . . If the Union be not a mockery, there exists no such thing as an English treasury . . . How are these expectations to be realized, how are these pledges to be fulfilled, if the partnership is only to be one of loss and never of profit to us? if, bearing our share of all imperial burdens – when calamity falls upon us we are to be told that we then recover our separate existence as a nation, just so far as to disentitle us to the state assistance which any portion of a nation visited with such a calamity has a right to expect from the governing power? If Cornwall had been visited with the same scenes that have desolated Cork, would similar arguments have been used?

Isaac Butt, April 1847[1]

I THE WHIGS AND THE BLIGHT: STRATEGIES AND TENSIONS

The unavoidable fact of continuing famine in Ireland overshadowed much of Russell's first administration, posing particular problems for the Whig-Liberal leadership. The making of relief policy was interconnected with the struggles of ideological factions in government and parliament (with the participation of

1 [Isaac Butt], 'The famine in the land. What has been done, and what is to be done', *Dublin University Magazine*, XXIX (April 1847), 514.

articulate and influential groups in civil society) to implement the policies each thought appropriate to address the crisis. Although there emerged a broad consensus view that any 'solution' to the Famine must include a rural transition encompassing the commercialisation of agriculture, the righting of the perceived capital-labour imbalance, and the creation of a tripartite division of labour in the countryside, sharp divisions existed within the political elite over appropriate strategies and the extent to which the immediate humanitarian objective of preserving life could be disregarded in the pursuit of social 'transition'.

The Whig-Liberal leadership had given little thought to the question of famine relief policy for most of the 1846 parliamentary session. Criticism of Peel's relief policy had been muted, and a broadly bi-partisan consensus maintained; indeed Russell thought further relief legislation unnecessary in July.[2] The Whig leader's attentions were instead directed to the 'comprehensive measures' he aspired to introduce once Peel had dealt with the 'temporary' famine conditions of 1845–6.

The sudden and catastrophic second failure of the potato crop thus came as more of an unexpected shock to the incoming than the outgoing ministers. The reappearance and spread of the blight was reported through official channels in mid-July, but it was not until the first week of August that it became clear that the great bulk of the main crop had been lost.[3] Unlike the previous year, the disaster was sudden and final, the blight coming 'by one sweeping blast in one and the same night'.[4] The *Freeman's Journal* echoed the official reports with its own observation at the end of that devastating week that 'Providence had again visited our land with a blight, and was about to perish our people, by depriving them of the fruits of the earth.'[5]

The unprecedented and unforeseen scale of the disaster was outside the bounds of Irish experience and the imagination of the government and its officials.[6] The full consequences were thus not initially realized in England. In the resulting confusion Charles Trevelyan's position was enhanced; the Assistant Treasury

---

2 *Hansard's Parliamentary Debates*, 3rd ser., LXXXIII, 1085 [17 Feb. 1846: Russell]; ibid., LXXXVII, 1176–85 [16 July: Russell]; Russell to Bessborough, 29 June 1846, Russell Papers, Public Record Office, London, PRO 30/22/5A, fols. 312–13.

3 Routh to Trevelyan, 14 July 1846, *Correspondence explanatory of measures adopted by Her Majesty's government for the relief of distress arising from the failure of the potato crop in Ireland (Commissariat series)*, P.P. 1846 [735], XXXVII, 260; Routh to Trevelyan, 6, 7 Aug. 1846, Treasury Papers, Public Record Office, London, T 64/366C/1.

4 Fr Mathew to Trevelyan, 7 Aug., Hewetson to Trevelyan, 19 Aug. 1846, *Correspondence, from July 1846 to January 1847, relating to the measures adopted for the relief of distress in Ireland (Commissariat series)*, P.P. 1847 [761], LI, 3–4, 15.

5 *Freeman's Journal*, 10 Aug. 1846.

6 The 1846 potato failure was far beyond the norms for European subsistence crises in the nineteenth century. See Peter Solar, 'The Great Famine was no ordinary subsistence crisis', in E. Margaret Crawford (ed.), *Famine: the Irish experience, 900–1900. Subsistence crises and famines in Ireland* (Edinburgh, 1989), pp. 112–29.

Secretary had already made himself master of the Irish relief mechanism, and was ready to proffer advice to the inexperienced new ministers on how to proceed.[7] One of Trevelyan's recommendations, the withdrawal of state interference from the external food trade, was not immediately contentious in Britain as Peel's ministry had already been moving towards such a disengagement.[8] A second, for overhauling the relief works system to make it more amenable to state sanctions, also commanded a substantial degree of acquiescence at Westminster, due to burgeoning public criticism of the behaviour of local relief committees and presentment sessions.[9] The decision to devolve the responsibilities of Peel's Relief Commission solely upon Sir Randolph Routh[10] also tended to increase the centralization of power, as the Commissariat was directly subordinate to the Treasury, although the new Irish executive under Bessborough soon began to challenge Whitehall's dominance.

Once it was clear that a second year of famine was inevitable, the government rushed a new Poor Employment Act through parliament in August 1846.[11] Responding to the public outcry over the 'abuse' of Peel's works relief, it included clauses for strengthening the powers of the Commissioners of Public Works to regulate and control the projects recommended by baronial sessions. Trevelyan's hand was also evident in the decision to abandon the half grant system of financing relief works – a change he had been pressing since the spring.[12] The Bill's so-called 'labour rate clause' – placing ultimate responsibility for the repayment of relief loans on the local rates – was intended as a move towards making 'Irish property support Irish poverty', but it was softened by a grant of £50,000 in the first instance for relief works in the most impoverished western districts. Russell ostentatiously put no limit on the loans that would be made available under the new 'Labour Rate Act', stating to the Commons that 'the whole credit of the Treasury and means of the country are ready to be used as it is our bounden duty to use them . . . to avert famine, and to maintain the people of Ireland.' Irish Chief Secretary, Henry Labouchere, also urged the Commons to remember that 'their first duty was to take care that the people did not starve'.[13] These public commitments of humanitarian

7 Trevelyan memo, 1 Aug. 1846, Treasury Papers, T64/358A.

8 The centrist *Spectator* was defensive of Peel's interference in 1845–6, but argued that now a 'totally new trade' had been introduced, all 'nursing aid' should be withdrawn, *Spectator,* 22 Aug. 1846.

9 Reports of abuses of the relief system, often to the detriment of the genuinely needy, punctuated the reports of administrators throughout the 1846 session. See Jones to Lincoln, 9 April, Commissioners of Public Works to Trevelyan, 5 June, 7 July, 8 Aug., *Correspondence explanatory . . . (Board of Works ser.),* P.P. 1846 [735], XXXVII, 365, 372–5, 384–6, 403–5.

10 Treasury minute, 31 Aug. 1846, *Correspondence, from July 1846 to January 1847, relating to the measures adopted for the relief of distress in Ireland (Board of Works series),* P.P. 1847 [764], L, 70

11 9 and 10 Vict. c. 107.

12 Trevelyan memo: 'Grants for the relief of distress in Ireland', 15 April 1846, *Corr. explan. (Bd. of Works ser.),* P.P. 1846 [735], XXXVII, 356.

13 *Hans.*, LXXXVIII, 772–8, 781–4 [17 Aug. 1846].

intent would later be derided by Irish observers angered by the government's subsequent failure to honour its own pledges.[14]

There were sharp disputes in cabinet on the details of the Relief Bill, and particularly over the proposal that the Lord Lieutenant have the power to compel recalcitrant baronial sessions to present for relief works. This intrusion into the powers of the local landed elite was strongly resisted by the moderates Clanricarde and Palmerston, but insisted upon by Bessborough and Labouchere.[15] Morpeth summed up the point at issue; the compulsory clauses amounted to 'the nucleus of a compulsory Poor Law with outdoor relief'.[16] Russell endorsed this construction, and it was adopted in a modified form in the Bill. Not only were the sessions to be 'empowered and required' to present where necessary, the assessments for repayments were to be levied on the Poor Law valuation, thus shifting the ultimate burden for relief from the occupiers of landholdings valued below £4 per annum, who were exempted from poor rates.[17] Despite Wood's official claims to the contrary, this amounted to an infringement of Peel and Graham's dictum that relief be kept strictly separate from the Poor Law.[18]

No Peelite opposition was offered to any aspect of this legislation. Russell had consulted Goulburn before the Bill was introduced, but had received only vague comments and a warning of the need 'to secure us against the permanent maintenance of the poor of Ireland out of the national purse'.[19] Peel himself also saw 'all the difficulty in providing a second time against famine in Ireland by the intervention of the Government. It stamps a character of permanency on a relief which was only tolerated from the hope of its being casual and temporary.' The government was, he added, obliged to do what it could, if only to satisfy English humanitarian feeling and to pre-empt a rising in Ireland.[20] No doubt this unwillingness to criticize Russell's relief policy reflected Peel's relief at being released from the trials of Irish governance.

The relief measures of August 1846 were thus an adaptation of previous legislation rather than a radical departure. This continuity was rational, as the minority Whig government remained dependent on the goodwill of its predecessors and

14 *Cork Examiner*, 7, 21 Dec. 1846.

15 Broughton Diary, Broughton Papers, British Library, London, Add. MS 43,749, fols. 23, 26 [8, 13 Aug. 1846].

16 Morpeth Diary, 13 Aug. 1846, Castle Howard Papers, Castle Howard, N. Yorkshire, J19/8/12.

17 *Hans.*, LXXXVIII, 775–6 [17 Aug. 1846].

18 Ibid., 797. The *Freeman* declared that the Bill did indeed constitute an effective extension of the Poor Law, and that its true object had been 'the realization of the Elizabethan principle in Ireland'. It welcomed the discomfiture of the landlords, who had long ignored O'Connell's warnings on the subject, *Freeman's Journal*, 22, 26 Aug. 1846.

19 Goulburn to Peel, 13 Aug. 1846, Peel Papers, British Library, London, Add. MS 40,445, fols. 365–6.

20 Peel to Goulburn, 14 Aug. 1846, Goulburn Papers, Surrey Record Office, Kingston, SHS 304, box 42.

had few specific policy formulations of its own in this area. The major shift in policy lay less in the formal structure of relief than in the manner in which it was implemented, and in the responses considered to meet the threatened breakdown of the system. To understand the forces at play in relief policy-making requires a survey of the ideological forces operating within the government.

Much of the attention of historians of the Famine has been focused on the record of Charles Trevelyan, leading to something of an exaggeration of his role. For all his administrative importance, Trevelyan was never 'virtually dictator of relief for Ireland', at least not in his own right, nor was he ever in a position to be 'a Victorian Cromwell'.[21] The Assistant Secretary to the Treasury operated within a political context that at times assisted him and at others circumscribed his activities. He was at all times a subordinate, if assertive and self-willed, government official, whose power was largely dependent on the ministerial balance of forces within the government and the disposition of British public opinion. It was the influx of a group of like-minded men into government in 1846 which empowered him, and he is best considered as an untiring and dedicated member of this 'moralist' ideological grouping. While it is true that Trevelyan's evangelical work ethic and obsessive attention to detail (which included a reluctance to delegate any executive decision to his subordinates) made him the lynch-pin of relief operations, his influence over policy was heavily dependent on his entente with the Chancellor of the Exchequer, Charles Wood, and the Colonial Secretary, Earl Grey.[22]

The moralist perspective on the famine crisis was set out in autumn 1846 in a series of letters by Charles Wood lecturing the Irish government on the correct interpretation of the crisis and on how relief should be managed. For Wood, the potato failure was not accidental or temporary, but was the necessary harbinger of a 'social revolution in Ireland'. The relief measures of the previous session had already had profound permanent effects in raising the expectations of the poor with respect to employment and money wages; returning to any *status quo ante* was both impossible and undesirable. It was the responsibility of the administration to prepare Ireland for this permanent change by stamping out the 'present habit of dependence on Government' shared by peasants and landowners. The Irish wages fund would have to meet the obligations imposed by the proven redundancy of potato subsistence, as 'wages must come from the funds of the persons paying rates, for that is the only fund from whence they can come'. The moral impetus behind Wood's insistence on these points came from his conviction

21 Cecil Woodham–Smith, *The great hunger: Ireland 1845–1849* (London, 1987 edn), p. 105; J.M. Hernon, 'A Victorian Cromwell: Sir Charles Trevelyan, the Famine and the age of improvement', *Éire-Ireland*, XXII (1987), 15–29.

22 For Trevelyan's exhaustive workload during the Famine, see Trevelyan to Sheil, 11 Sept. 1846, Trevelyan Letterbooks, Bodleian Library, Oxford (microfilm), vol. 8, fols. 50–1; Jennifer Hart, 'Sir Charles Trevelyan at the Treasury', *English Historical Review*, LXXV (1960), 92–110.

that this catastrophe was both inevitable and natural; the blight had 'precipitated things with a wonderful impetus, so as to bring them to an early head'. Reading the situation through the lens of evangelical theodicy, Wood concluded that the seeming disaster had been willed by a higher power: 'A want of food and employment [was] a calamity sent by Providence'.[23] This visitation might entail considerable short-term suffering, but its intention was merciful and ameliorative, for the destruction of the 'curse' of a potato-based social system would entail the ultimate eradication of excessive competition for land, rack-renting and agrarian outrages.[24]

Trevelyan was also anxious to disseminate his sincere conviction that the crisis was divinely ordained. He lectured Monteagle on the meaning of the second infliction of the potato blight:

> I think I see a bright light shining in the distance through the dark cloud which at present hangs over Ireland. A remedy has been already applied to that portion of the maladies of Ireland which was traceable to political causes . . . The deep and inveterate root of Social evil remained, and I hope I am not guilty of irreverence in thinking that, this being altogether beyond the power of man, the cure has been applied by the direct stroke of an all wise Providence in a manner as unexpected and unthought of as it is likely to be effectual. God grant that we may rightly perform our part and not turn into a curse what was intended for a blessing.[25]

Trevelyan was never shaken from this reading of the famine crisis, and expressed impatience at the impiety of those who failed to grasp its true meaning. These moralist themes were systematically and triumphally restated at the beginning of 1848 when Trevelyan announced categorically and publicy that in Ireland 'Supreme Wisdom has educed permanent good out of transient evil'.[26] For Wood, Trevelyan and other adherents of moralist discourse, alleviating the famine-related sufferings of individuals could never be the prime concern of government, particularly if it impeded the necessary inducements to self-help.[27] Their 'optimistic' construction of the crisis was founded on anti-Malthusian premisses; moralists believed that Ireland must move rapidly from potato to grain cultivation, and were convinced that Irish resources were adequate to support that transition. Exertion, Trevelyan told Labouchere, was all that was needed: 'If the cultivable land of Ireland were tolerably cultivated, there would be an abundance of employment, according to a higher standard of living, for an even larger population than the present.'[28]

---

23 Wood to Bessborough, 16 Sept. 1846, Hickleton Papers, Cambridge University Library (microfilm), A4/185/1.
24 Wood to Labouchere, 22 Sept., ibid.
25 Trevelyan to Monteagle, 9 Oct. 1846, Monteagle Papers, National Library of Ireland, Dublin, MS 13,397/11.
26 C.E. Trevelyan, *The Irish crisis* (London, 1848), p. 1.
27 Trevelyan to Routh, 21 Sept. 1846, Trevelyan Letterbooks, vol. 8, fols. 93–5.
28 Trevelyan to Labouchere, 5 Sept., ibid., fols. 11–14.

Moralism was firmly entrenched in the Treasury bloc centred on Trevelyan, Wood and Earl Grey, and it received the fervent support of the *Times*. Public pressure was actively cultivated by moralist ministers, who were well aware of growing British restiveness about heavy relief expenditure and were ready to play this card to bolster their ideological position.[29] Indeed, the paper was regularly supplied by Treasury sources with selected information on Irish operations.[30] The power of the *Times* in forming British opinion and closing the options available to the government was recognized and lamented by moderate figures such as Lord Devon.[31] The *Times* held that while some assistance to meet Irish distress was acceptable in the specific circumstances of 1846–7, this should be strictly limited and controlled; echoing Trevelyan, it adopted the line that Irish relief expenditure imposed a 'poll-tax amounting to a shilling a head for every man, woman and child' in England. What was required was 'a parliament . . . sufficiently patriotic to put the screw on the landowner and make him do his duty'.[32] Moralist pamphleteers were also ready to employ populist rhetoric against the 'lavish waste of public money, already so inefficiently applied, to the performance of a duty which ought to be performed by the Irish, and the Irish only'.[33]

Significant sections of British opinion continued to interpret the Irish crisis in providentialist language. While the repeal of the Corn Laws had been regarded as a necessary step towards creating a more 'natural' social structure, the second failure was seen by many as pointing out the culpable reluctance of Irish landlords and peasants to abandon the potato system and embrace a more progressive system of agriculture. Botanists were no more agreed on the 1846 blight than they had been on the previous season's, but analysis tended increasingly to stress the operation of 'natural laws' over any extraordinary intervention, and hence to place greater onus on the subjects of the visitation. The English author of one botanical tract commented:

> Almighty Providence has said, in the works of his creation, that all was good, and if evil exists in the world it arises rather from the improvidence of man, which makes a bad use of the blessings bestowed upon him, than from the means within his reach of obtaining good. Thus, in most cases, it may be

---

29 Ellice to Wood, 27 Oct., Wood to Labouchere, 2 Oct., Hickleton Papers, A4/103, A4/185/1. Ellice explicitly welcomed the arrival of the '*Times* Commissioner' (T.C. Foster) in the Highlands of Scotland in September, and hoped that he would produce an exposé of landlordism there similar to his previous work on Ireland, Ellice to Wood, 30 Sept. 1846, Hickleton Papers, A4/103.

30 Trevelyan to Delane, 14 Nov., Trevelyan Letterbooks, vol. 9, fol. 181.

31 Devon to Monteagle, 21 Dec., Monteagle Papers, MS 13,396/3.

32 *Times*, 17, 27 Aug., 17 Oct.

33 [Anon.], *Irish improvidence encouraged by English bounty; being a remonstrance against the government projects for Irish relief . . . by an ex-member of the British parliament* (London, n.d. [1847]), p. 3.

> doubted, whether in the diseases which affect the human species, or in those which affect the vegetable world, the creator has inflicted a fatality, from which it is not in the power of human prudence to escape.[34]

What Ireland needed, he concluded, was agricultural improvement in the form of systematic thorough-draining, subsoiling and waste-land reclamation, and greater use of green crops and 'cold manure', all of which were impeded by the conacre system. Above all, the Poor Law should be extended to force the landowner 'to do that justice that God and nature has imposed'.[35]

The *Times* was more certain that the reappearance of the blight was intended not as a further ministration to Britain, but as a direct judgement on the evils of Irish society.[36] The refusal of the Irish to accept this truth and to abandon their 'abuse' of British generosity was both erroneous and impious:

> Alas! The Irish peasant had tasted of famine and found it was good. He saw the cloud looming in the distance . . . to him it teemed with goodly manna and salient waters. He wrapped himself up in the ragged mantle of inert expectancy and said he trusted to Providence. But the deity of his faith was the Government. He called his submission a religious obedience, and he believed it to be so. But it was the obedience of a religion which, by a small but material change, reversed the primaeval decree. It was a religion that holds: 'Man shall not labour by the sweat of his brow'.[37]

The task of government was to disabuse the labourer and landlord of such fallacies and compel them to submit to the will of heaven. Active self-improvement would have to replace the resignation to divinely ordained suffering which relief officials observed among the peasantry in the wake of the 1846 failure.[38] What was required, moralists concluded, was not the total abandonment of Ireland to *laissez-faire*, but the creation of moral mechanisms that would enforce obedience to moral law. This was the fundamental paradox at the heart of the moralist agenda. While stressing the moral superiority of local responsibility, and denouncing the 'Russian

---

34 L. Rawstorne, *The cause of the potato disease ascertained by proofs; and the prevention proved by practice* (London, 1847), p. 4.

35 Ibid., p. 29. Rawstorne was, however, reluctant to abandon completely the idea of some shared responsibility in January 1847. While 'it may be going too far to consider this great calamity sent as a judgment upon us', the relief grants could be seen as the price for past neglect of Ireland, making amends by an 'ample and liberal atonement', ibid., pp. 17, 31.

36 *Times*, 8 Sept. 1846.

37 Ibid., 22 Sept. The target of this attack was a *Freeman* article which had accused a *Times* correspondent of impiety in hesitating to admit that Irish distress was the result of a 'visitation of the living God', *Freeman's Journal*, 4 Sept. In this Catholic construction, the action of providence demanded humility and patience from the sufferer, and charity from the observer.

38 William Henry Smith, *A twelve month's residence in Ireland, during the Famine and the public works, 1846 and 1847* (London, 1848), pp. 18–20.

despotism' of extended government, moralists depended on the manipulative use of the Treasury's powers over the administration in Ireland to break the 'cancer' of dependency.[39]

Moderate liberals held views antithetical to such moralist dogmatics, and in general regarded the Irish situation in a more secular light. After suffering a rebuff in the cabinet on the terms of the Poor Employment Bill, the moderates put their energies into resisting any further moves towards an extension of the Poor Law. Nassau Senior articulated their fears in an *Edinburgh Review* article of October 1846.[40] This was directed ostensibly against Poulett Scrope's 'anarchical' proposals for extending the Irish Poor Law, but it was also implicitly critical of moralist assumptions and their popularity with the British public. While agreeing with the Treasury that compulsory charity to relieve the poor 'must be rendered less eligible than independence', Senior defended the record of Irish landlords. He assailed moralist and radical assumptions of a high wages fund, and insisted that landlords should not be compelled to bear the burdens of relief alone: following the failure of the potato the produce of Ireland was insufficient to support the country's poor, a fact confirmed rather than contradicted by the export of provisions.[41]

Senior's call for respect to be accorded to the opinions of 'Irish representatives', and his criticism of those who treated 'them as if *they* were ignorant of their own country, and *we* understood it, [and acted] as if our superiority of strength implied that of knowledge on their affairs',[42] appears to have been an indirect reference to the increasingly bitter row between moderates and the Treasury. This began as a dispute over Monteagle's claim that the government had 'broken its pledge' in refusing to complete the road works begun in the 1845–6 season, but rapidly escalated into an acrimonious dispute over the principles of relief.[43] Treasury 'lectures' on 'sound principle' merely incensed Monteagle. Although 'both an Economist and a Treasury man', he argued that 'the Government must be prepared to face much responsibility if they wish to keep society together'.[44] The landowning

39 Wood to Monteagle, 10, 19 Oct., Monteagle Papers, MS 13,396/6; Wood to Bessborough, 5 Oct. 1847, Hickleton Papers, A4/185/1. An intermediate tier between government and the masses had to be maintained as the arena for 'enabling all persons to follow their respective avocations in the social system', Trevelyan to S. Spring Rice, 6 Nov. 1846, Trevelyan Letterbooks, vol. 9, fols. 118–22.

40 As in 1843, Senior produced his text in collaboration with Lansdowne and Monteagle. All were in a state of 'utmost anxiety' about the intentions of the cabinet regarding the Poor Law, Lansdowne to Napier, 3 July, Senior to Napier, 5, 14 Aug. 1846, Macvey Napier Papers, British Library, London, Add. MS 34,626, fols. 268–9, 330–3, 347–8.

41 [Nassau W. Senior], 'Proposals for extending the Irish Poor Law', *Edinburgh Review*, LXXXIV (Oct. 1846), 267–314.

42 Ibid., p. 268.

43 Monteagle to Wood, 14 Sept., Wood to Russell, 22 Sept. 1846, Russell Papers, PRO 30/22/5C, fols. 237–48.

44 Monteagle to Bessborough, 1 Oct., Monteagle Papers, MS 13,396/8.

class was, he insisted, as much the victim of the upheavals and misgovernment of Irish history as the peasantry, and could not be held responsible for Irish backwardness. The moralist slogan of self-help was, in these conditions, fundamentally flawed; they would do 'as well to ask a child why he does not perform the functions of a man, or Hindustanis why they do not build Manchester at Benares'. In the context of the unprecedented catastrophe, Irish landowners had a right to expect assistance in promoting reproductive works and providing effective relief. Monteagle quoted approvingly Senior's dictum of the previous year that the scarcity should be treated like the invasion of a foreign army, which all should aid in resisting.[45] Unlike Senior, Monteagle did allow for the role of 'God's providence' in the potato failure, although he placed no burden of public interpretation upon it. This fatalist attitude to the 'dispensations of providence' was common in the statements of Irish public bodies and landowners, and was usually coupled with appeals to treat the disaster as a shared UK experience.[46]

Monteagle's attitude towards the government became steadily more embittered as the Famine advanced.[47] Those moderates who remained within the government were also unhappy with the tendency of policy, but sought to restrain it from within. Lansdowne tried to balance Wood's influence by presenting the Prime Minister with benign interpretations of landlord conduct.[48] He agreed with Palmerston's view that the moralist programme would have disastrous conseqquences, and that the Irish poor were mostly responsible for their own predicament:

> the only thing clear is, that if the landed income of Ireland is to be compelled for any length of time to maintain a Pauper nation which has grown up without any relation to the demand for labour or to the amount of the funds applicable for the employment of labour, the landowners will in the end be as well qualified as the cottiers to demand admission to the union houses.[49]

This Malthusian sentiment chimed with the increasingly shrill appeals of the Irish landed classes for assistance in coping with Ireland's 'surplus population', but was at odds with majority opinion in Great Britain. Crucially however, British moderates shared liberal common ground with moralists regarding the commercialization of Irish agriculture, and were equally welcoming of the 'social revolution' sweeping

---

45 Monteagle to Trevelyan, 1 Oct., ibid., MS 13,396/9.

46 'Memorial of the Poor Relief Committee of Carrigaline' (Sept. 1846), *Correspondence . . . relief of distress (Comm. ser.)*, P.P. 1847 [761] LI, 66; *Dublin Evening Mail*, 13 Jan. 1847; ['Anglo-Hibernicus'], *A letter to the Rt. Hon. Lord John Russell, on the future prospects of Ireland* (London, 1847), pp. 4, 12.

47 Monteagle believed that Wood and Trevelyan were responsible for priming the *Times* with official information for its attacks on his record as a proprietor in County Limerick, *Times*, 7 Nov.; Monteagle to Bessborough, 17 Nov. 1846, Monteagle Papers, MS13,396/8, Monteagle to Empson, n.d. (Jan. 1847), ibid., MS 13,397/7.

48 Lansdowne to Russell, 18 Oct. 1846, Russell Papers, PRO 30/22/5D, fols. 233–5.

49 Palmerston to Monteagle, 14 Oct., Monteagle Papers, MS 13,396/4.

away the cottier system that had been ushered in by the second potato failure.[50] This mutual agreement combined with shared hostility towards Protectionists and ultra-radicals to hold together what could only be described as an ideologically heterogenous administration.

As Prime Minister, Russell was the focus of these competing pressures. Both moderates and moralists frequently expressed alarm at the policy options which he and his allies were prepared to consider, and they often shared an anxiety to restrain such initiatives. It was the susceptibility of Foxites to populist pressure that was most feared. The Irish government had gone out of its way in the autumn of 1846 to conciliate O'Connell and to begin the preparation of what it hoped would be popular reform legislation. Consequently O'Connell enthusiastically commended the Poor Employment Act to the Repeal Association as 'unlimited in the extent of relief that it affords', and was anxious that it should be interpreted in a favourable way.[51] He urged Dublin Castle to grasp the political necessity of extensive action:

> You cannot conceive how fretful people are here at the *smallness* of any relief this session. I am doing the best I can for you but I cannot perform miracles. There is a *famine* imminent. There is no exaggeration in the accounts of the loss of the potato crop. The *feeding* of the people must be provided for by the government *no matter at what cost* and without delay.[52]

Russell assured O'Connell that the Lord Lieutenant would be given discretionary powers to act as he thought necessary,[53] and cordial relations were retained with the Irish government during the autumn. O'Connell continued to worry that the government was not 'sufficiently terrified by the actual state of the country', but it was Westminster and not Dublin Castle he held to be at fault: Bessborough's 'paternal assistance' was vital, but the Treasury and its subordinates in the Board of Works and Commissariat were greatly at fault.[54] It was this very responsiveness

---

50 *Spectator*, 22 Aug. 1846. This weekly was 'moderate' in its economic views, but nevertheless reflected the impatience with the Irish landowners and sympathy for an extended Poor Law widespread amongst its English readership. It attacked Senior's views on the Poor Law as redundant, ibid., 24 Oct. 1846.

51 *Freeman's Journal*, 8 Sept. 1846. The only Repeal MP to speak in the debate also fulsomely praised Russell's speech on the new relief policy, as did the temperance campaigner Fr Mathew, *Hans.*, LXXXVIII, 779–80 [17 Aug. 1846: Browne]; Mathew to Trevelyan, 22 Aug. 1846, *Correspondence . . . relief of distress (Comm. ser.)*, P.P. 1847 [761], LI, 19–20.

52 O'Connell to Pigot, 13 Aug. 1846, Maurice R. O'Connell (ed.), *The correspondence of Daniel O'Connell* (8 vols., Dublin, 1972–80), VIII, 83. O'Connell soon found himself under pressure from Young Ireland over his public confidence in the government's willingness to respond, Ray to O'Connell, 12 Sept., ibid., p. 97; *Nation*, 9 Sept. 1846.

53 Russell to O'Connell, 13 Aug. 1846, Russell Papers, PRO 30/22/5B, fols 364–5.

54 O'Connell to Labouchere, 29 Sept., 4 Oct., Bessborough to O'Connell, 6 Oct., O'Connell, *Correspondence*, VIII, 104, 108, 112; Fermoy speech, reported in *Spectator*, 31 Oct. 1846. O'Connell's personal efforts for employment and improvement on his Iveragh estates – which included a drainage project – were welcomed by the government as exemplary, Russell to Bessborough, 30 Sept., Russell Papers, PRO 30/22/5C, fols. 375–8.

of the Irish government to Irish opinion that moralists saw as a potentially serious threat to their reconstructive agenda.[55]

Demands that the government adopt a popular policy came from other directions. In October the Revd Charles Gibson of Mallow warned the government that O'Connell's position in the country, with which Whig popularity was bound up, was becoming untenable under existing policies.[56] The problem lay in the application of the principles of political economy to circumstances in which they were not applicable. The situation, Gibson warned, was serious but still salvageable: 'It is not too late for the Whigs to gain back the full confidence of the country, and the entire support of O'Connell. *They have not the food to keep down the markets but they have the money.*'[57] Such views led moralists to fear that 'sound principle' might be undermined by an engagement with popular politics.[58]

Another potential threat was that posed by Poulett Scrope's call for an extended Poor Law giving a right to relief to the able-bodied. He prefaced his argument by stating his personal and political loyalty to Russell and appealed to what he believed to be the Whig leader's favourable views on the subject. Famine, Scrope argued, was unlikely to be confined to one year, and only the guaranteed security provided by the right to relief would prevent the collapse of the agrarian economy. The country could easily afford such a system, as 'it is notorious that Ireland possesses the means within herself of maintaining and employing twice or four times the number of her existing population.' Neither England nor Ireland could, on the other hand, afford the alternative of mass starvation and social breakdown.[59]

Senior's broadside reflected the seriousness with which Scrope's views were regarded by their opponents, particularly as the Prime Minister was thought to be susceptible to such heterodoxy. Russell had inherited from Holland and Fox a suspicion of political economy which was not seriously reconsidered until the 1840s. Only when the politics of corn came to dominate the political agenda did he engage in intensive reading on economic matters.[60] It is unlikely that his grasp

55 Trevelyan to Routh, 20 Sept., Trevelyan Letterbooks, vol. 8, fols. 88–9.

56 Gibson had been a member of the County Cork delegation which visited London in September to appeal directly to ministers for higher public works wages. He was stung into writing by being fobbed off by Wood, who had given him a lecture on the designs of providence and the need for ameliorative self-help, *Spectator*, 26 Sept.; Gibson to Wood, 24 Sept., Wood to Gibson, 29 Sept., Hickleton Papers, A4/181, A4/185/1.

57 Gibson to Wood, 10 Oct., ibid., A4/181. Gibson later argued that emigration was the best form of immediate relief for Ireland, but held that the Famine had failed to resolve the key problem – the low rate of Irish wages, C.P. Gibson, *The history of the County and City of Cork* (London, 1861), p. 528.

58 Wood replied that the government could not create food when a providential dispensation had destroyed it, Wood to Gibson, 14 Oct., Hickleton Papers, A4/185/1.

59 Scrope to Russell, 2 May, 23 June 1846, Russell Papers, PRO 30/22/5A, fols. 201–4, 267–74. These arguments were later published in G.P. Scrope, *Letters to the Rt. Hon. Lord John Russell, on the expediency of enlarging the Irish Poor Law* (London, 1846).

60 Peter Mandler, *Aristocratic government in the age of reform: Whigs and Liberals, 1830–1852* (Oxford, 1990), pp. 26–7, John Prest, *Lord John Russell* (London, 1972), pp. 191–2.

of the subject was ever much more than superficial, and it sat ill with his continuing adherence to traditional Foxite objectives; however, the result was that he became more susceptible to arguments couched in classical economic language, and more cautious about whole-heartedly espousing alternatives. This encouraged moralists and moderates to focus their attentions on him, and led to a degree of distancing from Bessborough and a failure to engage fully with popular alternatives in relief policy. Yet Lansdowne and Senior remained worried by Russell's vacillation on the question of outdoor relief. While Russell eventually allowed himself to be persuaded by Senior's arguments, he objected strongly to the anti-Foxite tone of the *Edinburgh Review* article, and was keen to embrace the outdoor relief principle again in early 1847.[61]

Russell's outlook remained fundamentally anti-Malthusian. Like Scrope, he believed that Ireland was capable of producing sufficient food to provide for its existing population and leave a considerable surplus for exports, and that this could be attained without substantial external investment. He wrote to Wood in October: 'The future is no doubt perilous. But if there is capital in Ireland as I believe there is, the country will be made to produce food for eight millions of Irish, and four millions of English in a few years.' Where he disagreed with the moralists was on the necessity of providing sufficient relief aid to meet the existing crisis, for 'the destruction of £10,000,000 of food' could not be treated 'as if it were an ordinary calamity'.[62] Russell's readiness to countenance large-scale expenditure to meet the Irish crisis left Wood 'aghast'.[63] While Russell's response to the potato failure was relatively free from providentialist exegesis, it was not without some religious character. Russell's conventional liberal Anglicanism inclined him towards expressions of formal piety, and he approved the preparation of a special form of prayer to avert scarcity to be read in the established Churches of England and Ireland.[64]

---

61 Senior to Napier, 14, 21, 22 Aug., Russell to Napier, 8 Sept., Macvey Napier Papers, Add. MS 34,626, fols. 347–8, 364–5, 368–9, 404–5.

62 Russell to Wood, 15 Oct., Hickleton Papers, A4/56/1. This opinion had not altered by January 1847, when Russell told the Commons that he agreed with Sir Robert Kane's opinion that with proper security for investments, and exertion and co-operation on the part of all classes, the present population of Ireland was not excessive for its resources, *Hans.*, LXXXIX, 449 [25 Jan. 1847].

63 Wood to Russell, 11 Aug. 1846, Russell Papers, PRO 30/22/5B, fol. 343.

64 Russell to Archbishop of Canterbury, 8 Sept. 1846, Bishop of Durham to Russell, 15 Sept., Russell to Bessborough, 16 Sept., ibid., PRO 30/22/5C, fols. 78–9, 158–61, 167–8; Broughton Diary, Add. MS 43,749, fol. 50 [26 Sept.]. There was some scepticism in the cabinet as to the utility (and the piety) of such a prayer so long as trade was not entirely free, ibid., fols. 57–8 [29 Oct.].

II PUBLIC WORKS AND 'SOUND PRINCIPLE'

Conflict over the implementation of relief policy began in September. The initial point of focus was the continuation of the public works begun under Peel's Relief Acts. A Treasury minute of 21 July had ordered the closing by 15 August of all current works, 'except where extraordinary circumstances prevailed'; Trevelyan's intention was to use this 'breathing time' to overhaul the Board of Works mechanism in preparation for the ensuing season.[65] The intensity of distress and a spate of popular disturbances during August and September made such a general cessation impossible, and Bessborough used his discretionary powers to re-open works already sanctioned under Peel's Act in the first week of September. The new system was unready, but he could not 'allow the people to starve in the mean time'.[66] Wood, however, expressed irritation at this capitulation to 'exaggerated' reports and landlord pressure.[67]

This was the overture to a more fundamental dispute on the nature of 'public' works. Bessborough proposed that in the absence of sufficient profitable and remunerative 'public' works to meet the demand for employment, 'other works than those which would be strictly called public works' should be allowed, so long as interested proprietors made a fair contribution.[68] In the view of Dublin Castle, works should meet two objectives simultaneously – the prevention of starvation by the provision of wages, and a permanent increase in the field of employment. Bessborough admitted his sympathy for the local delegations which had pressed such an amendment upon him, but indignantly rejected the moralist charge that he was acting as the spokesman of Irish landlordism. The works would, he argued, continue to be closely supervised by the Public Works Board, whose chief administrators had endorsed his views.[69] The Lord Lieutenant was optimistic that he could persuade the cabinet to enact this 'labour rate on property' with no restrictions on reproductive works, but underestimated both the obstinacy of the Treasury and Russell's vacillation.[70]

Bessborough's proposals were anathema to the Treasury. Wood regarded the function of public works as being essentially penal:

---

65 Treasury minute, 21 July 1846, Treasury Papers, T 64/368/A; Trevelyan, *Irish crisis*, pp. 51–7.

66 Bessborough to Russell, 8 Sept., Russell Papers, PRO 30/22/5C, fols. 59–60.

67 Wood to Monteagle, 10 Sept., Monteagle Papers, MS 13,396/5. A Treasury minute of 5 October criticized Bessborough's action, *Correspondence . . . relief of distress (Board of Works ser.)*, P.P. 1847 [764], L, 98–9.

68 Bessborough to Russell, 13 Sept., PRO 30/22/5C, fols. 144–8. Labouchere agreed that this case was 'unanswerable', Labouchere to Morpeth, 24 Sept., Castle Howard Papers, J19/1/40/70.

69 Bessborough to Russell, 18, 28 Sept., Russell Papers, PRO 30/22/5C, fols. 365–6.

70 Bessborough to Russell, 19, 20 Sept., ibid., fols. 204, 212, Bessborough memo, n.d. (1846), ibid., 5G, fols. 198–9; Bessborough to Monteagle, 25 Sept., Monteagle Papers, MS 13,396/2. The opinion of many liberal Irish landlords was strongly in favour of such a 'labour rate' as a temporary expedient. Devon and Monsell led Limerick proprietors in demanding this in late August, *Freeman's Journal*, 27 Aug.

> a sort of test like the workhouse test here – I mean for the proprietors – 'If you don't support your people by wages on your own estates, you will have to pay the county cess, to repay the advances for wages on the relief works' . . . the time has come when the Irish proprietor must learn to depend upon himself. Hitherto we have oppressed the people and bribed the landlords. We have given up the first and ought also to give up the latter.[71]

His threat that British opinion would not tolerate additional Irish subsidies or any outdoor relief based on public loans was promptly reinforced by explosions of 'English prejudice' against Irish landowners in the *Times.*[72] The Treasury view was that the existing drainage legislation represented the utmost limits of state assistance to private improvement, and that further intervention would destroy individual exertion. Trevelyan was convinced that only by holding the unremunerative public works over the proprietors 'in terrorem' would they be forced to 'employ the great majority of the starving people, leaving only a manageable minority to be employed by us on the relief works'.[73]

Equally alarmingly, Russell also appeared hostile, arguing that Bessborough had confounded 'two things essentially distinct' – relief and agricultural improvement; his plan was quite inadmissible, as it would raise unwarranted landlord expectations in Britain as well as Ireland.[74] Yet Russell's perspective was not identical to the Chancellor of the Exchequer's. The Prime Minister was anxious to summon parliament as soon as possible to consider the new administration's substantial remedial measures,[75] and his objection to the Lord Lieutenant's plan was based not on any insistence on non-remunerative works, but on the fear that an expanded relief system might damage the prospects of the reconstructive measures. In the interval, he favoured the extension of public works beyond the existing roads and bridges, even if some private interests might incidentally benefit.[76]

Russell was more ready to concede some of Bessborough's demands once the prospect of a November session faded.[77] Yet despite the Premier's support, and warnings of the political dangers of intransigence, the cabinet rejected Bessborough's proposals on 25 September.[78] The result was a political crisis. The Irish executive

---

71 Wood to Labouchere, 21, 22 Sept., Hickleton Papers, A4/185/1.

72 *Times*, 26 Sept.

73 Trevelyan to Routh, 12 Sept., *Correspondence . . . relief of distress (Comm. ser.)*, P.P. 1847 [761] LI, 68–9, Trevelyan to Labouchere, 2 Oct. 1846, Trevelyan Letterbooks, vol. 8, fols. 149–55.

74 Russell to Wood, 2 Sept., Russell Papers, PRO 30/22/5C, fol. 14; Russell to Wood, 20 Sept., Hickleton Papers, A4/56/1.

75 Russell to Bessborough, 18 Sept., Russell Papers, PRO 30/22/5C, fols. 183–4.

76 Russell to Bessborough, 21 Sept., ibid., fols. 222–3.

77 Russell memo: 'On public works in Ireland', 24 Sept., ibid., fols. 288–98.

78 Ministers were warned that if no such concession was made, Bessborough's popularity would evaporate, and the starving masses and disaffected landowners would unite in a violent Repeal agitation, Connellan to Morpeth, 27 Sept., Castle Howard Papers, J19/1/42/74. Bessborough himself continued to stress the importance of O'Connell's support, Bessborough to Russell, 2 Oct., Russell Papers, PRO 30/22/5D, fols. 20–1.

was unwilling to accept such a repudiation of its recommendations, and Redington was despatched to Westminster with a memo stating the unanimous insistence of its senior officers on their plans for reproductive works.[79] George Grey, closely advised by Trevelyan, remained hostile, but Russell was sympathetic and declared his willingness to give the Lord Lieutenant full discretionary powers until an amending bill could be introduced.[80] Bessborough's threat to resign as Viceroy, and Russell's refusal to continue in office without him, forced the question to a head. Despite some reservations, the Foxites closed ranks in support of their colleague.[81] Isolated in a cabinet meeting from which both Greys were absent, Wood found that the decision went unanimously against him, and was unable to prevent an amended form of Redington's paper being accepted.[82] Moderate ministers, sympathetic towards Irish proprietors and increasingly antagonized by the Treasury's insistence on unproductive works, fell into line.[83] What was agreed fell short of the Irish government's original demands – only drainage works were to be included, and the parish or electoral division rather than the townland was to be the unit of taxation, the sum available for remunerative works was restricted to one million pounds, and all works would cease on 15 August 1847 – but the Lord Lieutenant accepted it as a sufficient compromise.[84] The policy changes were proclaimed in the 'Labouchere letter' issued to the Board of Works on 5 October. This outcome was regarded by the Irish press and some landlords as a personal triumph for Bessborough. Monteagle rather prematurely hailed it as 'a coup d'état – practically a new Act of Parliament'.[85]

This was a temporary setback rather than a decisive blow to the Treasury. Wood denounced the scheme as a second great step in the demoralization of Ireland, but was determined to 'protect the Treasury to the utmost of my power' and was sure that the Viceroy would 'find himself in almost inextricable confusion when he comes to develop his notions'. While assuring Bessborough that 'you shall have all the help we can give you to make the scheme work', he privately

79 Russell to Bessborough, 25 Sept., Bessborough to Russell, 27 Sept., Memo, signed by Bessborough, Maziere Brady, Labouchere and Moore, urging amendments to Act 10 Vict. c. 107, 27 Sept., ibid., 5C, fols. 312–17, 340–3.

80 G. Grey to Russell, 28 Sept., Russell to Bessborough, 30 Sept., ibid., fols. 357–8, 375–7; Memo: 'Redington's proposals on drainage work in Ireland with Lord John Russell's note thereon', n.d. (Oct. 1846), ibid., 5D, fol. 6.

81 Labouchere to Morpeth, 4 Oct., Castle Howard Papers, J19/1/42/84; Morpeth memo, n.d. (Oct. 1846), Russell Papers, PRO 30/22/5G, fol. 196; Fortescue to Russell, 9 Oct., ibid., 5D, fol. 196.

82 Wood to Grey, 30 Sept., Hickleton Papers, A4/195/1; Diary of the third Earl Grey, 2, 3, 5 Oct., Grey of Howick Papers, Durham University Library; Morpeth Diary, 1, 2 Oct., Castle Howard Papers, J19/8/13.

83 Lansdowne to Bessborough, 10 Oct., Russell Papers, PRO 30/22/5D, fols. 147–50.

84 Russell to Bessborough, 2 Oct., Bessborough to Russell, 4 Oct., ibid., fols. 38–41, 46–7.

85 *Freeman's Journal*, 7 Oct.; Monteagle to Wood, 13 Oct., Monteagle Papers, MS 13,396/9.

looked forward to its ignominious collapse: 'as some English and Scotch men refuse to pay any longer, and this will be before very long, this system must come to a sudden end'.[86] The Treasury subsequently fought Bessborough's attempts to allow any work of improvement to be undertaken and to provide employment for up to two million people.[87] In the face of such resistance the Labouchere letter proved of limited use; the dual system of relief works was excessively complex, insufficient Board of Works staff were available to oversee private works, and proprietors continued to demand these be structured on smaller territorial divisions coinciding with estate boundaries or townlands.[88] Only around £180,000 was advanced under the letter, employing a maximum of 27,000 labourers in May 1847.[89] Official observers were convinced that most landowners preferred to rely on the unremunerative public works because of the widespread assumption that the government would never enforce the repayment of the vast sums laid out on them, while landowners themselves objected to the rigid control exercised by the Board, and the high costs of pauper labour.[90]

The most significant legacy of the Labouchere letter was the further alienation of the Treasury from the Irish government. Trevelyan believed the first principle of relief had been broken: 'Every system of poor relief must contain a penal and repulsive element, in order to prevent its leading to the disorganization of society. If the system is such as to be agreeable either to those who relieve or to those who are relieved, and still more if it is agreeable to both, all test of destitution must be at an end.'[91] The task of the Treasury subsequently would be to insist more strictly on 'sound principle', and Trevelyan was quick to crow over the letter's failure and its unpopularity in Britain.[92] The articulation of similar sentiments in the *Times* was not without effect. Bessborough was 'most annoyed' at the paper's observations, and Russell believed them deeply injurious. With a general election approaching, he could not afford to ignore the political repercussions of his actions: 'our defence must be before Englishmen and Scotchmen – who will complain of their taxes

---

86 Wood to Labouchere, 2 Oct., Wood to Grey, 4 Oct., Wood to Bessborough, 3 Oct., Hickleton Papers, A4/185/1. Ellice – who attributed the setback to 'the tutelage of little Rice' over Lansdowne – was also confident that an English backlash would overturn the 'monstrous machine' of the relief system, Ellice to Wood, 27 Oct., ibid., A4/103.

87 Russell to Bessborough, 10 Oct., Bessborough to Russell, 12, 23 Oct., Russell Papers, PRO 30/22/5D, fols. 176–8, 182–3. The Labouchere letter permitted the Board of Works to undertake only drainage works.

88 Labouchere to Russell, 12 Nov., ibid., 5E, fols. 82–3; R.J. Montague, 'Relief and reconstruction in Ireland 1845–9: a study of public policy during the Great Famine' (unpublished D.Phil. thesis, University of Oxford, 1976), pp. 116–17.

89 Trevelyan, *Irish crisis*, p. 68.

90 Capt. O'Brien to Trevelyan, 26 Dec. 1846, *Correspondence . . . relief of distress (Comm. ser.)*, P.P. 1847 [761] LI, 423–5; Robert Collins, *Two letters addressed to the Rt. Hon. Henry Labouchere . . . on the extreme destitution of the poor* (Dublin, 1846), pp. 13–20.

91 Trevelyan to Monteagle, 9 Oct. 1846, Monteagle Papers, MS 13,397/11.

92 Trevelyan to Labouchere, 14 Nov., Trevelyan Letterbooks, vol. 9, fols. 182–4.

being laid out on private estates and demand the same benefits.'[93] Under such pressure, Russell felt obliged to insist on a more rigid interpretation of the Act.[94] Caught between the contradictory forces of the Treasury and Dublin Castle, the government adopted a compromise policy that satisfied neither, and which was inadequate in the face of the descent of Ireland into appalling misery.

The costs of transition

In contrast to the ideological certainty characteristic of the moralists' interpretation of the potato blight, the views of Russell and Bessborough were somewhat ambiguous. Russell was uncertain about the nature of the potato disease, and was confused by the differences of opinion between the 'men of science'. If anything he tended towards the more optimistic view, yet he and Bessborough were perplexed as to what advice should be given to Irish farmers regarding the next harvest, and ultimately shifted the burden of advice onto the shoulders of the Royal Agricultural Society of Ireland. Russell took some comfort from the recovery of the Belgian potato crop in 1846, and cited 'Danish botanists [who] think the disease is like cholera, and will disappear in time', but this was speculation, and uncertainty over the long-term health of the potato was of central importance in the debate on the viability of small farms and the reclamation of estates.[95]

Russell and Bessborough agreed that whether or not the potato returned, the system of paying potato truck wages in the form of conacre or cottier plots had been demonstrated to be illegitimate. Bessborough believed as sincerely as Wood that some degree of 'social revolution' was inevitable, and that 'many of those who now call themselves farmers must fall into their natural position, that of labourers.' Cottiers would no longer be satisfied with wages in truck after the experience of earning them in money, and even if they were, farmers would thenceforth resist granting conacre.[96] Unlike other commentators, however, the Lord Lieutenant's use of the term 'cottier' applied to a specific social grouping and was not equivalent to small farmer. 'Cottier' had at least three distinct meanings in 1840s Ireland, but Bessborough used it in the sense prevalent in his native Kilkenny, that is, as 'one

93 *Times*, 26 Sept., 9 Oct.; Bessborough to Russell, 6 Oct., Russell to Bessborough, 4 Oct., Russell Papers, PRO 30/22/5D, fols. 64–7, 84–7.

94 Russell to Bessborough, 10 Oct., ibid., fols. 151–3.

95 Russell to Bessborough, 22 Oct., Bessborough to Russell, 23 Oct., ibid., fols 270–1, 282–3; Russell to Leinster, 17 Oct. 1846, G.P. Gooch (ed.), *The later correspondence of Lord John Russell, 1840–1878* (2 vols., London, 1925), I, 155–8.

96 Bessborough to Russell, 3, 14 Nov. 1846, Russell Papers, PRO 30/22/5E, fols. 17–20, 107. For the contemporary critique of the system, see Jasper W. Rogers, *The potato truck system of Ireland the main cause of her periodical famines and of the non-payment of her rents* (2nd edn, London, 1847).

who paid all or part of his rent in labour service'.[97] The poor labourers raising potatoes on a quarter to two acres of land had 'existed by a sort of artificial means which hardly any person who does not live in this country can understand'. This system had now failed completely and could not be revived; a man on less than five to ten acres could not grow enough of any alternative crop to support his family.[98]

The matter now at issue was, in Russell's words, how Ireland was 'to be carried through its present transition, and brought into a state of harmony within itself, productive of industry, and good will towards other parts of the United Kingdom'.[99] Auxiliary measures were required in the fields of the Poor Law, public works, emigration, and, most of all, waste-land reclamation. All these reforms would be directed at enabling Ireland to maintain the bulk of her existing population, by means of an improved and more productive agriculture. Exports should be increased to pay for 'clothing and colonial products', but Ireland should be self-supporting in terms of food consumption: 'she will require in future a large supply of food of her own growth or produce which the labourer should be able to buy with his wages.'[100]

The Foxite ministers believed this improvement possible in the context of a mixed or 'Prussian' structure of agriculture, involving a combination of peasant proprietors (or long leaseholders) on reclaimed lands and a tripartite division of labour on landed estates, in which tenants would have legal protections and the labourers the security of some form of effective poor law.[101] They agreed that relief measures should not promote clearances; Russell insisted that those who entered the workhouse should not be deprived of their cottages, and Bessborough protested vigorously against a Treasury minute which sought to confine public works relief to those who held no land. While he agreed that those on holdings rated above £5 should be discouraged, the Lord Lieutenant predicted that: 'It would either be nugatory or would lead to deception, perjury and everything in the shape of the transfer of land that for years we have tried to put a stop to.'[102] Bessborough later began to take a more pessimistic view, fearing that a 'large portion' of the small farmers would eventually have to become labourers, but he believed that the transition must be slow and that protection against destitution should be given to

97 Michael Beames, 'Cottiers and conacre in pre-famine Ireland', *Journal of Peasant Studies*, II (1975), 352–4.

98 Bessborough to Russell, 1 Dec. 1846, Russell Papers, PRO 30/22/5F, fols. 38–40.

99 Russell to Bessborough, 6 Nov., ibid., 5E, fols. 34–5.

100 Russell to Leinster, 17 Oct., Gooch, *Later correspondence*, I, 155–8.

101 See above, pp. 204–9.

102 Russell to Bessborough, 17 Sept., Russell Papers, PRO 30/22/5C, fols. 171–2, Bessborough to Russell, 27 Nov., ibid., 5E, fols. 196–8; Treasury minute, 24 Nov., *Correspondence . . . relief of distress (Comm. ser.)*, P.P. 1847 [761], LI, 288–9.

them 'until improved cultivation compels the farmer to employ more labourers'.[103] He continued to reject mass evictions, and was sceptical about the benefits of large-scale assisted emigration, although he was prepared to advocate a certain amount of state assistance for those families to emigrate from specific 'overgrown townlands'.[104]

Russell and Bessborough did not see the relief system as the primary mechanism for promoting social change, but relegated it to a supplementary role. Russell was as insistent as any moralist that the Board of Works should pay labourers by task work rates to enforce 'a fair day's wage for a fair day's work'.[105] This would, he believed, not only deter the unneedy and thus minimize interference in the labour market, but would begin the essential task of inculcating the discipline of wage labour into the mind of the Irish cottier-labourer. Yet his vision was fundamentally melioristic and tinged with paternalism. He hoped much of the burden of moral improvement would fall to the private efforts of 'good patriots' such as the Duke of Leinster, who would teach the poor 'to take advantage of the favourable conditions of their soil, and surrounding sea, to work patiently for themselves in their own country as they work in London or Liverpool for their employers; to study economy, cleanliness and the value of time; to aim at improving the condition of themselves and their children.'[106]

The Premier and Viceroy agreed that social transition required the assistance of some permanent augmentation of the Poor Law, but disagreed on the form this should take. Bessborough preferred the adoption of a compulsory labour rate on the model of the old English Poor Law.[107] The Viceroy intended by this mechanism to extend and improve the principle already embodied in the Labouchere letter – making the relief system a means of directly improving the agricultural infrastructure of Ireland. He admitted that significant problems would be posed by the urban populations of country towns now swollen by clearances and migration, but that this was outweighed by the importance of inducing proprietors and farmers to give agricultural employment in their localities. From late November he began to concentrate the attentions of Irish administrators on the preparation of such a scheme.[108]

---

103 Bessborough to Russell, 18 Dec. 1846, Russell Papers, PRO 30/22/5F, fols 229–30.

104 Labouchere to Russell, 1 Jan., ibid., 6A, fols. 14–15; Bessborough to Grey, 4 Jan. 1847, Grey Papers. For the emigration debate, see below, pp. 299–301, 307–10.

105 *Hans.*, LXXXVIII, 772–3 [17 Aug. 1846]; Russell to Bessborough, 2 Oct., Russell Papers, PRO 30/22/5D, fols. 28–9. The Irish government was aware of the difficulties involved, but was also firm about implementing the task-work system, Labouchere to Morpeth, 8 Nov., Castle Howard Papers, J19/1/43/5; Labouchere to Russell, 11 Nov., Gooch, *Later correspondence*, I, 160.

106 Russell to Leinster, 17 Oct., Russell Papers, PRO 30/22/5D, fols. 228. This letter, which was released to the press, was intended as something of a government manifesto, Russell to Bessborough, 29 Oct., ibid., fols. 321–2, Bessborough to Russell, 3 Nov., Fortescue to Russell, 4 Nov., ibid., 5E, fols. 16–20, 26–7.

107 Bessborough to Russell, 19 Nov., Russell Papers, PRO 30/22/5E, fols. 138–9.

108 Bessborough to Labouchere, 23 Nov., Bessborough Papers, F. 336. Montague cites

Russell looked instead to the reformed model of the 1834 English new Poor Law. He thought the baronial sessions and local relief committees had demonstrably failed to remain calm, resist popular clamour and make rational proposals, and it followed that the more controllable boards of guardians should manage relief in their place. Bessborough dismissed the latter as 'inefficient squabbling tumultuous' bodies and defended the ability of the sessions, with proper precautions, to provide relief. His opposition to the guardians reflected a residual paternalism, but also a concern that popular election made them 'party bodies' and therefore unable to provide the social and religious co-operation essential if Ireland was to meet the crisis of famine.[109] Russell was as yet reluctant to advocate the granting of a right to relief for the able-bodied 'unless very much guarded', and was also conscious of strong opposition from the moderates on this head. He grasped for a compromise in the form of the 'Scotch Poor Law', which 'with the aid of the workhouse, and plenty of public works, and great facilities for borrowing by individual landlords' would prove the optimum system. Bessborough was sceptical and unsure about what was meant by this term, but it seems that Russell intended to give a right to relief to all but the able-bodied, either in or out of the workhouse.[110] Yet despite his concern that Bessborough's plan would result in the immobility of labour in pauperized districts, Russell felt obliged by the Viceroy's insistence to include it in his legislative plan for 1847.[111]

For his part, Trevelyan expressed the opinion that a 'comprehensive and complete poor law' was desirable as a permanent outcome of the Irish crisis, and argued that it was already being accomplished by gradual steps. He was, however, reluctant to abandon too early the penal mechanism of the public works, which he believed would bring about the agricultural and behavioural improvements vital for such a poor law to succeed. Care was also essential to preserve the Poor Law mechanism as a bastion of the 'sound principle' with regard to self-government and local taxation: it was vital that no Treasury money be used to underpin it.[112]

Bessborough's insistence on the labour-rate principle as evidence that he was the 'quintessential proponent of the principles of 1822'. But while Bessborough's adherence to relief by productive employment did reflect some desire for continuity, it also involved something novel – a compulsory and permanent rating for the relief of the able-bodied poor of Ireland. This was something that the framers of the relief measures of 1822 and 1845–6 had sought to avoid. See Montague, 'Relief and reconstruction', pp. 117–25.

109 Russell to Bessborough, 22 Nov., Bessborough to Russell, 24 Nov., 1 Dec. 1846, Russell Papers, PRO 30/22/5E, fols. 157, 178–9, 5F, fols. 38–41.

110 Russell to Bessborough, 1 Dec., Bessborough to Russell, 4 Dec., ibid., fols. 33, 72. This was in line with Russell's earlier support for More O'Ferrall's suggestion that the children of men on the public works with large families be temporarily admitted to or fed from the workhouses, Russell to Bessborough, 11 Oct., ibid., 5D, fols. 172–3; G. Grey to Wood, 11 Oct., Hickleton Papers, A4/58/1.

111 Russell to Bessborough, 8 Dec., Russell Papers, PRO 30/22/5F, fols. 101–4.

112 Trevelyan to Russell, 25 Nov., Trevelyan Letterbooks, vol. 9, fols. 252–3; Trevelyan to Labouchere, 15 Dec., ibid., vol. 10, fols. 140–5.

In the circumstances of the winter of 1846–7 Russell admitted that he found a 'good deal of sense' in Smith O'Brien's view that 'the landlords ought not to be made to bear all the burden of supporting the destitute'.[113] Yet as the meeting of parliament approached political considerations began to become paramount. Given the huge costs of the relief operation, it appeared that some greater imposition would have to be placed upon Irish property to 'reconcile the English and the Scotch to make the exertions which are necessary in Ireland'. Extending the income tax to Ireland seemed impractical, and Russell confessed to Lansdowne that he could see no alternative 'but the extension to Ireland in some shape or other of the English Poor Law'.[114] With much of the British press urging tax-payers to refuse to continue subsidizing improvident Irish landowners, and demanding the introduction of 'a permanent system [of poor laws] such as that which has worked so well in this country for 300 years',[115] there were strong inducements to take this path.

These tensions were evident in the policy debates in December 1846 and early January 1847. Russell reluctantly admitted the principle of the labour rate and Bessborough hoped that little real difference now existed between them on the permanent Bill.[116] Yet doubts remained, particularly over the temporary relief measure that would continue in operation until August 1847. This was intended, in Labouchere's words, to do 'little more than legalize what has been done already', but the Treasury put strong pressure on the government to introduce a rate for current expenditure or repayments, and was generally hostile towards the continuation of the existing works policy.[117] Wood remained insistent that a moralist agenda be worked out through the relief measures. The government must not, he told Russell:

> relax in any point which relieved any portion of the Irish community from the duties that they are respectively called upon to perform. We must bear a great deal, see a great deal done wrong, aid them a great deal, but *by* them and *through* them, in the end, the work must be done . . . Permanently we *cannot* and they *must*: and the sooner this is practically understood, the better for all parties.[118]

---

113 Russell to Bessborough, 1 Dec., Russell Papers, PRO 30/22/5F, fol. 33; William Smith O'Brien, *Reproductive employment: a series of letters to the landed proprietors of Ireland; with a preliminary letter to Lord John Russell* (Dublin, 1847), pp. 3–6, 12–17.

114 Russell to Lansdowne, 2 Dec. 1846, Gooch, *Later correspondence*, I, 162–3.

115 *Times*, 2, 25 Nov., 18 Dec.; *Spectator*, 12 Dec. 1846.

116 Bessborough to Russell, 16 Dec. Russell Papers, PRO 30/22/5F, fols. 197–8; Russell to Bessborough, 16 Dec., Gooch, *Later correspondence*, I, 164–5.

117 Wood to Labouchere, 5 Dec., Bessborough Papers, F. 340; Labouchere to Wood, 22 Dec., Russell Papers, PRO 30/22/5G, fols. 24–5; Wood to Bessborough, 21 Dec., ibid., 5F, fols., 246–51.

118 Wood to Russell, 2 Dec., ibid., fols. 50–5.

Despite his doubts, Russell refused to overrule his Lord Lieutenant, and hoping that the auxiliary schemes would lift the bulk of the burden from the labour rate.[119]

The vexed questions of townlands as taxation units and exemption from general rating remained unresolved and a serious point of contention to mid-January. Russell rejected these proposals on the grounds that they would 'have ended the *general* interest for provision for the destitute; and would allow the grazier and clearer to escape their responsibilities, while ruining others'.[120] Beneath the apparent stalemate, however, Bessborough's position was being steadily eroded. The defection of Labouchere on the principle of a permanent labour rate was a major blow. The Chief Secretary's vigorous advocacy of stronger relief measures had been an important asset for Bessborough, but now Labouchere argued along similar lines to Russell that 'any permanent measure must separate relief from industry'.[121] Bessborough's proposed temporary measure also began to face considerable problems. From mid-November the Irish government had been concerned about the disruption of 'ordinary' agricultural labour by the collapse of the old agricultural system under the weight of the potato failure.[122] George Grey felt the fault lay in the 'indisposition' of the occupiers to employ labour, but the Irish government responded in quite a different way by authorizing Griffith's plan for 'family task work' under 'Circular 38' of the Board of Works. This proposed the employment of small farmers and their families on field drainage and sub-soiling, while allowing them sufficient time to cultivate their own plots once their tasks were completed.[123] Although welcomed in Ireland, the circular provoked another clash, and Russell voiced the cabinet's alarm and warned that the ministry could not defend such a proceeding.[124] Any possible wavering on Russell's part was quashed

---

119 Russell to Bessborough, 26 Dec., ibid., 5G, fols. 71–3; Russell to Wood, 26 Dec., Gooch, *Later correspondence*, I, 165–6.

120 Bessborough to Russell, 4 Jan. 1847, Wood to Russell, 6 Jan., Russell Papers, PRO 30/22/6A, fols. 42–3, 72–5; *Hans.*, LXXXIX, 431 [25 Jan. 1847]. His argument drew heavily on a paper prepared by W.T. Mulvany of the Board of Works, 'Poor employment: memo on the proposition to reduce the unit of taxation to townlands', 22 Oct. 1846, *Correspondence . . . relief of distress (Board of Works ser.)*, P.P. 1847 [764], L, 264–5.

121 Bessborough to Russell, 6 Jan., Labouchere to Russell, 8 Jan. 1847, Russell Papers, PRO 30/22/6A, fols. 69–71, 76–7.

122 Labouchere to Russell, 19 Nov. 1846, ibid., 5E, fols. 134–5.

123 G. Grey to Bessborough, 9 Dec. 1846, Home Office Papers, Public Record Office, London, HO 122/19, fols. 196–7; Board of Works, Relief Department Circular No. 38, 9 Dec. 1846, Treasury Papers, T 64/362B.

124 *Cork Examiner*, 18 Dec.; Russell to Bessborough, 17 Dec. 1846, Gooch, *Later correspondence*, I, 165. The cabinet's obstinacy was reinforced by the revelation of an increase in savings bank deposits in the west of Ireland, indicating to vigilant moralists that the wages fund was less drained than had been claimed, and that ratepayers were wilfully avoiding their obligation to employ labour. This information was leaked to the *Times* at Wood's behest, Trevelyan to Delane, 4 Nov., Trevelyan Letterbooks, vol. 9, fols. 98–9; *Times*, 6 Nov.; Wood to Russell, 24 Dec., Russell Papers, PRO 30/22/5G, fols. 36–9; G. Grey to Twisleton, 21 Dec., Home Office Papers, HO 122/19, fols. 203–207.

by Wood's vehement denunciation of what amounted to 'paying a man for the ordinary cultivation of his ground'. Bessborough's defence was overruled, and the circular was suppressed by Treasury order.[125]

Defeated on the circular, Bessborough attempted to include its principle in his Temporary Relief Bill, which he believed should make 'the cultivation of farms under 10 acres' a priority.[126] A loan for land tillage and the provision of seed was also included in the draft prepared by Redington. Bessborough went so far as to propose that on the estates of absentees, the state should intervene directly to encourage the small farmers to till the land and provide them with seed.[127] Despite Russell's sympathy, the cabinet thought the plan 'too absurd', and it was on the specific point of the cultivation of small plots that Bessborough's Bill was dropped on 16 January.[128] Bessborough found himself in the political situation that he had managed to avoid in late September. An alliance was struck between the moralists and moderates at the Bowood summit in December. Those present – including Wood, Clarendon, Lansdowne and Devon (the latter brought in a moderate 'expert' on Ireland) – agreed amongst other things that the workhouse test must be offered to the able-bodied before they could be employed on the public works. Lansdowne, in common with many Irish landowners, insisted on this test as the only means of keeping down the numbers on relief.[129] Wood endorsed it for the different reason that the moral responsibility for selecting the destitute should be put upon the local authorities.[130] Bessborough's acquiescence in the cabinet's decision to put his painfully constructed relief scheme aside, was, he believed, the price of extracting a more generous temporary relief system.

Food policy

Bessborough's scheme was also being undercut on the more palpable grounds of the failure of the existing relief works to prevent mass starvation. The Lord Lieutenant had recognized in September that public works relief would prove futile should the market fail to provide food at a price in line with the rate of wages. Yet while he lamented the failure of the much vaunted 'small dealers' to

---

125 Wood to Labouchere, 16 Dec., Bessborough Papers, F. 340; Bessborough to Wood, 19 Dec., Russell Papers, PRO 30/22/5F, fols. 233–4; Lords of the Treasury to the Commissioners of the Relief Department of the Board of Works, 21 Dec. 1846, *Correspondence . . . relief of distress (Board of Works ser.)*, P.P. 1847 [764], L, 398. Grey hoped that this snub would provoke Labouchere's resignation, Grey Diary, 16 Dec. 1846, Grey Papers.

126 Bessborough to Russell, 4 Jan. 1847, Labouchere to Russell, 8 Jan., Russell Papers, 6A, fols. 42–3, 83–4.

127 Bessborough to Russell, 10, 15 Jan., ibid., fols. 118–20, 144–6.

128 Russell to Wood, 7 Jan., Hickleton Papers, A4/56/2; Grey Diary, 19 Jan., Grey Papers; Russell to Bessborough, 17 Jan., Russell Papers, PRO 30/22/6A, fols. 167–8.

129 Lansdowne to Wood, 23 Dec. 1846, Hickleton Papers, A4/107.

130 Wood to Bessborough, 10 Dec., ibid., A4/185/1; Wood to Bessborough, 21 Dec., Russell Papers, PRO 30/22/5G, fols. 248–9.

supply cheap grain, he did not challenge the opinion that parliament could not regulate the price.[131] Russell, fresh from his espousal of free trade, also failed to question Treasury dogma on this point.[132]

Russell's two proposals for further action within the free trade paradigm – an immediate suspension of Peel's transitional Corn Law, and encouragement to local relief committees to sell food at subsidized prices – were overruled in cabinet in the autumn. Orthodox opinion declared the former politically inexpedient given the government's minority status, and of little practical significance to Ireland.[133] While it was probably true that the continuance of duty on higher grades of grain had 'only the remotest bearing on Irish "famine"', particularly at a time of international shortage,[134] Russell was aware of the growing pressure in England for measures to compensate for Irish relief expenditure.[135] The government may have been more at fault for delaying the suspension of the Navigation Acts' restrictions on 'third party' ships importing corn.[136] The Treasury also vetoed the idea of relief committees selling meal to the poor at a loss.[137]

The combination of Wood's committed backing and the closure of the food debate by the repeal of the Corn Laws gave Charles Trevelyan *carte blanche* in this vital area of relief policy. The government did not withdraw entirely from the food trade, but from August 1846 restricted itself to acting as supplier of last resort in the western districts of Ireland. The Treasury was insistent that the progress already attained in commercializing the food trade should not be compromised by state interference; depots were not to be opened while food could be obtained from private dealers at 'reasonable' prices, and even when opened, prices were to be set at rates which would permit private traders to sell with a 'reasonable profit'.[138]

---

131 Bessborough to Russell, 13 Sept., G. Grey to Russell, 23 Sept., ibid., 5C, fols. 144–8, 253–4.

132 Russell to Bessborough, 15 Oct., Gooch, *Later correspondence*, I, 154.

133 Russell to Bessborough, 21 Oct., Russell Papers, PRO 30/22/5D, fols. 266–7; Russell to Lansdowne, 22 Oct., Gooch, *Later correspondence*, I, 158; Clarendon to Wood, 18 Oct., Hickleton Papers, A4/57/1; Broughton Diary, Add. MS 43,749, fols. 57–8 [29 Oct.].

134 *Spectator*, 10 Oct. 1846.

135 The editor of the *Economist* put it bluntly: 'It is impossible that the English, so much free traders as they now are, will see the money market drained month after month for Ireland . . . and suffer any restriction to remain here.' James Wilson to Clarendon, 10 Oct., Clar. Dep., c.523.

136 The Navigation Acts permitted ships from exporting countries to carry goods directly to the UK, but prohibited those of other countries doing so, a particular problem given that the British and American fleets were considered inadequate to tranship the 1846 American harvest to the UK, Routh to Trevelyan, 16 Dec. 1846, *Correspondence . . . relief of distress (Comm. ser.)*, P.P. 1847[761] LI, 379. The Acts were suspended in January, and in the six months to June more than half of all grain imports to the UK were by third party carriers, Sarah Palmer, *Politics, shipping and the repeal of the Navigation Laws* (Manchester, 1990), pp. 87–88, 105.

137 Wood to Bessborough, 16 Oct., Hickleton Papers, A4/185/1.

138 Treasury minute, 31 Aug. 1846, *Correspondence . . . relief of distress (Board of Works)*, P.P. 1847 [764] L, 67–70.

To this was added the strict enforcement of the pledge extracted from Russell by the mercantile interest in August, that the Treasury would buy only in the UK market, so as not to interfere with the international grain trade.[139] This restrictive ordinance, coupled with the refusal to countenance any prohibition of food exports from Ireland, left the administration with a very limited supply of food stocks with which to face the winter of 1846–7.[140]

The shortfall did not unduly trouble the Assistant Secretary, who was initially confident that the private trade, accompanied by the incentives to utilize remaining food resources in the localities, would tide the country over.[141] Any 'artificial' control over prices – whether by extensive state purchase, control of local markets by issues from depots, or subsidized sale to the poor by relief committees – would be counterproductive, as it would merely draw the available supplies to higher markets (either abroad or in Britain) and prevent the economizing of local reserves. 'Famine', in Trevelyan's construction, was in general an artificial condition, brought about by state meddling at times of scarcity; high prices were a providential mechanism designed to diminish the disequilibrium, 'a mercy disguised under the appearance of a judgment'.[142]

The recognition in late September that the bulk of the American maize crop would not be available for export until the new year thus did not significantly alter Treasury thinking.[143] There was, Trevelyan informed Jones, certainly no question of artificially transferring famine from Ireland to Great Britain by buying up supplies in the British market.[144] Nevertheless, Trevelyan was extremely reluctant to recognize the existence of objective famine conditions in Ireland, and resorted to mechanisms of mental distancing: distress was, he declared, the consequence neither of the will of God nor of government miscalculation, but of deviation from 'sound principle' and the absence of responsible exertion on the part of individuals and public bodies in the localities.[145] His belated admission in late

---

139 Trevelyan to Routh, 24 July, Trevelyan to T. Baring, 24 Aug. 1846, Trevelyan Letterbooks, vol. 7, fols. 143–4, 237–8

140 Trevelyan to Hewetson, 3 Sept., ibid., vol. 8, fols. 1–3; Trevelyan to Routh, 1 Oct. 1846, *Correspondence . . . relief of distress (Comm. ser.)*, P.P. 1847 [761], LI, 106. To Trevelyan's disgust, several other European governments facing subsistence crises in 1846 were active in pursuing food imports and prohibiting exports while the UK was embracing *laissez-faire*, Trevelyan to Routh, 11 Jan. 1847, Trevelyan Letterbooks, vol. 11, fols. 95–6, 103–4. See also Peter Gray, 'Famine relief policy in comparative perspective: Ireland, Scotland and North-Western Europe, 1845–49', *Éire-Ireland*, XXXII (1997), 86–108.

141 Trevelyan to Labouchere, 11 Aug. 1846, Trevelyan Letterbooks, vol. 7, fols. 196–7.

142 Trevelyan to T.F. Kennedy, 17 Sept., Trevelyan to Routh, 11 Sept. 1846, ibid., vol. 8, fols. 74–6, 46–50. In the version of the latter published in the 1847 blue book, Trevelyan's description of price rises as a 'great blessing' was rendered into the more anodyne 'advantage', *Correspondence . . . relief of distress (Comm. ser.)*, P.P. 1847 [761], LI, 64.

143 Trevelyan to Routh, 29 Sept., 1 Oct. 1846, Trevelyan Letterbooks, vol. 8, fols. 112–13, 133–6

144 Trevelyan to Jones, 5 Oct., ibid., 162–4; see also Treasury minute, 29 Sept., *Correspondence . . . relief of distress (Comm. ser.)*, P.P. 1847 [761], LI, 63.

145 Trevelyan to Routh, 12 Dec. 1846, Trevelyan Letterbooks, vol. 10, fols. 115–17.

December that Ireland was indeed facing a 'stark, staring, downright, actual famine' did not lead him to question his minimalist view of the role of the state.[146]

This self-justifying assurance in the face of impending calamity created increasing stress between the Treasury and its subordinate officers in Ireland. While Routh and Jones shared many of Trevelyan's preconceptions, particularly with inculcating a disciplined work culture in Irish labourers and an ethic of responsible exertion among the proprietors, their position closer to the realities of the disintegrating relief mechanism made them increasingly uncertain about a rigid adherence to Treasury policy.[147] As early as September, Jones expressed scepticism as to the ability of free trade to fill the subsistence vacuum created by the potato failure, doubts which were shared by at least some senior Commissariat officers.[148] Routh was instinctively closer to the official dogma that 'the failure of this crop will commence [Ireland's] cure',[149] but even in his case the administrative logic of the Commissariat and a serious belief in the pledge made to supply the west began to temper his adherence to reconstructive priorities.[150] By mid-December he was advocating the use of warships to transport supplies from America – a measure supported even by some private traders – and was warning Trevelyan of the consequences of the failure of supply: 'this is the principal point, "food", to which everything else is subordinate, and in which, if we fail, all our other successes will count for nothing.'[151] Neither the protests of Commissariat officers at blatant profiteering by Irish corn merchants, nor the graphic official reports of cases of starvation, moved the Treasury.[152]

Faced with such wavering on the part of his agents, Trevelyan's response was twofold. The first was to bolster their resolution through the employment of evangelical rhetoric. Hewetson was upbraided for his lack of faith:

---

146 Trevelyan to J. Thornton, 30 Dec., ibid., fols. 277–8.

147 For the 'Benthamite' ideas operating particularly on the Board of Works officers, see Montague, 'Relief and reconstruction', pp. 80–1.

148 Jones to Trevelyan, 1 Sept., 1 Oct., *Correspondence . . . relief of distress (Board of Works ser.)*, P.P. 1847 [764], L, 74, 94; Dobree to Trevelyan, 19 Aug. 1846, *Correspondence . . . relief of distress (Comm. ser.)*, P.P. 1847 [761], LI, 16; c.f. Dobree to Trevelyan 14 Sept., ibid., pp. 73–4

149 Routh to Trevelyan, 16 Sept., ibid., p. 77.

150 Routh to Trevelyan, 21 Sept. 1846, ibid., pp. 62–3.

151 Routh to Trevelyan, 16, 22 Dec., ibid., p. 379, 403; Trevelyan acknowledged the problem, but insisted that Wood had vetoed any increase in the state's activities, Trevelyan to Routh, 18, 26 Dec., ibid., pp. 380–2, 409–10; see also 'Petition to the Treasury from Richardson Bros. & Co., Belfast', 26 Aug., ibid., pp. 33–4.

152 Hewetson to Trevelyan, 30 Dec., ibid., 439–40. On 21 December Assistant-Commissary General Inglis reported from Skibbereen that 197 had died in the poorhouse since 5 November, with many more in their cabins or on the roads. Like many officials, he transmitted his eye-witness accounts to his superiors: 'On my arrival on Saturday, a girl about nine years old was found lying on a heap of dirt near the police barracks, dead, her father and mother having died a few days previously. Also two men were discovered dead in a miserable hut, partly rat-eaten, and no-one to remove them.' Inglis to Hewetson, 21 Dec., *Correspondence . . . relief of distress (Comm. ser.)*, P.P. 1847 [761], LI, 420.

> Dearness is synonymous with scarcity, and it is the check which God and nature have imposed on the too rapid consumption of an insufficient supply of any article . . . 'Let me now fall into the hand of the Lord, for very great are His mercies; but let me not fall into the hand of man' – this is a feeling common to all mankind. It is hard upon the poor people that should be deprived of the consolation of knowing that they are suffering from the infliction of God's Providence, to mitigate which much has been done by the Government and the upper classes, while nothing, as far as I am aware, has been done to aggravate it . . . [153]

Trevelyan's firm adherence to this optimistic theodicy was not to alter for the remainder of the Famine period. He was, however, conscious of the need to reassure his wavering subordinates, and bombarded them with didactic literature. The 1845–6 relief correspondence was weeded on 'the principle of making it a magazine of our past experience', and distributed as a blue book to all relief officers.[154] Not content with this, a special edition of Adam Smith's 'Digression concerning the corn trade and corn laws' – in Trevelyan's view 'the most strikingly practical part of the "Wealth of Nations"' – was issued in October to every Commissariat officer and clerk.[155] Trevelyan was particularly impressed by Smith's arguments that it was price controls which produced 'instead of the hardships of a dearth, the dreadful horrors of a famine'.[156] Extracts from Edmund Burke's *Thoughts and details on scarcity* were also employed to ram home the non-interventionist dogma.[157] Officials who remained openly critical of the official line were eased out of Irish service.[158]

This blend of 'moderate' evangelical providentialism with an optimistic reading of Smithian economics gave Trevelyan and his allies not only a resilient and intellectually satisfying paradigm through which to interpret the Irish catastrophe, but also a moralistic device for directing responsibility away from the state and its agents to the failings of the Irish as individuals and as a nation. Trevelyan denied any racist intent in this, not least because his critique extended to the Anglo-Irish landowning elite, and because he believed fervently in the possibility of the

---

153 Trevelyan to Hewetson, 6 Jan. 1847, ibid., pp. 440–1.

154 Trevelyan to J. McCulloch, 16 Sept. 1846, Trevelyan Letterbooks, vol. 8, fols. 68–9.

155 Trevelyan hoped this 'would do as much good in Ireland as in England and Scotland, where it has furnished the staple of all the arguments which have led to the present enlightened and beneficial state of feeling on the subject', Trevelyan to Routh, 30 Sept., ibid., fol. 118.

156 [Adam Smith], *Extract from the fifth chapter of the fourth book of Adam Smith's 'Wealth of Nations'* (London, n.d. [1846]), p. 4.

157 Trevelyan to Routh, 2 Oct. 1846, *Correspondence . . . relief of distress (Comm. ser.)*, P.P. 1847 [761], LI, 107–8; see above, p. 104. For Burke's relationship to Smith, see Gertrude Himmelfarb, *The idea of poverty: England in the early industrial age* (London, 1984), pp. 66–73.

158 Trevelyan to Col. Archer, 23 Nov. 1846, 4 Jan. 1847, Trevelyan to Routh, 9 Dec. 1846, Trevelyan Letterbooks, vol. 9, fols. 226–7, vol. 10, fols. 76–81, vol. 11, fols. 48–9.

salvation of Irish society through its own efforts (albeit with firm guidance from its moral superiors).[159] The proprietors of the Scottish Highlands, facing similar difficulties after the potato failure, were increasingly held up as a model for what their Irish counterparts could and should achieve; the smaller scale of the Highland crisis and different position of Scottish landowners was conveniently overlooked.[160]

Nevertheless, Trevelyan remained supremely confident that suffering would bring the Irish to their senses. He assured the over-stretched officers of the Board of Works:

> If the discovery be not soon made that the great body of the landed proprietors have by neglecting their own duties thrown upon the Board of Works a task which is utterly beyond the power of mortal man to perform, the country must pass through fearful calamities.[161]

The didactic dimension of the relief system was continually stressed; Trevelyan vetoed Jones' suggestion that the local relief committees be wound up as inefficient, on the grounds that 'the upper and middle classes are now beginning to be trained, through the medium of these local committees, to the local administration of their affairs.'[162] Such arguments clashed with the centralizing ethic of the Board – which criticized its masters for placing them in an impossible situation – but were at the heart of the moralist agenda.[163] The incomprehension and hostility expressed by the Irish landlord class towards Trevelyan's policies merely reinforced his determination to re-educate them.[164]

By December a number of ministers were also growing increasingly uneasy about Trevelyan's ideologically-driven campaign. The Irish administration, closer to the real horrors of the localities, sought a more interventionist policy. Labouchere

---

159 Trevelyan disliked the *Times'* attacks on the racial deficiencies of the 'Celts': 'I myself boast to be of Celtic origin; I have always regarded with peculiar interest the Celtic branch of our national family. However superior the German race may be in some points, I would not have Ireland Anglo-Saxon if I could; and it has always appeared to me, that in the infinitely varied distribution of the rich gifts of Providence, the Celtic race has no reason to complain of its share.' Trevelyan to S. Spring Rice, 10 Nov. 1846, Trevelyan Letterbooks, vol. 9, fols. 144–8.

160 Trevelyan to Monteagle, 9 Oct. 1846, Monteagle Papers, MS 13,397/11; Trevelyan to G. Grey, 17 Oct., Trevelyan Letterbooks, vol. 8, fols. 267–8. On the Highland crisis, see T.M. Devine, *The Great Highland Famine: hunger, emigration and the Scottish Highlands in the nineteenth century* (Edinburgh, 1988), esp. pp. 33–55, 83–145.

161 Trevelyan to Larcom, 17 Oct. 1846, Larcom Papers, National Library of Ireland, Dublin, MS 7745.

162 Jones to Trevelyan, 28 Nov., 5 Dec., Trevelyan to Jones, 2 Dec., *Correspondence . . . relief of distress (Board of Works ser.)*, P.P. 1847 [764], L, 289, 306–7, 291–2.

163 *Final report from the Board of Public Works, Ireland, relating to the measures adopted for the relief of distress in July and August 1847*, P.P. 1849 [1047], XXIII.

164 For Irish landed anger at the operation of the Labour Rate Act, see [Mortimer O'Sullivan], 'State of Ireland', *Quarterly Review*, LXXIX (Dec. 1846), 238–69.

pressed the matter strongly on the cabinet, contrasting its record adversely with Peel's, and called for 'decisive measures'.[165] Russell responded by authorizing outdoor relief to the impotent, inducing the Treasury to increase donations, and pressed Wood to take steps to bolster the overall food supply. The Chancellor, however, denounced further 'meddling' and announced that, at any rate, the American maize crop – which represented the only substantial source available on the world market – would not be available before May.[166] Despite Wood's objections, the Prime Minister did at last get his way on suspending the Navigation Acts and opening UK ports to all grains completely free of duty, but this appears to have made little immediate impact on supply.[167]

Faced with a blockage of supply, Russell turned to the mechanism of distribution. Bessborough admitted by mid January 1847 that with prices so high 'all hope of giving employment to enable the poor to purchase food is out of the question', and that the government's food policy – particularly with respect to the non-regulation of private enterprise – had proved a disaster. He thought that although soup kitchens would be no panacea, the government had no option but to resort to them.[168] Changing British perceptions of the Irish crisis opened the way for such a dramatic shift in policy.

III PROVIDENCE AND THE POOR LAW, 1847

Charity and atonement

By the end of 1846, British perceptions of the Famine had taken a more concrete form. Graphic reports of the horrors of mass mortality from starvation and disease, most notoriously at Skibbereen, began to fill the pages of the press.[169] Pamphlets containing affective famine narratives by Quakers and other humanitarian travellers also brought home the extremity of the crisis to a wide audience.[170] A growing awareness of the human consequences of the potato failure altered the context in which political decisions were made. The British response was complex and variable; a genuine if ill-focused humanitarianism was widespread, but was constrained by previously determined interpretations of the crisis.

---

165 Labouchere to Russell, 11, 16 Dec., Russell Papers, PRO 30/22/5F, fols. 151–2, 195–6.

166 Russell to Wood, 25, 26 Dec., Hickleton Papers, A4/56/1; Wood to Labouchere, 17 Dec., Bessborough Papers, F. 340; Wood to Russell, 24, 26 Dec. 1846, Russell Papers, PRO 30/22/5G, fols. 36–9, 67–70.

167 Broughton Diary, Add. MS 43,749, fol. 83 [13 Jan. 1847].

168 Bessborough to Russell, 14, 18, 19 Jan. 1847, Russell Papers, PRO 30/22/6A, fols. 140–3, 171–3, 180–1.

169 *Times*, 24 Dec. 1846; *Illustrated London News*, 16, 23 Jan. 1847.

170 Elihu Burritt, *A journal of a visit of three days to Skibbereen, and its neighbourhood* (London, 1847); William Bennett, *Narrative of a recent journey of six weeks in Ireland, in connexion with the subject of supplying small seed in some of the remoter districts* (London, 1847); [Anon.], *A brief account of the famine in Ireland* (London, 1847).

Peel had believed that there was little private sympathy in Great Britain for the Irish, and had made no efforts to stimulate charitable activity outside Ireland. His Whig successors were also slow to recognize such a possibility, and it was Trevelyan who first took the idea seriously in early December. Again, evangelical morality was paramount in his thinking; while state intervention was by its essence an evil, private charity was scripturally enjoined, and would be beneficial to the donor and to the recipient, so long as it was appropriately channelled.[171] Conscious of the success of the collections raised spontaneously in India and Ceylon for Irish relief in 1846, he began to regard a more general fund as a safety net for the most distressed, allowing the government to adhere rigidly to its relief rules for the majority of the population. Routh agreed that the expenditure of such a private subscription should be tightly controlled by the state.[172]

Shortly after, the idea of issuing a Queen's letter to promote such a charitable fund was raised publicly by the Anglican clergymen of the devastated Skibbereen district. George Grey was initially dismissive, but Trevelyan used the opportunity to promote his own scheme, arguing that the Irish crisis placed a duty of private philanthropy on all. He insisted, however, that two conditions be attached – that leading Irish magnates should set a public example, and that the Treasury should retain a high degree of control over the use of the fund.[173] Wood remained sceptical that the British public would respond positively, but Trevelyan was more sensitive to the changing mood of the country, arguing that anti-Irish feeling would subside as 'further horrifying accounts are received'.[174] Despite the reluctance of Irish proprietors to contribute on the grounds of inability or that it was a distraction from public relief,[175] the appeal proved successful, and other ministers acquiesced in Trevelyan's strategy.[176]

At the beginning of January 1847, the 'British Association for the Relief of Extreme Distress in the Remote Parishes of Ireland and Scotland' was established

---

171 Trevelyan to T. Hankey, 17, 24 Dec. 1846, Trevelyan Letterbooks, vol. 10, fols. 157, 218.

172 Trevelyan to Routh, 5 Dec., Routh to Trevelyan, 7 Dec. 1846, *Correspondence . . . relief of distress (Comm. ser.)*, P.P. 1847 [761], LI, 332, 336. For the Indian subscription, which raised nearly £14,000, see [Indian Relief Fund], *Distress in Ireland. Report of the trustees of the Indian Relief Fund* (Dublin, 1847).

173 G. Grey to Revs. C. Caulfield and R. Townsend, 9 Dec., Home Office Papers, HO 122/19, fols. 197–200; Trevelyan to Labouchere, 15 Dec. 1846, Bessborough Papers, F. 338. Despite official reports confirming the extremity of distress and the collapse of the relief committee at Skibbereen, the Treasury insisted that no additional assistance be given to the locality until a number of conditions had been met by the local proprietors, Trevelyan to Routh, 18 Dec., *Correspondence . . . relief of distress (Board of Works ser.)*, P.P. 1847 [764], L, 381.

174 Wood to Russell, 21 Dec., Russell Papers, PRO 30/22/5F, fols. 248–9; Trevelyan to Russell, 26 Dec., Trevelyan Letterbooks, vol. 10, fols. 235–6.

175 Devon to S. Spring Rice, 31 Dec., Monteagle Papers, MS 13,396/3; Lansdowne to Russell, 30 Dec. 1846, Russell Papers, PRO 30/22/5G, fols. 121–2. Lincoln was also suspicious, Lincoln to Peel, 5 Jan. 1847, Peel Papers, Add. MSS 40,481, fol. 398.

176 Labouchere to Russell, 1 Jan. 1847, Russell Papers, PRO 30/22/6A, fols. 14–15.

in the City of London, largely at Trevelyan's and Russell's instigation.[177] It immediately attracted considerable support and incorporated local appeals already begun in British provincial cities; the public subscription of the Queen and her ministers did much to stimulate interest in Britain, by making Irish charity 'fashionable'.[178] Trevelyan was intent on moralising the philanthropy of the British Association, and was helped by its association with the evangelical philanthropic ethos and the fact that the committee included several Claphamites such as Henry Kingscote and Samuel Jones Loyd. From the beginning the committee was in constant communication with Trevelyan at the Treasury and George Grey at the Home Office.[179] Before the month was out, Trevelyan was already giving firm guidance on how and where the Association should deploy its resources.[180]

This identification became stronger when the Queen's letter, calling for parochial collections, was issued in January; from the beginning the government intended its proceeds to be channelled through the British Association.[181] Charity sermons had begun before its circulation, stimulated by accounts from Skibbereen and other places, but became more widespread thereafter.[182] These frequently preached the need for charity not only for the sake of the Irish, but in atonement for the sins of the English. Some ultra-Protestants insisted on anathematizing official toleration of Catholicism as the prime 'national sin',[183] but the majority chose to

177 Trevelyan to Routh, 22 Dec. 1846, *Correspondence . . . relief of distress (Comm. ser.)*, P.P. 1847 [761], LI, 402; Memo: 'London Committee on Irish relief', 24 Jan. 1847, Monteagle Papers, MS 13,397/10. Monteagle's son Stephen Spring Rice became its secretary, and occasionally clashed with Trevelyan, Trevelyan to Spring Rice, 9 Jan., Trevelyan Letterbooks, vol. 11, fols. 85–6.

178 Wood to Russell, 6 Jan. 1847, Russell Papers, PRO 30/22/6A, fols. 72–5. Russell gave £300, Wood £200, and the Queen doubled her subscription to £2000 'in consequence of Scotland being included', Russell to Spring Rice, 1 Jan., Monteagle Papers, MS 13,397/5; G. Grey to Wood, 4 Jan., Hickleton Papers, A4/58/1.

179 British Association Minute Book, National Library of Ireland, Dublin, MS 2022, fols. 8, 11, 21–2 [4, 5, 8 Jan. 1847]; Trevelyan to Kingscote, 4 Jan., Trevelyan Letterbooks, vol. 11, fols. 32–6.

180 Trevelyan to Jones Loyd, 26 Jan. 1847, *Correspondence . . . relief of distress (Comm. ser.) second part*, P.P. 1847 [796], LII, 19. A full analysis of the British Association's activities in Ireland has yet to be published, but Devine's account of its operations in the Scottish Highlands indicates that Trevelyan's influence, though surreptitious, was effective in ensuring that the expenditure in Scotland met with moralist social aims, Devine, *The Great Highland Famine*, pp. 102–45. For the moralists' preference for assisting Scotland to Ireland, see T.B. Macaulay to T.F. Ellis, Jan. 1847, T. Pinney (ed.), *The letters of Thomas Babington Macaulay* (6 vols, Cambridge, 1974–81), VI, 332.

181 British Association Minute Book, MS 2022, fols. 40–1, 43, 200–2 [12, 13 Jan., 3 March 1847].

182 T. Walker to Wood, 7 Jan. 1847, Hickleton Papers, A4/181. For an example of the direct use of Irish reports to stimulate charitable pathos, see Leslie Badham, *A sermon, preached in St Stephen's Chapel, Frensham . . . in aid of the Irish relief funds* (Godalming, n.d. [1847]).

183 For examples of retributive Anti-Catholic readings see C. Vansittart, *A sermon on famine: the expediency of a public fast, and the duty of personal abstinence in the present time of dearth* (London, 1847), J.C. Crosthwaite, *The unfruitful fig-tree. A sermon, preached at the church of St Mary-at-Hill, London* (London, 1847).

emphasize pious introspection or the ultimate benefits to be expected from Divine visitation. To many, the Famine was as much as a warning to its observers as a visitation on the sufferers; providence required humility and renunciation of luxury from the former, while the Irish, if properly guided, would learn to exert themselves and undertake their responsibilities, and would ultimately be blessed with an improved diet and a more productive agriculture.[184]

The cabinet decided, with Bessborough's approval, to encourage the subscription by setting apart a national day of fast and humiliation on Wednesday 24 March.[185] This appears to have been well kept; newspaper accounts from major British cities claimed a very high degree of compliance and capacity crowds at religious services, while Morpeth observed that 'all the churches were very full, the shops shut, and little appearance of pleasuring'.[186] The Queen's letter and day of fast had two major consequences. Firstly, they gave official sanction to a providentialist interpretation of the potato failure, which became remarkably widespread amongst the English political classes. A very high proportion of parliamentary speeches in 1847 attributed the crisis to divine intervention in one form or another.[187] Few elements in British society publicly opposed the national fast. J.S. Mill's argument that 'no persons with any pretensions to instruction now see a special interposition of Providence in a blight, any more than in a thunder storm', was more a statement of secularist polemic than of representative opinion.[188]

The second consequence was ambiguous. The Queen's letter and associated appeals raised nearly £435,000 for distribution by the British Association,[189] but were accompanied by demands for reciprocal exertions in Ireland. The *Times* had initially rejected the British subscription as 'a shabby excuse . . . for staving off [a]

---

184 For this 'liberal' interpretation, see Henry W. Sulivan, *Christian compassion: a sermon, preached in obedience to the Queen's letter, in behalf of the starving Irish* (2nd edn, London, 1847); C.H. Gaye, *Irish famine, a special occasion for keeping Lent in England: a sermon, preached in obedience to the Queen's letter* (London, 1847).

185 Russell to Bessborough, 1 March, Bessborough to Russell, 3 March, Archbishop of Canterbury to Russell, 6 March, Russell Papers, PRO 30/22/6B, fols. 172–3, 184–6, 203–6.

186 *Observer*, 28 March; *Illustrated London News*, 27 March; *Leeds Mercury*, 27 March; Morpeth Diary, 24 March, Castle Howard Papers, J19/8/14.

187 Even Greville, whose religious opinions were heterodox, recorded his responses to the crisis in religious language. While critical of mainstream evangelical interpretations, he wrote of the 'mysterious operations of providence' demanding humility from observers, Greville, *Journal*, III, 69–70, 73–4 [14 March, 2 April].

188 [John Stuart Mill], *Morning Chronicle*, 23 March 1847, in Ann P. and John M. Robson (eds.), *Collected works of John Stuart Mill, Vol. XXIV: Newspaper writings, January 1835 to June 1847* (London, 1986), pp. 1073–5.

189 Trevelyan, *Irish crisis*, pp. 115–29. This did not include additional sums raised by religious bodies or the substantial relief aid sent from America. The government welcomed private donations from the latter and agreed to pay the costs of freight, Palmerston to Pakenham, 19 April 1847, Palmerston Papers, Foreign Office Letterbooks, British Library, London, Add. MS 48,547, fol. 39.

real poor law', and condemned those who continued to publicize the plight of Skibbereen for not taking direct action themselves.[190] In the wake of Russell's parliamentary commitment to extending the Irish Poor Law, the paper endorsed the national humiliation, but warned that England's duty of sacrifice should not exonerate the Irish:

> The afflicted country should have helped to work out its own redemption, ere it reposed in confident security on the vicarious activity of its wealthier neighbour . . . Deep, indeed, has the canker eaten; not into the core of a precarious and suspected root – but into the very hearts of the people, corrupting them with a fatal lethargy and debasing them by a fatuous dependence! Not the subsistence of this year alone – but the hope of many years is at stake; the honour, the industry, and the independence of a million of men.[191]

England's atonement for its past neglect of Ireland thus included the charitable collection of March, but this would be meaningless without stern moral guidance thereafter: 'we must educate and elevate Ireland, by teaching her people to educate and elevate themselves.'[192]

Radical nonconformist opinion was similarly double-edged, endorsing charitable generosity, but denouncing state aid as taxation of the British poor for the indolent Irish aristocracy.[193] Greville noted in March that in London people were 'animated by very mixed and very varying feelings . . . and are tossed about between indignation, resentment, rage, and economical fear on the one hand, and pity and generosity on the other.' Harrowing accounts had stimulated English charity, but these had been accompanied by reports of exploitation, idleness and importunity.[194] A letter from a Cambridgeshire clergyman to the Prime Minister summed up the popular mood in England; his parishioners had been generous, 'but we must not have it again'.[195]

One religious group that had ignored the day of fast, objecting to temporal injunctions in religious matters, was the Society of Friends. John Bright typically denounced the proclamation on behalf of radical Quakerism as 'an insult to religion, and calculated to engender, on the one hand, gross superstition, and gross infidelity on the other'.[196] Quaker interpretations of the Famine also looked to providence, but many were more benign and optimistic in outlook, and less judgmental towards the Irish poor. The visitation, Jacob Harvey explained to Morpeth, was not a punishment to Ireland: 'Divine Providence has spoken to

190 *Times*, 6 Jan., 8 March 1847.
191 Ibid., 26 March.
192 Ibid., 14 April.
193 *Nonconformist*, 13, 27 Jan., 3 Feb. 1847.
194 Greville, *Journal*, III, 71 [23 March].
195 Rev. A. Peyton to Russell, 20 March, Russell Papers, PRO 30/22/6B, fols. 271–2.
196 *Hans.*, XCI, 336–7 [23 March 1847].

Great Britain on behalf of Ireland, in the potato blight. She must now be raised from her degradation – it required the "voice from the dead" to open the eyes of the English nation!'[197] It was intended not as retribution but to encourage ameliorative human action. Harvey expressed this in terms compatible with Foxite Whiggery: '*You* . . . are suffering for the sins of your ancestors towards Ireland – but with unbounded confidence in the mercy of the Almighty, I trust your endeavours to mitigate all the evils of former bad government will be considered by Him as an atonement, sufficient to correct the human errors of politicians and permit success to crown your efforts!' The intention of the Almighty was 'to open the eyes of landowners and Government to the un-Christian state of social life in Ireland', and 'to raise the poor peasantry and labourers of all classes from their present low condition.'[198]

With regard to the immediate question of relief, many Quakers held that 'when famine stares you in the face, political economy should be forgotten.' In November 1846 the Central Relief Committee of the Society of Friends in Dublin began the systematic establishment of soup kitchens in distressed areas, and effectively publicized these activities in England, exposing the failure of the public works to keep the starving alive in the west. The message of James Hack Tuke's narrative of William Forster's journey in the west was explicit: 'Who would have ventured to recommend us *to wait* for the operations of the poor-laws and labour rates, however desirable these provisions may be and are in themselves? Whilst these methods are discussing, the people are dying . . . How then can anyone doubt that it is the imperative duty of all to endeavour to relieve those who are thus perishing?'[199]

Morpeth, who had close connections with the Quakers of Yorkshire and Ireland, was kept well informed of these developments and brought his correspondence to the attention of Russell.[200] The Quakers were not alone in setting up soup kitchens,[201] but their effective propagandizing and shaming won the attention and interest of ministers, administrators and the public. Russell, convinced by

---

197 Harvey to Morpeth, 14 Nov. 1846, Castle Howard Papers, J19/1/43/10. Harvey, an Irish Quaker, was agent for the National Loan Fund Life Assurance Company in New York, and the co-ordinator of the Friends' relief activities in North America; for his work see *Transactions of the Central Relief Committee of the Society of Friends during the Famine in Ireland in 1846 and 1847* (Dublin, 1852), pp. 216–328.

198 Harvey to Morpeth, 30 Dec. 1846, 16 Feb. 1847, Castle Howard Papers, J19/1/43/31, 46.

199 [James Hack Tuke], *James Hack Tuke's narrative describing the second, third and fourth weeks of William Forster's journey in the distressed districts in Ireland* (London, n.d. [1847]), p. 3. For a detailed survey of Quaker relief during the Famine, see Helen E. Hatton, *The largest amount of good: Quaker relief in Ireland 1654–1921* (Kingston and Montreal, 1993), pp. 79–222.

200 Morpeth to Russell, 24 Dec. 1846, Tuke to J. Bewley, 15 Dec., Russell Papers, PRO 30/22/5G, fols. 28–31.

201 One was established by Assistant Commissary-General Inglis at Skibbereen on his own initiative, Caulfield to Monteagle, 29 Dec. 1846, Monteagle Papers, MS 13,396/1; Inglis to Hewetson, 21 Dec. 1846, *Correspondence . . . relief of distress (Comm. ser.)*, P.P. 1847 [761], LI, 420.

early January that 'the pressing matter at present is to keep the people alive', drew the conclusion that 'soup kitchens appear the most immediate relief'.[202]

Soup kitchens

Morpeth and Russell carried these convictions into the cabinet committee which met on 13 January and proposed the radically altered programme accepted unanimously by the cabinet three days later.[203] A shift in public opinion opened the door to a more interventionist and direct relief policy, but humanitarianism was by no means the only element in the decision to abandon public works for soup kitchens, and was certainly not responsible for the cabinet's unanimity on the matter. Orthodox objections to Bessborough's proposed labour rate focused minds on viable alternatives.[204]

Perhaps more important was the growing criticism of the public works system by senior Irish administrators. By the end of the year it was transparent that, despite vast and increasing expense, it was failing to fulfil any of its objectives adequately.[205] The Board of Works lacked the capacity to cope with the vast numbers employed: the task-work system was unworkable in many circumstances, and operated against the interests of the weaker and infirm labourers. Payments were often irregular, and discontent on the crowded work-sites was leading to outbreaks of violence. Frustration with the limitations of the system led some field-officers to attack the principle of unreproductive works.[206]

Routh had initially opposed gratuitous distribution of cooked food as likely to prevent the promotion of 'habits of domestic economy', but came to acknowledge the success of local experiments in the localities and the much lower cost of this mode of relief.[207] By early January, senior administrators were pushing for the

---

202 Russell to Bessborough, 5 Jan. 1847, Russell Papers, PRO 30/22/6A, fols. 48–9. Both Clanricarde and the Irish government endorsed this view, Clanricarde to Russell, 17 Dec. 1846, Bessborough to Russell, 2 Jan. 1847, ibid., 5F, fols. 208–10, 6A, fols. 19–20.

203 Cabinet memo, 15 Jan. 1847, Palmerston Papers, CAB/46/A; Broughton Diary, Add. MS 43,749, fol. 85 [16 Jan.]. At the same time, Russell prevailed on his clearly reluctant Home Secretary to allow the Lord Lieutenant discretionary powers to issue loans of food to workhouses in unions where insufficient rates could be collected, Somerville to the secretary of the Poor Law Commissioners, 14 Jan., G. Grey to Bessborough, 18, 23 Jan., Home Office Papers, HO 122/19, fols. 224–8, 230–4, 246–9.

204 See above, pp. 246–50.

205 Commissioners to Trevelyan, Jan. 1847, *Correspondence . . . relief of distress (Board of Works ser.)*, P.P. 1847 [764], L, 523; Trevelyan to Wood, 6 Jan. 1847, Hickleton Papers, A4/59.

206 Smith, *Twelve month's residence*, pp. 23–4, 79–96. Smith, who expressed much sympathy for the plight of both labourers and landlords, had volunteered to serve as a Board of Works engineer in the belief that he was joining 'a crusade, in fact, against famine', ibid., p. v.

207 Routh to Trevelyan, 5, 9, 30 Dec., Stanley to Rosse, 24 Nov. 1846, *Correspondence . . . relief of distress (Comm. ser.)*, P.P. 1847 [761], LI, 333, 352, 437, 347. By the new year, administrators were urging relief committees to establish soup kitchens as a matter of urgency, but still insisted on the sale of rations to the able bodied, 'Circular: augmented ratio of donations

abandonment of public works relief, and a strict separation of relief from the labour market in future.[208]

Moralists accepted the logic of this argument, but also saw the soup kitchens as offering an opportunity to impose a novel set of moral checks in place of those of the relief works which had patently failed. The two-tiered administrative structure introduced in the new Bill created a central Relief Commission with a professional and active inspectorate, which would exercise considerable discipline over the officially-appointed local finance committees, while leaving the reformed local relief committees responsible for the physical provision of food. Expenditure was to be regulated by a greater insistence on the raising of local rates, and importunity checked by a 'cooked food test'. The scheme would facilitate the transition to an extended Poor Law, not least by forcing proprietors to confront the reality of paying directly for outdoor relief when no private employment was offered.[209] In addition to these considerations, Wood was also anxious for any instrument that would ratchet down the spiralling relief expenditure.[210]

The Irish government accepted that the unforeseen scale of the distress had made a departure from original intentions inevitable. Redington feared that such outdoor relief would have adverse consequences in discouraging emigration and in encouraging dependency, but accepted it as a necessary evil given the failure of the public works:

> I never thought that anything approaching to this [new] system would be considered. Time has, nevertheless, by making apparent the magnitude of the disaster, reconciled everyone to the consideration of what under other circumstances would appear monstrous propositions . . . the wretched labour now afforded for public money will no longer be asked for; and the peasantry, being fed without this demand upon their time or exertion, it is hoped will devote themselves to the ordinary pursuit of agriculture. This will be a blessing, as breaking up the demoralizing public works which have promised fairly to render anarchy perfect and overturn society in this country.[211]

Bessborough was also attracted to the prospect of a new Commission that would, he hoped, be less tightly controlled by the Treasury, and he approved Russell's choice of the experienced administrator Sir John Burgoyne as its head.[212] Instructions for

---

on subscriptions for affording gratuitous relief', 20 Jan., Routh to Trevelyan, 23 Jan. 1847, *Correspondence relating to the measures adopted for the relief of distress (Comm. ser.) second part*, P.P. 1847 [796], LII, 13–14.

208 Larcom to Trevelyan, 6 Jan. 1847, Larcom Papers, MS 7745.

209 Trevelyan to Larcom, 6 Jan., Trevelyan Letterbooks, vol. 11, fols. 68–9; Trevelyan to Jones, 14 Jan. 1847, Larcom Papers, MS 7745; Trevelyan, *Irish crisis*, pp. 84–8.

210 Wood to Palmerston, n.d. [Dec. 1846], Palmerston Papers, GC/WO/19/1–2.

211 Redington to Labouchere, 19, 20 Jan. 1847, Bessborough Papers, F. 337.

212 Bessborough to Labouchere, 18, 24 Jan., Bessborough Papers, F. 336; Russell to Bessborough, 24 Jan., Bessborough to Russell, 27 Jan. 1847, Russell Papers, PRO 30/22/6A, fols. 204–5,

the operation of the new temporary relief measure were issued on 28 January, but the Lord Lieutenant was frustrated in his hopes that it would have greater financial independence from the Treasury.[213]

When parliament met on 25 January, Russell announced the new temporary relief mechanism as part of his 'comprehensive scheme' of Irish measures.[214] Immediate distress would now be met by gratuitous outdoor relief without a labour test; pauperization would not be enforced as it was necessary to encourage the poor to cultivate their own or others' plots for the coming harvest. The government would also subsidize the distribution of seed with a £50,000 loan – a measure which Bessborough had long been pursuing.[215] The state would advance loans and make donations in aid of subscriptions for immediate relief, and would remit half the debt owed under the Poor Employment Act, although responsibility would remain primarily with local rate-payers and proprietors.

The Irish debates of January 1847 put pressure on the government to remove the financial and political embarrassment of the unproductive public works as quickly as possible. The temporary Soup Kitchen Bill passed into law in February with relatively little debate, and the cabinet urged the freezing and rapid reduction of the numbers on the works.[216] Russell feared that the concurrent operation of the two relief systems would overturn the fragile financial structure hammered out in parliament, and that the vast numbers on the public works (up to 714,000 in early March) would prevent the sowing of much of the land.[217] Alarm on this head displaced the Prime Minister's earlier concern that 'it would be a dreadful thing to have the men suddenly turned off the roads without the means of procuring food.'[218] Bessborough had also been extremely reluctant to begin cutting

---

219–20. Burgoyne had been head of the Irish Board of Works 1831–45, and had previously taken a robustly interventionist line on railway development. Bessborough found him 'an excellent man', although 'rather slower than suits me', Burgoyne to Monteagle, 4 April 1843, Monteagle Papers, MS 13,394/1; Bessborough to Labouchere, 3 March 1847, Bessborough Papers, F. 336.

213 G. Grey to Bessborough, 28 Jan., Home Office Papers, HO 122/19, fols. 254–63. The new Commission also included Redington, Twisleton, Jones, McGregor and Routh.

214 *Hans.*, LXXXIX, 426–35 [25 Jan. 1847]. He cited the authority of Col. Jones as to the expediency of abandoning the existing system, Jones to Trevelyan, 19 Jan. 1847, *Correspondence relating to the measures adopted for the relief of distress in Ireland (Board of Works series), second part*, P.P. 1847 [797], LII, 28–9.

215 Labouchere to Parker, 10 Oct. 1846, *Correspondence . . . relief of distress* (*Comm. ser.*), P.P. 1847 [761], 166.

216 *Morning Chronicle*, 16 Feb.; Broughton Diary, Add. MS 43,749, fols. 128–9 [3, 5 March]; G. Grey to Bessborough, 4 March 1847, Home Office Papers, HO 122/19, fols. 284–8.

217 Russell to Bessborough, 5, 8, 9 March, Russell Papers, PRO 30/22/6B, fols. 194–5, 213–15, 219–20. The need for cultivation was stressed in the Treasury minute of 10 March, *First report of the Relief Commissioners*, P.P. 1847 [799], XVII, 19.

218 Russell to Bessborough, 18 Jan., Russell Papers, PRO 30/22/6A, fols. 176–7.

the numbers on the works before the new Act was fully in operation, yet was also pressurized into abandoning his protests by the vital question of cultivation. The production of as much food as possible for the following season became his priority, and the social costs of curtailing public employment were set aside.[219] Yet the government failed to make more than a token quantity of seed available to farmers, again bowing to Treasury dogma on the need to free the private trade.[220] Reports that landowners were deliberately withholding seed from their small tenants to induce them to emigrate were conveniently ignored.[221]

To the outrage of the nationalist press,[222] mass dismissals from the relief works began from 20 March, and despite sporadic resistance from many workers, all had been discharged by the end of June except for 28,000 retained to render safe any works left in a dangerous condition.[223] The consequent loss of relief entitlements was offset in the interim only by private charity and donations to local subscriptions for soup kitchens.[224] The existing Poor Law system was already overwhelmed by the end of 1846 and a number of western unions were on the verge of bankruptcy. The Poor Law Commissioners advised a number of boards of guardians not to admit those still clamouring at the gates into the already grossly overcrowded and pestilential workhouses, and declared that outdoor relief from the poorhouse was both illegal and unaffordable.[225] The limited state aid that was available during the spring of 1847 thus made a negligible impact on the calamitous plight of the Irish poor.[226]

Bessborough found that the implementation of the new Relief Act proved more difficult than at first anticipated.[227] Many landlords strongly opposed the new 'dictatorial' scheme and some deliberately impeded the establishment of the new

---

219 Russell to Bessborough, 18 March, 2 April, Russell Papers, PRO 30/22/6B, fols. 258–63, 6C, fols. 7–8; Redington to Labouchere, 11, 16 May, Bessborough Papers, F. 337.

220 An appeal by the Catholic clergy of Mayo for grain seed for small farmers was rejected by Labouchere, *Freeman's Journal*, 12 March.

221 Col. William Clarke to Clarendon, 4 April, Clarendon Deposit, Bodliean Library, Oxford, c.561/2.

222 *Freeman's Journal*, 15, 16 March.

223 Russell had hoped to retain more for useful works such as arterial drainage, but his position was weakened by Bessborough's death and the fiscal crisis of April-May 1847, Russell to Bessborough, 8 May, Russell Papers, PRO 30/22/6C, fols. 256–7; Redington to Labouchere, 5 June, Bessborough Papers, F. 337.

224 This was done at Skibbereen, but was not permitted in places without an active or solvent relief committee, Somerville to Townsend, 19 Jan., Home Office Papers, HO 122/19, fols. 237–8

225 *Thirteenth annual report of the Poor Law Commissioners*, P.P. 1847 [816], XXVIII, 22–30.

226 One individual story may be taken as emblematic: 'Last Thursday a man aged around 60 applied for admission to the Dungarvan poorhouse, *whilst the Board of Guardians was sitting*, but was refused. Shelley, the porter, offered him some of his own stirabout – but the poor fellow was unable to partake of it, was left outside the gate and died in the night. *There was grass in his stomach and bowels.*' *Waterford Mail*, cited in *Freeman's Journal*, 4 June 1847.

227 Griffith to Monteagle, 26 March, Monteagle Papers, MS 13,397/3; Gilbert to Jones, 10 April, Treasury Papers, T 64/363B; *Second report of the Relief Commissioners*, P.P. 1847 [819], XVII, 75.

local committees.[228] Moreover, the Commission itself proved tardy in organizing and approving the local mechanism, leading the *Freeman's Journal* to denounce it in April for having produced thus far nothing but 'fourteen tons *of paper!*'[229] Burgoyne was successful in neutralizing the Treasury's demand that relief rates be levied in advance, but found his freedom of manoeuvre greatly circumscribed.[230] On the ground, relief officials complained that the 'great multiplicity of forms to be observed' were combining with landlord apathy to frustrate efforts to assist communities where the people 'were literally howling with hunger'.[231]

It was not until the early summer that the soup kitchen system became universal and local resistance from ratepayers and the poor alike was overcome. The Commission's insistence that 'a thick stirabout of meal, rice etc.' be introduced in place of the 'thin soup' initially distributed by some local committees was important in winning popular acceptance for the system.[232] By July over three million daily rations were being issued in 1,826 electoral divisions at a cost of around 2d per head – an administrative achievement that gave Trevelyan and Burgoyne genuine grounds for self-congratulation:

> This enterprise was in truth the 'grandest attempt ever made to grapple with famine over a whole country' . . . neither ancient nor modern history can furnish a parallel to the fact that upwards of three millions of persons were fed every day in the neighbourhood of their homes, by administrative arrangements emanating from and controlled by one central office.[233]

Workhouse mortality rates, which give some indication of the health of the wider population, fell from a peak of 25 per 1,000 weekly in early April to one third that level at the start of September.[234] The soup-kitchen regime gave some indication of what the early Victorian state was capable of when it mobilized its human and financial resources. However, it is difficult to avoid the observation that it was implemented too late to save tens of thousands of those who had perished in the spring, and that its utility was circumscribed by the provision of only the minimum

---

228 *Dublin Evening Mail*, 29 Jan., 19 March; *Freeman's Journal*, 8 April 1847.

229 Ibid., 21 April.

230 Burgoyne to Trevelyan, 18 June 1847, George Wrottesley (ed.), *Life and correspondence of Field Marshall Sir John Burgoyne, Bart.* (2 vols., London, 1873), I, 456–9. More than half of the Commission's expenditure took the form of grants in aid of rates and subscriptions, *Examiner*, 11 Sept. 1847.

231 Col. W. Clarke to Clarendon, 11 April, Clar. Dep., c.561/2.

232 *Third report of the Relief Commissioners constituted under the Act 10th Vict., cap. 7*, P.P. 1847 [836], XVII, 3–5. Popular resistance had generally been led by those who had done better on the public works, see *Freeman's Journal*, 29 May 1847.

233 Trevelyan, *Irish crisis*, p. 90; *Fifth, sixth and seventh reports of the Relief Commissioners*, P.P. 1847–8 [876], XXIX, 27.

234 [Alfred Power], *The Irish Poor Law: past, present and future* (London, 1849), pp. 8–9.

nutrition required for life, and the refusal to contemplate its continuation beyond the harvest of 1847.

Falling food prices in the wake of large imports of Indian corn from late March pushed down the ultimate cost of the soup-kitchen relief to well under the amount anticipated by the Treasury.[235] This decline was trumpeted by liberals as a vindication of the firm adherence to private enterprise principles over the winter.[236] The controversy over 'political economy' and its applicability to the Irish situation did not abate, but there was now a triumphalist feeling in the liberal camp. Alexander Somerville, the Cobdenite radical and *Manchester Examiner* correspondent who toured Ireland in the winter and spring of 1847 as a self-appointed missionary for free trade in both food and land, confirmed his English readers' preconceptions concerning the misdemeanors of Irish landlordism. Somerville summarily dismissed any resistance to the ascendant doctrine: 'Political economy is in itself the very essence of humanity, benevolence, and justice. It is its conflict with selfishness, error, ignorance, and injustice that makes it appear otherwise to some eyes at some times.'[237]

At a rather more elevated level, W.N. Hancock responded to the criticism of orthodox 'political economy' articulated by Isaac Butt and echoed in the Irish press. Reflecting the Whateleian bias of the Dublin school of economics (he was Whately Professor of political economy at Trinity College in 1846–51), Hancock defended the discipline of political economy as an objective 'science of value' relatively autonomous from moral objectives. Free trade was the only effective means of maximizing food resources, and was intended by the 'Divine economy' to play a yet more vital role in famine than in 'normal' years.[238] While there was a shared core of ideas common to these defences of 'political economy', there were also marked discrepancies mirroring the ideological divergences of its various schools. Hancock's 'moderate' approach was relatively uncritical of Irish landowners and remained fundamentally opposed to any outdoor relief to the able-bodied poor.[239] The gulf between this version and the moralism exemplified in Somerville's

---

235 *Freeman's Journal*, 26 March, 28 April 1847.

236 *Illustrated London News*, 10 April 1847. Parts of the free trade press argued that even in the winter there had been 'famine in the midst of plenty', caused by moral inertia and the rottenness of the social system rather than any subsistence shortfall, *Observer*, 14 March 1847.

237 Alexander Somerville, *Letters from Ireland during the famine of 1847* (ed. K.D.M. Snell, Blackrock, 1994), p. 134. See also pp. 97–8, 171–6, 188. Somerville explicitly rejected Malthusian population theory as a part of true political economy, ibid., pp. 181–2.

238 W. Neilson Hancock, *Three lectures on the questions, should the principles of political economy be disregarded at the present crisis? and if not, how can they be applied towards the discovery of measures of relief?* (Dublin, 1847), pp. 10–11, 46–56. For context of this work, see Thomas A. Boylan and Timothy P. Foley, '"A nation perishing of political economy"?', in Chris Morash and Richard Hayes (eds.), *Fearful realities: new perspectives on the Famine* (Blackrock, 1996), pp. 138–50.

239 Hancock, *Three lectures*, pp. 41–6. Such constructions allowed a Malthusian proprietor to comment that 'the reasoning of the political economists is the only safe guide through the

letters would become explicit during the Poor Law reform debates. Irish popular opinion remained unconvinced by both strands, for, as the *Freeman's Journal* pointed out, while political economy always looked to things '"in the long run" . . . life or death depends on the "*short* run".'[240]

If the food crisis was easing in the spring of 1847, this was more than compensated for by the concurrent famine fever and dysentery epidemics.[241] Here the government's response was equally hesitant. Peel's temporary Central Board of Health was dissolved amidst accusations of widespread abuse and needless expense in August 1846. In early 1847 Bessborough re-established the Central Board on his own authority to deal with the virulent fever epidemic, but was hampered by the shortage of funds and limited administrative powers at his disposal. A temporary Fever Bill passed in April allowed for cash advances, but again was slow to come into operation and relied on local voluntary co-operation. This insistence on local responsibility, along with Treasury parsimony and a belief in the 'providential' aspect of Irish suffering, contributed to such assistance coming too late and in too small a degree to mitigate suffering before the summer.[242] Ultimately, it was only the provision of a minimum ration of nutritious cooked food in the localities that began to lower the population's susceptibility to famine-related diseases such as dysentery, and curb the mortality rate of fever victims.[243]

The humanitarianism so manifest in Britain in early 1847 thus failed to be translated effectively into the means of preventing mass mortality until the summer. This was largely due to the dominant form of this response, which drew justification from providentialist interpretations of the famine crisis and the presuppositions of classical economic thought and its derivatives. No relief system could have coped fully with the scale of social catastrophe of 1846–7, but the power of providentialism was strong enough to hinder and qualify philanthropic reactions. As Wood lectured the Commons: 'No exertion of a Government, or, I will add, of private charity, can supply a complete remedy for the existing calamity. It is a national visitation, sent by Providence'.[244]

---

difficulties with which we are surrounded.' Earl of Rosse, *Letters on the state of Ireland* (2nd edn, London, 1847), p. 10.

240 *Freeman's Journal*, 22 April 1847.

241 Ibid., 15 June.

242 *Hans.*, LXXXIX, 460–3 [25 Jan.: Lincoln, Russell, Labouchere], XCI, 332–4 [23 March: Labouchere]; Redington to Labouchere, 19 Jan., Bessborough to Labouchere, 5 March, 16 April, Bessborough Papers, F. 337, 336; Woodham-Smith, *Great hunger*, pp. 196–205.

243 *Supplementary appendix to the seventh, and last report, of the Poor Law Commissioners, constituted under the Act 10 Vict. cap. 7*, P.P. 1847–8 (956), XXIX, 132–3. See also Laurence M. Geary, 'Famine, fever and bloody flux', in Cathal Póirtéir (ed.), *The Great Irish Famine* (Cork, 1995), pp. 74–85.

244 *Hans.*, LXXXIX, 689–90 [1 Feb. 1847].

Russell's 'comprehensive scheme'

Russell's Commons speech on 25 January had also set out a 'comprehensive scheme' of permanent reconstructive measures. These fell into three categories, but all drew a strict distinction between labour and relief. The government would advance loans for private agricultural improvements under a Land Improvement Bill, which would consolidate and replace the existing private drainage legislation and the Labouchere letter. Secondly, a scheme of remunerative public works would be introduced, featuring the state reclamation of waste lands and the arterial drainage of cultivated land. Thirdly, as a permanent means of meeting Irish destitution, the Poor Law would be extended to grant a right to relief to the infirm and disabled in or out of the workhouse, and to establish a separate Irish Poor Law Commission in Dublin, with powers to direct that outdoor relief be given to the able bodied in time of mass destitution when the workhouse was full. This interventionist programme contravened classical *laissez-faire*, but, Russell concluded, there were considerable limits to the state's power to raise the condition of Ireland; little could be achieved until the Irish adopted the maxim 'Help yourselves, and Heaven will help you.'[245]

Russell's speech was widely regarded as balanced and authoritative, and won the respect of the great majority of the house. Politicians as diverse as Disraeli, Roebuck, Bentinck and Bedford expressed admiration, and Clarendon commented that it had given the government a 'character of *durability*'.[246] Ministers were, however, disconcerted at the immediate hostility displayed by the *Times* and *Morning Chronicle*. Both papers denounced what they took to be gratuitous concessions to landlord importunity in the remittance of the relief debt and the land improvement loans. To the *Chronicle* the proprietors remained 'the spoiled and petted children of the Legislature', who were to be excused 'the penalties of past improvidence'. The quarrel of both papers with the government lay primarily in its relegation of their favoured panaceas (a punitive poor law and waste-land reclamation respectively) to subordinate places within a broader scheme, but each tapped the growing middle-class impatience with relief expenditure.[247] This dangerous mood was recognized even by observers sympathetic to the Irish proprietors, who warned that a purely negative reaction to the proposed measures would prove counterproductive.[248]

Alarmed by the growing scale of economic and social breakdown, angered by the abortive administrative response, and antagonized by the increasing hostility

245 Ibid., p. 452.

246 Broughton Diary, Add. MS 43,74, fol. 91 [25 Jan.]; Clarendon to Russell, 26 Jan., Bedford to Russell, 27 Jan., Russell Papers, PRO 30/22/6A, fols. 214–16, 221–2.

247 *Times*, 26 Jan.; *Morning Chronicle*, 26, 28 Jan. 1847.

248 James Ward, *Remedies for Ireland. A letter to the Rt. Hon. Lord Monteagle, on the fallacy of the proposed Poor Law, emigration, and reclamation of waste lands, as remedies* (London, 1847).

of British opinion, Irish politicians of all political persuasions found themselves drawn together. The ailing O'Connell implored all to co-operate as a means of exerting maximum influence on policy-makers, and was instrumental in organizing a meeting of twenty-six MPs in Dublin in January. This formed the potential nucleus of an 'Irish Party', but there proved to be few real points of positive agreement between its disparate elements.[249] Isaac Butt's attempt to create an anti-Whig platform on which Tory and Repealer could find common ground was also of limited success.[250] Many Catholic nationalists remained bitterly hostile towards the landlord class, to the extent of believing that the blight had been 'ordained for their especial destruction'.[251] Co-operation proved impossible under these circumstances.

Irish liberals and Repealers were to be bitterly disappointed with the limitations of government measures, but proved unable to provide consistent opposition; Russell's latent reputation as the man who could give 'justice to Ireland' kept alive a hope of more sympathetic treatment. One Irish Whig, Fitzstephen French, had come over 'vowing vengeance', but was placated by the Prime Minister's speech and hoped that regeneration would indeed flow from the measures promised.[252] Only a few, such as Monteagle and Smith O'Brien, consistently voiced strong opposition.[253] Some elements of the nationalist press yearned for the return of Peel, if only because any failure on his part would have united the nation in condemnation.[254] O'Connell himself, now physically weak, appealed directly to parliament to relieve the people who were 'starving in shoals, in hundreds – aye, in thousands and millions'.[255] His death three months later deprived Repeal MPs of the leadership and direction vital in the crucial session of 1847.[256]

---

249 O'Connell to F.W. Conway, 10 Dec. 1846, O'Connell, *Correspondence*, VIII, 152–3; Redington to Labouchere, 12, 15 Jan. 1847, Bessborough Papers, F. 337; Kevin B. Nowlan, *The politics of Repeal: a study of relations between Great Britain and Ireland, 1841–50* (London, 1965), pp. 125–7.

250 [Isaac Butt], 'The famine in the land. What has been done, and what is to be done', *Dublin University Magazine*, XXIX (April 1847), 501–40. The initially positive response of the nationalist press was not sustained, see *Freeman's Journal*, 31 March, 5 April.

251 Peter Carroll, *A letter from Peter Carroll to John Bull, on the origin, nature and conduct of the landlords of Ireland* (Liverpool, 1847).

252 Bessborough to Russell, 28 Jan., Russell Papers, PRO 30/22/5A, fols. 98–9; *Hans.*, LXXXIX, 453–8 [25 Jan.]. Bellew made similar noises, ibid., pp. 458–60.

253 *Hans.*, LXXXIX, 76–84 [19 Jan.], 635–44 [1 Feb.: W.S. O'Brien]; ibid., 1348–9 [15 Feb.: Monteagle]; 'Resolutions submitted to a meeting of Irish peers and MPs, 5 Feb. 1847', Monteagle to Downshire, 15 Feb., Monteagle Papers, MS 13,397/3.

254 *Limerick Examiner*, cited in *Cork Examiner*, 1 Feb. 1847.

255 *Hans.*, LXXXIX, 942–5 [8 Feb.]. O'Connell expressed his preference for a labour rate, but was ready to support 'any Bill which would afford one additional means of relief in the present calamity' – a significant deviation from his previous opposition to an extended Irish Poor Law.

256 Oliver MacDonagh, *The emancipist: Daniel O'Connell, 1830–1847* (London, 1989), pp. 312–18.

Shared circumstances and fears attracted many Irish landowners of all parties towards the British Protectionist leadership. Stanley, himself an Irish landowner, defended the record of proprietors and criticized the principle of an extended Poor Law, but his economic views remained generally Peelite. He declined to attack free trade, and, reflecting his concern for the strained Irish wages fund, argued that the 'great object' of government should be to encourage the introduction of capital into Ireland.[257] This muted response offered little of substance to Irish proprietors convinced that the Famine was 'a national judgment' and that a national (i.e. United Kingdom) response was required to mitigate the 'Divine infliction'.[258] It fell to Lord George Bentinck to propose an alternative to the government's scheme, in the form of a major Railway Bill. Supported by the Tory railway developer 'King' Hudson, he proposed advancing £16 million to Irish railway companies at a rate of three and a half percent to undertake a massive construction project.[259] Bentinck intended his Bill to serve as a point of cohesion for the Protectionist Party in parliament, to distinguish a true Tory social policy from 'the miserable peddling of Sir Robert Peel and Lord Lincoln in the last session'.[260]

The government's response to this initiative was initially ambiguous. A comprehensive railway construction programme had been proposed by the Whig-Liberals as late as 1843,[261] and both Russell and Bessborough had been favourable towards allowing presentments for railway earthworks under the 1846 Poor Employment Act. Russell had been considering a scheme offering employment for up to 110,000 unskilled labourers on railway 'public works', but by 25 January nothing had been finalized.[262] Given his interventionist sympathies, it is unsurprising that Russell did not oppose the introduction of Bentinck's Bill, and that he waived the rules of the House to allow it to proceed to discussion. While he dissented openly from its details, it was clear that he was favourable towards the discussion of its principle.[263] Moderates and Peelites feared that he would 'give way in whole or part' over this highly unorthodox venture; Graham and Peel were 'disgusted' at what they perceived as collusion between Russell and Bentinck, and warned the

---

257 *Hans.*, LXXXIX, 18–36 [19 Jan. 1847].

258 Ibid., 654–62 [1 Feb.: Bernard]; Butt, 'The famine in the land', pp. 514–16. Others stressed English responsibility for the underdeveloped condition of Ireland, [Anon.], *Thoughts on Ireland* (London, 1847), pp. 23–32.

259 *Hans.*, LXXXIX, 773–802 [4 Feb. 1847]. Stanley had been suspicious of such 'bubble schemes', but allowed Bentinck to proceed in February, Robert Stewart, *The politics of protection: Lord Derby and the Protectionist Party 1841–52* (Cambridge, 1971), pp. 102–4.

260 Bentinck to Stanley, 28 Sept. 1846, Derby Papers, Liverpool Record Office, 920 DER (14), box 132/13.

261 *Hans.*, LXX, 883–4 [10 July 1843: Howick].

262 Bessborough to Wood, 5 Sept. 1846, Hickleton Papers, A4/99; Russell to Bessborough, 15 Oct., Russell Papers, PRO 30/22/5D, fols. 201–2, 208–11; Russell to Wood, 26 Dec. 1846, 7 Jan., 1847, Gooch, *Later correspondence*, I, 166, 170; *Hans.*, LXXXIX, 453 [25 Jan. 1847].

263 Ibid., LXXXIX, 802–8 [4 Feb.].

government indirectly of the dire consequences that would follow.[264] Peel felt drawn to make a resounding defence of sound money, Treasury primacy and the principle of private enterprise, all of which he thought were under attack.[265] Free-trade radicals also declared outrage over the Bill, particularly as Bentinck made it no secret that his intention was to liquidate the capital of Irish proprietors tied up in existing railway stock, and to give them generous terms for the sale of land to railway companies.[266]

If Bentinck believed that a working alliance with the Whigs could be forged on the Irish railway question, he was to be sorely disappointed. Russell held out the hope of some future assistance to the railways, but argued that the scheme in hand was contradictory and did not complement the government's plan for immediate relief. Railway works could only employ the fittest and most skilled labourers, and would be concentrated in the less distressed east of Ireland.[267] Aware of the tightness of government finances, Russell was intent that immediate relief in food be given priority, and that waste-land reclamation remain at the top of the remedial agenda.[268] He made it clear that the government would treat the second reading as a vote of confidence, thus posing a considerable test of loyalty for many Irish representatives. In the end all but ten liberals voted with the government.[269]

This episode had several consequences. The idea of an independent and comprehensive 'Irish Party' was shattered by the division. While some semblance of organization survived in the shape of the Reproductive Employment Committee and its successor, the Irish Council, the movement was subsequently limited to the landed interest.[270] Bentinck's personal position was damaged by his displays of temper in the later stages of the debate and the defection of fifty-eight Protectionists to the 'no' lobby, and the chances of the Whig-Protectionist alliance envisaged by Bessborough were finally dashed.[271] As a result, relations between the Peelites and

---

264 Greville, *Journal*, III, 50, 54 [6, 8 Feb.].

265 *Hans.*, XC, 65–86 [16 Feb.].

266 Ibid., LXXXIX, 809–14, 818–21 [4 Feb. 1847: Roebuck, Hume]. Not all Radicals agreed; Osborne favoured the principle, and the interventionist Scrope thought some such plan might form a 'beneficial adjunct' to other measures, ibid., 808–9, 815–18.

267 Ibid., 802–8 [4 Feb.], XC, 116–22 [16 Feb.]. Russell's expert advisers questioned the proportion of the loan that would actually go towards wages, and the numbers of unskilled men that could be productively employed per mile. Isambard Kingdom Brunel specifically accused Hudson and the English railway interest of seeking to profit from Irish misfortune, Brunel to B. Hawes, 10 Feb., Hawes to Russell, 11, 16 Feb., Russell Papers, PRO 30/22/6B, fols. 61–2, 5A, fols. 131–2, 145–6.

268 Russell to Bessborough, 14 Feb., ibid., 6B, fols. 82–3.

269 Broughton Diary, Add. MS 43,749, fols. 104, 115 [11, 16 Feb.]; *Hans.*, XC, 123–6 [15 Feb.].

270 The Irish Council was primarily concerned with resisting or seeking amendment to the extended Irish Poor Law, but was to be disappointed by 'the subserviency to . . . political expediency' of Irish MPs and peers, [Irish Council], *Reports of the committee of the Irish Council* (n.p., n.d. [1847]), pp. 3–11.

271 Some British Protectionists were still reluctant to accept the reality of famine in Ireland, and attributed any signs of distress to the 'heedlessness and indolence' of the Irish. See

Whig-Liberals improved markedly.[272] Russell and Bessborough had not, however, abandoned their interventionism, and to Peelite irritation drew up an advance of £620,000 to three railways of proven financial reliability in April.[273] Russell defended the deviation from orthodoxy 'as only an act of justice' to Ireland. The amount was less than he would have wished, but even this limited sum was only disgorged by the Treasury in compensation for the abandonment of Russell's Waste Lands Bill. Even so, it was strongly condemned by Peel and Graham as an abandonment of 'sound principle'. Some fifty Peelites voted with the minority on Roebuck's motion against the proposal.[274]

This was the only occasion in the 1847 session when the Peelite leadership voted against the government. In retrospect Peelite opposition to Russell's Irish policy was a dog that failed to bark. It is not that the Peelites were wholly uncritical. Lincoln, who now regarded himself as a spokesman for Irish interests, had considerable personal animosity towards his successors and a deep loathing for 'our old incubus Trevelyan'. Letters written from Ireland to his erstwhile colleagues in autumn 1846 provoked sympathetic responses.[275] Graham rejoiced at 'our honourable escape from present responsibilities', but was also critical of Trevelyan and the operation of the Poor Employment Act, especially regarding deviances from Peelite practice on the stocking of depots and advances in aid.[276] He remained sceptical in private about the workability of the new Poor Law, but did not oppose it in parliament.[277]

Peel himself was damning of what he took to be the crude abuse of political economy embodied in the insistence on unproductive works. His greatest objection was, however, to the moral evil of making loans that were unlikely to be repaid. It would, he told Graham, be better 'for England to *give* a million to Ireland, rather than lend her half . . . I would rather *give* a million outright, and have the management of the gift, than make advances of £500,000 to be entrusted to Irish management – with Irish security for repayment.'[278]

[Archibald Alison], 'Lessons from the famine', *Blackwood's Edinburgh Magazine*, LXI (April 1847), 515–24.

272 Greville, *Journal*, III, 57–9 [19, 22 Feb.]; Frederick August Dreyer, 'The Russell administration, 1846–1852' (unpublished D. Phil. thesis, University of St. Andrews, 1962), pp. 84–98.

273 Bessborough to Russell, 11 Feb. 1847, Russell Papers, PRO 30/22/6B, fols. 66–7; Russell to Wood, 26 March, Hickleton Papers, A4/56/2.

274 *Hans.*, XCII, 213–30, 270–91 [30 April: Wood, Goulburn, Peel, Russell], XCIII, 982–9, 1019–27 [28 June: Russell, Graham]; Broughton Diary, Add. MS 43,750, fols. 30–1 [30 April 1847].

275 Lincoln to Peel, 12 Oct., 17 Nov. 1846, Peel Papers, Add. MS 40,481, fols. 366, 368–76.

276 Graham to Peel, 5 Oct., 23 Nov., 29 Dec. 1846, ibid., Add MS 40,452, fols. 172, 184, 195–7.

277 Graham to Lewis, 5 Feb., 26 Aug. 1847, Harpton Court Papers, National Library of Wales, Aberystwyth, C/673, C/675.

278 Peel to Goulburn, 17 Oct., 21 Nov. 1846, Goulburn Papers, SHS 304, box 42; Peel to Graham, 22 Nov. 1846, Graham Papers, Cambridge University Library (microfilm), bundle

However, only Lincoln was prepared to attack the government publicly. Peel reminded his former colleagues of the Irish tendency to exaggerate, and warned that British public opinion and the state of the poor at home placed considerable limits on the funds that could be allocated to Ireland.[279] What he objected to was the manner rather than the amount of expenditure, for he believed that the priority must be investment in private land improvement. Consequently, the former Prime Minister was largely placated by the government's Land Improvement Bill in 1847. Convinced of the innate profitability of land improvement works, he favoured the combination of relief with employment by private enterprise.[280]

Peel also publicly declared himself willing to make 'great allowances' for the difficulties facing the government and to support the new emergency measures; he praised Trevelyan and Routh by name for their exertions, although he emphasized that a 'wide discretionary authority' was required for the Irish government. His chief concern was that the proposed permanent measures should not impose crippling burdens on land, and that the principle of free enterprise be upheld. Yet he made it clear that it was the land rather then the existing class of landlords that he sought to protect from excessive taxation. If the latter failed to exert themselves and throw off old habits of dependency when they were offered favourable terms, they should not be saved from the consequences.[281] While by no means satisfied with Russell's Irish policy, Peel regarded the Protectionists as a more pressing danger to his primary political achievements of free trade and sound finance, and was prepared to support the Whigs in office.[282]

This rapprochement was promoted by Wood's espousal of Peelite fiscal rectitude.[283] Peel and the moralists found that they had in common a concern for Treasury primacy and unhindered private enterprise, which was reinforced by a shared economic liberalism and distaste for partisan loyalties. While Peel was reconciled by elements of Russell's broad plan, he was prepared to work with the

---

103. Goulburn was also concerned at the confiscatory and disruptive implications of huge unproductive loans, Goulburn to Peel, 24 Nov. 1846, Peel Papers, Add. MS 40,445, fols. 379–81.

279 Peel to Lincoln, 11 Dec. 1846, Newcastle Papers, Nottingham University Library, NeC 11,994.

280 *Hans.*, XC, 1049–50 [8 March 1847]; Peel to Monteagle, 27 Dec. 1846, Monteagle Papers, MS 13,396/4. Stanley also welcomed the Land Improvement Bill, Stanley to Bentinck, 7 Feb. 1847, Derby Papers, 177/1.

281 *Hans.*, LXXXIX, 758–64 [2 Feb.], XC, 65–86 [16 Feb. 1847]. Peel repeated his praise of Trevelyan's 'capabilities and . . . trustworthiness' in private, T.B. Macaulay to Mrs. C. Trevelyan, 3 Feb., Pinney, *Macaulay*, IV, 328–9.

282 Peel saw his role as a supra-party elder statesman and was antagonistic towards either seeking Conservative reunion or formalizing a distinct Peelite entity, Peel to Graham, 9 Jan., 3 April 1847, Graham Papers, bundle 104. He continued to make allowances for Russell's difficulties in his public speeches, Greville to Clarendon, 1 Aug. 1847, Clar. Dep., c.520.

283 Russell to Wood, 3 May, Hickleton Papers, A4/56/2; *Hans.*, XCII, 213–16 [30 April]. Wood's budget was praised by Peel, and by others who distinguished the Chancellor's achievement from that of his party, Greville, *Journal*, III, 64,69 [25 Feb., 13 March].

moralists to undermine those parts of it (such as the waste-land scheme) which he thought unorthodox. However, differences of opinion remained over the underlying dynamics of the economy, between a liberal Tory model that stressed equilibrium, and the more optimistic liberal-radical moralism that believed in vigorous capitalist development through exertion and self-reliance. The differences were obscured by Wood's vigorous defence of Peel's 1844 Bank Charter Act from attacks by Protectionists and Birmingham radicals in 1847, but were to be highlighted by Peel's plantation scheme of 1849.[284]

Radical opposition to the government's measures was more intolerant. Although they were limited in numbers and tended towards political atomization, the radicals' significance should not be underestimated. A few radicals pursued personal lines on Ireland: Bernal Osborne was defensive of the Irish landowning class of which he had become a minor member, but continued to spurn Smith O'Brien. Poulett Scrope, on the other hand, welcomed the government's 'great budget of measures' as an abandonment of 'the *laissez-faire* maxim [which if] applied to her would leave her to perish by the rapid destruction of all property, or to be overwhelmed in the ruin of some convulsive explosion!' He criticized only the extent to which some of these measures were to be taken.[285] These, however, were the exceptions; more typical was the absolute opposition expressed by the *Economist* to all Russell's proposals save the extension of the Poor Law and an encumbered estates bill.[286]

Most parliamentary radicals and the *Times* gave each other mutual support and publicity, with Roebuck praising the paper for casting a 'great light' on landlord iniquities.[287] Roebuck's rhetoric was intemperate – he denounced Irish landlords as 'slaveholders, with white slaves', but he knew there was little chance of defeating the Land Improvement Bill or reversing the remittance of half the relief debt. His aim was tactical – to rouse British opinion behind a campaign for 'a good poor law' for Ireland, and if possible for an extension of the income tax there, and more generally to use the Irish issue as a means of attacking the 'aristocratic' character of the British state. He was well aware of the balance of power within the cabinet,

---

284 See above, pp. 212–14. Peel's plan was prefigured by the prescriptions urged by Thomas Chalmers in 1847 to equalize the burden of famine throughout the United Kingdom, [T. Chalmers], 'Political economy of a famine', *North British Review*, VII (May 1847), 247–90. For Chalmers' thought in the context of Christian political economy and his relations with the liberal Tories, see Boyd Hilton, *The age of atonement: the influence of evangelicalism on social and economic thought, 1785–1865* (Oxford, 1988), pp. 57–70, 81–9, 108–14.

285 *Hans.*, LXXXIX, 622–35 [1 Feb.], 926–7, 950–1 [5, 8 Feb.]; G. Poulett Scrope, *Remarks on the Irish Poor Relief Bill* (London, 1847), pp. 9–32.

286 *Economist*, 30 Jan., 27 Feb. 1847. See also Ruth Dudley Edwards, *The pursuit of reason: the Economist 1843–1993* (London, 1993), pp. 48–55.

287 *Hans.*, XC, 1025–35 [8 March]. The paper was reciprocal in its praise, and Roebuck became a regular contributor, *Times*, 9 March; A.I. Dasent, *John Thadeus Delane, editor of 'The Times': his life and correspondence* (2 vols., London, 1908), I, 104.

and concentrated his attacks on the moderate landlords within it, while at the same time upbraiding Russell for his lack of courage, and bolstering the pro-Poor Law ministers.[288] He believed popular feeling on this question would have important repercussions now that a general election was imminent, and was certain that he had mass support for his anti-landlord crusade.[289] The *Times*' ever more vitriolic outpourings on 'those shameless and importune mendicants', the Irish landlords, seemed only to confirm radical anticipations.[290]

The Poor Law Bill in parliament

At the heart of Russell's reconstructive programme for 1847 was the Bill to extend the 1838 Irish Poor Law, creating a seperate Irish Poor Law Commission with the power to allow outdoor relief to the abld-bodied. This was the measure which provoked the most heated controversy both in cabinet and in parliament, yet, like its predecessor in 1838, it can be attributed to no single ideological initiative. Russell and George Grey prepared the draft of the Bill in January 1847, and Earl Grey strongly supported it both as a sound and moral measure in its own right, and as a necessary concession to British public opinion.[291] Bessborough's reservations about the extension of the Poor Law were overcome, partly through Russell's insistence that auxiliary measures would lift the burden of relieving the able-bodied from the rates, and partly from his hope that the reform would add to the Irish government's control over the local administration.[292] The strong support expressed by O'Connellites and much of the Catholic clergy for the principle of an extended Poor Law allowed it to be viewed as a popular 'Foxite' measure.[293] Lansdowne and the cabinet moderates were distinctly cool, but most realized that the state of British popular feeling made some extension of the Poor Law irresistible. Russell, faced with the collapse his government if the Bill failed in the Lords, made a number of parallel concessions, including the Land Improvement Bill and Lansdowne's pet project of a Vagrancy Bill to penalize mendicancy.[294]

---

288 Broughton Diary, Add. MS 43,749, fols. 130–1 [8, 9 March 1847].

289 Roebuck to Mrs. Roebuck, 21 Jan., 11 Feb., 28 May 1847, in R.E. Leader (ed.), *Life and letters of John Arthur Roebuck* (London, 1897), pp. 169–70, 172, 176–9.

290 *Times*, 10 March 1847. Archbishop Whately also feared that the inflamed state of British public opinion would be reflected in the election, Richard Whately, *Substance of a speech delivered in the House of Lords . . . on Irish Poor Laws* (London, 1847), pp. iv–vi.

291 G. Grey to Wood, 4 Jan. 1847, Hickleton Papers, A4/58/1; Russell to Wood, 7 Jan., Gooch, *Later correspondence*, I, 169–70; Paper by Lord Grey on Irish relief, 13 Jan. 1847, Grey Papers.

292 Russell to Bessborough, 16 Jan., Bessborough to Labouchere, 25, 29 Jan., 4 Feb., Bessborough Papers, F. 153, 336.

293 [W.B. McCabe], 'Measures for Ireland', *Dublin Review*, XXII (March, 1847), 230–60. John O'Connell denounced the 'Irish Party' for its opposition to the Bill, *Freeman's Journal*, 2 March.

294 Broughton Diary, Add. MS 43,749, fol. 95 [30 Jan.]; Lansdowne to Russell, (Feb. 1847), Russell Papers, PRO 30/22/6B, fols. 13–14; *Hans.*, XC, 625–6 [1 March 1847], XCII, 531. See also [Nassau Senior], 'Mendicancy in Ireland', *Edinburgh Review*, LXXVII (April 1843), 391–411.

Liberal public opinion invested great expectations in the Bill. The *Times* demanded a punitive Poor Law to systematize the reformation of Irish society, envisaging a self-regulating mechanism that would render further state intervention unneccessary. The measure would address the moral failings that posed a much greater danger to the country than mere famine. The paper discerned 'a dearth of those virtues and affections which enable men to brave national calamities with serenity and success', and prescribed the Poor Law to heal the national moral disease.[295] Irish landowners were demonized as 'a class without social humanity, without legal obligation, without natural shame'; only the imposition of outdoor relief supported by rates on the land would prevent them from transferring their deserved burdens to the British poor through higher taxes and the mass flight of paupers across the Irish Sea.[296]

Such was the growing public polarization between the representatives of Irish landlordism and their allies, and middle-class British opinion, that Russell's concessions were regarded as inadequate by one side and excessive by the other. As radicals railed against the limitations of the government's Bill and demanded the confiscation of Irish landed property, the remnants of the 'Irish Party' prepared to resist the Bill tooth and nail.[297] However, Stanley's intervention in the Lords prevented a straightforward clash and determined the fate of the Bill. Believing that an effective Poor Law was inevitable and that if properly guarded it could ease the transition to capitalized agriculture, he was prepared to let it pass on the condition that further substantial concessions were made to the propertied interest.[298]

Under pressure from Lansdowne, and with signs that many Peelites would support Stanley's demands, Russell felt obliged to accede to a number of important amendments. To Poulett Scrope's disgust it was announced on 1 March that 'very large' concessions to the landlords would be made; the government would delete the proposed discretionary power of the Commissioners to allow outdoor relief before the workhouse was full, increase the number of ex-officio guardians on the boards, and maintain the existing electoral divisions.[299] Most importantly, the question of the relief of small tenants was thrown open when the Peelite William Gregory introduced his amendment to exclude from relief the holders of more than a quarter of an acre of land and their dependants. Such smallholders were,

295 *Times*, 23 April 1847.

296 Ibid., 16, 20 April, 1 May.

297 *Hans.*, LXXXIX, 615–22, 644–54 [1 Feb. 1847: Williams, Roebuck]; 'Resolutions of a meeting of Peers and MPs connected with Ireland, 6 Feb. 1847', Clancarty to Monteagle, 13 Feb., Monteagle Papers, MS 13,397/11. For the fury of Irish landowners over attacks by the radicals and the *Times*, see *Hans.*, XC, 1300–3 [12 March: Shaw].

298 Ibid., LXXXIX, 1342–5 [15 Feb.].

299 Ibid., XC, 616–20, 622–3 [1 March: Russell, Scrope]. This announcement cost the Bill much Catholic support, Bishop Cantwell to Labouchere, 8 March, *Freeman's Journal*, 10 March; 'The Irish Poor Law', *Tablet*, 3 April 1847.

he argued, the class most given to fraud and imposture, and hence deserving of little sympathy:

> where a man held a large piece of land – half an acre, one, two or three acres – he was no longer an object of pity. He did not come before the public in *forma pauperis* – he has not given up his holding – he had not done that which, by the bankruptcy law, would entitle him to his certificate. When he did so he would be entitled to relief the same as any other destitute person, but not until then.[300]

This formulation attracted the support of a coalition of Protectionists, Peelites, Irish MPs and Whig-Liberal moderates.[301]

The government's decision to accept Gregory's amendment was a turning-point in the Poor Law debate. No such clause had been included in the original Bill, nor was there any parallel in the English Poor Law; but a general concern for the curbing of 'abuses' and a belief in the inevitable proletarianization of cottier smallholders, inclined most to accept it. This predisposition was strengthened in the spring of 1847 by reports that smallholders were refusing to sow their land as a result of disinclination or the intimidation of secret societies.[302] Ignorant of the acute problems caused by the shortage of seed, the Prime Minister accepted this interpretation, and declared himself prepared to force smallholders who would not cultivate to give up their land, adding that many must become labourers employed by improving farmers.[303] This general desideratum led him to swallow his doubts about the size of holdings that could be retained and the inapplicability of the clause to famine conditions.[304]

On 29 March the government incorporated the quarter-acre clause into the Bill. George Grey stated that the implementation of the clause might be delayed until November,[305] but this constraint was insufficient for Sharman Crawford and Poulett Scrope. Scrope predicted that 'Its consequence would be a complete clearance of the small farmers in Ireland – a change which would amount to a perfect social revolution in the state of things in that country.' Despite this plea, and the warning that the consequences would include a flood of pauperism into England, Gregory's amendment was carried by the huge margin of 117 to 7.[306]

---

300 *Hans.*, XC, 1273–7 [12 March], XCI, 585–7 [29 March: Gregory].

301 Lansdowne to Russell, (March 1847), Russell Papers, PRO 30/22/6B, fols. 338–41.

302 Bessborough to Labouchere, 17 Feb., Bessborough Papers, F. 336.

303 Russell to Bessborough, 28 Feb., 1 March, Russell Papers, PRO 30/22/6B, fols. 143–6, 172–3.

304 *Hans.*, XC, 617–18 [1 March].

305 Ibid., XCI, 587–8 [29 March].

306 Ibid., 588–93. The Gregory clause went some way towards reconciling improving landowners anxious to remove smallholders from their estates to the Poor Law, David Thomson and Moyra McGusty (eds.), *The Irish journals of Elizabeth Smith 1840–1850* (Oxford, 1980), pp. 135–6 [8 April 1847].

Scrope's comments illuminated some of the deep divisions in intention between Russell and the Irish promoters of the Gregory clause. Most Irish landowners believed the failure of the potato had rendered much of the cottier population permanently redundant; increased grain cultivation could not absorb them, and unless emigration could be promoted on a large scale, they would be 'an incubus, pressing heavily on the rate-payers'.[307] Russell's view was rather different. The productivity of the Irish soil was, he argued, a resource that had hardly been tapped as a result of previous dependency on the potato. Only the extended Poor Law could induce the mutual co-operation between classes required to promote sufficient alternative subsistence:

> no policy can be so good in the way of inducing the landowners and farmers to cultivate the land to the best advantage; for it is evident, that it is the interest of all who hold or who occupy land, that instead of having the population employed in useless works, to be paid for out of the rates, it will be better to employ labour in the cultivation of the soil. We must expect, if Ireland is to flourish, that a much greater extent of land shall be cultivated.[308]

Irish property was, he argued, considerably under-taxed, and the state was now obliged to make recalcitrant landowners bear an equitable burden during the period of transition.[309] The landlords would feel acutely the consequences of their own mismanagement at first, but ultimately all classes would benefit.[310] Russell's outlook was based on the assumption that the Irish wages fund was adequate in normal times to meet such a burden. Yet he was under no illusions that the Poor Law could be imposed in Ireland as the sole means of relieving distress such as that witnessed in 1846–7. Even if the following harvest was adequate, it was expected that 1847–8 would be a year of great, if not quite so severe, suffering, and Russell was convinced that substantial auxiliary measures were required if the Poor Law was to succeed. Labouchere also reminded the Commons that the Bill 'should be considered as a part of a general scheme for the amelioration of Ireland'.[311]

There were limits to the concessions which the government would allow to facilitate the passage of the Bill. Stanley had recommended that the entire burden of the rates be shifted onto the occupier by removing the existing right of the

---

307 *Hans.*, XC, 1285 [12 March: Bateson]. See also *Dublin Evening Mail*, 10 March 1847.

308 *Hans.*, XCI, 245–50 [19 March]. Russell cited Robert Kane's *Industrial resources of Ireland* in support of his claim that the unleashing of the productive power of the land could provide employment for more people, and that such employment would rapidly raise the character and skills of the Irish labourer.

309 *Hans.*, XC, 1255–61 [12 March]; Russell to Bessborough, 28 Feb., Russell Papers, PRO 30/22/6B, fols. 145–6.

310 Russell to Bessborough, 18 March, ibid., fols. 258–63. A number of Irish relief officials endorsed this view, see Col. W. Clarke to Clarendon, 9 April, Clar. Dep., c. 561/2.

311 *Hans.*, XC, 1393 [15 March].

tenant to deduct half his rates from his rent, but Bentinck's attempt to press this in the Commons was narrowly defeated.[312] Stanley threatened to pursue the amendment in the Lords, and warned the government that he would sell his Irish property if it was not carried. Bessborough steadied the cabinet waverers by predicting a backlash of increased class conflict and rate strikes in Ireland, and Wood spoke of British anger at what would be perceived as the exoneration of Irish landlords. The consequences, Wood warned, would be disastrous: 'We the *Government* shall have the odious task of enforcing the payment of rates by distress on the occupying tenantry, whilst the landlords are laughing at us coming into collision with the people – and getting their rents in full. We ought at least to be certain of that portion of the rate which is payable by the landlord.'[313] Unable to induce the government to accept the limiting of the act to five years as a *quid pro quo*, and finding many of his followers uneasy about both Irish popular reaction and the prospect of a Lords-Commons clash, Stanley reluctantly dropped his amendment on 10 May.[314]

More fundamentalist opposition was offered in the Lords by Monteagle, who was assisted by the ideological critique of outdoor relief provided by English moderates. Nassau Senior supplied his allies with arguments against the Bill. The potato failure, he told Archbishop Whately, had left Ireland over-populated by a redundant mass of two million people. Convinced that any 'safe' means of administering outdoor relief was impossible, and that it would invariably lead to three million paupers and insurrection, Senior declared that he would 'rather encounter all the miseries that will follow the rejection of the bill to those I anticipate from its passing'.[315]

Whately took his seat in the Lords with the specific intention of criticizing the government's Irish policy.[316] He deprecated the Poor Law Bill on the grounds that

---

312 Ibid., XCI, 600–11 [29 March: Bentinck]. Goulburn, Lincoln, and a number of other Peelites (although not Graham or Peel), voted with Bentinck. Graham continued to fear the immediate consequences of outdoor relief, but believed that 'in the temper of the House of Commons and the country, it was inevitable'. He admired Russell's handling of the matter and hoped that 'at a remote period, it will produce the regeneration of Ireland', Greville, *Journal*, III, 69–70 [14 March].

313 Broughton Diary, Add. MS 42,749, fol. 138 [20 March], 43,750, fols. 3–4, 14–15 [29 March, 16 April]; Bessborough to Russell, 5, 10 April, Russell Papers, PRO 30/22/6C, fols. 15–16, 51–2; Wood to Russell, 11 April, ibid., fols. 68–70. Wood for once agreed with Sharman Crawford, who had warned of a 'new rate war' in Ireland, *Times*, 7 April.

314 Broughton Diary, Add. MS 43,750 fols. 39–40, 42 [8, 10 May]; Grey Diary, 9 May, Grey Papers; Stanley to Portland, 12 May, Derby Papers, 920 DER (14) 177/2.

315 A copy of this letter was passed to Monteagle, Senior to (Whately), 20 April 1847, Monteagle Papers, MS 13,397/10. Senior was himself supplied with Malthusian criticisms of the Bill by his brother, a Poor Law official in Ulster, Edward Senior to Nassau Senior, 7 Feb. 1847, Senior Papers, E182.

316 Lansdowne and Senior had urged Whately to come over to speak on Irish matters, Senior to Whately, 18 Dec. 1846, Senior Papers, C662.

if a legal right to support was granted to the labourer, it would 'ruin his industry and independence of character for ever, and sink him, permanently, into the lowest degradation, physical and moral'. Whately's argument that it was the poor and not the landlords who would suffer most was regarded by many observers as the most cogent criticism made of the Bill, and it drew sharp replies from those with less pessimistic views of the inherent character of the Irish poor and the state of the Irish wages fund.[317] The elasticity of this fund remained at the heart of the Poor Law debate, and continued to be contested in the following years. Many who followed Whately were equally convinced that outdoor relief would drive out what was left of Irish capital and send the country into a Malthusian downward spiral.[318]

While Whately privately despaired of stopping the Bill, Monteagle clung to the hope that it could be shorn of all its dangerous clauses in the Lords. Stanley's compromise with the government posed considerable tactical difficulties for the Irish intransigents, but Monteagle hoped to construct a cross-party coalition against the Bill, and drew confidence from Lansdowne's and Palmerston's evident distaste for it.[319] Yet he underestimated the distrust and embarrassment now felt towards him by many leading Whig-Liberals, and the hostility generated by the language of some of his crudely pro-landlord allies.[320] Peelites such as Devon and St Germans rallied to the Bill, and many waverers were reconciled by Stanley's amendments. Nevertheless, Monteagle succeeded in defeating the government on his amendment to limit the Bill as a 'temporary experiment' to eighteen months duration.[321] This proved a tactical miscalculation, for when Monteagle revealed that his real aim had been to limit only outdoor relief, while retaining such landlord gains as the increase in ex-officio guardians, many peers reacted angrily. Fitzwilliam, who

---

317 Richard Whately, *Substance of a speech*; George Poulett Scrope, *Reply to the speech of the Archbishop of Dublin . . . and the protest against the Poor Relief (Ireland) Bill* (London, 1847); [James Godkin], 'Ireland and its famine', *British Quarterly Review*, V (May 1847), 504–40. Bessborough also thought Whately gave 'a very false picture of the character of Irish labourers', Bessborough to Russell, 30 March, Russell Papers, PRO 30/22/6B, fols. 324–5.

318 [Anon.], *The measures which can alone ameliorate effectually the condition of the Irish people* (London, 1847), pp. 9, 17–49; [Anon.], *Irish Poor Law question. A letter to the Rt. Hon. Lord John Russell from an Irish landlord* (London, 1847).

319 *Hans.*, XCII, 60–75 [29 April]; Broughton Diary, Add. MS 43,750, fol. 33 [1 May]; Monteagle to Fitzwilliam, 25 March, Monteagle Papers, MS 13,397/7; Fitzwilliam to Wood, 9 March, Hickleton Papers, A4/133; Palmerston to Russell, 26 March, Palmerston Papers, GC/RU/1010/1–2.

320 Broughton Diary, Add. MS 43,749, fols. 109–10 [14 Feb.]. The support of Lord Brougham, who believed that 'providence who sent the potato disease meant that many should be starved – and all attempts to prevent the inevitable result were foolish and futile', was not welcomed even by those who shared his presumptions, ibid., fol. 85 [16 Jan.]; *Hans.*, XCI, 456–65 [26 March], XCII, 124–5 [29 April]. For the Malthusian concerns of Fitzwilliam and Monteagle, see ibid., LXXXIX, 58–62 [19 Jan.: Fitzwilliam], Monteagle to Empson, n.d. (July 1847?), Monteagle Papers, MS 13,397/7.

321 *Hans.*, XCII, 430–49 [6 May 1847].

had favoured the amendment as a means of having the whole Bill brought again before parliament once the commons was free from 'hustings influence', warned that it looked 'as if we wanted to escape the burthen which they impose upon our estates – when we are all the while perfectly content to enjoy all the advantages derived from the *other* parts of the bill.'[322] Other lords indicated that they felt themselves tricked by Monteagle, and the Peelite Dalhousie thought him 'a dirty little dog' in his behaviour.[323] Once deserted by Stanley's followers, Monteagle found his majority evaporate when the government forced a second division.[324] The Poor Law Amendment Bill passed into law in June with no further major alterations; it was, however, considerably altered from that introduced at the start of the session. Any popular support surviving for it in Ireland arose more from a reaction against its opponents than from any enthusiasm about its final form.[325]

Despite the concessions made to the propertied interest, the Poor Law Bill remained popular in England, and redounded to the government's credit.[326] For many it was the correct response to the providential lesson of the Famine, and the only condition that could justify British self-sacrifice and financial assistance. That the 'salvation' of Ireland would flow from the moral regeneration consequent on the passage of the Poor Law was axiomatic to radical politicians.[327] To the *Times* this was the intention of divine wisdom:

> Society is reconstructed in disaster . . . In 'clouds and darkness' it is necessary to take a short and simple rule, the guidance of some great moral truth. The first law of nature, that the people must be fed, and that more particularly from the work of their hands, is the clue of this labyrinth. In the public weal an enlightened statesman will discern the cloud by day and the pillar of fire by night through this terrible wilderness; and public weal is an empty name unless it includes the relief of those who are ready to perish, and the employment of those who are able to work, but have not the opportunity.

The previously corrupt state of Irish society had now been dissolved – 'PROVIDENCE, not man, has put an end to that folly' – and it lay with the government to create the foundations of a more natural structure. Russell was assured of popular support so long as he adhered to this moralist agenda.[328] The sufferings of the 1846–7 season and the opposition of Irish landlords merely convinced moralists

322 Ibid., 494–5 [Monteagle]; Fitzwilliam to Monteagle, 12 May, Monteagle Papers, MS 13,397/3
323 Broughton Diary, Add. MS 43,749, fols. 37–8 [7 May].
324 *Hans.*, XCII, 811 [14 May].
325 The *Freeman* declared the Bill 'mutilated and diseased for good', but reacted strongly against an extended critique of outdoor relief published by the leading English Catholic peer, *Freeman's Journal*, 13, 18 May; Earl of Shrewsbury, *Thoughts on the Poor Relief Bill for Ireland* (London, 1847).
326 Le Marchant to Wood, 6 April, Hickleton Papers, A4/108.
327 *Hans.*, XC, 1294–5, 1324–5 [12, 15 March: Molesworth, Hall].
328 *Times*, 13 March, 19 May.

and radicals of the need to implement the Act in full as rapidly as possible. For Wood, as for the *Times* and much of British opinion, Ireland's regeneration through the instrumentality of the Poor Law had to begin in pain: 'except through a purgatory of misery and starvation', the Chancellor confided to the new Lord Lieutenant, 'I cannot see how Ireland is to emerge into a state of anything approaching to quiet or prosperity'.[329]

329 Wood to Clarendon, 23 July, Hickleton Papers, A4/185/2.

CHAPTER SIX:

'Between the Censure of the Economists and the Philanthropists': the Whigs and Famine Relief, 1847–50

> The popular members say the Poor Law is right and keeps the people – the landlords wish to shift the burthen on to British shoulders – and the British people have made up their minds to pay no more for Irish landlords. How this square is to be broken through I don't see . . . You must not suppose that I am at all insensible of what you urge on behalf of the Irish proprietors, whom it is desirable to keep well attached to the Government; but we can judge better of the feeling here; and there is the very strongest determination not to pursue the old system of buying the landlords to keep down the people . . . people here will not interpose their money between the Irish landlords and their losses.
>
> *Charles Wood*, 3 April 1848[1]

> Would to God that you could stand for one five minutes in our street, and see with what a troop of miserable, squalid, starving creatures you would be instantaneously surrounded, with tears in their eyes and with misery in their faces, imploring and beseeching of you to get them a place in the workhouse . . . The landlords expect the Government will interfere, and the Government with greater justice say the land must support those who dwell thereon, but vae victis alas the poor between both . . . Whatever be the cost or expense, or on whatever party it may fall, every Christian must admit, that the people must not be suffered to starve in the midst of plenty, and that the first duty of a Government is to provide for the poor under the circumstances such as they are placed . . .
>
> *Fr John O'Sullivan, Parish Priest of Kenmare*, 2 December 1847[2]

1 Wood to Clarendon, 3 April 1848, Hickleton Papers, Cambridge University Library (microfilm), A4/185/2.

2 O'Sullivan to Trevelyan, 2 Dec. 1847, Treasury Papers, Public Record Office, London, T64/368B.

I CUTTING THE 'GORDIAN KNOT', 1847–8

A number of developments in the summer and autumn of 1847 combined to alter British perceptions of the Irish crisis and to determine the character of the policies adopted in the following years. The first was the non-appearance of the potato blight and the unexpectedly productive Irish grain harvest of 1847. This coincided with the results of the general election in July, and the simultaneous mobilization of middle-class radicalism, to reinforce the moralist tendencies evident in the preceding years. The financial crisis of October, which was rapidly followed by a sharp commercial recession, closed the circle and dissipated what remained of the philanthropic enthusiasms of early 1847.

The prospects for the coming harvest had been a source of trepidation for much of 1847. Many officials expressed disappointment at what they perceived to be the obstinate and fatalistic adherence of the peasantry to the potato plant, although this was hardly surprising given the half-hearted distribution of turnip seed as an alternative.[3] Uncertainty persisted throughout the summer, with scientific botanists again unable to provide any authoritative guidance,[4] and it was not until September that the potato crop was declared to be largely free of blight. The potato's revival promoted complacency about the overall food situation, obscuring the reality that the harvest offered only a superficial respite to much of the island.[5] As Clarendon observed, less than a quarter of the usual amount had been planted, and the continuing high prices placed potatoes well beyond the reach of those without their own stocks.[6] This was particularly ominous, as the 1847 crop appears to have been disproportionately a commercial rather than a subsistence one, reflecting the success of stronger farmers in hoarding seed during the winter.[7]

Official attitudes towards the potato remained deeply ambivalent. Clarendon had feared that a good crop might encourage renewed reliance on the root by landlords and people, and that 'the experience of the last year would go *absolutely for nothing*'. If the potato failure heralded the social upheavals necessary for Ireland's 'salvation', the plant's revival would surely impede that process.[8] This

3 Griffith to Trevelyan, 8 June 1847, Cooper to Russell, 10 June, J. Wood to Trevelyan, 16 July, ibid., T64/369C/1. Despite reports from officials of the highly beneficial effects of gratuitous distribution of 'green crop' seed by the British Association and Quakers, the government refused to involve itself in such activity, F. Carleton to Trevelyan, 15 June 1847, ibid.; Report of Capt. O'Neill, 2 Dec. 1848, ibid., T64/366A; *Freeman's Journal*, 8, 25 March 1847.

4 Lindley to Trevelyan, 21 June, 7 July 1847, Treasury Papers, T64/369C/1.

5 For the graphic depiction of this perception, see 'Consolation for the million: the loaf and the potato', *Punch*, 11 Sept. 1847.

6 Clarendon to Reeve, 18 Sept., Herbert Maxwell (ed.), *The life and letters of George William Frederick, fourth Earl of Clarendon* (2 vols., London, 1913) I, 280.

7 Letter from an official of the Board of Works, *Times*, 3 May 1847.

8 Clarendon to Wood, 15 July, Clarendon to Normanby, 2 Aug. 1847, Clarendon Deposit Irish, Bodleian Library, Oxford, letterbook I.

view was an article of faith among moralists, but at the same time Wood was concerned that another major failure would herald a return to the policies of the preceding season, overthrowing 'all our calculations' by producing 'the same sort of pressure as we had last year, and to which Bessborough gave way too easily and too soon'.[9]

Trevelyan reassured his superior with the advice that by 'showing its teeth without biting too hard' the disease would continue to pose a benign threat without excessively diminishing the available food supply in the period of transition.[10] While the curse laid upon the plant and the social system it supported had evidently not been lifted, moralists believed that the absence of any specific visitation such as those witnessed in 1845 and 1846 meant that the 1847–8 season should not be categorized as exceptional. These points were further stressed when in early 1848 Trevelyan published his apologia for the Treasury's Irish policies. The food crisis was now over, he assured the public, and 'the appointed time of Ireland's regeneration is at last come'.[11] This predisposition to normalize the condition of Ireland in 1847–8 was greatly strengthened by reports that the country had also produced a bumper grain harvest.[12] A visit to Ulster left the secretary of the Royal Agricultural Society of Ireland so overwhelmed by the 'bountiful munificence of Providence' that he declared that the darkest hour was past and 'the crisis over in Ireland'. The *Times* predicted that the gloomy prognostications made about other parts of Ireland would be similarly contradicted by experience.[13] Ministerial optimism was further bolstered by the continuing influx of large quantities of Indian corn, and the collapse of its price by late August to less than half that of February 1847.[14] This not only appeared to vindicate the general policy of free trade and non-interference in food markets, but reinforced the presumption that the Irish poor could be fed on cheap imported maize paid for by agricultural exports. Relief officials were pleased to report that Indian corn consumption was continuing to make progress in Ireland, and believed that it would bring 'increased comfort to many homes'.[15] Official reports from America indicated that production of the grain for export was likely to continue to rise in line with Irish demand.[16] Convinced that it was no

9 Wood to Clarendon, 19, 23 July, Hickleton Papers, A4/185/2.

10 Trevelyan to Wood, 28 July, ibid., A4/59.

11 C.E. Trevelyan, *The Irish crisis* (London, 1848), pp. 41–2, 156, 183–5, 199.

12 Jones to Trevelyan, 19 June, Griffith to Trevelyan, 31 August, Treasury Papers, T 64/369C/1.

13 E. Bullen to the editor, 22 Aug., *Times*, 26 Aug. 1847.

14 The Board of Trade listed the amount of grain, meal and flour imported into Ireland in 1847 (the first year for which accurate figures were recorded) as the 'enormous quantity of 4,506,521 quarters', G.R. Porter to Trevelyan, 15 April 1848, Larcom Papers, National Library of Ireland, Dublin, MS 7743.

15 Trevelyan, *Irish crisis*, pp. 73–6, 163–4; Wood to Clarendon, 2 Sept., Hickleton Papers, A4/185/2; J. Wood to Trevelyan, 16 July 1847, Treasury Papers, T 64/369C/1.

16 Pakenham to Palmerston, 29 March 1847, Palmerston Papers: Foreign Office Letterbooks, British Library, London, Add. MS 48,547, fol. 59.

longer required, the government reduced the relief activities of the Commissariat to a minimum and finally phased them out in the course of 1848.[17]

The outcome of the 1847 harvest thus appeared to confirm the widespread view that the potato failures of 1845 and 1846 had been divine judgments against the potato 'system', rather than against Ireland *per se*. Such opinions were not confined to British moralists. The mouthpiece of the Royal Agricultural Society of Ireland argued along similar lines that the failure and its aftermath had resolved Irish society into its constituent elements preparatory to reconstruction. The conditions for rebuilding the country could only be attained when the people recognized 'this mighty and mysterious agency . . . [and] the proud heart of stubborn and rebellious man is forced to confess "Truly this was the Lord's doing, and it is marvellous in our eyes".'[18] Official sanction was again offered to a providential interpretation of events by the proclamation of a day of public thanksgiving for the plentiful harvest in Britain and Ireland.[19]

Other Irish voices were less sanguine. Clanricarde warned his ministerial colleagues that even the 'splendid harvest' would not be sufficient to feed the people beyond December, or allow the superior classes to meet their increased obligations.[20] Other landlord spokesmen denounced Trevelyan's complacency and prophesied disaster if the Poor Law burden was not lifted from the responsible members of the landed interest.[21] The Clare MP, Sir Lucius O'Brien, who shared with his brother, William Smith O'Brien, suspicions of crude Malthusianism and preference for reproductive improvements over mass emigration, attempted to use the language of providence and evidence of the physical prostration of the west to plead for the remission of relief debts in the face of the renewed famine threat.[22] Most ominously, Poor Law officials also warned that, in the absence of both potatoes and sufficient paid employment, the cottier population lacked an adequate entitlement to the available food supplies.[23] Such voices were drowned out by the more positive news that most in Britain wanted to hear.

---

17 Routh to T. Baring, 22 Jan. 1848, Treasury Papers, T64/368B. Despite a downturn in the food supply situation in autumn 1848, the depots were not re-activated, Erichsen to Trevelyan, 11 Oct. 1848, ibid., T64/366A.

18 Fitzherbert Filgate, 'The potato failure and its effects on Irish agriculture', *Agricultural and Industrial Journal*, I (Jan. 1848), 17–36.

19 Clarendon to Russell, 4, 13 Sept., Clar. Dep. Ir., letterbook I; Broughton Diary, Broughton Papers, British Library, London, Add. MS 43,751, fol. 25 [28 Sept. 1847].

20 Clanricarde to Clarendon, 16 Aug. 1847, Clar. Dep. Ir., box 9; Clanricarde to Wood, 17 Aug. 1847, Hickleton Papers, A4/96.

21 [Samuel O'Sullivan], 'The Irish crisis – the Poor Law', *Dublin University Magazine*, XXXI (April 1848), 537–52; A. Shafto Adair, *The winter of 1846–7 in Antrim, with remarks on out-door relief and colonization* (London, 1847), pp. 13–14, 28–58.

22 Lucius O'Brien, *Ireland in 1848: the late famine and the Poor Laws* (London, 1848), pp. 3–4, 19–22.

23 [Alfred Power], *The Irish Poor Law: past, present and future* (London, 1849), pp. 17–18.

The second significant development in the summer of 1847 was the general election at the end of July. While Protectionist members fell to below 230, with 'Liberal Conservatives' numbering around 100 early hopes of a workable Whig-Liberal majority proved illusory.[24] A number of ministers lost their seats in popular constituencies, and some eighty radicals were returned, many with little loyalty to the 'aristocratic' Whig-Liberal leadership.[25] The results in the popular constituencies reflected, in part, suspicion and hostility towards all aspects of the government's Irish policies, with high expenditure and favouritism towards landlords accompanying hostility to the Maynooth grant as subjects of considerable popular concern. Russell observed that it was 'very difficult to please England, Scotland and Ireland at the same time – we have in the opinion of Great Britain done too much for Ireland and have lost elections for doing so. In Ireland the reverse.'[26] In the absence of adequate mechanisms of party discipline or a powerful unifying idea, the government found itself incapable of managing the unruly House of Commons. By March 1848 it was clear to observers that 'war exists between the radicals and the government'.[27]

In Ireland the elections also produced considerable confusion. Repealers gained at the expense of Whig-Liberals, but under John O'Connell's weak leadership they lacked a party focus or much sense of direction. In the opinion of Wyse the Repeal movement had declined into a mere machine which, despite the violence of its rhetoric, was now directed solely at extracting patronage from the government.[28] The O'Connellite party now finally lost the remaining respect and weight it had previously carried with elements of the British Whig-Liberal leadership.

The upsurge of radicalism in Britain was further boosted by the fiscal crisis of autumn 1847 and the ensuing commercial slump. The causes of the crisis were complex, but Irish developments played a significant part. A cyclical downturn in the textiles and railway sectors was greatly exacerbated by the balance of payments crisis produced by the large imports of highly priced foodstuffs in the 1846–7 season. Large drains on bullion combined with the reluctance of the government to raise the bank rate while it was negotiating its Irish relief loan to provoke a City panic in April. The *Examiner* flippantly commented that 'the City is a Skibbereen'

---

24 John Prest, *Lord John Russell* (London, 1972), pp. 262–3; J.B. Conacher, *The Peelites and the party system 1846–52* (Newton Abbot, 1972), pp. 28–33.

25 Greville to Clarendon, 1 Aug. 1847, Clarendon Deposit, Bodleian Library, Oxford, c.520.

26 Russell to Clarendon, 2 Aug. 1847, Clar. Dep. Ir., box 43. Anti-Catholicism and nonconformist voluntarism also played a considerable part in the radical resurgence, indeed Roebuck lost his seat at Bath partly as a result of his hostility to voluntarism. See Diary of third Earl Grey, 31 July, 2 Aug. 1847, Grey Papers, Durham University Library; G.I.T. Machin, 'The Maynooth grant, the Dissenters and disestablishment, 1845–7', *English Historical Review*, LXXXII (1967), 61–85.

27 Greville to Clarendon, 4 March 1848, Clar. Dep., c.521.

28 Clarendon to Russell, 9, 16 Aug., Clar. Dep. Ir., letterbook I; Wyse to Russell, 10 Aug., Russell Papers, Public Record Office, London, PRO 30/22/6E, fols. 75–84; Prest, *Russell*, p. 263.

suffering from 'a famine of money'.[29] A more serious crash was triggered in October by the bankruptcy of a number of corn-dealing houses which had over-speculated and failed to anticipate the collapse in corn prices accompanying the market glut of mid-1847.[30]

In the general panic that followed the crash, Peel's Bank Charter Act became the immediate focus of political attention, but a general revulsion against easy credit (particularly with regard to railway speculation) ensued. Inevitably the costs of Irish relief in 1846–7 were identified as a contributory cause, and the campaign for retrenchment of government expenditure was bolstered.[31] These conditions rendered it extremely difficult for a government to raise a relief loan in 1847–8 on the scale of that previously floated to finance the public works. However, while the 1847 crash alarmed contemporaries, the scale of the slump should not be exaggerated; by 1849 commercial activity and the revenue had returned to the level of the mid-1840s.[32]

The shift in British public attitudes towards Ireland became obvious with the almost universally hostile response to a new Queen's letter for Irish relief issued to coincide with the national 'thanksgiving day' on 17 October. Trevelyan and Burgoyne publicly supported the appeal, the former on the grounds that further charity was needed to facilitate social transition, the latter for more explicitly humanitarian reasons, but the attempt to convince the English public that the Irish harvest would not do enough to relieve the western destitute had little impact.[33] The officiating clergy were particularly hostile, some refusing to read the Queen's letter, others requesting only nominal contributions, and most indicating that the charitable energies of England should now be directed to more deserving objects at home.[34]

The rhetoric of such journals as the *Times* went far to encourage this rejection; the paper declared Ireland to be a moral entity separate from Great Britain, and claimed that all its inhabitants shared an interest in obliging British workers to maintain the Irish poor in idleness. It followed that another British collection would be an act of misplaced humanity, diverting attention and energy from the

---

29 *Examiner*, 8 May 1847.

30 H.M. Boot, *The commercial crisis of 1847* (Hull, 1984), pp. 42–76.

31 Clarendon to Lewis, 5 Sept. 1847, Clar. Dep., c.532/1; G. Grey to Clarendon, 22 Oct., Clar. Dep. Ir., box 11; *Hansard's Parliamentary Debates*, 3rd series, XCV, 121 [23 Nov. 1847: Hall].

32 Palmerston to Clarendon, 6 Jan. 1849, Greville to Clarendon, 11 Oct. 1849, Clar. Dep., c.524, c.522.

33 Trevelyan to the editor, 7 Oct., Burgoyne to the editor, 6 Oct., *Times*, 12 Oct. 1847.

34 Daniel Moore, 'The Christian uses of national and individual chastisement. A harvest thanksgiving sermon . . . October 17, 1847', *Pulpit*, LII (1847), 327–8; Bedford to Clarendon, 17 Oct., Rev. G.S. Robinson to Bishop of Peterborough, 7 Oct., Clar. Dep. Ir., box 3. For Irish disgust at English clerical lack of charity, see Aubrey De Vere, *English misrule and Irish misdeeds* (1848, reprint Port Washington, 1970), pp. 27–30.

moral reformation and physical regeneration that would be attainable only through the full implementation of the extended Poor Law.[35] Writing in the paper, Thomas Campbell Foster welcomed England's 'burst of honest indignation' against the charitable appeal, and saw this as the fruit of the seed sown in his columns of 1845–6. To the former '*Times* commissioner' the collection smacked of gross impiety; it would 'thwart the providence of God' to 'degrade them into "contentment" with subsistence on charity'. Ireland's problems, he concluded, were no longer physical or legal, but solely moral, and thus the only answer that could be given to cries of starvation was to direct the Irish to self-exertion: 'let them work as we do, and their poverty will become wealth, and their distress will be changed into abundance.'[36] This rhetoric had the desired effect; only some £20,000 was collected in over 8000 parishes under the second Queen's letter.[37]

This evidence of strong public feeling over Irish relief in Britain combined with the acute difficulties of raising further credit to augment the moralists' case in cabinet. Russell noted that there was a general opinion that 'high prices of food in England and commercial panic are very much owing to the relief we gave to Ireland' and drew the lesson that government could not afford to repeat the same course 'and reap the same reward'.[38] He endorsed the view that Irish policy should be normalized in the interests of promoting social 'transition', and advised Clarendon that to 'dole out government rations when the visitation of providence has ceased would be to teach people never to use any exertion – and to be idle and beggarly all the rest of their lives.'[39]

The government had never intended to continue the soup-kitchen network into a new season, but the prevailing climate of opinion in Britain now rendered its rapid dismantling a priority. Harvest employment allowed the process of closure to proceed from mid-August without the mass unrest that Clarendon had initially feared. Some flexibility was shown in delaying the stoppage in more distressed areas, but Burgoyne was anxious to abandon relief to the able-bodied to curb abuses and shock proprietors and people into exertion.[40] The shut-down was completed on 12 September 1847.[41]

The government felt confident enough to disregard warnings that too sudden a dismantling of the system would result in thousands of deaths in the poorest districts, but the costs of abandoning direct feeding soon became evident. By mid-

35 *Times*, 8, 12 Oct. See also the moralist advocacy of *laissez-faire* in the *Examiner*, 16 Oct. 1847.
36 T.C. Foster to the editor, 12 Oct., *Times*, 13 Oct.
37 J. Mead to Trevelyan, 30 Oct., Treasury Papers, T64/367A/2.
38 Russell to Clarendon, 17 Nov., Clar. Dep. Ir., box 43.
39 Russell to Clarendon, 15 Aug., ibid.
40 Clarendon to Russell, 15 July, Clarendon to Sligo, 4 Aug., ibid., letterbook I; Burgoyne to Monteagle, 27 Aug., Monteagle Papers, National Library of Ireland, Dublin, MS 13,397/1; Wood to Burgoyne, 29 June, Burgoyne to Wood, 7 Aug., Hickleton Papers, A4/185/2, A4/158.
41 *Fifth, sixth and seventh reports of the Relief Commissioners*, P.P. 1847–8 [876], XXIX, 75–6.

October appeals were already being made for the re-opening of the kitchens in famine-devastated western districts such as Erris where the 'wretched population are living on turnip-tops boiled, with an occasional sprinkling of Indian meal'.[42] The fateful decision had, however, been made: in future only the Poor Law would be available as a safety net between the poor and starvation.

The Poor Law tested, 1847–8

Two largely incompatible tasks were expected of the extended Poor Law – the relief of immediate distress, and the promotion of social and economic development. The tensions between these objectives would form the focus of policy debates in the next three years. Clarendon came to Ireland convinced that the Act could achieve both and believed that it would eventually prove 'the salvation of the country'.[43] Yet while he continued to defend its principle vigorously in his public pronouncements, in private he soon began to question its competence to do either unaided. The moralist tone that had led some observers to identify him as one of the 'Grey Party', and which encouraged Wood to hint at a special relationship between the new Lord Lieutenant and the Treasury to the exclusion of Russell, evaporated rapidly once Clarendon found himself in the milieu of Dublin Castle.[44] Clarendon's impression of the Irish character was highly coloured by his fear of political rebellion and agrarian violence, and his private correspondence was peppered with expressions of supercilious abhorrence for peasants and proprietors alike; yet he came to regard himself as the spokesman for the interests of 'his' people before a government which gave priority to English interests.[45] The very 'backwardness' of the Irish rendered them, like the Spanish Clarendon had encountered during his time at Madrid, particularly in need of firm paternal government until such time as a mature 'public opinion' had been brought into existence.[46]

Reports from the west soon convinced Clarendon that 'we are very long way from those halcyon days with which Trevelyan winds up his article', and that the increasingly regional dimension of the crisis made necessary special provision to meet absolute destitution in areas where 'temporary' and 'ordinary' distress had become indistinguishable.[47] Fully aware of the political and ideological difficulties

42 Sligo to Clarendon, 5 Aug., Clar. Dep. Ir., box 57; R. Casey to J. Higgins, 18 Oct., Higgins to Trevelyan, 21 Oct., Treasury Papers, T64/367A/2.

43 Clarendon to Normanby, 2 Aug., Clar. Dep. Ir., letterbook I.

44 Clarendon to Brougham, 10 Aug., ibid.; Prince Albert memo, 6 July 1846, A.C. Benson and Viscount Esher (eds.), *Letters of Queen Victoria: a selection of Her Majesty's correspondence between the years 1837–1861* (3 vols., London, 1907), II, 102; Wood to Clarendon, 19 July 1847, Hickleton Papers, A4/185/2.

45 Clarendon to Wood, 28 Oct., Clar. Dep. Ir., letterbook I.

46 Clarendon to Lewis, 8 Aug., 20 Sept., Clarendon to Reeve, 18 Sept. 1847, Clar. Dep., c.532/1, c.534/1; Clarendon to Russell, 12 Oct., Clar. Dep. Ir., letterbook I.

47 Clarendon to Lewis, 3 Jan. 1848, Clar. Dep., c.532/1; Clarendon to Wood, 21 July, Clarendon to Russell, 18 Aug. 1847, Clar. Dep. Ir., letterbook I.

surrounding any extension of aid, Clarendon posed the question in a manner that revealed the duality of his own thinking:

> Esquimaux and New Zealanders are more thrifty and industrious than these people who deserve to be left to their fate instead of the hardworking people of England being taxed for their support, but can we do so? We shall be equally blamed for keeping them alive or letting them die and we have only to select between the censure of the Economists or the Philanthropists – which do you prefer?[48]

While he was convinced that in two-thirds of the country the Poor Law Act would succeed in 'developing a spirit of self reliance and self-exertion which is altogether new in Ireland', the Lord Lieutenant made clear his view that, with regard to the remainder, the censure of 'political economy' was the lesser evil and would have to be incurred.[49]

With the government reluctant to reopen the question of the structures of relief, the policy debate in 1847–8 resolved largely into a struggle over money. Under pressure from the Irish administration and Russell, the Treasury softened its insistence on levying additional rates for the repayment of advances, but was reluctant to make any further concessions beyond the deferral of payments.[50] The Chancellor defended his firmness by reference to the severe contraction of the revenue resulting from the slump, but it was clear that Wood's obstinacy was based on something deeper than the defence of an over-stretched Treasury. He lectured Clarendon in mid-August:

> Now financially, my course is very easy. I have no money, and therefore I cannot give it . . . assistance to Ireland means only a further loan, and in the present state of the money market and depression in all our manufacturing towns, this is out of the question. Ireland must keep herself somehow or other; this at least is certain, that the public funds of this country will not . . . Where the people refused to work or sow, they must starve, as indeed I fear must be the case in many parts. Ellice . . . says that all our difficulties arise from our impious attempt to thwart the dispensation which was sent to cut the Gordian knot in Ireland; and I believe that this must be the end of it.

The moralist agenda had not altered since autumn 1846. Wood was convinced that '*the struggle* in Ireland is to force them into self-government and that our song . . .

48 Clarendon to Russell, 10 Aug., ibid.

49 Clarendon to Russell, 22 Aug., Clarendon to Lansdowne, 26 Aug., ibid.

50 Twisleton to Clarendon, 24 July, ibid., box 29; Russell to Wood, 23 Aug., Russell memo, 31 Aug., Hickleton Papers, A4/56/2; Somerville to Wood, 12, 24 August, Somerville Letterbook (copy), Public Record Office of Northern Ireland, Belfast, T. 2982, fols. 1–3, 9–11. Wood admitted the expediency of leniency in the circumstances, Wood to Somerville, 27 Aug., Wood to Trevelyan, 29 Aug., Hickleton Papers, A4/185/2.

must be – "It is your concern, not ours";' only thus could the habitual Irish 'exaggeration' of distress be curbed.[51] The Chancellor was particularly irritated by the readiness of Clarendon and Twisleton to replace elected boards with paid vice-guardians where they believed this necessary to ensure the collection of rates, on the grounds that this substitution would weaken the didactic impact of the Poor Law on the Irish elite.[52] Trevelyan vetoed Twisleton's request for the supply of clothing and bedding to the workhouses for similar reasons: 'the Government is very reluctant to do anything which would tend to revive the mendicant spirit, and countenance a feeling of dependence upon the State instead of upon local exertion and contribution.'[53]

As the autumn of 1847 wore on, Clarendon could not ignore the evidence that the Poor Law was collapsing in much of the country, as contractors refused to supply workhouses, the banks refused further credit, and resistance to the collection of rates escalated. The Treasury, he told Trevelyan in October, would have to contribute public assistance to many unions before long.[54] Official reports from the localities explicitly stated the dangers of not granting financial assistance to the unions. One salaried vice-guardian wrote from Mayo:

> There is no doubt whatever that we should be able to work the Poor Law, so as to keep the destitute from starvation, had we the means at our disposal. Then comes the question, where are these means to be found? The government says, "From the rates." Doubtless much may be collected, but it remains to be proved, whether there can be any amount even approaching a sufficiency obtained to satisfy so great a demand.[55]

Quaker philanthropists echoed such warnings. James Hack Tuke returned to Ireland in autumn 1847 and published his concern that the Poor Law (which he had supported) could not work unaided in the west. Remunerative work was, he asserted, vital to keep the people alive and lift the burden from the rates.[56] Jonathan Pim agreed, reminding his readers that potatoes had formerly served as a 'circulating

---

51 Wood to Clarendon, 15 Aug., Hickleton Papers, A4/185/2; Wood to Russell, 1 Sept., Russell Papers, PRO 30/22/6F, fols. 9–10.

52 Wood to Clarendon, 9 July 1847, Wood to Somerville, 9 Sept. 1848, Hickleton Papers, A4/185/2, A4/111. Many western boards of guardians were suspended as their accounts slipped into chaos in later 1847, while others were content to cede responsibility to professional administrators, Sligo to Clarendon, 17 Aug. 1847, Clar. Dep. Ir., box 57.

53 Trevelyan to Twisleton, 13 Nov., ibid., box 29. This letter led Twisleton to complain sarcastically to the Lord Lieutenant about Treasury ignorance of the state of Connacht and its apparent willingness to contemplate the 'extinction of the Celtic Race', Twisleton to Clarendon, 15 Nov., ibid.

54 Clarendon to Trevelyan, 15 , 27 Oct., Treasury Papers, T64/367A/2.

55 W.R. Lecky to J. Pim, 27 Sept., ibid.

56 James Hack Tuke, *A visit to Connaught in the autumn of 1847* (London, 1847), pp. 4–5, 30–41.

medium'. Further Treasury advances were required alongside the investment of private capital.[57]

The government was not entirely without funds for Ireland, as because of falling food costs, over £530,000 had been saved from the sum voted in the spring for the Soup Kitchen Act.[58] Despite Clarendon's protests that this money had been earmarked for Irish relief, the Treasury vetoed its use for Ireland, and insisted that the remaining £170,000 in the British Association's coffers be hoarded until the winter, and then used in a manner that would reinforce the operation of the Poor Law.[59] This refusal to intervene became increasingly difficult to sustain in the face of adverse reports from the west and Clarendon's jeremiads, but when the Treasury did decide to make provision during the winter of 1847–8, it did so on its own terms. After a brief visit to Ireland in October, Trevelyan prepared a paper recommending that a line be drawn between twenty-two 'distressed' unions on the western seaboard and the others, and that the remaining government food stocks in Irish depots be sold to the British Association for distribution.[60] Clarendon at first reluctantly accepted this plan, but became increasingly critical as evidence accumulated of its inadequacy and the difficulty of excluding marginal unions. The Lord Lieutenant's motives were not wholly humanitarian, and arose as much from fear as sympathy. His growing concern over what he regarded as the incipient revolutionary threat in Ireland lay behind his conviction that the government could not 'allow above a certain number' to starve. Political considerations also dictated that the small gentry and the Catholic clergy be conciliated by increased aid.[61]

Russell's role in these disputes was pivotal. His anti-landlord instincts placed him close to Wood and Trevelyan on abstaining from 'extraordinary assistance',[62] and he shared the moralists' assumption of a high Irish wages fund which had now been augmented by the good grain harvest. Taking his figures from McCulloch, Russell believed the harvest to be worth some £40 million, of which £4 million

57 Jonathan Pim, *The condition and prospects of Ireland* (Dublin, 1848), pp. 106–34.

58 *Supplementary appendix to the seventh, and last report, of the Poor Law Commissioners, constituted under the Act 10 Vict. cap. 7*, P.P. 1847–8 (956), XXIX, 129.

59 Clarendon to Wood, 12 Aug., 7 Sept., Clarendon to Russell, 4, 23 Sept., Clar. Dep. Ir., letterbook I; Wood to Clarendon, 15 Aug., 11, 25 Sept., Wood to Trevelyan, 29 Aug., Hickleton Papers, A4/185/2; Trevelyan to Clarendon, 20 Aug., Clar. Dep. Ir., box 60.

60 The British Association complied with Trevelyan's view that 'supporting and strengthening the administration of the Poor Law . . . is the great point of all', Trevelyan to Jones Loyd, 20 Aug., Minutes of a meeting of the British Association, 20 Aug., Strzelecki to Trevelyan, 9 Nov. 1847, *Papers relating to the relief of distress and the state of the unions and workhouses in Ireland (fourth series)*, P.P. 1847–8 [896], LIV, 13–17.

61 Clarendon to Russell, 10 Nov. 1847, Clar. Dep. Ir., letterbook I, Clarendon to G. Grey, 22 March 1848, ibid., letterbook II. This political point was echoed in a number of pamphlets, see R.M. Martin, *Remedial measures suggested for the relief of Ireland* (London, 1848), p. 6.

62 Russell to Clarendon, 15 Aug., 18 Sept., Clar. Dep. Ir., box 43.

could easily be spared for the relief of the poor.[63] While he acknowledged the problem of the ill-distribution of the national income and the case for regional assistance, he warned Clarendon that this must be strictly circumscribed.[64]

Russell's moralistic tendencies on the question of relief remained strongly tinged with a Foxite insistence that proprietors ought to bear the greatest obligations. He had anticipated conflict between classes over the produce of the harvest, and subsequently over the primacy of rates or rents.[65] His personal sympathies were firmly with the tenantry:

> It is impossible to say that the land can support the people and pay rent – But in that case I think rent should be sacrificed. Proprietors and their tenants have raised up, encouraged, and grown rich upon a potato-fed population – Now that the question is between rent, and sustenance, and I think rent must give way, and the whole rental, if necessary, given to support the people. Farmers will look after their own profits; they will remain the real proprietors, and thus will keep down pauperism for their own sakes.[66]

This tallied with Russell's commitment to strengthening the position of tenants, but it revealed a lack of understanding of the actual dynamics of rural power. Wood agreed with the principle but had a sounder grasp of the practicalities, observing that the 'ruthless' landlords were already seizing the corn for rent, so as to 'pocket all they can get and laugh at the collector'.[67]

The frequency of evictions from autumn 1847 focused attention on the quarter acre clause, which was denounced by the nationalist press for turning the Poor Law into 'a law to enable landlords to evade their obligations and to *exterminate the poor*'.[68] Russell had hoped that the threat of the poor rate would act as a disincentive to clearances,[69] but events demonstrated this to be mere wishful thinking. By October Clarendon was expressing concern that an excessive stringency in enforcing this clause would create 'a permanent set of paupers who need not of necessity become so'.[70] As the winter progressed it became evident that many

---

63 Russell to Clarendon, 18, 22, 27 Sept., ibid.

64 Russell to Clarendon, 2, 25 Oct., ibid.

65 Russell to Wood, 25 June, Hickleton Papers, A4/56/2.

66 Russell memo: 'State of Ireland', July 1847, Russell Papers, PRO 30/22/6D, fols., 84–7. Trevelyan sought to implement this policy, Trevelyan to Twisleton, 14 Sept., Treasury Papers, T64/366A.

67 Wood to Clarendon, 12 Sept. 1847, Hickleton Papers, A4/185/2. In practice the authorities were legally obliged to enforce distraints and evictions in the face of widespread resistance to rents, *Cork Southern Reporter*, 9 Sept., reprinted *Times*, 13 Sept.; 'An Irish peer' to the editor, *Times*, 5 Nov. 1847.

68 *Freeman's Journal*, 2 Feb. 1848.

69 Russell to Clarendon, 9 Aug. 1847, Clar. Dep. Ir., box 43.

70 Clarendon to Russell, 8 Oct., ibid., letterbook I. Redington also recommended that exceptions be made, Clarendon to Russell, 18 Oct., ibid.

western proprietors had a 'settled design of clearing their estates' using the clause.[71] Russell expressed alarm that the spirit of the Act – to permit the labourer to retain his cottage and quarter acre when he applied for relief in 'virtual fulfilment of the law' – was being broken.[72] Proprietors were able to evade this provision due to the considerable confusions in practice over the legal distinctions between occupancy and tenancy, and guardians and relieving officers frequently refused to accept any surrender that did not include the applicant's cottage.[73] Clarendon, who found such activities 'very unjust and oppressive', recommended that they be checked, and with Russell's agreement the Irish Poor Law Commissioners issued a circular instructing boards to insist on only the surrender of occupancy of holdings over a quarter acre.[74] While paid vice-guardians in particular appear to have implemented this instruction, its observance was far from universal, and the practice of pulling down the cabins of those who sought poor relief, often without any legal authority, continued to be widespread in the west.

While ministers refused to accede to Sharman Crawford's demand that the Gregory clause be abolished as the only effectual way of curbing such abuses, the Irish authorities were gradually forced to admit that the clause was responsible for substantial mortality.[75] An unexpectedly large number of smallholders chose to risk starvation and put their last hopes in the return of the potato rather than surrender their land. The Act explicitly excluded these tenants from relief, but Clarendon supported Twisleton's attempt to alleviate the suffering of their dependents by allowing workhouse relief to their families.[76] Clanricarde, Lansdowne and Grey responded angrily to what was regarded as an arbitrary encouragement

---

71 Lynch to Commissioners, 14 Jan. 1848, *Papers relating to . . . the relief of the distress and state of Ireland (fifth series)*, P.P. 1847–8 [919], LV, 308; Trevelyan to Clarendon, 3 Feb. (1848), Clar. Dep. Ir., box 60. Several more humane proprietors were uneasy about the use of the clause for such purposes by their neighbours. See, for example Lord Sligo's anger at activities on the Lucan estate, Marquess of Sligo, *A few remarks and suggestions on the present state of Ireland* (London, 1847), pp. 15–16; *Telegraph, or Connaught Ranger*, 19 Jan. 1848.

72 Russell to Clarendon, 21 Oct. 1847, Clar. Dep. Ir., box 43.

73 *First report of the Commissioners for administering the laws for the relief of the poor in Ireland*, P.P. 1847–8 [963], XXXIII, 397–8. In some places the Catholic clergy attempted to uphold the letter of the law and frustrate landlord objectives, Sir. T. Ross to Commissioners, 18 April 1848, *Papers relating to . . . the relief of the distress (sixth series)*, P.P. 1847–8 [955] LVI, 203–4.

74 Clarendon to Russell, 4 Jan. 1848, Clar. Dep. Ir., letterbook II; Russell to Clarendon, 7 Jan., ibid., box 43; 'Surrender of land by applicants for relief where occupying more than a quarter of an acre – circular to unions, and opinion of counsel', 15 Feb., *First report of Commissioners*, P.P. 1847–8 [963], XXXIII, 471.

75 *Hans.*, XCVII, 338–62 [9 March 1848]. For Russell's attempts to curb illegal ejectments by law, see above, pp. 191–4.

76 *Copies of the correspondence upon which the Commissioners of Poor Laws in Ireland took legal advice as to the construction of the 10th section of the Act 10 Vict. c. 31, and the case submitted by them to counsel; and of the circular letters of the Commissioners thereupon*, P.P. 1847–8 [442], LIII, 519–23; Clarendon to Clanricarde, 7 June 1848, Clanricarde Papers, West Yorkshire Archive Service, Leeds, bundle 48.

to 'all the abuses of the old English system', and the circular was denounced by Monteagle in the Lords.[77] Faced with the threat of 'a batch of starvation brought before Parliament as a result of a too rigid adherence to the law', at a time when Crawford was ready to re-introduce his motion for abolition, and with Clarendon firmly supporting his subordinates, the cabinet gave way.[78] The concession was, however, limited by a second circular restricting such relief to 'extreme cases'.[79] The principle of the clause remained intact, and Russell laid down the limits to which he was prepared to go in his reply to an appeal for short-term aid on behalf of smallholders in the Tuam union:

> it may be a question with all of us whether holdings by persons of such small capital that they cannot live till their crops are gathered in ought to be relieved by artificial aid. Their becoming paupers and leaving their lands to those who can afford to hire as labourers those who now hold them is probably the best solution for society.[80]

Nothing could indicate more clearly the contradictions between Russell's land-reform and relief policies.

As the winter of 1847–8 worsened, and the workhouses became full to overflowing with the fever-racked destitute, the Dublin Poor Law Commissioners used their powers to permit outdoor relief to the able-bodied under the Poor Law. Landowners protested at the dilution of the 'test of destitution', but strict adherence to the test was impossible given the gross overcrowding, and irrelevant when masses of the poor continued in extremis to seek admittance to what were popularly regarded as 'slaughter asylums'.[81] Some attempt was made to make space for the able-bodied by removing other categories of inmates, but this proved of limited efficacy. Workhouse accommodation was increased by hiring auxiliary buildings, providing over 150,000 nominal places in September 1848 and about 250,000 a year later,[82] but the great majority of inmates remained those too infirm to be removed, along with thousands of orphaned or abandoned children.

---

77 Clanricarde to Clarendon, 5 June, Clar. Dep. Ir., box 9; *Hans.*, XCIX, 800–3 [19 June: Monteagle]; Grey Diary, 19 June 1848, Grey Papers. It was also unpopular with landowners and ratepayers generally, E. Ommanney to Trevelyan, 24 June, Treasury Papers, T64/366A.

78 Clarendon to Russell, 3 July, Clar. Dep. Ir., letterbook III; G. Grey to Clarendon, 27 June, ibid., box 12.

79 G.C. Lewis to Poor Law Commissioners, 30 June 1848, Home Office Papers, Public Record Office, London, HO 122/20, fols. 92–3. In July 1849 the Poor Law Commissioners conceded that few had actually been relieved under this regulation, *Second annual report of the Commissioners for administering the laws for the relief of the poor in Ireland*, P.P. 1849 [1118], XXV, 107.

80 Russell to Clarendon, 9 July 1848, Clar. Dep. Ir., box 43.

81 *Freeman's Journal*, 2 Feb. 1848.

82 George Nicholls, *A history of the Irish Poor Law, in connexion with the condition of the people* (London, 1856), p. 377.

Numbers on outdoor relief soared to over 800,000 by July 1848, two-fifths of these designated able-bodied and put to the unreproductive work-test of stone-breaking in relief yards.[83] Cooked rations were distributed in some unions, but the boards of guardians lacked the resources to reconstitute the soup-kitchen network of summer 1847, and the destitute were obliged to squat in the pestilential slums of county towns, or trek considerable distances for their food dole. The consequences of the Poor Law's failure in terms of famine mortality appalled travellers in the western part of the country in 1848.[84]

The crisis of the Poor Law further strained the relationship between the Irish administration and the Treasury. While the Poor Law Commissioners were committed to upholding the principle of less eligibility, they were equally convinced that the preservation of life was paramount, and that a degree of operational flexibility was vital to realize this end. However, Twisleton and Clarendon were powerless to force the Treasury to disgorge sums proportionate to the needs of the distressed unions and electoral divisions.[85] Wood and Trevelyan had no intention of allowing the Commissioners a free hand or of permitting the providential opportunity for reconstructing the Irish character to pass unseized.[86]

Remedial schemes and closing options

The point on which Russell differed most sharply with the Treasury in later 1847 was not the Poor Law, but auxiliary remedial schemes. His intention in July had been to support the Poor Law with advances for 'good profitable works' for 'permanent improvement'; he told Clarendon 'we must give very little for relief and much for permanent improvement – that is my programme for next year'.[87] The Prime Minister expressed his commitment to these schemes in the language of justice. Ireland, he insisted, 'has a right to expect advantage from the credit and capital of England'. On top of the sums already voted for land improvement, railways and harbours, other amounts would be available out of the savings made from the

83 *Second annual report of the Commissioners for administering the laws for the relief of the poor in Ireland*, P.P. 1849 [1118], XXV, 105–6. Clarendon unsuccessfully sought to put the able-bodied to reproductive work on local waste-land reclamations, Clarendon to Somerville, 13 Feb. 1848, Clar. Dep. Ir., letterbook II.

84 See, for example the vivid account of the Louisburgh district in spring 1848, in Asenath Nicholson, *Lights and shades of Ireland: part III. The Famine of 1847, '48 and '49* (London, 1850), pp. 356–61.

85 Twisleton to Trevelyan, 10 Aug. 1848, Treasury Papers, T64/367B/2; Clarendon to Wood, 30 March, Clar. Dep. Ir., letterbook II.

86 Wood to Clarendon, 3 April, Hickleton Papers, A4/185/2; Trevelyan to Twisleton, 13 June, Treasury Papers, T64/367B/1. For a detailed account of the growing antagonism between Twisleton and Trevelyan, see Christine Kinealy, *This great calamity: the Irish Famine 1845–52* (Dublin, 1994), pp. 227–31.

87 Russell to Clarendon, 17 July 1847, Clar. Dep. Ir., box 43; Russell memo: 'State of Ireland', July 1847, Russell Papers, PRO 30/22/6D, fols. 84–7.

1847 loans. All projects would be directed at promoting Irish agricultural development along the lines recommended by Sir Robert Kane.[88]

This optimism was soon shattered by the Treasury's insistence on retrenchment, which forced Russell to rule out all but the smallest of additional schemes until parliament reassembled.[89] The land improvement fund was granted priority, and Russell did all he could to secure it, but the Act proved to be ultimately only 'a trifle' as a means of national assistance. In March 1848 the Lord Lieutenant noted that a limited sum of only £150,000 had been expended on wages, and second instalments had been applied for very rarely.[90] Arterial drainage by the Board of Works was also declared a priority, but Clarendon was unhappy with the amounts made available and the mode of proceeding.[91] The Treasury begrudged every additional item of 'wholesale and indiscriminate' expenditure on drainage projects for reasons both of economy and the 'bad political effect' of raising expectations about state activity.[92] Similarly, the re-opening of road works was ruled out on the familiar grounds that this 'would be like breaking the main spring of a watch. The pressure which is now inducing landlords and tenants to exert themselves . . . would be greatly relaxed or entirely destroyed.'[93]

One of the most important remedial proposals suggested by Russell, and the greatest deviation from his previous views, was that of state assistance to emigration. Lord Grey had supported the principle of 'systematic colonization' in opposition, and Whig-Liberal landlords with western properties, such as Palmerston and Redington, continued to advocate this after the formation of Russell's government.[94] Grey, however, proved less enthusiastic once in office, fearing that mass Irish emigration would swamp and endanger the colonies. His 'naive and slovenly'

---

88 Russell: 'Notes on the condition of Ireland', Aug. 1847, Clar. Dep. Ir., box 43. Russell intended to give his programme a Foxite stamp by including legislation to popularize Irish institutions. Parliamentary and municipal reform would 'do more to strengthen the spirit and double the energy of Irishmen', than anything else.

89 Wood to Russell, 1 Sept., Russell Papers, PRO 30/22/6F, fols. 5–14; Russell to Clarendon, 2, 18 Sept., Clar. Dep. Ir., box 43.

90 Russell to Clarendon, 10 Sept. 1847, 9 April 1848, ibid.; Clarendon to Russell, 22 March 1848, ibid., letterbook, II.

91 Clarendon to Russell, 2 March 1848, ibid. The Board was allowed to raise loans under the Drainage Acts, but found this difficult with the money market so tight, Redington to Labouchere, 5 June 1847, Bessborough Papers, West Sussex Record Office, Chichester, F. 337.

92 Trevelyan to Clarendon, 9 June 1848, Clar. Dep. Ir., box 69. Mulvany's plan of draining some seven to eight million acres at first attracted some enthusiasm in Ireland, but ran into considerable difficulties from 1848. Proprietorial opposition became manifest when it emerged that the Board's aim was to drain the lowlands to the extent required for tillage farming rather than pasture, Montague, 'Relief and reconstruction', pp. 235–7.

93 Trevelyan to Clarendon, 16 Nov. 1847, Clar. Dep. Ir., box 60.

94 *Hans.*, LXX, 877–93 [10 July 1843]; Palmerston to Grey, 20 Dec. 1846, Grey Papers; Palmerston to Russell, 26 March 1847, Palmerston Papers, GC/RU/1010/1–2; Redington to Labouchere, 20 Jan. 1847, Bessborough Papers, F. 337.

1846 plan for village colonization in Canada was quickly abandoned in the face of Canadian opposition.[95] Grey was not sorry to see the scheme disappear, as he had become convinced that state intervention in this area was a moral evil. 'Nothing is so clear', he wrote to his cousin the Home Secretary, 'from what we know of the disposition of the people who emigrate as that if under regulations however strict the Government were to undertake to provide conveyances for emigrants to British America, the shoals who now find their own way there would at once throw themselves upon the public, and endeavour to get sent out for nothing.'[96] Economic moralism dominated his subsequent colonization policy.

Russell had initially been suspicious of assisted emigration proposals as a landlord manoeuvre, but later agreed with Bessborough that while state intervention would be impracticable on an extensive scale, some assistance might be given to destitute families in congested localities, possibly in the form of subsidized fares. Bessborough thought this the most just and humane mode of social amelioration in 'overgrown townlands'.[97] However, Russell continued to insist that the bulk of the cost should be raised in the first instance by the landowners themselves, as Palmerston had already done on his Sligo estate.[98]

By 1847 state-assisted emigration was regarded by Irish landlords as a vital precondition for agricultural improvement.[99] Their chief difficulty lay in appearing selfishly motivated, but in 1847 they found an able and widely-respected spokesman in John Robert Godley, who although 'a Tory in politics' was praised in the nationalist press for lacking 'the bigotry of the older generation'.[100] Godley's scheme for the state-assisted colonization of two million Irish in a 'New Ireland' in Canada, at a cost of £9 million over three years (two-thirds of this as a loan), became the favoured

---

95 T.F. Eliot, 'Memorandum on villages', 23 Jan. 1847, Grey to Elgin, 2 Feb. 1847, Arthur G. Doughty (ed.), *The Elgin-Grey Papers 1846–52* (4 vols., Ottawa, 1937), I, 10–12, III, 1110–13; Oliver MacDonagh, 'Irish overseas emigration during the Famine', in R.D. Edwards and T.D. Williams (eds.), *The Great Famine: studies in Irish history: 1845–1852* (Dublin, 1956), pp. 340–8.

96 Grey to Sir George Grey, 16 Nov. 1846, Doughty (ed.), *Elgin-Grey Papers*, III, 1079–81.

97 Russell to Grey, 15 Oct. 1846, Grey Papers; Bessborough to Russell, 3 Nov., Russell to Bessborough, 10 Nov. 1846, Russell Papers, PRO 30/22/5E, fols. 17–20, 60–1; Bessborough to Grey, 4 Jan. 1847, Grey Papers.

98 Russell to Palmerston, 27 March 1847, Palmerston Papers, GC/RU/141. For Palmerston's efforts to reduce the population on his Sligo estates by assisted emigration, see *Colonization from Ireland: report of the select committee of the House of Lords on colonization from Ireland; together with minutes of evidence*, P.P. 1847 (737), VI, 159–68 [Kincaid].

99 [Isaac Butt], 'The famine in the land. What has been done, and what is to be done', *Dublin University Magazine*, XXIX (April 1847), 529–35; T. St Leger Alcock, *Observations on the Poor Relief Bill for Ireland, and its bearing on the important subject of emigration* (London, 1847).

100 *Freeman's Journal*, 14, 15 April 1847. Godley had previously outlined his 'moral theory of emigration' in a book aimed at promoting a 'systematic colonization' of Canada, John Robert Godley, *Letters from America* (2 vols., London, 1844), I, 37–40.

option of the 'Irish Party', and drew support from some English Conservatives.[101] However Godley's success in articulating a coherent policy option, and its official recognition by Monteagle's House of Lords select committee on colonization, only succeeded in stoking up virulent controversy. Drawing on Canadian anger at the appalling condition of Irish 'voluntary' immigrants in 1847, the British liberal press denounced the very idea of the state adding to the exodus of Irish paupers to the British colonies.[102]

It was only when waste-lands reclamation was abandoned as a leading remedial measure that Russell turned to emigration in earnest, in the hope that the expressions of parliamentary sympathy for the principle would render it politically practicable. Having considered the best mode of assisting emigration, Russell prioritized the provision of work and wages on arrival in the colonies. Grey was instructed to prepare a plan to facilitate emigration through the creation of employment on the proposed Halifax-Quebec railway, as the first step towards a potentially more extensive programme.[103] Grey's reservations and financial difficulties ensured that little progress was made in 1847, but a developing *rapprochement* between Monteagle and some members of the government resulted in greater consideration being given to a comprehensive emigration scheme the following year.[104] Two great obstacles remained – finding the requisite funds and obtaining cabinet agreement to a coherent plan. Grey remained hostile on the grounds of the expense to Britain, the indignation of the colonies, and the continuing need for Ireland to be compelled to save herself through moral exertion.[105] Trevelyan endorsed this resistance, stiffening the ideological critique of state-assisted emigration.[106]

Russell's inclination was to raise the funds required for his Irish projects by extending the income tax to that country, while issuing loans from the Exchequer as *a quid pro quo*.[107] Despite resistance from the Treasury and the Irish lobby

---

101 John Robert Godley, *An answer to the question what is to be done with the unemployed labourers of the United Kingdom?* (London, 1847); *Colonization from Ireland : report of the select committee of the House of Lords*, P.P. 1847 (737), VI, 167–89, 202–16; *Hans.*, XCII, 899 [1 June 1847: Lincoln].

102 'Address from the City Council of Montreal', 23 June 1847, *Papers relative to emigration: part I. British provinces in North America*, P.P. 1847–8 (50), XLVII, 14; Elgin to Grey, 13 July, 12 Nov. 1847, Doughty (ed.), *Elgin-Grey Papers*, I, 34–7; *Times*, 16 March, 7 April, 14 Oct. Irish nationalist and Catholic opinion was also hostile to emigration, *Freeman's Journal*, 14 April.

103 Russell memo: 'State of Ireland', July 1847, Russell Papers, PRO 30/22/6D, fols. 84–7; Clarendon to Russell, 12 July, Clar. Dep. Ir., letterbook I; Russell to Grey, 2 Aug., Grey Papers.

104 Russell to Clarendon, 2 Oct. 1847, Clar. Dep. Ir., box 43; Clarendon to Grey, 29 Nov., ibid., letterbook I.

105 Grey to Clarendon, 4 Dec., Grey Papers.

106 Trevelyan, *Irish crisis*, pp. 147–50.

107 Russell to Wood, 25 Aug. 1847, Hickleton Papers A4/56/2.

respectively on the grounds of the difficulty of collection and the existing over-taxation of Ireland, a 3 percent levy was accepted by the cabinet in January 1848.[108] Yet Clarendon was prepared to accept the new tax only if the outstanding Labour Rate Act repayments (estimated at around £2.4 million) were written off, and when this was dismissed, he warned that Ireland would respond with violent agitation.[109] The balance swung decisively against the tax, which was postponed, along with its associated grants.[110]

This was but the first of a series of setbacks suffered in the 1848 session. Russell had threatened to resign if his spending estimates were defeated in January, but parliament was prepared to call his bluff in the absence of a credible alternative administration.[111] The Prime Minister also personally supervised and introduced the budget, which included a controversial proposal to renew the British income tax and raise it temporarily to 5 percent to meet the revenue deficiency. Widespread popular revulsion against the tax and a threatened radical-Protectionist alliance forced the government into a humiliating climb-down, and it was fortunate to salvage from the radical assaults even the renewal of the existing income tax for three years.[112] Persistent illness and exhaustion in the winter and spring of 1847–8 may have contributed to Russell's inability to obtain his political objectives in cabinet and parliament.[113] His personal prestige in parliament and with his own colleagues collapsed further with each successive failure.[114]

Wood was highly critical of the Prime Minister's performance, and believed that he should have raised the question of Irish expenditure to justify the tax increase, but he admitted that given the state of British opinion this would have been counter-productive.[115] British radicals argued that the weight of Irish expenditure in 1846–7 had entitled the British tax-payer to a remission in 1848, and then

---

108 Wood to Russell, 11 Sept. 1847, ibid., A4/185/2; Clarendon to Wood, 12 Oct., Clar. Dep. Ir., letterbook I; Lansdowne memo, 8 Jan. 1848, Hickleton Papers, A4/107; C.C.F. Greville, *The Greville memoirs (second part): a journal of the reign of Queen Victoria, from 1837 to 1852*, edited by H. Reeve, 3 vols. (London, 1885) III, 113–14 [7 Jan. 1848]; Broughton Diary, Add. MS 43,751, fol. 80 [1 Feb. 1848].

109 Clarendon to Wood, 2, 9, 13 Feb. 1848, Clar. Dep. Ir., letterbook II . For Clarendon's concern at the dangers of a harsh line on repayments, see Clarendon to Lewis, 19 May, Clar. Dep., c.532/1.

110 Russell to Clarendon, 11 Feb., Clar. Dep. Ir., box 43; Broughton Diary, Add. MS 43,751, fol. 88 [12 Feb.].

111 Greville to Clarendon, 24 Jan. 1848, Clar. Dep., c.521.

112 Prest, *Russell*, pp. 280–2; Frederick August Dreyer, 'The Russell administration 1846–52', (unpublished Ph.D. dissertation, University of St. Andrews, 1962), pp. 101–7.

113 Greville to Graham, 28 Feb., Graham Papers, Cambridge University Library (microfilm), bundle 105; Morpeth Diary, 18 Feb., Castle Howard Papers, Castle Howard, N. Yorks., J19/8/17.

114 Greville to Clarendon, 3 June 1848, Clar. Dep., c.521. Russell's critics considered the alternatives of a Clarendon ministry or a Peelite alliance, but these came to nothing, Greville to Clarendon, 2, 6 March 1848, ibid.

115 Wood to Clarendon, 3 April, Hickleton Papers, A4/185/2.

sought 'retaliation' against the Irish landlords who had voted for the continuation of the British income tax by proposing its extension to Ireland.[116] With distress in Britain, and Irish 'ingratitude' towards 'our superhuman exertions in the famine' brought vividly before parliament by the outdoor agitations in both countries, there appeared to be little sympathy for increased aid.[117]

The closing of the administration's financial options coincided with the further deterioration of the political and social situation in Ireland. A very high proportion of the western population was now dependent on outdoor relief in unions where the collected rate was insufficient to maintain the poor.[118] By the late spring of 1848 the British Association's remaining funds were also reaching exhaustion.[119] The Association was making grants in aid of rates and rationing some 200,000 children daily by the end of April 1848, and Russell pledged the government to make up any shortfall for this purpose until after the harvest.[120] This relatively modest contribution was as far as Russell could proceed on his own initiative.

Faced with the continuing crisis, Russell committed himself to raising substantial loans to cover the costs of relief and the development projects he thought necessary on the grounds of humanity, economy and political conciliation. His initial proposal of an Exchequer bill issue of one million pounds was later scaled back to an immediate loan of £150,000 each for relief and drainage, sums he argued that were 'too small to make much effect in the [money] market'.[121] In the following series of heated cabinet meetings the Prime Minister frequently found himself isolated, while the moralists exploited the perceived state of British opinion to resist such expenditure and the moderates rejected any additional impositions on Irish property. Labouchere, whose political opinions had now been remoulded in the 'dry' atmosphere of the Board of Trade, joined the moralists in raising the threat of a revolt of 'distressed English manufacturers' against Irish aid.[122]

A mixture of real alarm and political calculation led Clarendon to assert repeatedly that a massive Irish rebellion would occur in the absence of effective famine relief.[123] This strategy misfired, for in the summer of 1848 the government

116 *Hans.*, XCVII, 701–68 [17 March: Hall, Horsman]. Hall's motion for extension was defeated by 218 to 138, but had the backing of most British radicals and Protectionists.

117 Greville, *Journal*, III, 159–60 [2 April].

118 Jonathan Pim, *The condition and prospects of Ireland and the evils arising from the present distribution of landed property: with suggestions for a remedy* (Dublin, 1848), pp. 192–203.

119 Routh to Trevelyan, 1, 4 April 1848, Treasury Papers, T 64/365B.

120 Trevelyan to Clarendon, 10 May, Trevelyan to Jones Loyd, 2 May, Clar. Dep. Ir., box 69; Russell to Clarendon, 10 April, ibid., box 43.

121 Russell memo: 'State of Ireland', 30 March, Russell Papers, PRO 30/22/7B, fols. 158–61; Russell to Wood, 8 April, Hickleton Papers, A4/56/3.

122 Broughton Diary, Add. MS 43,752, fol. 15 [1 April].

123 The Lord Lieutenant was particularly worried by the bad example set to Ireland of the 'economic fallacies' adopted by the French revolutionary government, and shared Senior's hostility towards the 'socialist' doctrines inherent in the *ataliers nationaux*, Clarendon to Palmerston, 7 March 1848, Palmerston Papers, GC/CL/483/1; Nassau William Senior,

was as concerned at the danger of middle-class radicals in Britain making common cause with Chartists over the burden placed on 'the people' as it was with the amateurish plotting of Young Ireland. Wood proceeded to call Clarendon's bluff, arguing that if the advances of 1846–7 had not stimulated loyalty and gratitude, the much smaller amounts now under discussion would merely antagonize Britain without conciliating Ireland. Political expediency and moralist ideology now reinforced each other, and, with Russell 'benumbed' by the inertia of the Commons, Wood was in a position to take full advantage of the situation.[124] Despite the continuing protests of relief officials, only some £132,000 of public money was advanced for famine relief in 1847–8, less than 2 per cent of the sum expended in the previous season.[125]

II 'NATURAL CAUSES' 1848–9

'A winter of horrors'

In the summer of 1848 Ireland was shaken by another substantial potato failure. Ministerial policy had been premised on the need to promote 'transition' in the agricultural economy, but the breadth of land sown with potatoes in the spring of 1848 demonstrated just how limited this had been, and how desperate many smallholders were to retain their land. Tremendous sacrifices were made to procure potato seed (often the only variety available) in the hopes that the revival of 1847 would be repeated.[126] Clarendon, who had placed much confidence in the encouragement of green crops by his corps of peripatetic agricultural instructors, was concerned that potato cultivation had been encouraged by 'pauper landlords' out of a desperate desire for rent, and he feared that it would perpetuate the evils of the '*old system*'.[127] At the same time he was conscious that only a full revival of the potato could bring Ireland through its present crisis.[128]

'Sketch of the Revolution of 1848', in *Journals kept in France and Italy from 1848 to 1852* (edited by M.C.M. Simpson, 2 vols., London, 1871), I, 1–8.

124 Wood to Russell, 9 April, Russell Papers, PRO 30/22/7B, fols. 249–54; Wood to Clarendon, 3 April 1848, Hickleton Papers, A4/185/2; *Spectator*, 20 May 1848.

125 *Fourth report from the select committee on Poor Laws (Ireland)*, P.P. 1849 (170), XV, 296–7 [Twisleton].

126 Dobree to Trevelyan, 5 April 1848, Treasury Papers, T64/367B/1; Sligo to Clarendon, 19 Nov., Clar. Dep. Ir., box 57. 'Improving' agriculturalists in the east of Ireland were also critical of the west's apparent refusal to abandon the potato system, Sandham Elly, *Potatoes, pigs and politics: the curse of Ireland, and the cause of England's embarrassments* (London, n.d. [1848]).

127 Clarendon to G. Grey, 4 May, Clar. Dep. Ir., letterbook II. Twisleton supported the works of the agricultural instructors, but they were regarded with some contempt by the Chancellor, Twisleton to Trevelyan, 16 Sept., Wood to Trevelyan, 14 Sept. 1848, Treasury Papers, T64/366A.

128 Clarendon to Reeve, 21 Jan. 1848, Clar. Dep., c. 534/1.

Reports of the reappearance of the blight, 'more mysterious than ever', came before the government in July.[129] Trevelyan, who had committed himself to the view that the Famine was over, confidently predicted that 'the plant will outgrow [the disease] as it did last year', before responding to worsening reports by leaving matters in 'the hands of Providence'.[130] Clarendon, on the other hand, braced himself for the worst, believing that the failure would be greater than that of 1846, and that consequently 'nine tenths of the present ratepayers will be recipients of relief'.[131] The Viceroy's gloomy prognostications were partially realized. In mid September Somerville confirmed that around half the total crop had been lost, and that this was disproportionately weighted to the west and south.[132] The consequences for this region were indeed catastrophic; Clarendon anticipated that the poor whose 'constitutions are so broken that they are more than half rotten from all they have gone through', and who had 'been feeding more on hope than on meal', would 'now die in swarms'. Rentals had collapsed and the landlords and tenants rendered incapable of paying rates for poor relief.[133] Added to the threat of mass starvation was the arrival of a pandemic disease likely to devastate the weakened southern and western populations: '[they] will be swept away like Hindoos by the cholera', Clarendon informed his contact at the *Times*, 'and it will be almost a mercy that they should be spared more protracted suffering.'[134] The rest of the harvest offered little hope; the Irish wheat crop was mediocre and while oats and other grains were fairly good, little had been planted in the west.[135] Continuing huge grain imports kept food prices depressed throughout the British Isles, but Clarendon could only anticipate a 'winter of horrors' in the west of Ireland.[136]

The response of British public opinion to the 1848 failure was coloured by resentment over the 'ingratitude' most presumed to be embodied in the abortive Young Ireland rebellion of late July.[137] Greville shared the prevalent sense of

129 Broughton Diary, Add. MS 43,752, fols. 124 [8 July 1848]; R.W. Grey to Russell, 15 July, Russell Papers, PRO 30/22/7C, fols. 238–9; Clarendon to G. Grey, 7 Sept., Clar. Dep. Ir., letterbook III.

130 Trevelyan to Clarendon, 15 July, ibid., box 69; Trevelyan to Ommaney, 19 July, Trevelyan Letterbooks, Bodleian Library, Oxford (microfilm), vol. 22. Monteagle remarked sarcastically to the *Edinburgh's* editor that Trevelyan's next article should be entitled 'The Relapse', Monteagle to Empson, 23 Oct., Monteagle Papers, National Library of Ireland, Dublin, MS 13,398/6.

131 Clarendon to Russell, 5, 13, 14 Aug., Clar. Dep. Ir., letterbook III.

132 'Agricultural crops, Ireland, 1848', *Papers relating to . . . the relief of distress (seventh series)*, P.P. 1847–8 [999], LIV, 31–5; C.G. Gibbons to Jones, 20 Aug., Russell Papers, PRO 30/22/7C, fols. 363–4; Somerville to Wood, 11, 13 Sept., Hickleton Papers, A4/111; Clarendon to Russell, 28 Sept., Clar. Dep. Ir., letterbook III.

133 Clarendon to Russell, 15 Aug., Clarendon to Lansdowne, 18 Aug., ibid.

134 Clarendon to Reeve, 21 Aug., Clar. Dep., c. 534/1.

135 Wood to Russell, 6 Sept., Russell Papers, PRO 30/22/7D, fols. 7–13.

136 Erichsen to Trevelyan, 28 Nov., Treasury Papers, T64/366A; Clarendon to Lushington, 19 Nov., Clar. Dep., c.555.

137 *Illustrated London News*, 29 July.

'disgust . . . here at the state of Ireland and the incurable madness of the people'. Mass starvation was now, he believed, inevitable:

> the Irish will look in vain to England, for no subscription or parliamentary grants or aid of any sort, public or private, will they get; the sources of charity and benevolence are dried up; the current which flowed last year has been effectually choked by the brutality and ingratitude of the people, and the rancorous fury and hatred with which they have met our exertions to serve them. The prospect, neither more nor less than that of civil war and famine, is dreadful, but it is unavoidable.[138]

To the *Times* renewed famine was a further judgment of God, but of a different order to that of 1846. The continuing availability of cheap imported grain made the famine 'partial', and Ireland's aggregate wages fund would be sufficient to support the western destitute. 'John Bull' had learnt from the mistaken policy of seeking to conciliate 'Paddy', and would now insist on the imposition of strict moral and physical discipline for all classes.[139] Delane was at one with Wood in thinking that the habitual 'perversion' of British aid would make all but a minimalist policy unacceptable.[140] It was in vain that Fr Mathew protested to Trevelyan that 'we are not as we are represented'.[141]

Both the Prime Minister and Lord Lieutenant held Irish improvidence in the form of continued potato dependency to be a contributory factor in the renewed crisis. Clarendon sought to wean the people away from the belief that a 'revolutionary millennium' would end the catastrophe, while lecturing the landlords that, if the 1846 failure was 'a visitation of Providence against which no human foresight could guard', continued reliance on the potato was morally indefensible.[142] Despite these considerations, both ministers grasped the exigency of extraordinary assistance for the south and west.[143] News of the rebellion spurred Russell towards greater interventionism, in an attempt to compensate for such a spectacular failure of Foxite policy and to answer Tory and radical attacks on Whig 'misgovernment' of Ireland.[144]

---

138 Greville, *Journal*, III, 207–8 [21 July 1848].

139 *Times*, 28 Aug., 4 Oct.

140 Wood to Delane, 13 Sept., A.I. Dasent, *John Thadeus Delane, editor of 'The Times': his life and correspondence* (2 vols., London, 1908), I, 82–4.

141 Mathew to Trevelyan, 31 July 1848, Treasury Papers, T64/366A.

142 Clarendon to Oranmore, 4 Oct., Clar. Dep. Ir., letterbook III. Clarendon used secret service money to fund 'a weekly penny paper written in a popular style to shew how all the present evils of Ireland are caused or aggravated by agitation'. The paper's motto was 'Aid yourselves, and Heaven will aid you', Clarendon to Lewis, 1 Oct., Clar. Dep., c.532/1; Prospectus for *The Advocate: or Irish Industrial Journal*, Oct. 1848.

143 Clarendon to Russell, 25 Aug., Clar. Dep. Ir., letterbook III; Russell memo: 'On Mr. Gould's statement', 23 Sept., ibid., box 43.

144 [J.W. Croker], 'Ireland', *Quarterly Review*, LXXXIII (Sept. 1848), 584–614; W. Blanchard Jerrold, *An apology for the Irish rebels* (London, n.d. [1848]).

As soon as the blight was confirmed he urged the cabinet to agree to relief loans for those unions whose rates exceeded a certain maximum, or where it proved impossible to levy enough to feed the destitute, and to provide funds for useful public works and emigration.[145] The subsequent chain of events was depressingly similar to the previous year. Russell was unable to prevent the closing of the Commissariat's operations in Ireland by Treasury diktat, and the further curbing of drainage loans and other remedial projects on the grounds of retrenchment.[146]

It was now clear that Russell could only get further relief measures through his own cabinet and the Commons by building a wider political coalition around a common 'big idea'. Hence his decision in September to prepare a further 'comprehensive scheme' in collaboration with Clarendon and Redington that incorporated both Catholic endowment (acceptable to most Whigs, moderate liberals and Peelites), reproductive works, and assisted emigration (the favoured remedy of Irish landowners and many Protectionists).[147] Drawing on proposals made by Monteagle and Buller, Russell advocated a state subsidy to landlord-sponsored emigration from those western unions which unaided could 'never lift themselves out of the slough into which the loss of the potato has cast them'.[148] The announcement of his 'colonization' plans was enthusiastically welcomed by Monteagle and his allies, and supported even by some Irishmen sympathetic to the Treasury's position.[149] Monteagle provided Clarendon with blueprints for state assistance to landlord, Poor Law and voluntary efforts to promote emigration, and for ancillary public works in the colonies, and pointed to the success of the government's own emigration project from the crown estate of Ballykilcline as evidence of what could be done.[150] Hints of support from 'moderate' commentators in England for such a scheme may have persuaded Russell that it might pass through parliament.[151]

---

145 Russell to Wood, 11, 13 Aug. 1848, Hickleton Papers, A4/56/3.

146 Broughton Diary, Add. MS 43,753, fol. 22 [25 Aug.]; Trevelyan to Russell, 21 Aug., Russell Papers, PRO 30/22/7C, fols. 369–74; Trevelyan to Wood, 19 Sept., 1 Nov., Hickleton Papers, A4/59/1; Clarendon to Trevelyan, 21 Sept., Clar. Dep. Ir., letterbook III.

147 Clarendon to G. Grey, 25 July, ibid.; Russell to Clarendon, 11 Aug., Russell memo, 8 Sept., ibid., box 43. This grand plan was undermined by the collapse of the endowment proposals, see above, pp. 209–10.

148 Russell to Grey, 11 Sept., Grey Papers; Greville, *Journal*, III, 221 [5 Sept.].

149 'Propositions to be considered by the committee on colonization from Ireland', July 1848, Monteagle to Russell, 2 Nov., Russell Papers, PRO 30/22/7C, fols. 199–201, 7D, fols. 199–200; Monteagle to Russell, 18 Nov., Monteagle Papers, MS 13,398/6; More O'Ferrall to Trevelyan, 12 Oct., Treasury Papers, T64/366A.

150 Monteagle to Clarendon, 21 Oct., Nassau Senior Papers, National Library of Wales, Aberystwyth, C838. In 1847–8 the Woods and Forests Department spent some £2,500 to emigrate 409 people from Ballykilcline to New York. Despite 'systematic' planning and a much higher level of per capita expenditure than landlord-assisted emigrations, a considerable number 'disappeared' before reaching ship at Liverpool. For a detailed microstudy of the Ballykilcline case, see Robert J. Scally, *The end of hidden Ireland: rebellion, famine and emigration* (New York, 1995).

151 Pamphleteers concerned at the 'voluntary' Irish influx into Britain demanded overseas

Predictably, the new proposals ran into the blank wall of moralist dogma. Grey was quick to remind the cabinet of the spectre of disloyal Irish emigrants endangering the integrity of the colonies, especially now it was clear that both the United States and British colonies were hostile to the continuing Irish influx.[152] The financial arrangements also posed immediate and serious problems, but it was the ideological objections of moralists to a remedy that might allow Irish proprietors to slip off the hook that underlay their opposition. The Chancellor insisted on 'letting matters take their course' whatever the social consequences, and Grey argued that Ireland needed only 'energy, intelligence and industry in all classes of her inhabitants; the removal of artificial obstructions . . . to the occupation of land on terms favourable to industry, and confidence to induce capitalists to invest money in improvement', to allow her to support a far larger population. Russell's scheme would, he argued, disrupt healthy voluntary emigration and prove an expensive exercise in futility.[153] While he privately admitted that the clearance and emigration of small farmers was desirable for agricultural restructuring, Wood assured the Commons that the labouring population of even such notoriously distressed unions as Kilrush and Ballina was insufficient for their proper cultivation.[154]

While Russell and Clarendon rejected these 'extreme doctrines of the Economists', they were more alarmed when the *Times* ran a series of anti-emigration articles, which Clarendon believed to have been inserted 'at the express desire of the Colonial Office'.[155] Irish landlords also proved unexpectedly unwilling to contribute towards an emigration fund for the west; Clarendon anticipated as much trouble from the 'ignorant impatience of taxation' in Ireland as from the obstruction of Grey and Wood.[156]

The Lord Lieutenant's views on the subject were by late 1848 heavily influenced by western improving landlords, such as Monteagle and Redington, who hoped that the government would reverse the 'existing trend' of emigration of solvent tenants and undertake instead the removal of destitute smallholder and cottier

---

colonization as an 'imperial' remedy. See [Anon.], *An earnest plea for Ireland. By an Englishman* (London, 1848), pp. 8–16; [Anon.], *The Irish difficulty: addressed to his countrymen, by an Englishman* (London, 1848).

152 Grey to Russell, 6 Sept. 1848, Russell Papers, PRO 30/22/7D, fols. 16–17; *Times*, 5 Oct. 1847; Clarendon to Monteagle, 14, 20 Nov. 1848, Monteagle Papers, MS 13,398/2.

153 Greville, *Journal*, III, 237 (11 Nov.); Grey memo: 'Remarks on emigration, Poor Law and Ireland', 18 Dec. 1848, Grey Papers.

154 Wood to Trevelyan, 9 Sept. 1848, Treasury papers, T64/366A; *Hans.*, CII, 377–82 [7 Feb. 1849], ibid., CIII, 151–3 [2 March 1849].

155 Russell to Clarendon, 20 Dec., Clar. Dep. Ir., box 43; *Times*, 26 Dec. 1848, 3 Jan. 1849; Clarendon to Russell, 6 Jan. 1849, Clar. Dep. Ir., letterbook III. Delane acceded to Grey's preference for a 'slow and delicate' colonization, Grey Diary, 16 Jan., Grey Papers; *Times*, 16 Jan. 1849.

156 Clarendon to Monteagle, 26 Nov., Monteagle Papers, MS 13,398/2; Clarendon to Russell, 9 Dec., Clar. Dep. Ir., letterbook III.

families.[157] Clarendon had by the end of 1848 become persuaded that the west had been rendered permanently and absolutely over-populated with these classes, for whom no remunerative employment could be found in the future. Simply feeding the people would be futile, 'for if small holdings are abolished, farms are consolidated, and the rearing and feeding of cattle looked to as the profits of agricultural capital the population is undoubtedly redundant and must therefore be a pauper population.' In his view it had become necessary to 'sweep Connaught clean', through the removal of some 400,000 people, before regeneration could be possible.[158]

Russell was less indulgent towards the proprietors, whom he held responsible for the 'rottenness of the whole system', but he remained convinced of the economic and political expediency of some major remedial scheme.[159] Despite committing considerable political energy to his plan, he was unable to prevent it falling between the stools of moralist hostility to British advances, and Irish resistance to increased local taxation. To Clarendon's dismay, the Canadian railway plan was abandoned in mid-January, partly because of colonial reluctance to bear the bulk of the cost. Grey's initial support was too weak to withstand the moralist logic wielded by Wood and Trevelyan, while the rest of the cabinet was overawed by the difficulties of imposing a colonial timber duty to finance the railway, at a time when 'economy [was] all the rage' and free traders in the Commons highly sensitive to any hint of a Protectionist revival.[160]

This left only the option of an Irish rate in aid for emigration from the distressed unions coupled with a loan of one million pounds over three years. The Premier's threat to resign if the cabinet rejected this lesser scheme betrayed his deep frustration over Irish policy. He wrote to Clarendon: 'I feel that it is not right for you and me to go on with a policy with which we are not satisfied on the important question, "How is Ireland to be governed?".' Russell's adherence to the emigration loan was less the result of any fundamental attachment to the plan as such, than a reaction to the apparent bankruptcy of Foxite Irish policy, catalyzed by his acutely embarrassing admission to Graham that his government had no remedial proposals to balance the renewal of coercion in 1849.[161] It is symptomatic

---

157 Clarendon to Russell, 14 Dec., ibid.; Monteagle to Clarendon, 15 Dec. 1848, Monteagle Papers, MS 13,398/6. Many observers were alarmed at the flight of 'strong' tenant farmers to America under the combined weight of high rents, heavy poor rates and depressed agricultural prices, O'Sullivan to Trevelyan, 28 Aug. 1849, Treasury Papers, T64/366A.

158 Clarendon to Russell, 17, 26 Dec. 1848, Clarendon to Grey, 13 Jan. 1849, Clar. Dep. Ir., letterbook III.

159 Russell to Clarendon, 8 Dec. 1848, ibid., box 43.

160 Grey Diary, 20 Nov. 1848, Grey Papers; Russell to Clarendon, 25 Nov., 19 Dec. 1848, Clar. Dep. Ir., box 43; Clarendon to Russell, 18, 19 Jan. 1849, ibid., letterbook III; Clarendon to Monteagle, 28 Jan., Monteagle Papers, MS 13,399/6.

161 Graham to Peel, 16 Jan. 1849, Peel Papers, British Library, London, Add. MS 40,452, fols. 315–19; Russell to Clarendon, 5 Feb., Clar. Dep. Ir., box 26.

both of Russell's demoralization and the weakness of his position, that Clarendon dissuaded him from pressing his resignation by pointing out the relative insignificance of the already heavily circumscribed plan in the context of the 'great danger' facing the country.[162]

With moralists hostile to further grants, and moderates to the rate in aid, Russell was only able to secure a vague agreement that was subject to the concurrence of the forthcoming parliamentary committee on the Irish Poor Law.[163] Russell attempted to bring the income tax and emigration question before the cabinet again on 8 February, but faced with Grey's implacable opposition, and 'having nobody to give me real support', he 'was obliged either to submit, or break up the Government'. The abandonment of the government grant effectively neutered the proposal; instead of emigration being the government's '*cheval de bataille*' for 1849, it had been relegated to a 'mere palliative'.[164] Even the residual rate in aid for emigration ultimately fell victim to the Poor Law Committee's desire for the lowest possible rate, and to Treasury foot-dragging. Trevelyan remained hostile towards using any public money for such a purpose, as it 'would do much real mischief by encouraging the Irish to rely upon the Government for emigration which is now going on at a great rate from private funds'.[165]

The consequence of the failure of extraordinary aid and remedial projects was the abandonment in 1848–9 of the population of the west to sufferings that equalled or exceeded those of 'Black '47'. Trevelyan's attempts to enforce punitive rates and his order that all grants to Poor Law unions should cease from October 1848 caused great concern for many public officials in Ireland.[166] Some would eventually leave the service and attack their former masters, but others turned to ideological rationalizations of the sufferings they witnessed daily. Captain Pole, the Poor Law inspector at Sligo, was a personal friend and close ally of Trevelyan and a convinced evangelical.[167] His letters were written in a deeply religious tone

---

162 Russell to Clarendon, 17 Jan., Clar. Dep. Ir., box 43; Clarendon to Russell, 19 Jan., ibid., letterbook III.

163 Russell to Clarendon, 20, 27, 29 Jan., ibid., box 26. Lansdowne rejected the rate in aid and favoured only the use of rates raised by individual unions to assist the emigration of their own paupers, Lansdowne memo: 'On emigration', 31 Jan., Hickleton Papers, A4/107. For his own efforts to assist pauper emigration from his Kenmare estates in 1850–1, see W. Steuart Trench, *Realities of Irish life* (1868, reprint, London, 1966), pp. 64–74.

164 Russell to Clarendon, 8, 11 Feb. 1849, Clar. Dep. Ir., box 26; Clarendon to Russell, 21, 30 Jan., 3 Feb., ibid., letterbook III.

165 Grey Diary, 8 Feb., Grey Papers; Lansdowne to Wood, 27 June, Trevelyan to Wood, 31 Aug. 1849, Hickleton Papers, A4/107, A4/59/2.

166 Twisleton to Trevelyan, 17 Sept., 4 Oct. 1848, Treasury Papers, T64/366A. Trevelyan also vetoed the distribution of clothing from Ordnance stores on the grounds that it would 'prolong the habit of dependence on Government aid', marginal note on Twisleton to Trevelyan, 9 Nov., ibid.

167 In his opinion, Ireland's great misfortune was that the Reformation had never reached it, Pole to Trevelyan, 11 Nov. 1848, ibid.

and were suffused with moralistic justifications. In his opinion, the Poor Law was the 'saving principle' that would restore Ireland to a 'healthy social condition'. It had revealed the true corruption of that society:

> The veil which had so long concealed apparent wealth is withdrawn, and a mortgage-eaten bankruptcy is dissolved. The veil which hid specious prosperity is upheld and discovers hypocritical Pride labouring to deceive itself and the People: – the veil beneath which the pretended Reformer, the rampant Repealer, the imaginative Republican, and the desperate adventurer all worked, is torn aside; discovering to the country how near pretended Patriotism may be to real Poverty, and a love of Publicity to a dread of honest industry. The Power which has raised this veil is the Poor Law.

Pole was certain that the 'deceitful state of property and society' should be held responsible for shedding 'the blood of tens of thousands during the last few years'. However, the Poor Law was already transforming the country, and would produce prosperity and full employment within seven years.[168] Trevelyan endorsed Pole's optimism, adding only the typical evangelical reservation that '"ye have the poor *always* with you" – "The poor shall *never* cease out of the land".'[169]

The rate in aid

The collapse of Russell's land tax scheme had ominous consequences for the provision of food aid and employment in the west. In November 1848 Redington announced that the Poor Law Commissioners had again been obliged to reopen outdoor relief generally, and indicated that in twenty-two 'hopeless' unions extraordinary financial assistance would be required.[170] The British Association funds had run out in July 1848, and the Treasury grant extracted by Russell for the explicit purpose of feeding children in schools made up the shortfall only until October.[171] The consequences were predictable. In the western unions, it was reported in March 1849, 'deaths are now so frequent as almost to escape observation'. The parish priest of Swinford observed that as a result of the union's bankruptcy, those on relief were 'expected to live for a fortnight on an allowance scarcely sufficient for three days'.[172] The Protestant incumbent at Louisburgh, who was 'hourly beset with crawling skeletons begging for food', reported a similar state of affairs in Westport union.[173]

168 Pole to Trevelyan, 19 Dec. 1848, ibid.
169 Marginal note in Trevelyan's handwriting on Pole to Trevelyan, 16 May 1849, ibid.
170 Redington to Clarendon, 13, 17 Nov. 1848, Clar. Dep. Ir., box 24/2.
171 G. Grey to Clarendon, 19 Dec. 1848, ibid., box 12; *Second report of the Commissioners . . . for the relief of the poor in Ireland*, P.P. 1849 [1118], XXV, 109.
172 *Freeman's Journal*, 17, 23 March 1849.
173 Ibid., 17 Feb. 1849.

The government was well-informed of this human cataclysm, but believed it could not evade the fact that 'the patience and finances of England are dried up, and its assistance will be furnished with reluctance and parsimony;' it was thus extremely wary of risking further advances.[174] As a result, Clarendon's warnings that 'the Religion and charity of John Bull will in the end revolt' against the consequences of 'leaving things "to the operation of natural causes"', fell on stony ground. The Viceroy was reduced to endorsing the Irish fury 'with C. Wood and Trevelyan who sit coolly watching and applauding what they call "the operation of natural causes".'[175] Russell despairingly pointed out that it was less the 'crude Trevelyanism' of the moralists than feelings lying 'deep in the breasts of the British people' that made substantive intervention politically impracticable.[176]

A Prime Minister heading a weak administration with little control over the Commons could not ignore the political climate. In the wake of the *Times*' warning that 'there is no such card in the pack as another great Irish grant', and to believe otherwise would prove fatal to the ministry, Greville noted that the government was so uneasy about the threat posed by the 'new economical agitation' that they 'are moving heaven and earth in the way of reduction'.[177] With Cobden channelling his energies into a new Financial Reform Association agitation in early 1849, it became clear that the elimination of 'financial extravagance' had 'taken a firm hold on the opinion of the country'.[178]

The parliamentary reaction to Russell's proposal in February of a £50,000 grant for urgent food aid to distressed areas dispelled any lingering doubts.[179] With Russell again threatening resignation if it failed, only a core of radicals voted against; but Graham, Disraeli and the *Times*, who all represented 'constituencies which [had] become savage and hard-hearted towards the Irish', insisted that there

---

174 Lewis to Head, 24 Nov. 1848, Gilbert Frankland Lewis (ed.), *Letters of the Rt. Hon. Sir George Cornewall Lewis, Bart., to various friends* (London, 1870), pp. 188–9. Wood derived some amusement from Russell's caution, Wood to Russell, 16 Dec. 1848, Russell Papers, PRO 30/22/7D, fols. 296–303.

175 Clarendon to G. Grey, 13, 16 Dec. 1848, Clarendon to Russell, 6 Dec., Clar. Dep. Ir., letterbook III; Clarendon to Lewis, 29 Dec., Clar. Dep., c.532/1.

176 Russell to Clarendon, 8 Dec. 1848, Clar. Dep. Ir., box 43; Russell to Clarendon, 24 Feb. 1849, ibid., box 26.

177 *Times*, 12 Jan. 1849; Greville *Journal*, III, 260 [19 Jan.]. John O'Sullivan tried in vain to persuade the *Times*' editorial team to change their line on Ireland: 'I could plainly see . . . that the "*Times*" was England. I found the most extravagant absurd monstrous stories regarding my unhappy country received with implicit credence simply because it was in the "*Times*", and I longed to make the acquaintance of some if its proprietors to try and find way occasionally into it for some statements on which the English people might depend.' O'Sullivan to Trevelyan, 2 April 1849, Treasury Papers, T64/366A.

178 *Illustrated London News*, 6, 13 January.

179 Clarendon approved Russell's 'refusal to take the pledge' that this would be the last, Clarendon to Russell, 10 Feb., Clar. Dep. Ir., letterbook III; *Hans.*, CII, 433–6 [7 Feb.: Russell].

must be no more.[180] The *Times*' leader on the subject throws particular light on the government's relationship with the press. The rhetoric was familiar:

> 'It is the last ounce that breaks the camel's back,' and it must be confessed that this fresh grant of 50,000*l.* to Ireland has almost broken the back of English benevolence . . . We believe the real reason to be the total absence not merely of gratitude, not merely of respectful acknowledgements, but of the barest 'receipt' for all these favours.[181]

What is of interest is the authorship of the leader, which was 'put in' by Wood, and published by Delane in preference to the more conciliatory article requested by Clarendon. Despite the Lord Lieutenant's personal connections with the paper's staff, and their willingness to endorse his calls for coercion, ideological commitment combined with a sense of what the public wanted to read to determine a hostile editorial line.[182]

The price exacted for the parliamentary grant was a declaration that in future the burden of relief would fall on a 'local' fund, a rate in aid imposed on all Irish unions to support those distressed unions whose rates exceeded a certain maximum.[183] Russell, in common with the Irish government, would have preferred the imposition of the income tax, but found that the difficulties of creating the necessary machinery in the limited time available, and the resistance of much of Irish opinion to this more permanent tax, again made this impossible.[184] Lansdowne threatened resignation over the rate in aid, but was dissuaded when Russell pointed out that with the prevailing opinion in the cabinet against an income tax, it would be very difficult to get through the Commons.[185] Clarendon acceded reluctantly to Russell's observation that without the rate in aid, nothing further could be extracted from parliament,[186] but, as he had predicted, the Bill was strongly

---

180 Greville, *Journal*, III, 266–8 [9 Feb.]; Broughton Diary, Add. MS 43,753, fols. 99, 101, 102 [8, 12, 16 Feb.]; *Hans.*, CII, 374–433 [7 Feb.]; *Times*, 8, 9, 10 Feb.

181 *Times*, 12 Feb.

182 Greville to Clarendon, 13 Feb., Clar. Dep., c.522. The paper did subsequently carry a Clarendonian piece criticizing the use of Ireland as a party shuttlecock, but rapidly returned to demanding an acceleration of reconstructive measures and punishment of the landowners, *Times*, 13, 19 Feb.

183 Graham's strong advocacy of this option was seized on by moralists in vindication of their own preferences, Greville to Graham, 9 Feb., Graham Papers, bundle 106; G. Grey to Clarendon, 8 Feb., Clar. Dep. Ir., box 13; Wood to Russell, 11 Feb., Russell Papers, PRO 30/22/7E, fols. 278–81.

184 Clarendon to Russell, 3, 14 Nov. 1848, Clar. Dep. Ir., letterbook III; Russell to Clarendon, 22, 25 Jan. 1849, ibid., box 26; *Hans.*, CIII, 313 [6 March: Russell].

185 Russell to Lansdowne, 9, 12 Feb., Lansdowne to Russell, Feb. 1849, 15 Feb., G.P. Gooch (ed.), *The later correspondence of Lord John Russell, 1840–78* (2 vols., London, 1925) I, 233–5.

186 Clarendon to Russell, 14 Feb., Clar. Dep. Ir., letterbook III; Russell to Clarendon, 17 Feb., ibid., box 26. Palmerston reluctantly agreed, Palmerston to Clarendon, 3 March, Clar. Dep., c.524.

opposed in Ireland and was fought bitterly at each stage as an unfair imposition, a threat to the solvency of the north and east, and a denial of the integrity of the Act of Union.[187]

Two unexpected shocks provoked the cabinet into a reconsideration of its minimalist policy in March 1849. The first was the sudden resignation of Edward Twisleton as Chief Poor Law Commissioner on the grounds 'that the destitution here is so horrible, and the indifference of the House of Commons to it so manifest that he is an unfit agent of a policy that must be one of extermination.'[188] Twisleton's disillusionment with the relief regime had been growing over the winter, and he made it clear that Treasury interference with the Commission's activities and sole reliance on the rate in aid had placed him in a position 'that no man of honour or humanity can endure'.[189] A strong advocate of a regional policy, and a believer in 'imperial' responsibility for the fate of Ireland, he had previously urged Clarendon to press for continued state assistance to the distressed western unions for another two or three years, accompanied by a maximum rate and assisted emigration.[190] In the context of extensive famine mortality, Clarendon could only echo Twisleton's charge and condemn the 'constant negatives' of the legislature and Treasury, while Russell sympathized with Twisleton's motives and thought his opinions had 'great weight'.[191]

Once unfettered by public office, Twisleton was able to state unreservedly his opinions before the parliamentary select committees on the Irish Poor Law.[192] He reserved his sharpest censure for the Treasury and its rhetoric of 'natural causes':

> there are many individuals of even superior minds who now seem to me to have steeled their hearts entirely to the sufferings of the people of Ireland, and who justify it to themselves by thinking it would be going contrary to the provisions

187 Clarendon to Russell, 12 Feb., Clar. Dep. Ir., letterbook III; Monteagle to Clarendon, 24 Feb., Monteagle Papers, MS 13,399/8; Isaac Butt, *The rate in aid: a letter to the Rt. Hon., the Earl of Roden* (Dublin, 1849); James Grant, 'The Great Famine and the Poor Law in Ulster: the rate-in-aid issue of 1849', *Irish Historical Studies*, XXVII (1990), 30–47.

188 Clarendon to Russell, 10, 12 March 1849, Clar. Dep. Ir., letterbook IV.

189 Twisleton to Clarendon, 9, 10, 13 March, ibid., box 29.

190 Twisleton to Clarendon, 2 Jan., ibid. Twisleton also complained of the 'wonderfully small' expenditure on outdoor relief, adding that 'Mr Poulett Scrope and others might say that we were slowly murdering the peasantry by the scantiness of the relief. The weak point is that nothing whatever . . . is allowed for clothes, fuel, soap, or any thing else except food. This is defensible perhaps in the very peculiar circumstances of Ireland – but it is altogether contrary to the principle on which relief is administered in England, and affords consequently a topic for animadversion.' Twisleton to Trevelyan, 21 Jan. 1849, Treasury Papers, T64/366A. See also Twisleton to Trevelyan, 15 Nov. 1848, 26 Feb., 24 March 1849, ibid.

191 Clarendon to Russell, 26, 28 April, Clar. Dep. Ir., letterbook IV; Russell to Clarendon, 11, 13 March, ibid., box 26.

192 Even before his resignation Twisleton had made it clear that he would place the responsibility for mass mortality on the Commons, Twisleton to Wood, 22 Feb., Hickleton Papers, A4/181.

> of nature to give any assistance to the destitute in that country. It is said that the law of nature is that those persons should die . . . and that you should let them alone; there is thus a sort of philosophical colour given to the theory or idea, that a person who permits the destitute Irish to die from want of food is acting in conformity with the system of nature. Now my feeling is, that it is wholly the contrary; that it is part of the system of nature that we should have feelings of compassion for those people, and that it is a most narrow-minded view of the system of nature to think that those people should be left to die; that because the material elements do not produce sufficient food for them at the time, they are to perish, and their brothers in the rest of the empire are to look on and let them die . . . I believe it is part of the system of nature that we should feel compassion for them and assist them.[193]

This was one of the clearest statements of ethical humanitarianism of the Famine era, made by a senior official who refused to put the transformation of Irish society before the preservation of life in the face of an unprecedented catastrophe.[194]

Twisleton was not the only senior Poor Law official to speak out against the prevailing policy in 1849. John Ball, who had already resigned from ill-health as Assistant Poor Law Commissioner, attacked moralist assumptions in print. Trevelyan and his allies in the British press, about whom Ball was particularly scathing,[195] were upbraided for consistently under-rating the scale of the losses suffered by Ireland over the previous four years. For Ball, the already vulnerable Irish wages fund had now been stretched to breaking point by the imposition of the full costs of famine relief, a policy that combined the 'grossest infraction of justice, and the most insane defiance of common sense'. The solution lay not in abandoning relief to the able-bodied, but in making the workhouse test again practicable through a combination of relieving proprietors who employed pauper labour, estate-rating, a maximum rate (with top-up funds supplied by the Treasury where necessary), and relieving the burden through state assistance to emigration and arterial drainage.[196]

---

193 *Fourth report from the select committee on Poor Laws (Ireland)*, P.P. 1849 (170), XV, 299. For Twisleton's public reasons for resignation, see *Fifth report from the select committee on Poor Laws (Ireland)*, P.P. 1849 (148), XV, 329–33.

194 Twisleton insisted that the crisis be treated as a temporary aberration, noting that the potato disease had ceased to be virulent in North America, and suggesting that it would also pass in Ireland, *Fourth report*, P.P. 1849 (170), XV, 314; *Sixth report from the select committee on Poor Laws (Ireland)*, P.P. 1849 (194), XV, 370, 400.

195 'When the history of the time is fairly written, the same stern condemnation which awaits those who, forgetful of recent benefits, could only seek to excite in Ireland a blind hostility against England, will not less surely be awarded to those who contributed to the same object by embittering the feelings of Englishmen towards Ireland, and by making the very benefits conferred by them wear the garb of injuries.' John Ball, *What is to be done for Ireland?* (2nd edn, London, 1849), p. 26.

196 Ibid., pp. 32–42, 49–86.

In the wake of Ball's critique, even the more compliant Assistant Commissioner, Alfred Power, was prepared to criticize Trevelyan's *Irish crisis*, albeit anonymously.[197]

The second shock to the government was the announcement of Peel's 'plantation scheme', which exposed the remedial vacuity of government policy, and drew the support of many concerned at the apparent *laissez-faire* dogmatism of the administration.[198] The remedial projects envisaged by Peel – drainage, land improvement, road and harbour building – mirrored much of what Russell had been attempting to get piecemeal through the cabinet in the previous months, and the scheme generally reflected Ball's concerns over the wages fund. Where it differed markedly from both was in the proposal to abandon outdoor relief under the Poor Law and immediately restore a rigorous and mandatory workhouse test to curb pauperism. Even if Peel's infrastructural works had been accepted by parliament (and the prospects for this were poor in early 1849),[199] relief officials were aware that the scheme threatened to return the west to the disastrous conditions witnessed during the later stages of the Labour Rate Act works.[200] Many of the western 'able-bodied' were in fact severely malnourished and disease-prone after four years of hunger, and another major upheaval in the relief mechanism would probably have consigned to death many of those then barely clinging to life. Peel, like many of his contemporaries, gave a higher priority to reconstructing the Irish economy, and maintaining the value of Irish landed property, than to preserving life. His 1849 'plantation' proposals were intended primarily as auxiliaries to facilitate the operation of an Encumbered Estates Bill, but when the government took up the latter, he quietly dropped his insistence on a superintending 'commission' for Connacht.[201]

Whatever Peel's intentions, some government ministers felt shamed by the absence of a ministerial remedial project. Clarendon, who came over from Dublin to throw his personal weight behind a new departure, responded by presenting

---

197 [Power], *Irish Poor Law*, p. 18. Power was, however, prepared to see a rate in aid replace direct parliamentary grants, which he considered demoralizing, ibid., pp. 46–7.

198 *Hans.*, CIII, 179–92 [5 March], CIV, 87–117 [30 March 1849]; Clarendon to G. Grey, 10 March, Clar. Dep. Ir., letterbook IV; *Illustrated London News*, 10, 31 March, 7 April.

199 Stanley had rejected any extensive scheme of state emigration or waste-land reclamation, looking instead to local or individual initiative, *Speech of Lord Stanley, February 9, 1849, on the . . . appointment of a select committee to consider the operation of the Irish Poor Law* (London, 1849), pp. 27–35.

200 For the hostility of relief officials to any return to primary relief by public works, see *Final report from the Board of Public Works, Ireland, relating to the measures adopted for the relief of distress in July and August 1847*, P.P. 1849 [1047], XXIII, 725; [Power], *Irish Poor Law*, pp. 48–50; *Fourth report from the select committee on Poor Laws (Ireland)*, P.P. 1849 (170), XV, 315 [Twisleton].

201 Poulett Scrope's alternative proposal of a 'labour rate' was open to similar charges. See G. Poulett Scrope, *A labour rate recommended in preference to any reduction in the area of taxation, to improve the operation of the Irish Poor Law* (London, 1849); *Fourth report . . . on Poor Laws*, P.P. 1849 (170), XV, 316–22 [Twisleton].

the cabinet with memoranda by Redington and the Commissioners of Public Works for major railway and arterial drainage projects. If supported by the income tax, these would, he declared, be 'the best rate in aid we can contribute'.[202] The cabinet's support was at best half-hearted, and Russell felt that he had no mandate to press ahead with the scheme on his own authority. The initiative subsequently collapsed, to the disgust of Clarendon, when Russell placed the choice of income tax or rate in aid before a special meeting of Irish members. Despite the strong lobbying of Monteagle and Fitzwilliam for the former, the Irish MPs were unable to agree in private, and subsequent divisions in the House carried only the latter.[203] The struggle over the rate in aid continued to the end of the session, with parliament grudging any advances while it remained in limbo despite the exhaustion of the £50,000 grant in April, and there was radical opposition even to the £100,000 eventually advanced on the credit of the rate.[204] The western and southern poor, meanwhile, were left to the mercy of a system that was collapsing into 'a chaos of insolvency' and which lacked the means to cope with the added burden of a cholera pandemic and the consequences of mass evictions.[205]

Individual or collective responsibility?

One consequence of throwing the relief of distress on to the rate in aid was to exacerbate the already growing political polarization over the Poor Law system. Pressure for the amendment of the Law had been building amongst the Irish landowners for some time, particularly with respect to the most contentious issues of 1847 – the rating of smallholdings, the provision of outdoor relief, and the size of unions and electoral divisions.[206] Their campaign took on momentum with the publication of Nassau Senior's swingeing critique of the operation of the Act in the *Edinburgh Review*, and the adherence of Stanley to the view that 'the Poor Law in the south and west had broken down, and had been proved a failure from first to last.' Outdoor relief and the activities of the Dublin Poor Law Commissioners and their paid vice-guardians were condemned as impediments to the concentration of the landowner's resources on the improvement of his property. The 'individualizing of responsibility', through making boundaries coterminous with estates, reinstating elected boards, and removing all obstacles to proprietorial control over his land, tenantry and labourers, was demanded by these advocates of orthodox

202 Clarendon to Russell, 14, 16 March, Clar. Dep. Ir., letterbook IV; Russell to Clarendon, 16 March, ibid., box 26; Redington to J. Wood, 6 April, Redington to C. Wood, 12 April, C. Wood to Redington, 10 April, Hickleton Papers, A4/61.

203 Fitzwilliam to Monteagle, 10, 17 April, Monteagle Papers, MS 13,399/7; *Times*, 17, 20 April.

204 *Hans.*, CIV, 467–70 [19 April 1849: Wood, Hume].

205 Clarendon to Russell, 14 May, Clar. Dep. Ir., letterbook IV; G. Grey to Clarendon, 24 July, ibid., box 13; Power to Wood, 26 May, Hickleton Papers, A4/181.

206 Clancarty to Monteagle, 10 Oct. 1848, 'Resolutions of the provincial meeting in Ballinasloe', 6 Oct., Monteagle to Bourke, 23 Oct., Monteagle Papers, MS 13,398/1.

economics.[207] Irish landowners met in February 1849 to co-ordinate their attacks on Twisleton and the Commission and to prepare for the coming session, although Trevelyan's informant at the 'Poor Law Parliament at Dublin' kept the government abreast of their plans.[208]

The government resorted to select committees of inquiry into the Poor Law in both Houses as a calming measure, in the hope that 'when they had quarrelled over their different panaceas and one nostrum had neutralized the other, the Government might have more chance of interposing with effect and extracting something practical out of incoherent ideas and contradictory evidence.'[209] Whately was sure that they would 'be merely a blind, to quash all discussion in the House', but, like Senior, had he had no overarching remedy to offer in place of what he regarded as a fundamentally flawed Poor Law.[210]

The government was, however, actively considering some amendments. Although critical of Senior's article, Clarendon found himself persuaded by the appeals of 'improving and energetic landlords', and argued that it was now vital to amend the Poor Law mechanism in such a way as to distinguish between good and bad landlords, and to assist the former.[211] The enlightened public opinion represented by Lord Devon and John Pitt Kennedy should, he thought, be indulged by the adoption of smaller taxation districts.[212] An increase in the number of unions had already been accepted in principle, but the implementation of this was expected to be complex and slow.[213] More contentious was the matter of making the electoral

207 Monteagle to Empson, 23 Oct. 1848, ibid., MS 13,398/6; [N.W. Senior], 'The relief of distress in 1847 and 1848', *Edinburgh Review*, LXXXIX (Jan. 1849), 221–68; *Speech of Lord Stanley, Feb. 9, 1849, on the . . . Irish Poor Law.* Senior was more blunt than most moderates in asserting the absolute character of Irish over-population and insisting on the necessity of diminishing the number of people by any means. The article was privately endorsed by Lansdowne and Whately, Senior to Lansdowne, 2 Dec. 1848, Whately to (?), 8 Jan. 1849, Senior Papers, C218, C868.

208 W. Fairfield to Trevelyan, 17 Feb. 1849, Treasury Papers, T64/366A.

209 Clarendon to Russell, 7 Dec. 1848, Clar. Dep. Ir., letterbook III. For the success of the committee in doing this, particularly on the contentious question of outdoor relief, see Montague, 'Relief and reconstruction', pp. 216–26.

210 Whately to Senior, 23 Jan. 1849, Senior Papers, C689.

211 Whately to Senior, 30 Jan. 1849, ibid., C690; Clarendon to Lewis, 12 May 1848, Clar. Dep., c.532/1; Clarendon to Russell, 18 Dec. 1848, Clar. Dep. Ir., letterbook III. The Viceroy was particularly influenced by the writings of John Hamilton of St Ernans, Donegal. See H.C. White (ed.), *Sixty year's experience as an Irish landlord: memoirs of John Hamilton* (London, n.d.), pp. 220–33.

212 Kennedy had waged a sustained campaign for the individualization of responsibility since the spring of 1847 on the grounds that proprietorial investment in land improvement in the west and south was futile as long as the responsible landowner was obliged to carry the burden of the negligence of his neighbours, John Pitt Kennedy, *Correspondence on some of the general effects of the failure of the potato crop, and on the consequent relief measures, with suggestions as to the re-construction of the Poor Law electoral and rateable divisions* (Dublin, 1847), pp. 21–48, 51–7.

213 Clarendon to Somerville, 13 Feb., Clarendon to Russell, 30 Oct. 1848, Clar. Dep. Ir., letterbooks II, III.

6. While the crop grows Ireland starves, *The Puppet-Show*, 13 May 1849. To some observers in spring 1849 neither Russell's rate-in-aid plan nor Peel's plantation scheme appeared to offer much in the way of immediate aid to a country suffering a fourth year of famine.

7. The new Irish still: showing how all sorts of good things may be obtained (by industry) out of peat, *Punch*, Aug. 1849. John Leech's Smilesian allegory epitomised the moralist attitude towards Irish poverty and famine, and coincided with the optimism accompanying the Queen's visit to Ireland: industry alone was required to render Irish people prosperous and contented.

divisions coterminous with estates, as this raised the disputed issue of whether Irish proprietors were to be held responsible as individuals for their own properties, or as a class for the general state of society. At the end of 1848 the Irish government agreed on Twisleton's plan of a number of moderate reforms, stopping short of anything that might encourage further clearances.[214]

Stiff ideological opposition to concessions came from Wood and Grey, who argued that closed electoral divisions would lead to the sort of increased inertia and indolence of the labourers and oppression by the landowners which had characterized the 'reign of pauperism' under the old English Poor Law.[215] Moralists and radicals declared the landlords to be responsible as a class, and reminded them that it was the exposure of their flawed agricultural system by a 'dispensation of Providence', and not the Poor Law, which was causing Ireland's misery.[216] Any weakening of the integrity of the Act, which was based on 'a principle of nature', was rejected. The 'wonderful social revolution' believed to be under way in Ireland was not to be impeded by vain attempts to save the landowners from the bankruptcy and removal they deserved.[217] Moralists believed in the localization but not the individualization of responsibility, as they held peer pressure under the weight of shared taxation to be the most effective spur to moral improvement.

Russell's gut reaction was also strongly anti-landlordist. Historical forces were, he told Clarendon, at the root of the present situation: 'The grinding treatment of the poor by the landlords of the last century has brought down a heavy retribution on the well-meaning proprietors of the present day.' The landlord campaign against the Poor Law provoked a strong outburst of frustrated Foxism:

> Time out of mind the landlords of Ireland have exercised the rights of property, squeezing by means of agents, police and military the utmost rents out of their tenants and performing none of the duties of property . . . In receiving rent and in collecting rent, began, continued, and ended their work as proprietors. Suddenly the foundation of the whole system the potato fails – and at the same time Parliament by a righteous law provided that the whole calamity should not fall on the wretched poor but should be shared by the proprietors. Hence the tears and groans of the Irish landlords – their own recklessness, cruelty and extravagance are made the scourges to flog their backs – and they make an outcry against the Government – and English legislation.[218]

It was this conception of the extended Poor Law as an act of social justice to the Irish poor, which co-existed in Russell's mind with more conventional justifications,

214 Clarendon to Lewis, 29 Dec. 1848, Clar. Dep., c.532/1.

215 Grey memo: 'Remarks on emigration, Poor Law and Ireland', 18 Dec. 1848, Grey Papers. George Grey's inclination towards giving way on the question was seen as weakness, Grey Diary, 5 Dec. 1848, ibid.

216 *Hans.*, CII, 374–8 [7 Feb. 1849: Wood].

217 *Times*, 4, 11 Jan. 1849; Trevelyan to Clarendon, 26 Feb., Clar. Dep. Ir., box 60.

218 Russell to Clarendon, 1 Oct., 20 Dec. 1848, ibid., box 43.

that Senior went to some length to refute in 1849. In his view the doctrine at the heart of Foxite Whiggery, that 'popular' English political and social institutions should be extended to Ireland as an act of 'justice' was a dangerous fallacy. The very Irish social backwardness highlighted by famine – 'a calamity which cannot befall a civilized nation' – made the English Poor Law inapplicable there.[219]

Although Russell's condemnation of Irish landlordism did still find an echo in the words of some representatives of the 'popular' interest in Ireland,[220] it lacked the analytical depth and coherence required to answer the imperative questions of 1849. Other priorities in Irish policy, apparently more urgent than the provision of 'justice', made him susceptible to Clarendon's case for a number of moderate concessions to help those proprietors prepared to 'turn away from the wickedness they have committed'.[221] The Prime Minister continued to believe that 'a transition from a state of the population living upon their own plots of ground, to a state of the population consisting chiefly of farmers and labourers' was unavoidable, and would ultimately remove the causes of 'the perpetual war of one class against another'. Yet he argued that this process would be gradual and that government was obliged to further it as much as possible.[222] Appealing to the Prime Minister, the Irish government also concentrated on the importance of encouraging employment. Redington reported that high rates dissuaded tenants from taking or remaining on the uncultivated tracts of the west, and Clarendon urged that the errors of the 1847 Act – the inevitable result of 'groping in the dark' – be admitted and rectified.[223]

The meeting of parliament drew Clarendon and Russell together. The Lord Lieutenant expressed disgust at the behaviour and language of many Irish MPs, but at the same time he impressed on Russell the necessity of showing 'some deference to the wishes of honest Irishmen' as a *quid pro quo* for the rate in aid.[224] To meet these just complaints Russell agreed to set a maximum rate on electoral divisions, supplemented when the rate was five and seven shillings respectively by union and national rates in aid, to provide greater security to the occupier, and to allow some reduction in the size of electoral divisions and unions along the lines recommended by Thomas Larcom's Boundary Commission.[225] These were proposed

219 Senior, 'The relief of Irish distress in 1847 and 1848', *Journals*, I, 208–28.

220 See, for example the savagely anti-landlord views expressed by Fr John O'Sullivan of Kenmare. O'Sullivan supported the Poor Law – 'the only poor man's law that was ever passed for Ireland' – which 'while it may press hard upon us, it must needs be utter ruin and destruction in the end to that heartless class who countenanced, and fostered, and encouraged the unnatural state of things in which we hitherto moved.' O'Sullivan to Twisleton, 10 Dec. 1848, O'Sullivan to Trevelyan, 5 Feb. 1849, Treasury Papers, T64/366A.

221 Clarendon to Russell, 22 Dec. 1848, Clar. Dep. Ir., letterbook III.

222 *Hans.*, CII, 617–18 [12 Feb. 1849].

223 Clarendon to Russell, 1, 9 Jan. 1849, Clar. Dep. Ir., letterbook III.

224 Clarendon to Russell, 10 Feb., ibid.

225 For the rationale of Larcom's commission, see *First report of the select committee of the House*

to the committee as being vital for 'the encouragement of industry and the promotion of the cultivation of the soil'. There was, however, no question of introducing 'estate rating', a system which would discriminate against the class of small proprietors Russell was anxious to promote, and which would provide a further inducement to bad landlords to proceed with mass evictions rather than give employment or assist emigration. The suggestion of a law of settlement to mitigate the latter danger was, however, rejected by Russell as an impediment to the voluntary circulation of labour, and as an attempt to reduce the population to 'the miserable condition of absolute serfs'.[226] The Prime Minister had come to share Torrens McCullagh's opinion that it was wise to preserve the western landlords from bankruptcy, as 'they could not destroy one class of the community without ruining others, dependent upon them to a greater or less extent.' Sound policy required that they let 'them remain where they were, but compel them to do their duty'.[227]

Moralists were less magnanimous towards the existing owners, but acquiesced in the Poor Law amendments out of a desire to promote the sale of estates unencumbered with excessive rate arrears.[228] Smaller electoral divisions were also accepted as likely to provide greater discipline and restraint in the provision of relief – a concern which united moralists and moderates against the central Poor Law authorities.[229] Wood's obsession with the moral superiority of 'self-government' and local responsibility provoked him into campaigning against the rule of appointed vice-guardians in Ireland. Twisleton's Benthamite concern for administrative order had resulted in the appointment of 'really efficient individuals' to these posts and a staunch defence of their records, but following his replacement as Chief Poor Law Commissioner by the weaker Alfred Power in March 1849 many elected boards were restored.[230] Humanitarian observers deplored the corruption and abuse that ensued; Sidney Godolphin Osborne identified the worst failings of the Poor Law in 1849–50 as resulting from the neglect of the 'green book' of workhouse regulations by the poorly supervised elected boards.[231]

The passage of the Poor Law Amendment Bill in July 1849 was seen by some as an unexpected success, but Russell was disappointed that the Lords had struck

---

of Lords, appointed to inquire into the operation of the Irish Poor Law, and the expediency of making any amendment in its enactments, P.P. 1849 (192), XVI, 831–43 [Larcom].

226 *Hans.*, CIII, 99–105 [2 March]. Russell continued to regard evictions as an obstacle to his vision of Irish 'improvement', but saw no practicable way of countering them, Russell to Clarendon, n.d. (May 1849), 15 June 1849, Clar. Dep. Ir., box 26.

227 *Hans.*, CIII, 285–8 [6 March 1849: McCullagh]; Russell to Clarendon, 24 Dec. 1848, Clar. Dep. Ir., box 12.

228 *Hans.*, CIII, 228 [5 March 1849: G. Grey].

229 Wood to Power, 25 May 1849, Hickleton Papers, A4/185/2.

230 Wood to Somerville, 9 Sept. 1848, ibid., A4/111; Clanricarde to Clarendon, 31 Dec. 1848, Clar. Dep. Ir., box 9; Twisleton to Trevelyan, n.d. (1848), 13 Sept. 1848, Treasury Papers, T64/368B, 366A; Wood to Russell, 6 Jan. 1850, Russell Papers, PRO 30/22/8C, fols. 203–8.

231 S.G. Osborne, *Gleanings in the west of Ireland* (London, 1850), pp. 118–39.

out both the union rate in aid and statutory maximum rate.[232] British and Irish public opinion was equally damning of the Act's perceived pro-landlord bias. The report of the Lords committee had been denounced by the *Times* as an attempt to evade the proprietorial responsibility for the state of the country proclaimed by the 1847 Act: 'From that providential enforcement it is impossible that we should ever recede; and when the Lords start with reminding us of the original Poor Law, we only remember how signally PROVIDENCE has convicted and reproved their own miserable shortcomings, and how little they are entitled to special consideration in the amendment of the Poor Law.'[233] Russell and Clarendon subsequently pressed for a rapid redivision of unions, but were hampered by Treasury obstructiveness over the allocation of union debts and the issuing of bridging advances until new rates could be levied. It was not until later in 1849 that construction began on the first of the thirty-three new union workhouses.[234]

III 'DISPOSED OF BY A HIGHER POWER', 1849–50

The established pattern of Russell's response to the continuing problem of Irish famine – bursts of enthusiasm for remedial schemes alternating with gloomy and fatalistic public declarations of the inevitability of suffering and the limitations of government capabilities – continued in the following season. His despair focused on the apparent inability of the government to address 'that general question which lies at the root of much of the distress of Ireland, the excessive cultivation of the potato on small patches, and the excessive reliance on that produce.'[235] Faced with the continuation of the crisis following a fourth potato failure in summer 1849, Russell drew the pessimistic lesson that it was impossible 'to invert the natural order, and to create employment for the people instead of allowing the people to grow up for employment.'[236]

As in 1848, two incompatible attitudes towards the potato crop co-existed uneasily. While Clarendon dreaded 'the results of a good potato harvest and all the false hopes and bad habits it will entail', he could only agree with Russell's opinion that 'a good crop of all kinds this year is the only thing which can save

232 Grey Diary, 31 July 1849, Grey Papers; Russell to Clarendon, 9 Aug., Clar. Dep. Ir., box 26; *Hans.*, CVII, 297–323 [13 July: Monteagle], ibid., 365–6 [16 July: Stanley].

233 *Times*, 10, 28 July 1849. For an Irish echo, see [Patrick McMahon], 'Ireland – spirit of recent legislation', *Dublin Review*, XXVII (Dec. 1849), 346–62.

234 Russell to Clarendon, 14 Aug., Clar. Dep. Ir., box 26; Clarendon to Wood, 31 Oct., ibid., letterbook V; Somerville to Wood, 30 Oct., Hickleton Papers, A4/111; Wood to Clarendon, 2, 23 Nov., ibid., A4/185/2. By 1849 union debts were often huge; in April the leading corn dealer in Limerick was owed £45,000 by nine unions and had ceased supplying them, J. Russell to Trevelyan, 26 April 1849, Treasury Papers, T64/366A.

235 *Hans.*, CIV, 214–27 [2 April 1849].

236 Russell to Clarendon, 4 Sept. 1849, Clar. Dep. Ir., box 26.

Ireland from dreadful scenes in the next two or three'.[237] The government had been advised that early planting on well-drained land could limit the damage of the blight, but neglected to make this widely known for fear of encouraging 'planting of potatoes in any quantity'.[238] The reappearance of the blight, 'this calamitous infliction of the will of the Almighty, ruler and disposer of events', was reported by a Poor Law inspector in Skibbereen as early as the end of May.[239] A failure to the extent 'which may be useful in keeping alive the recollection of what a precarious resource it is', was welcomed by some ministers, but the disproportionate distribution of the loss to the south-west ensured another season of suffering there.[240] The consequences for the poor in such unions as Kilrush threw the Lord Lieutenant into despair, as he believed that they were now beyond the reach of remedial assistance. 'The wretched people', he wrote to Russell, 'seem to be human potatoes, a sort of emanation from "the root" – they have lived by it and will die with it.'[241]

Prospects for British expenditure on relief aid or remedial schemes did not improve despite the ending of commercial recession. As in 1847, a good grain harvest and a largely sound potato crop in most of the country appeared to indicate the cessation of famine and hence the redundancy of extraordinary aid.[242] Yet localized failures and the effects of clearance perpetuated famine conditions in some places. In May 1850 County Clare still had 30,000 on outdoor relief and 12,000 workhouse inmates.[243] The continuation of localized distress appeared to British moralists to be self-inflicted, and at the same time necessary for the 'working of a gigantic remedy'. Trevelyan rejected intervention in the western counties using the medical metaphor employed so frequently about Ireland in the period: 'what the patient now requires in *rest and quiet and time for the remedies which have been given to operate.* Continual dosing and dependence upon physicians is not good either for the body politic or corporate.'[244]

---

237 Clarendon to Russell, 26 July, ibid., letterbook IV; Russell to Clarendon, 29 July, ibid., box 26. Peel also feared the return of a 'delusive' prosperity, which would 'check that tendency to permanent improvement – which is the one counter-balancing good, engendered by severe suffering', Peel to Monteagle, 14 Sept., Monteagle Papers, MS 13,399/2.

238 Lindley to Trevelyan, 14 May, Trevelyan to Russell, 14 May, Treasury Papers, T64/366A. Lindley gave his final opinion on the subject in June: 'None but the Irish would be "alarmed" at the consequences of their own imprudence. They have been warned often enough: and I see no prospect of further advice being of the slightest utility.' Lindley to Trevelyan, 5 June, ibid.

239 J.F. Robertson's report, 29 May, ibid.

240 Lansdowne to Wood, 19 Aug., 12 Sept., Hickleton Papers, A4/107; Clarendon to Russell, 2 Aug., Clar. Dep. Ir., letterbook IV.

241 Clarendon to Russell, 14 Oct., ibid.

242 Clarendon to Russell, 21 Aug., ibid.; Russell to Clarendon, 3 Dec. 1849, ibid., box 26.

243 *Third annual report of the Commissioners for administering the laws for the relief of the poor in Ireland,* P.P. 1850 [1243], XXVII, 467.

244 *Times,* 5 July; Trevelyan to Wood, 16 Sept., 20 Oct. 1849, Hickleton Papers, A4/59/2.

Wood's insistence on the political and fiscal necessity of a budgetary surplus for 1849–50 was given added weight by the continuation of the retrenchment campaign, in which radicals had now been joined by Protectionists protesting against the agricultural distress brought on by the collapse in agricultural prices.[245] The government anticipated, and suffered, a number of defeats on its financial measures as a result of this political realignment.[246] Nevertheless, some observers complained that Irish expenditure was being sacrificed to protect more politically popular items. Greville found it 'disgusting to see Wood and Trevelyan worrying everybody to death with twopenny halfpenny economies, straining at gnats', while swallowing the 'huge camel' of Palmerston's pet policy of the anti-slave trade African naval squadron.[247]

In this context it was hardly surprising that Irish landowners' efforts to reopen the colonization debate using the language of imperial destiny fell on deaf ears.[248] Attempts to revive the Redington proposals also foundered, despite Clarendon's appeal for added employment on land improvement, arterial drainage and railway construction to give the country 'breathing space' for recovery, to conciliate Irish opinion, and to attract 'Saxon capitalists'.[249] As before, the cabinet refused to contemplate Russell's renewed suggestions for a land or income tax on Ireland, and the issuing of loans secured on the anticipated surplus.[250] All that was conceded, and that after 'great difficulty', was the rescheduling of repayments of relief loans over forty years and a delay in the first instalment until after the 1850 harvest.[251] Russell later extracted an additional £300,000 loan to liquidate the debts owed to contractors by the bankrupt unions, and to facilitate the formation of the new unions.[252] However, in 1852 Ireland still remained subject to a Famine-related annuity debt of £4,422,951 (with an additional £3.3 million in anticipated interest charges), a burden which many regarded as unsustainable.[253]

---

245 Wood to Russell, 1 Sept., Russell Papers, PRO 30/22/8A, fols. 124–9; Russell cabinet memo, 3 Dec. 1849, Clar. Dep. Ir., box 26. The price depression was due in part to 'immense imports from America', Greville to Clarendon, 17 Sept. 1850, Clar. Dep., c.522.

246 Greville, *Journal*, III, 321–2 [8 March 1850].

247 Greville to Clarendon, 17 Jan., 19 March 1850, Clar. Dep., c.522.

248 [Aubrey De Vere], 'Colonization', *Edinburgh Review*, XCI (Jan. 1850), 1–62.

249 Clarendon to Russell, 29 Nov., 8 Dec. 1849, Clarendon to Wood, 11 Dec. 1849, Clar. Dep. Ir., letterbook V. Russell was enthusiastic about state railway construction, Russell to Wood, 12 Nov., Hickleton Papers, A4/56/4

250 Russell to Clarendon, 18 Nov. 1849, Clar. Dep. Ir., box, 26; Russell to Wood, 19 Jan. 1850, Hickleton Papers, A4/56/4. Another 'grand scheme' involving Catholic endowment was again raised and dropped as politically inexpedient, Russell to Clarendon, 8, 22 Nov. 1849, Clar. Dep. Ir., box 26.

251 Russell to Clarendon, 13, 17 Dec. 1849, 2 Feb. 1850, ibid.

252 *Hans.*, CVIII, 823–33 [15 Feb. 1850].

253 The Labour Rate Act debt, which comprised over half the total, was singled out as particularly unjust, *Report from the select committee of the House of Lords on the Treasury minute, providing for the debts due from counties and unions in Ireland by the imposition of a consolidated annuity*, P.P. 1852 (585), VI, 1.

Unable to induce the cabinet to comply with Clarendon's requests for something more than 'such palliatives . . . unsuited to the magnitude of the crisis', Russell remained prey to those 'evils still haunting me . . . [which] include the state of Kilrush union'. He continued to denounce the 'harsh Trevelyanism' of the moralists, and took a critical view of the measures adopted previously: 'It is idle to talk of "natural causes" – the acts of Parliament of 1846 and 1847 are no doubt the efficient causes of much of the present difficulty'.[254] Yet when checked he found it easy to adopt convenient rationalizations. One was to voice despair over the efficacy of intervention in Ireland and to put faith in *laissez-faire* and the stimulation of voluntary migration by 'a flourishing state of Lancashire and Belfast'.[255] Like many contemporaries, Russell was tempted to look for glimmers of hope from the Encumbered Estates Act – the single major Irish Act of 1848–9. Even the British Association's former agent Count Strzelecki voiced similar sentiments:

> Considering the salutary change which has taken place within the last three years in the Irish character, as regards the opinions, tendencies, habits, and general spirit of the various classes of the community, the prosperity of Ireland can be but a matter of time. No doubt its attainment may be accelerated, and in great measure will depend upon the rate at which the transfer of the encumbered property proceeds; that change is an essential preliminary to the full development of the resources of the soil, and to the profitable employment of that large class of able-bodied labourers who, now maintained on out-door relief, press severely upon the community at large, and upon the solvent ratepayers in particular.[256]

Another, perhaps more congenial resort, was to place the responsibility firmly on the shoulders of the proprietors, whom Clarendon was more reluctant to defend in the wake of the 1849 harvest and their continued toleration of the 'potato mania'.[257] Differing reports from the west, contrasting the peaceable and solvent condition of well-managed estates such as Redington's and Gregory's, with the troubled state of properties owned by some of the more vociferous proprietors, added to this impression. Clanricarde's apocalyptic accounts of the state of County Galway were undermined by Clarendon's observations on the 'wretchedly managed' state of his Portumna estate.[258] Clarendon himself was prepared to wash

---

254 Clarendon to Russell, 31 Dec. 1849, Clar. Dep. Ir., letterbook V; Russell to Clarendon, 28 Dec., ibid., box 26. The sufferings of the poor at Kilrush were associated with the notoriously harsh evictions carried out in the previous two years. These were publicly and graphically exposed in the *Illustrated London News*, 15, 22, 29 Dec. 1849; Osborne, *Gleanings*, pp. 14–35; *Report of the select committee appointed to enquire into the administration of the Poor Law in the Kilrush Union since 19 September 1848*, P.P. 1850 (613), XI, 529.

255 Russell to Clarendon, 19 Oct. 1849, Clar. Dep. Ir., box 26.

256 Strzelecki, 'To the subscribers of the fund raised in June 1849, for the relief of distress in Ireland', 3 Oct. 1849, Treasury Papers, T64/366A.

257 Clarendon to Bedford, 25 Aug., Clarendon to Russell, 27 Aug., Clarendon to Peel, 2 Sept. 1849, Clar. Dep. Ir., letterbook IV.

258 Clarendon to Russell, 19 Dec. 1849, 16 Jan. 1850, ibid., letterbook V; Clanricarde to Russell,

his hands of the continuing social crisis in the impoverished west once it was clear that 'more potatoes than ever' had been sown in 1850. 'The Irish', he concluded, 'are a nation of devils from the highest to the lowest'.[259]

Perhaps the most damaging case of all to the western lords was the circulation of a lengthy account of his tour of the west by Lord Dufferin, the young Ulster landlord of Peelite persuasions who as a student had helped expose the appalling condition of Skibbereen in early 1847.[260] Dufferin spared nothing in his denunciation of western landlordism:

> If ever the parable of Dives and Lazarus had an antitype, it is in Ireland. Providence has placed in the hands of these gentlemen the education and existence of a numerous tenantry – it was evidently their lot in life, as it might have been their glory, like Noah of old, to have mitigated the curse upon the earth and gradually to have made them capable of all those joys and happiness which are still within the reach of men, instead of which they thought only of themselves and their own enjoyment. They left their people to grow up and multiply like brute beasts, they stifled in them by their tyranny all hope and independence and desire of advancement, they made them cowards and liars, and have now left them to die off from the face of the earth.

He concluded that, in general, 'the present class of proprietors must and will be swept off the surface of the earth', and replaced with men who would employ and improve the people.[261] Such views confirmed Russell's prejudices, and appeared to endorse the idea of the Encumbered Estates Act as Ireland's panacea.

Russell's response to the continuing appeals from the west of Ireland was, he believed, in line with that of English public opinion. Responsibility, he argued, lay not with the state but with the proprietors both as individuals and as a class, and also with the people insofar as they continued to take the unwarranted risk of depending upon the potato.[262] Rather than publicly acknowledge that the government had pursued policies that had exacerbated Irish suffering and social conflict, particularly in the latter years of the Famine, Russell sought refuge in public self-justifications that obscured his own private doubts, confusion and defeats. A

---

11 Jan. 1850, Russell Papers, PRO 30/22/8C, fols. 171–2; Clarendon to G. Grey, 11 Jan. 1850, Clar. Dep. Ir., letterbook V.

259 Clarendon to Lewis, 17 March 1850, Harpton Court Papers, National Library of Wales, Aberystwyth, C/1047.

260 Lord Dufferin and G.F. Boyle, *Narrative of a journey from Oxford to Skibbereen during the year of the Irish Famine* (2nd edn, Oxford, 1847).

261 Lord Dufferin to Lady John Russell, 10 Sept. 1849, Russell Papers, PRO 30/22/8A, fols. 181–4 (incomplete), also in Desmond MacCarthy and Agatha Russell (ed.), *Lady John Russell* (London, 1910), pp. 104–5. Dufferin, 'an indulgent and a generous landlord . . . [who had] met the present difficulties of his tenantry by a voluntary sacrifice of rent', was appointed by Russell to a place in the royal household and a representative Irish peerage shortly afterwards, Graham to Russell, 26 Oct. 1849, Russell Papers, PRO 30/22/8B, fols. 167–8, Dufferin to Russell, 28 Dec. 1849, ibid., 8C, fols. 115–16.

262 Russell to Clarendon, 13 Jan., 26 Oct. 1850, Clar. Dep. Ir., box 26.

fatalistic and passive reliance on providence was evident when he stated to the Commons in February 1850 his belief that Ireland was best left to be 'disposed of by a higher Power'.[263]

Attacks on the government's record, particularly from the respected English philanthropic publicist and clergyman, Sidney Godolphin Osborne, were particularly embarrassing. Clarendon had welcomed Osborne to Ireland in summer 1849 as 'a witness whom the British public are disposed to believe',[264] but despite praise for Clarendon's administration and concentration on the misdeeds of local authorities and landowners, Osborne did not absolve the government of responsibility for its failures:

> I do not see how any policy of a government could have done more than was done at the early stages of this wretched crisis . . . I cannot, however, acquit the Government of all blame, in those matters I am now seeking to expose. This is not a year of famine; the people have starved in many hundreds, I believe, within the last twelvemonth, *in the face of an abundance of cheap food.* They have starved under the working of a law especially directed to meet the case of the destitute. I have no hesitation in adding my firm conviction, that very many have been *done to death* by pure tyranny . . . I cannot get rid of a very strong impression I entertain . . . that there was a sort of tacit determination to let things take their course, at any cost.[265]

This was a damning but accurate verdict on the Russell administration's handling of the Famine.

The government had chosen through a combination of commission and omission to pursue policies originating in the moralist agenda which philanthropists such as Osborne denounced. Its rationale was articulated by Anthony Trollope, who had served as a Post Office official in Munster during the Famine years, and who wrote to the *Examiner* in 1849 to defend the government's record against Osborne's charges. Trollope declared bluntly that the 'severity of circumstances ordained by Providence' had been necessary to promote the anglicization of Ireland's morals and society. The task of government, and of the English capitalist and improving commercial farmer prepared to take land under the Encumbered Estates Act, was to complete the work begun by the Famine: 'to encourage industry, to do battle with sloth and despair; to awake a manly feeling of inward confidence and reliance on the justice of Heaven.'[266] It was such popular moralist sentiments, rather than Russell's residual ideals of 'justice to Ireland', or the orthodox political economy of Senior and Lansdowne, that dominated the making of relief policy between 1847 and 1850.

---

263 *Hans.*, CVIII, 828–33 [15 Feb. 1850].

264 Clarendon to Russell, 28 June 1849, Clar. Dep. Ir., letterbook IV.

265 Osborne, *Gleanings*, pp. 254–6.

266 Anthony Trollope, *The Irish Famine: six letters to the Examiner 1849–50* (ed. L.O. Tingay, London, 1987) pp. 13, 29.

Conclusion

> [T]he poverty of the Exchequer . . . [is], I should say, but a relative term, as money can be got if the Nation wills it, and would be forthcoming if the necessity of it were proved either for foreign war or internal famine. It surely is equally the office of the Executive to protect from the latter as from the former and deliberately to allow a man innocent of all crime to perish for economy's sake would amount almost to an abdication of government.
>
> *Marquess of Sligo*, 19 November 1848[1]

> The remedies have been due partly to the Divine Providence and partly to human exertions. Many years ago the Political Economy Club of London came, as I was told, to a resolution that the emigration of two millions of the population of Ireland would be the best cure for her social evils. Famine and emigration have accomplished a task beyond the reach of legislation or government; and Providence has justly afflicted us by the spectacle of the results of the entire dependence on potato cultivation, and by the old fires of disaffection which had been lighted in the hearts of Irishmen, and are now burning with such fierceness on the banks of the Hudson and the Potomac.
>
> *John, Earl Russell*, 1868[2]

The lasting impression of the 1840s as an era in Anglo-Irish relations is one of failure and lost opportunities, particularly in the related fields of land reform and famine relief. This is all the more significant given the apparent fluidity of Irish policy in the middle years of the decade. Peel's dramatic 'conversion' to Irish reform in 1844 raised (temporarily) the possibility of a political *rapprochement.* O'Connell's land reform platform, assembled amid the social and political excitements of the immediate pre-Famine years, represented an important development in his politics. The positive response of the Foxite Whigs and a handful of British radicals, exhibited in defiance of economic orthodoxy and against the trend towards cross-party liberal consolidation in Britain, created the potential for a reform initiative that pre-dated by some twenty years the next serious attempt to solve the Irish land

1 Sligo to Clarendon, 18 Nov. 1848, Clarendon Deposit Irish, Bodleian Library, Oxford, box 57.
2 John, Earl Russell, *A letter to the Rt. Hon. Chichester Fortescue, MP, on the state of Ireland* (2nd edn, London, 1868), pp. 11–12.

question through interference with landed property rights. The abortive outcome was due in part to the onset of the potato failure and the consequent upheavals of the Great Famine. The catastrophe had the effect of setting the public opinion of each country against the other over the costs of relief, and of prioritizing questions of economic development that appeared antithetical to land reform proposals couched in the language of 'justice'. The more radical economic prescriptions advanced at the time proved incapable of displacing orthodox opinions now reinforced by the language of evangelical providentialism. The immediate political consequence of the Famine was to compromise the political traditions in Ireland and Britain that had been involved in the renewed reformist compact of 1846; Foxism and O'Connellism were among the many victims of the potato blight.

The failure of land reform was also due in part to its internal contradictions and to the political limitations of its proponents. The inclusiveness of O'Connell's Repeal movement from 1843 led him to gloss the social frictions within Irish Catholic community and the 'peasantry' by phrasing his demands in the amorphous rhetoric of 'justice to Ireland' and evading potentially divisive points of detail. This strategy was not of itself an impediment to political success – Parnell was later to hold the fissiparous class alliance of the Land League together by similar means in 1879–82 – but amid the sharpening social tensions associated with famine conditions, and in the less capable and distinctly uncharismatic hands of his immediate successors, O'Connellite rhetoric proved inadequate.

Russell's position was also beset with confusion. From 1846 he faced a cabinet deeply divided over the meaning and direction of Whiggery, and containing a majority sceptical towards the Foxite tradition. He never commanded more than the conditional allegiance of many of his colleagues, and the premiership visibly accentuated the flaws of his leadership style – his coolness towards all but his closest political intimates, his tendency to seize radical policy initiatives unilaterally and without much deliberation or preparation, and to show a lack of determination and resolution when checked. His unwillingness (or inability) to articulate publicly the strong opinions often expressed in his private correspondence disappointed some of his colleagues.[3] The repeated demonstration of these flaws combined with differences over the substance of his policies to alienate liberal moderates and moralists within his party coalition. Illness throughout much of 1848 compounded Russell's problems by reinforcing the underlying perception that he was 'weak and inefficient *as a leader*'.[4] By 1850 Russell remained head of the Whig-Liberal Party and Prime Minister largely by default.

3 Clarendon complained: 'if he will only speak in the House of Commons as he has written to me, he will . . . lead the malcontents into co-operating with him instead of drawing them into open hostility.' Clarendon to Lewis, 29 Dec. 1848, Clarendon Deposit, Bodleian Library, Oxford, c.532/1.

4 Greville to Clarendon, 3 June 1848, ibid., c.521.

The content of Russell's Irish policy was also problematic. The Foxite style was to a great degree reactive – an attempt to respond positively and constructively to 'just' Irish demands. A reform agenda was agreed in 1846 through the Bessborough-O'Connell entente, with some additional contributions from radical British economists, and the Lord Lieutenant's Waste Lands Bill and his proposed landlord-tenant measure were attempts to implement as far as was practicable a shared programme of 'justice to Ireland'. The death of Bessborough and the collapse of Irish popular politics into incoherent atomism and conspiratorial plotting set Russell adrift; his subsequent initiatives – particularly the tenant right proposals of late 1847, and the comprehensive Prussian land bank, Farmers' Estate Society and Encumbered Estates Bill schemes of 1848 – contained elements of social radicalism, but these were quickly abandoned in the face of orthodox hostility. Any hopes that a British middle-class public opinion radicalized by its struggle against protection and sympathetic to O'Connell's demand for 'justice' would promote Irish reform proved premature. Anti-landlord feeling transferred instead into a campaign for 'free trade in land' that was hostile to Russell's proposals for an extension of state interference with private contracts and private enterprise.

Perhaps the most significant aspect of Russell's failure was his inability to grasp the changing character of the land question during the Famine once many landlords expressed their determination to clear their lands for pasturage.[5] Although Clanricarde and Palmerston made no secret of their opinion that tillage farming, particularly in the west, was to be discontinued as economically unviable, Russell clung to the hope that 'improved' mixed farming would provide employment for most of the 'surplus' population of Ireland.[6] It is clear from his private correspondence that he was convinced of the need for state intervention to promote this end, ideally through the emulation of the 'Prussian agricultural system', but he lacked the weight to push land reform through a reluctant cabinet and parliament, and responded to his failure with a series of public rationalizations which fell back upon orthodox conceptions. Russell was confused by the tensions between his inherited Foxite conception of popular government and the more sophisticated and hegemonic language of *laissez-faire* liberalism, from which he was not immune. As Peter Mandler has indicated, social and political changes in the later 1840s contributed to the creation of an environment in which Foxite ideas appeared increasingly redundant.[7]

5 *Hansard's Parliamentary Debates*, 3rd series, CV, 1359–60 [11 June 1849]; CVI, 1042 [28 June: Glengall]. Some landowners were more calculating than others. See Donald E. Jordan, *Land and popular politics in Ireland: County Mayo from the Plantation to the Land War* (Cambridge, 1994), pp. 111–18.

6 Peel was also obstinate in his belief in the efficacy of 'high farming' as the solution to Irish agricultural difficulties, and James Caird's advocacy of such a settlement received the imprimatur of both Peel and Clarendon as late as 1850, James Caird, *The plantation scheme; or, the west of Ireland as a field for investment* (Edinburgh and London, 1850).

7 Peter Mandler, *Aristocratic government in the age of reform: Whigs and Liberals 1830–1852* (Oxford, 1990), pp. 267–82.

It is unquestionable that during the Famine the Russell administration failed the people of Ireland in what it publicly accepted as being the first duty of government – preventing mass famine mortality. This is not just the judgment of hindsight, but an opinion shared by many well-informed contemporaries within and outside the administration, including, in their more introspective exchanges, both the Prime Minister and the Irish Viceroy.

Of course full allowance must be made for factors beyond government control: the sheer scale and unpredictability of the ecological disaster, the unfortunate correspondence with a period of European food shortage and domestic financial difficulty, and the relatively unsophisticated administrative mechanisms available. State intervention to secure an entitlement to food for the most vulnerable sections of Irish society often encountered fierce resistance from local elites and self-interested imposture from individuals who were far from destitute.[8] Yet despite these obstacles the inescapable conclusion remains that the state failed to make optimum use of its resources to contain the number of deaths, especially in the later stages of the Famine from the autumn of 1847.

This policy failure was due in large measure to the success of the dominant faction in the government in prioritizing another, ideologically-driven, agenda – that of grasping the heaven-sent 'opportunity' of famine to deconstruct Irish society and rebuild it anew. Liberal moralists were prepared to play a deadly game of brinkmanship in their campaign to impose a capitalist cultural revolution on the Irish.[9] Their intention was not genocidal, nor was it grounded in any Malthusian assumption of the necessity of Irish depopulation; rather it was the fruit of a powerful social ideology that combined a providentialist theodicy of 'natural laws' with a radicalized and 'optimistic' version of liberal political economy. God and nature had combined to force Ireland from diseased backwardness into healthy progressive modernity; any unnecessary suffering incurred in the transition was the result of human folly and obstruction, and could not be attributed to the will of God or to those who understood his purposes and acted accordingly.[10]

The regular references made to the 'abuse' of the relief mechanisms need also to be read in this context. In an environment of social collapse and acute individual competition for scarce resources, some maldistribution and 'wastage' of relief

8 David Fitzpatrick, 'Famine, entitlements and seduction: Captain Edmond Wynne in Ireland, 1846–1851', *English Historical Review*, CX (1995), 596–619. Fitzpatrick uses the case of Wynne to highlight the local pressures exerted on relief officials and the temptations for them to abuse their powers. The very singularity of the case (Wynne was the subject of two parliamentary enquiries, in 1847 and 1850) suggests the need for caution in generalizing from such microstudies.

9 For the obsession with the breaking of the 'false principle [of dependency] which eats like a cancer into the moral health and physical prosperity of the people', see C.E. Trevelyan, *The Irish crisis* (London, 1848), pp. 158–63, 183–91.

10 Wood to Bessborough, 16 Sept. 1846, Hickleton Papers, Cambridge University Library (microfilm), A4/185.

goods was inevitable. The state recognized this as a problem, and gave a high priority to reducing it by introducing disincentive elements directed at the poor and property owners alike. Many of these innovations were ill-advised, but it is clear that the shift from public works to direct feeding by soup kitchen did prove to be the most effective form of delivering relief entitlements to those most in need. For moralist administrators and opinion-formers, however, identifying and eradicating 'abuse' acquired a higher priority than saving lives. Their fetishization of the idea directly reflected their behaviouralist construction of the underlying 'Irish problem'. Dealing with what was ultimately a marginal problem was elevated to the organizing principle of state policy.[11]

This moralist fixation was recognized and vigorously attacked by some contemporary commentators who attributed the scale of the human catastrophe to a combination of the imposition of a delusive social theory and the avarice of ruthless landlords. One such was the *Illustrated London News*' Irish correspondent, who wrote from amid the ruins of the cleared villages of west Clare in late 1849:

> The present condition of the Irish . . . has been mainly brought on by ignorant and vicious legislation. The destruction of the potato for one season, though a great calamity, would not have doomed them, fed as they were by the taxes of the state and the charity of the world, to immediate decay; but a false theory, assuming the name of political economy, with which it has no more to do than the slaughter of the Hungarians by General Haynau, led the landlords and the legislature to believe that it was a favourable opportunity for changing the occupation of the land and the cultivation of the soil from potatoes to corn. When more food, more cultivation, more employment, were the requisites for maintenance of the Irish in existence, the legislature and the landlords set about introducing a species of cultivation that could only be successful by requiring fewer hands, and turning potato gardens, that nourished the maximum of human beings, into pasture grounds for bullocks, that nourished only the minority.

Measures allegedly introduced to give 'justice' to the people had merely added to their suffering:

> The Poor Law, said to be for the relief of the people and the means of their salvation, was the instrument of their destruction. In their terrible distress, from that temporary calamity with which they were visited, they were to have no relief unless they gave up their holdings. That law, too, laid down a form for evicting the people, and gave the sanction and encouragement of legislation to exterminating them. Calmly and quietly, but very ignorantly – though we

11 This obsession blinded officials to the counter-productive consequences of their policies. Wood and Trevelyan's insistence that 'responsibility' for Poor Law relief be restored to elected boards of guardians in 1848–9 led to a marked increase in local corruption and abuses in the west. See S. Godolphin Osborne, *Gleanings in the west of Ireland* (London, 1850), pp. 6–13.

> cheerfully exonerate all parties from any malevolence – they not only committed a great mistake, a terrible blunder, which in legislation is worse than a crime – but calmly and quietly from Westminster itself, which is the centre of civilization, did the decree go forth which has made the temporary but terrible visitation of a potato rot the means of exterminating, through the slow process of disease and houseless starvation, nearly half of the Irish.[12]

This sense that Ireland had been betrayed by the British government and parliament was by no means restricted to the nationalist zealots of Young Ireland.[13]

Contemporaries frequently contrasted the relatively meagre expenditure by the state on Irish relief with both the large outlay on the military establishment and the £20 million voted in 1833 to compensate the West Indian planters for the emancipation of their slaves.[14] The total state expenditure for Irish famine relief in 1845–50 amounted to around £8 million (over half of this advanced as loans),[15] a fraction of the £69 million expended on the Crimean War of 1854–6.[16] The unhindered expenditure on imperial adventures in southern Africa and the Indian subcontinent in the later 1840s was contrasted by Ireland's senior relief official with the Treasury's refusal to disgorge even 'the comparatively trifling sum with which it is possible for this country to spare itself the deep disgrace of permitting any of our miserable fellow subjects . . . to die of starvation'.[17] It is difficult not to sympathize with Twisleton's despairing comment that compared with keeping the Irish poor alive, 'of how much less permanent importance is the conquest of Scinde or of the Punjaub for the greatness of the Empire!'[18]

---

12 *Illustrated London News*, 15 Dec. 1849. This paper was one of the few in Britain to pursue a humanitarian line in the later stages of the Famine. This account, with its accompanying series of sketches, was probably by the same James Mahony of Cork who had exposed the state of Skibbereen in early 1847.

13 The classic nationalist 'history' of the Famine used similar language but attributed malign intention to the government, John Mitchel, *The last conquest of Ireland (perhaps)* (London, n.d. [1860]), pp. 219–20.

14 Sligo to Clarendon, 18 Nov. 1848, Clar. Dep. Ir., box 57; *Cork Examiner*, 16 Dec. 1846; William Henry Smith, *A twelve month's residence in Ireland* (London, 1848), pp. xi–xii. Despite the 'rage of economy' the military budget suffered only marginal reductions in the period, M.S. Partridge, 'The Russell cabinet and national defence, 1846–1852', *History*, 72 (1987), 231–50.

15 *Report from the select committee of the House of Lords on the Treasury minute, providing for the debts due from counties and unions in Ireland by the imposition of a consolidated annuity*, P.P. 1852 (585), VI, 4. The remaining debt was forgiven in 1853, in return for Gladstone's extension of the income tax to Ireland. The concession was opposed in the cabinet by Charles Wood, *Hans.*, CXXV, 1402–3 [18 April 1853: Gladstone]; John Morley, *The life of William Ewart Gladstone* (2 vols., London, 1905), I, 465–7.

16 Joel Mokyr, *Why Ireland starved: a quantitative and analytical history of the Irish economy, 1800–1850* (London, 1985 edn), p. 292.

17 *Second report of the select committee of the House of Lords, appointed to inquire into the operation of the Irish Poor Law, and the expediency of making any amendment in its enactments*, P.P. 1849 (228), XVI, 717 [Twisleton].

18 Twisleton to Clarendon, 10 March 1849, Clar. Dep. Ir., box 29.

Russell's conspicuous Irish failures, compounded in 1850–1 by his insensitive handling of the ecclesiastical titles issue, contributed to his loss of prestige and ultimately of the Whig-Liberal leadership after 1852. The liberal amalgamation looked for by so many 'moderates' in the 1840s did not come smoothly, but as Russell was eclipsed it was liberalism of the Palmerstonian and Peelite varieties that dominated the following decade and a half.[19] As Britain entered a period of sustained economic boom after the upheavals of the 1830s and 1840s, economic moralism lost its edge and was also absorbed into the liberal mainstream. Charles Wood concluded that the heroic age of free-trade reform had ended with the repeal of the Navigation Acts in 1849 and henceforward the role of government had ceased to be pro-active.[20]

Irish land legislation in this period was marked by a reassertion of orthodoxy, with popular moralist writers enthusiastically joining the campaign to negate the Irish tenant right movement.[21] Carlisle returned to Ireland as Viceroy in 1855, but his role was largely decorative, and he was unable to promote constructive reforms in the face of Palmerston's implacable resistance to such 'meddling'.[22] The Cardwell-Deasy land legislation of 1860 implemented many of the 'moderate' proposals of the 1840s, including a full contractualization of the landlord-tenant relationship, and the allowance of compensation for specified improvements made only after the landlord's consent had been given.[23] In effect, a period in which a degree of coexistence between 'English' and 'Irish' conceptions of landed property relations had appeared politically possible had been succeeded by one in which the British model of absolute ownership of the soil and *laissez-faire* in landlord-tenant relations was vigorously applied. As Philip Bull has suggested, the consequence of this breakdown in communication was the emergence of an ever closer nexus of land agitation and a less accommodating form of nationalist politics.[24]

When a shift of British public opinion rendered some form of 'popular' land reform again politically practicable in the wake of the 1867 Reform Act, it was Gladstone, Bright and Mill, rather than the aged and cautious Russell, who were ready to accept the legalization of Ulster tenant right as a mode of granting 'justice', and to take the first steps towards facilitating tenant purchase.[25] Russell was now prepared to go no further with state interference than Chichester

---

19 For this desire, see Whately to Senior, 24 Sept. 1849, Nassau Senior Papers, National Library of Wales, Aberystwyth, C699.

20 Wood memo: 'The function of government', n.d. [*c*.1867], Hickleton Papers, A4/202.

21 Harriet Martineau, *Letters from Ireland* (London, 1852), pp. 41–8.

22 Diana Davids Olien, *Morpeth: a Victorian public career* (Washington, 1983), pp. 395–478.

23 R.D. Collison Black, *Economic thought and the Irish question, 1817–70* (Cambridge, 1960), pp. 45–6.

24 Philip Bull, *Land, politics and nationalism: a study of the Irish land question* (Dublin, 1996), pp. 4–9.

25 E.D. Steele, *Irish land and British politics: tenant right and nationality, 1865–70* (Cambridge, 1974), pp. 43–68.

Fortescue's mild bill to compensate tenants for improvements – a concession which by 1868 was irrelevant to Irish circumstances.[26] The resonances of the revived rhetoric of 'justice to Ireland' were Gladstonian rather than Foxite,[27] but even Gladstone's Land Acts of 1870 and 1881 proved to be 'too little, too late', failing to satisfy higher Irish expectations, and further strengthening nationalist feeling.[28]

If the 1840s were in one respect a dead end in the politics of Irish land, these were also in some respects formative years for subsequent land agitations. Although the Famine produced an agricultural system substantially altered in terms of the structure of production and rural class relationships, the language of later movements owed much to the experience of the 1840s. The post-Famine social order was characterized by the predominance of larger holdings and the decline, outside the west, of the smallholder. Much of the surviving agricultural labourer class continued to depend on conacre and cottier plots, but it was steadily attenuated in numbers, and became increasingly differentiated from the farming community.[29]

This led to a divergence in the path of land agitation. The substantial tenantry who formed the core of the Tenant League in the 1850s demanded 'fixity of tenure' but eschewed mass mobilization and looked in vain to the agency of the Independent Irish Party in parliament. While this movement owed its origins to a reaction against the high level of evictions throughout Ireland, and to the perceived threat to the Ulster custom in the north, it was essentially one of 'strong' tenants who had survived the Famine relatively unscathed and believed they had something to lose in the new economic conditions.[30] The rapid decline of evictions after the early 1850s, and the gradual revival of economic prospects for those capable of investing in the pasture-orientated export market, meant that the agitation of this class concentrated primarily on the 'fair rent' component of the '3Fs', as a means of clawing back from the landlords the bulk of the profits realized from the agricultural boom of the 'age of equipoise'.[31]

---

26 John, Earl Russell, *Recollections and suggestions, 1813–73* (London, 1875), pp. 176–89; Russell, *Letter to C. Fortescue*, pp. 30–4.

27 This distinction was not absolute. Lord Granville, 'the most talented youngster of Grand Whiggery' in the 1840s, became Gladstone's political confidant and closest cabinet ally during the Irish Land Bill crisis of 1870, Mandler, *Aristocratic government*, p. 268; Steele, *Irish land*, pp. 156–9.

28 Bull, *Land, politics and nationalism*, pp. 46–93.

29 David Fitzpatrick, 'The disappearance of the Irish agricultural labourer, 1841–1912', *Irish Economic and Social History*, VII (1980), 66–92.

30 J.H. Whyte, *The Independent Irish Party, 1850–9* (Oxford, 1958), pp. 1–13; Paul Bew and Frank Wright, 'The agrarian opposition in Ulster politics, 1848–87', in Samuel Clark and James S. Donnelly (eds.), *Irish peasants: violence and political unrest* (Dublin, 1983), pp. 192–200.

31 The 'revisionist' orthodoxy that it was the farmers who took the lion's share of these profits, as established in the 1970s by B.L. Solow and W.E. Vaughan, has been sharply criticized in recent writing. A number of historians have suggested that the post-Famine prosperity of all but the most substantial graziers was highly precarious, and that this helps explain the

Yet it was in the west that social tensions were greatest and the legacy of the Famine most keenly felt. Large-scale clearances to create grazing ranches on the better land had resulted in the creation of congested districts of smallholders living in insecurity, and left a bitter social memory of the Famine that persisted for decades.[32] The Ribbon-Fenianism that provided much of the early dynamic of the Land War became deeply entrenched here in the late 1860s, and drew on the Lalorite rhetoric of social revolution.[33] The western movement was boosted by the threatened return of famine conditions following the potato failure of 1879, sharpening memories of the 1840s. Charles Stewart Parnell, himself the heir of the Buttite critique of British policy during the Famine, explicitly used the threat of a recurrence of the Great Famine to mobilize the west, and subsequently advocated 'undoing the work of the Famine' as the ultimate aim of the Land League.[34]

The Land League alliance was made possible by the existence of an inclusive rhetoric of land reform that identified the tenantry with the 'people', and allowed the relatively cautious eastern farmer (and western grazier) to participate in a 'national' campaign. This owed much to the O'Connellite legacy and to the radicalization of the Catholic clergy and of the organs of Catholic middle-class opinion that occurred in this formative period. The shift of opinion within the *Dublin Review*, in many ways the voice of Maynooth, from its cautious and conservative suggestion of ameliorative action in 1842, to a full-blooded denunciation of landlordism and endorsement of 'fixity of tenure' for all tenants by 1848, illustrated this development. The trajectory of the *Freeman's Journal*, which became the dominant mouthpiece of moderate Catholic nationalism after the Famine, was another. This radicalization owed much to the respectability granted to the ideas of peasant proprietorship, a small farm structure, and some form of 'fixity of tenure' by the radical English economists. The debt was acknowledged by the *Dublin Review* in 1848:

> only a study of the writings of Scrope, Thornton and Mill . . . removed all doubt from our minds. They were not enthusiasts or visionaries, or foreigners, not knowing our laws or surplus natives . . . but cool and unimpassioned Englishmen, proficient in the only science which exterminating landlords affect to value, and

---

continuing undercurrent of agrarian unrest in the mid-Victorian period, Cormac Ó Gráda, *Ireland before and after the Famine: explorations in economic history, 1800–1925* (Manchester, 1988), pp. 128–53; Michael Turner, *After the Famine: Irish agriculture 1850–1914* (Cambridge, 1996), pp. 196–216; K. Theodore Hoppen, *Ireland since 1800: conflict and conformity* (Harlow, 1989), pp. 90–4.

32 For the folk memory of clearance in the west, see Cathal Póirtéir, *Famine echoes* (Dublin, 1995), pp. 230–43

33 Jordan, *Land and popular politics*, pp. 182–9.

34 T.W. Moody, *Davitt and Irish revolution, 1846–82* (Oxford, 1981), p. 305; Paul Bew, *Land and the national question in Ireland* (Dublin, 1978), pp. 82–3.

> who regard their own suggestions for our relief, as a means of promoting the best interests of England.[35]

One of the consequences of the 1840s debates was a continuing openness in Ireland to the ideas on land reform of Mill and other British radicals.

Many of the proposals aired in the 1840s resurfaced subsequently in various configurations; the Prussian land model was incorporated into Land League rhetoric in the 1870s, and in 1882 Michael Davitt revived the idea of a waste-land reclamation scheme, financed by a land tax, to settle the labourers as peasant proprietors.[36] The superiority of tillage farming to pasture, which was a central (if highly ambiguous) element of nationalist-agrarian rhetoric in the century following the Famine, also owed its emotional and moral power to the experience, either direct or inherited through popular tradition, of the Famine years.[37]

The shadow cast by the Famine thus extended beyond the specific sphere of the land question into the entire Anglo-Irish relationship. The intimacy and trust that existed between O'Connell and the Foxite Whigs was inconceivable in the wake of the culpable failure of Russell's government to fulfil its pledge to make the relief of Ireland its chief priority. The consequent mass mortality was regarded even by members of the government as amounting to the 'extermination' of the Irish poor by neglect. The abandonment of Ireland to its fate was interpreted by many members of the Protestant ascendancy as demonstrating the failure of the Union.[38]

It has not been the intention of this book to attribute blame for the catastrophe, but to explain the circumstances and motives that lay behind the policies adopted, with particular reference to the preoccupation of ministers and the public with the future of the Irish land system. If any general conclusion can be drawn, it is that the Whig-Liberal government as a whole, and even its moralist ideologues, were less responsible for the social sufferings of the later 1840s than an attitude of mind that suffused the British political public, and set the parameters of state activity. The belief that the blight was a providential visitation, sent to bring Ireland into a higher state of social and moral organization through a necessary measure of pain, shaped contemporary attitudes and subsequent apologetics. The dominant British 'memory' of the Famine thus centred on the notion that the physical and moral condition of Ireland had indeed been raised as a consequence

---

35 [Patrick McMahon], 'Measures for Ireland: tillage – waste lands – fixity of tenure', *Dublin Review*, XXV (Dec. 1848), 331–2.

36 Moody, *Davitt*, pp. 292, 305, 521.

37 Paul Bew, *Conflict and conciliation in Ireland, 1890–1910: Parnellites and radical agrarians* (Oxford, 1987), pp. 1–12.

38 Some, such as De Vere, demanded the reconstruction of the Union on a basis of equitable partnership; Butt feared it was beyond repair, Aubrey De Vere, *English misrule and Irish misdeeds* (London, 1848), pp. 115–19, 227–36; Isaac Butt, *The rate in aid: a letter to the Rt. Hon. the Earl of Roden* (Dublin, 1849), pp. 65–8.

of the providential advent of the potato blight, primarily through 'free trade in land' and (somewhat euphemistically) mass voluntary emigration.[39] As one Scottish commentator proclaimed in 1872, 'the famine year, with all its calamities, has proved the dawn of a better era . . . by compelling the "depopulation"' of the country.[40] Even the tired and increasingly conservative Russell of later years was prepared to endorse this truism, albeit with the acknowledgment that the price had been the creation of an Irish diaspora with a very different and embittered memory of the Famine.[41]

The British 'memory' was nowhere more powerfully expressed than in a justificatory comment inserted by Anthony Trollope into his 'Famine' novel *Castle Richmond*:

> If one did in truth write a tale of the famine, after that it would behove the author to write a tale of the pestilence; and then another, a tale of the exodus. These three wonderful events, following each other, were the blessings coming from Omniscience and Omnipotence by which the black clouds were driven from the Irish firmament. If one, through it all, could have dared to hope, and have had from the first that wisdom which has learned to acknowledge that His mercy endureth for ever! And then the same author going on with his series would give in his last set, – Ireland in her prosperity.[42]

The focus of Trollope's providentialist apology of 1860 had shifted somewhat from his Trevelyanite polemics of 1849, but the underlying message remained the same: the catastrophe had been imperative to break the barriers to progress in Ireland.[43] Even had Ireland's vaunted 'prosperity' proved less ephemeral, the historian would find it impossible to conclude that the ends of policy justified the appalling and unnecessary cost in human life.

---

39 See, for example, *British Standard*, 11 Nov. 1859; John Locke, *Ireland's recovery, or, excessive emigration and its reparative agencies in Ireland* (London, 1853), pp. 10–11.

40 James Macaulay, *The truth about Ireland. Tours of observation in 1872 and 1875, with remarks on Irish public questions* (London, 1876), pp. 38–40. For modern echoes of this 'memory', see Magnus Magnusson, *Landlord or tenant? A view of Irish history* (London, 1978), pp. 90–1.

41 Russell, *Letter to C. Fortescue*, pp. 12, 17–23. For the making of the Irish nationalist interpretation, see James S. Donnelly, 'The construction of the memory of the Famine in Ireland and the Irish diaspora, 1850–1900', *Éire-Ireland*, XXXI (1996), 26–61.

42 Anthony Trollope, *Castle Richmond* (1860, edited by Mary Hamer, Oxford, 1989), p. 489.

43 See above, pp. 327. For the narrative of progress in Trollope's novel, see Christopher Morash, *Writing the Irish Famine* (Oxford, 1995), pp. 35–6, 39–51.

Bibliography

I UNPUBLISHED PAPERS

National Library of Wales, Aberystwyth
Harpton Court Papers
Nassau Senior Papers

Public Record Office of Northern Ireland, Belfast
Sharman Crawford Papers
Somerville Letterbook (copy)

Cambridge University Library
Sir James Graham Papers (microfilm)
Hickleton Papers (microfilm)

West Sussex Record Office, Chichester
Bessborough Papers

National Library of Ireland, Dublin
British Association Letterbooks
Larcom Papers
Monteagle Papers

Durham University Library
Grey of Howick Papers

Devon Record Office, Exeter
Fortescue of Castle Hill Papers

Surrey Record Office, Kingston
Goulburn Papers

West Yorkshire Archive Service, Leeds
Clanricarde Papers

Liverpool Record Office
Derby Papers

British Library, London
Bright Papers
Broughton Papers
Macvey Napier Papers
Palmerston Papers (Foreign Office Letterbooks)
Peel Papers

Public Record Office, London
Colonial Office Papers
Home Office Papers
Treasury Papers
Russell Papers

Nottingham University Library
Newcastle Papers

Bodleian Library, Oxford
Clarendon Deposit
Clarendon Deposit Irish
Trevelyan Letterbooks (microfilm)

Hartley Library, University of Southampton
Palmerston (Broadlands) Papers

Castle Howard, North Yorkshire
Castle Howard Papers

II PARLIAMENTARY DEBATES AND PAPERS

Hansard's Parliamentary Debates, third series

Third report of Her Majesty's Commissioners for inquiring into the condition of the poorer classes in Ireland, with appendix and supplement. P.P. 1836 [43], XXX

Papers relating to improvements on crown lands at King William's Town. P.P. 1836 (315), XLVII

Letter from Nassau W. Senior, esq., to Her Majesty's principal Secretary of State for the Home Department on the third report from the Commissioners for inquiring into the condition of the poor in Ireland. Dated April 14th 1836. P.P. 1837 (90), LI

Further reports of Richard Griffith, esq., dated 15 July 1839, to the Commissioners of Her Majesty's Woods, etc., on the progress of the roads and land improvement on the crown estate of King William's Town, Co. Cork. P.P. 1839 (515), XLVII

A Bill for the amendment of the law relating to landlord and tenant in Ireland. P.P. 1843 (490), III

Report of Her Majesty's Commissioners of Inquiry into the state of the law and practice in respect to the occupation of land in Ireland, together with minutes of evidence, parts I–V. P.P. 1845 [605], [606], XIX; [616], XX; [657], XXI; [672], [673], XXII

Copy of the report of Dr Playfair and Mr Lindley on the present state of the Irish potato crop and on the prospect of the approaching scarcity, dated 15 November 1845. P.P. 1846 (28), XXXVII

Instructions to committees of relief districts, extracted from minutes of the proceedings of the Commissioners appointed in reference to the apprehended scarcity. P.P. 1846 (171), XXXVII

A Bill for facilitating the sale of encumbered estates in Ireland. P.P. 1846 (634), IV

Correspondence and accounts relating to the different occasions on which measures were taken for the relief of the people suffering from scarcity in Ireland between the years 1822 and 1839. P.P. 1846 [734], XXXVII

Correspondence explanatory of the measures adopted by Her Majesty's government for the relief of distress arising from the failure of the potato crop in Ireland. P.P. 1846 [735], XXXVII

A Bill to secure the rights of occupying tenants in Ireland, and thereby to promote the improvement of the soil, and the employment of the labouring classes. P.P. 1847 (127), IV

A Bill intitulated an act to facilitate the sale of incumbered estates in Ireland. P.P. 1847 (355), II

Report of the select committee of the House of Lords on colonization from Ireland; together with minutes of evidence. P.P. 1847 (737), VI

Correspondence, from July 1846 to January 1847, relating to the measures adopted for the relief of distress in Ireland (Commissariat series). P.P. 1847 [761], LI

Correspondence, from July 1846 to January 1847, relative to the measures adopted for the relief of distress in Ireland (Board of Works series). P.P. 1847 [764], L

Correspondence relating to the measures adopted for the relief of distress in Ireland (Commissariat series), second part. P.P. 1847 [796], LII

Correspondence relative to the measures adopted for the relief of distress in Ireland (Board of Works series), second part. P.P. 1847 [797], LII

First report of the Relief Commissioners constituted under the Act 10th Vict., cap. 7. P.P. 1847 [799], XVII

Thirteenth annual report of the Poor Law Commissioners; with appendix. P.P. 1847 [816], XXVIII

Second report of the Relief Commissioners constituted under the Act 10th Vict., cap. 7. P.P. 1847 [819], XVII

Third report of the Relief Commissioners constituted under the Act 10th Vict., cap. 7. P.P. 1847 [836], XVII

Papers relative to emigration: part I. British provinces in North America. P.P. 1847–8 (50), XLVII

A Bill intitulated an Act to facilitate the sale of incumbered estates in Ireland. P.P. 1847–8 (319), III

A Bill [as amended by select committee] intitulated, an Act to facilitate the sale of encumbered estates in Ireland. P.P. 1847–8 (373), III

Copies of the correspondence upon which the Commissioners of the Poor Laws in Ireland took legal advice as to the construction of the 10th section of the Act 10 Vict. c. 31, and upon the case submitted by them to counsel; and of the circular letter of the Commissioners thereupon. P.P. 1847–8 (442), LIII

A Bill [as amended by the select committee] to amend the law of landlord and tenant in Ireland. P.P. 1847–8 (459), IV

A Bill for the establishment of the Farmers' Estates Society, Ireland. P.P. 1847–8 (534), II

Report from the select committee on the Farmers' Estate Society (Ireland) Bill, together with minutes of evidence. P.P. 1847–8 [535], XVII

Fifth, sixth and seventh reports of the Relief Commissioners constituted under the Act 10th Vict., cap. 7, and correspondence connected therewith. P.P. 1847–8 [876], XXIX

Papers relating to the relief of distress, and the state of the unions and workhouses in Ireland (fourth series). P.P. 1847–8 [896], LIV

Papers relating to proceedings for the relief of distress and state of the unions and workhouses in Ireland (fifth series). P.P. 1847–8 [919], LV

Papers relating to proceedings for the relief of distress and state of the unions and workhouses in Ireland (sixth series). P.P. 1847–8 [955], LVI

Supplementary appendix to the seventh, and last report, of the Poor Law Commissioners, constituted under the Act 10 Vict. cap. 7. P.P. 1847–8 (956), XXIX

First report of the Commissioners for administering the laws for the relief of the poor in Ireland, with appendices. P.P. 1847–8 [963], XXXIII

Papers relating to proceedings for the relief of distress and state of the unions and workhouses in Ireland (seventh series). P.P. 1847–8 [999], LIV

Fifth report from the select committee on Poor Laws (Ireland). P.P. 1849 (148), XV

Fourth report from the select committee on Poor Laws (Ireland). P.P. 1849 (170), XV

Reports of the select committee of the House of Lords, appointed to inquire into the operation of the Irish Poor Law, and the expediency of making any amendment in its enactments. P.P. 1849 (192), (228), XVI

Sixth report from the select committee on Poor Laws (Ireland). P.P. 1849 (194), XV

Second report from the select committee on receivers, Courts of Chancery and Exchequer (Ireland). P.P. 1849 (494), VIII

Final report from the Board of Public Works, Ireland, relating to the measures adopted for the relief of distress in July and August 1847; with appendices. P.P. 1849 [1047], XXIII

Second annual report of the Commissioners for administering the laws for the relief of the poor in Ireland. P.P. 1849 [1118], XXV

Report of the select committee into the administration of the Poor Law in the Kilrush Union since 19 September 1848. P.P. 1850 (613), XI

Third annual report of the Commissioners for administering the laws for the relief of the poor in Ireland. P.P. 1850 [1243], XXVII

Report from the select committee of the House of Lords on the Treasury minute, providing for the debts due from counties and unions in Ireland by the imposition of a consolidated annuity. P.P. 1852 (585), VI

Return from the Court for the sale of encumbered estates in Ireland, up to the 1st day of April 1853. P.P. 1852–3 (390), XCIV

III NEWSPAPERS AND PERIODICALS

Advocate: or Irish Industrial Journal
Agricultural and Industrial Journal of the Royal Agricultural Improvement Society of Ireland
Annual Register
Belfast Newsletter
Blackwood's Edinburgh Magazine
British Quarterly Review
British Standard
Christian Observer
Citizen
Cork Examiner
Daily News
Dublin Evening Mail
Dublin Review
Dublin University Magazine
Economist
Edinburgh Review
Examiner
Fraser's Magazine
Freeman's Journal
Illustrated London News
Leeds Mercury
Morning Chronicle
Nation
Nonconformist
North British Review
Observer
Pulpit
Punch
Quarterly Review
Spectator
Tablet
Tait's Edinburgh Magazine
Telegraph, or Connaught Ranger
Times
Truth-Seeker and Present Age
Westminster and Foreign Quarterly Review
Westminster Review

IV BIOGRAPHIES, COLLECTIONS OF LETTERS AND DIARIES

[Anon.] (ed.), *Correspondence between the most Revd Dr MacHale, Archbishop of Tuam, and the most Revd Dr Murray, Archbishop of Dublin, relative to an address to be presented to Her Majesty Queen Victoria, on the occasion of her visit to Ireland in 1849*. Dublin, 1885

Ashley, Anthony Evelyn, *The life of Henry John Temple, Viscount Palmerston, 1846–1865*. 2 vols., London, 1876

Auchmuty, James Johnston, *Sir Thomas Wyse 1791–1862: the life and career of an educator and diplomat*. London, 1939

Benson, A.C., and Esher, Viscount (eds.), *The letters of Queen Victoria: a selection from Her Majesty's correspondence between the years 1837 and 1861*. 3 vols., London, 1907

Broughton, Lord, *Recollections of a long life, with additional extracts from his private diaries*. Edited by Lady Dorchester, 6 vols., London, 1909–11

Creighton, Mandell, *Memoir of Sir George Grey, Bart.* London, 1901

Dasent, A.I., *John Thadeus Delane, editor of* 'The Times': *his life and correspondence*. 2 vols., London, 1908

Doughty, Arthur G. (ed.), *The Elgin-Grey Papers 1846–1852*. 4 vols., Ottawa, 1937

Fogarty, L. (ed.), *James Fintan Lalor, patriot and political essayist – collected writings*. Dublin, 1947 edn

Foot, M.R.D., and Matthew, H.C.G. (eds), *The Gladstone Diaries, vol. III, 1840–1847*. Oxford, 1974

Fry, Edward, *James Hack Tuke: a memoir*. London, 1899

Gooch, G.P. (ed.), *The later correspondence of Lord John Russell, 1840–78*. 2 vols., London, 1925

Greville, Charles Cavendish Fulke, *The Greville memoirs (second part): a journal of the reign of Queen Victoria, from 1837 to 1852*. Edited by H. Reeve, 3 vols., London, 1885

Jennings, Lewis J. (ed.), *The correspondence and diaries of the late Rt. Hon. John Wilson Croker*. 3 vols., London, 1884

Leader, R.E. (ed.), *Life and letters of John Arthur Roebuck, PC, QC, MP, with chapters of autobiography*. London, 1897

Lewis, Sir Gilbert Frankland (ed.), *Letters of the Rt. Hon. Sir George Cornewall Lewis, Bart., to various friends*. London, 1870

MacCarthy, Desmond, and Russell, Agatha (eds.), *Lady John Russell: a memoir, with selections from her diaries and correspondence*. London, 1910

McCullagh, W. Torrens (ed.), *Memoirs of the Rt. Hon. Richard Lalor Sheil*. 2 vols., London, 1855

MacDonagh, Michael, *Bishop Doyle 'J.K.L.': a biographical and historical study*. London, 1896

Maxwell, Herbert (ed.), *The life and letters of George William Frederick, fourth Earl of Clarendon*. 2 vols., London, 1913

Mill, John Stuart, *Autobiography.* London, 1924 edn

O'Connell, Maurice R. (ed.), *Correspondence of Daniel O'Connell.* 8 vols., Dublin, 1972–80

Morley, John, *The life of William Ewart Gladstone.* 2 vols., London, 1905

Parker, C.S. (ed.), *Life and letters of Sir James Graham, second Baronet of Netherby.* 2 vols., London, 1907

——, (ed.), *Sir Robert Peel from his private papers, with a chapter on his life and character by his grandson, the Hon. George Peel.* 3 vols., London, 1891–9

Peel, Sir Robert, *Memoirs.* Edited by Lord Mahon and Edward Cardwell, 2 vols., London, 1856–7

Pinney, T. (ed.), *The letters of Thomas Babington Macaulay.* 6 vols., Cambridge, 1974–81

Reid, Thomas Wemyss (ed.), *Memoirs and correspondence of Lyon Playfair.* London, 1899

Robinson, Tim (ed.), *Connemara after the Famine: journal of a survey of the Martin estate by Thomas Colville Scott, 1853.* Dublin, 1995

Robson, Ann P., and Robson, John M., (eds.), *John Stuart Mill, collected works, vol. XXIV: newspaper writings, 1835–47.* London and Toronto, 1986

——,(eds.), *John Stuart Mill, collected works, vol. XXV: newspaper writings, 1847–73.* London and Toronto, 1986

Rolleston, T.W. (ed.), *Prose writings of Thomas Davis.* London, n.d. [1889]

Russell, Lord John (ed.), *Correspondence of John, fourth Duke of Bedford, selected from the originals at Woburn Abbey.* 3 vols., London, 1842–6

Russell, Lord John (ed.), *Memorials and correspondence of Charles James Fox.* 4 vols., London, 1853–7

Russell, John, Earl, *Recollections and suggestions, 1813–73.* London, 1875

Russell, Rollo (ed.), *Early correspondence of Lord John Russell, 1805–40.* 2 vols., London, 1913

Senior, Nassau William, *Journals kept in France and Italy from 1848 to 1852.* Edited by M.C.M. Simpson, 2 vols., London, 1871

Somerville, Alexander, *Letters from Ireland during the famine of 1847.* Edited by K.D.M. Snell, Blackrock, 1994

Thomson, David, and McGusty, Moyra (eds.), *The Irish journals of Elizabeth Smith 1840–1850.* Oxford, 1980

Trench, W. Steuart, *Realities of Irish life.* [1868]. Reprint, London, 1966

Trevelyan, G.M., *Sir George Otto Trevelyan: a memoir.* London, 1932

Trollope, Anthony, *The Irish Famine: six letters to the Examiner, 1849–50.* Edited by L.O. Tingay, London, 1987

Villiers, G.W.F., *A vanished Victorian: being the life of George Villiers, fourth Earl of Clarendon 1800–70.* London, 1938

Walling, R.A.J. (ed.), *The diaries of John Bright.* London, 1930

Whately, E. Jane (ed.), *Life and correspondence of Richard Whately, late Archbishop of Dublin.* 2 vols., London, 1866

White, H.C. (ed.), *Sixty years' experience as an Irish landlord: memoirs of John Hamilton, DL, of St Ernan's, Donegal.* London, n.d.

Wrottesley, George (ed.), *Life and correspondence of Field Marshall Sir John Burgoyne, Bart.* 2 vols., London, 1873

V CONTEMPORARY BOOKS, PAMPHLETS AND ARTICLES

Adair, A. Shafto, *The winter of 1846–7 in Antrim, with remarks on out-door relief and colonization.* London, 1847

Alcock, Thomas, *The tenure of land in Ireland considered.* London, 1848

Alcock, T. St Leger, *Observations on the Poor Relief Bill for Ireland, and its bearing on the important subjects of emigration; with some remarks on the great public works projected in the British North American colonies.* London, 1847

[Alison, Archibald], 'Lessons from the famine', *Blackwood's Edinburgh Magazine,* LXI (April 1847), 515–24

['Anglo-Hibernicus'], *A letter to the Rt. Hon. Lord John Russell, on the future prospects of Ireland,* London, 1847

[Anon.], *A brief account of the famine in Ireland.* London, 1847

——, *Cases of tenant eviction, from 1840 to 1846, extracted from public journals.* n.p., n.d. [1843]

——, *An earnest plea for Ireland. By an Englishman.* London, 1848

——, *The emancipation of the soil and free trade in land, by a landed proprietor.* Edinburgh, 1845

——, *The farmer's guide: compiled for the use of the small farmer and cottier tenantry in Ireland.* 2nd edn, Dublin, 1842

——, *A few words of remonstrance and advice to the farming and labouring classes of Ireland, by a sincere friend.* Dublin, 1848

——, *God's laws versus Corn Laws: a letter to His Grace the Archbishop of Canterbury. From a dignitary of the English Church.* London, 1846

——, *Ireland in reality, or the true interest of the labourer.* 2nd edn, Dublin, 1848

——, *Ireland. Observations on the people, the land and the law, in 1851; with especial reference to the policy and practice of the Incumbered Estates Court.* Dublin, 1851

——, *The Irish difficulty: addressed to his countrymen, by an Englishman.* London, 1848

——, *Irish improvidence encouraged by English bounty; being a remonstrance against the government projects for Irish relief, and suggestions of measures by which the Irish poor can be speedily and effectually fed, relieved, employed, and elevated above their present degraded position, without taxing English industry for this purpose. By an ex-member of the British parliament.* London, n.d. [1847]

——, *Irish Poor Law question. A letter to the Rt. Hon. Lord John Russell from an Irish landlord.* London, 1847

——, *The measures which can alone ameliorate effectually the condition of the Irish people.* London, 1847

——, *Memorandum in regard to the use of Indian corn as an article of food.* Dublin, 1846

——, *Notices of the viceroyalty of the late Earl of Besborough.* Dublin, 1847

——, 'Registration of landed property', *Westminster Review,* XCV (March 1846), 107–32

——, *Remarks by a junior to his senior, on an article in the* Edinburgh Review *of January 1844, on the state of Ireland, and the measures for its improvement.* London, 1844

——, *Remarks on Ireland; as it is; – as it ought to be; – and as it might be: Sir Robert Peel's plantation scheme, etc . . . by a native.* London, 1849

——, 'Tenant-right and the Tenant League', *Dublin University Magazine,* XXXVII (Feb. 1851), 159–76

——, *Thoughts on Ireland.* London, 1847

[Anster, John], 'Agrarian outrages in Ireland', *North British Review,* VII (Aug. 1847), 505–38

——, 'Colonization from Ireland', *North British Review,* VIII (Feb. 1848), 421–64

——, 'The state of Ireland', *North British Review,* VI (Feb. 1847), 509–50

[Aytoun, W.E.], 'Ministerial measures', *Blackwood's Edinburgh Magazine,* LIX (March 1846), 373–84

Badham, Leslie, *A sermon, preached in St Stephen's Chapel, Frensham, diocese of Winchester, in aid of the Irish relief funds.* Godalming, n.d. [1847]

[Baines, Edward], 'Overpopulation and its remedy', *British Quarterly Review,* IV (Aug. 1846), 115–42

Ball, John, *What is to be done for Ireland?* 2nd edn, London, 1849

[Bancroft, –], '"Fixity of tenure" historically and economically considered', *Dublin University Magazine,* XXIII (May 1844), 605–15

Beamish, N. Ludlow, *Remedy for the impending scarcity; suggested by a visit to the Kilkerrin estate of the Irish Waste Lands Improvement Society,* Cork, 1846

Bennett, William, *Narrative of a recent journey of six weeks in Ireland, in connexion with the subject of supplying small seed in some of the remoter districts: with current observations on the depressed circumstances of the people, and the means presented for the permanent improvement of their social position.* London, 1847

Bermingham, Thomas, *Letter addressed to the Rt. Hon. Lord John Russell, containing facts illustrative of the good effects from the just and considerate discharge of the duties of a resident landlord in Ireland.* London, 1846

Blackall, S.W., *Suggestions for relieving distress, by stimulating private and public employment.* Dublin, 1848

Blacker, William, *An essay on the improvement to be made in the cultivation of small farms, by the introduction of green crops and housefeeding the stock thereon.* Tenant's edn, Dublin, n.d. [1834]

[Brady, J.D.], 'Ireland and the ministerial measures', *Blackwood's Edinburgh Magazine*, LXIII (Jan. 1848), 113–26

——, 'Ireland – its condition – the life and property bill – the debate, and the famine', *Blackwood's Edinburgh Magazine*, LIX (May 1846), 572–603

——, 'Ireland: the landlord and tenant question', *Blackwood's Edinburgh Magazine*, LV (May 1844), 638–64

Burke, Edmund, *Thoughts and details on scarcity, originally presented to the Rt. Hon. William Pitt, in the month of November 1795*. London, 1800

Burritt, Elihu, *A journal of a visit of three days to Skibbereen, and its neighbourhood.* London and Birmingham, 1847

[Butt, Isaac], 'The famine in the land. What has been done, and what is to be done', *Dublin University Magazine*, XXIX (April 1847), 501–40

——, 'Measures for Ireland', *Dublin University Magazine*, XXIX (May 1847), 656–74

——, *The rate in aid: a letter to the Rt. Hon. the Earl of Roden, KP.* Dublin, 1849

Caird, James, *High farming under liberal covenants the best substitute for protection.* 3rd edn, Edinburgh, 1849

——, *The plantation scheme; or, the west of Ireland as a field for investment.* Edinburgh, 1850

Carroll, Peter, *A letter from Peter Carroll to John Bull, on the origin, nature and conduct of the landlords of Ireland, and on the best method of preventing them in future from starving 'Patrick' and robbing 'John'.* Liverpool, 1847

de Cavour, Camille, *Considerations on the present state and future prospects of Ireland.* London, 1845

[Chalmers, Thomas], 'Political economy of a famine', *North British Review*, VII (May 1847), 247–90

Collins, Robert, *Two letters addressed to the Rt. Hon. Henry Labouchere, Chief Secretary of Ireland, on the extreme destitution of the poor, in consequence of the total loss of the potato crop; with suggestions as to sources of employment, and other measures for their relief.* Dublin, 1846

Conner, William, *The true political economy of Ireland: or rack-rent, the one great cause of all her evils, with its remedy*. Dublin, 1835

——, *Two letters to the editor of the* Times *on the rackrent oppression of Ireland, its source – its evils – and its remedy – in reply to the* Times *commissioner*. Dublin, 1846

Crawford, William Sharman, *A defence of the small farmers of Ireland.* Dublin, 1839

——, *Depopulation not necessary: an appeal to the British members of the imperial parliament against the extermination of the Irish people.* 2nd edn, London, 1850

[Croker, J.W.], 'Ireland', *Quarterly Review*, LXXXIII (Sept. 1848), 584–614

——, 'Repeal agitation', *Quarterly Review*, LXXV (Dec. 1844), 222–92

Crosthwaite, J.C., *The unfruitful fig-tree. A sermon, preached in the church of St Mary-at-Hill, London, on Wednesday March 24, 1847, being the day appointed for the general fast.* London, 1847

[Davis, Thomas], 'Emigration – no remedy', *The Citizen*, I (Dec. 1839), 73–83

Desmond, Daniel, *Project for the reclamation of one million acres of waste lands in Ireland, by colonies for her surplus and unemployed population.* Cheltenham, 1847

[De Vere, Aubrey], 'Colonization', *Edinburgh Review*, XCI (Jan. 1850), 1–62

——, *English misrule and Irish misdeeds: four letters from Ireland addressed to an English member of parliament.* [1848]. Reprint, Port Washington, NY, 1970

[Devon, Earl of], *Letter from an Irish proprietor to the ministers of religion of the district.* London, 1847

——, *Paper on Ireland: read at the Dublin Society in March, 1849.* London, 1849

Dobbs, Conway E., *Some observations on the tenant-right of Ulster: a paper read before the Dublin Statistical Society.* Dublin, 1849

Douglas, John, *Life and property in Ireland assured as in England by a poor-rate on land to provide employment for the destitute poor on the waste lands of Ireland.* London, 1846

Doyle, James W., *Letter to Thomas Spring Rice, esq., MP, on the establishment of a legal provision for the Irish poor, and on the nature and destination of Church property.* Dublin, 1831

Doyle, Martin, *The labouring classes in Ireland: an inquiry as to what beneficial changes may be effected in their condition by the legislature, the landowner and the labourer respectively.* Dublin, 1846

Dufferin, Lord, and Boyle, the Hon. G.F., *Narrative of a journey from Oxford to Skibbereen during the year of the Irish Famine.* 2nd edn, Oxford, 1847

[Duncan, Jonathan], 'Tenure of land in Ireland', *Dublin Review*, XXIV (June 1848), 349–80

Elly, Sandham, *Potatoes, pigs, and politics: the curse of Ireland, and the cause of England's embarrassments.* London, n.d. [1848]

Ensor, Thomas, *Ireland made happy and England safe: two letters addressed to the Rt. Hon. Sir Robert Peel, Bart., MP, and a letter to Daniel O'Connell, Esq., MP.* London, 1846

Fagan, James, *Waste lands of Ireland: suggestions for their immediate reclamation, as a means of affording reproductive employment to the able-bodied destitute.* Dublin, 1847

Filgate, Fitzherbert, 'The potato failure and its effects on Irish agriculture', *Agricultural and Industrial Journal of the Royal Agricultural Improvement Society of Ireland*, I (1848), 17–36

Foster, Thomas Campbell, *Letters on the condition of the people of Ireland.* London, 1846

Francis, G.H., *Orators of the age.* London, 1847

[Friends, Society of], *Address to the public from the Relief Association of the Society of Friends in Ireland.* Dublin, n.d. [1849]

——, *Transactions of the Central Relief Committee of the Society of Friends during the Famine in Ireland in 1846 and 1847.* Dublin, 1852

Gaye, C.H., *Irish famine, a special occasion for keeping Lent in England: a sermon, preached in obedience to the Queen's letter, on the first Sunday of Lent, 1847, at Archbishop Tenison's chapel, St. James, Westminster.* London, 1847

Gibson, C.P., *The history of the County and City of Cork.* London, 1861

[Godkin, James], 'Ireland and its famine', *British Quarterly Review,* V (May 1847), 504–40

Godley, John Robert, *An answer to the question what is to be done with the unemployed labourers of the United Kingdom?* London, 1847

——, *Letters from America.* 2 vols., London, 1844

Goold, Henry, *Thoughts on a judicious disposition of land in Ireland. Calculated to promote the best interests of landlord and tenant, whilst securing equitable remunerative employment for the entire labouring population. Communicated in a letter to Richard S. Guinness, esq., an Irish landlord and land agent.* London, 1847

Gore, Montague, *Suggestions for the amelioration of the present condition of Ireland.* London, 1847

[Graydon, William], *Suggestions on the best modes of employing the Irish peasantry as an anti-famine precaution: a letter to the Rt. Hon. Sir Robert Peel, Bart.* London, 1845

[Greville, Charles Cavendish Fulke], *The past and present policy of England towards Ireland.* London, 1845

Hancock, W. Neilson, *Statistics respecting the sales of incumbered estates in Ireland.* Dublin, 1850

——, *The tenant right of Ulster, considered economically: being an essay read before the Dublin University Philosophical Society.* Dublin, 1845

——, *Three lectures on the questions, should the principles of political economy be disregarded at the present crisis? and if not, how can they be applied towards the discovery of measures of relief?* Dublin, 1847

Henchy, John, *Observations on the state of Ireland, with remarks on her resources and capabilities, and plans for carrying into effect the remedies necessary for the Commissioners' report under the late Land Commission.* Dublin, 1845

Hill, Lord George, *Facts from Gweedore.* [Facsimile of fifth edn, 1887], Belfast, 1971

Hole, James, 'Social science: lecture V. the land', *Truth-Seeker and Present Age: a Catholic Review,* I (1849), 421–43

[Indian Relief Fund], *Distress in Ireland. Report of the trustees of the Indian Relief Fund showing the distribution of the sum of £13,919 14s. 2d. Commencing the 24th April and ending the 21st December 1846.* Dublin, 1847

Inglis, Henry D., *A journey throughout Ireland during the spring, summer and autumn of 1834.* 3rd edn, 2 vols., London, 1835

[Irish Council], *Reports of the committee of the Irish Council.* n.p., n.d. [1847]

Jerrold, W. Blanchard, *An apology for the Irish rebels.* London, n.d. [1848]

Kane, Robert, *The industrial resources of Ireland.* 2nd edn. Dublin, 1845

——, 'The agricultural banks of Prussia', *Agricultural and Industrial Journal of the Royal Agricultural Improvement Society of Ireland*, I (1848), 125–34

——, 'The large or small farm question considered in regard to the present circumstances of Ireland', *Agricultural and Industrial Journal of the Royal Agricultural Improvement Society of Ireland*, I (1848), 147–71

Kennedy, John Pitt, *Correspondence on some of the general effects of the failure of the potato crop, and the consequent relief measures, with suggestions as to the reconstruction of the Poor Law electoral or rateable divisions, as a means of arresting the impending national dangers, by substituting reproductive enterprise and industry for almsgiving.* Dublin, 1847

——, *Instruct; employ; don't hang them: or Ireland tranquillized without soldiers, and enriched without English capital.* London, 1835

——, (ed.), *Digest of evidence taken before Her Majesty's Commissioners of inquiry into the state of the law and practice in respect to the occupation of land in Ireland.* 2 vols., Dublin, 1847–8

Laing, Samuel, *Observations on the social and political state of the European people in 1848 and 1849.* London, 1850

de Lavergne, Leonce, *The rural economy of England, Scotland and Ireland.* Edinburgh, 1855

Lewis, George Cornewall, *On local disturbances in Ireland; and on the Irish Church question.* London, 1836

Locke, John, *Ireland's recovery, or, excessive emigration and its reparative agencies in Ireland. An essay, read September 10, 1853, before the British Society for the Advancement of Science.* London, 1853

[Loyal National Repeal Association], *Reports of the parliamentary committee of the Loyal National Repeal Association.* 2 vols., Dublin, 1845

Maberley, Katherine C., *The present state of Ireland, and its remedy.* 2nd edn, London, 1847

Macaulay, James, *The truth about Ireland. Tours of observation in 1872 and 1875, with remarks on Irish public questions.* London, 1876

[McCabe, W.B.], 'Measures for Ireland', *Dublin Review*, XXII (March 1847), 230–60

[McCollum, R.], *Sketches of the highlands of Cavan and of Shirley Castle, in Farney, taken during the Irish Famine.* Belfast, 1856

[McCulloch, J.R.], 'Cottage system', *Encyclopaedia Britannica Supplement*, Edinburgh, 1824, III, 378–9

McKnight, James, *The Ulster tenant's claim of right, or land ownership a state trust; the Ulster tenant right an original grant from the British crown, and the necessity of extending its general principle to the other provinces of Ireland demonstrated: in a letter to Lord John Russell.* Dublin, 1848

[McMahon, Patrick], 'Depopulation – fixity of tenure', *Dublin Review*, XIII (Nov. 1842), 512–60

——, 'Ireland – spirit of recent legislation', *Dublin Review*, XXVII (Dec. 1849), 345–431

——, 'Measures for Ireland: tillage – waste lands – fixity of tenure', *Dublin Review*, XXV (Dec. 1848), 284–345

McNeile, Hugh, *The famine a rod of God; its provoking cause – its merciful design. A sermon preached in St Jude's Church, Liverpool, on Sunday February 28 1847.* London, 1847

Mahony, Pierce, *Incumbered Estates Act (Ireland) . . . case and opinion.* Dublin, 1849

[Maley, Andrew John], *Observations upon the inutility of exterminating the resident landlords of Ireland, by act of parliament, or otherwise, and some suggestions for their self-preservation.* Dublin, 1849

Manners, Lord John, *Notes of an Irish tour in 1846.* New edn, Edinburgh and London, 1881

[Mansion House Committee], *Report of the Mansion House Committee on the potato disease.* Dublin, 1846

Martin, R.M., *Remedial measures suggested for the relief of Ireland.* London, 1848

Martineau, Harriet, *Letters from Ireland.* London, 1852

Meekins, Robert, *Plan for the removal of pauperism, agrarian disturbances, and the poor's rate in Ireland, by liberally providing for the destitute, free of expense.* Dublin, 1847

[Mill, John Stuart], 'Ireland', *Parliamentary History and Review*, II (1827), 599–613

——, *Principles of political economy with some of their applications to social philosophy.* London, 1848. Edited by J.M. Robson in *Collected Works of John Stuart Mill, II–III.* Toronto, 1965

Moore, Daniel, 'The Christian uses of national and individual chastisement. A harvest thanksgiving sermon . . . preached in Camden Church, Camberwell, on Sunday morning, October 17, 1847. Being the day appointed for a general thanksgiving for the late abundant harvest', *Pulpit*, LII (1847), 321–8

[Monteagle, Lord], 'Distress in the manufacturing districts – causes and remedies', *Edinburgh Review*, LXXVII (Feb. 1843), 190–227

Naper, J.L.W., *An appeal to Irishmen to unite in supporting measures formed on principles of common justice and common sense for the social regeneration of Ireland.* London, 1848

[National Anti-Corn Law League], *Corn Laws. Selections from a plea for the poor. By the Hon. and Revd Baptist W. Noel.* Manchester, 1842

——, *Corn Laws. Selections from Mrs Loudon's Philanthropic Economy.* Manchester, 1842

Nevile, C., *The justice and expediency of tenant-right legislation considered, in a letter to P. Pusey, esq.* London, 1848

Newman, C., *On the importance of a legislative enactment uniting the interest of landlord and tenant, to facilitate the culture of the land and promote an increase of food and employment for the millions.* 2nd edn, London, 1848

Nicholls, George, *A history of the Irish Poor Law, in connexion with the condition of the people.* London, 1856

——, *Poor laws – Ireland: three reports by George Nicholls, esq., to Her Majesty's principal Secretary of State for the Home Department.* London, 1838

Nicholson, Asenath, *Lights and shades of Ireland: part III. The Famine of 1847, '48 and '49.* London, 1850

Niven, N., *The potato epidemic and its probable consequences; a letter to His Grace the Duke of Leinster, as president of the Royal Agricultural Improvement Society of Ireland.* Dublin, 1846

O'Brien, Lucius, *Ireland in 1848: the late famine and the Poor Laws.* London, n.d. [1848]

O'Brien, William Smith, *Reproductive employment: a series of letters to the landed proprietors of Ireland; with a preliminary letter to Lord John Russell.* Dublin, 1847

O'Connell, Daniel, *Observations on the Corn Laws, on political pravity and ingratitude, and on clerical and personal slander, in the shape of a meek and modest reply to the second letter of the Earl of Shrewsbury . . . to Ambrose Lisle Phillipps, esq.* Dublin, 1842

O'Connell, John, 'Ireland and her present necessities', *Tait's Edinburgh Magazine,* XIV(Jan. 1847), 39–44

——, *The Repeal dictionary, part I.* Dublin, 1845

Osborne, Sidney Godolphin, *Gleanings in the west of Ireland.* London, 1850

[O'Sullivan, Mortimer], 'Ireland – Repealers and landlords', *Dublin University Magazine,* XXI (Feb. 1843), 156–67

——, 'State of Ireland', *Quarterly Review,* LXXIX (Dec. 1846), 238–69

[O'Sullivan, Samuel], 'Condition of Ireland', *Dublin University Magazine,* XXXII (Aug. 1848), 228–43

——, 'The Irish crisis – the Poor Law', *Dublin University Magazine,* XXXI (April 1848), 537–52

——, 'Irish landlords – the Land Commission report', *Dublin University Magazine,* XXX (Oct. 1847), 481–96

——, 'Irish proprietorship', *Dublin University Magazine,* XXXII (Sept. 1848), 356–70

——, 'Land Commission in Ireland', parts I and II, *Dublin University Magazine,* XXV (April, May 1845), 471–85, 616–30

——, 'Tenant-right', *Dublin University Magazine,* XXXI (April 1848), 498–512

Pim, James, *Ireland: 'Incumbered Estates Commission' – a letter to Sir John Romilly, MP.* London, 1850

Pim, Jonathan, *The condition and prospects of Ireland, and the evils arising from the present distribution of landed property; with suggestions for a remedy.* Dublin, 1848

——, *Observations on the evils resulting to Ireland from the insecurity of title and the existing laws of real property; with some suggestions towards a remedy.* Dublin, 1847

Pizey, Edward, 'National sins, the cause of national judgments; or, Israel and England compared. A sermon . . . preached in St. Peter's Church, Saffron Hill, on . . . Nov. 16, 1845', *Pulpit,* XLVIII (1845–6), 348–53

[Power, Alfred], *The Irish Poor Law: past, present and future.* London, 1849

Rawstorne, Lawrence, *The cause of the potato disease, ascertained by proofs; and the prevention proved by practice; with some remarks added on Irish affairs.* London, 1847

Reade, Philip, *Whig and Tory remedies for Irish evils, and the effects a repeal of the Corn Laws would have on the legislative union.* Dublin, 1844

Robinson, D., *Practical suggestions for the reclamation of waste lands, and improvement in the condition of the agricultural population of Ireland, with an introductory letter to the Chancellor of the Exchequer, from the Earl of Devon.* London, n.d. [1847]

Rogers, Jasper W., *The potato truck system of Ireland the main cause of her periodical famines and of the non-payment of her rents.* 2nd edn, London, 1847

Rosse, Earl of, *Letters on the state of Ireland.* 2nd edn, London, 1847

Russell, Lord John, *The government of Ireland: the substance of a speech, delivered in the House of Commons, on Monday, April 15th, 1839.* London, 1839

Russell, John, Earl, *An essay on the history of the English government and constitution from the reign of Henry VII to the present time.* New edn, London, 1865

——, *A letter to the Rt. Hon. Chichester Fortescue, MP, on the state of Ireland.* 2nd edn, London, 1868

[Savage, M.W.], 'Lord Clarendon's administration', *Edinburgh Review*, XCI (Jan. 1851), 208–303

Scrope, George Poulett, *Extracts of evidence, taken by the late Commission of Inquiry into the occupation of the land in Ireland, on the subject of waste lands reclamation, with a prefatory letter to the Rt. Hon. Lord John Russell.* London, 1847

——, *How is Ireland to be governed?: a question addressed to the new administration of Lord Melbourne in 1834, with a postscript in which the same question is addressed to the administration of Sir Robert Peel in 1846.* 2nd edn, London, 1846

——, 'Irish clearances and the improvement of waste lands', *Westminster and Foreign Quarterly Review*, L (Oct. 1848), 163–87

——, 'The Irish difficulty and how it must be met', *Westminster and Foreign Quarterly Review*, L (Jan. 1849), 436–61

——, *The Irish relief measures, past and future.* London, 1848

——, *A labour rate recommended in preference to any reduction in the area of taxation, to improve the operation of the Irish Poor Law. In three letters to the editor of the* Morning Chronicle. London, 1849

——, *Letters to Lord John Russell, MP, etc., etc., etc., on the further measures required for the social amelioration of Ireland.* London, 1847

——, *Letters to the Rt. Hon. Lord John Russell, on the expediency of enlarging the Irish Poor Law, to the full extent of the Poor Law of England.* London, 1846

——, *Remarks on the Irish Poor Relief Bill.* London, 1847

——, *Reply to the speech of the Archbishop of Dublin, delivered in the House of Lords, on Friday, 26th March, 1847, and the protest signed R. Dublin, Monteagle, Radnor, Mountcashel, against the Poor Relief (Ireland) Bill.* London, 1847

[Senior, Nassau William], 'Ireland', *Edinburgh Review*, LXXIX (Jan. 1844), 189–266

——, *Journals, conversations and essays relating to Ireland.* 2 vols., London, 1868

——, *A letter to Lord Howick on a legal provision for the Irish poor; commutation of tithes, and a provision for the Irish Roman Catholic clergy.* London, 1831

——, 'Mendicancy in Ireland', *Edinburgh Review*, LXXVII (April 1843), 391–411

——, *On national property and on the prospects of the present administration and of their successors.* 2nd edn, London, 1835

——, 'Proposals for extending the Irish Poor Law', *Edinburgh Review*, LXXXIV (Oct. 1846), 267–314

——, 'The relief of Irish distress in 1847 and 1848', *Edinburgh Review*, LXXXIX (Jan. 1849), 221–68

Shrewsbury, Earl of, *Thoughts on the Poor Relief Bill for Ireland, together with reflections on her miseries, their causes, and their remedies.* London, 1847

Simpson, W.W., *A defence of the landlords of Ireland, with remarks on the relation between landlord and tenant.* London, 1844

Skilling, Thomas, *The science and practice of agriculture.* Dublin, 1846

Sligo, Marquess of, *A few remarks and suggestions on the present state of Ireland.* London, 1847

Smiles, Samuel, *History of Ireland and the Irish people under the government of England.* London, 1844

[Smith, Adam], *Extract from the fifth chapter of the fourth book of Adam Smith's 'Wealth of Nations'.* London, n.d. [1846]

——, *An inquiry into the nature and causes of the wealth of nations.* Edited by Kathryn Sutherland, Oxford, 1993

Smith, William Henry, *A twelve month's residence in Ireland, during the Famine and the public works, 1846 and 1847.* London, 1848

[Stanley, Lord], *Speech of Lord Stanley, February 9, 1849, on the motion of the Marquis of Lansdowne, for the appointment of a select committee to consider the operation of the Irish Poor Law.* London, 1849

Storey, Thomas George, *A short address as a word of advice to the small farmers and peasantry of the County of Tipperary.* Dublin, 1843

Sulivan, Henry W., *Christian compassion: a sermon, preached in obedience to the Queen's letter, in behalf of the starving Irish, on Sunday, 31st January, 1847.* 2nd edn, London, 1847

Thornton, William Thomas, *Over-population and its remedy; or, an inquiry into the extent and causes of distress prevailing among the labouring classes of the British Islands, and into the means of remedying it.* London, 1846

——, *A plea for peasant proprietors, with the outline of a plan for their establishment in Ireland.* London, 1848

[The Times], *The Great Irish Famine of 1845–6. A collection of leading articles, letters and parliamentary and other public statements, reprinted from the* Times. London, 1880

Torrens, Robert, *Systematic colonization: Ireland saved, without cost to the Imperial Treasury.* 2nd edn, London, 1849

Townshend, William R., *Directions on practical agriculture, originally addressed to the working farmers of Ireland.* 2nd edn, Dublin, 1843

Trevelyan, Charles Edward, *The Irish crisis.* London, 1848

Trollope, Anthony, *Castle Richmond.* [1860]. Edited by Mary Hamer, Oxford, 1989

[Tuke, James Hack], *James Hack Tuke's narrative describing the second, third and fourth weeks of William Forster's journey in the distressed districts in Ireland.* London, n.d. [1847]

——, *A visit to Connaught in the autumn of 1847. A letter addressed to the Central Relief Committee of the Society of Friends, Dublin.* London, 1847

Vansittart, C., *A sermon on famine: the expediency of a public fast, and the duty of personal abstinence in the present time of dearth.* London, 1847

Venedey, Jacob, *Ireland and the Irish during the Repeal year.* Dublin, 1844

[Waller, J.F.], 'Incumbered Estates Court', *Dublin University Magazine,* XXXVI (Sept. 1850), 311–28

Ward, James, *Remedies for Ireland. A letter to the Rt. Hon. Lord Monteagle, on the fallacy of the proposed Poor Law, emigration, and reclamation of waste lands, as remedies.* London, 1847

Weightman, George, *A treatise on the true nature and cause of the present destructive disease of potatoes, with the means of cure.* London, 1846

Whately, Richard, *Substance of a speech delivered in the House of Lords, on Friday, the 26th of March, 1847, on the motion for a committee on Irish Poor Laws.* London, 1847

Wiggins, John, *The 'monster' misery of Ireland; a practical treatise on the relation of landlord and tenant.* London, 1844

VI LATER WORKS

Akenson, D.H., *A Protestant in purgatory: Richard Whately, Archbishop of Dublin.* Hamden, CT, 1981

Beames, Michael, 'Cottiers and conacre in pre-Famine Ireland', *Journal of Peasant Studies,* II (1975), 352–4

——, *Peasants and power: the Whiteboy movements and their control in pre-Famine Ireland,* Brighton, 1983

——, 'Rural conflict in pre-Famine Ireland: peasant assassinations in Tipperary 1837–47', *Past and Present,* 81 (1978), 75–91

Bentley, Michael (ed.), *Public and private doctrine: essays in British history presented to Maurice Cowling.* Cambridge, 1993

Bew, Paul, *Conflict and conciliation in Ireland, 1890–1910: Parnellism and radical agrarianism.* Oxford, 1987

——, *Land and the national question in Ireland 1858–82.* Dublin, 1978

Bew, Paul, and Wright, Frank, 'The agrarian opposition in Ulster politics, 1848–87', in Samuel Clark and James S. Donnelly (eds.), *Irish peasants: violence and political unrest 1780–1914*. Dublin, 1983, pp. 192–229

Black, R.D. Collison, *Economic thought and the Irish question, 1817–70*. Cambridge, 1960

Boot, H.M., *The commercial crisis of 1847*. Hull, 1984

Bourke, Austin, 'The Irish grain trade, 1839–48', *Irish Historical Studies*, XX (1976), 156–67

——, '*The visitation of God*'? *The potato and the Great Irish Famine*. Edited by Jacqueline Hill and Cormac Ó Gráda, Dublin, 1993

——, 'The scientific investigation of the potato blight in Ireland, 1845–6', *Irish Historical Studies*, XIII (1962–3), 26–32

Bourne, Kenneth, *Palmerston: the early years 1784–1841*. London, 1982

Boyce, D. George, *Nationalism in Ireland*. London, 1982

Boylan, Thomas A., and Foley, Timothy P., '"A nation perishing of political economy"?', in Chris Morash and Richard Hayes (eds.), *Fearful realities: new perspectives on the Famine*. Blackrock, 1996

——, *Political economy and colonial Ireland: the propagation and ideological function of economic discourse in the nineteenth century*. London, 1992

Brent, Richard, 'God's Providence: Liberal political economy as natural theology at Oxford 1825–1862', in Michael Bentley (ed.), *Public and private doctrine: essays in British history presented to Maurice Cowling*. Cambridge, 1993, pp. 85–107

——, *Liberal Anglican politics: Whiggery, religion and reform 1830–1841*. Oxford, 1987

Buckley, David N., *James Fintan Lalor: radical*. Cork, 1990

Bull, Philip, *Land, politics and nationalism: a study of the Irish land question*. Dublin, 1996

Burn, W.L., 'Free trade in land: an aspect of the Irish question', *Transactions of the Royal Historical Society*, 4th series, 31 (1949), 61–74

Clark, Samuel, and Donnelly, James S. (eds.), *Irish peasants: violence and political unrest 1780–1914*. Dublin, 1983

Conacher, J.B., *The Peelites and the party system 1846–52*. Newton Abbot, 1972

Connell, K.H., 'The colonization of waste land in Ireland, 1780–1845', *Economic History Review*, 2nd series, III (1950), 44–71

Connolly, S.J., 'The Catholic question, 1801–12', in W.E. Vaughan (ed.), *A new history of Ireland, vol. V: Ireland under the Union, I, 1801–70*. Oxford, 1989, pp. 24–47

Corish, P.J. (ed.), *Radicals, rebels and establishments: Historical Studies XV*. Belfast, 1983

Crawford, E. Margaret, 'Food and famine', in Cathal Póirtéir (ed.), *The Great Irish Famine: the Thomas Davis lecture series*. Cork, 1995, pp. 60–74

——, 'Indian meal and pellagra in nineteenth-century Ireland', in J.M. Goldstrom and L.A. Clarkson (eds.), *Irish population, economy and society*. Oxford, 1981, pp. 113–33

——, (ed.), *Famine: the Irish experience 900–1900. Subsistence crises and famines in Ireland.* Edinburgh, 1989

Crossman, Virginia, 'Emergency legislation and agrarian disorder in Ireland, 1821–41', *Irish Historical Studies*, XXVII (1991), 309–23

Cullen, L.M., *An economic history of Ireland since 1660.* 2nd edn, London, 1987

Curtis, L.P., 'Incumbered wealth: landed indebtedness in post-Famine Ireland', *American Historical Review*, LXXXV (1980), 332–67

Daly, Mary E., *The Famine in Ireland.* Dundalk, 1986

Davis, Richard, *The Young Ireland movement.* Dublin, 1987

Devine, T.M., *The Great Highland Famine: hunger, emigration and the Scottish Highlands in the nineteenth century.* Edinburgh, 1988

Devine, T.M., and Dickson, David (eds.), *Ireland and Scotland, 1600–1850: parallels and contrasts in economic and social development.* Edinburgh, 1983

Dewey, Clive J., 'The rehabilitation of the peasant proprietor in nineteenth-century economic thought', *History of Political Economy*, VI (1974), 17–47

Donnelly, James S., 'The construction of the memory of the Famine in Ireland and the Irish diaspora, 1850–1900', *Éire-Ireland*, XXXI (1996), 26–61

——, 'Famine and government response, 1845–6', 'Production, prices and exports, 1846–51', 'The administration of relief, 1846–7', 'The soup kitchens', 'The administration of relief, 1847–51', 'Landlords and tenants', 'Excess mortality and emigration', in W.E. Vaughan, (ed.), *A new history of Ireland, vol. V: Ireland under the Union, I, 1801–70.* Oxford, 1989, pp. 272–371

——, *The land and the people of nineteenth-century Cork: the rural economy and the land question.* London, 1975

——, 'The land question in nationalist politics', in T.H. Hachey and L.J. McCaffrey (eds.), *Perspectives on Irish nationalism.* Lexington, KY, 1989

——, 'Mass eviction and the Great Famine', in Cathal Póirtéir (ed.), *The Great Irish Famine: the Thomas Davis lecture series.* Cork, 1995, pp. 155–73

——, 'The social composition of agrarian rebellion in early nineteenth-century Ireland: the case of the Carders and Caravats, 1813–16', in P.J. Corish (ed.), *Radicals, rebels and establishments: Historical Studies XV.* Belfast, 1983, pp. 151–70

Dreyer, Frederick August, 'The Whigs and the political crisis of 1845', *English Historical Review*, LXXX (1965), 514–37

Duffy, Sir Charles Gavan, *Four years of Irish history, 1845–1849.* London, 1883

Edwards, R.D., and Williams, T.D. (eds.), *The Great Famine: studies in Irish history, 1845–1852.* Dublin, 1956

Edwards, Ruth Dudley, *The pursuit of reason:* The Economist *1843–1993.* London, 1993

Fairlie, Susan, 'The Corn Laws and British wheat production 1829–76', *Economic History Review*, 2nd series, XXII (1969), 88–116

——, 'The nineteenth-century Corn Law reconsidered', *Economic History Review*, 2nd series, XVIII (1965), 562–75

Fitzpatrick, David, 'The disappearance of the Irish agricultural labourer, 1841–1912', *Irish Economic and Social History*, VII (1980), 66–92

——, 'Famine, entitlements and seduction: Captain Edmond Wynne in Ireland, 1846–1851', *English Historical Review*, CX (1995), 596–619

——, 'Unrest in rural Ireland', *Irish Economic and Social History*, XII (1985), 98–105

Freeman, T.W., 'Land and people, *c.*1841', in W.E. Vaughan (ed.), *A new history of Ireland, vol. V: Ireland under the Union, I, 1801–70*. Oxford, 1989, pp. 342–71

Garvin, Tom, 'Defenders, Ribbonmen and others: underground political networks in pre-Famine Ireland', *Past and Present*, 96 (1982), 219–43

Gash, Norman, *Mr Secretary Peel: the life of Sir Robert Peel to 1830*. Harlow, 1985 edn

——, *Reaction and reconstruction in English politics, 1832–52*. Oxford, 1965

——, *Sir Robert Peel: the life of Sir Robert Peel after 1830*. Harlow, 1986 edn

Geary, Laurence M., 'Famine, fever and bloody flux', in Cathal Póirtéir (ed.), *The Great Irish Famine: the Thomas Davis lecture series*. Cork, 1995, pp. 74–85

Ghosh, R.N., 'The colonization controversy: R.J. Wilmot-Horton and the classical economists', *Economica*, n.s. XXXI (1964), 385–400

——, 'Malthus on emigration and colonization: letters to Wilmot-Horton', *Economica*, n.s. XXX (1963), 45–62

Goldstrom, J.M., 'Richard Whately and political economy in school books 1833–80', *Irish Historical Studies*, XV (1966–7), 131–46

Goldstrom, J.M., and Clarkson, L.A. (eds.), *Irish population, economy and society: essays in honour of the late K.H. Connell*. Oxford, 1981

Graham, A.H., 'The Lichfield House compact, 1835', *Irish Historical Studies*, XII (1960–1), 209–25

Grampp, William D., *The Manchester school of economics*. Stanford, CA, 1960

Grant, James, 'The Great Famine and the Poor Law in Ulster: the rate-in-aid issue of 1849', *Irish Historical Studies*, XXVII (1990), 30–47

Gray, Peter, 'British public opinion and the Great Irish Famine, 1845–49', in Breandán Ó Conaire (ed.), *Comhdháil an Chraoibhín: conference proceedings 1995*. Boyle, 1996, pp. 56–74

——, 'Famine relief policy in comparative perspective: Ireland, Scotland and North-Western Europe, 1845–49', *Éire-Ireland*, XXXII (1997), 86–108

——, 'Potatoes and Providence: British government's responses to the Great Famine', *Bullán: an Irish Studies Journal*, I (1994), 75–90

Griffiths, A.R.G., 'The Irish Board of Works in the Famine years', *Historical Journal*, XIII (1970), 634–52

Guthrie-Jones, Winston, *The Wynnes of Sligo and Leitrim*. Manorhamilton, 1994

Hart, Jennifer, 'Sir Charles Trevelyan at the Treasury', *English Historical Review*, LXXV (1960), 92–110

Hatton, Helen E., *The largest amount of good: Quaker relief in Ireland 1654–1921*. Kingston and Montreal, 1993

Haury, D.A., *The origins of the Liberal Party and liberal imperialism: the career of Charles Buller 1806–1848*. New York, 1987

Hawkins, Angus, 'Lord Derby and Victorian Conservatism: a reappraisal', *Parliamentary History*, VI (1987), 280–301

——, '"Parliamentary Government" and Victorian political parties, *c.*1830–*c.*1880', *English Historical Review*, CIV (1989), 638–669

Hernon, J.M., 'A Victorian Cromwell: Sir Charles Trevelyan, the Famine and the age of improvement', *Éire-Ireland*, XXII (1987), 15–29

Hilton, Boyd, *The age of atonement: the influence of evangelicalism on social and economic thought, 1785–1865*. Oxford, 1988

——, *Corn, cash, commerce: the economic policies of the Tory governments 1815–1830*. Oxford, 1977

——, 'Peel: a reappraisal', *Historical Journal*, XXII (1979), 585–614

——, 'The ripening of Robert Peel', in Michael Bentley (ed.), *Public and private doctrine: essays in British history presented to Maurice Cowling*. Cambridge, 1993, pp. 63–84

——, 'Whiggery, religion and social reform: the case of Lord Morpeth', *Historical Journal*, XXXVII (1994), 829–59

Himmelfarb, Gertrude, *The idea of poverty: England in the early industrial age*. London, 1984

Hollander, Samuel, *The economics of John Stuart Mill*. 2 vols., Oxford, 1985

Hoppen, K. Theodore, *Elections, politics and society in Ireland, 1832–1885*. Oxford, 1984

——, *Ireland since 1800: conflict and conformity*. Harlow, 1989

Jenkins, Brian, *Sir William Gregory of Coole: a biography*. Gerrard's Cross, 1986

Jordan, Donald E., *Land and popular politics in Ireland: County Mayo from the Plantation to the Land War*. Cambridge, 1994

Kemp, Betty, 'Reflections on the repeal of the Corn Laws', *Victorian Studies*, V (1961–2), 189–204

Kennedy, B.A., 'The tenant right agitation in Ulster, 1845–50', *Bulletin of the Irish Committee for Historical Sciences*, 34 (1944), 2–5

——, 'Tenant right before 1870', in T.W. Moody and J.C. Beckett (eds.), *Ulster since 1800: a political and economic survey*. London, 1954, pp. 39–49

Kennedy, Liam, and Ollerenshaw, Philip (eds.), *An economic history of Ulster, 1820–1940*. Manchester, 1985

Kerr, Donal A., *'A nation of beggars'? Priests, people and politics in Famine Ireland 1846–1852*. Oxford, 1994

——, *Peel, priests and politics: Sir Robert Peel's administration and the Roman Catholic Church in Ireland, 1841–6*. Oxford, 1982

Kinealy, Christine, *This great calamity: the Irish Famine 1845–52*. Dublin, 1994

Kinzer, Bruce L., 'J.S. Mill and Irish land: a reassessment', *Historical Journal*, XXVII (1984), 111–27

Kriegel, A.D., 'The Irish policy of Lord Grey's government', *English Historical Review*, LXXXVI (1971), 22–45

Lane, Padraig G., 'The Encumbered Estates Court, Ireland, 1848–9', *Economic and Social Review*, 3 (1972), 413–53

——, 'The general impact of the Encumbered Estates Act of 1849 on Counties Galway and Mayo', *Journal of the Galway Archaeological and Historical Society*, XXXII (1972–3), 44–74

——, 'The impact of the Encumbered Estates Court upon the landlords of Galway and Mayo', *Journal of the Galway Archeological and Historical Society*, XXXVIII (1981–2), 45–58

Lee, Joseph, 'The Ribbonmen', in T.D. Williams (ed.), *Secret societies in Ireland.* Dublin, 1973, pp. 26–35

——, 'The social and economic ideas of O'Connell', in Kevin B. Nowlan and Maurice R. O'Connell (eds.), *Daniel O'Connell: portrait of a radical.* Belfast, 1984, pp. 70–84

Levy, S. Leon, *Nassau W. Senior, 1790–1864: critical essayist, classical economist and adviser of governments.* Newton Abbot, 1970

Locker Lampson, G., *A consideration of the state of Ireland in the nineteenth century.* London, 1907

McCaffrey, L., *Daniel O'Connell and the Repeal year*, Lexington, KY, 1966

McCord, J.N., 'The image in England', in Maurice R. O'Connell (ed.), *Daniel O'Connell: political pioneer.* Dublin, 1991, pp. 57–71

MacDonagh, Oliver, *The emancipist: Daniel O'Connell 1830–47.* London, 1989

——, *The hereditary bondsman: Daniel O'Connell 1775–1829.* London, 1988

——, 'Irish emigration to the United States of America and British colonies during the Famine', in R.D. Edwards and T.D. Williams (eds.), *The Great Famine: studies in Irish history 1845–1852.* Dublin, 1956, pp. 319–88

——, 'Politics 1830–45', in W.E. Vaughan (ed.), *A new history of Ireland, vol. V: Ireland under the Union, I, 1801–70.* Oxford, 1989, pp. 169–92

——, *States of mind: a study of Anglo-Irish conflict 1780–1980.* London, 1983

McDowell, R.B., *The Irish administration, 1801–1914.* London, 1964

——, *Public opinion and government policy in Ireland, 1801–1846.* London, 1952

Machin, G.I.T., 'The Maynooth grant, the Dissenters and disestablishment, 1845–1847', *English Historical Review*, LXXXII (1967), 61–85

Macintyre, Angus, *The liberator: Daniel O'Connell and the Irish party 1830–47.* London, 1965

Magnusson, Magnus, *Landlord or tenant? A view of Irish history.* London, 1978

Mandler, Peter, *Aristocratic government in the age of reform: Whigs and Liberals, 1830–1852.* Oxford, 1990

——, 'The making of the new Poor Law *redivivus*', *Past and Present*, 117 (1987), 131–57

——, 'Tories and paupers: Christian political economy and the making of the new Poor Law', *Historical Journal*, XXXIII (1990), 81–103

Martin, David, *John Stuart Mill and the land question.* Hull, 1981

——, 'Land reform', in Patricia Hollis (ed.), *Pressure from without in early Victorian England.* London, 1974, pp. 131–58

——, 'The rehabilitation of the peasant proprietor in nineteenth-century economic thought: a comment', *History of Political Economy*, VIII (1976), 297–302

Matthew, H.C.G., *Gladstone, 1809–1874.* Oxford, 1986

Mitchell, Austin, *The Whigs in opposition 1815–30.* Oxford, 1967

Mitchell, L.G., *Charles James Fox.* Oxford, 1992

——, *Holland House.* London, 1980

Mokyr, Joel, 'Uncertainty and pre-Famine Irish agriculture', in T.M. Devine and David Dickson (eds.), *Ireland and Scotland, 1600–1850: parallels and contrasts in economic and social development.* Edinburgh, 1983, pp. 89–101

——, *Why Ireland starved: a quantitative and analytical history of the Irish economy, 1800–1850.* London, 1985 edn

Mokyr, Joel, and Ó Gráda, Cormac, 'Poor and getting poorer? Living standards in Ireland before the Famine', *Economic History Review*, 2nd series, LXI (1988), 209–35

Molony, John N., *A soul came into Ireland: Thomas Davis 1814–1845, a biography.* Dublin, 1995

Moody, T.W., *Davitt and Irish revolution, 1846–82.* Oxford, 1981

Moore, D.C., 'The Corn Laws and high farming', *Economic History Review*, 2nd series, XVIII (1965), 544–61

Morash, Christopher, *Writing the Irish Famine.* Oxford, 1995

Morash, Christopher, and Hayes, Richard (eds.), *Fearful realities: new perspectives on the Famine.* Blackrock, 1996

[Morison, Stanley], *The history of the Times: Vol. II – The tradition established 1841–84.* London, 1939

Morley, Tom, '"The arcana of that great machine": Politicians and the *Times* in the late 1840s', *History*, 73 (1988), 38–54

Munsell, F. Darrell, 'Charles Edward Trevelyan and Peelite Irish famine policy, 1845–1846', *Societas – a Review of Social History*, I (1971), 299–315

——, *The unfortunate duke: the life of Henry Pelham, fifth Duke of Newcastle, 1811–1864*, Columbia, MO, 1984

Murphy, Antoin E. (ed.), *Economists and the Irish economy: from the eighteenth century to the present day.* Dublin, 1984

Newbould, Ian, 'Whiggery and the growth of party 1830–1841: Organization and the challenge of reform', *Parliamentary History*, IV (1985), 137–56

Nowlan, Kevin B., *The politics of Repeal: a study in the relations between Great Britain and Ireland, 1841–50.* London, 1965

Nowlan, Kevin B., and O'Connell, Maurice R. (eds.), *Daniel O'Connell, portrait of a radical.* Belfast, 1984

O'Brien, D.P., *The classical economists.* Oxford, 1975

O'Brien, Gerard, 'The establishment of Poor Law Unions in Ireland, 1838–43', *Irish Historical Studies,* XXIII (1982), 97–120

O'Connell, Maurice R., 'John O'Connell and the Great Famine', *Irish Historical Studies,* XXV (1986), 138–43

——, (ed.), *Daniel O'Connell: political pioneer.* Dublin, 1991

Ó Gráda, Cormac, *The Great Irish Famine.* London, 1989

——, *Ireland: a new economic history 1780–1939.* Oxford, 1994

——, *Ireland before and after the Famine: explorations in economic history, 1800–1925.* Manchester, 1988

——, 'Malthus and the pre-Famine economy', in Antoin E. Murphy (ed.), *Economists and the Irish economy from the eighteenth century to the present day.* Dublin 1984, pp. 75–95

——, 'Poverty, population and agriculture, 1801–45', 'Industry and communications, 1801–45', in W.E. Vaughan (ed.), *A new history of Ireland, vol. V: Ireland under the Union, I, 1801–70.* Oxford, 1989, pp. 108–57

Olien, Diana Davids, *Morpeth: a Victorian public career.* Washington, 1983

Ó Muirithe, Diarmaid, 'O'Connell in Irish folk tradition', in Maurice R. O'Connell (ed.), *Daniel O'Connell: political pioneer.* Dublin, 1991, pp. 72–85

O'Neill, Thomas P., 'The Irish land question, 1830–50', *Studies,* XLIV (1955), 325–36

——, 'The organization and administration of relief, 1845–52', in R.D. Edwards and T.D. Williams (eds.), *The Great Famine: studies in Irish history 1845–1852.* Dublin, 1956

Opie, Redvers, 'A neglected English economist: George Poulett Scrope', *Quarterly Journal of Economics,* XLIV (1929), 101–37

Ó Tuathaigh, M.A.G., *Ireland before the Famine 1798–1848.* Dublin, 1972

——, *Thomas Drummond and the government of Ireland, 1835–41.* Dublin, 1978

Palmer, Sarah, *Politics, shipping and the repeal of the Navigation Laws.* Manchester, 1990

Partridge, M.S., 'The Russell cabinet and national defence, 1846–1852', *History,* 72 (1987), 231–50

Perkin, H.J., 'Land reform and class conflict in Victorian Britain', in J. Butt and I.F. Clarke (eds), *The Victorians and social protest.* Newton Abbot, 1973, pp. 177–217

Póirtéir, Cathal, *Famine echoes.* Dublin, 1995

——, (ed.), *The Great Irish Famine: the Thomas Davis lecture series.* Cork, 1995

Pomfret, John E., *The struggle for land in Ireland, 1800–1923.* Princeton, 1930

Prest, John, *Lord John Russell.* London, 1972

——, *Politics in the age of Cobden.* London, 1977

Read, Donald, *Peel and the Victorians*. Oxford, 1987

Ryder, Sean, 'Reading lessons: Famine and the *Nation*, 1845–1849', in Chris Morash and Richard Hayes (eds.), *Fearful realities: new perspectives on the Famine*. Blackrock, 1996, pp. 151–63

Scally, Robert James, *The end of hidden Ireland: rebellion, famine and emigration*. New York, 1995

Smith, E.A., *Lord Grey 1764–1845*. Oxford, 1990

Solar, Peter, 'The Great Famine was no ordinary subsistence crisis', in E. Margaret Crawford (ed.), *Famine: the Irish experience 900–1900*. Edinburgh, 1989, pp. 112–29

Solow, B.L., *The land question and the Irish economy, 1870–1903*. Cambridge, MA, 1971

Spring, David, 'A great agricultural estate: Netherby under Sir James Graham, 1820–1845', *Agricultural History*, XXIX (1955), 73–81

Steele, E.D., *Irish land and British politics: tenant right and nationality, 1865–70*. Cambridge, 1974

Steele, E.D., 'J.S. Mill and the Irish question: the principle of political economy, 1848–1865', *Historical Journal*, XIII (1970), 216–36

Stewart, Robert, *The politics of protection: Lord Derby and the Protectionist Party 1841–52*. Cambridge, 1971

Taylor, Miles, *The decline of British radicalism 1847–1860*. Oxford, 1995

Thompson, F.M.L., 'Land and politics in England in the nineteenth century', *Transactions of the Royal Historical Society*, 5th series, 15 (1965), 22–44

Turner, Michael, *After the Famine: Irish agriculture 1850–1914*. Cambridge, 1996

Vaughan, W.E., *Landlords and tenants in Ireland. 1848–1904*. Dublin, 1984

——, (ed.), *A new history of Ireland, vol. V: Ireland under the Union, I, 1801–70*. Oxford, 1989

Wadsworth, A.P., *Newspaper circulations, 1800–1854*. Manchester, 1955

Waterman, A.M.C., *Revolution, economics and religion: Christian political economy 1798–1833*. Cambridge, 1991

Whyte, J.H., *The Independent Irish Party, 1850–9*. Oxford, 1958

——, *The Tenant League and Irish politics in the eighteen-fifties*. Dundalk, 1972

Williams, T.D. (ed.), *Secret societies in Ireland*. Dublin, 1973

Woodham-Smith, Cecil, *The great hunger: Ireland 1845–1849*. London, 1987 edn

Wright, Frank, *Two lands on one soil: Ulster politics before Home Rule*. Dublin, 1996

Zastoupil, Lynn, 'Moral government: J.S. Mill on Ireland', *Historical Journal*, XXVI (1983), 707–17

VII UNPUBLISHED THESES

Crossman, Virginia, 'The politics of security: a study of the official reaction to rural unrest in Ireland 1821–41', University of Oxford, D.Phil., 1989

Dreyer, Frederick August, 'The Russell administration 1846–52', University of St. Andrews, Ph.D., 1962

Job, R., 'The political career of the third Earl Grey', University of Durham, M.Litt., 1959

Jowitt, John Anthony, 'Sir Charles Wood (1800–85): a case study in the formation of Liberalism in mid-Victorian England', University of Leeds, M.Phil., 1981

Montague, R.J., 'Relief and reconstruction in Ireland 1845–9: a study in public policy during the Great Famine', University of Oxford, D.Phil., 1976

Index

Aberdeen, 4th Earl of (Foreign Secretary, 1841–6; Prime Minister, 1852–5) 108n.
Advocate 306n.
agrarian unrest 10–11, 13, 27, 34–5, 37, 42–5, 53, 73–4, 84–6, 90, 92, 112, 138–9, 144n., 173–4, 181–3, 187n., 210–11, 222, 278, 291. See also Ribbonism, Whiteboys
Albert, Prince 79n., 147, 291n.
Alcock, Thomas 177
Althorp, Viscount (3rd Earl Spencer, 1834) 22
America, South 115n.
America, United States of 98, 103, 113–14, 116n., 123, 172, 180, 208n., 251n., 252–3, 256, 259n., 261n., 286, 308, 309n., 315n., 322n., 324n., 328
Anglesey, 1st Marquess of (Lord Lieutenant, 1828–9, 1830–3) 27, 28n.
Anster, John 177n., 178n., 200–1
Anti-Corn Law League 25, 69, 89n., 96n., 97, 105–6, 108, 146, 151
Antrim, County 136n.
Armagh, County 161
Auckland, 1st Earl of (First Lord of the Admiralty, 1846–9) 22, 26, 148

Ball, John 315–16
Ballina 308
Ballinasloe 89, 317n.
Ballykilcline 193n., 307
Bank Charter Act (1844) 275, 289
Baring Brothers 113–14, 123
Baring, Sir Francis (Chancellor of the Exchequer, 1839–41; First Lord of the Admiralty, 1849–52) 22, 26, 34, 148
Barrington, Sir Matthew 207, 208n.
Barron, Sir Winston 134, 161n., 176
Beaumont, 8th Baron 116n., 177
Bedford, 6th Duke of (Lord Lieutenant, 1806–7) 19–20, 22, 169n.
Bedford, 7th Duke of (Marquess of Tavistock to 1839) 22, 23n., 26, 55n., 67n., 79n., 150, 181n., 269; declines the Lord Lieutenancy, 169–70
Belfast 8, 72n., 174n., 221, 253n., 325
Belgium 200, 244
Benthamism 15, 25, 35n., 44, 59, 197, 253n., 321
Bentinck, Lord George 146–7, 269, 271–2, 280
Bessborough, 4th Earl of (Viscount Duncannon to 1844; Home Secretary, 1834–5; First Commissioner of Woods, 1835–41; Lord Lieutenant, 1846–7) 19, 75n., 149, 165–8, 239, 330; Foxite Whig, 19–20, 26, 167–8, 242; party organizer, 20, 147, 168, 272; and O'Connell, 22, 28–9, 60, 145–6, 150–1, 167–8, 237, 241n., 330; as Commissioner of Woods, 29, 147, 159; and Irish Poor Law, 33, 245, 246–50, 262, 276, 280; and land reform, 59–60, 66, 88, 153, 164–5, 179, 186, 198n., 199n., 330; and Devon Commission, 74–5, 160; and coercion, 145–6; and free trade, 146–7; as Lord Lieutenant, 147–51, 153, 167–8, 170, 229, 242, 259; and waste lands, 153, 159–60, 164–5, 330; and franchise reform, 163–4; and public works relief, 240–3, 246, 248–50, 262, 264–5, 271, 273, 286; on Irish society, 244–6, 281n.; and emigration, 246, 300; and food policy, 250–1, 256; and soup kitchens, 256, 263–5; and seed, 264; and fever, 268
Bianconi, Charles 120n.
Birmingham 275
Blackburne, Francis (Attorney General, Ireland, 1830–4, 1841–2) 44
Blake, Sir Valentine 38

Board of Works 10, 27, 133–7, 159–60, 237, 240–3, 249, 255, 262, 264n., 299, 317
botanists 100n., 102, 233–4, 244, 285
Bowood 12, 22, 25, 62, 65, 160, 170, 198, 250
Brady, Maziere (Solicitor General, Ireland 1837–9; Attorney General, Ireland 1839–40; Lord Chancellor, Ireland, 1846–52) 149–50, 164, 179, 216–17, 219, 242n.
Bright, John 201–2, 218, 225, 260, 334
British Association 191, 257–9, 285n., 294, 303, 311, 325
Brougham, 1st Baron 177, 219, 281n.
Brunel, Isambard Kingdom 272
Buller, Charles (Judge Advocate General, 1846–7; Chief Poor Law Commissioner, England, 1847–8) 26n., 54, 59, 163, 307
Burgoyne, Sir John Fox (Chairman of Board of Works, 1831–45; Chairman of Relief Commission, 1847) 263, 264n., 266, 289, 290
Burke, Edmund 21, 34, 80, 104n., 125, 254
Butt, Isaac 161n., 227, 267, 270, 271n., 300n., 314n., 336, 337n.
by-elections 37, 149, 178n.

Caird, James 81n., 221–2, 224, 330n.
Campbell, 1st Baron (Lord Chancellor, Ireland, 1841; Chancellor of Duchy of Lancaster, 1846–50) 59, 203, 219
Canada 12, 163n., 182, 198, 299–301, 308–9
Canningites 23, 27, 168
Cardwell, Edward (Secretary to the Treasury, 1845–6; Chief Secretary, 1859–61) 119, 334
Carlisle, 7th Earl of. See Morpeth, Viscount
Carlow, County 19
Carrick-on-Suir 120–1
Cashel 172
Catholic Church 3, 56, 68, 78; clergy and politics, 11, 45–6, 55, 63, 68, 79, 209; and land agitation, 49, 73, 90, 137, 172–4, 182, 184, 336; state endowment of, 11–12, 62–5, 79–80, 153, 203, 209–10, 307, 324n.; and Devon Commission, 68; and famine relief, 101n., 112–13, 122, 172–3, 265n., 284, 294, 311; and Irish Poor Law, 276, 277n., 296n.; and Queen's visit, 221. See also Maynooth College, Maynooth grant.
Catholic emancipation 11, 21–2, 30, 37, 44, 80, 97, 169n.
Cavan, County 86, 112n., 178n.
Central Board of Health 268
Ceylon 257
Chads, Captain 126–8
Chalmers, Revd Thomas 14, 15, 275n.
Chancery, Irish Court of 84, 199, 203, 206–7, 212, 217–18, 222
Chartists 304
Cholera 244, 305, 317
Christian economists 14–16
Christian Observer 110
Church of England, prayers read in, 239; and charity, 258–9, 260, 289
Church of Ireland, reform of, 11–12, 25, 28, 51, 53–4, 56, 59, 62–3, 65, 79n., 94, 148; and Devon Commission, 68; sale of lands, 210; prayers read in, 239; and Queen's letter, 257–8; and famine relief, 311
Clanricarde, 1st Marquess of (Postmaster-General, 1846–52) moderate liberal, 23, 26, 62, 148, 167n.; Irish landowner, 23, 177, 244n., 325, 330; and land legislation, 66, 87, 88n., 91n., 175, 177–9, 185, 192–3; and coercion, 144–5; and Encumbered Estates Act, 198, 202, 205, 220; and famine relief, 230, 262n., 287, 296–7, 325
Clapham Sect 15, 24, 110, 258
Clare, County 37, 85n., 181, 211, 287, 323, 332
Clare, 2nd Earl of 112
Clarendon, 4th Earl of (George Villiers to 1838; President of Board of Trade, 1846–7; Lord Lieutenant, 1847–52) 240, 244; as Lord Lieutenant, 3, 168–70, 179, 327; and land reform, 3, 67, 160, 171–2, 178–9, 181, 184–5, 187–93, 206–8, 219–20, 225; Canningite, 23, 168; moderate liberal, 23, 26, 160, 168, 170–1, 179, 269; and Irish Church reform, 79n.; at Board of Trade, 148; relationship with

Clarendon (*contd.*)
moralists, 148, 149n., 171, 216, 291, 312; and Repealers, 150, 169n., 171, 179; and Russell, 168–9, 171, 178–9, 181–91, 193, 202–3, 205–6, 209–10, 216, 220–1, 269, 290–2, 294–8, 302, 306–10, 313, 317, 319–20, 322–3, 325, 329; and *Times*, 169, 182, 189–90, 221, 305, 308, 313; and Irish Poor Law, 170–1, 250, 291–8, 318, 320, 322; and famine relief, 171n., 285, 290–2, 294, 296, 298, 303–5, 307–9, 312, 314, 325, 331; and Catholic Church, 172, 173n., 209–10, 294, 307; and coercion, 180, 182, 186–7, 190; and parliament, 195; and Encumbered Estates Bills, 198n., 202–3, 205–7, 216, 219–22, 224; and Peel, 215–16, 220–1; and Queen's visit, 221–2; and Caird, 222, 224, 330n.; and Spain, 291; and rebellion, 291, 294, 303–4; and waste lands, 298n.; and public works, 299, 316–17, 324–5; and taxation, 302, 308, 317; suggested as Prime Minister, 302n.; and France, 303n.; and agricultural instructors, 304; and propaganda, 306; and emigration, 307–10; and clearances, 309; and rate in aid, 313–14, 317, 320; and S.G. Osborne, 327
clearances 10, 13–14, 43, 45, 47, 65, 70, 72, 75, 89n., 91, 132, 139, 155, 157, 177, 180–1, 183, 187, 191–2, 193n., 194, 197, 206n., 208, 210, 224, 245–6, 249, 278, 295–6, 308, 317, 319, 323, 330, 332, 336
Clements, Lord 51
Clonmel 120–1
Coast Guard 114, 126
Cobden, Richard 24, 105, 312
Cobdenites 215, 267
coercion 21, 24, 27–8, 30, 32, 37, 48, 51, 53, 56n., 60–1, 77, 82–3, 90–2, 96, 138–41, 143–6, 151–2, 182–3, 185–7, 195, 205, 209, 210, 309, 313; Arms Act (1843), 51; Protection of Life Bill (1846), 90–2, 96, 138–40, 143–6; Crimes and Outrages Act (1847), 186–7; Suspension of Habeas Corpus Act (1848), 195, 210n., 309
Coffin, Commissary-General Edward Pine 125n., 140n.
Coleraine 173
Commissariat 114, 118–25, 128, 229, 237, 253–4, 287, 307
conacre 71, 73, 118, 123–4, 165, 181, 234, 244, 335
Connacht 140, 191n., 192, 212–14, 293n., 309, 316
Connellan, Corry (Secretary to the Lord Lieutenant, 1846–7) 149
Connemara 216, 220n., 221
Conner, William 47, 52, 175
Conservative Party 17, 35, 37–40, 48, 61, 67n., 78, 80, 94, 109–10, 128, 143, 274n., 288, 301. See also Peelites, Protectionists, Tory Party
consolidation 5, 8, 10, 43, 49–50, 54, 68, 70, 75, 164, 178, 179n., 180–1, 219, 224, 309
Cork 103, 118, 221
Cork, County 4, 103, 166n., 174n., 227, 238n.
Cork Examiner 214
Corn Laws 16, 25, 79, 83, 90, 96–106, 107–119, 125, 130, 134, 138, 144, 145–6, 147, 196–7, 201, 213, 233, 238, 239n., 251, 254, 256. See also Anti-Corn Law League
Cottenham, 1st Baron (Lord Chancellor, 1836–41, 1846–50) 198–9, 203
cottiers 8, 9–10, 11, 68, 71, 72, 123, 156–7, 165, 175, 177, 180–1, 183, 188, 191–2, 194, 211, 237, 244–6, 278–9, 287, 308–9, 335
Crawford, William Sharman 14, 49; and Irish Poor Law, 32–3, 49, 132, 278, 297–7; and tenant right, 47–50, 166n., 173; proposes land reform bills, 49–50, 52, 66, 71, 75, 87–9, 165–6, 190; support for, 52, 175–6; criticism of, 67, 60, 166, 189; and emigration, 54n.; and government land bills, 89, 92–3, 189, 193, 208n.; and free trade, 117–18; and waste lands, 154–5; censures Russell, 194–5
Crimean War 333
Croker, John Dillon 103, 104n.
Croker, John Wilson 101, 306n.

Daily News 192, 203–4, 211, 214
Dalhousie, 10th Earl of (President, Board of Trade, 1845) 282

Davis, Thomas 34, 46, 72, 149
Davitt, Michael 337
de Grey, Earl (Lord Lieutenant, 1841–4) 44, 48, 57, 78
Delane, John Thadeus 169, 182, 216n., 306, 308n., 313
Denison, Evelyn 101
Devon Commission (1843–5) 3, 42, 56–9, 62, 66–7, 68–76, 77, 78, 82–4, 85, 89, 92, 94, 95, 129, 133, 138, 153–4, 158–9, 196, 214
Devon, 10th Earl of, advises Peel, 57–8, 82–3; as Irish landlord, 57–8, 82, 240n.; and Foxite Whigs, 67, 160; and Irish opinion, 72; as moderate liberal, 78, 233, 250; and land legislation, 85, 87, 89–90, 92–3, 186; on potato failure, 105; and waste lands, 153; and Wood, 160, 198; at Bowood, 160, 186, 198, 250; and Encumbered Estates Bill, 198, 217; and Farmers' Estates Society, 206–8; and Times, 233; and 'labour rate', 240n.; and Irish Poor Law, 250, 281, 318; as Peelite, 281
Devonshire, 6th Duke of 19
Dillon, John Blake 46, 72
Disraeli, Benjamin 213, 269, 312
Dobree, Assistant Commissary-General 120–1, 125n.
Doheny, Michael 174
Donegal, County 126, 140
Down, County 49
Doyle, James Warren, Bishop of Kildare 14, 32, 33
drainage 50, 87, 130, 134–5, 194, 210, 215, 234, 241–2, 249, 265n., 269, 299, 303, 307, 315–17, 324
Drogheda 175
Drummond, Thomas (Under-Secretary, 1835–40) 31, 32–3, 34, 35, 59, 126
Dublin 36, 113, 169n., 199, 221, 226, 261
Dublin Evening Mail 71–2, 208, 214
Dublin Review 56, 141n., 172, 174n., 181n., 215n., 223, 276n., 322n., 336–7
Dublin University Magazine 4n., 48n., 72, 161n., 178n., 179n., 201n., 223, 225n., 227, 270n., 287n., 300n.
Dufferin, Lord 326
Duffy, Charles Gavan 46, 175n., 209
Duncan, Jonathan 172, 174n.
Duncannon, Viscount. See Bessborough, 4th Earl of
Dundalk 149, 176
Dungarvan 265n.

East India Company 156n.
Easthope, Sir John 75n., 211n.
Ebrington, Viscount. See Fortescue, 2nd Earl
Ecclesiastical Titles Bill (1851) 226, 334
Economist 75–6, 251n., 275
Edinburgh letter 107
Edinburgh Review 16, 22, 41n., 62–5, 156n., 165n., 204, 208n., 235, 239, 276n., 305n., 317–18, 324n.
education 10, 27, 39n., 62, 81, 117, 171n., 184, 208n., 260
Eliot, Lord (3rd Earl of St Germans, 1845; Chief Secretary, 1841–5) 44, 57, 68, 281
Ellice, Edward (Secretary at War, 1832–4) 24, 26, 145n., 198, 212, 218, 233n., 243n, 292
emigration, landlord-assisted 182, 183n., 300, 307, 321
emigration, state-assisted 12, 54, 70, 86, 193n., 210, 212, 238n., 245–6, 299–301, 307–10, 314–15, 316n., 324
emigration, voluntary 117, 149n., 180–1, 210–11, 263, 265, 277–9, 287, 301, 307n., 308–10, 325, 328, 338
Encumbered Estates Bills 70, 73, 77, 83–4, 139–40, 158, 177, 195–8, 199–202, 207, 212–14; 1847 Bill, 198–9; 1848 Act, 202–6, 208–9, 211–12, 216–17, 330; 1849 Act, 3, 40, 217–24, 316, 325–7
Encumbered Estates Commission 222–3
Ensor, Thomas 106n., 349
Erris 291
evangelicalism 14–16, 24, 81n., 98–101, 102, 104–6, 110, 148, 231–2, 253–4, 257–8, 310–11, 329
Examiner 288–9, 290n., 327
famines, threat of, 7; in 1816–17, 8, 37, 110, 126; in 1822, 8, 110, 126; Malthus on, 8; in 1831, 39, 126–8; in 1835, 126; in 1837, 126; in 1836, 126–7; in 1839, 126–8; pattern of, 142; in Scottish Highlands, 198, 255; in Europe, 225, 244

Farmers' Estate Society 207–9, 219, 224, 330
Farnham, 7th Baron 86
Fenianism 336
Ferguson, Sir Robert 58, 64, 72, 87n., 89
fever 268, 297
Financial Reform Association 218, 312
FitzPatrick, P.V. 151
Fitzwilliam, 5th Earl (Viscount Milton to 1833) 22, 26, 35n., 66, 147, 203, 221, 281–2, 317
fixity of tenure 47, 49–50, 51–2, 53, 55–6, 59, 64, 70–1, 73, 86, 92, 157, 165, 172, 175, 335–6
Flanders 225n.
food riots 120–2
Forster, William 261
Fortescue, 2nd Earl (Viscount Ebrington to 1841; Lord Lieutenant, 1839–41) Foxite Whig, 20, 26, 242n.; evangelical, 20n.; as Lord Lieutenant, 29, 35; and land reform, 53, 64n., 67, 85n., 88–9; and Church reform, 63; as Lord Steward, 147; and waste lands, 159; and franchise reform, 163; on O'Connell, 166; and Encumbered Estates Bill, 198; and Queen's visit, 221n.
Fortescue, Chichester (Chief Secretary, 1865–6, 1868–70) 334–5
Foster, Thomas Campbell 7n., 76–8, 112n., 139n., 156, 233n., 290
Fox, Charles James 18–19, 21, 30, 66, 238
Fox, William John 105–6
Foxites, faction in Whig-Liberal Party, 18–22, 26, 28–9, 36, 80, 146–7, 196, 242, 329–30; and Lord Holland, 19–21; and Russell, 19–22, 26, 59, 143, 146, 170, 195–6, 239, 295, 299n., 306, 309, 319, 329–30; and Bessborough, 19–20, 26, 167–8, 242, 330; and Ireland, 21–2, 27, 30, 61, 65, 80, 151, 168, 203, 224, 261, 306, 309, 320; and O'Connell, 22, 28–30, 33, 54, 61, 67, 168, 237, 276, 330, 337; and coercion, 22, 24, 28, 30, 32, 35, 145, 195; and Morpeth, 20, 26, 170–1; and Fortescue, 20, 26, 198; and Irish Church reform, 28–9, 31; and Irish government (1835–41), 29–36, 65; and Irish landlords, 31–2, 295, 319; and economic heterodoxy, 31, 237, 239, 328; and Irish Poor Law, 32–3, 239, 276, 319–20; and Devon Commission, 59, 74; and land reform, 88, 245, 328–30; and Lady John Russell, 143; and 1846 government, 147, 149; and franchise reform, 163, 226, 299n.; and Alexander MacDonnell, 171; Clarendon hostile to, 181n.; and Encumbered Estates Act, 198; and Queen's visit, 221; victims of potato blight, 329; and Gladstone, 335
France 190, 303n.
franchise reform 3, 19, 35n., 51, 53–4, 65, 89n., 147n., 153, 163–4, 210, 217n., 226, 299n.
Fraser's Magazine 138
Freeman's Journal 72, 78n., 85, 87n., 88, 92, 122, 141n., 145n., 151n., 153n., 158, 162, 167n., 170n., 189, 208, 214, 228, 230n., 234n., 265n., 266, 268, 270n., 282n., 295n., 300n., 301n., 336
Fremantle, Sir Thomas (Chief Secretary, 1845–6) on agrarian disturbances, 90, 112; resignation, 90; against English 'tenant right', 93n.; and Peel, 100; and potato failure, 101n.; on Catholic clergy, 112; doubts about Lucas, 128; and drainage loans, 134; and public works relief, 136
French, Fitzstephen 270
Friends, Society of. See Quakers

Galway, County 91, 122, 192–3, 325
general elections (1841), 36, 97; (1847), 21n., 97, 175–6, 178n., 201, 218, 243, 276, 285, 288
Gerrard evictions 91, 132, 152n.
Gibson, Revd Charles 238
Gibson, Thomas Milner 26n.
Gladstone, William Ewart (Colonial Secretary, 1845–6; Chancellor of Exchequer, 1853–5, 1859–65, Prime Minister, 1868–74) and land reform, 5, 184, 334–5; and Corn Law crisis, 101, 105n., 108n.; and Peelites, 212; and 1853 budget, 222, 333n.
Glengall, 2nd Earl of 82, 103, 206, 219
Godley, John Robert 300–1

Gore, Charles 159
Goulburn, Henry (Chief Secretary, 1821–7; Chancellor of Exchequer, 1841–6) liberal Tory, 15, 39, 97; evangelical, 15; as Chief Secretary, 39, 111; and Corn Laws, 97, 111; and Indian corn purchase, 113n., 121; defends Trevelyan, 121, 136–7; and public works relief, 136–7, 274n.; consulted by Russell, 230; and Irish Poor Law, 280n.
Graham, Sir James (First Lord of the Admiralty, 1830–4; Home Secretary, 1841–6) leaves Whigs, 28–9; and Peel, 39, 100–1, 213n.; and 1831 famine, 39, 126–7; and land reform, 55–7, 85–6, 90–1; and Church reform, 56; and Russell, 56, 271, 273, 280n., 309; on Lalor, 56n.; and Encumbered Estates Bills, 56, 206, 213n.; and Catholic endowment, 56, 210n.; and Devon Commission, 56–8, 82, 85; on Mahony, 74n.; and Greville, 79n.; and high farming, 81–2, 91n.; and coercion, 83, 91, 122, 138–40; on clearances, 91; and 1845 potato failure, 95, 97–103, 107, 115; and Corn Laws, 97, 99–100, 107, 108–9, 113–14, 117–18, 130; evangelicalism, 98, 101; providentialism, 98–101, 106, 115, 129, 131; and agrarian disturbances, 112–13, 122, 139; and O'Connell, 113, 146; and Relief Commission, 113, 127–33; and food policy, 113, 115, 118, 120, 125, 273; and public works relief, 113, 133, 136–7, 273; and seed, 115; and emigration, 117; and Trevelyan, 120–1, 137, 273; and 1846 potato failure, 124; and Burke, 125; and Irish Poor Law, 129–33, 230, 273, 280n.; and wages fund, 130, 133; and agricultural improvement, 130–1, 139; and Lincoln, 137; resignation, 140; and Whigs, 146, 210n.; and waste lands, 155; and Clarendon, 169; and rate in aid, 212n., 313n.; and West Indies, 213n.; and railway bills, 271, 273; against 1849 relief grant, 312
Granville, 2nd Earl of 335n.
Grattan, Henry 21
Gregory, William 109, 277–8, 325
Greville, Charles Cavendish Fulke 1; Clerk of the Privy Council, 23; moderate liberal, 23; on O'Connell, 23–4, 168; and coercion, 24; on Russell, 55, 66, 144, 216; on land reform, 55n.; on party politics, 68, 79; on Peel, 79; his book on Ireland, 79n.; on Bessborough, 145, 168; on Clarendon, 216; providentialism, 259n.; on British public opinion, 260, 305–6; on Irish ingratitude, 305–6; on retrenchment, 312; on Wood and Trevelyan, 324
Grey, 2nd Earl (Prime Minister, 1830–4) 20, 21, 24, 27–8, 61
Grey, 3rd Earl (Viscount Howick to 1845; Secretary at War 1835–9; Colonial Secretary, 1846–52) moralist liberal, 18, 24–6, 54, 231, 233, 300, 308; rivalry with Russell, 24; and Whig Party, 24; and Wood, 24–5; and Irish Church reform, 25, 54, 148; and political economy, 25; and Irish Poor Law, 25, 54, 186, 276, 196–7, 319; and wages fund, 25; and Corn Laws, 25; and land reform, 54, 179, 185–6; and franchise reform, 54; and public works, 54, 242; and assisted emigration, 54, 299–301, 308, 310; and Peel, 54; and O'Connell, 67n.; as Colonial Secretary, 147–8; and Palmerston, 148; and Bessborough, 149; and Labouchere, 149, 250n.; and Clarendon, 216n., and Trevelyan, 231; and Canada, 300–1, 308
Grey, Sir George (Home Secretary, 1846–52) evangelical, 16, 24, 148; liberal moralist, 16, 24, 26, 148; and Earl Grey, 24, 148; Home Secretary, 148; and Wood, 148; and land reform, 188; on Lincoln, 190n.; against Farmers' Estate Society, 208; on Peel's scheme, 215; and public works relief, 242; critical of farmers, 249; and Queen's letter, 257; and British Association, 258; and Irish Poor Law, 276, 278, 319n.
Griffith, Richard 123, 136, 153, 249

Halifax-Quebec railway 301, 309
Hall, Benjamin 303n.

Hamilton, George Alexander 56–7, 138n., 225n.
Hamilton, John 318n.
Hancock, W. Neilson 88n., 223n., 267
Hargreave, Charles James 222
Harvey, Jacob 150, 200n., 260–1
Hatherton, 1st Baron (Edward Littleton to 1835; Chief Secretary 1833–4) 217
Herbert, Sidney (Secretary at War, 1845–6) 108n., 211n.
Hewetson, Commissary-General 118–19, 253–4
Heytesbury, 1st Baron (Lord Lieutenant, 1844–6) advised by Peel, 38; Peelite, 78–9; and Constabulary, 83; and agrarian disturbances, 84–5, 121–2; and Devon Commission, 85; and clearances, 91; and potato failure, 99; on Bianconi, 120n.; on Repeal agitation, 122, 146; on 1846 harvest prospects, 123–4; and Relief Commission, 127n.; on Bessborough, 146
high farming 10, 81–2, 108, 117, 134, 222, 224, 330n.
Hill, Lord George 140
Hill, Sir John 126–7
Hilton, Boyd 14–16, 20n., 98n., 109n.
Hobhouse, Sir John Cam (Lord Broughton, 1851; Chief Secretary, 1833; President of Board of Control, 1846–52) 26, 80n., 148, 150, 162n., 167–8, 188n., 192, 196n.
Holland, 3rd Baron 19–21, 31, 187, 238
Holycross meeting 174–5, 181
Horner, Francis 22
Horsman, Edward 187
Horton, R.J. Wilmot 12
Howick, Viscount. See Grey, 3rd Earl
Hume, Joseph 54, 134, 161, 201

Illustrated London News 132, 194, 214n., 221n., 332–3
income tax 248, 275, 301–3, 310, 313, 317, 324, 333n.
Independent Irish Party 335
India 236, 257, 305, 333
Indian corn (maize) 105, 109, 110n., 113–14, 115–16, 118–25, 252, 256, 267, 286, 291
Inglis, Assistant Commissary-General 253n., 261n.
Inglis, Sir Robert 98n.
Irish Constabulary 32, 45, 82–3, 114, 117, 138, 180
Irish Council 272
Irish Felon 196
Irish Party 270, 272, 276n., 277, 301
Irish Society 221

Jones, Colonel Harry (Chairman of Board of Works, 1845–50), 136, 252–3, 255, 264n.
Jones, Richard 13, 156
'Justice to Ireland' 23, 28–36, 44, 51, 59, 64–5, 73, 74n., 79–80, 108, 144, 145n., 151n., 152, 168, 181, 200n., 270, 273, 298, 320, 327, 329–30, 332, 334–5

Kane, Sir Robert 115n., 129, 131–2, 206–7, 208n., 239n., 279n., 299
Kenmare 284, 310n.
Kennedy, John Pitt 6, 58, 70, 82, 129, 154, 217n., 318
Kerry, County 43, 66n., 136n.
Kilkenny, County 120, 244–5
Kilmacthomas 176
Kilrush 308, 323, 325
King's County 84
Kingscote, Henry 258

Labouchere, Henry (Chief Secretary, 1846–7; President of Board of Trade, 1847–52) moderate liberal, 22, 26, 148; on Indian corn purchase, 125n.; influenced by Bessborough and Morpeth, 148–9, 171; and land reform, 164, 166; on famine relief, 229–30, 255–6; and 'labour rate', 230, 249; and Trevelyan, 232; and public works, 240n., 248–9; and Grey, 250n.; and seed, 265n.; and Irish Poor Law, 279; and moralists, 303
Labouchere letter 242–3, 246, 269
Laffan, Archdeacon 172
Laing, Samuel 225
laissez-faire 10, 34, 37, 75, 80, 81, 124, 208, 212, 214n., 234, 252n., 269, 275, 290n., 316, 325, 330, 334
Lalor, James Fintan 46, 56, 174–5, 196, 336
Land Improvement Act 269, 274–6, 298–9
Land League 329, 336–7

Langdale, Lord 206
Lansdowne, 3rd Marquess of (Lord President of the Council, 1830–4, 1835–41, 1846–52) and political economy, 16, 327; religious sceptic, 20; moderate liberal, 22–3, 26, 148; and 'Bowood set', 22, 62, 160, 250; and Monteagle, 22, 243n.; Irish landowner, 23, 144, 310n.; and Foxites, 29; and railway schemes, 34; and Irish reforms, 62–4; and Senior, 62–4, 235n., 318n., 327; and land reform, 88n., 179, 185, 188, 193; and coercion, 144; and Repealers, 150; and waste lands, 159–60; and franchise reform, 164; and Clarendon, 168; and Lord Lieutenancy, 169–70; and Farmers' Estates Society, 208; and Encumbered Estates Bills, 217, 219n.; criticises moralists, 236; on Irish pauperism, 236; and Irish Poor Law, 239, 250, 276–7, 280n., 281, 296; and Vagrancy Act, 276; and Whately, 280n.; and rate in aid, 310n.; and assisted emigration, 310n.
Larcom, Thomas 136, 149, 320
Leinster, 2nd Duke of 67n., 150, 246
Leitrim, County 57, 85n.
Lewis, George Cornewall (Under-Secretary for Home Affairs, 1848–50) 1, 11, 13, 22, 32–3, 35n., 79n., 168, 179
liberal Anglicans 20, 239
liberal Tories 21, 37, 44, 80, 109n., 275
Lichfield House Compact 29, 67, 143, 145
Limerick 112, 123, 322n.
Limerick, County 58, 181, 236n., 240n.
Limerick Examiner 215n.
Lincoln, Earl of (Chief Secretary, 1846) appointed Chief Secretary, 90; and land reform, 91–3, 153, 166n., 178–9, 190, 206n.; on Graham, 101; and Corn Laws, 108n.; on potato failure, 115n.; alarm at food riots, 120–1; criticizes Trevelyan, 120–1, 136–7, 273; on Whig food policy, 125; on drainage loan, 134n.; and public works relief 135–7, 274; and Catholic clergy, 137; criticized by G. Grey, 190n.; Peelite, 206n., 211n., 212, 271, 280n.; buys *Morning Chronicle*, 211n.; on Queen's letter, 257n.; criticized by Bentinck, 271; and Irish Poor Law, 280n.
Lindley, John 116n., 323
Linen industry 8, 42–3
Liverpool 121, 246, 307n.
Liverpool, 2nd Earl of (Prime Minister, 1812–27) 15
London 152, 203, 220, 246, 258, 288
Londonderry, 3rd Marquess of 87, 91n.
Longfield, Mountifort 222
Lord Lieutenancy, abolition of 30, 62, 169–70, 226
Louisburgh 298n., 311
Loyd, Samuel Jones 258
Lucas, Edward (Under-Secretary, 1841–5; Chair of Relief Commission, 1846) 44, 128–30, 134
Lyndhurst, 1st Baron (Lord Chancellor, 1841–6) 61

Maberley, Katherine 149
Macaulay, Thomas Babington (Paymaster-General, 1846–8) 26, 80n., 258n.
McCullagh, William Torrens (Secretary to the Lord Lieutenant, 1847–52) 149, 176–7, 206, 224n., 321
McCulloch, John Ramsay 8, 9n., 294
MacDonnell, Alexander 171
MacHale, John, Archbishop of Tuam 68, 172, 221
McKenna, Theobald 129
McKnight, James 173–4, 177
Maginn, Edward, Bishop of Derry 174, 208n.
Mahon, Major Denis 182–3
Mahony, James 333n.
Mahony, Pierce 73–4, 90, 216n.
Malthus, Revd Thomas Robert 8, 10, 12
Malthusianism 12–13, 15, 72, 102, 155, 232, 236, 239, 267n., 280n., 281, 287, 331
Manchester 106n., 201, 218n.
Manchester School 16, 76, 201
Mandler, Peter 14, 15, 17–20, 148, 330
Mansion House Committee 113
Marx, Karl 26
Mathew, Revd Theobald 237n., 306
Maunsell, Henry 202, 208n.
Maynooth College 65, 79, 81n., 336
Maynooth grant 65, 74, 79, 83n., 85, 94, 97, 102, 288

Mayo, County 180, 191, 265n., 293
Meath, County 171n.
Melbourne, 2nd Viscount (Chief Secretary, 1827–8; Home Secretary, 1830–4; Prime Minister 1834, 1835–41) 23, 26–7, 29–30, 35, 61, 146, 148
middlemen 9–10, 43, 54, 60, 70, 71, 77, 175, 180, 185n., 186, 206, 223
Mill, John Stuart, heterodox economist, 6, 13, 156; newspaper articles on Ireland, 7n., 156–7; against Irish Poor Law, 13, 156; advocates peasant proprietorship, 13, 156–9, 198, 214, 225; *Principles of Political Economy*, 156; on waste lands, 156–8, 162; and Russell, 156, 158, 162; and cottier system, 156–7; on land reform, 157, 172n., 334; and European opinion, 157n.; and Scrope, 158; criticized by Clarendon, 179; and *Daily News*, 211, 214; against national fast, 259; and *Dublin Review*, 336–7
Milnes, Richard Monckton 134
Minto, 2nd Earl of (Lord Privy Seal, 1846–52) 26
Mitchel, John 46, 209, 333n.
moderate liberals, faction in Whig-Liberal Party, 18, 22–4, 27, 148, 329; and Lansdowne, 22–3, 26, 145, 148, 185, 217, 236, 276; and 'Bowood set', 22, 170; and *Edinburgh Review*, 22, 62; and Senior, 22, 62, 78, 235, 280, 318n.; and Monteagle, 22–3, 26, 62, 87, 146, 165, 235; and Auckland, 22, 26, 148; and Baring, 22, 26; and Lewis, 22; and Labouchere, 22, 26, 148; and Fitzwilliam, 22, 26, 35n., 66, 147; and Bedford, 22, 26; and Canningites, 23; and Clarendon, 23, 26, 170; and Melbourne, 23; and Palmerston, 23, 26, 53, 148, 185, 192, 230; and political economy, 23, 170; and Church reform; 23; and Catholic endowment, 23, 62, 307; and Irish landlords, 23, 242; and Clanricarde, 23, 26, 66, 87, 148, 185, 192, 202, 230; and party politics, 23, 334; and O'Connell, 23, 145; and Greville, 23–4; and coercion, 24, 146, 210n.; and Hobhouse, 26, 148, 167; and Foxites, 29, 237; and Ferguson, 58n.; and Devon, 78, 233, 250; and land reform, 87, 165, 185–6, 192, 334; critical of Bessborough, 147, 149, 167; and 1846 government, 148, 236, 276; and franchise reform, 164; and moralists, 185–6, 235–6, 250; and Encumbered Estates Bills, 202, 217; and Maunsell, 202; and wages fund, 217; and public works relief, 230, 235–6, 242; and Irish Poor Law, 235, 237n., 247, 250, 276, 278, 280, 321; against Trevelyan, 235; and Malthusianism, 236, 318n.; and cottier system, 237; and Russell, 237, 239, 329; and *Spectator*, 237n.; and Hancock, 267; and railway schemes, 271; and Irish taxation, 303; and assisted emigration, 307; and rate in aid, 310
Monaghan, County 45
Monahan, James Henry (Solicitor-General, Ireland, 1846–7; Attorney-General, Ireland, 1847–50) 149, 166
Monsell, William 208, 240n.
Monteagle, 1st Baron (Thomas Spring Rice to 1839; Chancellor of Exchequer, 1835–9) and political economy, 16, 168n., 235; and Whately, 16, 280–1; moderate liberal, 22, 26, 62, 165, 280; and Lansdowne, 22, 62; and 'Bowood set', 22, 62; and *Edinburgh Review*, 22, 62, 235n., 305n.; Irish landowner, 22–3, 144, 235–6; and Irish reform, 62; and Senior, 62, 235n., 236, 280; and Irish Poor Law, 62, 280–2, 297; and land reform, 62, 87–8, 164–5, 193; and Relief Commission, 127n.; and Peel, 127n., 168n., 217; and coercion, 144, 146; on social subordination, 164–5; and 1846 government, 165, 236, 270, 281, 301; and Clarendon, 168n., 307; criticizes Russell, 193; on Ballykilcline, 193n., 307; and Encumbered Estates Bills, 200, 203, 217, 219; and Farmers' Estate Society, 208n.; against Queen's visit, 221; and Trevelyan, 232, 236n., 235–6, 305n.; and public works relief, 235–6, 242; and providentialism, 236; and Wood, 236n.; and *Times*, 236n.; and Fitzwilliam, 281–2;

Malthusianism, 281n.; criticized by Dalhousie, 282; and assisted emigration, 301, 307–8; and income tax, 317
Moore, Richard (Attorney General, Ireland, 1846–7) 149
moralists, faction in Whig-Liberal Party, 16, 18, 24–6, 147–8, 231, 329, 337; and evangelicalism, 16, 24, 148, 254; and providentialism, 16, 232–3, 254, 286, 319, 331, 337; and Trevelyan, 16, 24, 160, 163, 204, 224n., 231–3, 254–5, 258n., 286–7, 309, 312, 323; and Wood, 16, 24–6, 54, 148, 160, 186, 197, 231–3, 248, 292, 308–9, 312; and Grey, 16, 18, 24–6, 54, 148, 185, 233, 308–9; and George Grey, 24, 26, 148, 208; and Edward Ellice, 24, 26, 121, 218; and Ireland, 25; and political economy, 25, 234, 274–5, 331; and Irish Poor Law, 25, 54, 185, 263, 283, 315, 319, 321; and wages fund, 25, 54, 77, 231–2, 249n., 294; and Corn Laws, 25, 233; and party politics, 25, 274; and Macaulay, 26, 258n.; and Church reform, 54; and franchise reform, 54; and public works, 54, 246, 248, 250, 255, 263; and assisted emigration, 54, 308; and British opinion, 77, 151, 233, 285, 290, 303, 312, 337; and *Times*, 77, 212, 218, 233, 282, 323; and Clarendon, 148, 170–1, 216, 291, 312; and potato failures, 151, 231–2, 244, 286; and Irish landlords, 160, 171, 185, 197–8, 231, 255, 308, 319, 321; and Peel, 161, 212, 274–5; and waste lands, 163, 275; and land reform, 185, 189, 334; and moderates, 185–6, 235–6, 250; and Encumbered Estates Acts, 185, 197–8, 204, 216, 218, 321; and Farmers' Estate Society, 208; and coercion, 210n.; and Queen's visit, 221; and pastoralism, 224n.; and 'dependency', 231–2, 235, 331n.; anti-Malthusianism, 232, 308, 331; and local responsibility, 234–5, 292, 319; and cottier system, 236; and Russell, 237–9, 282, 312, 325, 329; and O'Connell, 238; and Bessborough, 240; and Smith, 254; and Scotland, 258n.; and British Association, 258n.; and soup kitchens, 263; and fiscal rectitude, 274, 304, 309–10; and Labouchere, 303; and rate in aid, 313n.; and Trollope, 327, 338; and cultural revolution, 331–2; and 'abuses', 332; decline of, 334
Morning Chronicle 74, 75, 78, 89, 151, 156, 211, 269
Morpeth, Viscount (7th Earl of Carlisle, 1848; Chief Secretary, 1835–41; First Commissioner of Woods, 1846–50; Lord Lieutenant, 1855–8, 1859–64) Foxite Whig, 20, 26, 170; and evangelicalism, 20n., 170; as Chief Secretary, 29, 35, 49; and Irish Poor Law, 33, 230; and railway scheme, 34; and O'Connell, 36; and land reform, 49; and Staunton, 144; denied Home Office, 147; at Woods and Forests, 147, 159, 170; and Labouchere, 148; and Irish appointments, 149; and Harvey, 150, 200n., 260–1; denied Lord Lieutenancy, 170–1; and public works relief, 230; on national fast day, 259; and Quakers, 260–2; and soup kitchens, 262; as Lord Lieutenant, 334
Mulgrave, 1st Earl of. See Normanby, 1st Marquess of
Mulvany, W.T. 249n., 299n.
Murray, Daniel, Archbishop of Dublin 221

Napier, Joseph 205
Napier, Macvey 62–5
Nation 45–6, 112n., 174
national fast day (1847) 259–60
national thanksgiving day (1847) 287, 289
Navigation Acts 251, 256, 334
New York 261n., 307n.
New Zealand 292
Newry Examiner 45
Newson, George 103
Nicholls, George 32–3, 35n.
Normanby, 1st Marquess of (Viscount Normanby to 1831, 1st Earl of Mulgrave to 1838; Lord Lieutenant, 1835–9; Home Secretary, 1839–41) Foxite Whig, 20, 26, 61, 145; and Russell, 20; as Lord Lieutenant,

Normanby (*contd.*)
29–30, 34–5, 65, 94, 147; and O'Connell, 30, 67n.; and Irish Poor Law, 32; and coercion, 34–5, 145; and Irish reforms, 61, 66–7, 75, 88; and Devon Commission, 66–7; criticized, 69n.; and Corn Laws, 147; given Paris Embassy (1846), 147
Norreys, Sir Denham J. 52

oats and oatmeal 107, 110n., 118–19, 121, 123, 305
O'Brien, Sir Lucius 205, 287, 353
O'Brien, William Smith, Young Irelander, 46, 167; and land reform, 46, 52–3, 91n., 175n., 189n.; and Irish motion (1843) 51–3; and food exports, 121; and O'Connell, 144, 146, 151; and waste-lands reclamation, 161; and rebellion, 167; and relief policy, 248, 270, 287; and Bernal Osborne, 275
O'Connell, Daniel, and land reform, 5, 47–9, 59, 72–4, 90, 92, 118, 151–2, 179, 328; and Catholic clergy 11, 68; and Bessborough, 22, 28–9, 60, 146, 150–1, 167–8, 237, 241n., 330; and Foxite Whigs, 22, 27–8, 30, 36, 54, 61, 67, 74, 150, 168, 337; and moderates, 23, 145; Greville on, 23–4, 168; and Stanley, 27–8; and Repeal, 27–9, 35, 41, 43–4, 47, 57, 74, 79–80, 143–4, 146, 149–51, 270; and 'justice to Ireland', 28–31, 36, 44, 73–4, 80, 108, 168, 330; and coercion, 28, 60, 143, 145–6; and Lichfield House Compact, 29, 67, 143, 145; and Orangeism, 29, 36, 44; and Russell, 30, 34–5, 54, 60–2, 66–7, 80, 143–4, 150, 166; and Irish Poor Law, 33, 46, 230n., 270n.; as landlord, 33, 43–4, 78, 118, 237n.; and political strategy, 35–6, 44, 47, 54, 60, 67, 113, 142–4, 149–51; and Peel, 36–7, 44–5, 74; Lord Mayor of Dublin, 36; and Irish elections, 36, 149; and Scully, 43; economic ideas of, 43–4, 117; and agrarian violence, 43–4, 49, 73–4, 146; and Benthamism, 44; and Devon Commission, 58–9, 72–3; and Palmerston, 60; trial and imprisonment, 61–2, 66–7; Senior on, 64; and radicals, 67, 74; and Young Ireland, 68, 151, 237n.; and Corn Laws, 108, 117–18; and *Times*, 78; 112n.; and famine relief policy, 113, 117–18, 141, 142–3, 151, 166, 237–8, 270, 337; Heytesbury on, 146; 'friends of', 149; and patronage, 150, 166; illness and death, 166–9, 209; followers of, 171; and Irish Party, 270; legacy of, 336
O'Connell, John 167, 175–6, 276n., 288
O'Connell, Maurice 150
O'Connell, Morgan John 92
O'Connor, Feargus 189n., 208n.
O'Conor Don, The (Lord of Treasury, 1846–7) 150
O'Ferrall, Richard More (Governor of Malta, 1847–51) 26n., 51, 94, 148n., 186, 247n.
Orangeism 29, 36, 38, 44, 56–7, 78, 111–12
Ordnance Survey 136, 149, 197n.
Oregon dispute 123
Osborne, Ralph Bernal 92, 161, 195, 201, 205, 218, 272, 275
Osborne, Revd Sidney Godolphin 194n., 321, 327, 332n.
O'Sullivan, Revd John 284, 312n., 320n.
over-population 4, 6, 8–9, 12, 13, 155–6, 236, 280, 309, 318n.

Palmerston, 3rd Viscount (Foreign Secretary, 1830–4, 1835–41, 1846–51; Prime Minister, 1855–8, 1859–65) moderate liberal, 23, 26, 236; Canningite, 23; and political economy, 23, 185; Irish landlord, 23, 53–4, 185, 192, 299–300; and O'Connell, 36, 60–1; and land reform, 53–4, 185, 188–9; and party politics, 80n.; and 1846 government, 148; and Clarendon, 168; and coercion, 182, 185; and Irish Poor Law, 185, 236, 281; on clearances, 192, 330; and Farmers' Estate Society, 208; and relief policy, 230, 236, 313n.; and assisted emigration, 299–300; and anti-slavery squadron, 324; and Liberalism, 334
Parnell, Charles Stewart 329, 336
peasant proprietors 5, 13, 52, 64, 70, 73, 154–63, 172, 198, 200, 206n., 207–8, 214, 220n., 245, 336–7

Peel, Sir Robert (Chief Secretary, 1812–18; Home Secretary, 1821–7, 1828–9; Prime Minister, 1834–5, 1841–6) as Prime Minister 3, 23, 36, 44, 97; liberal Tory, 15, 37, 80, 97–8, 109n., 275; evangelical, 15, 81n., 98, 99n., 110; and party politics, 24, 38–9, 44, 54, 56, 68, 79–80, 94, 97, 108–9, 146, 212–13, 274, 328; as Home Secretary, 27, 37, 110n.; and Stanley, 27, 39–40, 86, 107; and fiscal orthodoxy, 34, 37, 272–4; and O'Connell, 36–7, 48–9, 55, 74, 79, 111–13, 141; as Chief Secretary, 37–8, 110n.; and coercion, 37, 48–9, 51, 83, 91–2, 138–40, 143–5, 187; and famine relief policy, 37, 96, 108–10, 113, 125–9, 132n., 134, 136–7, 140, 212, 228–30, 240, 256, 271, 273–4, 316; and Irish landlords, 37–9, 81–3, 86n., 93, 117, 133n., 138–40, 214, 274; and railway schemes, 37–8, 80–1, 271–3; and Irish Catholics, 37–9, 55–6, 78–81, 94, 137, 142, 214–15, 270; and Heytesbury, 38, 78–9; and Repeal, 38, 79, 81, 111, 150; and Orangeism, 38, 78, 111–12; and providentialism, 38–9, 54, 97, 99n., 102, 108–9, 111, 213–14; and Goulburn, 39, 111, 121, 136–7; and Graham, 39, 99–101, 127; and Encumbered Estates Bills, 40, 84, 139–40, 161, 197–8, 200, 212–18, 316; and Devon Commission, 42, 57, 82, 84; and land reform, 42, 44, 52, 55–6, 69, 80–1, 84, 86, 89–93, 139–40, 225; and Lalor, 56; and Devon, 57, 82, 89; and Maynooth Act, 79, 97; and Queen's Colleges, 79, 81; and Senior, 79; and Corn Laws, 79, 96–7, 99, 105, 107–11, 114–17, 124, 134, 138, 213, 251, 274; and Catholic endowment, 79, 210; and Russell, 79–80, 107, 144, 187, 210, 215, 230, 273–4; and Burke, 80; and *laissez-faire*, 80–1, 124, 161–2, 212, 272, 316; and high farming, 81–2, 94, 108, 117, 134, 213, 222, 224, 330n.; fall of government, 93, 96, 140, 146, 210; and food policy, 96–7, 108–9, 113–14, 116, 118–19, 121–5, 212n., 229; and potato failure, 98–9, 101–3, 116, 106–8, 116–17, 134, 137–8, 213, 323n.; and seed, 115–16; and social reconstruction, 116, 118, 212, 214, 316; and Lincoln, 121, 136, 274; and America, 123; and Irish Poor Law, 132n., 212n., 280n., 316; and drainage, 134–5, 316; and Lord G. Hill, 140; and waste lands, 161–2, 275; and Bessborough, 167n.; and Clarendon, 169, 215–16; and Wood, 198, 274–5; and Pim, 200; and plantation scheme, 212–18, 220, 275, 316; and emigration, 213; and private charity, 257; and Board of Health, 268; and Bentinck, 271–2, 280n.; and Land Improvement Act, 274; and Trevelyan, 274; and Routh, 274; and Chalmers, 275n.; and Bank Charter Act, 275, 289

Peelites 21, 78, 94n., 102, 108n., 109, 125, 128, 134, 146, 147n., 181, 194, 196, 197n., 206, 211–12, 218n., 230, 271, 272–4, 277–8, 280n., 281–2, 302n., 307, 326, 334

penal laws 2, 21, 174

Pennefather, Richard (Under-Secretary, 1846) 127, 128

Perceval, Captain 124n.

Pigot, David Richard 61, 148n., 149, 167n.

Pim, James 224

Pim, Jonathan 199–201, 204–6, 224, 293–4

plantation scheme 212–14, 218, 220–1, 222n., 275, 316

Playfair, Lyon 101, 107, 116

Pole, Captain 140–1, 204n., 216n., 310–11

Poor Inquiry Commission (1834–6) 11, 27, 32

Poor Law, English 8, 11, 13, 14, 15, 32, 35n., 131, 246–8, 278, 297, 314n., 319–20

Poor Law, Irish, proposed, 11, 13, 25, 49; opposed, 11, 13, 32; Poor Law Act (1838), 14, 32–5, 49, 62, 117, 276; resistance to, 46–7; demands for stronger, 54, 59–60, 132–3, 156, 158, 163, 234, 238, 245–8, 250, 260, 269, 275–7; opposition to extension, 235, 238–9, 270n., 271, 272n., 277, 280–2; as famine relief measure, 129–31, 230, 261, 265; and 'labour rate', 131, 246–50, 270n., 316n.; Poor Law Extension Act (1847), 170–1, 198, 201, 215n., 263, 268,

Poor Law, Irish (*contd.*)
269, 273, 276–83, 320, 325; operation of, 170–1, 185–6, 193–4, 211, 284, 290–8, 303, 305, 307, 309n., 310–11, 314–17, 319; demands for reform, 180, 205n., 217n., 284, 287, 295–7, 314–20; committees of inquiry, 310, 314–15, 318, 320, 322; Poor Law Amendment Act (1849), 224n., 320–2; operation of, 321–5, 327, 332–3. See also quarter-acre clause, rate in aid, workhouses
Poor Law, Scottish 76, 247
Poor Law Commissioners, Irish 123, 265, 269, 276–7, 296–8, 311, 314–17, 321
Portman, Lord 93, 186
potato blight 95, 98–9, 101–3, 107–8, 115–16, 120, 124, 153, 213, 227–8, 232–4, 244, 259, 261, 270, 281n., 285–6, 305, 307, 315n., 329, 333, 337–8
potatoes, failure of, 7, 98, 329, 332; in 1816, 37; in 1845, 90, 94, 95–6, 98–114, 117, 127, 134, 286–7; in 1846, 115, 124, 142–3, 151, 153, 199, 228–9, 231–3, 235–7, 239, 245, 253, 255, 259, 279–80, 285–7; in 1848, 213, 304–6; in 1849, 322–3, 325; in 1879, 336; criticism of, 8, 103–4, 115–16, 119, 120n., 213; and population, 8, 178, 183, 280; and conacre, 71, 123–4, 244; Irish dependency on, 71, 104, 110, 115–16, 124, 279, 285, 296, 306, 322–3, 326, 328; and social structure, 110, 116, 119–20, 123, 125n., 155, 178, 183, 199, 213, 215–16, 227, 231–3, 236–7, 244–5, 249, 261, 270, 279, 285–7, 293–5, 304, 307, 323, 332; seed, 115–16, 285, 304, 319; nutritional value of, 118, 120n.; planting of, 123–4, 285, 304, 323, 326
Power, Alfred (Chief Poor Law Commissioner, Ireland, 1849) 316, 321
Presbyterian Church 68, 173
Protectionists 40, 103, 114, 117, 139, 146, 147n., 186, 205–6, 213, 218, 237, 271–2, 274–5, 278, 288, 302, 303n., 307, 309, 324
Providentialism 15–16, 54, 95, 97–8, 173–4, 255n., 327, 331; and 1845 potato failure, 98–100, 102–6, 108–11, 115–17, 119–20, 129, 131, 134; and 1846 potato failure, 199, 228, 232–4, 236, 238n., 239, 259–61, 268, 281n., 306; and 1847 harvest, 286–7; and 1848 potato failure, 305–6; and social reconstruction, 174n., 178, 192, 197, 199, 201, 213–14, 232–4, 282–3, 290, 298, 319, 322, 327, 328–9, 331, 337–8; and markets, 252, 254
Prussia 48, 184, 206–7, 245, 330, 337
Prussian land bank 206–8, 220, 330
public works 10–11, 14, 27, 32, 34, 54, 81–2, 210, 212, 269, 299, 307, 316; as relief measure (1845–6), 121, 131, 133–7; as relief measure (1846–7), 229–30, 235, 240–50, 255, 273, 289; abandonment of, 262–5, 266n., 332; Public Works Act (1846), 133–6; Poor Employment (Labour Rate) Act (1846), 229–30, 235, 237, 264, 273, 302, 316. See also Board of Works, Labouchere letter
Pusey, Philip 93, 186

Quakers 150, 199–200, 204, 206, 224, 256, 260–1, 285n., 293–4
quarter-acre clause 180, 205n., 277–9, 295–7
Queen's Colleges 79, 81, 83n., 85
Queen's letter 257–9, 289–90

'race' 77n., 174n., 189n., 254–5, 293n.
radicals, Benthamite 26, 59, 163, 197
radicals, Birmingham 275
radicals, free-trade 16–18, 24–5, 26n., 29, 39, 51, 54, 67, 69, 74, 92, 96n., 118, 134, 151, 155n., 161–2, 166, 169, 181, 195, 197, 201–5, 213, 218, 225n., 235, 237, 260, 267, 272, 275–7, 282–3, 285, 288, 302, 303n., 304, 306, 312, 317, 319, 324
radicals, heterodox 6, 13, 49, 102n., 154–6, 158n., 166, 169, 192–3, 196, 201, 203, 211, 235, 275, 328–30, 336–7
radicals, Irish 14, 34, 39, 43, 46, 49, 51, 123, 130, 149, 154, 174, 275
railways 10, 34, 35n., 37–8, 81, 195n., 210, 264n., 271–3, 288–9, 298, 301, 309, 317, 324
rate in aid 212n., 214–15, 309–11, 313–14, 317, 320–2
rebellion 22, 36, 209, 211, 291, 294, 303–4, 305–6

Redington, Thomas (Under-Secretary, 1846–52) Whig-Liberal, 26n., 58; Devon Commissioner, 58, 72; Galway landlord, 58n., 215, 299, 308, 325; and Repeal, 72, 149, 167n., 171; as Under-Secretary, 149; and land reform, 187–8, 191n., 193n., 216–17; and Catholic endowment, 210n., 307; and plantation scheme, 215; and Encumbered Estates Bills, 215–17; and relief policy, 242, 250, 263, 295n., 317, 320, 324; and emigration, 299, 307–8; Irish Poor Law Commissioner, 311
Reeve, Henry 182
Reform Club 52
Relief Commissions (1816), 110n.; (1846), 119, 127–33, 135, 229; (1847), 263, 266
relief committees 110n., 120, 132, 229, 236n., 247, 251–2, 255, 257n., 262n., 263, 265n.
Repeal, clergy and, 11, 46, 49, 73, 79, 122, 176; O'Connell and, 27–30, 35–6, 43–4, 46–9, 58–9, 67–8, 72–4, 78–9, 143–6, 149–52, 167–8, 237, 270, 329; rhetoric of, 27–8, 51, 67, 288; Whigs and, 28, 30, 35–6, 44, 51, 62, 68, 72, 74, 143–6, 149–51, 167–8, 171, 191n., 209, 237, 241n., 270; popular support for, 30, 36, 41, 43, 46–8, 51, 74, 79, 112, 144; Peel and, 38–9, 44, 48–9, 79, 81, 84, 111–12, 150; and land reform, 41–2, 43–4, 46–9, 51, 56n., 68, 72–4, 89n., 112, 144, 151–2, 157–8, 175–6, 181, 189, 329; 'Repeal rent', 43; and Irish Poor Law, 46–7, 311; and Young Ireland, 46, 68, 72, 151; and monster meetings, 47–8, 67, 80n., 112; and agrarian violence, 49, 73–4, 84, 112, 122, 182, 241n.; and Smith O'Brien, 51n., 144, 146, 151; and Lalor, 56n.; and famine relief, 122, 134, 151, 237, 241n., 270; and coercion, 144–5; and Bessborough, 146–7, 150, 167–8, 241m.; and patronage, 150, 171, 288; 'Repeal magistrates', 150–1; and Clarendon, 171, 184; and John O'Connell, 175–6, 288; and Encumbered Estates Act, 218
Repeal Association 35, 41, 46–7, 51n., 59, 67, 72–4, 149, 151, 209, 237
Repeal Party 36, 134, 145, 149, 176, 218, 270, 288
Ribbonism 42n., 46, 85n., 112, 210, 336
Ricardo, David 8–9, 14, 16, 25
rice 110n., 114
Rice, Stephen Spring 258n.
Rice, Thomas Spring. See Monteagle, 1st Baron
Richards, Baron 222
Ripon, 1st Earl of 28
Roden, 3rd Earl of 87, 203
Roebuck, John Arthur 54, 161, 201, 269, 273, 275–6, 288n.
Romilly, Sir John (Solicitor General, 1848–50; Attorney General, 1850–1) 205–6, 216–17, 219n., 223–4
Roscommon, County 85n., 182
Routh, Sir Randolph, and Commissariat, 119–20, 124, 128, 229, 253; Relief Commissioner, 119, 128, 131–2, 229, 264n.; on potato, 119; on Indian corn, 119; and Irish society, 119, 123, 253; and food depots, 120–4, 253; and Treasury, 128, 229, 253; and Irish Poor Law, 131; and Trevelyan, 253; and Queen's letter, 257; and soup kitchens, 262, 264n.; praised by Peel, 274
Royal Agricultural Society of Ireland 190–1, 206, 208, 244, 286–7
Russell, Lady John 143, 196n.
Russell, Lord John (Earl Russell 1861; Paymaster General, 1830–4; Home Secretary, 1835–9; Colonial Secretary, 1839–41; Prime Minister, 1846–52, 1865–6) and land reform, 3, 31, 52–3, 56, 59, 61, 65, 80, 93, 142, 153, 163, 165–6, 178–9, 181–95, 207–8, 210, 220, 225, 245, 295, 330, 334–5; and 'comprehensive measures', 3, 152, 187, 195, 198, 210, 228, 241, 264, 269, 279, 298–9, 307, 309, 316–17, 322; Foxite Whig, 19–22, 26, 61, 146–7, 167, 187, 195–6, 203, 226, 237–9, 242, 245, 295, 299n., 306, 309, 319, 330; and Whig-Liberal Party, 19–21, 24, 28–9, 52, 54–5, 61–3, 66, 80, 144–5, 148, 196, 208, 272, 329, 334; and Fox, 19–20, 30, 66, 238; and franchise reform, 20, 65, 153, 164, 195n., 210, 226, 299n.;

Russell, Lord John (*contd.*)
liberal Anglican, 20, 239; and party politics, 20–2, 24, 55, 68, 143, 272, 276, 302, 312; and Catholic emancipation, 22, 30; and moderates, 23, 185, 237, 239, 271, 303, 310; and Grey, 24, 148, 186, 301, 308, 310; and Irish Church reform, 28, 63, 65, 195n., 210; and coercion, 28n., 30, 144–6, 182–4, 186–7, 191, 195, 210, 309; and 'justice to Ireland', 28, 31, 34–5, 64, 80, 181, 270, 273, 298, 327; and O'Connell, 29–30, 34, 36, 54, 60–1, 66–8, 80, 144–5, 148, 166, 209, 237; at Home Office, 29, 148; and Union, 30, 54, 169, 221; and political economy, 31, 179, 188, 206, 208, 238–9, 269, 273, 308, 322, 325, 330, 338; and Irish landlords, 31, 33–4, 162, 182–5, 191–2, 241, 247–8, 279, 294–5, 300, 309, 319–21, 326; and waste lands, 31, 155–6, 158–61, 195n., 245, 269, 272–3, 301; and Irish Poor Law, 32–3, 35, 238, 245–9, 260, 262n., 269, 275–7, 292, 295–8, 307, 309–10, 319–22, 324–5; and public works, 32, 210, 241–7, 264, 269, 271, 298–9, 307; and Scrope, 33n., 158, 193, 196, 238–9, 275, 277; and agrarian violence, 34–5, 65, 181, 183, 186, 191; and Normanby, 34–5, 145–7; at Colonial Office, 35; and Graham, 56, 271, 273, 280n.; and Peel, 59, 61, 79–80, 94, 144, 197n., 210, 212–13, 215, 228, 271, 273–4, 316; and Devon Commission, 59; and Bessborough, 59, 75, 145–8, 159, 167, 239, 241–2, 244–50, 265n., 273, 276, 300, 330; and Melbourne, 61; and Stanley, 61, 277; and *Edinburgh Review*, 63–4, 239; and Senior, 63–6, 238–9, 320; and Catholic endowment, 63, 65n., 79–80, 153, 203, 209–10, 307, 324n.; and clearances, 65, 181, 183, 191–2, 245, 249, 295, 321, 330; and More O'Ferrall, 94, 247n.; and Edinburgh letter, 107; and Corn Laws, 107–8, 144, 238, 251; and 1845 potato failure, 107; failure to form government, December 1845, 108, 143–4; and food policy, 124, 251–2, 256, 307; and public opinion, 142, 156, 169, 191–2, 194, 237, 243–4, 248, 251, 269, 275, 282, 288, 290, 303, 312, 326, 330; and 1846 potato failure, 142, 239, 244; and Lady John, 143; and Anti-Corn Law League, 146; and Bentinck, 147, 269, 271–2; and Fortescue, 147; and Morpeth, 147, 170, 261–2; and English reforms, 147; and Wood, 148, 186, 220, 239, 241, 248, 256, 291, 294, 302, 304; as Prime Minister, 148, 210, 213, 216, 220, 227, 237, 302, 307, 310, 312, 329; and Labouchere, 148, 170, 249; and Repealers, 149, 183, 209, 270; and relief policy (1846–7), 151, 162–4, 228, 237, 239–50, 256, 261–2, 264, 269–70, 330, 337; and elections, 152, 243, 288; and Mill, 156, 158, 162; and Irish society, 160–1, 192, 195, 202–3, 207, 244–6, 278–9, 290, 297, 319–20; and Buller, 163; and Monteagle, 164, 193; and Crawford, 165–6, 194–5; and Clarendon, 168–9, 171, 178–9, 181–91, 193, 202–3, 205–6, 209–10, 216, 220–1, 269, 290–2, 294–8, 302, 306–10, 313, 317, 319–20, 322–3, 325, 329; and Lord Lieutenancy, 169–70, 226; and Bedford, 169, 269; and *Times*, 169, 243, 269, 276, 282, 308; and Prussia, 184, 207–8, 245, 330; and education, 184; and Clanricarde, 185; and Lansdowne, 185, 188, 239, 248, 276–7, 313; illness, 188, 302, 329; Ejectments Bill, 191–5; and parliamentary obstruction, 195, 304; and Bernal Osborne, 195; on small farms, 195, 244; on Tuscany, 195; and Encumbered Estates Bills, 195–6, 198, 202–3, 205–6, 216–19, 223–4, 275, 325–6, 330; and railways, 195n., 210, 271–3, 298, 324n.; considers resignation, 196, 210, 242, 302, 309–10; and Pim, 205; and 'improvidence', 205, 290, 306; and Kane, 206, 239n., 279n., 299; and Farmers' Estates Bill, 208, 330; and Young Ireland rebellion, 209, 306; and drainage, 210, 265n., 269, 299, 303, 307; and emigration, 210, 245, 299–301, 307–10, 321, 325, 328; and rate in aid, 215, 309–10, 313, 317; and

potatoes, 216, 244, 279, 306, 322, 326; and Queen's visit, 221; and Ecclesiastical Titles Bill, 226, 334; and moralists, 237, 239, 244, 246, 294–5, 303, 308–10, 312, 325; anti-Malthusian, 239; and providentialism, 239, 290, 327, 328; and Royal Agricultural Society, 244; and task-work, 246; and Leinster, 246; and Smith O'Brien, 248; and income tax, 248, 301–2, 309–10, 313, 317, 324; and British Association, 258, 303, 311; and Quakers, 261–2; and soup kitchens, 262–4, 272; and Burgoyne, 263; and seed, 264–5, 278; and Land Improvement Act, 269, 276, 298–9; and radicals, 269, 302, 306, 312; and George Grey, 276; and wages fund, 279, 294; and relief policy (1847–8), 279, 290, 294, 298–9, 303–4, 330; and Trevelyan, 294, 299, 310, 312, 325; and 1848 potato failure, 306–7; and relief policy (1848–9), 306–7, 309–12, 317, 330; and Redington, 307; and Twisleton, 314; and McCullagh, 321; and relief policy (1849–50), 322, 324–6, 330; and Kilrush, 325; and Dufferin, 326

Sadler, Michael Thomas 32
St Germans, 3rd Earl of. See Eliot, Lord
Scientific Commission (1845) 101–2, 104, 107, 115
Scotland 197–8, 233n., 255, 258n.
Scrope, George Poulett, popular radical, 13, 91n., 196, 275; heterodox economist, 13–14, 155, 238, 336; and Irish Poor Law, 13–14, 32, 33n., 132, 156, 158, 215n., 235, 238–9, 277–9, 314n., 316n.; on population, 13, 155, 238–9; and land reform, 13–14, 91n., 92, 155, 158, 177, 193, 198, 208, 215n.; and waste lands, 14, 154–5, 158, 161n., 162n.; and Russell, 33n., 158, 193, 196, 238–9, 275; and Encumbered Estates Bills, 158; and clearances, 192n., 193, 278; popularity in Ireland, 215n., 336; on railway schemes, 272n.; on *laissez-faire*, 275
seed 110n., 115–16, 142, 250, 264–5, 278, 285, 304
Senior, Nassau William, classical economist, 8–9, 15, 64–5, 327; and population, 9, 280, 318n.; and Irish society, 9, 11, 41, 63–4; and education, 10, 62, 64; and public works, 10–11; and Irish Poor Law, 11, 13, 25, 33, 47n., 62, 235–6, 237n., 238–9, 280, 317–18, 320; and Catholic Church, 11–12, 62–3, 209; and Whig-Liberal Party, 12, 22, 62–6, 209; and Lansdowne, 12, 22, 62, 64, 235n., 318n., 327; and Whately, 15, 62, 280, 318; moderate liberal, 22, 78, 235, 280; and *Edinburgh Review*, 22, 62–5, 235, 238–9, 317–18; and abolition of Lord Lieutenancy, 62; and Repeal, 62, 64; and party politics, 62, 65, 79; and Monteagle, 62, 235–6, 280; and land reform, 62, 64, 165n.; and Russell, 63–6, 238–9, 320; on O'Connell, 64–5; and Peel, 79; and famine relief policy, 235–6, 280, 318, 327; on France, 303n.
Shaw, Frederick 92, 116n.
Sheil, Richard Lalor (Master of the Mint, 1846–50) 26n., 33, 51, 67, 148n., 149–50
Shrewsbury, Earl of 282n.
Skibbereen 253n., 256–8, 261n., 265n., 288, 323, 326, 333n.
Skilling, Thomas 158n.
Sligo 310
Sligo, County 53–4, 57, 192, 300
Sligo, 3rd Marquess of 179n., 180, 208n., 296n., 328
Smiles, Samuel 69
Smith, Adam 7, 10, 14, 15, 254
Smith, Elizabeth 45, 48n., 278n.
Smith, Thomas Berry Cusack (Attorney General, Ireland, 1842–6) 84, 90
Somerset, Lord Granville 85
Somerville, Alexander 267–8
Somerville, Sir William Meredyth (Under-Secretary for Home Affairs, 1846–7; Chief Secretary, 1847–52) Whig-Liberal, 26n.; and Coercion Bill, 145; suggested as Chief Secretary, 148n.; at Home Office, 150, 171; as Chief Secretary, 171; and 1847 elections, 175–7; and tenant right, 176–7; and

Somerville, Sir William (*contd.*)
land bills, 179, 189–90, 225; on Mahon, 183; and Encumbered Estates Bill, 215n.; on 1848 potato failure, 305
soup kitchens 256, 261–8, 290–1, 294, 298, 332
Spain 291
Spectator 49, 65, 229n., 237n.
Stanley, Lord (14th Earl of Derby 1851; Chief Secretary, 1830–3; Colonial Secretary, 1841–5; Prime Minister, 1852) defects from Whigs, 23, 28–9, rivalry with Russell, 23, 28, 61; as Chief Secretary, 27–8, 37, 126; as Conservative, 39; and Peel, 39; Irish landlord, 39, 86, 107, 271; and Devon Commission, 58; and land bill, 74, 86–90, 92, 155, 190n.; and economic education, 81; and political economy, 86–7; resignation, 90; and potato failures, 107, 117; Protectionist leader, 117, 271; and waste lands scheme, 161, 316n.; and Encumbered Estates Bills, 203, 206, 219; and Irish Poor Law, 271, 277 279–82, 317; and Land Improvement Bill, 274n.; and emigration, 316n.
Staunton, Michael 144
Stein-Hardenberg reforms 48
Stewart, Dugald 23
Storey, Thomas 48
Strzelecki, Count Paul Edmund de 191, 325
Subletting Act 10
Sugden, Sir Edward (Lord Chancellor, Ireland, 1841–6) 44, 57, 84
Sumner, John Bird, Archbishop of Canterbury (1848) 14, 98
Swinford 311
Switzerland 200

Tait's Magazine 152
Tenant League 151, 174n., 224–5, 335
tenant right 4, 14, 47, 49–50, 64, 68, 70, 72–3, 77, 86, 88, 92, 93–4, 151–2, 157, 165–6, 171, 173–8, 181, 183–4, 188n., 189n., 190–1, 202, 224–5, 330, 334
Thornton, William Thomas 12–13, 155–6, 162n., 225, 336
Thurles 112, 311
Times 76–8, 89, 91n., 95, 103–5, 112n., 113, 132, 139n., 156, 158, 169, 174, 182, 189, 192, 194–6, 201, 210n., 211–12, 214, 216n., 218, 221, 227, 233–4, 236n., 241, 243, 249n., 255n., 259–60, 269, 275, 277, 282–3, 286, 289–90, 305–6, 308, 312–13, 322
Tipperary, County 32, 39, 48, 82, 107, 112n., 120, 121, 174–5, 181, 184, 208, 211
Tipperary Vindicator 194, 210n.
Torrens, Robert 8, 12
Tory Party 18–22, 110. See also Conservative Party
Trench, W. Steuart 45, 153n., 310n.
Trevelyan, Charles Edward (Assistant Secretary to Treasury, 1840–59) moralist, 16, 24, 26, 163, 204, 224n., 231–2, 255, 258, 286, 309, 325, 331n.; and evangelicalism, 16, 24, 231, 253–4, 257–8, 311; at Treasury, 24, 114n., 120, 228–9, 231–2, 240, 243, 252–3, 257, 286, 299n., 324; Whig-Liberal, 24, 26, 137; and Indian corn purchase, 114n.; and Peel government, 120–1, 135–7; and Commissariat, 120, 124, 125n., 229, 253–4; and Routh, 120, 124, 229, 253; and food policy, 120–1, 123–4, 229, 251–4, 294; and providentialism, 120, 174n., 232, 252, 254, 298, 305; and Irish society, 120, 163, 204, 224n., 232, 235n., 255, 286, 319, 331n.; and potato, 120, 232, 286, 305; and Lincoln, 120–1, 136–7, 273; *Irish crisis*, 120n., 163, 232, 286, 291, 305n., 316, 331n.; and Burke, 125, 254; and relief policy (1845–6), 135–7, 228–9, 254; and Irish landlords, 135–6, 160, 241, 253, 255, 257, 287, 318–19; and public works, 136–7, 229, 240–3, 247, 255; and waste lands schemes, 160, 163; and Encumbered Estates Bills, 204–5, 216n.; and Pim, 205; and relief policy (1846–7), 205, 228–9, 231–2, 240–3, 247, 251, 253, 257, 263n., 266; and coercion, 205; and Russell, 207, 294, 312, 325; and high farming, 224; and public opinion, 231, 243, 257, 315; and Wood, 231–2, 251, 253n., 298, 309; and Grey, 231–2; and Monteagle, 232,

236n., 305n.; anti-Malthusian, 232; and *Times*, 232, 236n., 255n.; and George Grey, 242; and Labouchere letter, 243; and Irish Poor Law, 247, 293–4, 295n., 298, 310, 318–19, 332n.; and definition of famine, 252–3, 286, 305; and European governments, 252; and Jones, 253, 255; and blue books, 254; and Adam Smith, 254; and race, 254–5; and Scotland, 255, 258n.; and Queen's letters, 257–8, 289; and British Association, 257–8, 294n.; and soup kitchens, 263n., 266; and Graham, 273; and Peel, 274; and relief policy (1847–8), 286, 293–4, 298; and Clarendon, 291, 312; and Twisleton, 293, 298n., 311n., 314n.; visits Ireland, 294; and drainage, 299n.; and emigration, 301, 309–10; and Fr Mathew, 306; and relief policy (1848–9), 310, 332n.; and Pole, 310–11; and 'natural causes', 312; and Ball, 315; and Power, 316; and relief policy (1849–50), 323–4; and Trollope, 338
'Trevelyanism' 312, 325
Trinity College, Dublin 267
Trollope, Anthony 327, 338
Tuam 297
Tuke, James Hack 191, 200n., 261, 293
Tuscany 195
Twisleton, Edward (Chief Poor Law Commissioner, Ireland, 1847–9) as Poor Law Commissioner, 123, 314, 333; on maize, 123; Relief Commissioner, 131–2, 264n.; and Irish opinion, 215n., 318; and vice-guardians, 293, 321; and Trevelyan, 293, 298n., 314–15; and Irish Poor Law, 293, 298, 314, 319, 321; and Clarendon, 293n., 298, 314; and quarter-acre clause, 296; and agricultural instructors, 304n.; resignation, 314–15; and emigration, 314; and Russell, 314; humanitarianism, 315, 333; and potato disease, 315n.; on public works, 316n., 318–19; Benthamism, 321; and imperialism, 333
Tyrone, County 43

Ulster 14, 45, 49, 50n., 64, 72–3, 77n., 86, 88, 151–2, 166, 173–5, 177–8, 183–4, 189, 212, 214, 221, 225, 280n., 286, 326, 334
Ulster custom 49, 70, 88n., 166n., 173–4, 177, 183–4, 191, 195, 225, 335
Union, Act of 2, 7, 21, 28, 38, 44, 51, 54, 111, 169, 209, 221, 227, 314, 337

Vagrancy Bill 33, 276
Venedey, Jacob 48
Victoria, Queen 111, 221, 258
Villiers, Charles 205

wages fund 25, 33, 71, 76–7, 130, 133, 155n., 217, 231, 235, 249n., 271, 279, 281, 294, 306, 315–16
Wakefield, Edward Gibbon 12
waste-land reclamation 5, 14, 52, 66n., 70, 73, 144n., 153–63, 164–5, 195n., 198, 214, 234, 245, 269, 272–3, 275, 298n., 301, 316n., 330, 337
Waterford 121, 176
Waterford, County 176
Wellington, 1st Duke of (Prime Minister, 1828–30, 1834; Minister without Portfolio, 1841–6) 27, 37, 57n., 101, 107, 113
West Indies 213n., 333
Westmeath, County 112n.
Westmeath, Marquess of 177, 225n.
Westminster Review 197
Westport 124n., 311
Wharncliffe, 1st Baron (President of the Council, 1841–5) 93n., 101
Whately, G.N. 103
Whately, Richard, Archbishop of Dublin, chairs Poor Inquiry Commission (1834–6), 11–12, 27, 32, 34; and Christian political economy, 15–16, 27, 32; and Senior, 15, 62, 280, 318; and economic education, 15, 27, 267; and Whig-Liberals, 16, 32, 280, 334n.; and Monteagle, 16, 280; and Stanley, 27; and Irish Poor Law, 32, 280–1, 318; moderate liberal, 62; and Hancock, 267; and public opinion, 276n.; and wages fund, 281; and Bessborough, 281n.

Whig-Liberal Party 12, 16, 17–27, 29–31, 35–6, 39, 44–5, 51–5, 58–60, 62–9, 74, 79–80, 87, 91–2, 94, 97, 108, 120, 124n., 125, 128, 133, 137–9, 141, 142–7, 149–51, 166–9, 171, 175–6, 181, 190, 195–7, 209, 216n., 217–18, 221, 225, 227–8, 230, 238, 257, 261, 270–4, 278, 281, 288, 299, 306–7, 320, 328–9, 334, 335n., 337. See also Foxites, moderate liberals, moralists
Whiteboys 42n.
Wicklow, County 45
Wiggins, John 66, 69n.
William IV, King 29, 30
Wilson, James 76, 251n.
Wood, Sir Charles (Chancellor of Exchequer, 1846–52) moralist, 16, 24–6, 54, 160, 185n., 197, 231–5, 248, 274–5, 286, 291–3, 304, 308–9, 312, 319, 334; evangelical, 16, 232; and Grey, 24–5, 148, 216n., 231; and Irish reforms, 25, 54; and political economy, 25, 234, 238n., 274–5; and wages fund, 25, 231; and Whig-Liberal Party, 25, 274; and radicals, 25, 202, 218; and land reform, 54, 185n., 186, 188; and Irish Poor Law, 54, 230, 280, 283, 284, 293, 298, 319, 321, 332n.; and Church reform, 54; and franchise reform, 54; and emigration, 54, 308–9; as Chancellor, 148, 159, 218, 233, 235, 242, 274, 292, 304, 324; and Russell, 148, 160, 161n., 186, 207, 236, 239, 256, 291, 294, 302, 304, 312; and Repealers, 150; and Bessborough, 150, 242–4, 286; and waste-lands schemes, 159–61, 162n.; and Devon, 160, 198; at Bowood, 160, 186, 198, 250; and Irish landlords, 160, 197, 202, 206n., 231, 240–1, 280, 284, 295, 319; and providentialism, 174n., 231–2, 238n., 268, 292, 298, 319; and Irish society, 197–8, 201, 231–2, 283, 308; and Encumbered Estates Bills, 197–8, 201–2; and Peel, 198, 274–5; and Prussian land bank scheme, 207, 220; and *Times*, 216n., 233, 236n., 249n., 283, 306, 313; and 1848 budget, 218, 302; and relief policy (1846–7), 230–2, 239–43, 248, 250, 253n., 256, 263, 268; and Trevelyan, 231–3, 251, 253n., 298, 312, 324; and potatoes, 231–2; anti-Malthusian, 232, 308; and Monteagle, 236n.; and Gibson, 238n.; and public works, 240–3, 250; and public opinion, 243, 257, 280, 283, 284, 302, 304; and Queen's letter, 258n.; and soup kitchens, 263; and Bank Charter Act, 275; and Crawford, 280n.; and relief policy (1847–8), 286, 292–3, 298, 304; and Clarendon, 291–3, 304, 308, 312; and Ellice, 292; and Twisleton, 293; and vice guardians, 293, 321, 332n.; and 'natural causes', 312; and relief policy (1848–9), 312–13; and relief policy (1849–50), 324; opposes waiver of famine debt, 333n.
Woodham-Smith, Cecil 96
workhouses 11, 14, 115n., 172, 241, 247, 250, 262n., 265n., 266, 269, 277, 284, 293, 296–8, 315–16, 321–3
Wynne, Captain Edmond 331n.
Wynne, John 57, 87n., 214
Wyse, Sir Thomas 52–3, 67n., 150, 155, 176n., 288

Young Ireland 46, 68, 142, 151, 167, 174–6, 194, 209, 237n., 304–6, 333